VAT Deductions
A Comprehensive Guide to Recovery of VAT in the UK

VAT Deductions
A Comprehensive Guide to Recovery of VAT in the UK

First Edition

Contributing Editor

Greg Sinfield,
MA (Cantab), solicitor
Partner, Lovells, London

Contributors

John Davison
BA LLDip DMS CTA (Fellow) AIIT
VAT Partner, Baker Tilly, London

Maric D Glaser,
BSc CA(SA) CTA
Senior Manager, Tax Services
PricewaterhouseCoopers LLP, Edinburgh

Hugh Love
CTA
Director, Tax Services
PricewaterhouseCoopers LLP, London

Chistopher P Orchard
B Ed (Hons) ATT AIIT
Manager, Tax Services
PricewaterhouseCoopers LLP, London

Martin Sharratt
Director
Smith & Williamson Limited, London

Alan Sinyor
BA (Oxon) PhD (Cantab) ACA CTA Barrister
Director of International VAT
Freshfields Bruckhaus Deringer, London

LexisNexis™ UK

Members of the LexisNexis Group worldwide

United Kingdom	LexisNexis UK, a Division of Reed Elsevier (UK) Ltd, Halsbury House, 35 Chancery Lane, LONDON, WC2A 1EL, and 4 Hill Street, EDINBURGH EH2 3JZ
Argentina	LexisNexis Argentina, BUENOS AIRES
Australia	LexisNexis Butterworths, CHATSWOOD, New South Wales
Austria	LexisNexis Verlag ARD Orac GmbH & Co KG, VIENNA
Canada	LexisNexis Butterworths, MARKHAM, Ontario
Chile	LexisNexis Chile Ltda, SANTIAGO DE CHILE
Czech Republic	Nakladatelství Orac sro, PRAGUE
France	Editions du Juris-Classeur SA, PARIS
Germany	LexisNexis Deutschland GmbH, FRANKFURT and MUNSTER
Hong Kong	LexisNexis Butterworths, HONG KONG
Hungary	HVG-Orac, BUDAPEST
India	LexisNexis Butterworths, NEW DELHI
Ireland	LexisNexis, DUBLIN
Italy	Giuffrè Editore, MILAN
Malaysia	Malayan Law Journal Sdn Bhd, KUALA LUMPUR
New Zealand	LexisNexis Butterworths, WELLINGTON
Poland	Wydawnictwo Prawnicze LexisNexis, WARSAW
Singapore	LexisNexis Butterworths, SINGAPORE
South Africa	LexisNexis Butterworths, Durban
Switzerland	Stämpfli Verlag AG, BERNE
USA	LexisNexis, DAYTON, Ohio

First published in 2004

Published by LexisNexis UK

A CIP Catalogue record for this book is available from the British Library.

ISBN 07545 19910

Typeset by Letterpart Ltd, Reigate, Surrey

Printed and bound in Great Britain by The Cromwell Press Limited, Trowbridge, Wiltshire

Visit LexisNexis UK at www.lexisnexis.co.uk

Preface

There are only two questions in relation to VAT that people really care about:
Do I have to pay it?
and
Can I recover it?

This book attempts to answer the second question. The intention of the authors is to help businesses and their advisers to understand how and when VAT can be deducted. The book starts with an overview of the VAT system and the right to deduct. Key concepts, the treatment of specific transactions and the application of the right to deduct to specific businesses are then considered in greater detail in subsequent chapters. The book also provides a detailed examination of topics such as:

- the capital goods scheme
- the partial exemption override
- tax avoidance and VAT deductions
- recovery of VAT by businesses established outside the member state.

The rules are examined in the light of cases decided in the UK tribunals, higher courts and as the European Court of Justice with some cases from courts in other member states. Many of these decisions challenge existing views on the scope and application of the right to deduct VAT. Cases considered in detail in the text include evergreen favourites such as Rompelman and Lennartz as well as more recent cases such as Royal and Sun Alliance, Seeling and KapHag. As well as being discussed in detail in the text, the most important cases are summarised in an appendix.

I owe an enormous debt of gratitude to my contributors John Davison, Maric Glaser, Hugh Love, Chris Orchard, Martin Sharratt and Alan Sinyor who accepted my comments and suggestions with good grace and, most importantly, maintained (under often trying circumstances) their enthusiasm and commitment to producing this work. Without their hard work, support and encouragement this book would never have been completed. I should also thank the Tolley's editorial team (Alison Lovejoy, Sabrina Kuhn, Kim Hutchings and Rajni Boswell) who took up my idea for the book and then forgave me when I missed deadlines I had imposed on myself. I would also like to acknowledge my gratitude to my partners, both business and marital, for making it possible for me to devote a substantial part of my time to the project at the expense of time which should have been devoted to them. Finally, I would also like to record my gratitude to my secretary, Susan Linton, for the important role she has played throughout the prolonged gestation of this book, from producing the first outline up to and including typing this preface.

Greg Sinfield
Lovells
London
June 2004

Contents

Table of Statutes

Table of Statutory Instruments

Table of Cases

A

B

C

D

E

F

G

H

I

J

K

L

M

N

O

P

R

S

T

U

V

W

Y

Decisions of the European Court of Justice are listed below numerically. These decisions are also included in the preceding alphabetical table.

Table of EC Legislation

Chapter 1

Overview

Introduction

1.1 Value added tax ('VAT') is a European tax imposed throughout the European Union ('EU') by the First VAT Directive (Directive 67/227 11 April 1967) and the Sixth VAT Directive (Directive 77/388 17 May 1977) and implemented in the United Kingdom by the Value Added Tax Act 1994 ('VATA 1994') and various statutory instruments made under it. VAT is a tax on the value of transactions not on the profit derived from them. VAT is chargeable on the taxable supply of goods and services at each stage of the chain of production and distribution. In this way, VAT is ultimately borne by the person at the end of the chain of supply (usually the final consumer). In order to prevent either double taxation or the absence of taxation, the fundamental principle which underlies the VAT system is that VAT applies to each transaction by way of production or distribution after deduction of the VAT borne directly by the various cost components of the transaction (see First VAT Directive, art 2(1) and *BP Supergas Anonimos Etairia Geniki Emporiki-Viomichaniki kai Antiprossopeion v Greece (C-62/93) [1995] STC 805, para 16).* This principle is the fountain-head from which all the rules on deduction of VAT flow.

Scope of VAT

1.2 The Sixth VAT Directive provides that VAT is chargeable on:

(a) the supply of goods for consideration by a taxable person in the course of carrying out an economic activity (Sixth VAT Directive, arts 2(1) and 4(1));

(b) the acquisition of goods from another Member State for consideration (Sixth VAT Directive, art 28a(1));

(c) the supply of services for consideration by a taxable person in the course of carrying out an economic activity (Sixth VAT Directive, arts 2(1) and 4(1)); and

(d) the importation of goods (Sixth VAT Directive, art 2(2)).

1.3 The UK has implemented the above by providing that VAT is chargeable on:

(a) the taxable supply of goods or services in the UK by a taxable person in the course or furtherance of any business carried on by that person (VATA 1994, ss 1(1)(a) and 4(1);

(b) the taxable acquisition of goods from another Member State by a taxable person (VATA 1994, ss 1(1)(b) and 10); and

(c) the importation of taxable goods into the UK from outside the EU by any person (VATA 1994, s 1(1)(c)).

1.4 Although it may seem that VAT must be chargeable on everything that a business does, this is far from correct. Many areas of activity undertaken by businesses fall outside the scope of VAT because either they are not an economic activity (eg passive or private investment, see **1.10** below) or because the turnover of the business is below the registration threshold (£58,000 in the UK for 2004–2005) and it chooses not to register for VAT. Further, many transactions are specifically exempted from the VAT system by the legislation. If all transactions carried out by businesses were subject to VAT then, in theory, businesses should be entitled to deduct all the VAT that they incur and this would be a very short book. Unfortunately (or fortunately, depending on your point of view), the situation is not that straightforward and the right to deduct is subject to a number of rules which determine whether and how the right can be exercised.

The right to deduct – a summary

1.5 It follows from the First, Second and Sixth VAT Directives that a taxable person has a right to deduct VAT:

(a) which the taxable person has paid or is liable to pay (Sixth VAT Directive, art 17(2));

(b) in respect of goods and services supplied to the taxable person (Sixth VAT Directive, art 17(2), VATA 1994, s 24(1));

(c) to the extent that the goods and services are used for the purposes (ie are cost components) of the taxable person's taxable transactions (ie supplies of goods and services other than exempt supplies) or transactions treated as such carried out in the course of an economic activity (Sixth VAT Directive, arts 17(2) and (3), VATA 1994, ss 25 and 26).

1.6 To determine whether or not VAT is deductible, it is essential to understand the meanings of the various elements of the right to deduct. In fact, whether or not a taxable person has paid for a supply and whether or not a supply has been made to the taxable person are fairly easy to determine save in unusual situations (eg see *Customs and Excise Comrs v Redrow Group plc [1999] STC 161* (**Case Summary 31**), *Goldsmith Foundation for European Affairs v C & E [2000] V & DR 97, WHA Ltd v C & E Comrs [2003] EWHC 305 (Ch), [2003] STC 648)*. The concept which gives the most difficulty in relation to the right to deduct is 'used for the purpose of taxable transactions' (see para **1.37–1.40** below).

1.7 Member states are entitled to restrict the right to deduct VAT on certain goods and services where there might be some element of private use (Sixth VAT Directive, art 17(6), VATA 1994, ss 24(3), (7) and 25(7)).

1.8 Businesses established outside the UK either in another Member State or outside the EU also have a right to deduct VAT subject to the same rules as those that apply to UK taxable persons. There is also a refund procedure for businesses not required or entitled to be registered (see paras **1.81–1.85**).

Key VAT concepts

1.9 An understanding of the key concepts of VAT contained in the Directives is essential before looking at the specifics of the deduction of VAT in relation to particular transactions. It is also important to understand how these concepts have been implemented in the UK legislation. The concepts described below are the elements of the equation which determines whether or not VAT is chargeable and deductible.

Economic activity or business

1.10 Economic activity means the activities of producers, traders and persons supplying services as well as the exploitation of property for the purpose of obtaining income on a continuing basis (Sixth VAT Directive, art 4(2)). The ECJ has stressed that the concept of economic activity must be given a wide scope but does not extend to the mere exercise of rights of ownership by the holder as a private investor (*Polysar Investments Netherlands BV v Inspecteur der Invoerrechten en Accijnzen, Arnhem (C-60/90) [1993] STC 222* (**Case Summary 16**), *para 13* and *Wellcome Trust Ltd v C & E Comrs (C-155/94) [1996] STC 945, paras 31–32)* (**Case Summary 23**). In the *Wellcome Trust* case, the ECJ held that neither the scale of a transaction nor the employment of professional advisers in connection with the transaction constituted criteria for distinguishing between the activities of a private investor and economic activities. The ECJ has held that the receipt of dividends by a holding company is not consideration for an economic activity and is thus outside the scope of VAT (*Satam SA v Ministre chargé du Budget (C-333/91) [1997] STC 226, para 13)* (**Case Summary15**) whereas interest received by a property management company on money placed on deposit with a bank does not arise simply from ownership of the asset but is consideration for placing capital at the disposal of a third party and cannot be excluded from the scope of VAT *(Régie Dauphinoise-Cabinet A Forest SARL v Ministre du Budget (C-306/94) [1996] STC 1176)* (**Case Summary 24**). Economic activity includes investment activity preparatory to actually making supplies and the status of economic activity is retained even if no supplies are ever made (*Intercommunale voor Zeewaterontzilting (in liquidation) v Belgian (C-110/94) [1996] STC 569)* (**Case Summary 20**). Where activities are deemed not to be economic activities for the purposes of VAT legislation, input tax attributable to those activities is not deductible. Where tangible property is available partly for business purposes and partly for non-business purposes, the input tax on expenses must be apportioned between the use of the goods for business purposes, which is deductible, and the use for non-business purposes which is not deductible (*Enkler v Finanzamt Homburg (C-230/94) [1996] STC 1316)* (**Case Summary 25**).

1.11 The distinction between economic activity and non-economic activity is crucial in determining whether or not a transaction is within the scope of VAT and thus whether or not VAT incurred in relation to such transaction can ever be deductible. For this purpose, transactions may be classified as follows:

- Economic activity
  - Taxable
    - Standard rate
    - Reduced rate
    - Super reduced or zero rate
  - Exempt
  - Exempt with refund
  - Non-supply (TOGC or free supply of services)
- Non-economic activity
  - Private or non-business (ie not acting as taxable person)
  - Occasional or one-off business activity

Fig. 1

1.12 The UK legislation does not use the term 'economic activity' but instead refers to 'business' which is not exhaustively defined but includes any trade, profession or vocation (VATA 1994, s 94). If an activity is not business then it is outside the scope of VAT. There is no single test for determining whether or not an activity is a business but in *C & E v Lord Fisher [1981] STC 238*, six criteria were approved as indicating that an activity is a business. The criteria are that an activity should:

(a) be a serious undertaking earnestly pursued, not necessarily a commercial or profit-making activity;

(b) be actively pursued with recognisable or reasonable continuity;

(c) have a certain measure of substance i e value;

(d) be conducted in a regular manner and on sound and recognised business principles;

(e) be predominantly concerned with making taxable supplies for a consideration;

(f) consist of making taxable supplies of a kind commonly made by those who seek to profit by them.

The six indicia should not be regarded as exhaustive and none of them is conclusive. The ECJ has held that criterion (e) is not relevant in deciding whether or not an activity is a business activity (or an economic activity in the terms of Sixth VAT Directive, art 4) and that the scale of the transaction is also irrelevant (*Wellcome Trust Ltd v C & E Comrs (C-155/94) [1996] STC 945, para 30)*.

Taxable person

1.13 Any person who independently carries out any economic activity is a taxable person (Sixth VAT Directive, art 4(1)). The UK implements this provision by defining (VATA 1994, s 3(1)) a taxable person as anyone who makes or intends to make taxable supplies and is registered for VAT or is required to be registered for VAT (ie has exceeded the compulsory registration thresholds). The status of 'taxable person' is objective, in the sense that it is determined by whether or not the person carries out an economic activity without regard to its purpose or the results of that activity. A person who carries out an economic activity on a one-off or occasional basis does not thereby become a taxable person but a Member State may treat such a person as a taxable person (Sixth VAT Directive, art 4(3)).

1.14 The term 'person' for these purposes includes an individual, a company or an unincorporated association. In the UK, a partnership is treated as a single person for VAT purposes (VATA 1994, s 45). Customs and Excise also treat co-owners of immovable property, eg joint tenants or tenants in common; and the trustees of a fund or charity as single persons for VAT purposes. The use of 'independently' excludes employees and other persons from being taxable persons and, therefore, no VAT is chargeable on the supply by a person under a contract of service, eg a contract of employment or one which creates a relationship of employer and employee.

1.15 Member states may treat persons who are legally independent but are closely bound to one another by financial, economic and organisational links as a single taxable person (Sixth VAT Directive, art 4(4)). This permits VAT group registration of companies. In the UK, companies under common control may (but need not) register together as members of a VAT group (VATA 1994, s 43). Companies registered as a VAT group are treated much as a single company for VAT purposes. In particular, supplies between companies in the VAT group are ignored for VAT purposes. Where there is a VAT group registration, supplies between members of the group and third parties are treated as made to or by a nominated company in the group, known as the 'representative member'. A VAT group registration need not include all companies in a corporate group.

Taxable supply

1.16 There is no separate concept of a taxable supply in the Sixth VAT Directive: all supplies are taxable but certain supplies are exempted from the VAT system. The UK defines a taxable supply as a supply of goods or services made in the UK other than an exempt supply (VATA 1994, s 4(2)). Accordingly, all other supplies are taxable supplies. This includes supplies on which VAT is charged at 0 per cent (the zero rate), 4 per cent (the farmer's flat rate), 5 per cent (the reduced rate applicable to goods and services specified in VATA 1994, Sch 7A) and 17.5 per cent (the standard rate). Certain supplies that would otherwise be subject to VAT are not so subject because they are outside the scope of UK VAT altogether. A supply may be outside the scope of VAT in one of two ways: conceptually (eg supplies not made in the course or furtherance of a business); or geographically (eg supplies not made or not treated as made in the UK). A transfer of a business as a going concern is not outside the scope of VAT but is deemed to be neither a supply of goods nor a supply of services and, as there is no other category of supply, it is, therefore not a supply (Sixth VAT Directive, art 5(8), VAT (Special Provisions) Order 1995, art 5, SI 1995/1268). Even though VAT is not chargeable in any case, it is important to distinguish between exempt supplies, zero-rated supplies and supplies which are outside the scope of VAT (conceptually or geographically) as the VAT treatment of each is different and has different consequences in relation to the ability to deduct VAT.

Supply

1.17 Curiously, there is no definition of supply in the Sixth VAT Directive. The only definition of supply in UK legislation is that it includes all forms of supply but not anything done otherwise than for a consideration (VATA 1994, s 5(2)(a)). In the context of VAT, consideration has a European law meaning rather than an English law meaning: there must be a direct link between consideration and the supply; the consideration must be able to be expressed in monetary terms; and the consideration must have a subjective value to the supplier.

Supply of goods

1.18 It is important to determine whether a supply is of goods or services as the place of supply and the time of supply, which determine whether and when VAT is chargeable and thus deductible, may differ according to the nature of the supply.

1.19 Supply of goods is defined as the transfer of the right to dispose of tangible property as owner (Sixth VAT Directive, art 5(1)). For there to be a supply of goods, it is not necessary for title in the goods to pass. It is sufficient if the seller gives the buyer the power to dispose of the goods as if he were the owner (*Staatsecretaris van Financiën v Shipping and Forwarding Enterprise Safe BV (C-320/88) [1991] STC 627*). Goods for VAT purposes means tangible property but a number of non-tangible items are considered to be tangible property for these purposes, including:

(a) the transfer of ownership of property by order of a public authority or law against payment of compensation (Sixth VAT Directive, art 5(4)(a));

(b) the transfer of possession of goods under a hire purchase or conditional sale agreement (Sixth VAT Directive, art 5(4)(b));

(c) the transfer of goods under a commissionaire arrangement (Sixth VAT Directive, art 5(4)(c)); and

(d) electric current, gas, heat and refrigeration (Sixth VAT Directive, art 5(2)).

1.20 In addition, Member States may consider certain transactions to be supplies of goods (Sixth VAT Directive, art 5(3) and (5)) and the UK has done so in relation to the grant, assignment or surrender of leasehold interests of more than 21 years in land (VATA 1994, Sch 4, para 4). Additionally, certain dealings by a taxable person with his own goods (eg transferring them to another Member State or removing them from the business) are treated as a supply of goods even though carried out for no consideration.

Supply of services

1.21 A supply of services is any transaction which does not constitute a supply of goods (Sixth VAT Directive, art 6(1)). VAT is only chargeable where the services are provided for a consideration (Sixth VAT Directive, art 2(1)). The Sixth VAT Directive provisions in relation to services are implemented in the UK by VATA 1994, s 5(2)(b). In *Trinity Mirror plc v C & E Comrs [2000] STC 156*, the High Court adopted the submissions of Customs and Excise and held that six characteristics must be present for there to be a supply of services. In summary, a supply of services exists where there is something which is:

(a) a transaction;

(b) something done by the supplier;

(c) not a supply of goods;

(d) capable of being used by and for the benefit of an identified recipient;

(e) capable of being regarded as a cost component of the activity of another person in the commercial chain; and

(f) for consideration.

The right to deduct – general principles of EU Directives

1.22 A taxable person has the right to deduct VAT charged on the cost components of his taxable transactions (ie transactions that are within the scope of VAT and not exempt), which he has paid or is liable to pay, at the time the VAT becomes chargeable, subject to specific exceptions. The deduction system is meant to relieve the taxable person entirely of the burden of VAT paid or payable in the course of his economic activities, provided that such activities are themselves, in principle, subject to VAT. The right to deduct VAT is derived from general EC law principles (most importantly, the principle of neutrality) and applied to VAT by the main VAT Directives. To ensure complete neutrality, VAT is deducted and charged at each stage in the chain of supply until the supply to the final consumer. This mechanism ensures that VAT is levied on the price of the goods to the consumer without regard to the number of transactions in the production and distribution process and that tax is not levied upon tax. An essential part of the mechanism is the right to deduct.

1.23 The First VAT Directive contains a statement of the general objective and a broad description of the structure of the tax of which the right to deduct is a fundamental part. The objective is to achieve neutrality. The eighth recital to the First VAT Directive states that:

> 'Whereas the replacement of the cumulative multi-stage tax systems in force in the majority of member states by the common system of value added tax is bound, even if the rates and exemptions are not harmonised at the same time, to result in neutrality in competition, in that within each country similar goods bear the same tax burden, whatever the length of the production and distribution chain …'

1.24 The structure of the tax is expressed in the First VAT Directive, art 2, which provides that:

> 'On each transaction, value added tax, calculated on the price of the goods or services at the rate applicable to such goods or services, shall be chargeable after deduction of the amount of value added tax borne directly by the various cost components.'

1.25 The ECJ and UK courts have made frequent reference to the First VAT Directive, art 2 in interpreting the provisions of the Sixth VAT Directive concerning the right to deduct VAT. Although useful as a general statement of principle, the First VAT Directive, art 2 raises several difficult questions: what is meant by 'borne directly'? what is meant by 'cost components'? and how is the deductible VAT to be deducted? The answers to these questions were left to the Second and Sixth VAT Directives, national legislation and the ECJ.

1.26 The general statements of the First VAT Directive were turned into a detailed structure and procedures by the Second VAT Directive (Directive 67/228, 11 April 1967). The scope and extent of right to deduct were set out in the Second VAT Directive, art 11 as follows:

> '(1) Where goods and services are used for the purposes of his undertaking, the taxable person shall be authorised to deduct from the tax for which he is liable:
>
> (a) the value added tax invoiced to him in respect of goods supplied to him or in respect of services rendered to him …
>
> …
>
> (2) Value added tax on goods and services used in non-taxable or exempt transactions shall not be deductible.
>
> …
>
> As regards goods and services which are used both in transactions giving entitlement to deduction and in transactions which do not give entitlement to deduction, deduction shall only be allowed for that part of the value added tax which is proportional to the amount relating to transactions giving entitlement to deduction (pro rata rule).
>
> (3) The deduction shall be made from the value added tax due for the period during which deductible tax is invoiced in the case of paragraph 1(a) or paid in the case of paragraph 1(b) and (c) (immediate deductions).

In the case of a partial deduction under paragraph 2 the amount of the deduction shall be provisionally determined in accordance with criteria established by each Member State and finally adjusted after the end of the year when the pro rata figure for the year of acquisition has been calculated …'

(4) Certain goods and services may be excluded from the deduction system, in particular those capable of being exclusively or partially used for the private needs of the taxable person or of his staff.'

The emphasis on 'each transaction' in the First VAT Directive, art 2 means that it is necessary to look at each supply and identify its cost components. Cost components can be specific, i e costs which are directly attributable to transactions, or general, i e costs which form part of the overheads of a business.

1.27 The Second VAT Directive was superseded by the Sixth VAT Directive in 1977. Although no longer in force, the provisions of the Second VAT Directive are important for the light they cast on the general right expressed in the First VAT Directive and the subsequent implementation in the Sixth VAT Directive.

1.28 The provisions of the Sixth VAT Directive relating to deductions are contained in arts 17–20. The Sixth VAT Directive provisions are longer and more detailed than those contained in the Second VAT Directive. Article 17 of the Sixth VAT Directive is headed 'origin and scope of the right to deduct' and provides as follows:

'(1) The right to deduct shall arise at the time when the deductible tax becomes chargeable.

(2) In so far as the goods and services are used for the purposes of his taxable transactions, the taxable person shall be entitled to deduct from the tax which he is liable to pay:

[VAT due or paid on supplies to him, imports and certain self-supplies].

(3) Member States shall also grant every taxable person the right to the deduction or refund of the value added tax referred to in paragraph 2 in so far as the goods and services are used for the purposes of [certain international transactions]:

…

(5) As regards goods and services to be used by a taxable person both for transactions covered by paragraphs 2 and 3, in respect of which value added tax is deductible, and for transactions in respect of which value added tax is not deductible, only such proportion of the value added tax shall be deductible as is attributable to the former transactions.

This proportion shall be determined, in accordance with Article 19, for all the transactions carried out by the taxable person.'

Credit for input tax – UK law

1.29 A taxable person (eg a business which is registered for VAT) can recover input tax incurred on:

(a) supplies of goods and services;

(b) imports of goods from outside the EU; and

(c) acquisitions of goods from other Member States;

provided the goods or services are used or to be used for the purpose of any business carried on or to be carried on by the business. The UK legislation employs the word 'use' in setting out rules for the deduction of VAT in the same way as the Sixth VAT Directive and the term must be interpreted consistently with that Directive.

1.30 The taxable person can recover input tax attributable to:

(a) taxable supplies of goods and services by the taxable person;

(b) supplies by the taxable person outside the UK which would be taxable supplies if made in the UK;

(c) supplies by the taxable person of exempt insurance services or financial services to a person in a non-EU country or directly linked to the export of goods outside the EU or the making of arrangements for such services.

1.31 Input tax attributable to exempt supplies or to a non-business activity is not recoverable. Special rules (VAT Regulations 1995, regs 99–111) apply to determine how much input tax may be recovered where a taxable person makes both exempt and taxable supplies, namely:

(a) input tax incurred on supplies used exclusively for making taxable supplies is recoverable in full;

(b) input tax incurred on supplies used exclusively for making exempt supplies or for an activity other than making taxable supplies is irrecoverable;

(c) input tax incurred on supplies used for making both taxable supplies and exempt supplies (or non-business use) is recoverable in the same proportion as the value of the taxable supplies bears to the value of all supplies.

An additional step is required where the taxable person makes 'out of country' supplies (see VAT Regulations 1995, reg 103 and *Liverpool Institute for Performing Arts v C & E Comrs [2001] STC 891)*(**Case Summary 40**).

1.32 Where input tax is eligible for recovery, it is recovered on the VAT return for the accounting period in which the input tax is incurred. Input tax cannot be reclaimed unless a valid tax invoice is held (although input tax can be reclaimed on supplies from a person who is not registered but is required to be registered even though invoices are not issued – see *Greenall* (1987) VAT decision 2362 and *Ellen Garage (Oldham) Ltd [1994] VATTR 392* but also see *C & E Comrs v Pennystar Ltd [1996] STC 163)*. Customs will in some circumstances permit recovery of tax purported to have been charged by an unregistered trader who is not required to be registered (Notice 48 Extra-statutory Concessions (March 2002) para 3.9).

What VAT is deductible?

1.33 The categories of potentially deductible VAT are set out in article 17(2) of the Sixth VAT Directive. Assuming all other conditions for deduction are met, a taxable person is entitled to deduct VAT due or paid on:

(a) goods or services supplied or to be supplied to the taxable person by another taxable person;

(b) goods imported by the taxable person;

(c) a self-supply on use of own goods or services by a taxable person (Sixth VAT Directive, arts 5(7)(a) and 6(3)) and dispatch and acquisition of own goods between Member States (Sixth VAT Directive, art 28A(6));

(d) an intra-Community acquisition of goods (Sixth VAT Directive, art 28A(1)(a)).

1.34 The UK legislation uses the term 'input tax' to cover VAT which is deductible and VAT which is not deductible. VAT which is not input tax can never be deducted. Input tax is a term which does not appear in the First VAT Directive and appears in the Sixth VAT Directive only in the context of special schemes or situations (see article 12(3) final paragraph on the gold scheme, art 28(3)(g) derogating from the tour operators margin scheme and Annex E paragraph 11 referring to transitional arrangements for buildings supplied other than before first occupation). Input tax means (VATA 1994, s 24(1)):

(a) VAT on supplies to a taxable person (ie a person registered or required to be registered for VAT in the UK) of goods or services which are used or to be used for the purpose of any business carried on or to be carried on by the taxable person (VATA 1994, s 24(1)(a));

(b) VAT on the acquisition by a taxable person (ie a person registered or required to be registered for VAT in the UK) from another EU member state of any goods which are used or to be used for the purpose of any business carried on or to be carried on by the taxable person (VATA 1994, s 24(1)(b));

(c) VAT on the importation by a taxable person (ie a person registered or required to be registered for VAT in the UK) from outside the EU of any goods which are used or to be used for the purpose of any business carried on or to be carried on by the taxable person (VATA 1994, s 24(1)(c)).

VAT arising on deemed supplies and acquisitions is also treated as input tax (eg VAT chargeable under the reverse charge procedure – VATA 1994, s 8(1)).

1.35 In addition, VAT charged on supplies of goods or services in and importations of goods into a Member State is potentially deductible by a taxable person (as defined in the Sixth VAT Directive) in another Member State or even in a non-EU country under the procedures laid down in the Eighth VAT Directive (which is implemented in the UK by VAT Regulations 1995, Regs 173–184) for repayments to EU taxable persons and the Thirteenth VAT Directive (which is implemented in the UK by VAT Regulations 1995, Regs 185–197) for repayments to non-EU taxable persons. Eligibility for a refund is subject to the conditions set out in Sixth VAT Directive, art 17. See **1.131** below for further details.

1.36 For VAT to be deductible, the goods or services on which the VAT is charged must have a direct and immediate link with (i e be cost components of and used to make) one of the following:

- Taxable transactions (i e supplies of goods or services made in the country and subject to VAT at the standard rate or a reduced rate) (Sixth VAT Directive, art 17(2)).
- Supplies in another country which would be taxable if made in the country (out of country taxable supplies) (Sixth VAT Directive, art 17(3)(a)).
- Certain exempt supplies (exempt with refund supplies) (Sixth VAT Directive, art 17(3)(b)).
- Certain exempt insurance and financial services either supplied to persons established outside the EU or directly linked with goods for export outside the EU (out-of-country specified exempt supplies) (Sixth VAT Directive, art 17(3)(c)).

The provisions of article 17 of the Sixth VAT Directive are implemented in the UK by VATA 1994, s 26(1)–(2) which provides that input tax is allowable to the extent that it is attributable to:

- Taxable supplies (i e supplies in the UK which are subject to VAT at the standard rate, a reduced rate or the zero rate).
- Supplies outside the UK which would be taxable if made within the UK (out-of-country supplies).
- Specified exempt supplies outside the UK.

VAT on supplies that are 'used or to be used' in making the supplies listed above is recoverable. This means that it is not only activities that have taken place that need to be identified in determining whether or not VAT is deductible but also activities intended for the future need to be taken into account.

What is meant by 'used'?

1.37 The use of the word 'used' in article 17 and its linkage with the taxable activity of the taxpayer seeking a deduction indicates that a cost item must be a component of a taxable supply of goods or services for the VAT incurred to be deducted. The ECJ has consistently stressed that use implies a 'direct and immediate' link between the supply on which the VAT sought to be deducted is incurred (the 'cost component') and the activity that gives the right to deduct.

1.38 In *Midland Bank plc v C & E Comrs (C-98/98) [2000] STC 501* (**Case Summary 35**), the dispute before the national court concerned whether Midland

Bank, which carried out both exempt transactions and taxable transactions, could deduct in full VAT incurred on legal services in relation to defending a claim for damages brought against it in relation to a previous supply in respect of which VAT was fully recoverable. The ECJ held in *Midland Bank* that (paragraph 26):

> 'A taxable person who makes transactions in respect of which VAT is deductible and transactions in respect of which it is not may deduct the VAT in respect of the goods or services acquired by him, provided that such goods or services have a direct and immediate link with the output transactions in respect of which VAT is deductible, without it being necessary to take into account art 17(2), (3) or (5) of the Sixth Directive. However, such a taxable person cannot deduct in its entirety the VAT charged on input services where they have been utilised not for the purpose of carrying out a deductible transaction but in the context of activities which are no more than the consequence of making such a transaction, unless that person can show by means of objective evidence that the expenditure involved in the acquisition of such services is part of the various cost components of the output transaction.'

1.39 The ECJ explained that (paragraph 30):

> 'It follows from [the principle in article 2 of the First VAT Directive] as well as from the rule enshrined in the judgment of *BLP Group plc v C & E Comrs (C-4/94) [1995] STC 424 at 437, paragraph 19* according to which, in order to give rise to the right to deduct, the goods or services acquired must have a direct and immediate link with the taxable transactions, that the right to deduct the VAT charged on such goods or services presupposes that the expenditure incurred in obtaining them was part of the cost components of the taxable transactions. Such expenditure must therefore be part of the costs of the output transactions which utilise the goods and services acquired. That is why those cost components must generally have arisen before the taxable person carried out the taxable transactions to which they relate.'

Since the ECJ in *Midland Bank* said that it was for the national court to apply the test and decide whether or not the appellant could by objective evidence show that the expenditure in question was linked with the output tax of a specific transaction, it is clear that some costs that are incurred subsequent to a transaction may be cost components of a particular transaction rather than of a part of the business or business as a whole. The distinction appears to be that a cost that is an inevitable concomitant of doing business (even if the extent is unknown at the time the output transaction is concluded) is a cost component while a transaction which is the simply a consequence of entering into any transaction is an overhead of the business as a whole and not of the particular transaction in respect of which it arose.

1.40 In *C & E Comrs v Wiggett Construction Ltd [2001] STC 933*, the High Court, applying *Midland Bank* and other cases, held that the correct test for attribution of input tax is that:

(a) the input must be 'objectively linked' to the taxable transaction;

(b) the link must be 'direct and immediate'; and

(c) the input must be a cost component of the taxable transaction.

The High Court held that the Tribunal's decision was based on its facts and, as the Tribunal had used the correct test, it could not be disturbed. Customs and Excise did not appeal *Wiggett* further.

What VAT is not deductible?

1.41 Article 17(2) of the Sixth VAT Directive describes the scope of the right to deduct in positive terms in that all VAT incurred by a taxable person on goods and services is deductible in so far as it is used for the purposes of the taxable person's taxable transactions. From the terms of article 17(2) it is possible to state the scope of the right to deduct negatively and determine what VAT is not deductible. VAT incurred by a taxable person on goods and services is not deductible in so far as the goods and services are:

(a) supplied or to be supplied to someone other than the taxable person; or

(b) used by the taxable person for:

- Non-business transactions (eg private use and goods imported from outside the EU for private purposes (VATA 1994, s 27));
- Exempt transactions (subject to the partial exemption de minimis limits, Value Added Tax Regulations 1995, SI 1995/2518, reg 106);
- Outside the scope transactions (eg non-supplies, passive investment activities).

1.42 VAT incurred on certain categories of expenditure is never eligible for deduction even if the expenditure is for business purposes. The Sixth Directive, art 17(6) provides that member states may agree what expenditure will not give rise to a deduction. While the intention was that this should be determined within a period of six years from the coming into force of the Directive (ie about 1984), no such agreement has been reached although a number of proposals have been put forward. In any event, art 17(6) states that:

> 'Value added tax shall in no circumstances be deductible on expenditure which is not strictly business expenditure, such as that on luxuries, amusements or entertainment.'

Pending agreement, article 17(6) gives member states the power to retain exclusions from deductions that were in force when the Directive came into force. When the Directive came into force in 1978, the UK had provisions disallowing the deduction of VAT incurred on the purchase of cars and on business entertainment. There is also a block on recovery of input tax on articles of a kind not ordinarily installed by builders as fixtures in new houses. Since then, a further restriction has been brought into effect, ie the restriction on the deduction of VAT on directors' accommodation. Each of these restrictions is discussed below.

1.43 There are further exceptions to the right to deduct contained in special measures (Sixth VAT Directive, art 28(3)(d) and (g)) and derogations under Sixth VAT Directive, art 27. In addition, the deduction rules have been modified in relation to certain special schemes, eg the margin and flat rate schemes

Motor cars

1.44 VAT on the supply, acquisition or importation of a motor car is not deductible unless certain conditions are met. The provisions (VAT (Input Tax) Order 1992, art 7) are extremely complex and have given rise to numerous disputes in the VAT and Duties Tribunal and the Courts. In general terms, VAT is not deductible unless the car cannot be available for any non-business use. VAT on the motor car is deductible if the car is to be used exclusively for business purposes and will not be available for private use. It is important to note that it is availability for private use and not actual use for private purposes that determines whether or not the VAT will be deductible.

In *C & E Comrs v Upton (t/a Fagomatic) [2002] STC 640* (**Case Summary 43**), *CA* the Court of Appeal upheld the judgment of the High Court which had overturned the decision of a VAT and Duties Tribunal that Mr Upton's Lamborghini was used exclusively for purposes of his business as a cigarette vending machine operator. The Court distinguished between article 7(2E) of the 1992 Order, which refers to the use that a car is put to, and article 7(2G), which refers to intention to make available for private use. Peter Gibson LJ observed:

> 'The very fact of [an individual taxable person's] deliberate acquisition of the car whereby he makes himself the owner of the car and controller of it means that at least ordinarily he must intend to make it available to himself for private use, even if he never intends to use it privately.'

In summary, where an individual taxable person acquires a car it will always be regarded as made available for private use unless the taxable person takes steps to make private use of the car impossible. Mr Upton had sought motor insurance which covered business use only and forbade private use but was told that the insurer did not have policies that exclude private use.

1.45 VAT on the supply, acquisition or importation of a motor car is also deductible if the motor car is to be used for specified purposes, namely:

i. as stock in trade, ie it is held for resale by a motor manufacturer or dealer;

ii. for letting in connection with the Motability scheme for disabled drivers;

iii. as a mini-cab, self-drive car or for driving instruction.

The block on deduction of input VAT applies to the VAT on the car and also any accessories fitted at the time of purchase. Input tax on accessories fitted subsequently may be deductible if they are for business purposes.

1.46 If the vehicle is not a motor car, VAT will be deductible subject to the normal rules. The blocking provisions do not apply to other types of vehicles eg a company van or a motorcycle. In respect of such vehicles, if there is any private use the business can either disallow a proportion of VAT on the purchase of the motor vehicle as representing the VAT on private use or can deduct all VAT on purchase and then account for VAT on the deemed output, being the cost of providing the private use. The question of what is a motor car is therefore important. Motor car is defined in VAT (Input Tax) Order 1992, art 2 as any motor vehicle of a kind normally used on public roads which has three or more wheels and either:

- is constructed or adapted solely or mainly for the carriage of passengers; or
- has roofed accommodation to the rear of the driver's seat that is fitted with side windows or adapted for the fitting of rear windows.

The following are not motor cars:

- vehicles that are capable of carrying only one passenger or can carry ten or more seated passengers;
- vehicles that weigh more than three tonnes unladen or which are designed to carry a payload of more than one tonne;
- ambulances, prison vans and caravans;
- certain special purpose vehicles.

Business entertainment

1.47 A deduction is not allowed on goods or services on which VAT is incurred if the goods or services are used for the purposes of business entertainment (VAT (Input Tax) Order 1992, art 5(1)). Business entertainment is defined as entertainment including hospitality of any kind provided by a taxable person in connection with a business carried on by him but excluding entertainment of employees and directors (provided the entertainment of the employees and directors is not merely incidental to the entertainment of others).

1.48 What does or does not constitute business entertainment is a complex issue of fact and law that has resulted in over 50 appeals to the VAT and Duties Tribunal and beyond. Examples of what has been held to be business entertainment include:

- Food and accommodation supplied to trainee agents of a pyramid selling organisation (*C & E Comrs v Shaklee International [1981] STC 776, CA*.
- The lease of a hospitality box at a rugby league ground *(Cockcroft & Co (Travel) Ltd v C & E Comrs (1995) VAT decision 11800)*.
- A party for a premiere of a film (*Entertainment Group of Companies Ltd v C & E Comrs [2000] V & DR 447*).

Examples of what has not been held to be business entertainment include:

- Hotel expenses of visiting football teams taking part in the European Football Cup which were met by the home club (*Celtic Football and Athletic Club Ltd v C & E Comrs [1983] STC 470*).

- Meals and refreshments provided to delegates nominated by sponsors of a conference organised by the appellant (*Webster Communications International v C & E Comrs [1997] V & DR 173*)
- Meals provided by a television company to participants in a television show where the appellant had a legal obligation to provide the meals (*C & E Comrs v Kilroy Television Co Ltd [1997] STC 901, QB* (**Case Summary 28**).

The cases indicate that business entertainment does not include entertainment or hospitality which is:

(a) provided under a contractual obligation (even if the recipients of the hospitality provide no consideration); or

(b) incidental to some business objective; or

(c) paid for even if the amount charged is only nominal provided it is not so small that the entertainment is effectively supplied free (*Ernst & Young v C & E Comrs [1997] V & DR 183* (**Case Summary 29**)*)*

1.49 Where input tax is used partly for business entertainment and partly for other purposes, it should be apportioned (*Thorn EMI v C & E Comrs [1995] STC 674, CA*). In that case, the company had stands at air shows that were used both for hospitality and to hold discussions with potential purchasers. The Court of Appeal held that article 17 of the EC Sixth Directive did not permit the exclusion of all credit for input tax where VAT was incurred partly for business purposes.

Directors' and staff accommodation

1.50 VAT on goods and services supplied, acquired or imported by a company in connection with the provision of accommodation for domestic purposes to a director or a person connected with a director is not deductible. VATA 1994, s 24(3) provides that such supplies are not treated as used or to be used for the purposes of business. A director is broadly defined but only in relation to a company. Connected person is also widely defined and includes the director's wife or husband and any relative of the director or director's wife or husband as well as the husband or wife of such a relative. Relative is not defined. It is only the VAT on domestic accommodation that is not deductible. The VAT on accommodation provided when a director travels on the business of the employer company will be deductible in the same way as VAT on any other employee's expenditure.

Business gifts

1.51 Gifts of goods or services are not, in principle, subject to VAT because they are not provided for consideration but Sixth VAT Directive, arts 5(6) and 6(2) provide that free supplies by a taxable person are treated as supplies made for consideration. In the case of free supplies of or using goods, the supply is only treated as made for consideration if the VAT on the goods or their component parts was wholly or partly deductible. Samples or gifts of small value provided by a taxable person for the purposes of his business are not to be treated as made for consideration. In the UK, a business gift is not treated as a supply of goods provided that the cost of all business gifts made by the taxable person to the same person in the same year is not more than £50. Samples are not treated as supplies of goods except that where a number of identical samples are given to the same person (even if on different occasions), only one is not treated as a supply of goods. VAT incurred on goods to be used as business gifts or samples is deductible.

1.52 If VAT is chargeable on the gift or sample (e g where the £50 limit has been breached), the recipient can deduct that VAT as input tax subject to the normal rules. The donor cannot issue a VAT invoice because there has not been a supply but Customs and Excise accept a tax certificate as evidence to support a claim for recovery of input tax. The certificate should describe the goods, give the amount of output VAT and state: 'No payment is necessary for these goods. Output tax has been accounted for on the supply.'

Margin schemes and flat-rate schemes

1.53 There are a number of special schemes which aim to reduce the administrative burden of VAT. One type of scheme is the margin scheme by which a taxable person is subject to VAT not on turnover but on the margin or profit on each transaction (or, in certain cases, on transactions globally). The VAT is calculated by reference to the margin, i e the difference between the cost, including VAT, of goods and services supplied to the taxable person and the total amount received by the taxable person from the customer. There are margin schemes for travel agents and dealers in second hand goods, works of art, collectors' items and antiques (Sixth VAT Directive, arts 26 and 26A). Article 4 of the VAT (Input Tax) Order 1992, SI 1992/3222, excludes VAT on the supply, acquisition or importation of goods to be sold under the second hand goods schemes and article 12 of the VAT (Tour Operators) Order 1987, SI 1987/1806, does the same in relation to supplies to tour operators.

1.54 There are also flat-rate schemes for small businesses and farmers. Subject to certain conditions, a taxable person using a flat-rate scheme calculates VAT due by applying a flat-rate percentage, which differs according to the category of business, to total turnover. A taxable person using a flat-rate scheme cannot deduct VAT on supplies, imports or acquisitions as the flat-rate percentage includes an allowance for input tax.

Second hand goods schemes

1.55 VAT legislation provides for the value of taxable supplies of second hand goods to be determined by reference to the margin between the selling price of such goods and the cost of purchase or other acquisition of the goods. No deduction is allowed in respect of the cost of purchase or acquisition but VAT on the cost of repairs to goods, selling expenses and business overheads will be deductible in the normal way.

Tour operators margin scheme

1.56 Tour operators are required to use a margin scheme in respect of designated travel services. The VAT (Tour Operators) Order 1987, SI 1987/1806, provides that VAT on the costs of a designated travel service is not deductible. However, VAT on other costs, such as selling costs and business overheads, is deductible.

Flat-rate schemes

1.57 The flat-rate scheme for small businesses allows businesses that have a taxable turnover of £100,000 or less to account for VAT on the basis of a fixed percentage of their total turnover (including any other supplies and income). The flat-rates applicable to the different business are lower than the standard rate but a business that applies to join the scheme is not allowed any deduction for input tax incurred. There are, however, two exceptions to this for small businesses using the flat-rate scheme.

(a) VAT incurred on goods costing more than £2,000, including VAT, is recoverable provided the goods are of a capital nature and were not acquired:

- for the purpose of resale or incorporation into goods supplied by him,
- for consumption by him within one year, or
- to generate income by being leased, let or hired.

(b) A business can recover VAT incurred before registration on stocks and assets on hand at registration subject to certain conditions.

1.58 A business within the scheme must nevertheless issue tax invoices in respect of any taxable supply in the normal way, i e if the recipient of any supply by a small business is a taxable person, he can require a tax invoice and recover the VAT incurred in the normal way. The rate of tax to be applied on any tax invoice will be that which would have applied had the flat rate not been in force, i e 17.5% unless the supply would be subject to the reduced rate.

1.59 The flat-rate scheme for farmers is different because it is not a simplified method for accounting for VAT but is an alternative to VAT registration for farmers. A farmer cannot join the scheme if the value of his non-farming supplies is above the VAT registration threshold. A flat-rate farmer does not charge and account for VAT and therefore is not required to submit returns. The flat-rate farmer simply charges and keeps a flat rate addition of 4% on goods or goods and services, even where these sales would be zero-rated for VAT, sold to VAT registered customers. The flat-rate addition is not VAT but the VAT registered customers can deduct the addition on their VAT returns as if it were input tax and subject to the normal rules. The flat-rate addition is not charged to customers who are not registered for VAT or are themselves flat-rate farmers because they are unable to reclaim the addition. The flat-rate farmer cannot deduct any VAT incurred on purchases as the flat-rate addition is intended to be compensation for losing VAT on purchases.

Car mileage

1.60 Customs and Excise allow businesses to deduct an amount of VAT in respect of mileage allowances paid to employees for use of their own cars for business purposes. The allowance is intended to cover VAT on the supply of petrol – there is no allowance in respect of the actual cost of the car. It is understood that the European Commission is considering the question of whether or not the principles established by the ECJ in *EC Commission v Netherlands (C-338/98) [2001] ECR I-8265* are applicable. The ECJ found in that case that the Netherlands had failed to comply with its obligations under the Sixth VAT Directive by allowing taxpayers to deduct the underlying VAT on mileage allowances paid by employers. The two cases are not identical since in *Commission v Netherlands*, the facts show that an allowance was made in respect of the employees' costs of acquiring the cars. Since the employees did not acquire the cars as taxable persons, the VAT was clearly not deductible. The situation may well be different in the case of the UK where VAT on the petrol would be deductible if purchased by the employer.

Deduction of VAT attributable to non-supplies

1.61 Difficult questions arise where VAT is incurred on supplies of goods and services used in respect of a transaction that is not a supply by the taxable person at all. The two most common types of transaction to cause such difficulty are:

- the sale or purchase of a business by way of transfer as a going concern ('TOGC');
- the acquisition of a business or shares in a company, particularly when the consideration given is the issue of shares or debentures.

Sale of business as TOGC

1.62 The ECJ provided guidance on the correct approach to deduction of VAT incurred on the expenses of a sale by way of TOGC in *Abbey National plc v C & E Comrs (C-408/98) [2001] STC 297* (**Case Summary 39**). There the ECJ concluded that:

> 'Where a member state has made use of the option in article 5(8) of the Sixth Directive, so that the transfer of a totality of assets or part thereof is regarded as not being a supply of goods, the costs incurred by the transferor for services acquired in order to effect that transfer form part of that taxable person's overheads and thus in principle have a direct and immediate link with the whole of his economic activity. If, therefore, the transferor effects both transactions in respect of which VAT is deductible and transactions in respect of which it is not, it follows from article 17(5) of the Sixth Directive that he may deduct only that proportion of the VAT which is attributable to the former transactions. However, if the various services acquired by the transferor in order to effect the transfer have a direct and immediate link with a clearly defined part of his economic activities, so that the costs of those services form part of the

overheads of that part of the business, and all the transactions relating to that part of the business are subject to VAT, he may deduct all the VAT charged on his costs of acquiring those services.'

1.63 The decision of the ECJ in *Abbey National* showed that Customs' previous policy on recovery of input tax by the vendor of a TOGC was wrong and that input tax incurred on the sale of businesses as going concerns had not been recovered correctly in the UK. Following the decision of the ECJ in *Abbey National,* Customs adopted a new policy (see Business Brief 8/2001, 2 July 2001) as follows:

> 'VAT incurred on services that wholly relate to the transfer of part of a business, should be treated as an overhead of that part of the business.
>
> Where that part of the business makes only taxable supplies, then the VAT incurred is deductible. Conversely, where only exempt supplies are made then the VAT incurred is not deductible. In instances where both taxable and exempt supplies are made then the VAT incurred is partly deductible, determined by reference to the partial exemption method in place. If the partial exemption method in place fails to achieve a fair and reasonable result Customs may be prepared to approve an alternative method.'

The new policy applies to transfers on or after 1 August 2001 but businesses may apply it from an earlier date, subject to the three-year limit, provided they do so consistently.

Purchase of a business as TOGC

1.64 Business Brief 7/96 of 3 May 1996 stated that, from 1 June 1996, the policy on recovery of input tax in relation to the acquisition of assets by way of a transfer of a business as a going concern changed. Input tax attributable to the purchase of a business as a TOGC is recoverable as follows:

(a)	Purchase of taxable business:	recoverable in full
(b)	Purchase of exempt business:	not recoverable
(c)	Purchase of mixed use business:	recoverable at same rate as purchaser's general overheads

The decision of the Court of Appeal in *C & E Comrs v UBAF Bank Ltd [1996] STC 372* confirmed that the revised view of the recoverability of input tax on purchases of businesses as going concerns was not a concession but simply an application of the law on recovery of VAT.

Purchase of shares in a company

1.65 The issue in relation to deduction of VAT incurred in relation to the acquisition of shares is always whether the VAT is attributable to the purchaser's general business activities, a future exempt supply of the shares or an investment activity such as the receipt of dividends which is outside the scope of VAT. If the VAT is attributable to either of the two latter activities, it is not deductible.

1.66 In *C & E Comrs v UBAF Bank Ltd [1996] STC 372* (**Case Summary 21**), *CA* a bank incurred input tax on professional fees in acquiring shares in leasing companies. It arranged for the leasing companies to transfer the leasing business to itself on the following day and claimed to deduct the input tax in full as attributable to the taxable supplies to be made by its leasing business. The Court of Appeal agreed that the input tax was correctly attributable to the bank's leasing activities, since as a matter of fact the purpose underlying the acquisition of shares was to expand those leasing activities. The acquisition of the shares and subsequent transfer of the businesses were so closely linked as to be regarded as one and as, in turn, directly linked to the making of taxable supplies by the bank. The fact that the input tax was at one remove from the taxable supplies did not prevent it being purposively connected with them since there was no intervening supply by the bank between the acquisition of shares and businesses and the subsequent use of the acquired assets in making taxable supplies.

1.67 In *Cibo Participations SA v Directeur régional des impots du Nord-Pas-de-Calais (C-16/00) [2002] STC 460* (**Case Summary 41**), the French tax authority refused to allow Cibo to deduct input tax on various services in connection with the acquisition of shares in its subsidiaries. The services in question included the auditing of the companies, assistance with the negotiation of the purchase price of the shares, organising the take-over of the companies and legal and tax services. The ECJ held that, following *Floridienne SA and Berginvest SA v Belgian (C-142/99) [2000] STC 1044* (**Case Summary 37**), the involvement of a holding company in the management of companies in which it has acquired a shareholding constitutes an economic activity where it entails carrying out transactions such as the supply by a holding company to its subsidiaries of administrative, financial, commercial and technical services. The ECJ considered whether a holding company can deduct VAT charged on expenditure incurred on services obtained in connection with the acquisition of a shareholding in a subsidiary. The ECJ held that, although there was no direct and immediate link between the services and any output transaction in respect of which VAT is deductible, the costs of those services are part of the taxable person's general costs and as such, are cost components of an undertaking's products. Such services have, in principle, a direct and immediate link with the taxable person's business as a whole and are deductible in accordance with its partial exemption calculation.

1.68 In *Southampton Leisure Holdings plc v C & E Comrs [2002] V & DR 235* (**Case Summary 44**), Southampton Leisure Holdings ('SLH') sought to acquire the share capital of Southampton Football Club ('the Club'). SLH issued shares to the Club's shareholders in exchange for their own shares in the Club. SLH and the Club remained separately registered for VAT. SLH incurred VAT on professional fees which it sought to recover in part on the basis that the VAT was partly attributable to management services provided by SLH to the Club. The Tribunal held the appeal raised three questions, namely:

(a) Was there a direct link between the services supplied to SLH and the supply of management services by SLH?

(b) Was there a direct link between the services supplied to SLH and SLH's business as a whole?

(c) Were all the services used by SLH for the share issue?

In relation to the first issue, the Tribunal accepted that *Cibo Participations* (see above) was a binding decision that there is no direct and immediate link between the costs of acquiring a subsidiary company and a subsequent supply of management services. In relation to the second issue, Customs argued that an exempt supply of shares prior to making an acquisition constituted a chain-breaking event as a result of which there was a direct link between the services and the exempt supply of the shares. The Tribunal held, following *Cibo*, that if there had been only an acquisition without any issue of shares then the services would have been directly linked to SLH's business as a whole allowing SLH to treat the VAT as residual input tax. The final issue was whether the services were wholly used in connection with the share issue. The Tribunal followed *RAP Group plc v C & E Comrs [2000] STC 980* (**Case Summary 36**) and looked at each of the invoices in turn and concluded that, for the most part, the services received were not used exclusively in the exempt supply of shares and should therefore be treated as part of SLH's residual input tax.

1.69 Customs and Excise decided not to appeal the tribunal's decision in *Southampton Leisure Holdings* (Business Brief 23/02, 20 August 2002) and have revised their policy. Customs now accept that, in a merger and acquisition or management buy-out, VAT on any supplies of professional services which include:

(a) acting as financial adviser;

(b) the drafting of service contracts for the directors;

(c) the due diligence review of the target company's affairs the investigation of title and/or the valuation of that company's property; or

(d) coordinating the transaction

is residual input tax and recoverable in accordance with the person's partial exemption method. In the case of an issue of shares to persons within the EU and to persons belonging outside the EU, then the deductible proportion of tax is to be determined on a 'use' basis under VAT Regulations 1995, reg 103(2).

1.70 Customs' view is that the decision in *Southampton Leisure Holdings* has no application where shares are issued for subscription (eg an IPO or rights issue) because, in such cases, the services are used exclusively for the exempt supply of an issue of shares. This view has not been accepted by the VAT and Duties Tribunal when challenged by appellants with good evidence of alternative or additional purposes for the issue of shares. In *Halladale Group plc v C & E Comrs [2003] SWTI 1803, (VAT decision 18218* (**Case Summary 50**)*)*, the Tribunal allowed Halladale to recover all the input VAT on its Alternative Investment Market ('AIM') listing because the input supplies were not used exclusively for the purposes of the exempt supply of shares but partly for the exempt supply and partly for the general purposes of the business (raising profile, making shares tradable etc). The same treatment should apply to any listing, not just one on AIM. Halladale won on a question of fact, namely what were the input supplies used for? The case turned on its facts and therefore is of limited value as a precedent but it indicates a possible line of argument to take where the facts are right and evidence is available.

Abortive transactions

1.71 An abortive transaction raises the issue of whether or not an adjustment has to be made in respect of VAT deducted on the basis that the transaction would proceed as intended. There are two circumstances in which the issue may arise: where nothing happens and where something different happens.

1.72 The situation of a business not making any supplies commonly occurs where a person starts a business with the intention of making taxable supplies but events intervene and no supplies are made. The original UK legislation providing for 'intending trader' registration allowed Customs and Excise to claw back any input tax recovered if the intended activity did not take place. That provision was challenged in the case of *Merseyside Cablevision Ltd v C & E Comrs [1987] VATTR 134* (**Case Summary 6**). In *Merseyside*, the taxpayer was a company that had been set up to provide cable services. However, it was unable to proceed with the intended undertaking and Customs and Excise sought to recover the VAT originally claimed. The Tribunal followed *DA Rompelman & EA Rompelman-van-Deelen v Minister van Financiën (C-268/83) [1985] ECR 655* (**Case Summary 4**) in which the ECJ held that a person who carried on activities which were preparatory to the carrying on of an economic activity was to be treated as a person carrying on that economic activity.

1.73 The ECJ reached a similar conclusion in the case of *Intercommunale voor Zeewaterontzilting (in liquidation) v Belgian (C-110/94) [1996] STC 569* ('*INZO*') (**Case Summary 20**). Inzo had reclaimed VAT in respect of a study into the economic feasibility of a project to build a desalination plant. The study showed that the project was not viable and the company went into liquidation. The Belgian tax authorities sought to recover the VAT charged on the basis that no taxable supplies had been made. The ECJ held that once a person was a taxable person, that status could not be retroactively withdrawn. INZO was therefore a 'taxable person' under the Sixth Directive, art 4 and the input tax on that activity was deductible and could not be clawed back.

1.74 In both *Merseyside* and *INZO*, the taxpayers made no taxable supplies and aborted the intended activities. There was therefore no question of whether or not any input tax has to be adjusted on the basis that the underlying supplies were used for another purpose. The issue of what happens when an activity is aborted and another takes its place was considered in the case of *Belgium v Ghent Coal Terminal NV (C-37/95) [1998] STC 260* (**Case Summary 30**). The company had set out to develop a piece of land as a coal terminal but prior to starting the work, it was required to exchange the land for another piece of land and so never made the intended taxable supplies. The Belgian tax authorities, as in *INZO*, sought to claw back the tax deducted by the taxpayer. The ECJ upheld the taxpayer's right to deduct but observed that a subsequent supply may give rise to a requirement to adjust under article 20 of the Sixth Directive.

1.75 The principles that emerge from these cases are that once a person is able to establish that he is acting as a taxable person, he is entitled to be registered for VAT and to deduct VAT on any taxable activity. Once the right to deduct has been exercised, there is no provision allowing the VAT to be clawed back. However, in certain circumstances, there may be a requirement to adjust input tax incurred.

1.76 VAT Notice 706/1 Partial Exemption states at paragraph 8.2:

> 'Abortive supplies
>
> In addition to changes of intention before the goods or services are used (the "clawback" and 'payback' provisions), there may be occasions when an intended supply does not take place because a project is aborted. In such circumstances, when the goods and services are not used to make any supply, no adjustment to the initial claim of input tax is required.
>
> However, where a project is aborted and the goods and services are used to make a different supply to that originally intended, an input tax adjustment will still usually be appropriate, using the "clawback" and "payback" provisions above.
>
> Note: the above reflects a revised Customs and Excise policy where a project is aborted or frustrated. This follows the European Court decision in the case of Ghent Coal Terminal NV. Previously, the UK had always treated the input tax on such goods and services as residual input tax to be apportioned in accordance with the partial exemption method of the business. This is no longer correct and the new procedure should now be followed.'

1.77 The change of policy is bad news for fully taxable companies which call off share issues, although it may be good news for certain exempt businesses. The new policy may, in any event, be an over-simplification of the ECJ's decision in *Ghent Coal Terminal* as it ignores the fact that the ECJ specifically ruled:

> 'Article 17 of the Sixth Directive must be construed as allowing a taxable person acting as such to deduct the VAT payable by him on goods or services supplied to him for the purpose of investment work intended to be used in connection with taxable transactions. The right to deduct remains acquired where, by reason of circumstances beyond his control, the taxable person has never made use of those goods or services for the purpose of carrying out taxable transactions. A supply of investment goods during the adjustment period, where such occurs, may give rise to an adjustment of the deduction under the [capital goods scheme].'

The High Court in *Tremerton Ltd v C & E Comrs [1999] STC 1039* (**Case Summary 32**) declined to follow *Ghent Coal Terminal* in a similar case that dealt with adjustments to input tax recovery where intended taxable supplies were not made but the capital goods scheme did not apply. Carnwath J held that the *Ghent*

Coal Terminal case only considered the original right to deduct under article 17 and was not binding in relation to article 20(1) because the issue of adjustments under article 20(1) was not in terms before the ECJ.

1.78 In *Grundstückgemeinschaft Schloßtrasse GbR v Finanzamt Paderborn (C-396/98) [2000] ECR I-4279* (**Case Summary 34**), a company acquired development rights in respect of building land. It subsequently elected to waive exemption in respect of the land. It began construction work in January 1994 and reclaimed input tax. The tax authority issued assessments to recover the tax, on the basis that the possibility of waiving exemption in such cases had been withdrawn by an amendment to German law which came into force on 1 January 1994 and had retrospective effect. The company appealed, contending that the retrospective restriction of its right to opt for taxation was a breach of the Community law principle of legitimate expectation. The case was referred to the ECJ, which held that the effect of EC Sixth Directive, art 17 was that input tax incurred on intended taxable supplies was deductible despite the subsequent change in the law. The ECJ observed that, under art 17(1), the right to deduct arose at the time when the deductible tax became chargeable. The ECJ held that 'in the absence of fraud or abuse and subject to any adjustments to be made' under the conditions laid down in art 20, the right of deduction was 'retained even if the taxable person has been unable to use the goods or services which gave rise to a deduction in the context of taxable transactions by reason of circumstances beyond his control'. In such circumstances, 'the taxable person is entitled immediately to deduct the VAT due or paid on the goods or services supplied with a view to the performance of the economic activities which it envisages carrying out'. The principles of the protection of legitimate expectations and of legal certainty 'preclude its being deprived retroactively of that right by a legislative amendment post-dating the supply of those goods or services'.

1.79 In the *Paderborn* case, the ECJ confirmed the principles established in *INZO* and *Ghent Coal Terminal* that a taxable person's right to deduct VAT under article 17 is retained, even where a legislative amendment after the date of supply of the inputs, but before any outputs are supplied by the person, deprives the taxable person of the ability to make taxable supplies. Unfortunately this is yet another example of a case where the ECJ chose not to explain precisely how article 17 interacts with article 20. In paragraph 42 of its judgment, the ECJ stated that:

> 'In the absence of fraud or abuse and subject to any adjustments to be made under the conditions laid down in article 20 of the Sixth Directive, entitlement to deduct, once it has arisen, is retained even if the taxable person has been unable to use the goods or services which gave rise to a deduction in the context of taxable transactions by reason of circumstances beyond its control.'

1.80 *Finanzamt Goslar v Brigitte Breitsohl (C-400/98) [2001] STC 355* (**Case Summary 33**) was released on the same day as the *Paderborn* case and makes an interesting comparison piece. The facts of *Breitsohl* are much closer to those of *Tremerton*. Mrs Breitsohl was unable to proceed with her business because she could not obtain sufficient bank finance. The main distinguishing feature between the *Breitsohl* and *Tremerton* cases is that Mrs Breitsohl elected to waive exemption in relation to her partially built property before selling it. Mrs Breitsohl always intended to use the premises for her taxable business but was prevented from doing so by her inability to raise the necessary finance. Mrs Breitsohl, therefore, sold the partially completed premises (a taxable supply of building works and an exempt supply of land) and made a tax return claiming repayment of the VAT incurred in relation to the initial construction of the buildings after it had become clear that she would not engage in her intended economic activity. The ECJ stated that the right to deduct, once it has arisen, is retained even where the economic activity is not taken up provided there is no fraud or abuse and subject to adjustment under art 20. In paragraph 52, the ECJ indicated that if Mrs Breitsohl had not elected, she would have had to carry out an adjustment of her deductions in accordance with the Sixth VAT Directive, art 20(3). This supposes that Mrs Breitsohl's property was a capital item. Unfortunately, there is no discussion of what the position would be if the premises were not a capital item. This decision appears to show that the inability to obtain finance may be regarded as circumstances beyond a person's control in the same way as the compulsory purchase order in the *Ghent Coal Terminal* case.

VAT incurred prior to registration for VAT or prior to incorporation

1.81 A taxpayer may incur VAT prior to the time when he is required to be registered and also before he is in fact registered for VAT (VAT Regulations 1995, reg 111). In addition, a person may incur VAT on expenditure in relation to a business prior to its incorporation. In both cases, provision exists under which Customs and Excise may allow the respective taxpayers to deduct VAT incurred prior to registration or incorporation as the case may be. In both cases, the VAT incurred is treated as input tax but according to the UK definition of input tax is not input tax because the taxpayer was not a taxable person at the time the VAT was incurred. This has some significance, eg in relation to the partial exemption de minimis limits, which only apply to input tax (VAT Regulations 1995, reg 106). A taxpayer cannot therefore make a claim to deduct pre-registration VAT on the basis that it is de minimis.

1.82 The VAT that may be deducted and the main conditions that have to be fulfilled for the VAT to be deductible are summarised in the table below:

Circumstances	Conditions
VAT incurred prior to registration for VAT on goods purchased for the purpose of a business carried on at the time or to be carried on	The goods had not been supplied by or consumed by the business prior to registration The normal rules (described above) allow the VAT to be deducted The VAT was incurred no more than three years prior to registration
VAT incurred prior to registration for VAT on services purchased for the purpose of a business carried on at the time or to be carried on	The services had not been supplied for the business or used by the business or goods supplied by it prior to registration The VAT was incurred within six months prior to registration (although this requirement is sometimes waived) The normal rules (described below) allow the VAT to be deducted
Supplies of goods and services supplied prior to incorporation	Must be supplied to a person who becomes a director, member or employee The recipient must not be a taxable person at the time The normal rules of deduction allow the VAT to be deducted

1.83 Because of the restrictions on recovering VAT incurred while not registered, it can be the case that an application for registration to be effected prior to the date of application can allow a better recovery of VAT. However, it should be noted that Customs and Excise will not always allow retrospective registration and, in any event, will never allow registration going back more than three years. Accordingly, where significant VAT is incurred, a business needs to ensure that it is registered at the correct time (see eg *P J & M L Edwards v C & E Comrs [1998] SWTI 1330 (VAT decision 15533).*

1.84 It should be noted that Customs and Excise take the view that only input tax that is directly attributable to taxable supplies made or intended to be made after registration is deductible (see eg *GN Byrd v C & E Comrs (1994) VAT decision 1275*; *Mark Jenkins Lifetime Financial Services t/a v C & E Comrs (1997) VAT decision 14784*; and *Trustees of Park Avenue Methodist Church v C & E Comrs [2001] SWTI 794 (VAT decision 17443)*. This is arguably correct under EC VAT law since it is arguable that prior to registration, the taxable person makes only exempt supplies (because the EC Sixth VAT Directive, art 24 rules for small businesses provide for their turnover to be exempted for VAT rather than excluding the small business from being a taxable person).

VAT incurred subsequent to deregistration

1.85 A business that ceases trading and deregisters would not normally be able to recover any VAT incurred after deregistration. However, provision is made for a refund procedure in certain cases (VAT Regulations 1995, SI 1995/2518, reg 111(5)–(7)). The deregistered person can claim VAT on services (but not goods) supplied to him after the date from which he ceased to be (or to be required to be) registered provided the services relate to taxable supplies of the business made before deregistration. A claim must be made on Form VAT 427 and must be made within three years of the date on which the supply of services was made.

How much VAT is deductible?

1.86 If goods or services are used both for purposes that entitle the taxpayer to deduct VAT and purposes in respect of which no entitlement exists, it must be apportioned (see Sixth VAT Directive, arts 17(5) and 19 and VATA 1994, s 26(3)). For some taxable persons, no difficulties arise because all their activities are taxable business activities and therefore there is no need to make any apportionment. However, for many other taxpayers some form of apportionment process is required.

Apportionment of VAT

1.87 The apportionment process can be summarised as follows:

Step 1 Determine the extent to which supplies, acquisitions and imports on which VAT is incurred are used for non-business purposes and exclude this from the deduction calculation completely (VATA 1994, s 24(1)).

Step 2 Determine the extent to which supplies, acquisitions and imports on which VAT is incurred are used or to be used to make either out of country taxable supplies (i e supplies outside the UK that would be taxable if made in the UK) or out-of-country specified exempt supplies (i e exempt supplies that are specified as giving a right to recovery when supplied to non-EU persons) – that VAT is deductible (VAT Regulations 1995, SI 1995/2518, reg 103(1)).

Step 3 Determine the extent to which supplies, acquisitions and imports on which VAT is incurred are used or to be used exclusively to make taxable supplies in the UK – that VAT is deductible (VAT Regulations 1995, SI 1995/2518, reg 101(2)(b)).

Step 4 Determine the extent to which supplies, acquisitions and imports on which VAT is incurred are used or to be used exclusively in making exempt supplies (including supplies made outside the UK that would be exempt if made in the UK but are not out-of-country specified exempt supplies) and other than in making taxable supplies – that VAT is not deductible (VAT Regulations 1995, SI 1995/2518, reg 101(2)(c)).

Step 5 Multiply any remaining VAT by the fraction produced by the value of taxable supplies in the UK over the value of all supplies (excluding out-of-country taxable supplies but including supplies made outside the UK that would be exempt if made in the UK and non-business supplies) (VAT Regulations 1995, SI 1995/2518, regs 101(2) or 102).

1.88 Although technically European VAT law only requires an apportionment to determine what VAT is deductible, in practice (as seen in steps 1 and 4 above) it is often easier to identify the non-deductible VAT first. However, the fact that there is no specific requirement to identify non-deductible VAT does have implications for record keeping since it means that there is no need to record separately VAT that is not deductible – it can simply be charged in the accounting records to whatever expenditure (capital or revenue) it relates. The only occasion when it may be necessary to identify non-deductible VAT will be when there is a need to determine whether it is within the de minimis provisions (VAT Regulations 1995, SI 1995/2518, reg 106).

Annual adjustment

1.89 At the end of each 'longer period' (usually, a VAT tax year but it can be shorter), the VAT originally deducted in each of the quarterly or monthly periods comprising that longer period must be re-calculated for the longer period as a whole using the method used in the quarterly or monthly periods (VAT Regulations 1995, SI 1995/2518, reg 107). The result of the re-calculation must be compared with the aggregate amount of VAT deducted in each of the quarterly or monthly periods. If there has been any over-deduction or under-deduction, the amount of the difference must be accounted for in the return for the accounting period after the end of the longer period.

Partial exemption override

1.90 In certain cases the initial turnover-based attribution must be adjusted according to use. The adjustment is known as the partial exemption override (VAT Regulations 1995, SI 1995/2518, regs 107A–E). The partial exemption override applies where a taxable person has residual input tax in excess of £50,000 (£25,000 for group undertakings not in a VAT group) and uses the partial exemption standard method to calculate the deductible amount. If the deductible amount so calculated differs substantially from one calculated according to the extent to which the goods or services are used or to be used by the taxable person or a successor in making taxable supplies, an adjustment must be made in the return for the accounting period after the end of the longer period. A difference is substantial if it exceeds £50,000 or 50 per cent of the amount of residual input tax for the longer period but is not less than £25,000. A successor is a person to whom a business is transferred as a going concern so that it is not a supply of goods or services.

1.91 There is no statutory or even recommended method of determining the use or intended use for the purpose of the override. Customs state that any calculation will be acceptable if it provides a fair and reasonable attribution of input tax (VAT Information Sheet 04/2002). Notwithstanding the introduction of the partial exemption override, Customs and Excise still consider that in the vast majority of cases, turnover will be an appropriate measure of use except that the turnover used should take into account any turnover that will accrue outside the current VAT accounting year that uses supplies made in the period. It is important to note that the 'partial exemption override' is not an adjustment based on a change in use of the inputs but an adjustment intended to reflect the taxpayer's original intended use of the inputs in question. The application of the override does not depend on any change in use or intended use but on the use or intended use at the time the VAT is incurred.

Adjustments of deductions

1.92 Both EU and UK VAT legislation contemplate only a limited right to adjust the amount of any input tax deducted. The principal situations where the taxpayer is either obliged to make an adjustment or might be able to choose to make an adjustment if favourable to him are limited to:

- When the inputs on which the VAT is borne are, before first use for the original intended purpose, applied to a purpose other than that originally intended, the original deduction must be adjusted (VAT Regulations 1995, SI 1995/2518, regs 108 and 109).
- If the VAT was incurred on any capital item as defined, then in each year during a specified adjustment period following the original deduction, an adjustment must be made if necessary to reflect any change in the level of use from the original period.

Adjustment of use

1.93 Article 20(1) of the Sixth VAT Directive provides that:

> 'The initial deduction shall be adjusted according to the procedures laid down by the Member States, in particular:
>
> (a) where that deduction was higher or lower than that to which the taxable person was entitled;
>
> (b) where after the return is made some change occurs in the factors used to determine the amount to be deducted, in particular where purchases are cancelled or price reductions are obtained; however, adjustment shall not be made in case of transactions remaining totally or partially unpaid and of destruction, loss or theft of property duly proved or confirmed, nor in the case of applications for the purpose of making gifts of small value and giving samples specified in Article 5(6). However, Member States may require adjustment in cases of transactions remaining totally or partially unpaid and of theft.'

1.94 The UK has implemented art 20(1) by VAT Regulations 1995, SI 1995/2518, regs 108 and 109. Regulation 108 applies where a taxable person has deducted VAT on the basis of an intention to make taxable supplies and reg 109 applies where a taxable person has not deducted VAT because the intention was to make exempt supplies. Where, before the intention is fulfilled, the actual use differs from the intention or the intention changes then regs 108 and 109 provide for an adjustment of the original deduction. The adjustment is only required if the change in intended use occurs within six years of the first day of the prescribed accounting period in which the attribution was determined. In the case of reg 108, the adjustment is effected by an entry on the VAT return accounting for the VAT which is no longer attributable to taxable supplies and is thus repayable to Customs and Excise. Regulation 109, which applies when the taxable person is entitled to a further deduction, provides that the adjustment is made by a separate application for a refund of the VAT. In fact, Customs and Excise have indicated that the taxable person should write to the local VAT office claiming repayment and when the amount to be repaid has been confirmed, enter that amount on the next VAT return.

1.95 The adjustment processes above are aimed only at changes in use for exempt and taxable supplies and do not apply to changes from intended business use to non-business use. The reason for this can be seen in the discussion on the treatment of non-business use of goods and services. If VAT has been deducted and an asset is subsequently allocated to non-business use, then VAT law provides that there is a supply of goods or services at the cost to the taxpayer of making that asset available for private use. If no VAT was deducted in the first place, then of course, the asset would not be a business asset and no VAT adjustment would be required

1.96 There is no provision permitting subsequent deduction of VAT that was not deducted when the asset was originally bought because at that time it was intended for private use, even if it is subsequently used for business use. The point was recently reinforced in the decision in *EC Commission v Netherlands (C-338/98) [2001] ECR I-8265* in which the European Court of Justice upheld a complaint by the European Commission that by allowing VAT to be deducted on flat rate allowances paid by employers to employees who used their cars for the purposes of the employer's business where the allowance included an element of depreciation, the Netherlands was in breach of its obligations under the Sixth VAT Directive.

1.97 Difficulties arise where when an asset is purchased, the taxpayer decides to disallow 50 per cent of any VAT as reflecting his intended private use. Subsequently, that use turns out to be significantly above or below the 50 per cent claimed. If the private use exceeds the original 50 per cent, it would appear to be possible to make a charge for private use of the business portion (ie the element on which VAT was recovered) but there does not appear to be any provision for an adjustment of the VAT disallowed downwards to reflect lower private use.

Capital items

1.98 Article 20(2) of the Sixth VAT Directive provides that:

> 'In the case of capital goods, adjustments shall be spread over five years including that in which the goods were acquired or manufactured. The annual adjustment shall be made only in respect of one-fifth of the tax imposed on the goods. The adjustment shall be made on the basis of the variations in the deduction entitlement in subsequent years in relation to that for the year in which the goods were acquired or manufactured.
>
> By way of derogation from the preceding sub-paragraph, Member States may base the adjustment on a period of five full years starting from the time at which the goods are first used.
>
> In the case of immovable property acquired as capital goods, the adjustment period may be extended up to 20 years.'

The remaining provisions of art 20 give member states considerable latitude in implementing the adjustment regime.

1.99 The UK has implemented art 20(1) by VAT Regulations 1995, SI 1995/2518, regs 112–116, known as the Capital Goods Scheme although the regulations refer to 'capital items'. The Capital Goods Scheme is a special scheme for adjusting the initial deduction of input tax in relation to certain defined capital items over a period of five or ten (usually annual) intervals where there is a change in the taxable person's VAT recovery rate.

1.100 The defined capital items within the scheme are:

(a) a computer or item of computer equipment of a value of £50,000 or more purchased, imported or acquired on or after 1 April 1990 (VAT Regulations 1995, SI 1995/2518, reg 113(a));

(b) an interest in any land, building (or part of a building) or civil engineering work (or part of a civil engineering work) acquired on or after 1 April 1990 by way of standard rated supply with a value of £250,000 or more excluding VAT and so much of that value as may consist of rent (other than rent payable, paid or invoiced for more than 12 months) (VAT Regulations 1995, SI 1995/2518, reg 113(b));

(c) an interest in, or right over, or licence to occupy, a building (or part of it) acquired for a relevant residential or a relevant charitable purpose which becomes treated as a taxable self-supply on or after 1 April 1990 by reason of a change of use and where the value of the initial zero rated supply is £250,000 or more (VAT Regulations 1995, SI 1995/2518, reg 113(c));

(d) where, on or after 1 April 1990 but before 1 March 1997, a developer is treated as receiving a self-supply of £250,000 or more by virtue of their granting an exempt right over, or licence to occupy a building or work, or themselves occupying or using it when not fully taxable (this refers to properties subject to the developer's self-supply which has been abolished and will become obsolete on 30 April 2010 at the latest) (VAT Regulations 1995, SI 1995/2518, reg 113(d));

(e) a building, other than one subject to a self-supply charge under (c) or (d) above, constructed by the owner, which is first used by them on or after 1 April 1990 and where the value of all standard-rated supplies of the land, and goods and services in the course of construction of the building incurred on or after 1 April 1990 is £250,000 or more (VAT Regulations 1995, SI 1995/2518, reg 113(e));

(f) a building which is altered or extended or to which an annex is added thereby increasing the floor area by 10 per cent or more, where the value of the standard-rated supplies made on or after 1 April 1990 in connection with the alteration, extension or annex is £250,000 or more (VAT Regulations 1995, SI 1995/2518, reg 113(f)); and

(g) a civil engineering work constructed by the owner and first brought into use by them on or after 3 July 1997 where the value of all standard-rated supplies of the land and goods and services in the course of construction of the civil engineering work made to the owner on or after 3 July 1997 is £250,000 or more (VAT Regulations 1995, SI 1995/2518, reg 113(g)); and

(h) a building refurbished or fitted out by the owner where the value of all standard-rated supplies of services and goods affixed to the building made to the owner on or after 3 July 1997 in connection with the refurbishment or fitting out is £250,000 or more (VAT Regulations 1995, SI 1995/2518, reg 113(h)).

1.101 The extent to which the capital item is used for making taxable supplies must be reviewed over an adjustment period of five intervals for computer equipment and ten intervals for all other capital items (or five intervals in the case of an interest in land for less than ten years). An interval is usually one year but may be less. If there is any change in the extent to which the capital item is used for making taxable supplies during the adjustment period, the person must make an input tax adjustment. The scheme is, therefore, of no concern to a person who makes only taxable supplies throughout the adjustment period. If taxable use increases, the person may deduct more input tax than was originally deducted. If the taxable use decreases, the person must repay a proportion of the input tax originally deducted.

1.102 Initially, input tax on the capital item acquired is recoverable in accordance with the normal rules. Where, however, there is a change in taxable use of the capital item or a change in the level of the owner's partial exemption recovery during the adjustment period, an adjustment has to be made. If appropriate, this is done annually in the second VAT accounting period after the end of each adjustment interval.

1.103 The first adjustment interval commences on the day on which the asset is acquired (or used by the owner under the above provisions if the acquisition itself does not fall within the rules) and runs until the end of the owner's longer period or, if none is applicable, the tax year. The longer period and tax year are defined in and determined by reference to the VAT Regulations 1995 SI 1995/2518. There are subsequently four or nine adjustment intervals. The adjustment is calculated as follows:

$$\frac{\text{Total input tax on capital item}}{\text{Number of intervals in adjustments periods (either 10 or 5)}} \times \text{adjustment \%}$$

1.104 The adjustment percentage is the difference, if any, between the extent to which the item is used in making taxable supplies in the first interval and the extent to which it is so used in the subsequent interval in question. If taxable usage has increased, a further amount of VAT is deductible; if taxable usage has decreased, a further amount of VAT is payable to Customs.

1.105 If during an interval the asset in question ceases to be used wholly in making either a taxable or exempt supply and starts to be used on a partially (or wholly) exempt basis, the degree of taxable use for the interval is computed on a daily basis by reference to actual usage.

1.106 If the capital item is disposed of (or deemed to be disposed of eg on deregistration) before the end of the adjustment period, the adjustment for that period is generally calculated as follows:

(a) the use to which the asset has been put in that interval until disposal is treated as being for the whole of that interval;

(b) if the disposal is itself a taxable supply the trader is treated as using the asset for each of the remaining complete intervals wholly for taxable purposes; and

(c) if the disposal is an exempt supply, the land or building is treated as being used for each of the remaining complete intervals wholly for non-taxable purposes.

However, the amount recoverable in respect of the remaining complete periods cannot exceed the output tax chargeable by the owner on the relevant disposal (VAT Regulations 1995, SI 1995/2518, reg 115(3)). Further, if all the input tax deducted in respect of the past together with the input tax deductible in respect of the remaining complete periods exceeds the output tax chargeable by the owner on the relevant disposal, the owner must pay the excess to Customs and Excise (VAT Regulations 1995, SI 1995/2518, reg 115(3A) and (3B)).

1.107 Because of the above method of calculation, the timing of any disposal may be important. Generally, if a sale is taxable it should take place on or before the end of the tax year whereas, if it is to be exempt, it should be deferred until the next tax year.

1.108 Where a business is transferred as a going concern, the then current interval is brought to an end and the transferor must make any adjustment in the normal way. The new owner then becomes responsible for the next interval which runs from the date of the transfer to the end of the new owner's longer period or tax year, as the case may be. Where, however, the new owner takes over the vendor's VAT registration number, the interval during which the transfer takes place continues without a break and the new owner is responsible for making any adjustment for that interval. New owners by way of TOGCs must ensure that they obtain the information required to make adjustments (or have access to such information).

1.109 If a company owning land or buildings subject to the Capital Goods Scheme joins or leaves a VAT group during the adjustment period, the interval is brought to an end and an adjustment is made in the normal way. Responsibility for making future adjustments passes in the former case to the representative member of the group and in the latter to the company itself. If a company leaves a VAT group but does not register for VAT, the representative member's adjustment for the interval in which the company leaves the group is the final adjustment.

1.110 Where input tax is incurred on capital items, the taxpayer will need to maintain records showing the amount of such input tax that was incurred, the amount deducted in the initial period and the subsequent adjustments under the Capital Goods Scheme.

Who can deduct VAT?

1.111 As stated above, in most cases the person entitled to deduct VAT will be obvious but there have been a number of cases in which the issue has arisen. The decision of the House of Lords in *C & E v Redrow Group plc [1999] STC 16* (**Case Summary 31**) provides guidance on how to identify the recipient of a supply of services where the services are supplied to more than one person. In summary, the correct test for deciding to whom a service is supplied is a subjective test which takes as its starting point the person who is claiming to deduct the input VAT. In relation to that person, one then asks the following questions:

(a) Did that person instruct the supplier to do something?

(b) Was something done for or obtained by that person;?

(c) Did that person use that something in the course or furtherance of its business?

(d) Did that person pay consideration for the something which included VAT?

If the answer to all four questions is yes, then the person can treat all the VAT which it has paid as its input VAT.

1.112 The fact that someone else (who has not paid for it) also receives a service as part of the same transaction does not deprive the person who paid of the right to deduct. Even the apportionment of benefit between recipients of services does not matter, as Lord Millett emphasised when he formulated one of the questions of the new test as 'Did he obtain anything – anything at all – used or to be used for the purposes of his business in return for that payment?'

1.113 Customs' interpretation of the *Redrow* decision is contained in Business Brief 27/99 of 21 December 1999. Customs' view is that the decision only applies where the circumstances are similar to the *Redrow* case, ie where there is a claim to input tax credit by a taxable person who has commissioned goods or services and contracted with the supplier for them. Customs specifically reject the idea that payment for a supply means that the payer is a recipient of a supply. Usefully, Customs also state that they do not accept that a taxable person must have paid for a supply in order to be entitled to recover the input tax.

1.114 The *Redrow* case was applied by the VAT Tribunal in *British Airways plc v C & E [2000] V & DR 74* which was a re-hearing of the High Court case of *British Airways plc v C and E Comrs [1996] STC 1127* (meals provided to delayed airline passengers were held to be supplied to the passengers rather than the airline company). The Tribunal held that British Airways received a supply of services (the right to have the delayed passengers fed at its expense) from the restaurants and could treat the tax charged as input tax. The Tribunal held that in order to give rise to an input tax deduction under *Redrow*, there must be:

(a) a prior agreement that goods or services should be supplied to a third party; and

(b) the agreement and supplies must be for the purposes of the paying party's business.

How is VAT deducted?

1.115 To claim a deduction, the taxpayer must comply with certain formalities but the tax authorities may provide for alternative procedures where it is not possible to comply with the primary procedures (Sixth VAT Directive, art 18, VATA 1994, s 24(6)).

1.116 Where VAT is deductible, this is done by setting it against the output tax which a taxable person accounts for on the VAT return or, if the input tax exceeds the output tax on that return, claiming a repayment. A credit or a repayment may be obtained or claimed in full in the return for the period in which the VAT is incurred: there is no need to wait until there is sufficient output tax to set against the input tax. The maximum delay between paying VAT to a supplier and obtaining a credit or repayment, where the entitlement arises, should be about four months for a person with a quarterly accounting period.

Accounting and records

1.117 The right to deduct is subject to the requirement that the taxpayer must have adequate evidence of the input tax that he seeks to deduct. The evidence required for input tax is summarised in the table below.

Nature of supply	Type of evidence	Customs and Excise Notice Reference/VAT Regulations
Supply received from a UK supplier (other than those described below)	Tax invoice addressed to taxpayer or, if the taxpayer is a VAT group, a company within that group	C & E Notice 700, para 19.7.1 VAT Regulations 1995, reg 29(2)(a)
Supply of construction services from building contractor (alternative)	Tax invoice, as above, or authenticated receipt	C & E Notice 708, para 13.2 (NB The supplier can only issue receipt after payment)
Expenditure that does not exceed £25 (inclusive of VAT) that relates to telephone calls from public or private telephones, purchases through coin-operated machines or car park charges	No evidence required if within limits	C & E Notice 700, para 19.7.5(b)
Employee expenses, eg subsistence expenditure	Tax invoice–may be made out to employee instead of employer	VAT Regulations 1995, reg 29(2)(a) C & E Notice 700 para 19.7.5(a)
Acquisition of goods from a taxable person established in another EU member state	Equivalent of tax invoice issued by EU business.	
Importation of goods from a country outside the EU or removal of goods from a bonded warehouse	Monthly VAT certificate (C79) Authenticated document in respect of removal of goods from warehouse	C & E Notice 700, para 19.7.3 VAT Regulations 1995, reg 29(2)(c)
Postal imports	Authenticated copy of 8SAD document if more than £2,000, otherwise declaration	VAT Regulations 1995, reg 29(2)(c)
Services received from abroad to which the 'reverse charge' applies	Invoice from supplier (will not necessarily be a 'tax invoice')	C & E Notice 700, para 19.7.4 VAT Regulations 1995, reg 29(2)(b)

1.118 Although the normal rule is that the relevant evidence must be available in order to support a deduction, Customs and Excise have the power to accept alternative evidence (VAT Regulations 1995, SI 1995/2518, reg 29(2)).

Timing of right to deduct

1.119 The first paragraph of article 17 of the Sixth Directive provides that 'The right to deduct shall arise at the time when the deductible tax becomes chargeable'. The Second VAT Directive provided that a taxable person may only exercise the right to deduct if the tax in respect of the relevant transaction has become chargeable. VAT generally becomes chargeable when goods are delivered or services are performed but may be chargeable on receipt of payment or issue of an invoice if earlier. In the case of intra-Community acquisitions of goods, VAT is chargeable on the 15th day of the month following that in which the supply was effected or on issue of an invoice if earlier.

1.120 Although the right to deduct may arise when the deductible tax becomes chargeable, the exercise of that right will usually not be possible until some time later. In the UK, VAT Regulations 1995, SI 1995/2518, reg 29(1) provides that a person claiming deduction of input tax shall do so on the return made by him for the accounting period in which the VAT became chargeable subject to holding the required documentary evidence and save as Customs and Excise may otherwise allow or direct. Customs and Excise state that if a taxable person does not hold the necessary evidence to support deduction in the proper period, the taxable person can claim it on a return for a later period provided the return is made within three years of the date that the return for the proper period was due (Notice 700, para 10.5).

1.121 Where the supplier and the recipient of a supply are both taxable persons but with different VAT accounting periods, careful timing of supplies, submission of VAT returns and payment of VAT (both between parties and to Customs and Excise) can generate a cashflow advantage. Equally, a disregard for matters of timing can increase the cashflow cost to a purchaser and on a large transaction (e g property transactions) this can exhaust a buyer's loan facility.

Special arrangements and schemes

1.122 The UK has implemented a number of measures that relieve some public bodies from the VAT on certain activities in the public interest. There are three special provisions that do not create a right to deduct but a right to a refund of VAT incurred by particular bodies in certain circumstances. The bodies entitled to refunds are:

- local authorities and certain other public bodies such as the BBC (VATA 1994, s 33);
- certain national museums (VATA 1994, s 33A);
- government departments in respect of VAT incurred on certain specified services (VATA 1994, s 41).

In each case, the refund provision is a means provided by the UK Government of funding the relevant bodies. Although these provisions are not part of the deduction system, the UK Government has adapted the deduction system to provide funding in particular circumstances.

Local authorities

1.123 Local authorities and certain other bodies (such as the BBC) do not make taxable supplies when carrying out their statutory duties. This is in accordance with the Sixth VAT Directive, art 4(5). When VAT was introduced in the UK in 1973, it was appreciated that local authorities would have to increase their rates or receive increased Government funding to take into account the fact that they would have to pay VAT on supplies that they receive. To avoid this, the Finance Act 1972 made provision for VAT paid by local authorities on their non-business supplies ie those supplies that they make as local authorities. The legislation provided for a refund of the VAT so incurred.

1.124 The legislation has been reproduced in subsequent VAT legislation and is now contained in VATA 1994, s 33. As with other businesses, local authorities cannot recover the VAT that they incur on exempt supplies. However, VATA 1994, s 33(2) allows Customs and Excise to refund the VAT on exempt supplies if it is insignificant. Customs and Excise Notice 749, para 8.2 currently provides that a local authority can recover all its input tax (except that on which VAT is not deductible under the rules discussed in **1.60**) provided that the VAT on its exempt supplies does not exceed the greater of:

- £625 on average per month or £7,500 per annum; and
- 5 per cent of all VAT incurred on both business and non-business activities but excluding non-deductible VAT such as that on cars etc.

Despite these very generous de minimis limits, some authorities can still encounter difficulties because they make significant exempt supplies such as sale or letting of property.

1.125 Because VAT reclaimed under VATA 1994, s 33 is not input tax, there is no right of appeal under VATA 1994, s 83(c), against a refusal by Customs and Excise to repay the tax. There may however be other judicial remedies available see *R (on the application of Cardiff County Council) v C & E Comrs [2002] EWHC 2085 (Admin), [2002] STC 1318).*

Museums and galleries

1.126 As part of Government policy of encouraging national galleries and museums to allow free admission to their premises, the Government introduced VATA 1994, s 33A. This provides a refund of VAT to certain specified galleries and museums. The galleries and museums are specified in the VAT (Refund of Tax to Museums and Galleries) Order 2001, SI 2001/2879.

1.127 The VAT refundable is such VAT as is attributable to the free admissions made by the museum or gallery. VAT on those items discussed **1.41–1.60** above is never deductible, even if it is attributable to free admissions or taxable supplies.

1.128 VAT reclaimed under VATA 1994, s 33A is also not input tax and therefore there is no right of appeal under VATA 1994, s 83(c) although other remedies may be available.

Contracted out services by Government departments

1.129 Section 41 of VATA 1994 was introduced to provide a level playing field when the Government decided to promote the contracting out of services. The aim of the provision was to ensure that an external provider of services was not disadvantaged from bidding for contracts with Government departments merely because the VAT cost took its bid above the cost that would be incurred if the services were provided internally.

1.130 The current provisions allow Government departments (eg the NHS) to acquire services that are specified in the London Gazette and to claim the VAT incurred on them as a refund from Customs and Excise. There are strict rules as to when the VAT can be recovered.

VAT deductions and non-UK taxable persons

1.131 It is not only UK taxpayers that can deduct UK VAT; taxpayers from other Member States and taxpayers from outside the EU are entitled to a refund of the VAT they incur in the UK in connection with their taxable activities outside the UK. The Sixth VAT Directive, art 17(4) states:

'The refund of value added tax referred to in paragraph 3 shall be effected:

- to taxable persons who are not established within the territory of the country but who are established in another member state in accordance with the detailed implementing rules laid down in Directive 79/1072/EEC [EC Eighth Directive];
- to taxable persons who are not established within the territory of the Community, in accordance with the detailed implementing rules laid down in Directive 86/560/EEC [EC Thirteenth Directive].'

1.132 Subject to certain exclusions (see below), a claim for refund for VAT may be made in relation to any supply of goods or services made in the UK to a non-UK business or any importation of goods into the UK from outside the EU by a non-UK business provided that, in the period of the claim, the non-UK business:

(a) was not established in the UK; and

(b) did not make any supplies of goods and services in the UK other than freight transport (and ancillary services) and reverse charge services.

1.133 Refunds cannot be claimed on VAT incurred on:

(a) a supply, or part of a supply, which is not used for the purposes of the business;

(b) any supply of goods or services used or intended to be used for the purpose of making a supply in the UK;

(c) certain supplies of motor cars;

(d) certain second-hand goods;

(e) all business entertainment and hospitality expenses.

(f) Unless Customs allow otherwise, repayments will not be made to non-EU businesses established in a country with a comparable system of turnover taxes to VAT unless that country provides reciprocal arrangements for refunds to be made to UK businesses.

1.134 The claim for refund must be made not later than six months after the end of the claim year in which the VAT is incurred. For businesses that are established outside the UK but elsewhere in the EU, the claim year runs from 1 January to 31 December. For businesses that are established outside the EU, the claim year runs from 1 July to 30 June. The maximum claim period is 12 months and the minimum period is three months, which is not restricted to calendar quarters. A period shorter than three months is allowed where the claim relates to the final part of a year. The minimum amount of a claim for any period of less than one year is £130. The minimum amount of a claim for a whole year or the final part of a year is £16.

1.135 Claims must be made on the prescribed form (VAT 65 or VAT 65A) in English and must be accompanied by original VAT invoices. If an invoice is in the name of an employee, there must be appropriate proof that the person to whom the invoice is addressed is an employee. The claimant must have a certificate either that it is a taxable person in the EU or that it carries on a business outside the EU. Completed claim forms must be sent to:
HM Customs & Excise VAT Overseas Repayments
Eighth/Thirteenth Directive
Customs House
PO Box 34
Londonderry
Northern Ireland
BT48 7AE

1.136 The refund is normally made within six months of receiving a claim by payable order issued directly to the non-UK business or its agent. Alternatively, payments can be made directly into a UK bank account.

1.137 In relation to taxable persons established in countries outside the EU, entitlement to claim may depend on there being reciprocal refund arrangements for the refund of indirect taxes to UK businesses by the claimant's country of establishment.

Chapter 2

Taxable Person and Economic Activity

Introduction

2.1 Input tax deduction is a key element of the VAT system and was incorporated to remove the problems of the cumulative tax systems that had preceded VAT. Prior to VAT, most European countries had cumulative multi-stage systems, where each producer in the chain of transactions charged tax and this tax was not deductible by the recipient. This meant that more tax accumulated when goods were processed through more and more stages. This led to vertical integration of businesses and also to subsidies being paid on export to repay tax accumulated. Deduction of VAT by each taxable person in the chain of distribution and supply was, therefore, a vital component to remove this problem.

EU legislation

2.2 This right to deduction is given in article 17 of the Sixth VAT Directive:

> '17(2) In so far as the goods and services are used for the purposes of his taxable transactions, the taxable person shall be entitled to deduct from the tax which he is liable to pay.'

Articles 5, 6 and 7 of the Directive define taxable transactions as supplies of goods, supplies of services and imports.

Taxable person

2.3 Taxable person and economic activity are defined in article 4 of the Sixth VAT Directive:

> **'Taxable persons**
>
> 4(1) "**Taxable person**" shall mean any person who independently carries out in any place any economic activity specified in paragraph 2, whatever the purpose or results of that activity.
>
> 4(2) The **economic activities** referred to in paragraph 1 shall comprise all activities of producers, traders and persons supplying services including mining and agricultural activities and activities of the professions. The exploitation of tangible or intangible property for the purpose of obtaining income therefrom on a continuing basis shall also be considered an economic activity.

4(3) Member states may also treat as a taxable person anyone who carries out, on an occasional basis, a transaction relating to the activities referred to in paragraph 2 and in particular one of the following:

(a) the supply before first occupation of buildings or parts of buildings and the land on which they stand; member states may determine the conditions of application of this criterion to transformations of buildings and the land on which they stand.

Member states may apply criteria other than that of first occupation, such as the period elapsing between the date of completion of the building and the date of first supply or the period elapsing between the date of first occupation and the date of subsequent supply, provided that these periods do not exceed five years and two years respectively.

"**A building**" shall be taken to mean any structure fixed to or in the ground;

(b) the supply of building land.

"**Building land**" shall mean any unimproved or improved land defined as such by the member states.

4(4) The use of the word "**independently**" in paragraph 1 shall exclude employed and other persons from the tax in so far as they are bound to an employer by a contract of employment or by any other legal ties creating the relationship of employer and employee as regards working conditions, remuneration and the employer's liability.

Subject to the consultations provided for in article 29, each member state may treat as a single taxable person persons established in the territory of the country who, while legally independent, are closely bound to one another by financial, economic and organisational links.

4(5) States, regional and local government authorities and other bodies governed by public law shall not be considered taxable persons in respect of the activities or transactions in which they engage as public authorities, even where they collect dues, fees, contributions or payments in connection with these activities or transactions.

However, when they engage in such activities or transactions, they shall be considered taxable persons in respect of these activities or transactions where treatment as non-taxable persons would lead to significant distortions of competition.

In any case, these bodies shall be considered taxable persons in relation to the activities listed in Annex D, provided they are not carried out on such a small scale as to be negligible.

Member states may consider activities of these bodies which are exempt under article 13 or 28 as activities which they engage in as public authorities.'

Taxable person – UK legislation

2.4 The UK legislation is not an exact translation of the EU legislation. Taxable person is defined in VATA 1994, s 3 as follows:

> '3(1) A person is a **taxable person** for the purposes of this Act while he is, or is required to be, registered under this Act.'

Thus, any person who is, or must be, or volunteers to be registered is a taxable person. The definition of person, however, is a little more difficult. A person includes a natural person (that is an individual) and legal persons (eg a company). The Interpretation Act 1978, Sch 1 provides that a person includes a body of persons corporate or unincorporate unless the context requires otherwise. VATA 1994, ss 41 and 42, ensure that the VAT legislation applies to Crown bodies and local authorities and other public bodies.

2.5 A partnership is not a legal person in England and Wales (though it is in Scotland – Partnership Act 1890, s 4), but is a group of persons trading jointly and thus creating a joint tax liability. VATA 1994, s 45, however, has ensured that the partnership as notified to Customs and Excise is treated as a taxable person, and that body (and the partners constituting the partnership as notified) has the obligation to account for VAT and the right to deduct VAT. This obligation continues until Customs and Excise are notified otherwise, and not when the partnership ends.

2.6 Where the partnership conducts more than one business then both business activities must be accounted for through the one VAT registration (*C & E Comrs v MJ & BJ Glassborow [1974] STC 142, QB*). A partner can act on behalf of the partnership and input tax incurred on expenses in their names can be deducted. If one of the partnerships has a different constitution (that is different partners), then the partnerships must be registered separately (assuming they are registrable, or wish to register).

2.7 A limited partnership is a partnership that consists of:

- one or more persons called general partners; and
- one or more persons called limited partners.

The limited partners contribute a capital sum, but are not liable for debts and obligations of the firm beyond the amount of capital contributed. Limited partners cannot take part in the management of the firm. Limited partnerships must be registered as such with the Registrar of Companies. Otherwise the limited partners are treated as general partners. Limited partnerships are registered in the names of the general partners and those treated as general partners. A general partner can act on behalf of the limited partnership, and input tax incurred on expenses in their names can be deducted.

2.8 Limited Liability Partnerships (LLPs) have a legal status distinct from their members. The members are protected from debts or liabilities of the LLP. An LLP is a corporate body and it is the legal entity for VAT purposes. An LLP can join a

VAT group (subject to the control provisions). The LLP has the right to deduct VAT and an obligation to account for VAT. A member of an LLP cannot act on behalf of the limited liability partnership and input tax incurred on expenses in their names cannot be deducted. The rules that apply to companies (and employees) apply to LLPs and their members.

2.9 Unincorporated persons (clubs, associations, organisations etc, called clubs hereafter) are a little more difficult to deal with. Clubs are not a person in England and Wales. VATA 1994, s 46(2) refers to clubs, associations or organisations the affairs of which are managed by its members or a committee or committees of members, and VAT Regulations 1995, reg 8 stipulates the persons responsible for complying with VAT obligations. The problem that arises is what constitutes the 'club'? Does it extend to sub-committees and sections? What is the exact relationship of the various bodies that make up the club? The decisions of *A G Hayhoe (for Watchet Bowling Club & Watchet Indoor Bowling Club (1981) VAT decision 1026* and *Old Parkinsonians Association (1993) STWI 1296 (VAT decision 10908)* give some guidance as to whether entities are separate or part of the same club.

2.10 It has also been argued that mutual trading by clubs (that is, where the club is trading with itself, as the members are also owners of the club) is not a taxable supply, not a supply at all. It was held, however, in *Carlton Lodge Club v C & E Comrs [1974] STC 507, QB* that supplies were made, despite the supplies being made to the member owners. In *Eastbourne Town Radio Cars Association v C & E Comrs [2001] UKHL 19, [2001] STC 606,* it was held that the activities of an association should not be excluded from VAT merely because it is unincorporated and not a legal person.

Right to deduct – UK legislation

2.11 Once the person has been defined and becomes registered or is liable to be registered, it is necessary to determine if the VAT incurred can be deducted. The right to deduct and the amount allowable is determined by VATA 1994, ss 24–26B and sundry regulations. The most important sub-section for the purpose of this chapter is s 24(1), which states:

> '**24(1)** Subject to the following provisions of this section, "**input tax**", in relation to a taxable person, means the following tax, that is to say–
>
> (a) VAT on the supply to him of any goods or services;
>
> (b) VAT on the acquisition by him from another member State of any goods; and
>
> (c) VAT paid or payable by him on the importation of any goods from a place outside the member States,
>
> being (in each case) goods or services used or to be used for the purpose of any business carried on or to be carried on by him.'

Business and economic activity

2.12 Thus, for VAT to be deducted it is necessary for it to be used for the purpose of the business carried on (though the Sixth VAT Directive requires the goods or services to be used for the purposes of taxable transactions – a small, and perhaps, irrelevant differentiation). Business is defined in the VAT legislation in VATA 1994, s 94:

> '**94 Meaning of "business" etc.**
>
> **94(1)** In this Act "**business**" includes any trade, profession or vocation.
>
> **94(2)** Without prejudice to the generality of anything else in this Act, the following are deemed to be the carrying on of a business –
>
> (a) the provision by a club, association or organisation (for a subscription or other consideration) of the facilities or advantages available to its members; and
>
> (b) the admission, for a consideration, of persons to any premises.
>
> **94(3)** [Repealed by FA 1999, s 20(1) and 139(1) and Sch 20, Pt II(2).]
>
> **94(4)** Where a person, in the course or furtherance of a trade, profession or vocation, accepts any office, services supplied by him as the holder of that office are treated as supplied in the course or furtherance of the trade, profession or vocation.
>
> **94(5)** Anything done in connection with the termination or intended termination of a business is treated as being done in the course or furtherance of that business.
>
> **94(6)** The disposition of a business as a going concern, or of its assets or liabilities (whether or not in connection with its reorganisation or winding up), is a supply made in the course or furtherance of the business.'

2.13 Whilst seemingly comprehensive, VATA 1994, s 94 does not actually give much assistance. A brief examination of relevant case law, however, gives some guidance on this matter:

- *Clwb Rygbi Nant Conway [1999] SWTI 316 (VAT decision 16376)* – a club charging admission fees was a business, the fact that it was non-profit making was not conclusive.
- *C & E Comrs v Morrison's Academy Boarding Houses Association 1997 [1978] STC 1, CS* – a non-profit making entity was a business. The supplies made were continued over an appreciable period, and with a frequency to amount to a recognisable and identifiable activity. Business does not mean that the activity needs to be undertaken commercially or with a view to making a profit.
- *Church of Scientology of California v C & E Comrs 1980 [1981] STC 65, CA* – a religious purpose does not make a business non-business.

- *DA Rompelman & EA Rompelman-van-Deelen v Minister van Financiën (C–268/83) [1985] ECR 655, ECJ* (**Case Summary 4**) – economic activity was being undertaken even where no taxable supplies had been made, so input tax could be deducted. See also *Merseyside Cablevision Ltd [1987] VATTR 134 VAT decision 2419* (**Case Summary 6**).
- *Whitechapel Art Gallery v C & E Comrs [1986] STC 156, QB* (**Case Summary 5**) – the gallery allowed visitors admission without charge, but made taxable sales of souvenirs. The gallery deducted all the VAT incurred on expenses but it was held that the input tax had to be restricted to the proportion that related to its taxable supplies.
- *Apple and Pear Development Council v (102/86) [1988] STC 221, ECJ* (**Case Summary 7**) –an activity could only constitute a business if it involved making taxable supplies for a consideration, and that for there to be supplies for consideration there must be a direct link between the service provided and the consideration received.
- *WM van Tiem v Staatssecretaris van Financiën (C–186/89) [1993] STC 91, ECJ* – the grant of a right of user over property for a specified period and in return for payment was an economic activity, so input tax incurred on the acquisition of the property was deductible.
- *Staatssecretaris van Financien v Heerma (C–23/98) [2001] STC 1437, ECJ* – the letting to a partnership of a property by a member of the partnership was an independent activity, and the individual was a taxable person.

It can be seen from these cases that for a matter to be regarded as business or economic activity there needs to be a degree of commerciality in the arrangements, even if the activities are undertaken for non-commercial reasons or where the profit motive is absent. Domestic or social arrangements can be excluded (see *C & E Comrs v Lord Fisher [1981] STC 238, QB*). Economic activity arises (and deductions are allowable) even when no taxable supplies have been made.

Unsocial or illegal activity

2.14 Activities that may not be regarded as socially acceptable (such as prostitution, *Adoui v Belgium (115/82) [1982] ECR 1665, ECJ*) or are illegal (such as the supply of counterfeit perfume, *R v Goodwin & Unstead (C-3/97) [1998] STC 699, ECJ*) are nevertheless an economic activity and subject to VAT (and suppliers are entitled to deductions). A supply that is subject to a total prohibition (eg narcotics, *Mol v Inspecteur der Invoerrechten en Accijnzen (C-269/86) [1988] ECR 3627, ECJ* and *Verenigiging Happy Family Rustenburgerstrat v Inspecteur der Omzetbelasting (289/86) [1988] ECR 3655, ECJ*) (**Case Summary 9**) is due to its nature absolutely precluded from release into economic and commercial channels in all member states, with the exception of strictly controlled scientific and medical channels (the same principle has been applied to counterfeit money). In *C & E Comrs v Polok [2002] STC 361*, it was held that the procurement of what was described as 'escorts' was a taxable business. It was held that 'a generalised differentiation between lawful and unlawful transactions was precluded. The decided cases show that the illegality exclusion is very narrow. In the only two cases where activities had been held outside the VAT system it was the inherently illegal nature of the activities which took them outside VAT'.

2.15 The same concepts have been applied in the UK (though these cases would not have been referred to, due to the age of the case) in *C & E Comrs v JRR Oliver [1980] STC 73, QB*, where the supply of stolen cars was held to be a taxable supply. Rather bizarrely, however, it was held in *CR Hudson (t/a 21st Century Demolition & Plant Hire) (1992) VAT decision 9666* that input tax was not deductible on stolen goods that had been supplied to a taxable person. It would seem that if a supply is made and output tax is properly deductible, then input tax should be deductible by the recipient of the supply. In this case, however, the police repossessed the goods, so it may be argued that the supply was for a temporary period only It is a difficult case to reconcile.

Holding companies and entities holding shares

2.16 Holding companies are a further area of difficulty. Over the years (at least the last 15 years) Customs and Excise have made several attempts to restrict the amount of VAT that can be reclaimed by holding companies. Customs and Excise have stated on occasions that they cannot understand why a holding company that is within a VAT group can reclaim VAT, but a holding company outside the VAT group cannot reclaim VAT. It is, of course, the effect of grouping, and if such a facility were not available it would force businesses to organise themselves in a different manner (perhaps in divisions instead of a holding company and subsidiaries, though this may not be an appropriate commercial solution). VAT should not force businesses to organise in a different manner; hence the facility for grouping that allows a holding company with no other activities to be able to reclaim all the VAT that it incurs. Other issues do, of course, arise, eg the commercial activities of the holding company.

2.17 It is well established that a company that does nothing but hold shares without any direct or indirect involvement in the management of the subsidiaries is not a taxable person (*Polysar Investments Netherlands BV v Inspecteur der Invoerrechten en Accijnzen (C-60/90) [1993] STC 222, ECJ* (**Case Summary 11**)). It is arguable that Customs and Excise should exclude such non-taxable entities from VAT groups, as their non-taxable status means that they should be afforded no opportunity to deduct, but grouping effectively allows this. A holding company with management activities should be able to deduct a proportion of the VAT incurred, whether it is in a VAT group or not.

2.18 It has also been held that a partnership is not carrying on an economic activity for VAT when it was only acquiring and holding bonds (*Harnas & Helm CV v Staatssecretaris van Financiën (C-80/95) [1997] STC 364, ECJ* (**Case Summary 26**)). Where activity consists of the purchase and sale of shares by a trustee in the course of managing of a charitable trust it is also not an economic activity for the purposes of VAT (*Wellcome Trust Ltd v C & E Comrs (C-155/94) [1996] STC 945, ECJ* (**Case Summary 23**)). This does not mean, however, that a person who holds shares or a holding company is not undertaking economic activity just by holding those shares or due to its status. There is economic activity where the share holding is accompanied by the performance of financial, administrative, commercial or technical services. Costs incurred (such as the cost of acquisition of subsidiaries) can be treated as general overhead costs, although the receipt of dividends is outside the scope of VAT (*Cibo Participations SA v Directeur regional des impots du Nord-Pas-de-Calais (C-16/00) [2002] STC 460, ECJ* (**Case Summary 41**)).

2.19 It would appear from this that VAT is deductible where a taxable person undertaking taxable supplies incurs the VAT. The definition of person being a taxable person is important to ensure that VAT can be deducted. As will be seen, this is wide-ranging. In summary, a person is a taxable person where he independently (that is, not as an employee) undertakes economic activity, and economic activity is all activities of producers, traders and persons supplying services.

Abortive costs, speculative ventures

2.20 Customs and Excise officers often believe that VAT is only deductible where it relates to taxable activities. This is not the case, but this misconception does not usually cause problems until there are abortive or speculative costs. As these costs do not relate to taxable supplies there is sometimes doubt regarding the ability to deduct the VAT incurred.

2.21 It would be thought that there is no problem with recovering VAT that relates to a future supply. VATA 1994, s 24(1) states that input tax is deductible where goods or services are used or are to be used for the purpose of any business carried on *or to be carried on*. It is assumed that the problem arises, or has arisen where the project is speculative or it is aborted, where the expenditure could be regarded as not relating to any business activity that has been or will be carried on.

2.22 In the UK the normal problem is convincing Customs and Excise that a taxable supply will be made and that the taxable person should be registered for VAT (See **Chapter 10**). Once the taxable person is registered then the VAT can be deducted subject to the normal rules. There have been instances where taxable persons registered for VAT have been subject to assessments for VAT on de-registration as the tax authorities believed that there was no entitlement to deduction as no taxable supplies were made. It was held, however, in *Inteercommunale voor Zeewaterontzilting (in liquidation) v Belgium (C-110/94) [1996] STC 569, ECJ* (**Case Summary 20**) that initial investment expenditure incurred for the purpose of a business could in principle be regarded as an economic activity. This right does not, however, preclude the tax authorities from requiring objective evidence to support the intention to make taxable supplies. The Court held that input tax incurred could be deducted where a tax authority had accepted that a person had declared an intention to commence economic activity and had the status of a taxable person. The status of a taxable person can only be withdrawn in cases of abuse or fraud.

Taxable or exempt project

2.23 It can be difficult to demonstrate that the proposed supply is taxable, so input tax can be deducted. This is a common problem with property transactions as these can be exempt and the input tax incurred cannot be deducted. Customs and Excise officers will sometimes express the view that the VAT incurred should not be deducted unless the election to waive exemption is made (and such an instruction is contained within the Guidance of Customs and Excise). This is a narrow view, but an understandable one. Businesses will, however, be reluctant to elect at an early stage as this reduces flexibility. There may be an intention to make a taxable supply, but an election may not be made, as there may be a later opportunity to make a greater profit through an exempt transaction. Just because a taxable person wishes to maintain this flexibility does not remove the intention to make a taxable supply. There is provision to claw back VAT where an intention changes.

2.24 Where a business wishes to maintain this flexibility it is essential that there is evidence that the intention is to make a taxable supply. In *Beaverbank Properties Ltd (2003) VAT decision 18099*, a property developer incurred speculative costs on a project that was abandoned because planning permission was unavailable. The developer had reclaimed the input tax incurred, but had not waived the exemption. Customs and Excise had argued that the supplies that the taxable person would have made would have been exempt, as no election had been made. The taxable person, who had never owned the land in question, persuaded the court that it had been its intention to opt to tax and make taxable supplies if the planning application had succeeded. The figures presented at the tribunal demonstrated that if the election had not been made, the profit would have been £1 million less and the transaction would have been unviable. The tribunal held that the absence of an election did not negate the intention of the taxable person. It is, of course, harder to demonstrate such an intention without making such an election.

2.25 An earlier decision (*Lawson Mardon Group Pension Scheme [1993] 3 CMLR 562*), has been held to be an authority by Customs and Excise that where a taxable person does not elect to waive exemption a property it is assumed that the intended supplies will be exempt. This is clearly not the case. Electing to waive exemption is an indicator of an intention (and will make supplies taxable except in a few restricted cases), but should not be held to be the only matter that determines intention.

2.26 *Royal & Sun Alliance Insurance Group plc v C & E Comrs [2003] UKHL 29, [2003] STC 832 (see* **3.71–3.81** *and* **Case summary 47**), however, put this in a slightly different light. It concerned a taxable person that was in the process of disposing of properties. The taxable person had a property that was empty and had been used for its own purposes (exempt activity). The landlord had elected to waive exemption and VAT was being incurred. When, some time later, a sub-tenant was found, the taxable person elected to waive exemption. It had not done so previously as it wished to maintain flexibility in respect of potential future tenants. The question arose as to whether the VAT incurred in the vacant period could be reclaimed. It was held, in a split judgment, by the House of Lords that the effect of regulations 85 and 90 of the VAT Regulations 1995/2518 was to treat each successive supply received as being different from the one before. In respect of the grant of a time-limited interest in land (eg a lease), the legislation treated the superior landlord as granting rights of occupation in successive units of time. Thus, the goods and services supplied during the vacant 'unelected' period were different from those supplied afterwards. Where there was then a change in the use of the leases, this was not a change of intention about the use of the leases in the past. The taxable person had undertaken an economic activity in the vacant unelected periods for which there were no outputs. It then undertook a different economic activity following the election. If there had been inputs from the previous activity that could be used in the new taxable activity, the taxable person would be entitled to an adjustment of the input tax under the capital items scheme (though it is likely this would not apply in this case). As the taxable person had not formed an intention for taxable or exempt use, the VAT had been consumed in the past and could not be related to future supplies.

2.27 It may be expected that Customs and Excise will use this decision to confirm its position that VAT cannot be reclaimed on speculative property transactions unless there has been an election to waive exemption. This would, it is suggested, be reading too much into this decision. In *Royal & Sun Alliance*, the taxable person had not formed an intention about the supply to be made. This is in contrast to *Beaverbank Properties Ltd*, where a firm intention had been formed but the election to waive exemption had not been made in case it was necessary to change that intention. Thus, in *Royal & Sun Alliance* the VAT could not be attributed to a future taxable supply, as it was not known what supply would be made.

2.28 In the *Royal & Sun Alliance* judgment it appears that it was thought that the input tax had been consumed by making no supplies and this equated to making exempt supplies. This is a disturbing thought. If no supplies are made, then surely the input tax should have been treated as being residual (and this would comply with Customs and Excise's Information Sheet 08/01 – see **2.33** below). In the *Royal & Sun Alliance* case, this would probably mean that there would be no, or little, VAT recovery. It does not, however, alter the position of a taxable person such as *Beaverbank Properties Ltd*, where a clear intention can be demonstrated to make taxable supplies, and the election to tax was irrelevant. It should be noted, however, that *Beaverbank Properties Ltd* was decided before the *Royal & Sun Alliance* decision was published.

Intention unknown

2.29 Where it is not known what the intention is and the proposed transaction is aborted, the VAT incurred is treated as residual input tax to be apportioned according to the taxable person's partial exemption method.

Change in intention

2.30 Where there is an intention to make a taxable supply, the VAT attributable to the proposed taxable supply can be deducted, even when the proposed supply is many years ahead. Should the supply actually made be an exempt supply the VAT deducted has to be repaid to Customs and Excise if the change in intention is within six years of reclaiming the VAT. Similarly, when it is expected that the supply that will be made will be an exempt supply any input tax incurred cannot be initially deducted. Where the intention changes within six years, the VAT can be deducted if the supply made is taxable. The VAT cannot, however, be reclaimed prior to notifying Customs and Excise though Customs and Excise are currently consulting on a change to this provision to allow automatic deduction on change in intention. (See VAT Regulations 1995 (SI 1995/2518), regs 108 and 109.) The time that the deduction arises (or the repayment to Customs and Excise occurs) is at the date intention changes, not the date the supply is made. In addition, where the input tax has been treated as residual because the nature of the expected supplies was uncertain, and a decision is taken to proceed with a particular project, the input tax must then be re-attributed according to the nature of the supplies that will result from the project.

2.31 On occasion the change of intention is forced upon the taxpayer. In *Belgium v Ghent Coal Terminal NV (C-37/95) [1998] STC 260, ECJ* (**Case Summary 30**), a taxable person acquired land that was to be used for taxable purposes. The taxable person was later required to sell the land (an exempt transaction) without having made the intended taxable supplies. This change in use was not a change in intention by the taxable person, but something forced upon it. Thus, the VAT originally incurred was deductible in full at the time it was incurred. There may, however, be a requirement to adjust the VAT claimed under the capital items scheme.

Legitimate expectation

2.32 The Advocate-General has given an opinion in *Gemeente Leusden v Staatssecretaris van Financien* and *Holin Groep BV c.s. v Staatssecretaris van Financien (C-487/01 and C-7/02)*, that where a taxable person has a legitimate expectation to deduct VAT and that expectation is frustrated, the VAT remains deductible. In the case of *Gemeente Leusden*, a local authority, refurbishment works were carried out to a property that was leased to a third party. VAT was charged on the lease. The Dutch Government amended the option to tax rules and the option became ineffective. The Dutch authorities sought to recover some of the input tax that had been deducted through the mechanism of the capital items scheme. The Advocate-General found that the principles of protection of legitimate expectations and legal certainty prevent a taxable person being subject to such adjustments where, due to amendment of regulations, the activity can no longer be subjected to VAT. Thus, it would appear (and the ECJ has yet to confirm the Advocate-General's opinion), that where a taxable person has a legitimate expectation to deduct input tax, the deduction should be allowed.

Customs and Excise Information Sheet – speculative costs

2.33 Customs and Excise has issued an information sheet (08/01 December 2001) in respect of speculative costs. This gives guidance on Customs and Excise's understanding and details of what evidence should be provided.

'VAT: Speculative property developers: input tax

This VAT Information Sheet explains Customs' policy on how a speculative property developer ("developer") should deal with input tax they incur on speculative costs.

1. Introduction

1.1 What has changed?

Previously Customs expected that developers would attribute input tax to either taxable or exempt supplies, depending on the supplies they intended to make. Although not wrong in itself, this policy did not recognise that there is an earlier stage where developers investigate many potential projects without having a clear intention as to what supplies they will make, where or when.

1.2 Comments

We would be pleased to receive any comments you may have about this publication. Please write or fax your comments or suggestions to:

Partial Exemption Team, HM Customs and Excise, 4th Floor West, New King's Beam House, 22 Upper Ground, London SE1 9PJ; Fax: 020 7865 4824

2. Background – attribution and adjustment of input tax

2.1 Attribution of input tax

A taxable person can deduct input tax on goods and services which he uses in making taxable supplies. Partial exemption methods specify how to calculate how much input tax can be deducted. A key stage in a partial exemption method is **attribution**:

- Input tax on goods and services which are used or will be used wholly in making taxable supplies is attributed to taxable supplies (and can be deducted in full).
- Input tax on goods and services which are used or will be used wholly in making exempt supplies is attributed to exempt supplies (and in principle cannot be deducted).

Other (**residual**) input tax is apportioned between taxable and exempt supplies as specified in the method.

2.2 Adjustment of input tax

The amount of input tax deducted may be adjusted under the "clawback" and "payback" rules (VAT Regulations 108 & 109). They apply when a trader has originally attributed input tax to an intended supply or supplies, but within 6 years of that attribution and before his intention is fulfilled the trader either changes his intention or actually makes a supply of a different VAT liability. If the conditions are met the trader must repay all or part of the input tax originally deducted ("clawback"), or may deduct all or part of the input tax not originally deducted ("payback"). No adjustment arises under regulations 108 or 109:

- once the goods or services have been used; or
- if the change of intention (or change from intended to actual) is to a supply or supplies of the same liability as the previous intention.

3. Speculative and abortive supplies

3.1 What are speculative and abortive supplies?

Developers spend a lot of time and effort investigating potential projects – looking at locations or sites, assessing their suitability, seeking customers, etc – without knowing what, if any, supplies they will eventually make. For the purposes of this Information Sheet these are called speculative supplies. Most speculative supplies are not followed through – no supplies are actually made. For the purposes of this Information Sheet these are called abortive supplies because the developer investigated the possibility of making some kind of supply for VAT purposes but then for some reason did not actually make a supply at all.

3.2 What if I know what supplies I will make?

If you know from the outset what supplies you intend to make then you should attribute input tax on speculative costs to the VAT liability of those supplies from the outset. So, for example, if your intention is only to build and sell new houses input tax on speculative costs is attributable to the intended taxable (zero-rated) supplies.

4. How should I deal with input tax relating to speculative supplies?

4.1 How to read this section and the Annex

The following paragraphs, together with the Annex, are a guideline for developers on how to attribute (and adjust, if appropriate) input tax in relation to developments. There is no "rule of thumb" which is applicable in all cases.

4.2 What if I have not yet decided what supplies I will make?

VAT incurred on speculative costs is input tax, because investigating potential projects is a business activity for business purposes. The input tax is residual at this stage because there is no firm intention to make either taxable or exempt supplies.

When a speculative supply is aborted, many of the associated costs will not be used to make any other supplies because they were specific to the particular project: input tax incurred on these costs should be left as residual (following the principles laid down by the European Court of Justice in *Ghent Coal*

Terminal). Where costs are used to make other supplies (for example, professional fees that relate to more than one development) the input tax should be adjusted if appropriate under the "clawback" and "payback" rules outlined in section 2.2.

4.3 What should I do when I have decided what supplies I will make?

At a later stage in a speculative supply a developer will decide to proceed with a development. They will have a clear intention as to what supplies they will make, and hence what the VAT liability of those supplies will be. The Annex assumes that this occurs at the point when land is acquired, as this is usually the case. In those cases where the decision to proceed comes a significant time before or after the acquisition of the land any adjustment of input tax should take place at that time.

At this stage input tax on the earlier speculative costs should be adjusted under the "clawback" and "payback" rules outlined in section 2.2 as the costs will now be used in making a taxable or an exempt supply (no adjustment is required if the developer intends to make both taxable and exempt supplies). Input tax on ongoing costs should be attributed to the expected taxable or exempt supplies.

Some supplies are exempt, but the developer can opt to tax them (see section 8 of VAT Notice 742 *Land and Property*). If a developer does not opt to tax the property it is assumed that his intended supplies will be exempt (VAT tribunal decision in *Lawson Mardon Pension Scheme*). Consequently a "clawback" adjustment should be made, and ongoing input tax should be attributed to exempt supplies. If the developer opts to tax the property, so that intended supplies would be taxable, a "payback" adjustment should be made and ongoing input tax attributed to taxable supplies. Where the intended supply is standard-rated (eg sale of a new commercial building) or zero-rated (sale of new dwellings) in its own right a "payback" adjustment should be made and ongoing input tax attributed to taxable supplies.

Annex: Decision-making stages for attribution and adjustment of input tax on speculative costs for developers

Stage 1 "Looking for opportunities"

Philosophy: "We are spending money looking for potential development opportunities but we have no real idea at this stage about what we might be able to do or whether we might actually do something"

Land held? – No.

Typical costs might be:

- looking for sites (eg finders fees)
- options to purchase land
- soil tests
- general feasibility/viability/research studies
- consultants/other professional fees.

Input tax treatment: residual.

Stage 2 "Projects in mind"

Philosophy: "We know what we want to try and do and are spending money to get ourselves into a position to be able to do it"

Land held? – Possibly.

Typical costs might be:

- options to purchase land
- detailed feasibility/viability/research studies
- seeking planning permission
- outline drawings/models
- consultants fees/other professional fees.

Input tax treatment:

(a) Review stage 1 input tax:

- leave input tax as residual on written-off costs for projects which will not proceed;
- leave input tax as residual if no land yet held;
- leave input tax as residual if land now held but taxable and exempt supplies are intended;
- adjust input tax if land now held and taxable or exempt supplies are intended.

(b) Stage 2 input tax:

- treat input tax as residual if no land yet held;
- treat input tax as residual if land now held but taxable and exempt supplies are intended;
- attribute input tax to taxable or exempt supplies if land now held.

Stage 3 "Projects in hand"

Philosophy: "We are in position to do what we want to do and we are spending money making it happen"

Land held? – Probably.

Typical costs might be:

- acquisition costs
- construction/development costs
- consultants fees/other professional fees
- success/kickback fees.

Input tax treatment:

(a) Review stage 1 and 2 input tax:

- leave input tax as residual on written-off costs for projects which will not proceed;
- leave input tax as residual if no land yet held;
- leave input tax as residual if land now held but taxable and exempt supplies are intended;
- adjust input tax if land now held and taxable or exempt supplies are intended.

(b) Stage 3 input tax:

- treat input tax as residual if no land yet held;
- treat input tax as residual if land now held but taxable and exempt supplies are intended;
- attribute input tax to taxable or exempt supplies if land now held.

Stage 4 "Making a supply"

Philosophy: "We are making a supply"

Land held? – Yes.

Typical costs might be:

- construction/development costs
- consultants/other professional fees
- marketing costs
- legal fees
- disposal costs
- success/kickback fees.

Input tax treatment:

(a) Review stage 1, 2 and 3 input tax:

- leave input tax as residual on written-off costs for projects which will not proceed;
- leave input tax as residual if land held but taxable and exempt supplies intended;
- adjust input tax if land held and taxable or exempt supplies are to be made.

(b) Stage 4 input tax:

- treat input tax as residual if land held and taxable and exempt supplies intended;

- attribute input tax to intended taxable or exempt supplies.

HM Customs and Excise (VAT Information Sheet 08/01) – December 2001.'

Clawback of input tax where the creditor is unpaid

2.34 A taxable person can, subject to the normal rules, deduct input tax when it has received a supply and obtained a valid tax invoice. Where, however, the creditor is unpaid the VAT is clawed back.

Supplies made before 1 January 2003

2.35 Where a valid claim for bad debt relief has been made by the supplier and the supplier has notified the recipient of the supply, the recipient has to repay any input tax that has been reclaimed. The entitlement to input tax expires at the date of the bad debt relief claim (VAT Regulations 1995/2518, regs 172C–E).

Where a business has been transferred as a going concern and the VAT number has also been transferred, the transferee takes over the transferor's obligation to repay the input tax.

By concession, insolvency practitioners need not repay the input tax after an insolvency procedure (eg bankruptcies, liquidations, receiverships etc) has been commenced. The effective date for the operation of this concession is the date of Customs and Excise's claim in the insolvency. The concession only applies to provisional liquidations if it is followed by permanent liquidation.

Where a payment is made in respect of the supply received, a claim can be made (a restoration of the input tax entitlement) for the input tax element of the payment.

Supplies made on or after 1 January 2003

2.36 Where a taxable person has not paid for a supply within six months of the date of supply or, if later, the due date for payment, any VAT that has been reclaimed must be repaid to Customs and Excise. If the supply has been part paid, an apportionment is made to calculate the input tax to be repaid (VAT Regulations 1995/2518, reg 172F–I).

The same insolvency concession as described at **2.35** above applies.

Where a payment is made in respect of the supply, a claim can be made (a restoration of the input tax entitlement) for the input tax element of the payment. This will, of course, create problems for businesses that do not introduce systems to capture information about unpaid expenses, for instance where there are disputed bills. The position for supplies made before 1 January 2003 was that a notification would be sent to the recipient of the supply and this would prompt the recipient to repay the input tax claimed. Now, there will be no notification and businesses should introduce a system of control in their creditors account to ensure that repayment of input tax is made where a debt is overdue by six months (and also to ensure that a claim is made after the debt is settled).

Deduction of VAT on third party consideration

2.37 To reclaim VAT as a deduction it is necessary for the VAT to be incurred by the taxable person. There are many instances where the taxable person does not receive the supply where this can be questioned. For instance, where an employee incurs an expense, it will normally be regarded as being incurred by the employing taxable person as the employee is acting for the employer (see **Chapter 4** for a more detailed analysis of this point, particularly with reference to invoicing).

2.38 Businesses will also frequently offer to pay another party's costs as part of the deal for the purchase or sale of an asset (typically a property). This VAT is not deductible by the person that has paid the costs, it is deductible (subject to the normal rules) by the person that received the supply.

Example 1

Company A sells a property that is subject to VAT (the election to waive exemption having been made). Company A incurs legal costs of £10,000 plus VAT on the sale.

Company B agrees to buy the property and pay the legal costs of Company A.

As Company A can reclaim the VAT incurred on the legal costs (because it is a taxable sale), it should reclaim the VAT and Company B will be required to pay £10,000 in costs to A. The law firm should issue the invoice to Company A. Company B will require a copy for its records but, as the invoice will be addressed to Company A, the VAT cannot be reclaimed by B. The £10,000 costs are, in fact, part of the consideration for the acquisition of the property. Thus, A will add an extra £10,000 to the sale price of the property and effectively charge £10,000 plus VAT.

If Company A had not elected to waive the exemption, its costs would have been £11,750 as it would not be able to reclaim the VAT incurred. Company B would be required to pay this amount to A, even if B can reclaim all the VAT it incurs. This is because the VAT charged is not VAT incurred by Company B, but by Company A.

As part of a settlement, Company Y may agrees to pay the legal costs of Company X. If the cost of the legal expenses to Company X £20,000 plus VAT, and X cannot reclaim VAT, the amount to be paid by Company Y would be £23,500. Company Y would not be able to reclaim the VAT element as the supply was made to X and not Y. If, however, Company X was a fully taxable person, then the cost to X would have been £20,000 and Y would only be liable to pay £20,000.

A (seeming) exception to the position of companies in the examples above where a company organises for the supplies to be made to it, even though the benefit is received by a third party. A house building company offered to assist purchasers of its properties with the sale of their own properties. It used its own solicitors and engaged estate agents to sell the properties owned by these third parties. The company reclaimed the VAT incurred on the estate agents' fees. It was held that it was eligible to reclaim this VAT as the supplies had been received by the company for the purpose of its business. The fact that another party also received the service did not deprive the taxable person that arranged the service from the benefit of input tax deduction (*C & E Comrs v Redrow Group plc [1999] STC 161, HL* (**Case Summary 31**)).

2.39 Customs and Excise have stated in Business Brief 27/99 that this decision only applies where there is a claim to input tax by a taxable person that has commissioned the goods or services and contracted with the supplier. There is no opportunity for a person to reclaim VAT where it is merely meeting the costs of another party, as in the example of companies X and Y shown above. Despite this being Customs and Excise's view, it still contested a claim for input tax where airline passengers were given meal vouchers to be exchanged at airport restaurants when flights were delayed. It was held in this decision that the input tax was deductible and no output tax was due, as it was all part of the single supply of zero-rated travel (*British Airways plc [2000] V & DR 74*).

2.40 Similarly, where an organisation (G) based in Liechtenstein arranged for a UK partnership (B) to supply advertisements in the UK calling for a referendum on European Union issues, B sent the invoices to G. These were treated as zero-rated invoices on the basis that G was outside the EU. Customs and Excise issued an assessment, as it believed that the benefit of the supplies accrued to a UK political party (R). The tribunal held that G was the recipient as it had arranged for the services to be supplied and the fact that R received a service or benefit was not relevant (*Goldsmith Foundation for European Affairs [2000] V & DR 97*).

Divisional registration

2.41 A corporate body that carries on its business in divisions can register in the names of the division (VATA 1994, s 46). Each division must be an independent accounting unit with a separate identity (either by geography, types of supply, or function). Each division is given a separate VAT number and makes its own VAT return. The divisions are *not*, however, separate taxable persons. The corporate body as a whole remains liable for all VAT debts and obligations of all of the divisions. VAT invoices are not permitted to be issued for transactions between divisions and no input tax can be reclaimed on 'supplies' made between divisions.

Divisional registration is only permitted where the corporate body as a whole is either fully taxable or treated as fully taxable. Any exempt input tax must remain below the de minimis limits.

Groups of companies

2.42 Article 4(4) of the Sixth VAT Directive allows member states to treat independent legal persons as a single taxable person provided such legal persons are closely bound to one another by financial, economic and organisational links. VATA 1994, s 43 enacts this provision in UK legislation.

2.43 Supplies between group members are not treated as supplies for VAT purposes. Thus, no VAT is charged on such supplies and no input tax can be deducted. The general principle that applies is that the VAT position of the group is determined by the activities of the group as a whole, the transactions external to the group, ignoring any internal transactions. It was found in *C & E Comrs v Kingfisher plc [1994] STC 63, QB* (**Case Summary 16**) that the representative member carried on all transactions for the group members: it was a single taxable person and there was not to be a separation of supplies, activities or functions within the group (but see below). All group members, however, are jointly and severally liable for any VAT due from the representative member and remain liable for the debts incurred whilst they were members of the group, even when they have left the group.

2.44 To be eligible for group treatment, one of the group must control each of the others, or one person must control all the members, or individuals in partnership must control each of them. Each member of the group must be a body corporate within the meaning of the Companies Act 1985. Each of the bodies must also be established or have a fixed establishment in the UK (VATA 1994, s 43A).

2.45 Input tax deduction is determined by the status of the group as a whole. Customs and Excise may, however, agree a special method where input tax deduction can be determined on a member-by-member basis, or any other method if it gives a fair and reasonable result.

2.46 Following the *Kingfisher* decision, Customs and Excise introduced legislation regarding special status companies. Where the status of an entity making a supply is relevant to the supply, then the group is not to be examined as a single taxable person. Thus, if a company is an insurance company, the supplies made by the insurance company will be exempt if they are insurance but insurance supplies made by other group members will not be exempt (unless they also qualify as insurers). In addition, the input tax recoverable will be determined by the entity incurring the VAT. Also, if a company in the group builds a dwelling, its sale can only be zero-rated if the person constructing makes the sale. Where the sale is made by another member of the group (following an intra-group transfer), the supply will be exempt and the group will suffer an input tax loss. This would appear contrary to the provisions in Article 4(4) of the Sixth VAT Directive, as the group is not treated as a single taxable person.

2.47 Several anti-avoidance provisions apply to VAT groups and these can affect the ability to deduct. Customs and Excise may direct that:

- a separately registered company eligible to be treated as a member of a VAT group will be treated as a member of the group from a specified date;
- a company that is in a group is removed from the group from a specified date; and
- a supply that was initially treated as being disregarded as being a supply is to be subject to VAT as if it were a supply made by a non-group member (VATA 1994, Sch 9(A)).

Clearly, this can affect deduction. For instance, if a supply is made to a group member that is not fully taxable, it would normally be ignored when the supplier is in the group. Where the supplier is outside the group, VAT would have to be charged and the full amount of VAT may not be deductible.

2.48 This provision was introduced to prevent exit (and other) schemes. This type of scheme was examined by the House of Lords in *Thorn Resources Ltd and Thorn Materials Supply v C & E Comrs [1998] STC 725, HL*. In this case, Thorn Resources and Thorn Materials were paid 90 per cent of the cost of cars to be purchased for the Thorn Group, whilst they were members of the Thorn VAT group. Normally the VAT on the purchase of these cars would not have been deductible. As the 90 per cent payment was made whilst the two prepayment companies were in the VAT group, it was disregarded for VAT purposes. After receipt of the payment, the two pre-payment companies left the VAT group. The companies then acquired the cars that were to be sold and deducted the input tax incurred (as they were cars bought for resale). The companies then received the 10 per cent payment and accounted for VAT on that 10 per cent. Customs and Excise were clearly concerned that this type of arrangement would work, and introduced VATA 1994, Sch 9(A) as described above. It was held, however, that the grouping provisions were not designed to confer exemption or relief from tax, but were to facilitate the collection of tax by treating all supplies made and received as if they had been made and received by the representative member of the group. It was held that the amount that was subject to VAT was the 10 per cent and the advance payment of 90 per cent that was received whilst the two prepayment companies were inside the group. The judgement forcibly finds against this type of avoidance. This has not, however, persuaded Customs and Excise to withdraw the avoidance provisions of VATA 1994, Sch 9(A).

2.49 In addition, Customs and Excise can refuse applications to group, to de-group or direct that a company should be removed from a group (VATA 1994, ss 43B and 43C). Customs and Excise are to exercise these powers to 'protect the revenue'. This does not mean that the Department can refuse to group a company merely because less VAT will be payable or more VAT can be deducted through the operation of grouping. The discretion is to be exercised to prevent avoidance, but not to prevent the normal operations of grouping where this results in a reduced amount of VAT payable (see *National Westminster Bank plc [1999] v & DR 201*).

2.50 Furthermore, Customs and Excise have a period of discretion regarding the date an entity can be de-grouped and this may have an adverse effect upon VAT deductions if the company to be de-grouped can claim a greater deduction when outside the group than when in the group (see *C & E Comrs v Barclays Bank plc [2001] EWCA Civ 1513, [2001] STC 1558* (**Case Summary 42**)). In the *Barclays* case, the Bank was anxious for a subsidiary to leave the group (as if it remained in the group it would adversely affect the Bank's partial exemption position) and gave the share capital of the subsidiary to a charitable trust on 27 February 1995. The gift of these shares meant that the subsidiary was no longer eligible to be a member of the group. Customs and Excise, however, did not remove the subsidiary until 1 July 1995. Barclays contended that the subsidiary was ineligible to be a member of the VAT group as a matter of law (as it was no longer controlled by a group member or anybody else that would entitle it to be grouped). The Court of Appeal, however, rejected this contention and held that whilst there was an obligation to inform Customs and Excise of any change in the constitution or ownership of group members of the group, Customs and Excise had discretion to determine the date that group treatment terminated. Group treatment did not begin with the onset of eligibility but with the beginning of a prescribed accounting period. The express provisions for the termination of such treatment did not provide that it should be coterminous with the cesser of eligibility to group.

2.51 Clearly, the timing of transactions will be important, as will ensuring that Customs and Excise have given a specified date for grouping or de-grouping to ensure that the VAT position of the group and subsidiaries can be determined.

2.52 Where a VAT group acquires a business as a transfer of a going concern (TOGC), a VAT charge MAY arise. Normally the acquisition of a business as a TOGC would not be treated as a supply but where a VAT group acquires a business as a TOGC, the representative member is deemed to make the supply (creating an output tax charge) and also to receive the deemed supply. The VAT incurred on the deemed supply can only be reclaimed in line with the partial exemption method of the VAT Group (VATA 1994, s 44). It may be necessary to agree a special method at this stage, if no special method has already been agreed. This is another avoidance provision to prevent partially exempt VAT groups acquiring assets without a VAT charge where another company previously used them for fully taxable purposes. The fully taxable company would have reclaimed all the VAT on the goods it owned and then transferred them to the group, which would need to continue the business of the old owner of the assets, but could also use them for their own exempt, non-business or partially exempt purposes.

2.53 The assets that are subject to the charge are all assets that would be taxable assets if supplied in the UK (except for any zero-rated supplies). The value of the charge would be the open market value of the assets. These provisions do not apply where:

- the representative member can deduct all VAT (VATA 1994, s 44(2));
- Customs and Excise are satisfied that the assets are more than three years old on the transfer (VATA 1994, s 44(3)); or
- the assets are capital items that are subject to the capital items scheme adjustments (these items will be subject to future adjustment according to their use – see **Chapter 7**) (VATA 1994, s 44(4)).

Where Customs and Excise are satisfied that the transfer or has not deducted all the VAT on the assets, they may reduce the charge (VATA 1994, s 44(9)).

2.54 As has been mentioned above, holding companies may not be regarded as a taxable person (see *Polysar Investments* at **2.17** above). Customs and Excise will, however, accept a holding company in a group if it complies with the requirements for grouping. The fact that this may enable more VAT to be deducted (for instance on the holding company expenses) than would be allowed if the holding company were outside the group is not a barrier to the holding company's inclusion in the VAT group.

Impact of change in liability: retrospective deductions

2.55 There are occasions where it has been accepted that a supply is either exempt or not a supply for VAT purposes, where it later transpires that the supply is taxable. The suppliers will not have charged VAT on these supplies, and on occasions Customs and Excise will not require the suppliers to account for VAT on income received in the past. These supplies, however, remain taxable.

2.56 Two examples may serve to demonstrate this position.

In *EC Commission v United Kingdom (C-359/97) [2000] STC 777, ECJ*, it was held that the UK was incorrect to fail to impose VAT on tolled roads and bridges unless the roads and bridges were operated by public authorities. As a consequence the UK has required VAT to be charged by privately owned bridge and road tolls since 1 February 2003 (details of these are given at **4.153**). Whilst VAT is being accounted for on these tolls from 1 February, it is arguable that these tolls were taxable supplies prior to 1 February and that the UK Government has taken a policy decision not to collect the VAT chargeable on these tolls.

In *Sinclair Collis Ltd v C & E Comrs (C-275/01) [2003] STC 898, ECJ*, it was held that the letting of a space for the installation of a vending machine was not a right over land. The commission received by the owner of the land from the owner of the machine was taxable. It is expected that Customs and Excise will announce that businesses that have treated these supplies as being exempt from VAT in the past, must account for VAT on the commission received from 1 January 2004. The supplies are, however, taxable and have been taxable since VAT was introduced in the UK (1 April 1973). In this instance, however, Customs and Excise are choosing not to collect the VAT that should have been charged.

2.57 It is, however, arguable in both instances described in **2.56** above that the supplies are, and have always been taxable. Thus, a taxable person that has received such supplies (the person using the toll bridge for their business purposes or the owner of the vending machine) should be able to reclaim the VAT that is included in the amount charged to him, even though this VAT did not have to be paid over to Customs and Excise. Although a VAT invoice will not have been received, it would be possible to reclaim the VAT using alternative evidence (expense forms for tolls or the payment sheets for the vending machines – see **Chapter 12** regarding alternative evidence). In addition, the right to deduct is not limited to instances where output tax has been paid, but also where it is payable (*Croydon Hotel & Leisure Co Ltd [1997] V & DR 245*).

Insolvency

2.58 Insolvency often occurs where a business does not have enough assets to cover its debts. The 'office holder' (the official receiver or the insolvency practitioner) will be liable to account for VAT in the normal way following their appointment. All normal rules, such as partial exemption, must be applied. The insolvency practitioner's fees do not relate to specific supplies but are a general overhead of the business. Thus, if the insolvent entity is partially exempt, full deduction will not be permissible. Where the business activities change it may be necessary to request a change in the partial exemption method.

2.59 Where a person becomes 'bankrupt or incapacitated' Customs and Excise may treat any person carrying on the business as a taxable person from the date of bankruptcy or incapacity (VATA 1994, s 46(4)) and this is termed the 'relevant date'.

2.60 Any VAT that is incurred in the running of the business is deductible by the office holder subject to the normal rules that apply to the taxable person before the bankruptcy or incapacity. Customs and Excise can, however, offer credits that arise from an insolvent person's VAT repayment claims arising before the relevant date to other Government Departments as Crown set-off. Customs and Excise only operate this procedure where the amount repaid exceeds £500, unless there is a fixed charge creditor to whom the repayment would have been made by the office holder.

2.61 Where a payment has not been paid to a creditor the recipient would normally be required to repay the input tax credit deducted subject to the Bad Debt Relief rules (see **above 2.36**). Insolvency practitioners, by concession, need not repay the input tax where there is a bad debt after an insolvency procedure (eg bankruptcies, liquidations, receiverships, etc) has been commenced. The effective date for the operation of this concession is the date of Customs and Excise's claim in the insolvency. The concession only applies to provisional liquidations if it is followed by permanent liquidation.

2.62 Bad debt relief can be claimed in insolvencies in the normal way. This will be made through a VAT return if the registration remains extant, but will be made on Form VAT 426 if it has been cancelled. A letter scheduling the claim, with copies of the relevant invoices, must be submitted to Insolvency Branch, Legal Recovery Unit for approval.

2.63 Where an office holder receives a credit note for supplies received in the pre-insolvency period, the VAT adjustment is related back to the period in which the supply was received (similar rules apply to credit notes issued for supplies made). To enable Customs and Excise to make the necessary adjustments, the credit notes must be declared to the local insolvency unit by letter or voluntary disclosure. A credit note adjustment cannot take place three years after the end of the accounting period in which the original supply was received due to the capping rules.

2.64 Input tax that has been incurred post de-registration can be claimed (again subject to the normal rules) using the Form VAT 426. This can be used by trustees in bankruptcy, trustees in sequestration, the official receiver, official assignees, liquidators or administrative receivers. This form cannot be used by solvent de-registered persons or for informal insolvencies.

2.65 The VAT that can be reclaimed is VAT incurred on:

- services received after de-registration that relate to the business carried on prior to de-registration;
- goods and services supplied before de-registration that have not been claimed on a VAT return;
- services of agents (eg solicitors, estate agents, etc), unless relating to an exempt supply; and
- realisation fees.

The form should be sent to: VAT 426 Claims Section, Insolvency Branch, Legal Recovery Unit, Queens Dock, Liverpool L74 4AA.

2.66 Normally claims will be paid within 30 working days unless there is a need for a verification visit, which will be made within 30 working days of receipt of the claim. Often verification visits will be made after payment of the claim.

Post-registration claims

2.67 Where the post-registration claim is for an insolvency the claim procedure described in the insolvency section at **2.58–2.66** above will apply, except where a liquidator has been appointed:

- in a members' voluntary liquidation and for all administration orders (where the claim form VAT 427 is sent to the VAT 426 Claims Section – see **2.65** above);
- in Scottish trust deeds or deeds or schemes of arrangement, where the form VAT 427 is sent to the de-registration unit; or
- in voluntary arrangements where the form VAT 427 is sent to the Voluntary Arrangement Service, Durrington Bridge House, Barrington Road, Worthing, West Sussex BN12 4SE.

2.68 Generally VAT cannot be reclaimed post-registration. Customs and Excise will, however, refund VAT on services supplied to the taxable person post-registration which relate to taxable supplies of the business carried on before de-registration. There is no time limit on the claim, but claims will not be paid more than three years after that date upon which the supply of services was made. Thus, if a taxable person de-registers on 1 January 2000 and a supply of services was made to that person on 1 January 2006, a claim must be submitted by 31 December 2008.

2.69 The normal expenses that are refunded are solicitors' and accountants' fees relating to the business whilst it was registered for VAT. It will *not* include VAT incurred on the disposal of assets that were held at the time of de-registration. Claims are paid subject to the normal rules (eg partial exemption).

2.70 Claims are made on Form VAT 427 and must be submitted with the original invoices.

Pre-registration and pre-incorporation deductions

2.71 Input tax can be reclaimed on goods on hand at the date of registration, if:

- the goods are for the purposes of the business that is or was carried on;
- the goods have not been supplied by the person, or consumed before the effective date of registration;
- the goods were acquired within the three years of the date of registration (note, the date of registration can be backdated by up to three years);
- all the normal input tax rules are applied; and
- a stock record is compiled showing the date of acquisition, a description, etc.

2.72 Input tax can be reclaimed on services received before registration where:

- the services are for the purposes of the business that is or was carried on;
- the services have not been supplied by the person before the effective date of registration;
- the services have not been performed on goods that have been supplied by or consumed by the taxable person before the date of registration (eg repairs to a vehicle sold before registration) or the services have not been performed on goods acquired more than three years before the date of registration;
- the services were received within six months of the date of registration (note, the date of registration can be backdated by up to three years);
- all the normal input tax rules are applied; and
- a record is compiled of the services showing the date of receipt, etc.

2.73 Input tax can also be deducted on supplies received before incorporation, despite them being supplied to another person, provided:

- the person to whom the supply was made or who paid the VAT:
  - (a) became a member, officer or employee of the corporate body and was reimbursed;
  - (b) was not a taxable person at the time; and
  - (c) acquired the goods or services for the purpose of the business;
- the normal rules for VAT deduction are followed.

2.74 It should be noted that Customs and Excise are conducting a consultation exercise on input tax deduction. Currently input tax is allowed for goods that are on hand that have been acquired in the previous three years and for services received in the previous six months. This, however, gives a disparate treatment between goods and services. Customs and Excise are proposing a three-year limit for services but there may be a need to introduce an apportionment of this VAT. This is because services may be 'consumed' in three years prior to registration. Thus, if a person registers for VAT on 1 November 2004, but signed a twelve-month maintenance contract for his computers on 1 January 2004, paying a one-off fee on 1 January of £12,000 plus VAT, he would currently be unable to reclaim any VAT. Customs and Excise are suggesting that the newly registered person should be able to reclaim £350 VAT (£12,000 × 2/12 × 17.5%).

2.75 Customs and Excise are also considering the contrasting treatment between a newly VAT-registered persons and an established taxable person where capital items are owned. Furthermore, there is a similar different treatment between established taxable persons and newly registered person where there is a change of intention. This currently works to the disadvantage of non-registered entities, as they cannot deduct any VAT where there is a change in intention or where a capital item was acquired outside the three-year time limit. It is proposed that there should be a Capital Goods Scheme type of adjustment for pre-registered input tax. It is assumed that this will also apply where there is a change in intention for items that are outside the current Capital Goods Scheme (that is, items other than a computer costing more than £50,000 or buildings costing more than £250,000). For example, if a newly registered person (that will only make taxable supplies) had purchased a property five years ago for £300,000 plus VAT of £52,500, it would not currently be able to reclaim any VAT. Customs and Excise are proposing that 50 per cent of this VAT should be recoverable (that is, 5/10 of the VAT incurred – ten years being the capital items adjustment period). Customs and Excise are consulting over whether this input tax should be claimed immediately or over a period of time.

Non-taxable persons

2.76 Non-taxable persons are, on occasion entitled to deduct input tax incurred.

Do-it-yourself house builders

2.77 A special VAT refund scheme operates for people construct their own dwellings. This is to put them in an equivalent position to persons purchasing a new dwelling from a commercial property developer. Customs and Excise will refund any VAT incurred on goods used in connection with the construction of a dwelling or the conversion of a non-residential building into a dwelling. There are a number of restrictions on what can be deducted and these parallel those for commercial developers (see **Chapter 4**).

2.78 Customs and Excise will also refund VAT incurred by a contractor, where the contractor is carrying out a conversion from a non-residential property to a residential property. Where VAT is due to be charged at the reduced rate on the conversion, VAT at the reduced rate only can be deducted, even if the contractor has charged 17.5 per cent. VAT incurred on services is not deductible on the construction of a new dwelling. VAT is not deductible on professional fees, or persons acting in a supervisory capacity.

2.79 A claim is submitted by using claim form VAT 431. This must be accompanied by: original invoices, a certificate of completion, documentary evidence of planning permission and a certificate from a surveyor or architect confirming that the goods shown in the claim would have been incorporated into the building.

2.80 There is no time limit on making a claim, but Customs and Excise prefer to receive the claim within six months of completion.

Non-UK businesses

2.81 A person established in another member state that incurs VAT in the UK can make a claim for refund where he is not undertaking taxable activity in the UK. This is claimed under the provisions of the Eighth VAT Directive. Similarly businesses established outside the EU can make similar claims under the provisions of the Thirteenth VAT Directive. See **Chapter 13** for further details.

Local authorities and the Crown

2.82 A local authority may, or may not be a taxable person. States, regional and local authorities and other bodies governed by public law are not taxable persons where they collect fees or other payments in connection with activities or transactions engaged in as public bodies (Sixth VAT Directive, art 4(5)). The UK has introduced provisions for Government, local authority and other public bodies to be able to deduct VAT so that VAT is not a burden upon local taxation or other public bodies (VATA 1994, ss 33 and 41). See **Chapter 9** for further information.

Other persons

2.83 Supplies may be zero-rated to diplomatic missions, 'international organisations', visiting NATO forces and their personnel based in other EU countries. The goods provided must be either for the personal use of the entitled persons or the official use of entitled bodies. The goods must not be new means of transport. The supplier must obtain sufficient documentation from the customer to claim the relief. Any goods provided must be removed from the UK. An international organisation means any organisation established by treaty between sovereign states or governments. See **Chapter 9** for further details.

Chapter 3

Use for the Purposes of Taxable Transactions

Introduction

3.1 **Chapter 1** outlined the basic principles of the deduction system. Although the detailed means of applying the deduction system are set out in the Sixth Directive, the courts have consistently referred to article 2 of the First Directive in interpreting those provisions.

The key principle underlying the VAT deductions system is that VAT is only deductible to the extent that it is incurred on *cost components* of a *taxable supply* or other supply in respect of which a VAT deduction is specifically allowed. The UK translates this principle into one that VAT is only deductible where the supply on which it arose is used or to be used for taxable purposes and certain other purposes.

In this chapter, the term cost component is examined first. This is followed by an examination of the detailed measures that are in place in order to ensure that only VAT incurred on cost components of a taxable supply or supplies is deducted.

Cost components

3.2 The term 'cost component' is found in the First Directive, art 2, but is not defined in either EU or UK VAT legislation. Thus, while the importance of the principle is well established by case law, a clear definition of precisely what is and what is not a cost component has tended to be elusive. In *C & E Comrs v Plantiflor Ltd [2000] STC 137, CA*, Ward LJ commented at page 153:

> '… My difficulty, and it may also be Laws J's difficulty as well, is that *Glawe Spiel* itself does not help identify what a cost-component is …'.

3.3 The term 'cost component' is used frequently in relation to cost accounting but, again, there does not appear to be a recognised standard definition of what constitutes a cost component from an accounting perspective. The reason for this is no doubt the fact that while certain costs will be readily recognised to be a cost of a particular activity, other more indirect costs are not as easily recognisable as such. Indeed, in commercial accounting, there is usually an element of subjectivity in determining which costs should be attributed to which cost centres. To some extent that same subjectivity is evident in the judicial decisions dealing with VAT deductions.

3.4 In his opinion in the case of *Lennartz v Finanzamt Mûnchen III (C-97/90) [1995] STC 514 at 526* (**Case Summary 12**), the Advocate-General outlines the VAT deductions system in the following terms:

> '7. Article 2 of EC Council Directive 67/227 (the First Directive) provides:
>
> "The principle of the common system of value added tax involves the application to goods and services of a general tax on consumption exactly proportional to the price of the goods and services, whatever the number of transactions which take place in the production and distribution process before the stage at which tax is charged.
>
> On each transaction, value added tax, calculated on the price of the goods or services at the rate applicable to such goods or services, shall be chargeable after deduction of the amount of value added tax borne directly by the various cost components."
>
> 8. The rules giving effect to the principle of deduction provided for in the second paragraph of that article were originally laid down in EC Council Directive 67/228 (the Second Directive), in particular in art 11 of that directive. The Sixth Directive, which superseded the Second Directive, laid down rather more detailed rules, which are set out in Title XI (arts 17–20).'

While the Advocate-General specifically notes that the Sixth VAT Directive supersedes the Second VAT Directive, it is clear from this quote that the purpose of the rules set out in the Sixth Directive, arts 17–20 is to ensure that the principles set out in the First Directive, art 2 are achieved. Other case law from the European Court of Justice supports this view.

3.5 This is demonstrated, for example, by the decision of the Court of Justice in the case of *BLP Group plc v C & E Comrs (C-9/94) [1995] STC 424 at 436* (**Case Summary 18**). At para 25, the Court answers the question of why the taxpayer would be entitled to deduct VAT on the raising of a loan to fund its business but cannot do so if it sells an investment to achieve the same economic objective in the following terms:

> '25. It is true that an undertaking whose activity is subject to VAT is entitled to deduct the tax on the services supplied by accountants or legal advisers for the taxable person's taxable transactions and that if BLP had decided to take out a bank loan for the purpose of meeting the same requirements, it would have been entitled to deduct the VAT on the accountant's services required for that purpose. However, that is a consequence of the fact that those services, whose costs form part of the undertaking's overheads and hence of the cost components of the products, are used by the taxable person for taxable transactions.'

3.6 The importance of the principle that VAT is only deductible if it is incurred on cost components of taxable supplies can be gauged from the consistent reference to the principle in UK Court decisions dealing with VAT deductions, including:

- *Schemepanel Trading Ltd v C & E Comrs [1996] STC 871, QBD*
- *C & E Comrs v Harpcombe [1996] STC 726, QBD*
- *C & E Comrs v UBAF Bank Ltd [1996] STC 372, CA* (**Case Summary 21**)

- *C & E Comrs v Redrow Group plc [1999] STC 161, HL* (**Case Summary 31**)
- *RAP Group plc v C & E Comrs [2000] STC 980, ChD* (**Case Summary 36**)
- *University of Sussex v C & E Comrs [2001] STC 1495*
- *Royal & Sun Alliance Insurance Group plc v C & E Comrs [2003] STC 832, HL* (**Case Summary 47**)
- *C & E Comrs v Southern Primary Housing Association [2004] STC 209, CA* (**Case Summary 51**).

Direct and immediate link

General principles

3.7 If the nature of what is a cost component is not defined, it can to a substantial extent be deduced from the relationship that the courts have said must exist between cost components and a taxable transaction or transactions for the relevant VAT to be deductible.

3.8 In *BLP Group plc v C & E Comrs [1995] STC 424* (**Case Summary 18**), the European Court of Justice noted at para 19 that:

> 'The use in that provision [Sixth Directive, Art 17(5)] of the words "for transactions" shows that to give the right to deduct under para 2, the goods or services in question *must* have a direct and immediate link with the taxable transactions, and that the ultimate aim pursued by the taxable person is irrelevant in this respect.' (Emphasis added.)

3.9 The need for a direct and immediate link was also referred to in *Abbey National plc v C & E Coms [2001] STC 297* (**Case Summary 39**). This case is considered in more detail at **3.20** below in relation to specific transactions. However, in essence, the European Court of Justice found that, in principle, where costs are incurred by a person *in the capacity* as taxable person (see **Chapter 2** – for what constitutes a taxable person) but are not related to a specific supply or supplies, those costs are linked to the whole of the activities of the business. At its lowest level therefore, all costs incurred as taxable person are intrinsically deductible. This is considered further in **3.20–3.23** below.

3.10 The nature of a direct and immediate link was also considered by the European Court of Justice in the case of *Midland Bank plc v C & E Comrs (C-98/98) [2000] STC 501* (**Case Summary 35**). The case concerned legal expenses incurred after an activity had taken place. The taxpayer sought to argue that because the expenses arose from defending a particular claim, the legal expenses were linked to the supplies made from the specific activity giving rise to the claim. Customs and Excise argued that the legal expenses had no link to the claim but were expenses of the whole business.

3.11 At para 29 of his opinion in *Midland Bank*, the Advocate-General effectively defines the expression 'direct and immediate link' in the following terms:

> 'So far as concerns the wording, I would mention first that the expression "direct and immediate link" was chosen by the Court, in the oft-cited *BLP* case, as a key to the interpretation of the terms used in Article 17 of the Sixth Directive. The use of the two adjectives "direct" and "immediate" cannot but refer to a particularly close link between the taxable transactions (in the present case, the financial transaction) carried out by a taxable person (in this case, the Midland) and the goods or services supplied by another taxable person (in the present case, Clifford Chance).
>
> In particular, the adjective "direct" means that there cannot be the appropriate link between two transactions where a third transaction takes place between them breaking the causal chain, or where the link between the two transactions is very distant in time. The example provided by the United Kingdom during the hearing seems apposite: A supplies a good to B; on delivery to B, an employee of A's drops the good on passer-by C's foot and injures him. C brings a claim for damages against A. The question then arises whether the legal costs incurred by A in defending itself against C could be seen as a cost component of the supply to B, or whether there is a different link with that supply. I am of the same view as the United Kingdom in that I believe that in such a case the link is too tenuous to be regarded as direct.
>
> The adjective "immediate" denotes a particularly close temporal proximity between the two transactions. That does not mean, however, as the Midland correctly observes in its submissions, that the tax on the input transaction must become chargeable before the output transaction is carried out (Any other solution might appear to run counter to the principles laid down by the Court, in particular in *Ghent Coal Terminal*, cited above. In that judgment, the Court held that the right to deduct remains where, by reason of circumstances beyond his control, the taxable person has never made use of those goods or services for the purpose of carrying out taxable transactions.); the only requirement is that the time which has elapsed between the two transactions should not be too long.'

The Advocate-General does, however, make it clear that the link may exist even where goods or services having been incurred with the intention of carrying out a taxable transaction are not in fact so used. Thus, in para 30 he continues:

> 'To that end, that requirement is met if the services received by B may be used for a deductible transaction or to prepare such a transaction or are capable of being so used. It is not inconceivable that such a link should exist where the services have not in actual fact been used for a deductible transaction by reason of circumstances beyond the control of company A, so long as neither fraud nor abuse is involved, for example circumstances in which company A falsely claims to wish to carry out a particular economic activity (see, to that effect, *Ghent Coal Terminal,* paragraphs 20, 21 and 22).'

The decision in *Ghent Coal Terminal* (see Case Summary 30) and related cases where the intended transaction was not carried out is considered in detail in **Chapter 2**. The Advocate-General then went on to point out:

'The corollary to such an interpretation is that there is no link, and thus no possible deduction of all the VAT, where it is objectively impossible to carry out the taxable output transaction at the time when taxable person B provides a service or a good to taxable person A.'

3.12 The European Court of Justice in its turn also stresses the need for a direct and immediate link in the following terms:

'30. A taxable person who makes transactions in respect of which VAT is deductible and transactions in respect of which it is not may deduct the VAT in respect of the goods or services acquired by him, provided that such goods or services have a direct and immediate link with the output transactions in respect of which VAT is deductible, without it being necessary to take into account art 17(2), (3) or (5) of the Sixth Directive. However, such a taxable person cannot deduct in its entirety the VAT charged on input services where they have been utilised not for the purpose of carrying out a deductible transaction but in the context of activities which are no more than the consequence of making such a transaction, unless that person can show by means of objective evidence that the expenditure involved in the acquisition of such services is part of the various cost components of the output transaction.'

The Court then concluded:

'1. Article 2 of the First Directive and art 17(2), (3) and (5) of the Sixth Directive must be interpreted as meaning that, in principle, the existence of a direct and immediate link between a particular input transaction and a particular output transaction or transactions giving rise to entitlement to deduct is necessary before the taxable person is entitled to deduct input VAT and in order to determine the extent of such entitlement.

2. It is for the national court to apply the 'direct and immediate link' test to the facts of each case before it. A taxable person who makes transactions in respect of which VAT is deductible and transactions in respect of which it is not may deduct the VAT in respect of the goods or services acquired by him, provided that such goods or services have a direct and immediate link with the output transactions in respect of which VAT is deductible, without it being necessary to take into account art 17(2), (3) or (5) of the Sixth Directive. However, such a taxable person cannot deduct in its entirety the VAT charged on input services where they have been utilised not for the purpose of carrying out a deductible transaction but in the context of activities which are no more than the consequence of making such a transaction, unless that person can show by means of objective evidence that the expenditure involved in the acquisition of such services is part of the various cost components of the output transaction.'

3.13 It will be clear from both the Advocate-General's opinion and the Court's judgment that there is no authority for concluding that all expenditure incurred subsequent to a supply is overhead VAT. The issue is whether the post-supply expenditure is a direct consequence of undertaking the particular work or is a consequence of a risk applying to the whole of the business or part of a business.

However, equally, the longer the period between when a supply is made and when costs are incurred, the less likely it is that there will be a specific link to the transactions undertaken.

3.14 By way of example, when a builder constructs a building it is inevitable that a number of faults are likely to disclose themselves only after occupation of the building. The customer will, therefore, normally retain some of the price until such faults are fixed. The costs of dealing with such faults will clearly be linked to that building and no other – in essence they are costs of constructing the building. The situation may well be different if legal costs were incurred in defending a claim by an employee for damages following injury on a site. Although the costs may have arisen on a particular site, the risk of such costs applies to the whole of the construction business and it would probably be a matter of chance that the injury incurred on a particular site.

3.15 The UK legislation dealing with the right to deduct refers extensively to the term 'use'. Thus, under UK legislation, VAT is only deductible to the extent that it is used or to be used for taxable transactions (or certain other similar transactions). In effect, therefore, what determines the question of whether or not there is a link between a particular supply of goods or services and any taxable transaction is the fact that the goods or services are *used* in order to make the taxable supply (or supplies) in question.

3.16 While the concept of use appears at first to be a relatively simple one, it is now common to find disputes before the VAT and Duties Tribunals and the courts that demonstrate the difficulty of deciding whether the necessary link exists. What constitutes use is discussed at paras **3.60–3.67** below.

Direct and immediate link where there is no immediate supply

3.17 The task of determining a direct and immediate link is relatively straightforward in the case of most on-going businesses. Direct costs and overheads can be more or less readily identified as forming part of the cost of supplies made. However, there are three particular circumstances where the link is more difficult to ascertain:

- the first is where a person sets out to undertake a business activity but that activity has to be aborted for any reason;
- the second is where costs are incurred on making supplies which by virtue of VAT legislation are not treated as a supply of goods or services, particularly the sale of a business as a going concern; and
- the third is where costs are incurred on the acquisition of a company or business.

The treatment of abortive transactions is considered in detail in **Chapter 2**.

Non-supplies – disposals of businesses

3.18 The Sixth Directive, art 5(8) provides that member states may consider that a transfer of a totality of assets or part of the totality of assets is not a supply of goods. Article 6(5) provides that art 5(8) also applies to services. Article 5(8) is a simplifying measure (see the Advocate-General's opinion at paras 22–24 in *Abbey National plc v C & E Comrs (C-408/98) [2001] STC 297*) (**Case Summary 39**). These provisions have been implemented in UK law.

3.19 Thus, provided that certain conditions are met, the disposal of a business as a going concern ('TOGC') is neither a supply of goods nor a supply of services (VAT (Special Provisions) Order 1995, art 5). Other transactions that would otherwise be regarded as supplies are also excluded from being taxable supplies by virtue of legislation, e g the disposal of repossessed goods (VAT (Case) Order 1992, art 4(1)(a)).

3.20 The question of whether the VAT on costs relating to non-supplies can be deducted was considered in *Abbey National plc*. The appellant was the representative member of a VAT group. One of its fellow group members, an insurance company, sold a building that it had let to commercial tenants. The property had been opted. The appellant's arguments are set out in the judgment of the European Court of Justice as follows:

> '17. Abbey National contends that, where a totality of assets or part thereof is transferred, the transferor is entitled to deduct the input VAT on the expenditure he has incurred for the services acquired in order to carry out the transfer.
>
> 18. It submits in particular that for VAT purposes, where the transferor and the transferee both, one before and one after the transfer, use the assets of the transferred business to make fully taxable supplies, the transferor may under art 5(8) of the Sixth Directive take account of the transferee's taxable supplies so as to recover the input VAT in full. In other words, although there is no taxable transaction as such, for the purposes of input VAT there is still a direct and immediate link with the transferee's taxable economic activities relating to the assets transferred.'

3.21 Customs and Excise (and the VAT and Duties Tribunal) had concluded that the VAT related to the business as a whole and so was to be treated as residual input tax and apportioned. The Court agreed with the arguments of Customs and Excise that the costs of concluding the disposal could not be related to the previous taxable business carried out with the assets. However, contrary to the arguments of Customs and Excise it concluded that:

> 'Where a member state has made use of the option in art 5(8) of the Sixth Directive, so that the transfer of a totality of assets or part thereof is regarded as not being a supply of goods, the costs incurred by the transferor for services acquired in order to effect that transfer form part of that taxable person's overheads and thus in principle have a direct and immediate link with the whole of his economic activity. If, therefore, the transferor effects both transactions in respect of which VAT is deductible and transactions in respect of which it is

not, it follows from art 17(5) of the Sixth Directive that he may deduct only that proportion of the VAT which is attributable to the former transactions. However, if the various services acquired by the transferor in order to effect the transfer have a direct and immediate link with a clearly defined part of his economic activities, so that the costs of those services form part of the overheads of that part of the business, and all the transactions relating to that part of the business are subject to VAT, he may deduct all the VAT charged on his costs of acquiring those services.'

3.22 The judgment in *Abbey National plc* is therefore authority for the principle that the costs incurred in disposing of all or part of a business will be overhead expenditure. Overhead expenditure is in principle linked to the whole of the business, but in some cases it might be regarded as overheads of a part of the business only. In the latter case, it is the liability of the supplies of that part of the business to which the overheads relate that determine whether or not the overheads are directly and immediately linked to taxable supplies or other supplies or both.

The point can be illustrated as follows.

Example 1

A taxable person owns various properties, each of which is let. He has exercised the option to tax in respect of some of the properties but has not done so in respect of others. Because the properties are all let, the sale of any single property should meet the conditions to be regarded as a TOGC subject to the requirement that any transferee must also opt to tax where the properties are already opted and meets the other conditions for TOGC treatment.

On a sale of any single property, the question will arise whether the costs of sale are to be regarded under the decision in *Abbey National plc* to be costs relating to:

- the whole business;
- a separate part of the business, being the single property, which, as noted, meets the conditions for TOGC treatment.

If the costs are referable to the whole business, the VAT incurred will be residual input tax. However, if the costs are referable to a part of the business, being the part sold, then they will be deductible according to the nature of the supplies made by that property (taxable, exempt or, in the case of a combined residential/commercial property where the option has been exercised, residual).

3.23 No doubt, in the example above, it may be possible to argue that notwithstanding that there is a sale of a single property that is capable of operation on its own, the costs are residual, eg if sold as part of a rationalisation scheme where the intent is to sell one or more properties without there being any fixed intent to sell a specific property or properties. In most cases, logic suggests that since the property sold would have been marketed as such, the entitlement to a deduction will depend on whether the property itself had been opted or not.

Acquisitions of businesses or shares in a company

3.24 Shares and interests in businesses are capital assets that are not normally consumed in production. Unlike other resources, the link with taxable or other supplies is more problematic. Customs and Excise accept that the costs relate to the acquisition of a business as a TOGC or shares in a company may be deductible (see **3.27** below).

3.25 The costs of acquiring shares in companies was considered in the case of *Polysar Investments Netherlands BV v Inspecteur der Invoerrechten en Accijnzen, Arnhem (C-60/90) [1993] STC 222, ECJ* (**Case Summary 11**). Polysar was a pure holding company. Its sole source of income was dividends. It took no active part in the management of its subsidiaries. It sought to deduct VAT incurred in the course of its activities. The European Court of Justice concluded that:

> 'Article 4 of the Sixth Directive must be interpreted as meaning that a holding company whose sole purpose is to acquire holdings in other undertakings, without involving itself directly or indirectly in the management of those undertakings, without prejudice to its rights as shareholder, does not have the status of a taxable person for the purposes of VAT and therefore has no right to deduct tax under art 17 of the Sixth Directive. The fact that the holding company belongs to a worldwide group of undertakings, which appears outwardly under a single name, is not relevant to the company's classification as a taxable person for the purposes of VAT.'

See also *Harnas and Helm CV v Staatssecretaris van Financiën (C-16/00) [1997] STC 364, ECJ* (**Case Summary 26**) in which the same principles were applied to bond holdings.

3.26 The decision in *Polysar* should be compared with the more recent decision of the Court in *Cibo Participations SA v Directeur régional des impôts du Nord-Pas-de-Calais (C-16/00) [2002] STC 460* (**Case Summary 41**). Cibo was also a holding company but in contrast to Polysar it received management fees from its subsidiaries. However, the facts set out in the Advocate-General's opinion make it clear that dividends comprised the majority of the taxpayer's income. The French tax authority refused a deduction for VAT incurred on the costs of the acquisition, including auditing of the companies, assistance with the negotiation of the purchase price of the shares, organising the take-over of the companies and legal and tax services, on the grounds that the VAT was not incurred in the capacity as taxable person. The European Court of Justice reaffirmed its conclusion in *Polysar* that the acquisition of shares in a company is in principle not an economic activity. However, the Court went on to distinguish this situation with that in *Polysar,* concluding as follows:

> '2. Expenditure incurred by a holding company in respect of the various services which it purchases in connection with the acquisition of a shareholding in a subsidiary forms part of its general costs and therefore has, in principle, a direct and immediate link with its business as a whole. Thus, if the holding company carries out both transactions in respect of which VAT is deductible and transactions in respect of which it is not, it follows from the first sub-paragraph of art 17(2) of the Sixth Directive that it may deduct only that proportion of the VAT which is attributable to the former.'

3.27 The *Cibo* case therefore affirms Customs and Excise's policy that the VAT incurred on the acquisition of shares in subsidiaries that are actively managed by a holding company is overhead input tax. However, it is possible that the overheads relating to the acquisition of the company relate to a particular part of the business rather than the business as a whole. In the latter case, the decision in *Abbey National plc* would suggest the costs would be cost components of that part of the business to which the acquisition relates. For example, a taxable person carries out a number of activities in divisions, one of which is leasing of assets. If the taxable person acquires a company that leases assets to augment its leasing business it may be argued that the acquisition costs relate only to the leasing division.

Multiple transactions

3.28 Difficulties have nevertheless arisen in the case of certain such transactions or combinations of such transactions and in others such as the issue of shares as consideration for shares or assets.

3.29 To understand the dilemma in the case of multiple transactions, it is necessary to consider the case of *BLP Group plc v C & E Comrs (C-4/94) [1995] STC 424* (**Case Summary 18**). BLP, a holding and management company, sold a German subsidiary. It incurred costs on the disposal of the shares and sought to deduct the VAT it had incurred on the costs. It argued that the VAT was deductible because the reason for the sale was to reduce debt that had arisen from its taxable transactions and that therefore the VAT was incurred for the purposes of its taxable transactions. The High Court referred three questions to the European Court of Justice for a preliminary ruling, ie:

> '(1) Having regard to art 2 of the First Directive and art 17 of the Sixth Directive, where a taxable person (A) supplies services to another taxable person (B), and those services are used by B for an exempt transaction (sale of shares) which was treated as an "incidental financial transaction" and whose purpose and result was to raise money to discharge all of B's indebtedness, are those services supplied by A:
>
> (a) services used for the purpose of an exempt transaction such that input tax thereon is not deductible;
>
> (b) services used for the purpose of taxable transactions (namely B's core business of making taxable supplies) such that input tax thereon is deductible in whole;
>
> (c) services used for both exempt and taxable transactions such that the input tax thereon is deductible in accordance with art 17(5) of the Sixth Directive?
>
> (2) … (not answered)
>
> (3) … (not answered).'

The European Court of Justice answered the questions as follows:

> 'Article 2 of the First Directive and art 17 of the Sixth Directive must be interpreted as meaning that, except in the cases expressly provided for by those directives, where a taxable person supplies services to another taxable person who uses them for an exempt transaction, the latter person is not entitled to deduct the input VAT paid, even if the ultimate purpose of the transaction is the carrying out of a taxable transaction.'

3.30 What is clear from *BLP Group plc* is, therefore, that there must be a causal link between the transaction on which the VAT sought to be deducted was incurred and a taxable transaction or transactions. Thus, in his opinion in *Abbey National plc* (**Case Summary 39**), the Advocate-General comments at para 35:

> 'Nevertheless, it remains clear from *BLP* that the "chain-breaking effect" which is an inherent feature of an exempt transaction will always prevent VAT incurred on supplies used for such a transaction from being deductible from VAT to be paid on a subsequent output supply of which the exempt transaction forms a cost component. The need for a "direct and immediate link" thus does not refer exclusively to the very next link in the chain but serves to exclude situations where the chain has been broken by an exempt supply. I agree here with the opinion delivered on 30 September 1999 by Advocate-General Saggio in *Customs and Excise v Midland Bank plc (Case C-98/98) at para. 29,* where he considers that the words "direct" and "immediate" refer to a "particularly close link between two transactions", in which no third transaction has taken place "breaking the causal chain".'

3.31 One of the immediate results of *BLP Group plc* was that Customs and Excise used the case to argue that no input tax was deductible on certain transactions such as a share for share issue or share for assets transaction. This was on the basis that since there was only one supply (the issue of shares), that was the only transaction to which the input tax on the costs of the whole transaction related.

3.32 The existence of or the extent to which a link can be established in transactions involving the acquisition or disposal of shares in exchange for an issue of shares has been considered in recent cases of *RAP Group plc v C & E Comrs [2000] STC 980* (**Case Summary 36**) and *Southampton Leisure Holdings plc [2002] V & DR 235* (**Case Summary 44**).

3.33 *BLP Group plc* and *Abbey National plc* were considered in *RAP Group plc*. In *RAP Group plc*, the appellant issued shares in consideration for the acquisition of shares in another company. Customs and Excise argued that to have regard to the acquisition was to look beyond the immediate supply (the exempt issue of shares) and that this was not permissible in terms of the decision in *BLP Group plc*. The Court held that the Tribunal had been wrong to reject evidence that part of the costs was related both to the acquisition of shares and to the issue of shares. Accordingly, the part of the VAT that was referable to costs incurred in relation to both the acquisition and the issue of shares was residual input tax and an apportionment was necessary to determine the deductible VAT.

3.34 The Customs and Excise argument in *RAP Group plc* contemplates a sequential set of transactions (Scenario 1 in the diagram below). In fact, there are parallel activities (Scenario 2 in the diagram below) and accordingly, the blocking effect encountered in *BLP Group plc* does not apply.

Scenario 1					
Costs		Exempt		Taxable	No deduction
Scenario 2					
		Exempt			No deduction
Costs					
		No supply			Residual

Fig. 2

3.35 A similar situation was considered in *Southampton Leisure Holdings plc [2002] V & DR 235* in which the taxpayer was more successful in providing evidence that costs related both to the acquisition carried out by the taxpayer and the issue of shares by the taxpayer.

3.36 The consequence of there being parallel rather than sequential transactions is that there is no 'chain-breaking transaction' as in *BLP Group plc*, and the normal rules relating to the deduction of VAT on the acquisition (no supply) must follow – it is overhead VAT. It is worth noting that had Customs and Excise succeeded in their argument, there could have been considerable scope for tax avoidance simply by ensuring that a taxable transaction preceded the exempt one.

Business v non-business use

General

3.37 There is no reference to the terms business and non-business in European VAT law. As noted in the discussion relating to abortive transactions in **3.11** above and in **Chapter 2** the key issue in European VAT law is rather the capacity in which a person undertakes an activity. If the person undertakes an activity as a taxable person, two basic consequences follow:

- first, the person must account for VAT on any consideration received in respect of supplies made unless the supplies are exempt;

- second, the person acquires a right to deduct VAT incurred in undertaking that activity insofar as the VAT is incurred on goods or services used for the purposes of taxable transactions.

Conversely, if VAT is incurred otherwise than in the capacity as taxable person, there is no right to deduct. Further, the disposal of an asset acquired otherwise than as taxable person is not a supply and is not subject to VAT (see *Finanzamt Uelzen v Armbrecht* (**Case Summary 19**) discussed in Chapter 2 above and at **3.46** below).

3.38 The term taxable person is defined in the Sixth Directive, art 4(1) as follows:

> ' "Taxable person" shall mean any person who independently carries out in any place any economic activity specified in paragraph 2, whatever the purpose or results of the at activity.'

Article 4(2) then defines an economic activity as:

> 'The economic activities referred to in paragraph 1 shall comprise all activities of producers, traders and persons supplying services including mining and agricultural activities and activities of the professions. The exploitation of tangible or intangible property for the purpose of obtaining income therefrom on a continuing basis shall also be considered an economic activity.'

3.39 The question of what is a taxable person has been considered by the European Court of Justice in a number of cases. They are considered in more detail in Chapter 2 above, but the key points that emerge are:

- the term economic activity extends to any activities undertaken that are preparatory to undertaking such activity; and
- once a person has been identified as a taxable person, the right to deduct cannot be withdrawn.

3.40 These principles were firmly established in the seminal case of *Rompelman v Minister van Financiën (268/83) [1985] ECR 655* (**Case Summary 4**). The case dealt with a partnership that sought to deduct VAT on its preliminary activities in the development of a property. The Dutch tax authorities refused a deduction for VAT incurred on those activities on the basis that exploitation of the property had not commenced. The European Court of Justice looked at the interaction of the Sixth Directive, art 4 (definition of taxable person) together with art 17(1) (the right to deduct VAT when it is incurred) and concluded that:

> 'Any other interpretation ... [i.e. one that did not regard the partnership as a taxable person when it commenced its preparatory activities] would burden the trader with the cost of VAT in the course of his economic activity without allowing him to deduct it in accordance with Article 17 ...'.

The Court then went on to comment that even a system that provided that input tax will be refunded once the activities actually commenced would be contrary to the Sixth Directive because there would be a financial charge that would encumber the property pending the commencement of exploitation.

3.41 In the later case of *Enkler v Finanzamt Homburg (C-230/94) [1996] STC 1316* (**Case Summary 25**), the European Court of Justice reaffirmed the principle that VAT incurred in the capacity as a taxable person is deductible (even if there is an intention that there will be some private use). However, it also noted that it was for the national courts to determine whether, in the particular circumstances of any case, a person is in fact a taxable person. The decision therefore makes it clear that member states can deny a deduction in the case where there is minimal business use aimed at securing a deduction for non-business VAT.

The principles that apply to private use

3.42 EC VAT law recognises that a person may acquire an asset or incur costs in both his capacity as taxable person and in a private capacity. The question of how to deal with cases where an asset is acquired both in the capacity as taxable person and as final consumer was the subject of specific consideration in the procedures leading to the adoption of the Sixth Directive. At the heart of the issue was the principle that a taxable person must be relieved of all the costs of VAT on expenditure used to carry out an economic activity – even the funding of VAT (see comments on *Rompelman* in **3.40** above).

3.43 The dilemma that faced the Community legislators is referred to in the case of *Lennartz v Finanzamt München III (C-97/90)[1995] STC 514* (**Case Summary 12**). In his opinion, the Advocate-General comments as follows:

> '58 … The provisions on the apportionment of input tax contained in article 17(5) … do not therefore apply. Consequently, such a person has, in principle, the right to full and immediate deduction of the input tax incurred on the acquisition of the assets.
>
> 59. Support for this view may be found in the Commission's commentary, in its proposal for the Sixth Directive (Bulletin of the European Communities, Supplement 11/73), on art 5(6) (or art 5(3)(a) as it was in the proposal), which is the equivalent provision, in art 5 ("supplies of goods"), to art 6(2)(a). The Commission stated: "The same aim [avoidance of unjustified advantages for taxable persons] could have been attained by means of adjustments to deductions already made, but the technique of treating these transactions as taxable supplies was chosen for reasons of impartiality and simplicity". Thus, the output tax charge was specifically chosen as an alternative to a restriction on the right to deduct input tax. Although the last sentence of art 6(2) permits member states, within certain limits, to derogate from the private use mechanism laid down in that paragraph, that sentence is not applicable here for reasons which I shall explain later (see para 75).'

3.44 Accordingly, it is provided that the whole of the VAT incurred on such expenditure is deductible but where there is any subsequent application to private use, there is an output tax charge. The relevant provisions are the Sixth Directive, art 5(6), which reads:

'The application by a taxable person of goods forming part of his business assets for his private use or that of his staff, or the disposal thereof free of charge or more generally their application for purposes other than those of his business, where the value added tax on the goods in question or the component parts thereof was wholly or partly deductible, shall be treated as supplies made for consideration. However, applications for the giving of samples or the making of gifts of small value for the purposes of the taxable person's business shall not be so treated.'

And the Sixth Directive, art 6(2), which reads:

'The following shall be treated as supplies of services for consideration:

(a) the use of goods forming part of the assets of a business for the private use of the taxable person or of his staff or more generally for purposes other than those of his business where the value added tax on such goods is wholly or partly deductible;

(b) supplies of services carried out free of charge by the taxable person for his own private use or that of his staff or more generally for purposes other than those of his business.

Member States may derogate from the provisions of this paragraph provided that such derogation does not lead to distortion of competition.'

3.45 The application of the Sixth Directive, art 6(2) has been considered in a number of other cases, most notably:

- *Kühne v Finanzamt München III (50/88) [1990] STC 749* (**Case Summary 10**)
- *Finanzamt Uelzen v Armbrecht (C-291/92) [1995] STC 997* (**Case Summary 19**)
- *Enkler v Finanzamt Homburg (C-230/94) [1996] STC 1316* (**Case Summary 25**)
- *Finanzamt München III v Möhsche (C-193/91) [1997] STC 195*
- *Wolfgang Seeling v Finanzamt Starnberg (C-269/00) [2003] STC 805* (**Case Summary 48**).

3.46 In *Armbrecht*, the European Court of Justice discussed the concept of whether a taxpayer must adopt the procedure in the Sixth Directive, art 6(2)(a) to deal with private use or whether it is possible to set aside part of an asset to private use and simply disallow the VAT on the private consumption when it is incurred. The Court stated:

'16. It is clear from the wording of art 2(1) of the Sixth Directive that a taxable person must act "as such" for a transaction to be subject to VAT.

17. A taxable person performing a transaction in a private capacity does not act as a taxable person.

> 18. A transaction performed by a taxable person in a private capacity is not, therefore, subject to VAT.
>
> 19. Nor is there any provision in the Sixth Directive which precludes a taxable person who wishes to retain part of an item of property amongst his private assets from excluding it from the VAT system.
>
> 20. This interpretation makes it possible for a taxable person to choose whether or not to integrate into his business, for the purposes of applying the Sixth Directive, part of an asset which is given over to his private use …'.

The European Court of Justice therefore sanctioned the blockage of input tax on the allocation of a part of an asset to private use in place of the use of article 6(2)(a). Customs and Excise basic guidance on private use is that taxpayers should apportion VAT incurred where it is incurred on goods or services that were partly to be used for business purposes and partly for private purposes. (See Customs and Excise Notice 700 at para 33). However, it is clear from *Armbrecht* that the Court considered that the taxpayer had a choice. A member state's power to derogate from the Sixth Directive, art 6(2) is limited, as the cases cited above show.

3.47 The UK has implemented the Sixth Directive, art 6(2)(a) in VATA 1994, Sch 4, para 5(4) as follows:

> '(4) Where by or under the directions of a person carrying on a business goods held or used for the purposes of the business are put to any private use or are used, or made available to any person for use, for any purpose other than a purpose of the business, whether or not for a consideration, that is a supply of services.'

However, FA 2003 modifies the provision above by adding the following provision:

> '(4A) Notwithstanding paragraph 9(1) below, sub-paragraph (4) above does not apply to –
>
> (a) any interest in land,
>
> (b) any building or part of a building,
>
> (c) any civil engineering work or part of such a work, or
>
> (d) any works incorporated or to be incorporated in a building or civil engineering work (whether by being installed as fixtures or fittings or otherwise).'

3.48 The effect of the provision is to impose upon a taxable person an obligation to determine the extent of any future use of an asset for non-business purposes and to disallow the VAT rather than use the provisions of the Sixth Directive, art 6(2) to account for private use. According to Customs and Excise, if at any point, the non-business use increases or the taxable person forms an intention to increase such use, a further adjustment has to be made.

3.49 It is understood that the UK Government considers that the provision above, which makes the treatment adopted in *Armbrecht* compulsory in the case of land applied to private use, is sanctioned by the last sentence of the Sixth Directive, art 6(2)(a). This allows member states to derogate from art 6(2)(a) provided that such derogation does not cause distortion of competition but, as noted above, member states have a limited power to derogate.

3.50 In the opinion of the authors, it is at least questionable whether the terms of the 2003 amendment are valid in EU VAT law. There are four main reasons for this:

- Firstly, while art 6(2) does allow a derogation from the requirements to treat private use as a supply of services for consideration, it can be argued that the amendment also represents a derogation from art 17. Since there is no automatic right to derogate from art 17, the only way in which such a provision can be permitted is if a specific derogation is sought from and granted by the European Commission under the Sixth Directive, art 27.
- Secondly, the effect of the derogation is to treat UK taxpayers as not acting as a taxable person in respect of the part allocated to private use. Since there is no provision in either EU or UK VAT law allowing adjustment of a deduction where an asset is not acquired as a taxable person, the result is that any subsequent decrease in the proportion of private use will result in a blockage of VAT referable to an economic activity.
- Thirdly, by making the right to derogate subject to the condition that any derogation must not distort competition, the wording of the derogation suggests that what is contemplated is that a simpler and more favourable regime can be adopted subject to the condition that it does not distort competition.
- Fourthly, it is clear that art 6(2) is intended as an anti-avoidance provision and that the form chosen was specifically chosen to ensure that other objectives of the VAT system were achieved including total relief from VAT on the use of goods and services in carrying out an economic activity. The new provision will in certain cases clearly go contrary to this principle.

3.51 The European Court of Justice judgment in *Enkler* (**Case Summary 25**) referred to in **3.41** above supports the view that the Sixth Directive, art 6(2) is itself intended as an anti-avoidance measure. The case dealt with a situation in which the taxpayer acquired a caravan – ostensibly for both business and private use. The facts of the case (see para 12 of the Court judgment at page 1331) make it clear, however, that the caravan was used primarily for private purposes. Even the business use comprised a substantial portion of letting to the appellant's husband. The Court concluded that:

- the letting of a caravan for consideration was in principle an economic activity but it was for the national court to determine whether in the particular circumstances of the case it was in fact such an activity; and
- the time spent on repairs must be regarded as partly for private and partly for business use and cannot be regarded as being solely incurred for business

purposes. Accordingly, the consideration for the private use, which under the Directive is to be determined on the basis of full cost is to be based on periods of actual use.

3.52 The new provision raises considerable practical difficulties. As already noted, in *Lennartz*, the European Court of Justice made it clear that once an asset is allocated to private use, there is no provision allowing an adjustment should the asset be used subsequently for business purposes. The capital items scheme is not applicable because the scheme deals only with input tax incurred, ie VAT incurred in the course or furtherance of a business (ie in the capacity as taxable person). By definition, if VAT is treated as being incurred otherwise than as a taxable person, it is not input tax and does not fall within the capital items scheme. The result of this is as noted at **3.50** above – where the initial apportionment of non-business input tax is greater than the actual future use, there will be a permanent disallowance of some input tax.

Nor is it fanciful to think that this can occur. A charity may well find that business use fluctuates from year to year. It is normally accepted that the life of a building prior to major refurbishment is usually about 40 years. Thus the impact of the new provision is also to require a business to predict the extent of any non-business use for a considerable period of time – something that will in a substantial number of cases be impractical. Further, on a disposal to a taxable person, there will be no ability to pass on to the taxable person any of the VAT.

3.53 At present, therefore, the UK law is that a person who uses goods or services for non-business purposes can always account for such use by disallowing the VAT on that private use at the point where the VAT is incurred. If an asset is later sold on which no VAT was deducted, there will be no VAT charge because the asset is treated as acquired otherwise than in the capacity as taxable person by the act of disallowing the VAT incurred. Except in the case of land and interests in land, UK law provides that VAT can be recovered on assets and accounted for as output tax on any subsequent private use.

3.54 In *Wolfgang Seeling v Finanzamt Starnberg* (**Case Summary 48**), at para 40, the Court reiterated the principles stated in previous decisions in the following terms:

> 'It must first be pointed out that it is settled case-law that a taxable person may choose whether or not to integrate into his business, for the purposes of applying the Sixth Directive, part of an asset which is given over to private use …'.

At para 54, the Court specifically rejected precisely the same arguments that the UK Government raised in support of its introduction of VATA 1994, Sch 4, para 5(4A) by the Finance Bill 2003, noting that the deferral of the tax and potential for untaxed private use once the capital items scheme adjustment period expires had been a deliberate choice of the Community legislature. The *Wolfgang Seeling* case strongly suggests that the UK provision might be ultra vires the Sixth Directive and that taxable persons retain the right to deduct VAT on assets used for both business and non-business purposes when it is incurred and to account for VAT on the non-business use when it occurs via an output tax charge.

3.55 Customs and Excise have subsequently issued Business Brief 22/03, dated 18 November 2003, in which they accept that, notwithstanding the Budget legislation, in certain circumstances taxable persons can choose to deduct VAT upfront as input tax and make changes for private use as and when it occurs. It remains arguable that there can be no restrictions on this treatment – it is the choice of the taxpayer whether an asset is appropriated to business or private use as accepted by the European Court of Justice in the *Armbrecht* case and reinforced in the more recent *Seeling* decision.

Apportionment generally

3.56 A person may incur costs that relate to more than one activity. The activities to which the costs relate may include business and non-business activities and also different types of business activities, some or all of which may have a different VAT liability to each other. It is implicit in article 2 of the First VAT Directive that some form of apportionment may be necessary to arrive at the VAT that is referable to taxable activities.

3.57 The Sixth Directive is clearer on the need for apportionment. Thus, art 17(2) provides (emphasis added):

> '*In so far* as the goods and services are used for the purposes of his taxable transactions, the taxable person shall be entitled to deduct from the tax which he is liable to pay: …'

The wording of the article clearly implies an apportionment that is reinforced by the specific provisions of art 17(5) and art 19(2). The corresponding UK law also contains both implicit provisions requiring apportionment (see VATA 1994, s 24(1)) and explicit provisions (see VATA 1994, s 25, particularly s 25(3)).

3.58 Similarly, there has been both EU and UK case law that makes it clear that apportionment is required. In EU law, there are two main processes:

- determine the extent to which VAT is incurred in the capacity as taxable person; and
- apportion VAT incurred as taxable person to determine the extent to which VAT is deductible.

In fact, the second process contains a number of sub-processes and the result is the five-step process outlined in **Chapter 1** at **1.87**, ie:

1 if there is any non-business use that is not dealt with by accounting for output tax, apportion the VAT incurred so as to determine the VAT that is input tax (ie is used for business purposes) and that which is not;

2 determine the extent to which any input tax on supplies, acquisitions and importations is used for out-of-country supplies or certain specified supplies;

3 determine the extent to which any input tax on supplies, acquisitions and importations is used wholly for taxable supplies;

4 determine the extent to which any input tax on supplies, acquisitions and importations is used for exempt and other non-taxable supplies;

5 apportion input tax on supplies, acquisitions and importations that are used both for taxable and exempt supplies so as to determine the extent to which they are used for taxable supplies.

3.59 Potentially, there is a further apportionment process. This will arise in certain businesses where there is substantial business entertainment. In a considerable number of cases business entertainment, business gifts, motor cars and other supplies of goods and services on which no VAT is deductible will be easily identifiable and the VAT attributable to them can be easily identified and excluded from deduction. However, it is clear from case law that apportionment may be required (See *Thorn EMI plc v C & E Comrs [1995] STC 674, CA*).

What constitutes use

The relevance of use

3.60 In **3.7** above, it was noted that it is the use to which expenditure is put that determines whether there is the necessary direct and immediate link to give a right to a VAT deduction. The term 'use' is also relevant to the capital items scheme where first use determines when an item becomes a capital item and changes in use determine the extent, if any, of the adjustment of input tax under the scheme.

Physical use

3.61 In the majority of cases, it might be fairly obvious what use means. Thus, if an oil company purchases oil to refine it into petrol and related products, it will be fairly obvious that physically the oil is converted into the refined product and is clearly used in the everyday physical sense to produce the saleable output

3.62 While use may be easily to identify with what accountants might refer to as direct costs, the issue becomes more problematic with indirect costs. In **3.9** above, reference was made to the case of *Abbey National plc v C& E Comrs [2001] STC 297, ECJ* (**Case Summary 39**) and the conclusion of the European Court of Justice that in principle overhead expenditure has a direct and immediate link to the whole of a business. However, the Court also notes that overheads may be linked to a specific part of the business.

3.63 From a practical perspective, it is sometimes easier to determine that a particular cost does not have any relationship with a particular output. This concept lies at the heart of the principle expressed in the Sixth Directive, art 19(2) in which it is provided that certain incidental transactions are to be excluded from the denominator used in determining the VAT deductible under the default partial exemption method contained in that article. By excluding the turnover applicable to incidental transactions from the fraction used in art 19(2), the legislators have accepted that there may be activities where there is at best a minimal relationship between overhead costs and incidental supplies. The result is effectively to accept that either no overhead expenditure or indeed very little overhead expenditure is used to make some supplies or carry out some activities within a business.

3.64 The UK apportionment provisions are based broadly on the Sixth Directive, art 17(5). This requires apportionment based on use. While VAT Regulations 1995, reg 101(3) provide similar provisions to those found in art 19(2) in relation to supplies within the UK, there is no directly similar provision excluding incidental transactions in relation to other supplies. Nevertheless, it is clear that in principle it is possible to identify overhead expenditure that is not used at all or is used to a de minimis extent to make certain supplies (eg out-of-country supplies).

3.65 Thus far, the question of what constitutes use has been predicated on the assumption that it is actual or physical use that is referred to in UK legislation. In fact, the VAT and Duties Tribunal has interpreted the term use differently.

Economic or legal use

3.66 The VAT and Duties Tribunal decision in *East Kent Medical Services LTd (1999) VAT decision 16095* concluded that the term 'use' in the capital items regulations was wide enough to cover use other than mere physical use or exploitation. The grant of an underlease in a building that had not been completed constituted use and that was sufficient to bring an item within the capital items scheme. The Tribunal also rejected the appellant's contention that if use did not mean physical use, then use must at least require economic use – that is to say there must be some use to earn income.

3.67 A number of practical difficulties arise in relation to the application of the capital items scheme under this view. The main ones are:

- because use can variously be physical, legal or economic use, there can be uncertainty as to what basis must be used for apportionment; and
- because the timing of the different bases of use can differ, the actual measurement of use can take place at different points in time.

By way of example:

Example 2

A company commences construction of a new building on 1 January 2001. On 1 January 2002 (before building is completed), it enters into a lease with a tenant. The construction is completed on 31 December 2002 and the tenant occupies the building on 1 January 2003.

It will be clear that physical use only takes place on 1 January 2003. However, legal use occurs when the lease is granted. It is also possible that economic use might take place later since there could be a rent free period.

The example makes it clear that overhead could be allocated to the building activity at several different times.

The issue will be considered in more detail in **Chapter 7**.

Measurement of use

3.68 The importance of determining what constitutes 'use' is that it is the factor that determines whether any VAT incurred is deductible or not. The most common method used to measure use is probably turnover since turnover is the default method of measuring use provided in both the Sixth Directive, art 19(2) and in VAT Regulations 1995, reg 101.

3.69 However, it will be evident that turnover is not necessarily the best measure of use. The main reasons for this are:

- The profit margin on different activities will differ. Thus, there will be a high percentage of VAT incurred in most manufacturing activities since much of the goods will be subject to VAT. However, this will not necessarily be the case in labour intensive services. Thus, in determining any measure of use, it will be important to have regard to the relative margins of taxable and exempt supplies made.
- The proportion of fixed costs that form a cost component of a particular activity will vary considerably depending on turnover. High turnover values will reduce the relative fixed cost per unit of goods or services sold while lower turnover will increase relative costs. Therefore, a turnover method may be an inappropriate measure of use in a business that has a high fixed cost base, eg if there are considerable opted rentals, particularly where turnover fluctuates considerably from year to year.

3.70 Care is needed in understanding what the basic cost components of all activities are in order to determine an appropriate measure of use. The application of the principles to given situations is considered in **Chapter 5 Partial Exemption**.

The Royal and Sun Alliance decision

3.71 The decision of the House of Lords in the case of *Royal and Sun Alliance v C & E Comrs [2003] STC 832, HL* (**Case Summary 47**), is perhaps the most important decision on the nature of use. However, the fact that in the course of hearings in the Tribunal and three courts, five judges found in favour of Customs and Excise while five found in favour of the taxpayer leaves the uneasy feeling that there remain doubts as to the exact principles to be applied.

3.72 The facts may be summarised as follows. Royal Sun Alliance ('RSA') carries out insurance business. It had acquired a number of properties under lease. As a result of changes in business need, the properties became surplus to requirements. Being unable to surrender the leases to the landlord, RSA determined to let the properties. The properties took some time to let so RSA incurred rentals in respect of periods in which the properties were vacant. RSA had not elected to waive exemption and therefore suffered a VAT cost on the rentals incurred in the periods when the properties were not let.

Once the properties were let under taxable leases, RSA sought to recover the VAT incurred. It argued that under VAT Regulations 1995, reg 109 it had incurred VAT on intended exempt supplies but those exempt supplies had not been made so it was now entitled to recover the VAT incurred because it was making taxable supplies instead.

3.73 In his judgment, Lord Hoffmann stated:

> '32 … There are two ways in which one could think of the grant of a time-limited interest in land … [o]ne is to regard it as a single supply of the leasehold estate in consideration of periodic payments of rent and the other lessee's covenants. That is how a real property lawyer would describe the grant of a lease …
>
> 33 But another way of looking at the matter is to treat the superior owner as granting rights of occupation in successive units of months, quarters, or whatever, depending upon the stipulated intervals for payment of the rent. In that case, the goods or services supplied during the vacant unelected period are different from those supplied afterwards and a change of plan about the use to be made of the leases in the future is not a change of intention about the use of the leases in the past.'

He then concludes at para 34 that VAT law has clearly adopted the second analysis. On this basis, both Lord Hoffmann and Lord Clyde decided that the second alternative was to be preferred and dismissed the appeal, Lord Steyn agreeing with them. In effect, both took the view that the input tax related to supplies that could only be used within the periods to which they related and that accordingly they could not have been used for the future taxable supplies.

3.74 Lords Woolf and Walker took the contrary view and decided that the supplies had not been used up and that accordingly because the ultimate supply was taxable, the input tax was deductible.

3.75 In the course of argument, both parties agreed that had the option to tax been exercised at the start the input tax would be deductible. Reference was also made, albeit indirectly to VATA 1994, s 94. This provides that:

> '(5) Anything done in connection with the termination or intended termination of a business is treated as being done in the course or furtherance of that business.'

Thus it was accepted that if RSA had been a taxable business, the input tax on the leases would have continued to have been deductible even if no letting had taken place.

3.76 The difficulty that the decisions of Lords Hoffmann, Clyde and Lady Arden (in the Court of Appeal) raise is that they appear to take the view that supplies whose time of supply is dealt with under VATA 1994, s 6(14) and VAT Regulations 1995, reg 85 necessarily relate to a specific period in time. Accordingly, it is said that once the time has expired, the use of those inputs would similarly have expired. Of course, it is well known that this is not necessarily the case. Thus, a landlord may grant a lease with a 'rent-free' period but arguably the existence of such period does not mean that there is no cost attributable to that period. If that were the case, it would be a relatively simple task for a person making exempt and taxable supplies to structure a lease so that input tax was incurred only in those periods when the highest claim for input tax could be made. Similar examples exist in respect of other continuous supplies, e g the lease of a motor car where there is either an upfront or terminal 'balloon' payment.

3.77 A further difficulty arises as can be seen by examining an example. A business rents properties in order to make taxable supplies. It is decided to close down the business. While it seeks to close down the business, the holding of the leases is undoubtedly used in carrying on activities that fall within VATA 1994, s 94(5) – see **3.75** above. Any VAT incurred on such leases is therefore deductible as input tax. If it then decides to let the properties, the holding of the leases can no longer be considered to be referable to the intended termination of a business – it has started a new business. Assuming the properties have never been opted by the business, it is then in the same position as RSA.

3.78 In order to let the buildings, it has to incur costs to bring the properties into a state in which they are fit to let. During such period, it is clear that the costs of holding the lease relate to the work preparatory to the future letting since clearly the property cannot be let without the work being done. Yet it would appear that the House of Lords' decision would hold that the costs are referable to an intended letting in the same period.

3.79 It is also the case that the fact that the business has not decided whether or not to opt, at that point in time, because it does not know who the future tenant is, does not mean that it intends to make either an exempt supply (which appears to have been conceded by RSA) or a taxable supply. It is incurring costs in holding the property to let (as argued by RSA). It should also be borne in mind that during this period, the business will no doubt undertake activities such as showing prospective tenants the property – a preparatory activity (in the *Rompelman* sense) aimed at the future letting of the property, which turns out to be taxable.

3.80 The *Royal Sun Alliance* decision also appears, to some extent, to nullify the partial exemption override provisions, since if input tax on continuous supplies can only be related to the period to which it relates, it cannot be related to future supplies – an essential component of the partial exemption override.

3.81 As noted, the roll call shows four judges and the tribunal chairman in favour of Customs and Excise and five judges in favour of RSA. There would appear to be a compelling case that this issue should have been referred to the ECJ to establish whether the Sixth Directive, art 10(2) has any relevance in deciding whether or not the VAT on any costs incurred on a continuous basis are cost components of a taxable supply. It should be borne in mind that art 10(2) is the basis for VATA 1994, s 6(14) and VAT Regulations 1995, reg 85.

Use for out-of-country supplies and certain other supplies

3.82 As noted at **3.1** above, it is not only use for taxable supplies that entitles a taxpayer to a deduction of input tax. Input tax on supplies, acquisitions and imports that are used for:

- supplies that would be taxable if made outside the UK; and
- certain supplies that are specified by order is also deductible.

The only supplies that have so far been specified under the second bullet point above are:

- certain insurance and financial services relating to the export of goods outside the EU to a person who belongs outside the member states; and
- certain investment gold supplies.

[VAT (Input Tax) (Specified Supplies) Order 1999.]

3.83 Although case law consistently refers to the need for there to be a direct and immediate link between the costs on which VAT is to be deducted and taxable supplies, that is merely a consequence of the fact that in general the issue has not arisen in respect of out-of-country and specified supplies. However, it is clear that the same principles apply. In the UK, different provisions apply to out-of-country supplies and specified supplies as opposed to taxable and exempt supplies.

3.84 In essence, it is always necessary to determine what VAT can be deducted on such supplies by applying a use-based method – see *C & E v Liverpool Institute of Performing Arts [2001] STC 891, HL* (**Case Summary 40**). The standard method as set out in VAT Regulations 1995, reg 101 does not apply. Further, while it is possible to agree with Customs and Excise that a particular method of apportioning VAT to out-of-country and specified supplies is a fair and reasonable method, such a method would not fall within reg 102. It would be an agreement that fell within Customs and Excise's general care and control powers. It is also the case that Customs and Excise have no powers to direct that a particular method be used to apportion VAT in relation to such supplies, since reg 102 represents an exception to reg 101 and has no bearing on reg 103.

3.85 Although the provisions of VAT Regulation 1995, reg 103 require a use-based method to be used to determine deductible VAT on out-of-country and specified supplies, this does not preclude a business from using a turnover-based method to determine use. Further, in making use of such a method, it is also acceptable for the business to exclude incidental supplies from any fraction if their inclusion would be distortive. The sole difference between using a turnover-based method under reg 103 compared with using one under reg 101 is that, in the latter case, the turnover method applies unless an alternative method is agreed or directed. If a business wishes to use a turnover based method under reg 103, it will need to be able to defend such method as being the best way of determining use should Customs and Excise not agree that it is a fair and reasonable method.

Use for taxable supplies

3.86 It has been seen at **3.84** above, that the only method by which deductible VAT can be determined in relation to out-of-country and specified supplies is a method based on use. In the case of taxable supplies, the default measure, usually referred to as the 'standard method', is a turnover-based method (VAT Regulations 1995, reg 101(2)). However, if the standard method does not approximate a method based on use, then the taxpayer must adjust his input tax deduction using the 'partial exemption override' (VAT Regulations 1995, regs 107A–107E).

3.87 A business can, instead of a turnover-based method, agree with Customs and Excise an alternative method (VAT Regulations 1995, reg 102). A special method must be a method based on use. In general, Customs and Excise are prepared to accept cost centre based methods where a business's allocation of costs to cost centres is a reasonable measure of use. In the event of disagreement with a proposed method, a business can appeal a decision by Customs and Excise not to allow a special method. If a special method does not give a fair and reasonable apportionment, the special method override may apply (see **6.35** below).

3.88 Where Customs and Excise are of the opinion that the standard method does not represent a fair measurement of use or where they form the opinion that an existing special method does not represent a proper measure of use, they can direct a taxpayer to use a special method (VAT Regulations 1995, reg 102). A direction can only be made on a prospective basis although because of the existence of the partial exemption override Customs and Excise now have an alternative method of dealing with what they see as an inappropriate method of input tax attribution. They could assess the taxpayer on the basis that an adjustment should have been made and leave it to the taxpayer to appeal any decision. **Chapters 5, 6** and 7 deal with the actual process of measuring use for taxable supplies.

Chapter 4

Non-Deductible VAT

Introduction

4.1 Input tax is VAT on goods or services supplied to the taxable person provided that the goods or services are used or are to be used for the purpose of any business carried on or to be carried on by the taxable person. This includes VAT on goods imported or acquired from EU member states. The input tax is not deductible or claimable by the taxable person unless the rules governing input tax recovery are met. In addition, the VAT on certain expenses is non-deductible, even where the VAT may be incurred for a business expense. This chapter examines the occasions where input tax is not deductible and also where a taxable person may choose not to reclaim input tax rather than charge VAT on a supply (gifts and certain items sold with dwellings).

4.2 The Sixth Directive, art 17(6) limits the right of deduction where an expense is not strictly a business expense, but a luxury, amusement or entertainment expense. This article states:

> 'Before a period of four years at the latest has elapsed from the date of entry into force of this directive, the Council, acting unanimously on a proposal from the Commission, shall decide what expenditure shall not be eligible for a deduction of value added tax. Value added tax shall in no circumstances be deductible on expenditure which is not strictly business expenditure, such as that on luxuries, amusements or entertainment.
>
> Until the above rules come into force, member states may retain all the exclusions provided for under their national laws when this directive comes into force.'

4.3 It should be noted that the Sixth Directive states that 'until the above rules come into force, member states may retain all the exclusions provided for under their national laws when this directive comes into force'. Thus, exclusions in force at the date of the introduction of the Sixth Directive (17 May 1977) can remain (and those of other member states are described in **Chapter 13**). The European Council has not, however, been able to agree on a proposal (and the Commission has submitted such a proposal on one occasion) and the restrictions in place when the Directive was introduced are still extant. New restrictions on deductions of input tax cannot, however, be introduced.

4.4 This issue was discussed in the case *EC Commission v France (C-40/00) [2003] STC 390, ECJ*. The French Government maintained an input tax block on diesel fuel purchased by businesses when the Sixth Directive was introduced in 1977. It later partially removed this block and allowed a deduction for a proportion of costs. This relief was later reversed and the total input tax block was re-introduced. It was held by the European Court of Justice that:

> 'National legislation does not constitute a derogation permitted by the second subparagraph of Article 17(6) of the Sixth Directive 77/388 on the harmonisation of the laws of the Member States relating to turnover taxes and infringes Article 17(2) thereof if its effect is to increase, after the entry into force of the Sixth Directive, the extent of existing exclusions, thus diverging from the objective of that directive. The same is true of any amendment subsequent to the entry into force of the Sixth Directive which increases the extent of exclusions applicable immediately before that amendment.
>
> Accordingly, a Member State which reintroduces from 1 January 1998 a total prohibition on the right to deduct value added tax on diesel used as fuel for vehicles and machines on the purchase of which no value added tax is deductible, after having introduced a partial right to deduct, has failed to fulfil its obligations under Article 17(2) of the Sixth Directive.'

Thus, a member state cannot extend the range or scope of any input tax block – even when this block had once existed. Therefore, in the UK the block on director's accommodation (inserted by FA 1990, s 12(2)) may, and the block on the entertainment of overseas customers (amended by VAT (Special Provisions) (Amendment) Order 1988) can, be seen to be illegal, but it would no doubt necessitate a challenge to enforce the right to deduction. As the VAT incurred is relatively small such a challenge is unlikely. The UK has attempted to get around this issue for directors' accommodation by denying the VAT incurred the status of input tax.

4.5 The Sixth Directive, art 17(6) gives the vires for the 'Blocking Orders' that have been introduced by the UK. The power to make statutory instruments that prevent input tax being reclaimed is contained in VATA 1994, s 25(7), which states:

> 'The Treasury may by order provide, in relation to such supplies, acquisitions and importations as the order may specify, that VAT charged on them is to be excluded from any credit under this section; and–
>
> (a) any such provision may be framed by reference to the description of goods or services supplied or goods acquired or imported, the person by whom they are supplied, acquired or imported or to whom they are supplied, the purposes for which they are supplied, acquired or imported, or any circumstances whatsoever; and
>
> (b) such an order may contain provision for consequential relief from output tax.'

4.6 The Treasury order that blocks input tax is the VAT (Input Tax) Order 1992, SI 1992/3222. The 1992 Order prevents deduction of input tax on second-hand goods, building materials incorporated in the new dwellings, cars and business entertainment.

4.7 Despite the importance of this area for basic VAT accounting (and the issue of the supply not being made to the taxable person), there is little guidance from Customs and Excise regarding the rules other than basic information on input tax recovery. Information regarding input tax recovery can be found in VAT Public Notice 700 in section 10. Section 12 gives some information regarding employee subsistence and entertainment. Section 17 of the same Notice gives information as to what will be acceptable as an invoice. The only notice that specifically covers employee expenses is Leaflet 700/64 Motor Expenses. Information can also be found in Customs and Excise's Internal Guidance V1–13, Chapter 2, para 3.

4.8 It should also be noted that for the amount to be deducted it has to be supplied to the taxable person. If the supply is made to Person A and Person B pays for it, then usually it is only Person A that can reclaim the VAT. This commonly occurs in property transactions where one party will pay the other party's costs. The 'other' party and not the paying party should reclaim the VAT. If the transaction is such that the VAT cannot be deducted the paying party has to pay the gross amount, as this is the cost incurred by the 'other' party. For more details see **2.37–2.38**.

Business and non-business

4.9 The Sixth VAT Directive, art 17 states (amongst other things):

> **'Origin and scope of the right to deduct**
>
> 17(1) The right to deduct shall arise at the time when the deductible tax becomes chargeable.
>
> 17(2) In so far as the goods and services are used for the purposes of his taxable transactions, the taxable person shall be entitled to deduct from the tax which he is liable to pay:
>
> (a) value added tax due or paid within the territory of the country in respect of goods or services supplied or to be supplied to him by another taxable person.'

This gives the right to deduct VAT where the VAT has been incurred for the purpose of taxable transactions. The primary provision in UK law is VATA 1994, s 24(1). This states:

> **'Input tax and output tax**
>
> 24(1) Subject to the following provisions of this section, "input tax", in relation to a taxable person, means the following tax, that is to say–
>
> (a) VAT on the supply to him of any goods or services;
>
> (b) VAT on the acquisition by him from another member State of any goods; and

(c) VAT paid or payable by him on the importation of any goods from a place outside the member States,

being (in each case) goods or services used or to be used for the purpose of any business carried on or to be carried on by him.'

4.10 The UK legislation states that VAT is only deductible where it is used or to be used for the purposes of any business carried on or to be carried on by the taxable person, whilst the EU legislation states that the VAT is deductible where it is used for the purpose of his taxable transactions. The Sixth VAT Directive does not require any business motive. Thus, a non-business entity can reclaim VAT where it relates to its taxable transactions, not necessarily its business transactions. In many situations this may be a moot point as a non-business entity's taxable transactions will normally be its business transactions.

4.11 For the purpose of this chapter only the issue of business transactions will be considered. In addition, there will only be a brief consideration of non-business entities (such as charities or Government bodies) as the issue is to determine whether their transactions are business or not (or taxable transactions or not). If they are business (or taxable) transactions then the VAT can be deducted.

Purpose of the business

4.12 There is no legal definition of whether goods and services have been supplied for the purpose of the business. The test for VAT as to whether the expense has been incurred for the purpose of the business is a subjective test; what purpose was in the mind of the taxable person at the time the expenditure was incurred (*Ian Flockton Developments Ltd v C & E Comrs [1987] STC 394*). This is at variance with the direct tax tests where the House of Lords has held that the motive of the taxable person is not determinative (see *Mallalieu v Drummond [1983] STC 665, HL*).

4.13 Thus, it is necessary to determine what the taxable person believed the expense was for when it was incurred. This is extremely important when considering VAT deduction of employee expenses as many expenses that can be incurred by employees may be regarded as either private or non-business expenditure.

4.14 It should not, however, be considered that just because the expense has been incurred and it is to the benefit of the business, that this will mean that it has been incurred for the purpose of the business. There is a requirement for a nexus between the expenditure in question and the business (see *C & E Comrs v FW Rosner [1994] STC 228*) (**Case Summary 17**) and para **4.123** below). This can be difficult to determine, and it would be of some assistance if Customs and Excise produced a list of the type of expenditure that they regarded as being closely connected and for the purpose of the business. In this way, the taxable person would have a clear understanding of Customs and Excise's views, even if there would undoubtedly be exceptions and differences of opinion. No such list, however, exists and there remains considerable uncertainty with principles being derived from case law.

4.15 An example of the need to establish a close nexus between the business and the expenses incurred is that of legal costs to preserve an employee's driving licence. It may be regarded as vital to the business, as without the driving licence the employee cannot work, but it is not regarded as providing a close enough nexus between the goods and services supplied by the taxable person and the expense (see *RN Scott (1987) VAT decision 2302*, *GM Child (t/a Child & Co (1992) VAT decision 6827* and *VW Evans (1997) VAT decision 14662*).

4.16 These cases differ from *SR Brooks (1994) VAT decision 12754*, where a gold dealer had been charged with evasion of customs duty on gold. The dealer had been acquitted and sought to reclaim the VAT incurred on his legal costs. The claim was allowed as 'the activities described in the indictment were all steps taken in the normal course of (the dealer) carrying on his gold dealing business'. The eligibility to reclaim VAT on expenses that may be regarded as either non-business or business expenditure will often differ according to the precise circumstances of the case. Thus, legal expenses may be deductible on some occasions but not on others. Examples of non-deductible and deductible items are detailed below.

4.17 Where such expenditure is to be incurred there is a need to document why the expense is necessary for the purpose of the business. For instance, there may be company policy regarding the type of overnight accommodation that is being used by employees or there may be board minutes documenting why costs for a legal action are to be paid by the company rather than by an individual. These will assist in demonstrating that the recovery of VAT is for the purpose of the business and the nexus between the expense and the business. A written explanation for an expense, however, will not convert a non-business expense into a business expense.

The Lennartz principle

4.18 Where an expense is incurred that is a private or non-business expense for which no charge is made for the use of the item, there are two methods of dealing with the VAT incurred (where a charge is made for the use, the supply will normally be a business supply though there may be a question over the valuation of the supply). The first option is to claim all the VAT and apply an output tax charge when the goods or services are supplied to a person other than for a consideration. Clearly, the valuation of the supply is important and this will be an open market value if the supply is made to a connected person and the recipient cannot reclaim all the VAT charged. This is called the *Lennartz* principal following the decision in *Lennartz v Finanzamt Munchen III (C-97/90) [1995] STC 514, ECJ* (**Case Summary 12**).

4.19 It should be noted that the 2003 Budget amendments (VATA 1994, Sch 4, para 5(4A), inserted by FA 2003, s 22(1), and the VAT (Supply of Services) Order 1993, SI 1993/1507, arts 3A and 3B, inserted by the VAT (Supply of Services) (Amendment) Order, SI 2003/1055, art 4, with effect from 10 April 2003) reduce the availability of this option. These measures prevent the *Lennartz* principal from applying to land, buildings, civil engineering works and goods incorporated in such buildings or works, by removing them from VATA 1994, Sch 4, para 5 and the VAT (Supply of Services) Order SI 1993, 1993/1507.

4.20 Customs and Excise have not obtained or sought a specific derogation to introduce this change as an anti-avoidance measure. Customs and Excise are relying upon the ability to derogate from the Sixth Directive contained in art 6(2). Article 6(2) states that the use of business goods for non-business purposes treated as supplies of services for consideration, as are free supplies of services to staff or the use of services for non-business purposes. The article then allows member states to derogate from this provided that the derogation does not lead to a distortion of competition. One question that will thus arise is whether there is a distortion.

4.21 There is, however, a considerable body of opinion that regards the 2003 Budget amendment as ineffective, due to the *Lennartz* and *Woolfgang Seeling v Finanzamt Starnberg (C-269/00) [2003] STC 805* (**Case Summary 48**) decisions. Customs and Excise have, however, taken Counsel's opinion regarding the changes and believe that the amendment is effective. Only time, and no doubt lengthy legal argument, will tell which of these opinions is correct. In the interim, it is necessary for anybody considering using a property for non-business activities to consider how they will deal with this problem; whether to challenge the amendment, claim back all input tax at the outset and account for VAT on the value of the use of the building or to apportion the VAT at the outset between business and non-business use. The issues that arise are briefly discussed here (but not the point regarding distortion of competition).

4.22 The recent ECJ decision in *Seeling* confirmed the principles established in the *Lennartz* decision: that a taxable person may reclaim all the input tax incurred on the cost of the purchase of a business asset and then account for VAT on the private use of that element. In *Seeling*, the taxable person had acquired a property, partly for use in the business and partly for use as a private residence. The input tax incurred was deducted, but the German tax authority believed that the VAT incurred should only be deductible in part. The German tax authority argued that the Sixth Directive, art 6(2) must be read as broadening art 13 (exemptions, including letting or property) and that it was established case law that exemptions were to be interpreted narrowly and, therefore, should not be extended to the exempt private use of a property. The private use of the residential part of the building in question must, in order to maintain equality of treatment, be regarded as having the same effect on input tax deduction as if it were an exempt supply. The ECJ rejected this argument as although art 13 was not applied to a fictional transaction (the own use by the taxable person in his private capacity), the private use by a taxable person constituted a leasing or letting of the property within that article.

4.23 Although a number of commentators have stated that decisions such as those in *Wolfgang Seeling* and *Lennartz* would seem to question the vires of the recent amendment to Sch 4 and the Supply of Services Order, it appears to the author that *Wolfgang Seeling* in particular would not prevent the 2003 Budget measure from being effective: any difficulty for this Budget amendment stemming from earlier decisions, in particular the *Lennartz* decision. Following the *Seeling* decision, full input tax recovery is secured where there is a charge for private use where there are fictional property transactions (that is, private use of a building by an individual or the mixed business and non-business use of a property by a charity). Customs and Excise may, however, seek to distinguish *Seeling*, as where a property is let for no consideration for use by an exempt entity (the type of transaction this measure is supposedly aimed at) the 2003 Budget amendment may still be considered to apply since such a transaction is not fictional, it is just being undertaken for no consideration. This may be a difficult line for Customs and Excise to pursue, give that at para 29 of the *Seeling* judgment it was found that from the point of final consumption it is immaterial whether a taxable person leases the residence or uses it himself.

4.24–4.25 A further difficulty for Customs and Excise is that the Sixth Directive, art 6.2 allows derogation from that article. That is, a derogation from the principle that free use of goods shall be treated as supplies for consideration. It does not allow derogation from the right to deduct. No doubt Customs and Excise would argue that, as they have derogated from art 6.2, the use of the goods is not a supply for consideration and there is no right to deduct any more, because the input tax incurred does not relate to any taxable activity. This view would appear untenable as in *Cookies World Vertriebsgesellschaft mbH iL v Finanzlandesdirektion fur Tirol (C-155/01) [2003] SWTI 1637* it was held at para 59 that the derogation in art 6(2) must be:

> 'interpreted as meaning that the Member States may refrain from treating certain supplies or use of services as services supplied for consideration. On the other hand, that provision in no way authorises Member States to provide for chargeable events not referred to in the first subparagraph of Article 6(2).'

It would, therefore, appear that, although this article gives Customs and Excise the power to not apply a tax charge, it does not give any subsidiary right to Customs and Excise to prevent input tax deduction.

4.26 Further difficulties for Customs and Excise arise from earlier cases (see paras 40 and 43 of the *Seeling* decision):

> 'It is settled case law that a taxable person may choose whether or not to integrate into his business, for the purpose of applying the Sixth Directive, part of an asset which is given over to his private use (see *Armbrecht*, paragraph 20, and Case C- 415/98 *Bakcsi* [2001] ECR I-1831, paragraph 25).
>
> If the taxable person chooses to treat capital goods used both for business and private purposes as business goods, the VAT due as input tax on the acquisition of those goods is in principle wholly and immediately deductible (see, *inter alia*, Case C-97/90 *Lennartz* [1991] ECR I-3795, paragraph 26, and *Bakcsi*, cited above, paragraph 25).
>
> It follows from Article (6)(2)(a) and from Article 11A(1)(c) of the Sixth Directive that the use of capital goods for the private use of a taxable person or of his staff or for the purposes other than those of his business, where the input VAT paid on such goods is wholly or partly deductible, is treated as a supply of

services for consideration and is taxed on the basis of the cost of providing the services (see *Lennartz*, paragraph 26, and *Backsi*, paragraph 30).

Accordingly, where a taxable person chooses to treat an entire building as forming part of the assets of his business and subsequently uses part of that building for private purposes, on the one hand, he is entitled to deduct the input VAT paid on all construction costs relating to that building and, on the other hand, he is subject to the corresponding obligation to pay VAT on the amount of expenditure incurred to effect such use.'

4.27 The element of choice is clearly demonstrated by the decisions of *Finanzamt Ulzen v Armbrecht (C-291/92) [1995] STC 997 ECT* (**Case Summary 19**) and *Bakcsi v Finanzamt Furstenfeldbruck (C-415/98) [2001] All ER (D) 114 (Mar), ECJ*. In *Armbrecht* it was held by the European Court that where an asset was sold by a taxable person (a guest house that had been used for private rather than business purposes) that had been part used for a private purpose, that part was outside the scope of the Sixth Directive, art 2(1) and was not subject to VAT. In *Bakcsi* it was held that where a vehicle had been used for both business and private use and the vehicle had been incorporated wholly into the business assets, then VAT was due on the sale, despite the fact that no VAT had been reclaimed as it had been bought from a non-taxable person. This element of choice is removed by the 2003 Budget changes and it is not understood why Customs and Excise, or their Counsel, believe that this choice is not to be permitted.

4.28 The cases that are, however, more difficult to reconcile to the Budget amendment are *Enkler v Finanzamt Homburg (C-230/94) [1996] STC 1316, ECJ* (**Case Summary 25**) and the *Lennartz* decision. In *Enkler* the wife of a taxable person started a business in 1984 of hiring out motor caravans. A motor caravan was purchased and hired to the business of her husband, who paid for the supply. The wife accounted for VAT on the supply. The motor caravan was also used for private purposes from 1986. Despite there being an avoidance motive, the ECJ held that the hiring out of tangible property was an 'economic activity' if it was done for the purpose of obtaining income on a continuing basis (and it was for the national courts to determine if it was continued on a continuing basis). The VAT incurred on the acquisition was deductible in full.

4.29 In *Lennartz* (**Case Summary 12**), a tax consultant purchased a car that was initially used mainly for private purposes. Later the vehicle was used more frequently for business purposes and the taxable person made a reclaim of the VAT incurred on acquisition. It held that deduction was determined at the time of purchase. Thus, if an item was purchased for private use, then no input tax is deductible, even where there is subsequent business use. Where, however, an item is purchased for both private and business use, the taxable person could deduct all the input tax incurred and would then be required to account for output tax on the private use (and this would be valued at the cost of providing the item, including all costs incurred during the period that the item was available for private or non-taxable use – see *Enkler*).

4.30 One of the problems of allowing deduction of input tax incurred on a capital item is that, after the period of adjustment (which in the UK is ten years), the item can be sold as exempt from VAT and there is no clawback of input tax deducted. This was one of the reasons for the objection to deduction of the German tax authority in *Seeling* (which also has a ten year period of adjustment). In *Seeling*, however, the European Court stated that it was up to the national authority to deal with this and suggested that as the Sixth Directive now allows immoveable property to be adjusted over 20 years this should not be a problem if this period of adjustment was adopted. It should also be noted that in the *Lennartz* judgment the European Court stated that art 20(2) contained no provisions concerning the origin of the right of deduction. It merely contained provisions detailing how to calculate adjustments to the initial deduction.

Alternative to the Lennartz method

4.31 The alternative to the *Lennartz* method is for the VAT incurred not be claimed. VAT on goods used partly for a business purpose and partly for a non-business purpose should be apportioned between the expected business and non-business use. This can be a particularly difficult apportionment as it relies upon knowing what the future use is; there being no mechanism for adjustment after initial deduction. Intention is always difficult to prove and it is necessary to prove that the claim is reasonable, to Customs and Excise's satisfaction, otherwise an assessment will be raised and it will be necessary to prove Customs and Excise's assessment is incorrect.

4.32 Clearly the taxable person is in a difficult position, trying to prove what the future will hold and this is a further argument for using the *Lennartz* principle rather than initial apportionment. This initial apportionment is, however, required if there is not, in the event , any taxable use as art 17 gives the time of deduction as being the time the VAT is chargeable. It is not, therefore, necessary to have actually made taxable supplies to enable the VAT incurred to be deducted. Indeed, if conditions change so that the original intention cannot be carried out then the VAT reclaimed is still reclaimable at the rate of the original intention (see *Belgium v Ghent Coal Terminal [1998] STC 260, ECJ* (**Case Summary 30**)). A recent Advocate-General's opinion (*Gemeente Leusden v Staatssecretaris van Financien and Holin Groep BV c.s. v Staatssecretaris van Financien (C-487/01 and C-7/02)*) has stated that the principles of legitimate expectation and legal certainty preclude a taxable person being subject to an adjustment on the grounds that an activity that was intended can no longer be carried out due to a change in regulations. When the input tax had been incurred there had been an intention to make a taxable supply and the VAT incurred could be reclaimed as input tax.

4.33 It should be noted that where a charge for the use of the goods is made neither the *Lennartz* principal nor non-claiming of input tax is appropriate. This is because a supply is made to the third party. All the VAT incurred can be reclaimed and output tax is due on the supply provided it is taxable. Where the third party is connected with the person making the supply (for instance, a sole proprietor's spouse or directors of a company) VAT is due on the open market value of the supply if this is more than the amount charged.

Business entertainment

4.34 VAT incurred on business entertainment is not deductible as input tax, except where this entertainment is of employees or, in relation to a company, directors and persons in management of the company (the VAT (Input Tax) Order 1992, SI 1992/3222, art 5 (the Input Tax Order)). Customs and Excise accept that the provision of entertainment is a part of business life and the VAT incurred would normally be deductible as input tax were it not for the application of the Input Tax Order, unless it was incurred for private purposes. This is because it is incurred for the purpose of the business.

Blocking order vires

4.35 The earlier blocking order for business entertainment (the VAT (Special Provisions) Order 1981) blocked input tax for the entertainment of UK customers. Prior to an amendment in 1988, VAT was reclaimable on entertainment of overseas customers (it was a provision to encourage exports). This included potential customers and the agents of customers and potential customers, but excluded overseas suppliers, other persons from overseas and persons normally resident in the UK or the Isle of Man. It is, therefore, arguable that the VAT incurred on the entertainment of overseas customers is recoverable despite the current UK legislation, as the amendment introduced by the VAT (Special Provisions) (Amendment) Order 1988 was subsequent to the adoption of the Sixth Directive (see paras 4.3–4.5 above).

Definition of employee

4.36 VAT is not reclaimable on goods and services purchased for the purpose of providing 'business entertainment'. The Input Tax Order defines business entertainment as the provision of any hospitality to persons who are not employees, directors or persons engaged in the management of a corporate body. The term 'employee' is defined by Customs and Excise's Internal Guidance V1–13, Chapter 2A, para 12.4 as 'a person currently employed by the taxable person (including temporary or casual staff)'. Included in the definition of employee are persons acting as agents or casual staff (but also see the sections below regarding employees acting as hosts, employee entertainment, staff entertainment and employee expenses). Excluded from the definition of employee are:

- pensioners;
- former employees;
- job applicants and interviewees;
- shareholders (unless also employees); and
- partners (eg spouses), relatives and friends of employees.

Definition of entertainment

4.37 The term 'entertainment' encompasses hospitality of any kind. The definition arises from the Court of Appeal decision *Shaklee International [1981] STC 776, CA*. The VAT Tribunal had accepted that free accommodation and meals that had been provided to self-employed persons at meetings and conferences was a business expense and was not done to entertain. The High Court, however, held that it was entertainment as:

> '… it was the provision of hospitality in connection with their business, and on a correct approach to the issue which was before them, it is my view that the tribunal could only come to one conclusion, namely, that this was expenditure which fell within the provisions of the Order.
>
> It seems to me that all that is required is for two questions to be asked. The first being: to what use did the trader put the goods or services which he provided? The second question, having answered the first, being: was the use one for the purpose of business entertainment as defined in the Order?'

The Court of Appeal agreed, stating:

> '… to give people free meals and to give them free accommodation is, to my mind to entertain them within the ordinary and natural meaning of the word. The proposition was strongly urged upon us, reliance being placed on a certain authority to which I do not intend to refer, that "entertainment" included hospitality. The reason I do not refer to the authority is because I should have thought that that was self-evident. Most people who receive free meals and are put up free at hotels would, I think, regard themselves as receiving hospitality. I certainly would so regard them as doing so. It seems to me that, whether the expression has been "business entertainment" or "business hospitality", the result would have been just the same.'

4.38 Entertainment can take many forms and this includes:

- the provision of food and drink;
- hotel accommodation and similar accommodation;
- shows, theatre and concerts;
- entry to sporting events, clubs or nightclubs; and
- use of luxury goods such as yachts, aircraft or motor cars for the purpose of entertaining.

4.39 Input tax has been disallowed for food provided at business discussion meetings, Elizabethan banquets, launch parties for the opening of offices (and docks!), entertainment at motor racing events, golf championships and sports grounds.

Occasions where input tax is deductible

4.40 Occasions where the input tax is deductible when food, drink or similar hospitality are offered are seen less frequently and some examples are given to illustrate when such the VAT is deductible.

4.41 The hotel expenses of a visiting sports club was seen to be deductible as it was held that entertainment should be hospitality that is freely given. In this instance the accommodation was not free as there was a contractual reciprocal arrangement (*Celtic Football and Athletic Club Ltd v C & E Comrs [1983] STC 470, CS* (**Case Summary 3**).

4.42 Where a payment is obtained, this is not entertainment, even if the payment is not directly for the food, drink or other hospitality. It was held in *City of Chicago Board of Trade (1992) VAT decision 9114*, that as delegates had paid to attend conferences, the expenses of the cocktail party and champagne reception were deductible.

4.43 In a case that was borderline, it was held that it was not business entertainment where persons participating in television programmes were provided with a modest meal as the television company had placed itself under a contractual obligation to provide the meal (*C & E Comrs v Kilroy Television Co Ltd [1997] STC 901*) (**Case Summary 28**). Also, where a market research company organised product trials of drink (which was accepted by Customs and Excise as not being business entertainment) that the food also provided was not business entertainment as it was a necessary part of the trial (*DPA (Market Research) Ltd (1997) VAT decision 14751*).

4.44 Customs and Excise have accepted that there are a number of occasions where input tax can be claimed even though it appears that hospitality has been offered. In Customs and Excise Internal Guidance V1–13, Chapter 2A, section 12.10 examples are given of when input tax can be recovered in respect of 'apparent business entertainment':

- Entertainment provided by clubs and associations that is available to all eligible members as a benefit of membership.
- Free drinks given to customers paying for meals at restaurants as the drink is regarded as being inclusive with the meal.
- Airlines (and presumably other forms of transport) providing catering or accommodation for delayed passengers.
- Free wine or beer tasting for trade customers or journalists which allow sampling (but not drinking), or a free glass of whisky following a tour of the distillery, etc. This would also presumably extend to other forms of hospitality such as catering at events that had been paid for.
- Free meals provided to coach drivers at motorway service stations. These are business gifts on which output tax may be due.

- Entertainment provided by local authorities at civic functions as this is a non-business activity, but if the entertainment was provided where the local authority was undertaking a business activity then the input tax incurred would be non-deductible.
- Entertainment of a non-personal nature (that is, to the public at large) provided freely by a store, or similar establishment. Examples given by Customs and Excise include hiring circus performers, musicians, or other entertainers to attract custom or advertise a business's premises. Input tax is not deductible where persons attend by invitation (such as a new car launch).

Apportionment of input tax costs

4.45 There can also be mixed motives where such expenditure is incurred. Where part of the motive is entertainment a proportion of the VAT incurred must be disallowed. In *Thorn EMI plc v C & E Comrs [1995] STC 674, CA* it was accepted by the Court of Appeal that the hire of chalets at air shows was for entertaining prospective clients and as the venue for holding business negotiations. Part of the chalet was furnished as office accommodation. It was held that the taxpayer was entitled to deduct VAT incurred to the extent that it can be established that it was incurred on the supply of goods and services for business use other than that of business entertainment.

4.46 The *Thorn* decision overturned an earlier High Court judgment in the case of *Plant Repair Services (South Wales) Ltd [1994] STC 232* where it was held that none of the input tax incurred on a hospitality suite at Cardiff Arms Park that was used on some weekdays as office accommodation and on match days for entertainment of customers was recoverable, as the Input Tax Order did not provide for apportionment. The *Thorn* decision has held that, where a business receives an 'indivisible supply of goods or services', VAT (Input Tax) Order, art 5 requires an apportionment to be made between business entertainment and other business, non-entertainment, use.

4.47 Apportionment of the input tax can be difficult and is a subjective matter. Customs and Excise has instructed officers to accept an apportionment only when they are satisfied that the non-entertainment use is genuine and not a contrivance to recover a proportion of input tax on supplies used for business entertainment. Any apportionment is to give a fair and reasonable result (which unfortunately is not defined, but see para **4.48** below). When considering an apportionment officers will consider what the taxable person is using the relevant goods or services for, other than to provide entertainment. Internal instructions state that there is to be no '... apportionment where the claimed "other business use" is something intangible such as "business promotion" or "marketing". All business entertainment is by way of marketing or promotion'. This would seem to be a restrictive interpretation and one that may not be sustainable.

4.48 Customs and Excise Internal Guidance V1–13, Chapter 2A, section 12.9 gives examples of where apportionment is allowed. These include:

- hire of a hospitality suite, a specific part of which is given over to use as an office conducting normal business;
- services connected with sponsorship of an event which are used partly to entertain customers and partly to advertise the trader to a wider audience attending or viewing the event;
- capital goods to be used partly to make taxable supplies (eg a yacht for charter) and partly for business entertainment; and
- consumable goods used partly for business entertainment and partly for other purposes.

A couple of these examples arise from Tribunal cases, but they do not give any clear guidance as to how the apportionment is to be made. Apportionment can be based upon use (hours used for business entertainment against business use – note that the time when the facility is not used at all may be treated as non-business use, (see *Teknequip Ltd [1987] STC 664*), number of persons attending, or the costs involved). When considering the apportionment, it is useful to relate this to the charge made for the facility. Thus, if the supplier charges for a facility by the hour or day, its apportionment should be on an hourly or daily basis, no matter how many people use the facility, as the volume of people will not affect the cost. The numbers attending, however, may determine catering costs, and a head count may be the most appropriate way of apportioning input tax. Thus for an apportionment it may be necessary to use more than one method to obtain a fair and reasonable result (time for room hire and numbers for catering).

Entertainment not provided free

4.49 Where a charge is made for entertainment it is not regarded as entertainment for the purposes of the Blocking Order (see *Shaklee International [1981] STC 776, CA*). Input tax can be reclaimed but output tax must be charged on the amount charged.

4.50 Problems, however, arise where the charge made is below the cost of providing the entertainment. It is Customs and Excise's policy to consider entertainment provided below cost to be 'free' hospitality. The non-deductible amount is the amount that represents the below cost element. Thus, if an event costs £1,000 in VAT and a charge is made on which £400 output tax is due, the free element is £600. Input tax of £600 is non-deductible. Support for this view comes from the High Court judgment in *BMW (GB) Ltd v C & E Comrs [1997] STC 824* (**Case Summary 27**). BMW arranged track days (and golfing and curling days). Dealers were charged an amount and members of the public were invited. The charge represented 17 per cent and 29 per cent of the cost of the days. Input tax of 17 per cent and 29 per cent respectively was allowed. This appears to be in conflict with the decision in *Ernst & Young [1997] VAT decision 15100* (**Case Summary 29**). That decision stated that the consideration was not to be insignificant, where it is less than cost. This is no doubt a subjective judgment and the *Ernst & Young* decision, being a VAT Tribunal, is not binding. It may, of course, be thought that the *BMW* arrangement was a scheme to reduce the VAT cost; it is difficult to say. The conflict, however, exists and Customs and Excise policy is clear following the *BMW* decision.

Employees acting as hosts

4.51 Input tax is recoverable where employees are entertained. In many instances, employees act as hosts of third parties that are being entertained. It is Customs and Excise policy that the VAT incurred on hosts entertaining the third party is non-deductible (see Public Notice 700/65, para 5). It has to be determined, however, if the employee is acting as a host or is being entertained. Where a company bought debentures for 130 seats at the All England Tennis Club, Customs and Excise assessed the input tax reclaimed as being incurred for business entertainment. It was held at a VAT Tribunal that 50 of the seats had been purchased for business entertainment and 80 for employees and their relatives. The VAT incurred on the 80 seats was allowed (though the reasoning for allowing the input tax where seats were for relatives is not understood) (*BTR Industries Ltd (1994) VAT decision 11828*).

Employee expenses

4.52 VAT on expenses of employees on business trips is reclaimable as input tax as it is a subsistence cost. Where, however, the trip is made for the purpose of business entertainment, the input tax is non-deductible. Where there are elements of subsistence and entertainment, there is a requirement to apportion the VAT incurred.

Staff entertainment

4.53 VAT incurred on the entertainment of employees is deductible. It must, however, be entertainment of employees (including directors) and not third parties, sole proprietors or partners. Where a cabaret was provided to partners in an accountancy firm the VAT was held to be non-deductible as it was entertainment and there was not a nexus with the purpose of the business (*Ernst & Young [1997] VAT decision 15100* (**Case Summary 29**)).

4.54 It should be noted that it is Customs and Excise's policy to treat directors as if they were not employees (and in an analogous situation to partners or sole proprietors). This is not correct as many directors are employees. For instance, Employment Appeals Tribunals have held that where directors have a service contract that they can be treated as an employee (though even then, regard has to be taken of the particular circumstances). Non-executive directors and controlling shareholder directors, though, may not be employees (and the facts will determine if they are employees or not). Where, however, there is expensive and gratuitous entertainment of directors (and no other employees) it is likely that a VAT Tribunal would hold that the VAT incurred was not recoverable because the expense did not have a close nexus to the purpose of the business. Entertainment of directors at the same time as staff (at, say, a staff Christmas party) should not be subject to any input tax restriction, though Customs and Excise may challenge this interpretation.

4.55 Spouses and partners of staff frequently attend staff parties. Customs and Excise used to operate a 50 per cent apportionment but this was held not to be justifiable (*Ernst & Young [1997] VAT decision 15100* (**Case Summary 29**)) and another form of apportionment is necessary. In this particular case, however, a charge was made for non-employees. Whilst this was not sufficient to cover the cost of the party, it was seen as not being insignificant. Hence, output tax was due on the amount charged and all the input tax incurred was deductible. This decision is contrary to the policy that is still maintained by Customs and Excise for hospitality provided below cost (see **4.50** above). This decision should, however, allow all the input tax incurred to be reclaimed as long as a charge is made that is not a notional charge.

4.56 The Tribunal found in *Ernst & Young* that there was no need for an apportionment as the employer is providing entertainment for the benefit of its staff; to reward them for good work, to maintain and improve staff morale, etc. This is done wholly for business purposes. Consequently VAT incurred on entertainment of staff (staff parties, team building exercises, staff outings and similar events) can be reclaimed in full. Where non-staff members attend, the VAT incurred is to be apportioned on the basis of the ratio of staff members to non-staff members (see *KPMG (No 2) [1997] VATDR 192 (1997) VAT decision 14962*).

4.57 It should be noted that an earlier decision (*KPMG Peat Marwick McLintock [1993] VATTR 118 VAT decision 10135*)) that held that all the input tax is reclaimable on the expense of a staff party where there is no charge for non-employees has been disapproved of in the subsequent Court of Appeal decision *Thorn EMI plc v C & E Comrs [1995] STC 674, CA*, which allowed apportionment, and in the Tribunal *KPMG (No 2)*. In the first *KPMG* case both parties agreed that the input tax was either wholly deductible or wholly blocked. This case can now be disregarded.

Other employee entertainment

4.58 Customs and Excise will deny input tax claims where an expense has been incurred for what it believes is private expenditure, ie expenditure that does not have a nexus with the purpose of the business. To enable the VAT incurred to be reclaimed it is necessary to demonstrate that there is a reason for incurring the expenditure that has a business purpose. In *Peugeot Motor Company (2001) VAT decision 16731* the company attempted (and succeeded) to improve attendance of its employees by awarding employees with a perfect attendance record the opportunity to win tickets to see football matches or motor racing events. Customs and Excise refused the claim for input tax but it was allowed by the Tribunal as it held that the taxable person 'acted for purely business reasons and that having regard to the requirements of its business the provision of tickets was necessary to improve absenteeism – in such circumstances, the personal benefit derived by its employees was of secondary importance compared with the needs of its business'.

Business gifts

4.59 The VAT charge on business gifts is an output tax charge. In practice, however, most taxable persons restrict input tax instead of accounting for output tax and business gifts are, therefore, considered in this chapter.

4.60 A gift is something that the 'giver' is not obliged to give and where the recipient is not obliged to do or give anything in return. Customs and Excise would regard as a business gift (see VAT Notice 700/35/97, para 1.1) the following:

- Brochures, posters, and advertising material.
- Executive presents.
- Long service awards.
- Retirement gifts.
- Goods supplied to employees under attendance of safety at work schemes.
- Items distributed to trade customers.
- Prizes from gaming machines and from gaming and free lotteries.

4.61 It seems odd that items supplied to employees attending safety at work schemes would be regarded as gifts if they were being supplied as a requirement for safety regulations. Presumably possession of the goods passes to the employee and as such they are regarded as gifts.

4.62 A supply of a gift of business assets is a supply of goods (VATA 1994, Sch 4, para 5(1)) and is taxable. Thus, input tax can be reclaimed, but VAT is due on the supply of the goods. No supply, however, arises unless the supplier has or will be able to claim an input tax credit or claim the VAT under the Eighth Directive or Thirteenth Directive mechanisms (see the Sixth Directive, art 13B(c) and *EC Commission v Italy (C-45/95) [1997] STC 1062*).

4.63 The value of the supply of a gift is the price the taxable person would have to pay (excluding VAT) at the time of the supply to purchase goods identical to the goods concerned. It is not the historic cost of the goods, but the cost to obtain the goods at the time of the gift, for goods of that age and condition. Where the value of identical goods cannot be ascertained, then the value is the value of similar goods and if that value is not possible to ascertain, it is the cost of production (VATA 1994, Sch 6, para 6).

4.64 There will also be no supply where the cost to the donor of the gift is £50 or less. This cost can be the cost of purchase or the cost of production, whichever is appropriate. Where a succession of gifts is made to the same person, the cost of the goods given in succession must be less than £50 in any 12-month period. Annual gifts (such as Christmas gifts), small items given to trade customers (eg ashtrays given away by breweries), advertising material and gifts distributed on a random basis are not regarded as gifts given in succession.

4.65 It should be noted that samples are not treated as gifts. No VAT is due on samples given away for testing purposes. Also, samples given to the public via an intermediary are not regarded as gifts. No VAT is due where there is no charge for the goods, the goods are supplied for business purposes and they are illustrative examples of the product, the samples remain the property of the supplier until given to the final consumer and any samples not used are returned or destroyed.

4.66 The recipient of the gift can reclaim any VAT charged (subject to the normal rules). A VAT invoice cannot, however, be issued by the supplier/donor as there is no consideration but a VAT certificate can be issued to support the claim for input tax deduction. This is essentially the same as a VAT invoice but must bear the words 'VAT Certificate' instead of 'VAT Invoice', and state: 'No payment is due on the supply of the goods. Output tax has been accounted for on the supply'. Most Customs and Excise officers will accept a 'VAT only invoice' even though it is not actually correct to do so.

4.67 Where services are gifted there is no supply and no VAT is due. This may, however, be regarded as being a private use of services if the services have been bought in. In such circumstances a taxable supply is regarded as taking place and VAT must be charged.

4.68 VAT is not due on gifts where no input tax has been claimed but if any VAT has been claimed (eg there has been an apportionment of the VAT incurred), VAT is due. Indeed, where a person is eligible to reclaim VAT but has chosen not to, output tax is technically due. It would probably not, however, be best judgement to assess for output tax and not allow a corresponding credit for input tax. Thus, many taxable persons do not reclaim VAT on the acquisition of gifts and do not account for output tax on the supply of the gift. A problem that frequently occurs, however, is forgetting to account for output tax on items gifted from stock held for resale.

Directors' and staff accommodation

4.69 The provision of accommodation to directors or persons connected with directors is prevented by VATA 1994, s 24(3) and this states:

> 'For the purposes of subsections (1) and (2) above, where goods or services are supplied to a company, goods are acquired by a company from another member State or goods are imported by a company from a place outside the member States and the goods or services which are so supplied, acquired or imported are used or to be used in connection with the provision of accommodation by the company, they shall not be treated as used or to be used for the purposes of any business carried on by the company to the extent that the accommodation is used or to be used for domestic purposes by–

(a) a director of the company, or

(b) a person connected with a director of the company.'

Thus, input tax is not blocked, as this restriction on a VAT deduction does not arise from the 'Blocking Order', but the VAT incurred is excluded from being input tax by this provision. The effect of this provision is to deny VAT credit and, consequently, it is strongly arguable that, as this provision was introduced after the introduction of the Sixth VAT Directive, the VAT incurred is properly deductible (see para **4.2–4.5** above).

Domestic accommodation

4.70 The provision of domestic accommodation is regarded as a private rather than business expense and, consequently, VAT cannot normally be recovered in respect of such costs (although the purchase price or rent will either be zero-rated or exempt, VAT is incurred on alterations, maintenance and repairs). Where, however, a taxable person is required to provide domestic accommodation to employees or such accommodation is necessary for the running of the business, the VAT on any expenditure incurred in providing the accommodation (such as maintenance and refurbishment costs) is regarded as having been incurred for a business purpose. This frequently arises in the farming (tied cottages) and hotel industries. In these and similar businesses, it is essential to have staff available at all times of the day. Alternatively, there may be little or no suitable accommodation available within reasonable distance or at a reasonable price locally.

4.71 Former employees may also be provided with accommodation, where this is a benefit of previous employment and traditional practice (in particular in farming). This treatment of past employees as employees differs from Customs and Excise's usual treatment of a past employee as no longer an employee (see para **4.36** above). The input tax incurred is regarded as incurred for the purpose of the business and is recoverable. If input tax is claimed on heat and light, telephone bills or goods that become the property of the employee, then an output tax charge is due on the value of the supply to the employee.

4.72 Any charges made for accommodation are exempt. Thus, the VAT incurred may not be deductible according to the partial exemption position of the business.

4.73 Customs and Excise may attempt to disallow VAT incurred for family members that are employees if Customs and Excise regard them as being 'nominally employed' and the expense is, in reality, a private expense. If the family member is a genuine employee then the input tax is deductible and the VAT is not blocked merely because they are family members (but see para **4.77** for corporate farming concerns).

4.74 A further problem arises where businesses are operated from domestic premises. Where a sole proprietor or partner carries on a business from home and uses a particular room, rooms or area for business the VAT incurred can reclaimed if it can be identified. VAT on domestic items is not recoverable. What is treated as domestic may differ and the circumstances and reasons for the purchase need to be examined. For instance, a stereo system would not normally be seen as a business expense but in *Woods and Seaton Ltd (1990) VAT decision 4640*, it was held that the input tax should be allowed as a deduction as the music centre was used for the purpose of the company's business as the appellant worked very long hours into the night and at weekends. The music centre enabled him (apparently) to work more effectively.

4.75 Where the VAT is not separately itemised, it may be apportioned or a VAT charge applied (as described in para **4.18–4.33** above concerning business and non-business use). Apportionment is likely to occur for costs such as heat and light, security systems and general maintenance. It has been agreed with the NFU that sole proprietors and partnerships who are full-time farmers may normally claim 70 per cent of the VAT incurred on repairs and maintenance, but it may be a greater or lesser amount for alterations depending on the part of the building to be altered (see Business Brief 18/96 (27 August 1996)).

Directors' accommodation

4.76 Although company directors are often employees of the companies they control they are unable to benefit from the input tax relief described at para **4.70** above.

4.77 The definition of 'director' and 'person connected' with a director are contained in VATA 1994, s 24(7):

> 'For the purpose of this section "director" means–
>
> (a) in relation to a company whose affairs are managed by a board of directors or similar body, a member of that board or similar body;
>
> (b) in relation to a company whose affairs are managed by a single person, that director or person;
>
> (c) in relation to a company whose affairs are managed by the members themselves, a member of the company,
>
> and a person is connected with a director if that person is the director's wife or husband, or is a relative, or the wife or husband of a relative, of the director or of the director's wife or husband.'

As can be seen, the scope is wider than simply a director of a limited company. Also, where a farm is run by a corporate entity if a director occupies the farmhouse or a person connected with the director, the VAT incurred cannot be reclaimed despite the agreement with the NFU noted at **4.75** above.

4.78 The restriction applies whether the accommodation is for a main residence, a second home, a weekend retreat or a flat available when directors are visiting London or other major city for a business meeting. It applies to all domestic accommodation for directors and persons connected with them. The restriction applies to VAT incurred on all expenses that relate to the accommodation such as repairs, refurbishment, furnishing, legal costs and estate agents' fees. The restriction does not apply to other costs such as telephone and heating bills but this VAT will not be recoverable if it is incurred for private purposes (or is recoverable in full where an output tax charge is made for private usage).

4.79 Where part of the domestic accommodation is put to a separate business use (such as storage) there may be a case for an input tax apportionment.

4.80 The input tax restriction does not, however, apply to hotel accommodation that is provided to a director. It is ironic that where a company purchases a flat in London for directors' accommodation to reduce costs, it cannot reclaim VAT but if they choose to use an expensive hotel, the VAT incurred can be reclaimed.

4.81 See below at para **4.105** for input tax treatment of removal expenses.

Hotel accommodation

4.82 Input tax incurred on hotel accommodation (and similar types of accommodation, such as motels, guesthouses, bed and breakfast accommodation, etc) is deductible as input tax (even where incurred by directors) where the expense is borne by the taxable person. The normal rules apply for hotel accommodation that it is incurred for the purpose of the business and a proper tax invoice is received. The restriction on director's accommodation discussed at para **4.76–4.80** above does not apply to hotel type accommodation. For employees, this includes accommodation near the normal place of work (for instance where staff are required to work late and there is no, or little, transport home). For other persons (sole proprietors, partners, etc) it will depend on the particular facts of the case. An overnight stay in London due to personal reasons would not be a deductible expense. Should, however, a director, sole proprietor or partner stay in a hotel due to transport strikes or other transport disruptions and the taxable person bears the cost as it is accepted as being for the purpose of the business, the VAT incurred is deductible.

4.83 When considering hotel accommodation, however, a number of issues need to be considered. First, has the expense been incurred for a business purpose or is the expense a private expense? This will depend upon the circumstances. Hotel accommodation may be seen to be used for private expenditure, such as prizes for employees (eg trips to London for valued employees), 'away days', bonding sessions or other social type gatherings. Such expenditure may be regarded as being private but if it is considered to be a genuine business expense the input tax is deductible and most of the examples given above should be eligible for input tax recovery.

4.84 Should the expenditure be regarded as entertainment or hospitality the input tax incurred on employees only is deductible (but see para **4.34** et seq above regarding entertainment). Whether there is a business motive is a subjective matter and it is necessary to determine what is in the taxable person's mind when incurring the expense (see para **4.12–4.17** above and *Ian Flockton Developments Ltd* *v C & E Comrs [1987] STC 394, QB*). It is also necessary to consider if an 'onward' supply is made to employees under VAT (Supply of Services) Order 1993, SI 1993/1507, art 3) when incurring expenses for staff incentive schemes. Other types of personal expenditure incurred at hotels will be mini-bar, bar drinks, videos, dry-cleaning and these are non-deductible as personal expenditure with insufficient nexus to the business.

4.85 The second issue to be considered is, has the supplier charged VAT? Many small hotel type establishments may be operating under the VAT registration threshold and not be VAT registered. Also, a number of supplies made by hotels will not bear VAT. For instance, charges for newspapers are zero-rated and room hire charges (for conferences etc) will be exempt unless there has been an election to waive exemption. It is necessary to examine the invoice carefully to determine if VAT is charged.

4.86 Finally, it is necessary to ensure that a tax invoice is obtained. As stated in Public Notice 700, para 19.7.5 and Customs and Excise Internal Guidance V1–13, Chapter 2, section 8.9, it is not necessary to have a tax invoice in the name of the business, it can be in the name of the employee. Unfortunately, many VAT officers (and occasionally Tribunal Chairmen) do not seem to agree with this contention and officers may raise an assessment. It is, therefore, prudent to obtain an invoice in the name of the taxable person wherever possible. Hotels, on occasion, produce invoices that are not proper tax invoices. Although most officers will exercise their discretion and allow input tax deduction, it is advisable to ensure a proper tax invoice is obtained.

4.87 VATA 1994, Sch 6, para 10 states that where accommodation is supplied to an employee the value will be taken as nil. This paragraph was intended to ensure that the VAT incurred on accommodation for employees who required accommodation (farm workers, hotel staff, etc) would be treated as a supply and the VAT incurred could be reclaimed. It could be considered that this is otiose, as the expenses were incurred for the purpose of the business and any input tax incurred should be deductible without the need for this deeming provision and that, as no consideration was supplied, no VAT is chargeable (and if it was a supply, it would be exempt).

4.88 Some practitioners had thought that this provision meant that any accommodation provided to an employee was a supply valued at nil. This would allow partially exempt persons to reclaim all the VAT incurred on hotel accommodation used by employees. It was held at Tribunal (*Co-operative Insurance Society Ltd (1997) VAT decision 14862*) that the taxable person is not making a supply of hotel accommodation to employees in such circumstances. It also held that, where accommodation was reserved by employees, the supply was made to the employee and not the company, so no input tax was reclaimable. Where the company reserved the hotel accommodation, the supply was made to the company and the input tax was to be treated as residual input tax.

4.89 The second part of this decision was, to say the least, an interesting interpretation, ignoring the fact that the expense was incurred for the purpose of the business and the VAT is, therefore, deductible. The point regarding the employer needing to book the hotel accommodation does not seem to have been taken up by Customs and Excise. It does, however, highlight the need for care, and it would be prudent for taxable persons to book such accommodation where possible.

Employee expenses

4.90 One of the more important differences between recovery of VAT generally incurred by a taxable person and the VAT incurred by an employee, is that employee expenses may not be regarded as being consideration for supplies to the taxable person but to the employee. Whilst the employee may be undertaking activities on behalf of the taxable person, the supply may be made direct to the employee, not the taxable person. For instance, where an employee eats food as subsistence, uses a hotel room during an overnight stay or puts petrol into the employee's own car for fuel used during a business trip, the supply has been made to the employee and not the taxable person. The expenses will have been incurred for a business purpose and a reimbursement of the expense made by the taxable person to the employee but the supply is not to the taxable person. Thus, the first requirement for the VAT incurred to be input tax is not met.

4.91 Similar issues have arisen in direct tax. For instance, in *Richardson v Worrall (58 TC 642)* it was held that the employee had a liability to pay for the fuel when he put it in the car and a subsequent payment through the use of a company credit card discharged the liability of the employee and it therefore constituted an emolument. This contention was upheld in *R v Department of Social Security, ex p Overdrive Credit Card Ltd [1991] STC 129.*

4.92 This issue has been a concern for VAT as VAT is a tax on consumption and VAT incurred on private expenditure is not deductible, but VAT incurred for the purpose of the business is deductible. When the Sixth VAT Directive was being drafted this issue was discussed at length. The working papers of the European Parliament state that it is necessary to determine if such deductions are to be allowed or not. The Committee on Budgets of the European Union considered that leisure and luxury expenditure should not qualify for deduction, as the consumption element was dominant, but that passenger transport and accommodation costs should be deductible. The European Parliament working papers, however, stated that VAT incurred on restaurants, food, drink and entertainment should be non-deductible but accommodation, lodging and passenger transport should be deductible. As it was not possible to agree a definitive list of non-deductible items it was decided to defer this issue for a period of four years and allow member states to determine what items were to be non-deductible (Sixth VAT Directive, art 17(6)). Although this period has expired, the European Council has not yet decided what items are to be non-deductible and, hence, the matter remains within the jurisdiction of the member state and the items not deductible on the introduction of the Sixth Directive remain extant.

4.93 Whilst the matter of what was to be deducted was considered when the Sixth Directive was being drafted, the issue of the supply being made to the employee and not to the taxable person did not merit a great deal of attention. It is clear from the legislation that the Sixth VAT Directive, art 17(2) and VATA 1994, s 24(1)(a) that the supply must be made to 'him' – the taxable person. The European Court of Justice has not, however, applied this strict interpretation. In *Leesportefeuille 'Intiem' CV v Staatssecretaris van Financiën (165/86) [1988] ECR 1471* (**Case Summary** 8), *ECJ* it was held that although art 17(2)(a) restricted a taxable person's right to deduct tax to amounts due or paid 'in respect of goods … supplied to him', the purpose of that provision could not be used to prevent a person deducting VAT paid on goods which were for use in his business. Thus, the input tax incurred on goods delivered to an employee that are used by a business for the purposes of its business can be deducted.

4.94 Customs and Excise do allow the deduction of input tax on expenditure that has been incurred by employees. The following are examples of some types of expenditure where the supply may be seen as being supplied to the employee but accepted by Customs and Excise as made to the employer provided the employer meets the full cost:

- road fuel and other motoring expenses;
- subsistence costs, ie meals and accommodation necessarily paid for whilst away from the normal workplace;
- removal expenses arising from company relocations or transfer of staff; and
- sundry items such as small tools, materials etc purchased 'on site'.

The above examples are not exhaustive but are illustrative of the type of expense that may be regarded automatically as being incurred by the business.

4.95 Where a tax invoice shows a supply is made to an employee of a taxable person (that is, the invoice is made out in the name of the employee), this invoice is satisfactory for input tax purposes provided the supplies were purchased for the purpose of the employer's business (see VAT Public Notice 700, para 19.7.5 and Customs and Excise Internal Guidance V1–13, Chapter 2, section 8.9).

4.96 VATA 1994, s 24(4) allows the Treasury to make an Order allowing supplies made to a third party to be treated as being supplied to a taxable person. This is to allow the input tax incurred by the third party to be treated as being supplied to the taxable business. Such an order has been made, the VAT (Input Tax) (Person Supplied) Order 1991, SI 1991/2306. This treats supplies of road fuel purchased by third parties as being supplied to the taxable business. Thus, the taxable person will be able to reclaim the VAT incurred, despite the invoice being made out to the third party. It should be noted that this Order is restricted to fuel only and does not encompass other supplies often incurred by employees or other third parties, such as accommodation or food. It is, however, wider than employees as it refers to third parties.

4.97 The Order allows the taxable person to reclaim VAT where the third party (the employee or other person) is reimbursed for the actual cost of the fuel expense or where an amount is paid by way of a mileage allowance. The mileage allowance paid is to be determined by the distance travelled and the cylinder capacity of the vehicle used. This is discussed in greater detail in the section discussing motor cars at para **4.146–4.152**.

4.98 It should be noted that there is no guidance from Customs and Excise regarding benefits provided to a spouse or partner of an employee. The assumption may be reasonably made that if the cost of the spouse is incidental (such as a spouse sharing a room in a hotel on a business trip) or the benefit is provided to the spouse as part of the employee's employment package then the VAT incurred is deductible. Where there is an additional non-contractual cost, the VAT incurred on the expense is not deductible. Where a charge is made to the spouse or partner and this is not a notional cost, output tax is due on the charge and the input tax incurred can be reclaimed.

4.99 Customs and Excise are less likely to allow input tax recovery for spouses of directors, partners or sole proprietors. The company often employs such spouses and Customs and Excise are likely to take into consideration the actual work done. Where the spouse undertakes no work, any VAT is likely to be denied as not having a nexus with the business.

Non-employees treated as employees

4.100 It is becoming increasingly common for businesses to use agents, contractors and the self-employed in the role of employees. In such instances the agent, contractor or the self-employed person should deduct any VAT incurred if VAT registered. This intermediary person can reclaim the VAT incurred, and make an onward charge plus VAT to the main business. Where the main business is a fully taxable person this VAT will be deductible. Problems will, however, arise where the main business cannot recover all the VAT incurred. It is common, however, for the agent, contractor or self-employed person to treat themselves as an employee, even though they are not legally an employee. Even where they are aware that they are not employees, they frequently do not wish to incur the burden of VAT registration to allow for the recovery of VAT on subsistence and travel expenses. Tribunals have disallowed the VAT recovery by a business where it has been incurred by an agent, contractor or self-employed person (see *Berbrooke Fashions [1977] VATTR 168 (1977) VAT decision 426*; *R Wiseman & Sons [1984] VATTR 168 (1977) VAT decision 1691* and *Stormseal (UPVC) Window Co Ltd [1990] VAT decision 4538*). There is, however, an element of entertainment in these cases, and entertainment is specifically blocked (see para **4.34 et seq** above).

4.101 There are instances where VAT incurred on non-employee expenses can be reclaimed. Where a taxable person wishes to run a conference or training event for non-employees, it may hire a hotel. This VAT would be recoverable by the taxable person if it can be regarded as being a supply for the purpose of the business made to the taxable person. The VAT is deductible if there is a single tax invoice from the hotel to the taxable person, even if some of the individuals are separately VAT registered. It is, however, necessary to consider the decision in

Shaklee International [1981] STC 776, CA. Here it was held that the food and accommodation supplied to trainee agents of a pyramid selling organisation was business entertainment. Input tax deduction is not permitted where the goods or services received are for the purpose of business entertainment (Input Tax Order 1992, art 5(1)). In addition, it may be considered that the supply is made directly to the individual and not the taxable person (see *Institute of Purchasing and Supply [1987] VATTR 207 (1987) VAT decision 2533)*.

4.102 Customs and Excise do allow input tax to be reclaimed where a non-employee incurs the VAT in a number of circumstances (see Customs and Excise Internal Guidance V1–13, Chapter 2, section 3.5). For instance, where a taxable person reimburses subsistence, road fuel or other motoring costs incurred by self-employed persons working for the business, the VAT incurred is deductible where:

- the individual is employed on the same basis as an employee;
- the expense is in respect of their 'employment';
- the individuals receive no payment from the end customer;
- the reimbursement is at cost, including VAT; and
- the amount is dealt with in the accounts in the normal way.

In such instances Customs and Excise treat these individuals as employees for the purposes of input tax deduction. Where the individual acts for a number of taxable persons, this concession cannot apply as their subsistence does not relate to any one 'employer'. Where the individual is registered for VAT in their own capacity, the VAT should be treated as incurred by the individual for the purpose of their own business.

4.103 Similarly, where a self-employed person buys tools or materials to use for a specific job for a taxable person, the VAT incurred is the taxable person's input tax provided the points above are complied with and the tools remain the property of the taxable person or the materials are incorporated into and become a cost component of the taxable person's supply to the end customer.

Specific employee expenses

4.104 In summary, VAT on an expense incurred by an employee can be deducted where it is an expense of the taxable person, it is used for the purposes of the business and a proper VAT invoice is held. Certain items are, however, non-deductible and these (with the exception of entertainment and accommodation, which are discussed at paras **4.34** and **4.69 above**) are detailed below. This section examines the potential for VAT recovery for specific items on commonly incurred employee expenses in detail and, in outline, for less commonly incurred employee expenses. Also, as they are closely linked, commentary is given on input tax deduction on expenses incurred by sole proprietors, partners and directors. Although directors are often employees, their dominant positions in a company merits special comment and receives special treatment by Customs and Excise.

Removal expenses

4.105 Customs and Excise's Internal Guidance V1–13, Chapter 2A, para 18.5 states that VAT incurred on the removal expenses of employees is deductible as input tax on:

- estate agents' and solicitors' fees;
- storage and removal of household and personal effects; and
- services, such as plumbing in washing machines or altering curtains.

4.106 Customs and Excise's guidance states that 'claims should not be rejected even if, as is usual, the relevant invoices are addressed to the employee rather than the taxable person'. Where a proportion of the expenditure is reimbursed, a pro-rata proportion of the input tax can be claimed. No input tax can be claimed where a fixed rate allowance is paid.

4.107 Input tax on removal expenses for directors, partners and sole proprietors is also deductible where the move is for the purpose of the business.

4.108 In *Michael Sellers & Co Ltd (LON/92/574X (unreported))* the VAT incurred on moving a director was allowed in full. Customs and Excise had argued for a 10 per cent recovery rate as it determined that there had been incidental use of the home for business purposes and that input tax was blocked (VATA 1994, s 24(3) (provision of domestic accommodation to a director, or a person connected with a director)). The Tribunal found that there was no provision of accommodation to Mr Sellers or his family as it was a removal expenditure and that the input tax was deductible.

Travel costs

4.109 Most travel costs (train, bus and airfares) do not bear VAT in the UK and, therefore, do not need to be considered. VAT is due on car hire, car leasing and car purchase, as well as repairs, servicing and petrol costs. These issues will be considered later in this section. It should be noted that Customs and Excise has issued a specific notice (VAT Notice 700/64, Motoring expenses (January 2002)), and this explains Customs and Excise's views on such costs (including input tax deduction on cars, petrol and output tax charges).

Subsistence

4.110 See paras **4.34–4.58** above in respect to business entertainment of customers and employees.

4.111 VAT incurred on employee meal expenses can be reclaimed (subject to the normal rules regarding invoices, etc). Meal expenses for other parties is not, however, always deductible. It can only be reclaimed where it is necessary for subsistence and is some distance from the normal working place of the individual. Customs and Excise quote in their internal guidance at V1–13, Chapter 2A, section 18.2, Subsistence, that:

> 'The Tribunal case of *D G Mutch (VAT decision 2,559)* is a useful precedent. It concerned a sole proprietor who was disallowed the VAT incurred on meals taken within two or three miles from his office. The Tribunal applied a test from *Strong and Co of Romsey Ltd v Woodfield* in which Lord Davey referring to the words "for the purpose of trade" said:
>
> "These words are used in other rules, and appear to me to mean for the purpose of enabling a person to carry on and earn profits in the trade. It is not enough that the (expenditure) is made in the course of, or arises out of, or is connected with the trade, or is made out of the profits of the trade. It must be made for the purpose of earning the profits."
>
> The Tribunal stated that the onus is upon the taxpayer to show that the expenditure for personal meals was for the purpose of the business and not for the "natural daily requirements for nourishment".'

Customs and Excise will not, therefore, allow meal expenses for a sole proprietor, partner and a director to be reclaimed unless it is away from their place of work on a business trip. Customs and Excise officers often use, as an unofficial guide, a five-mile radius from the office. This distance rule, however has no basis in law, it is only necessary to show that the meal was for the purpose of the business and not for ordinary nourishment, but this can be difficult to prove. Often, officers will attempt to apply this distance restriction to employees' meals, but this would not be a correct interpretation of the decision in *D G Mutch*.

Fixed allowances

4.112 Where a fixed cash allowance is paid to cover subsistence or overnight accommodation, no VAT is claimable. The VAT fraction is not to be applied to the amount paid. Where tax invoices are obtained to support the claim no VAT is payable even though an invoice is held. This is because the supply of the hotel accommodation was to the employee and not to the taxable person – the BBC in this case (*British Broadcasting Corp [1974] VATTR 100*). This seems contrary to the opinions outlined in **Chapter 3** and European principles that VAT should not be a burden upon a business. The Sixth VAT Directive requires the goods or services to be used for the purpose of the business, not actually supplied to the business. It is, therefore, suggested that this decision may be incorrect, and where an invoice is obtained the VAT should be deductible. The fact that, for administrative convenience (ease of administration and for economy), a business pays a fixed allowance should not be a bar to input tax recovery. Any claim for input tax, however, would be contrary to the practice adopted by Customs and Excise and is likely to be challenged.

Telephones

Home telephones

4.113 There is no guidance from Customs and Excise regarding home telephones and reclaiming input tax. The practice that has been established, however, is that if an employee, partner, sole proprietor or director uses a home telephone for business purposes, the VAT element that relates to business use can be reclaimed by the taxable person. Clearly, in most of these instances the telephone invoice will not be in the name of the taxable person but in the name of the employee or other third party. This is regarded as being sufficient for input tax deduction. It is usual to agree with a visiting VAT officer the percentage of private to business use of the home telephone.

Mobile telephones

4.114 Customs and Excise have, however, issued a Business Brief (14/99, 2 July 1999) regarding mobile telephones.

(a) The VAT incurred on the cost of providing and connecting a mobile telephone for business use and any standing or rental charge is fully deductible (but see (b) below).

(b) Where the rental charges allows for a certain amount of 'free' calls the VAT on the total package must be apportioned for business and private use.

(c) Where a business does not allow employees to make private calls, all of the VAT incurred on the call charges is input tax and is recoverable. Customs and Excise accept that in practice a small amount of private calls may be made and this will not prevent all the input tax from being reclaimed.

(d) If a business charges its employees for any private calls they make, then it may treat the VAT incurred on the calls as input tax, but must account for output tax on the amounts it charges.

(e) Where employees make private calls without a charge from the employer, then the input tax incurred must be apportioned. Any apportionment method may be chosen that produces a fair and reasonable result.

4.115 It should be noted that it is not the policy of Customs and Excise to apply the Supply of Services Order to mobile phones. Where there is sufficient private use to justify taxation, Customs and Excise do not treat the VAT incurred as input tax. This seems contrary to the *Lennartz v Finanzamt Munchen III (C-97/90) [1995] STC 514, ECJ* decision mentioned at **4.18–4.33** above.

4.116 Customs and Excise do not require apportionment to be a substantial burden on business and burdensome apportionment methods suggested by officers can be successfully resisted. A percentage apportionment based on a representative sample is acceptable.

Clothing

4.117 Clothing is a normal expense of the individual and, as VAT is a tax on consumption, the VAT incurred is not normally reclaimable. The principles outlined in the section regarding non-business use and business use at paras **4.9–4.33** are relevant here (particularly the differences between the direct tax and indirect tax treatment of such expenses) see *Ian Flockton Developments Ltd v C & E Comrs [1987] STC 394* and *Mallalieu v Drummond [1983] STC 665, HL* and output tax charges for private use where input VAT is claimed (see *Lennartz v Finanzamt Munchen III (C-97/90) [1995] STC 514, ECJ* (**Case Summary 12**)).

4.118 Where a uniform or protective clothing, or clothing that is appropriate for a job and not private use (such as entertainment or stage costumes) is provided, any VAT incurred will be deductible. A uniform should have the business's name or logo on it to identify it as a uniform, or it may be regarded as ordinary clothing. Where the clothing can be worn on private occasions (such as suits for television presenters) the VAT incurred will not be regarded as input tax (*JK Hill & SJ Mansell (t/a JK Hill & Co) (1988) VAT decision 2379*). Arguments that a high standard of dress is required to 'create a professional image' or that the clothing would not normally be worn is not sufficient to make the VAT incurred deductible. In *B J Brown (1992) VAT decision 6552*, the Tribunal dismissed the appellant's argument that an art consultant required a certain standard of dress in order to attract business.

4.119 VAT recovery on clothing expenses is a subjective test and the purpose in the individual's mind when incurring the expense is important. For instance, despite what is stated in the previous paragraph, where an actor bought clothing (a dress suit) for a particular role and did not wear it other than when acting, the Tribunal held that the input tax was deductible when Customs and Excise attempted to restrict the input tax to 50 per cent (*J Pearce (1992) VAT decision 7860*). Also an apportionment may be appropriate on occasions when the clothing does have a business use and can be worn privately. For instance, it was held that 75 per cent of the VAT incurred was reclaimable where an electrician bought suits that he wore to work and could not wear when not at work as they got dirty (*PR Younghusband (1992) VAT decision 7443*). A fur coat bought by an authoress for a business trip to New York was held to be part business and the VAT incurred was to be apportioned (*RA Sisson (1981) VAT decision 1056*). It should be noted that Customs and Excise's Internal Guidance V1–13, Chapter 2A, section 18.3, emphasises the non-deductibility of VAT incurred on clothing expenses. Hence, any claim for input tax is likely to be resisted.

4.120 It is ironic that despite the loss in the direct tax case (*Mallalieu v Drummond [1983] STC 665, HL*), input tax can be claimed where barristers claim that the dark clothing required in Court would not have been purchased if they did not have to attend court (*EM Alexander [1976] VATTR 107 (1976) VAT decision 251*). Also, the wig, gown and bands that a barrister is required to wear in Court are considered to be a uniform and the VAT recovered as input tax..

4.121 Where an employer provides employees with clothing (other than uniforms or protective clothing) as a perk, the VAT incurred is recoverable as input tax. The supply of this clothing is a supply by the business and an output tax liability will arise on the value of the supply.

Tools and materials

4.122 The VAT incurred on materials and tools bought on site by employees can be reclaimed. In addition, where these are bought by self-employed subcontractors to use for a specific job for a business, the VAT incurred is the business's input tax provided the points mentioned at para **4.102** above are complied with and the tools remain the property of the business or the materials are incorporated into and become a cost component of the business's supply to the end customer.

Legal expenses

4.123 Legal expenses of employees (and sole proprietors or partners) are rarely deductible for VAT purposes. The fact that the expense may have been incurred for a business purpose and the taxable person has benefited from the expenditure is not conclusive as there must be a real connection or a nexus between the expenditure and the business (*C & E Comrs v FW Rosner [1994] STC 228* (**Case Summary 17**)). In *Rosner*, the proprietor of an educational establishment had been convicted of a conspiracy to defraud. The proprietor believed there was a business purpose in defending himself as if he had been imprisoned the business would have closed. This was not regarded as being a close enough nexus between the expenditure and the business.

4.124 This decision has been followed in a number of appeals, particularly concerning speeding and drink drive offences (*RN Scott (1987) VAT decision 2302*; *GM Child (t/a Child & Co) (1992) VAT decision 6827* and *VW Evans (1997) VAT decision 14662*). It has been held in these cases, for example, that there is little connection between the supply of goods and services and the criminal offence of failing to provide a breath test to determine the level of alcohol in the blood.

4.125 A further reason for not allowing an input tax deduction is that the individual and not the business incurred the expense. These arguments have often been advanced where directors are concerned (*Wallman Foods Ltd (1983) VAT decision 1411* and *Britwood Toys Ltd (1987) VAT decision 2263*). This argument may be harder to sustain where the company contracts with the lawyers (see *Redrow Group Plc [1999] STC 161, HL*).

4.126 In an exceptional case (*P&O European Ferries (Dover) Ltd [1992] VATTR 221*), the taxable person was allowed to claim input tax in respect of legal fees incurred in the defence of employees against criminal charges (following the Herald of Free Enterprise disaster at Zeebrugge). Input tax recovery was allowed (by the decision of a VAT Tribunal) as the company considered that a guilty verdict on any of their employees would lead to a similar verdict being found against the company. Thus, there was a clear nexus to the business. The terms of engagement with the solicitors had the effect of making the company the client and the recipient of the services 'notwithstanding that the individual employee also received the benefit of those services'.

4.127 The *P&O* case was, however, exceptional. In *Plessey Co Ltd (1995) VAT decision 12814*, it was held that legal services that were initiated and paid for by the company were not supplied to it and therefore the VAT incurred was not deductible input tax.

4.128 The majority of the cases mentioned above are criminal cases but the same principles apply to civil cases, it being necessary to identify to whom the supply was made and establish a nexus between the expenditure and the business. It would appear, however, that it is more likely an apportionment of the VAT will be allowed in a civil than a criminal case. For instance, in a libel case, 25 per cent of the VAT incurred was allowed as an input tax deduction as there was some business purpose, even though the main purpose had been to clear the reputations of the directors (*Orrmac (No 49) Ltd (1991) VAT decision 6537*).

Motor cars and associated expenses

4.129 There are specific regulations regarding VAT deduction on cars (VAT (Input Tax) Order 1992, SI 1992/3222, art 7). This denies input tax recovery on the purchase, hire or lease of a car, except in certain specified circumstances.

Purchase of a car

4.130 VAT is not deductible on the purchase of a car except:

- a qualifying car;
- a car which is not intended to be made available for private use.

4.131 Where there is an intention at the time of purchase for the car to be available (not necessarily used) for private use (see *C & E Comrs v Upton (Fagomatic) [2002] EWCA Civ 520, [2002] STC 640, CA* (**Case Summary 43**)). The High Court (and the Court of Appeal upheld the High Court's decision) had reversed the Tribunal's decision which had accepted that the taxable person did not need to use the car privately; that was not a conclusive fact. This restriction applies even where the use is predominantly business use and there is only minor private use.

4.132 The High Court held in *Fagomatic* that the only cars that could be held to be used exclusively for business purposes were:

- those that were not physically available for private use (eg those used for leasing);
- cars that could not realistically be used for a private use (eg marked police cars); and

- cars that are insulated from the possibility of private use through the way they are allocated to staff (eg cars held in a pool).

4.133 Proving that the intention *at the time of purchase* was to use the car only for business purposes can be difficult. Normally, where a car is insured from the outset for business use only it is accepted that the car cannot be made available for private use. Board minutes, etc, to demonstrate that the car is to be used solely for business purposes will assist in demonstrating this intention. The very act of deliberately acquiring a car means that the taxable person must intend to make it available to him for private use even if he never intends to use it privately. Though the distinction between 'intends to use' and 'intends to make available' is a fine distinction, it is one that has great significance here. To ensure VAT recovery if a car is only to be used for business purposes, the taxable person must ensure that the car is only *available* for business use (eg through insurance restrictions, directives to staff not to use the car for private purposes, introducing a system of log books, etc).

4.134 To maintain the integrity of the input tax restriction, however, Customs and Excise will vigorously challenge any claim for input tax. In *Squibb & Davies (Demolition) Ltd (2002) VAT decision 17829*, Customs and Excise challenged input tax recovery on the purchase of a Range Rover (used to transport plant and machinery) and a Jaguar (used to transport customers). The vehicles were kept overnight on the premises, the cars had to be signed out when used and a mileage log was kept to ensure that there was no private use, but as they had not insured the cars for business use only, the input tax claim was open to challenge. The directors and their family all had their own vehicles (four convertible Mercedes, a Mercedes sports car and a Jeep) so had no need to use the Range Rover or Jaguar. It might be thought that in such circumstances that Customs and Excise would accept that the vehicles were intended for business use only, but Customs and Excise raised an assessment. In this instance though, the Tribunal found for the taxpayer. Claims for input tax incurred on the acquisition of cars will be determined on the specific facts of the respective case.

4.135 It has been held that even where other cars are available to the taxable person input tax is not deductible on cars, even when purchased for a specific business purposes (eg towing a trailer) (*Martinez (1999) VAT decision 16320*). Cases where the taxable person has been successful must be considered in the light of *Fagomatic* if they were heard before this decision (*Squibb* was heard after *Fagomatic*). In *Thompson (1997) VAT decision 14777* the taxable person successfully argued that the cars purchased were only available for business use as the cars were only insured for business purposes. Subsequent to this decision, Customs and Excise have regarded the insurance status of cars as determinative. This can cause difficulties where insurers give private use insurance as a matter of course or will not provide business only insurance.

4.136 Customs and Excise accept that VAT can be reclaimed on the purchase of cars bought which are:

- pool cars normally kept at the principal place of business, if they are not allocated to an individual and are not kept at an employee's home.

- cars bought for the purpose of sale and leaseback, which will not be treated as available for private use, provided output tax is accounted for on the sale to the lease company in the same VAT period as the input tax is claimed;
- cars bought for in-house leasing provided the lease amount is not less than commercial arm's length leasing charges.

(See VAT Notice 700/64/02.)

4.137 A motor car is a qualifying car where it is acquired by a taxable person and intends to use the car primarily for:

- carrying of passengers (taxis);
- self-drive hire; or
- driving instruction.

4.138 It should be noted that input tax is deductible even where there is some private use, though there would be an output tax charge on the private use element.

4.139 In addition, input tax is deductible for vehicles acquired as stock in trade by a motor dealer and vehicles provided to taxable persons who supply the vehicle under the Motability Scheme. Motor dealers must account for VAT on the private use by employees or similar persons who use cars that are part of the stock in trade.

Lease cars

4.140 Where a non-qualifying car is leased to a taxable person, 50 per cent of the VAT incurred cannot be reclaimed (but see para **1.144** below in relation to the maintenance charge). This includes the VAT on any charges for depreciation, hire, road fund licence, overheads and profit of the lease company. Where a separate charge is made for maintenance (and/or repairs, roadside recovery, overheads and profit of the lease company), all the VAT incurred on this charge is reclaimable if it is separately identified. If it is not separately identified, this will also be subject to the 50 per cent restriction. It should be noted that although this 50 per cent restriction was introduced after the introduction of the Sixth VAT Directive, the UK has obtained derogation from the European Commission for this restriction. This derogation is due to expire on 31 December 2003, but it is expected that it will be extended for a further 12 months.

4.141 One hundred per cent of the VAT incurred on a lease car is deductible where it is to be used exclusively for a business purposes or as a taxi, self-drive hire, or for motor instruction. A car is not regarded as being supplied for exclusively business purposes where it is supplied for hire at less than an arm's length commercial value or it is made available for private use.

4.142 Where a car is hired on a daily hire basis, the VAT is again non-deductible. By concession, Customs and Excise will allow the VAT incurred to be deductible if the hire is for a period of 10 days or less (before 1 January 2002, the period was five days). This concession does not apply where the hire is to replace a company car that is off the road (for instance, due to a need for repair).

Other vehicles

4.143 The input tax restriction does not apply to vehicles that are not cars. Thus, VAT in full can be claimed on motorbikes, vans and trucks. Vehicles that are not cars are those that meet any of the following criteria;

- they weigh three tonnes or more;
- have a payload of one tonne or more;
- can accommodate only one person;
- can accommodate 12 or more seated persons (ie mini-buses); or
- are constructed for a specified purpose (caravans, ambulances and prison vans) or special purpose other than the carriage of persons.

Repairs and maintenance

4.144 VAT on repairs and maintenance on cars, vans, etc, is deductible in full by companies even where there is substantial private use (Customs and Excise Internal Guidance V1–13, Chapter 2A, section 11.60), though sole proprietors and partnerships may need to apportion the VAT to reflect private use (*W G Tregenza (1985) VAT decision 1907*). It is prudent, though not essential, to ensure that the tax invoice is in the name of the business not the employee. As stated above, if a car is leased and the maintenance charge is not separately identified, 50 per cent of the VAT incurred cannot be reclaimed. If it is separately identified all the VAT incurred can be reclaimed.

Accessories and improvements

4.145 VAT on accessories cannot be reclaimed where the input tax on the purchase of the car is blocked (*Turmeau (1981) VAT decision 1135*). Where an accessory is purchased after the purchase of the car, the input tax can be reclaimed where the accessory has been purchased for the purpose of the business. For instance, the upgrading of a car's engine to enable it to travel at 175 mph was not seen as having any nexus to a management consultancy business (*Trade Development Associates (1994) VAT decision 12699*) and the renovation of old vans (using the company's livery) was seen as being incurred to allow the controlling director to enjoy his hobby rather than for the purpose of advertising the business (*Ron Miller Ltd (1990) VAT decision 5827*). It is suggested that car mats, mud flaps, etc, that preserve the value of the car would be a business expense and the VAT should be deductible if fitted after the car was acquired. Also, the fitting of a hands-free mobile telephone system so an employee can use a mobile telephone safely should be regarded as a business expense and the input tax deductible where the telephone is used for business purposes (see para **4.114 above**). The VAT is not deductible, however, where the accessory is fitted at the time of purchase (or lease) of the vehicle.

Petrol

4.146 VAT incurred on the cost of petrol is normally deductible in full – even where there is an element of private use. This is because a fuel scale charge is payable where fuel is purchased and the input tax is claimed on the purchase of the fuel. This scale charge is, in fact, payable where no input tax is claimed but Extra-Statutory Concession 3.1 (VAT Public Notice 48) allows no scale charge to be paid where no input tax is claimed at all. It should be noted that where VAT is claimed on business expenses (and none on private expenditure) the scale charge is applicable unless accurate records are kept of the mileage travelled for business and private purposes. VAT Officers would normally expect a specific agreement to be reached with the local VAT office regarding the necessary level of detail required (see Notice 700/64/02, paras 8.3 and 8.4).

4.147 It should be noted that the normal VAT rules apply where road fuel is used for private motoring in vehicles other than a car (eg a van). The VAT on fuel supplied to a taxable person for use by employees can either be treated as input tax and output VAT accounted for on any private use or the taxpayer may apportion the input tax. The scale charge is not applicable in such cases.

4.148 Where a taxable person charges employees for private use of road fuel at a value equal to or above cost, the VAT incurred on the road fuel purchased can be claimed in full. The taxable person, however, must account for output tax on the amounts charged and the scale charge does not apply in such cases. A fixed rate payment for private fuel is not sufficient to allow VAT to be reclaimed as input tax (and as no input tax has been claimed, no output tax will be due). Local VAT officers, however, may be able to agree a method for calculating the charge to be made to employees for private use based upon mileage records.

4.149 VAT can also be reclaimed where an employee (or third party) is reimbursed for the actual cost of the fuel expense or where an amount is paid by way of a mileage allowance (VAT Input Tax (Person Supplied) Order 1991, SI 1991/2306). The mileage allowance paid to the employee is to be determined by the distance travelled and the cylinder capacity of the vehicle used. It should be noted that there is an element of approximation in this as a mileage allowance can be used. Customs and Excise often state that the mileage rate to be used is that of the AA, RAC or other similar bodies. This is not a legislative requirement, but a good reason for using a different rate than these independently produced figures should be available to substantiate the claim. Where the mileage rate is for petrol, repairs, cost of the car, etc, only the element relating to the petrol (or other road fuel) can be reclaimed as a mileage allowance.

4.150 It was held in *Commission v Netherlands (C-338/98) [2003] STC 1506, ECJ* that the Netherlands had failed to comply with the Sixth Directive by allowing VAT to be claimed on a mileage allowance for the business use of a car. This has led many commentators to believe that the current UK provision will eventually have to be withdrawn. There are, however, differences between the UK and the Netherlands position. In the Netherlands the amount was paid for the use of a car and this car had not been supplied to a taxable person (but to the employee). Also, the sums were amounts paid in aggregate and did not take into account variations between vehicles. In the UK, the VAT can only be reclaimed for a mileage allowance for the petrol element and it does vary according to the type of car. These differences combined with the lack of purchase invoices, however, may not be sufficient for the European Commission and it may take infraction proceedings against the UK at a later date. Such infraction proceedings may also affect the entitlement of a taxable person to recover VAT on other supplies, eg hotel expenses, made to employees. However, until that time the mileage allowance can be used to substantiate a VAT reclaim.

4.151 It is also noteworthy that there is neither need for an invoice for a mileage allowance nor any need for a business/private apportionment. Many officers believe that the Department's prior permission needs to be obtained before using this method of input tax recovery. Clearly this is not the case as it is a statutory provision. (See Customs and Excise Internal Guidance V1–13, Chapter 2A, section 11.40.)

4.152 Where a mileage allowance is not paid to employees, it may be difficult to substantiate the re-imbursement of the actual fuel expense. If Customs and Excise believe that any private motoring as well as business motoring has been paid for, the scale charge will apply. Tax invoices must also be obtained from employees as evidence to support input tax claims (invoices addressed to employees are acceptable) where an actual re-imbursement is paid.

Tolls and congestion charges

4.153 Most tolls and the congestion charges are not subject to VAT because a local authority is providing the road, bridge or tunnel as part of its statutory duty. Tolls charged by other persons should have been subject to VAT, but the VAT charge was not imposed until 1 February 2003. Thus, as no VAT has been charged on local authority tolls or any tolls before this date, a question arises as to whether input tax can be claimed. From 1 February 2003, toll charges payable to use bridges, tunnels and roads operated by private persons became subject to VAT (with those operated by public authorities remaining outside the scope of VAT). Fees charged by private operators of bridges and tunnels that have not been individually contacted by Customs about the change to the VAT liability also remain outside the scope of VAT. Tolls not subject to VAT include the:

- Cleddau Bridge
- Dartford Crossing
- Erskine Bridge
- Forth Road Bridge

- Humber Bridge
- Itchen Bridge
- Mersey Tunnel
- Tamar Bridge
- Tay Bridge
- Tyne Tunnel

(See Customs and Excise Business Brief 03/03, 28 March 2003.)

4.154 Tolls of other bridges, roads and tunnels (unless operated by a local authority) will be subject to VAT (unless their turnover is below the VAT registration threshold). These include:

- Aldwark Bridge
- Clifton Suspension Bridge
- Dunham Bridge
- Rixton and Warburton Bridge
- Severn River Crossing
- Skye Bridge
- Swinford Bridge
- Shrewsbury (Kingsland) Bridge
- Whitchurch Bridge
- Whitney on Wye Bridge

4.155 VAT will be due on tolls paid to use wholly private roads and bridges. There is, apparently, no record of these wholly private bridges and roads. (See Customs and Excise News Release 108/02, 30 December 2002.)

4.156 Care needs to be taken when deducting VAT on tolls to ensure that VAT has been charged and an invoice is obtained, unless the toll is paid by a coin operated machine and the cost is less than £25.

Parking

4.157 VAT is due on most car parking (and excess charges). The issue with parking usually revolves around the VAT invoice. An exception to this, however, is car parking charges for parking on the roads. These charges are outside the scope of VAT as it is part of the local authority's statutory duty to keep the roads clear and not a business activity. Thus, off road parking is subject to VAT (even where provided by a local authority) and not subject to VAT where it is on road parking.

4.158 Care needs to be taken when deducting VAT on parking charges to ensure that VAT has been charged and an invoice is obtained, unless the toll is paid by a coin operated machine and the cost is less than £25.

Margin schemes

4.159 Margin schemes allow a taxable person who meets the necessary requirements to calculate VAT on 'profit margin' achieved on the sale. These requirements are not discussed here, other than where it relates to input tax deduction.

4.160 The main points regarding the margin scheme are as follows:

- The scheme is not compulsory.
- Taxable turnover for registration and other purposes is the full selling price, not the profit margin.
- Virtually all second-hand goods are eligible for inclusion in the scheme.
- There are specific rules for certain goods such as works of art, precious metals and stones, motor vehicles, caravans, horses and ponies, aircraft and boats.
- Most of the specific rules relate to record keeping.
- Where a loss is made, this loss on the sale of an item cannot be set off against the profit on other sales (except where a global scheme is permitted).
- A global scheme is available for the sale of low value goods (value less than £500) but excludes motor vehicles, caravans, horses and ponies, aircraft and boats.
- When using the global scheme VAT is accounted for on the profit margin of all sales in a VAT period aggregated together.

4.161 Any input tax incurred on the acquisition by a taxable person of an item that is to be sold through the margin scheme is ineligible for input tax credit (VAT (Input Tax) Order 1992, SI 1992/3222, art 4(4)). In addition, VAT charged on the supply of goods where VAT was calculated under the margin scheme is non-deductible by the purchaser, as the conditions of the scheme prevent a VAT invoice being issued (VAT Notice 718, paras 3.6 and 3.7).

4.162 Input tax on overheads and other expenses are reclaimable where a taxable person sells goods under the margin scheme. This includes the VAT on the costs of repairs and additions to the item that is being sold under the margin scheme.

Goods installed in new dwellings

4.163 There are several elements to the VAT position for the construction of dwellings (relevant residential buildings and relevant charitable buildings are referred to as dwellings in this section for simplicity). Zero-rating is available for a grant of a major interest in the dwelling (sale or lease over 21 years) (VATA 1994, Sch 8, Group 5, Item 1), a grant of a lease for a lesser period is exempt from VAT and any VAT incurred is non-deductible. Construction services to build dwellings are zero-rated (other than the professional services of architects, surveyors, etc) (Item 2). Building materials supplied by a person supplying construction services that are incorporated into the dwelling or its site are also zero-rated (Item 4).

4.164 Input tax:

- incurred on goods;
- incorporated into a dwelling (other than building materials (as defined – see para **4.169** below)); and
- incurred by a taxable person intending to grant a major interest in the building or any part of its site that is zero-rated (see **4.177** below regarding houses let on short-term leases),

is not deductible (VAT (Input Tax) Order 1992, SI 1992/3222, art 6).

4.165 Incorporated means goods that require fixing. That is they are attached through the use of tools or their fixing or removal will result in a need for remedial work to the fabric of the building or damage to the goods.

4.166 Where goods are not incorporated into the building (that is a free standing item) they are not zero-rated (unless they are goods regarded as building materials) and thus VAT is due on the supply of these goods. The value upon which VAT is charged will usually be the cost value if a separate amount is not charged. Where a separate amount is charged, VAT is due on that amount. It is the usual practice not to claim input tax and not to charge output tax on such items to simplify accounting.

4.167 Goods included in a show house are treated slightly differently. VAT cannot be reclaimed on items that are incorporated. The value for free-standing items will be the value of the goods at the time of sale (and the input tax can be reclaimed on these goods). As the goods will have been used and may have suffered a degree of deterioration during the period the building has been used as a show house, the value at the time of disposal may be considerably less than the cost value. VAT is due on the value at the time of disposal.

4.168 Goods that are removed from a house and disposed of are not subject to VAT if the input tax has not been reclaimed on its acquisition.

Building materials

4.169 Building materials means the goods that would ordinarily be incorporated or installed as fittings in buildings of that description. Thus, an altar would normally be incorporated into a church (a relevant charitable building) and the input tax incurred is deductible and zero-rated when supplied by a person who supplies construction services. Radiators and light fittings are normally incorporated in a dwelling and these are building materials for VAT purposes.

4.170 Customs and Excise distinguish between types of buildings for goods that will be installed (eg there is a distinction between dwellings, a church or a school). Customs and Excise do not, however, distinguish within that generic type. Thus, there is no distinction between goods that will be ordinarily installed in a flat, maisonette, a detached house or mansion house. Also, the 'quality' of the item will not affect zero-rating, or deduction of VAT. Thus, the VAT incurred on a tap that is to be incorporated into a building is deductible, whether it is a gold tap or a normal chrome tap.

4.171 The range of items that will be considered ordinarily installed will alter over time in line with changing trends and fashions. In addition, where building regulations require an item to be installed it will be regarded as ordinarily installed. For instance, smoke alarms will now be regarded as being ordinarily installed, whereas some years ago they would not have been.

4.172 Examples of items that would be regarded as being ordinarily installed in a dwelling are:

- air conditioning;
- bathroom fittings (towel rails, toilet roll holders, etc);
- curtain rails;
- dust extractors;
- electrical and gas appliances (but see **4.173** below);
- fencing that is permanently erected around the building;
- fire and burglar alarms;
- flooring materials (but not carpeting);
- heating systems;
- landscaping carried out at the time of construction;
- light fittings;
- plumbing installations;
- saunas;
- swimming pools (indoors);
- TV aerials; and
- wiring.

Certain items are specifically treated as not being building materials (VATA 1994, Sch 8, Group 5, note 22). These include electrical and gas appliances, finished or prefabricated furniture and carpets or carpeting material.

Electrical and gas appliances

4.173 Most electrical and gas appliances are not building materials for VAT purposes and are subject to VAT if free-standing (or, if incorporated, the VAT incurred cannot be reclaimed). A limited number of items can be zero-rated and these include:

- appliances to heat space or water;
- ventilation equipment, air cooling equipment and dust extractors;
- door entry systems (in buildings designed as a number of dwellings);
- waste disposal units (in buildings designed as a number of dwellings);
- lifts and hoists; and
- burglar alarms, fire alarms and fire safety equipment.

Electrical fittings (such as light switches and lamp pendants) are regarded as building materials. They are not, apparently, regarded as appliances.

Finished or prefabricated furniture

4.174 Finished or prefabricated furniture is not regarded as building materials other than furniture designed to be fitted in a kitchen. Customs and Excise have also indicated that a number of items are not regarded as being furniture and are, therefore, eligible for zero-rating and any VAT incurred can be reclaimed. These include airing cupboards, under-stair wardrobes and items that provide storage space as an incidental result of their primary purpose. Thus, where pipes in a bathroom are boxed in and shelving provided, there will not be a VAT cost. Elaborate vanity units are regarded as furniture and not building materials.

4.175 Basic wardrobes will not suffer a VAT cost (the VAT on their materials is deductible). Thus, where a wardrobe is constructed by using three walls of the building as the sides and back of the wardrobe and the wardrobe encloses a space bordered by walls, ceiling and the floor, where on opening the wardrobe the walls of the building can be seen, and the wardrobe features no more than a rail and a closing door, the materials used to construct the wardrobe will be treated as building materials. More complex wardrobes will be regarded as furniture and not building materials, for example, a bridge wardrobe over a bed, or where a dressing table is created.

Carpets and carpeting material

4.176 Carpets, carpet tiles and underlay are not building materials. Other floor coverings, such as lino, tiles and wood floor systems, are building materials.

Houses let on short-term leases

4.177 It would appear that persons building houses for short-term lets could gain an advantage regarding deduction of VAT on goods that are incorporated into the dwelling. These lets are exempt from VAT, so any VAT incurred cannot be reclaimed. The supply of construction services to the person making the let, however, is zero-rated. Thus, to minimise input tax costs, any professional services should be supplied to the person constructing the dwelling, not the person who is having the dwelling constructed.

4.178 In addition, the legislation (VATA 1994, Sch 8, Group 5, Item 4), allows building materials supplied by a person supplying construction services to a person having a dwelling constructed to be zero-rated. The building materials are subject to the normal restrictions that apply at VATA 1994, Sch 8, Group 5, note 22, (eg carpeting, fitted furniture and electrical and gas appliances will not be zero-rated). Item 4, therefore, allows materials supplied by a contractor, that are not part of his construction service, to be eligible for zero-rating, subject to the restrictions at note 22.

4.179 Any goods, however, that are supplied as part of the construction services will be zero-rated provided the goods are incidental to the service. It should be noted that the restrictions at note 22 do not apply to all supplies made under VATA 1994, Sch 8, Group 5, Item 2, only supplies made under VATA 1994, Sch 8, Group 5, Item 1. It would, therefore, appear that the goods specifically removed from the zero-rate relief by note 22 will benefit from zero-rating where supplied as part of an Item 2 construction service where the property is to be let on a lease of 21 years or less. Where the property is to be sold or let on a lease exceeding 21 years, VAT (Input Tax) Order 1992, art 6 applies to deny input tax deductions in respect of goods other than building materials to persons effecting works to the dwelling.

Goods imported for private purposes

4.180 VAT incurred on the importation of goods by a taxable person is non-deductible where, at the time of the importation, the goods belong wholly or partly to another person and they are to be used either partly or wholly for a private purpose either by the taxable person or the other party (VATA 1994, s 27(1)). Private purpose means not those of any business.

4.181 A claim can be made to Customs and Excise for repayment of the VAT incurred on the importation to the extent necessary to avoid a double charge to tax. Customs and Excise will repay an amount of VAT to the extent necessary to avoid the double charge to tax. It is necessary to demonstrate to Customs and Excise to their satisfaction that there will be a double charge to tax without this repayment (see VATA 1994, s 27).

Chapter 5

Partial Exemption

Introduction

5.1 This chapter considers the apportionment that must be made if a taxable person is partly exempt. The apportionment must be done in the individual periods in which the taxable person has to submit any VAT returns to Customs and Excise. A taxable person is 'partly exempt' if he incurs input tax that he uses or intends to use to make:

- exempt supplies; or
- both taxable and exempt supplies.

It is the intention, not the actual making of exempt supplies, that determines this status. However, the initial deduction of VAT is merely provisional and may have to be adjusted subsequently.

5.2 **Chapter 6** and **Chapter 7** describe the reasons for the various adjustments to the initial deductions and the mechanics of those adjustments.

The nature of partial exemption

What is 'partial exemption'?

5.3 The term 'partial exemption' is used to refer to the process by which a business that makes, or intends to make, both taxable and exempt supplies determines the quantum of input tax that can be deducted. Input tax is only that VAT which is incurred in the course or furtherance of a taxable person's business (VATA 1994, s 26(2)). Before the partial exemption process can commence, a taxable person must first identify what VAT he has incurred that can be treated as input tax. What is excluded from the term 'input tax' is considered in **Chapter 4** above.

5.4 Where input tax cannot be deducted because it relates to exempt supplies (whether in whole or in part), that input tax is 'exempt input tax' (VAT Regulations 1995, reg 99(1)(a)). Exempt input tax also encompasses input tax that is used or intended to be used by a successor of the taxable person in making exempt supplies. Thus, if input tax is incurred by one taxable person but used or intended to be used by a person to whom the assets of the business have been transferred as a transfer of a going concern, the input tax is still considered to be exempt input tax.

Partial exemption methods

5.5 A taxable person who incurs exempt input tax is referred to as 'partly exempt'. A partly exempt business will then have to operate a method (referred to as a 'partial exemption method') in order to determine how much of the input tax he incurs is attributable to taxable supplies or other supplies which entitle the taxable person to deduct input tax.

5.6 Whilst the technical position is that a taxable person is partly exempt only if that person incurs exempt input tax, in practice any taxable person that makes exempt supplies may be affected by the partial exemption legislation. This is because the taxable person who makes exempt supplies will need to apply the regulations to determine if any exempt input tax has been incurred. In some cases, a taxable person may still be able to deduct all of the input tax incurred (other than non-deductible input tax, such as that on business entertainment) even though he has made some exempt supplies.

The partial exemption process

5.7 The partial exemption process deals with two key aspects. The first is the attribution of input tax to specific categories of supplies, such as:

- taxable supplies;
- exempt supplies;
- taxable supplies made outside the UK;
- 'out-of-country' specified exempt supplies.

5.8 Where input tax can be attributed solely to a specific category of supplies, such as that input tax solely used in making taxable supplies, this attribution is referred to as direct attribution. Input tax that is not directly attributable is usually referred to as residual input tax or 'pot' input tax.

5.9 It should be borne in mind that the purpose of the partial exemption process is to determine what input tax has been 'used' for the purposes of taxable transactions and other supplies in respect of which there exists a right to deduct (see **Chapter 3**). As noted in **Chapter 3**, the term use is the means by which it is possible to determine whether VAT has been incurred on an activity that is a cost component of a supply in respect of which there is a right to deduct.

5.10 Once input tax has been attributed to specific categories of supplies, the next process is the apportionment process: that is determining the quantum of input tax in each category which can be deducted. For input tax directly attributable to taxable supplies, the quantum of recovery is 100 per cent. Similarly, for input tax directly attributable to exempt supplies, the quantum of recovery is nil (save for specific exceptions which will be elaborated upon later in this chapter). The apportionment process for the remaining input tax which is not directly attributable to either taxable or exempt supplies has to be carried out according to specific rules (as in the standard partial exemption method for UK supplies). The application of these rules is not straightforward. Furthermore, the default position may be overridden by agreement or direction with the result that a special partial exemption rather than the standard method is used.

5.11 Little difficulty arises where input tax can be directly attributed to a single type of activity, eg taxable or exempt, since the input tax will then be wholly deductible or not deductible at all. The same is true of out-of-country supplies in respect of which all the VAT incurred is deductible or not deductible as the case may be.

5.12 Whatever method is used, the purpose of the method is to ensure that all the VAT borne by the trader in making supplies with a right to deduct input tax and no more is deducted. To do otherwise would offend the principle of fiscal neutrality.

5.13 The primary legislation provides for the making of regulations to secure a fair and reasonable attribution of input tax to supplies carrying the right to deduct input tax (VATA 1994, s 26(3)). Customs and Excise explain their view of how the principles of fairness and reasonableness apply in the following terms:

> 'In broad terms, fair and reasonable means that the deduction of tax should most accurately reflect the use of the tax bearing goods and services in making supplies with a right to deduct tax. However in determining this, the question of trader's compliance costs and the best use of Departmental resources should not be ignored.'
>
> (Customs and Excise Manuals V1, Pt 15, Ch 1, para 2.)

5.14 As with all accounting, it is rarely possible to achieve a precise attribution of input tax to supplies with the right to deduct. Even where it is possible to achieve a precise attribution it may require excessive resources either on the part of the taxpayer or on the part of Customs and Excise themselves. Businesses and Customs and Excise alike take a pragmatic approach to partial exemption, where complex cost analysis would otherwise be time consuming, costly, and difficult to verify.

5.15 Irrecoverable input tax is a direct cost to affected businesses and, therefore, it is unsurprising that partial exemption is a fruitful area for contested interpretations of the law and subsequent litigation including referrals of significant questions to the European Court of Justice. The UK legislation which governs partial exemption has to implement the relevant articles of the Sixth Directive.

Legislation dealing with partial exemption

EC VAT legislation

5.16 The Sixth Directive provides the framework for partial exemption in arts 17, 18 and 19. Article 20 deals with changes of use and is dealt with later in this book, both in **Chapter 6**, where changes in use in respect of items not regarded as capital items are dealt with, and in **Chapter 7**, which deals with capital items adjustments. However, for the purposes of the partial exemption process arts 17 and 19 are of greatest significance. Article 18 deals principally with the formalities required for exercising the right to deduct (art 18(1)), and the process by which the deduction is effected (eg by subtracting deductible input tax from output tax payable) (art 18(2)).

5.17 The European Court of Justice has considered the relationship between the absolute right to deduct input tax as provided by the Sixth Directive, art 17(1) and the evidential requirements that a taxable person must meet in order to make a claim under the Sixth Directive, art 18. See *Reisdorf v Finanzamt Köln-West (C-85/95) [1997] STC 180* and the Advocate-General's opinions in *Terra Baubedarf-Handel GmbH (C-152/02)* and in *Finanzamt Gummersbach v Gerhard Bockemühl (C-90/02)*. Those cases reaffirmed the position that a taxable person must have a tax invoice to ensure his right to deduct. However, it should be noted that the Sixth Directive, art 18(3)(a) makes provision under which member states may make provision whereby taxable persons can use other satisfactory evidence in order to support a deduction.

5.18 Articles 17(2) and (3) provide for attribution to specific supplies which entitle the taxable person to deduction. Articles 17(5) and 19 provide for apportionment of input tax which is not directly attributable so that a proportion of such residual input tax is attributed to supplies with the right to deduct.

5.19 The time at which input tax is deductible is provided for by art 17(1), which provides:

> 'The right to deduct shall arise at the time when the deductible tax becomes chargeable.'

Thus in a given period in which the taxable person has to prepare a VAT return, there is an immediate entitlement to deduct any VAT which has been charged by his suppliers to him and which he is entitled to deduct. This is irrespective of whether the person will use the inputs immediately to make supplies with the right to deduct or whether the inputs are to be so used at a much later date.

5.20 Where preparatory expenditure is incurred with a view to carrying on an economic activity comprising the making of taxable supplies, any input tax incurred is deductible in the period in which it is incurred. In *DA and AE Rompelman v Minister van Financiën [1985] 3 CMLR 202* (**Case Summary 4**) the trader appealed against the disallowance of input tax on expenditure connected with the prospective exploitation of property (a commercial building). The ECJ held that the trader's contract demonstrated his intention to make taxable supplies, and gave him the right to deduct input tax immediately. The right to deduct arose when the tax had become chargeable and was not dependent upon the building being completed or occupied.

5.21 This immediate right to deduction is retained even if the anticipated economic activity does not arise, provided that there is objective evidence, provided in good faith, that there was an intention to carry on the economic activity (*Finanzamt Gosler v Brietsohl (C-400/98) [2001] STC 355* (**Case Summary 33**)). Adjustments to deductions when the anticipated economic activity does not materialise are considered in **Chapter 6**.

5.22 The authority for attribution of input tax to taxable supplies or other supplies with the right to deduct stems from art 17(2):

> 'In so far as the goods and services are used for the purposes of his taxable transactions, the taxable person shall be entitled to deduct from the tax which he is liable to pay:
>
> (a) value added tax due or paid within the territory of the country in respect of goods or services supplied or to be supplied to him by another taxable person;
>
> (b) value added tax due or paid in respect of imported goods within the territory of the country;
>
> (c) value added tax due pursuant to Articles 5(7)(a), 6(3) and 28a(6);
>
> (d) value added tax due pursuant to Article 28a(1)(a).'

Article 17(2) is then amplified by further provisions that determine how an apportionment is to be made where the tax cannot be directly attributed to supplies in respect of which a deduction is permitted.

5.23 In interpreting the provisions of arts 17 and 19, the courts have consistently noted that to be deductible, VAT must be incurred on cost components of the supply or supplies in respect of which a deduction is permitted. For an expense to be a cost component of a supply there has to be a direct and immediate link between them.

5.24 For example, in *BLP Group plc v C & E Comrs [1995] STC 424* (**Case Summary 18**) the question arose as to whether input tax was related to the activities of the business as a whole or whether it was linked to an exempt financial transaction. The European Court of Justice determined that there had to be a direct and immediate link with taxable transactions in order to give the right to deduct under art 17(2) and the ultimate aim pursued by the taxable person is irrelevant in this respect. There have been a number of cases subsequent to *BLP Group plc* where the nature of the necessary link with taxable transactions has been discussed (for example *Midland Bank plc [2000] STC 501* (**Case Summary 35**)).

5.25 Insofar as current case law developments on direct attribution are concerned, the case of *C & E Comrs v Southern Primary Housing Association Ltd [2003] STC 525* (**Case Summary 51**) highlights some of the current issues. In that case, the issue was whether input tax incurred on land purchased by the taxpayer was directly and immediately linked to an exempt sale of the land or to an overall transaction consisting of the sale of the land and the taxable supply of construction of residential dwellings. Following the decision of the High Court in *C & E Comrs v Wiggett Construction Ltd [2001] STC 933,* the High Court considered that the Tribunal had been entitled to take the view that, viewed objectively, the sale of the land and the building contract were part of one overall transaction. On applying a cost component analysis to the factual situation the High Court considered that the costs of the land were a cost component of the overall transaction and not solely a cost component of the exempt sale of the land. However, the Court of Appeal overturned the High Court decision, holding that the input tax incurred on the land was directly attributable to the exempt supply of the land rather than attributable to a transaction incorporating both the supply of the land and the supply of taxable construction services.

5.26 Plainly, if the link for direct attribution purposes is with a single supply, the Court of Appeal's approach gives a 'common sense' answer. However, it could equally be said that the approach in the courts below gave a 'common sense' answer where the transaction, viewed objectively, incorporated both the supply of the land and the supply of construction services and neither supply would occur without the other. Nonetheless, taxpayers and advisers alike have to deal with the Court of Appeal's interpretation on how such input tax should be attributed and this may require careful thought on how certain transactions are structured so that input tax cannot be directly attributed to any intervening exempt supply, in circumstances where the only reason the input tax is incurred is to make taxable supplies.

5.27 The terms of art 17(1) and (2) are sufficiently clear, precise and unconditional, that a taxpayer can rely upon their direct effect if a dispute arises regarding inconsistency between those articles and the relevant domestic legislation (*Sweden v Stockholm Lindöpark AB (C-150/99) [2001] STC 103*).

5.28 Input tax is also deductible where the supply on which it is incurred is a cost component of certain transactions conducted outside the UK (art 17(3)). These transactions include:

- supplies outside the UK which would be taxable if those supplies were made in the UK; and
- certain supplies of financial and insurance services which are made to non-EU recipients, or when they are directly linked with the export of goods to a country outside the EU.

5.29 Article 17(5) deals with the deduction of input tax which is not directly attributable to taxable supplies but is nonetheless used or intended to be used in making taxable supplies as well as other supplies which do not have the right to deduct. Thus overhead costs (such as head office costs, basic utility costs for a building put to taxable and exempt use, and any similar overheads) are deductible to the extent that they are cost components of taxable supplies. Article 17(5) provides permissive powers for member states to derogate from art 19, and art 17(5)(c) in particular provides permissive powers to compel taxable persons to operate a use-based method.

5.30 Article 17(5) states:

> 'As regards goods and services to be used by a taxable person both for transactions covered by paragraphs 2 and 3, in respect of which value added tax

is deductible, and for transactions in respect of which value added tax is not deductible, only such proportion of the value added tax shall be deductible as is attributable to the former transactions.

This proportion shall be determined, in accordance with Article 19, for all the transactions carried out by the taxable person.

However, Member States may:

(a) authorise the taxable person to determine a proportion for each sector of his business, provided that separate accounts are kept for each sector;

(b) compel the taxable person to determine a proportion for each sector of his business and to keep separate accounts for each sector;

(c) authorise or compel the taxable person to make the deduction on the basis of the use of all or part of the goods and services;

(d) authorise or compel the taxable person to make the deduction in accordance with the rule laid down in the first sub-paragraph, in respect of all goods and services used for all transactions referred to therein;

(e) provide that where the value added tax which is not deductible by the taxable person is insignificant it shall be treated as nil.'

5.31 It can be seen from art 17(5) that member states are permitted to authorise or compel a taxable person to make the deduction on the basis of use of all or part of the goods or services.

5.32 The UK has effectively implemented a use-based method in respect of input tax used for:

- foreign or specified supplies (reg 103, see paras **5.42** and 5.171 below); and
- input tax incurred in one year and used in a later year by taxable persons operating the standard method unless de minimis (the standard method override, regs 107A and 107B, see **Chapter 6**).

5.33 The interaction of the use-based method and the values-based standard method when input tax is incurred for making both supplies in the UK and out-of-country supplies was considered in *Liverpool Institute of Performing Arts* and is considered in detail at **paras 5.172–5.174** below.

5.34 Article 19 provides a values-based method for calculating the deductible proportion of residual input tax. Article 19 provides:

'1 The proportion deductible under the first sub-paragraph of Article 17(5) shall be made up of a fraction having:

— as numerator, the total amount, exclusive of value added tax, of turnover per year attributable to transactions in respect of which value added tax is deductible under Article 17(2) and (3),

— as denominator, the total amount, exclusive of value added tax, of turnover per year attributable to transactions included in the numerator and to transactions in respect of which value added tax is not deductible. The Member States may also include in the denominator the amount of subsidies, other than those specified in Article 11A(1)(a).

The proportion shall be determined on an annual basis, fixed as a percentage and rounded up to a figure not exceeding the next unit.

2 By way of derogation from the provisions of paragraph 1, there shall be excluded from the calculation of the deductible proportion, amounts of turnover attributable to the supplies of capital goods used by the taxable person for the purposes of his business. Amounts of turnover attributable to transactions specified in Article 13B(d), in so far as these are incidental transactions, and to incidental real estate and financial transactions shall also be excluded. Where Member States exercise the option provided under Article 20(5) not to require adjustment in respect of capital goods, they may include disposals of capital goods in the calculation of the deductible proportion.

3 The provisional proportion for a year shall be that calculated on the basis of the preceding year's transactions. In the absence of any such transactions to refer to, or where they were insignificant in amounts, the deductible proportion shall be estimated provisionally, under supervision of the tax authorities, by the taxable person from his own forecasts. However, Member States may retain their current rules.

Deductions made on the basis of such provisional proportion shall be adjusted when the final proportion is fixed during the next year.'

5.35 The standard method (see paras **5.48–5.84** below) only partly implements art 19 since:

- it applies only insofar as UK supplies are concerned; and
- the standard method override applies if the standard method does not provide a fair and reasonable attribution of input tax to taxable supplies.

5.36 In respect of foreign or specified supplies made by a taxable person, and where the standard method override applies, UK law requires that a use-based method is used.

UK VAT legislation

5.37 The UK primary legislation implementing the provisions of the Sixth Directive, arts 17 and 19 are found in VATA 1994, ss 25 and 26. The detailed provisions are primarily in the VAT Regulations 1995, regs 99–111 and in particular regs 101–106. Regulations dealing with adjustments to the provisional deduction, regs 107, 107A–E, 108, 109 and 110, are dealt with in **Chapter 6** below.

The attribution process

5.38 The attribution process is an allocation of input tax to certain categories of supplies. Where that attribution is to a category of supplies where there is a right to deduct input tax, such as input tax directly attributable to taxable supplies or to out-of-country supplies that would be taxable if made in the UK, then all of that input tax is deductible.

5.39 VATA 1994, s 26(1) and (2) provide:

> '(1) The amount of input tax for which a taxable person is entitled to credit at the end of any period shall be so much of the input tax for the period (that is input tax on supplies, acquisitions and importations in the period) as is allowable by or under regulations as being attributable to supplies within subsection (2) below.
>
> (2) The supplies within this subsection are the following supplies made or to be made by the taxable person in the course or furtherance of his business –
>
> (a) taxable supplies;
>
> (b) supplies outside the United Kingdom which would be taxable supplies if made in the United Kingdom;
>
> (c) such other supplies outside the United Kingdom and such exempt supplies as the Treasury may by order specify for the purposes of this subsection.'

Conversely, input tax directly attributable to exempt supplies is not deductible.

5.40 However, where input tax is incurred which is used or to be used in making both supplies with a right to deduct and supplies which carry no right to deduct, the quantum of input tax to be deducted has to be determined by apportionment. Such input tax which cannot be directly attributed to taxable or exempt supplies respectively is referred to as 'residual' or 'pot' input tax.

5.41 Where residual input tax is incurred wholly in respect of transactions in the UK, the default method for calculating the deductible proportion is that provided by reg 101(2)(d), the standard method which is considered in detail at paras 5.48–5.84 below. The standard method is a values-based method, that is it operates by reference to the comparative values of taxable supplies and all supplies.

5.42 By contrast, where input tax is incurred in respect of foreign or specified supplies, input tax is deducted under VAT Regulations 1995, reg 103. Regulation 103 is a use-based method and does not require the use of turnover values as a measure, although it could be that a turnover values-based method may be the most appropriate means of determining use. It can be the case that a values- or a use-based method produce very different results in the quantum of input tax recoverable. Although a specialised case, input tax incurred in relation to supplies of investment gold is also deducted on a use basis under reg 103A.

5.43 Problems can arise in determining whether input tax incurred has been incurred for use or intended use in making supplies of one description over another. For example there can be disputes over whether input tax is attributable solely to exempt supplies or whether the input tax is attributable to both taxable and exempt supplies. (see for example cases relating to merger and acquisition transactions such as *RAP Group plc v C & E Comrs [2000] STC 980* (**Case Summary** 3), *Southampton Leisure Holdings plc [2002] VAT decision 17716* (**Case Summary 44**), and *Halladale Group plc (2003) VAT decision 18218* (**Case Summary 50**)).

5.44 VAT Regulations 1995, reg 104 precludes direct attribution of input tax to taxable self-supplies. Thus where a taxable person makes a taxable self-supply (for example if they act as constructor of a property for own occupation), input tax cannot be directly attributed to that taxable supply but instead is treated as residual input tax.

Calculating the deductible proportion

5.45 The taxable person has to calculate the amount of deductible input tax in each accounting period. In any accounting period where exempt input tax is incurred, a partly exempt business has to calculate the deductible amount of input tax. Partly exempt businesses often submit returns on the standard quarterly basis so that each accounting period is three months long. However, taxable persons may have shorter periods, such as monthly returns, as is often the choice of taxable persons who regularly incur more recoverable input tax than the amount of output tax payable.

5.46 However, there may be seasonal fluctuations that distort the deduction when compared with the use to which inputs are put over a year long period. Because of this, the initial deduction in the particular accounting period is only provisional and each partly exempt business has to carry out a further annual adjustment (see **Chapter 6** below).

5.47 Because input tax is provisionally deducted in the accounting period in which it is incurred, the input tax may, in fact, be used in a different year when the circumstances of the business are quite different. There are various mechanisms to deal with this issue. The standard method override is considered below at **6.14–6.34**. This provision is to deal with a situation where in the tax year that input tax is incurred the business is fully taxable, or nearly so, and yet the input tax incurred in that year is used for primarily exempt purposes in a later year. There are also situations where the intended use does not materialise, and the inputs are used for an entirely different purpose. How this change of use of input tax is dealt with is considered in **Chapter 6**. Where input tax is incurred in respect of certain capital items with an enduring life span, adjustments are made over a period of ten years for land and buildings and five years for computers and computer equipment. This capital items scheme is considered in **Chapter 7**.

Standard method

5.48 The standard method is the default method which any business which incurs exempt input tax has to adopt. The standard method has to be used by all partly exempt businesses that have not either:

- agreed a special partial exemption method with Customs and Excise; or
- been directed by Customs and Excise to use a method other than the standard method.

5.49 If a business also has 'out-of-country' supplies, the input tax recoverable on such supplies must be determined separately (see PARA 5.171–5.178 below). Even though such input tax has to be determined separately there can be an interaction with the standard method.

5.50 Even though a business has incurred exempt input tax, it does not necessarily follow that such a business will suffer a restriction on the input tax that it is able to deduct beyond the usual restrictions on non-deductible input tax, on items such as cars put to private use and business entertainment. However, it is necessary for any business which is partly exempt to carry out the calculations required by the standard method to determine whether all of the input tax incurred is recoverable or whether a restriction of part of the input tax is required.

5.51 Whilst there is a theoretical possibility that a business which makes exempt supplies may not incur exempt input tax, in most cases any input tax relating to overheads of the business will include an element of exempt input tax and thus require that business to operate a partial exemption method. If the facts supported an assertion that no overhead input tax had been used to make exempt supplies, a taxable person could of course argue that no exempt input tax had been incurred.

How the standard method works

5.52 The standard method works by requiring the partly exempt business to carry out a provisional attribution to taxable supplies in each 'prescribed accounting period'. This means that on each VAT return (usually quarterly), an amount of input tax is claimed which is offset against the output tax payable. However, the amount of input tax claimed is only provisional, and can be adjusted later. The details of these later adjustments are considered in **chapter 6**. However, the purpose of such adjustments is to conform to the principles of fiscal neutrality and a fair and reasonable attribution of input tax to supplies with the right to deduct. Thus, where input tax is incurred but is used for a different purpose an adjustment would be required.

5.53 Where a business has seasonal fluctuations, it may be that the relative proportions of exempt supplies made vary significantly from one prescribed accounting period to the next. An annual adjustment is made to counter the effects of such seasonal fluctuations.

	Q1	Q2	Q3	Q4	Total
Taxable supplies	100,000	250,000	150,000	500,000	1,000,000
Exempt supplies	900,000	750,000	350,000	2,000,000	4,000,000
Per cent of taxable supplies	10 %	25 %	30 %	20 %	20 %
Residual input tax	200,000	50,000	50,000	200,000	500,000
Deductible residual input tax	20,000	12,500	15,000	40,000	100,000

5.54 It can be seen from the table above that there are fluctuations in the relative proportions of taxable to exempt supplies over the year. An adjustment is necessary at the year end, so that the taxpayer can deduct the 100,000 deductible residual input tax rather than the amounts he is able to deduct each quarter (20,000 + 12,500 + 15,000, + 40,000 = 87,500 in the above example).

5.55 Input tax incurred in one year might actually be used not in the year in which it was incurred, but in a later year when the proportion of taxable to exempt supplies might be radically different from the proportion in the year when the input tax was incurred. In certain circumstances this situation can also lead to an adjustment under the standard method override.

5.56 There are other circumstances which can affect the attribution of input tax, such as where a business is in an investment or start up phase significant inputs might be incurred when the outputs to which that investment is linked have yet to be generated.

5.57 Both the annual adjustment and the standard method override adjustment are required as part of the standard method.

5.58 Other adjustments may arise when input tax is incurred on costs for anticipated use in making one category of supplies, but is then used subsequently not for that original intention but for a different category of supply. Thus, adjustments can arise which lead either to an increased deduction of input tax (where the intention was originally exempt or overhead but the subsequent use is solely for taxable supplies) or a decreased deduction of input tax where the converse situation arises. These change of use adjustments are considered in **Chapter 6**.

Process of determining the provisional deduction

5.59 It will be apparent that a taxable person can incur VAT on costs that are referable to one or more of the following activities:

- personal or non-business activities;
- making taxable supplies;
- making exempt supplies;

- making out-of-country or specified supplies.

Even where VAT is referable to taxable or out-of-country supplies, it may nevertheless not be deductible, for example VAT incurred on cars put to private use, or business entertainment (see **Chapter 4**).

5.60 In most accounting systems it will be relatively easy to identify and debit to the VAT account, VAT on supplies used solely to make:

- taxable supplies;
- out-of-country supplies, in respect of which a deduction is permitted;
- specified supplies.

5.61 Similarly it should be possible to identify and exclude from deduction VAT incurred on supplies used *solely* to make:

- non-business supplies;
- exempt supplies;
- out-of-country supplies in respect of which no deduction is permitted;
- taxable supplies where the VAT is specifically non-deductible.

5.62 The remaining VAT will have to be apportioned but in some cases two or more apportionments may have to be made, eg:

- Total VAT on supplies received: TV
- Proportion of VAT incurred for non-business purposes: NB
- Identify input tax (TV – NB): IT
- Proportion referable to deductible out-of-country supplies: OV
- Proportion referable to deductible specified supplies: SV
- Remaining input tax (IT – OV – SV): RIT
- Directly attributable input tax (taxable and exempt): (DA)
- Residual input tax to be apportioned (RIT – DA): (ResIT)

The residual input tax is then subject to the apportionment contemplated by reg 101(2)(d) (see **5.72–5.84** below).

5.63 As noted, the standard method does not apply to out-of-country or specified supplies which are dealt with separately on a use basis under reg 103. Therefore, before any provisional attribution of input tax takes place, the following input tax is excluded from the calculation.

5.64 The input tax remaining, after removing that attributed to non-business, out-of-country and specified supplies and to non-deductible items, has to be attributed to taxable supplies. To do this, the first process is to directly attribute input tax to taxable supplies. This input tax is recoverable in full. Input tax directly attributable to exempt supplies is not recoverable.

5.65 The direct attribution process provided for by VAT Regulations 1995, reg 101(2)(b) for taxable supplies and reg 101(2)(c) for exempt supplies is deceptively straightforward. Disputes occur when there is a difference of opinion as to whether goods or services are properly directly attributable to taxable or exempt supplies.

5.66 There is a factual question, therefore, at the heart of the direct attribution process, namely was this input tax used solely for the making of taxable supplies or exempt supplies respectively. How input tax is determined to have been used for the purposes of taxable transactions has been considered in **Chapter 3**. It is nonetheless worth emphasising that there has to be a direct and immediate link between the input tax incurred and the taxable transactions in order for a deduction to be made (*BLP (C-4/94) Group plc v C & E Comrs ECJ [1995] STC 424* (**Case Summary 18**)).

5.67 However, in recent cases Customs and Excise's interpretation of the *BLP Group plc* case has been shown to be too restrictive when a direct and immediate link solely with exempt transactions has been alleged (see for example *RAP Group plc v C & E Comrs [2000] STC 980* (**Case Summary 36**); *Southampton Leisure Holdings plc [2003] VAT decision 17716* (**Case Summary 44**) and *Halladale Group plc (2003) VAT decision 18218* (**Case Summary 50**)).

5.68 There also appears to be no de minimis limit with regard to the test of whether input tax has been used exclusively for the making of taxable or exempt supplies. Thus if input tax has been incurred in making £1,000,000 of exempt supplies and only £100 of taxable supplies, provided that factually the input tax has been used to make both the exempt and taxable supplies, it is arguably sufficient for the input tax not to be directly attributable to exempt supplies.

5.69 However, there is still the factual question in direct attribution to either taxable or exempt supplies respectively, whether the input tax has been *exclusively* used to make either taxable or exempt supplies. In the *Britannia Building Society (1997) VAT decision 14886* case, the Tribunal held that input tax incurred on television adverts was not exclusively used for the making of exempt supplies of financial services. By contrast, in the *Royal Agricultural College (2002) VAT decision 17508* case, the Tribunal considered that input tax incurred in respect of prospectuses was exclusively used for the making of exempt supplies of education (even though the College did make some taxable supplies, such as supplies of catering).

5.70 Thus, whilst there is no apparent de minimis provision which counteracts the need for input tax directly attributed to be 'exclusively used', there is nonetheless a factual question of whether such input tax is exclusively used.

5.71 Once the input tax has been directly attributed to both taxable and to exempt supplies respectively, the remaining input tax (often referred to as 'residual' or 'pot') has to be apportioned to see how much of that input tax is attributable to taxable supplies.

Apportionment of residual input tax

5.72 VAT Regulations 1995, reg 101(2)(d) provides a values-based method for calculating the deductible proportion of residual input tax. This regulation requires the taxpayer to identify the input tax used to make both taxable and exempt supplies.

> 'there shall be attributed to taxable supplies such proportion of the input tax on such of those goods or services as are used or to be used by him in making both taxable and exempt supplies.'

5.73 The recoverable proportion of residual input tax is computed on a values-basis, ie by reference to the ratio that the value of taxable supplies made in the period bears to the aggregate of both taxable and exempt supplies. This calculation can be shown by the following formula:

$$\frac{\text{Value (exclusive of VAT) of taxable supplies}}{\text{Value (exclusive of VAT) of taxable and exempt supplies}} \times 100$$

The result is expressed as a percentage and rounded to the next whole number, eg 14.7 per cent will be rounded to 15 per cent (VAT Regulations 1995, reg 101(4)).

5.74 Both EU legislation and UK legislation make provision for the exclusion from values in the fraction of certain 'incidental transactions'. The rationale behind this exclusion is that such incidental supplies would distort the proportion of deductible input tax because only relatively small amounts of input tax may be consumed in making such supplies. These exclusions are:

- the grant of certain interests in land;
- the disposal of capital goods used in a taxpayer's business;
- certain financial transactions, eg making arrangements for credit; and
- self-supplies.

(VAT Regulations 1995, reg 101(3) and the Sixth Directive, art 19(2)).

5.75 It is perhaps arguable that absent the incidental provisions, the result would still be the same, since where there is incidental income there is arguably not even a marginal cost in making certain exempt supplies. For example, in certain circumstances there may be scarcely any costs involved in receiving certain exempt income such as interest on bank deposits.

5.76 The exclusion in relation to incidental transactions does not apply to such supplies made by a business as part of its core business activities.

5.77 There have been a number of disputes regarding what constitutes an incidental transaction in this context. In a High Court case concerning the sale of shares by a trading company, it was held that, as the taxpayer was not carrying on a business similar to an investment company, the sale of its shareholding was incidental to its business *(C & E Comrs v C H Beazer (Holdings) plc [1989] STC 549, QB*). In *Regie Dauphinoise-Cabinet A Forest SARL v Ministre du Budget (C-306/94) [1996] STC 1176, [1996] ECR I-3695* (**Case Summary 24**), the ECJ held that interest realised by a property management company on advances received from co-owners and lessees was not an incidental financial transactions and thus was included in the values in the formula determining the recoverable residual input tax.

5.78 Insofar as sales of capital assets are concerned, the High Court has held that sales of demonstrator cars were sales of capital assets and thus not included in the values of exempt supplies in the formula for determining recoverable residual input tax (*C & E Comrs v JDL Ltd [2002] STC 1*).

5.79 The deductible quantum of residual input tax is therefore made up of two elements insofar as VAT Regulations 1995, reg 101(2) is concerned: the input tax directly attributable to taxable supplies and the deductible proportion of residual input tax. There is also the deductible residual input tax referable, in part, to out-of-country or specified supplies, or to certain supplies of investment gold deductible under VAT Regulations 1995, regs 103 and 103A respectively.

5.80 However, if the amount of exempt input tax is less than £625 per month on average and does not exceed half of the total input tax incurred in the prescribed accounting period, then all of the input tax is treated as attributable to taxable supplies and the taxpayer is regarded as fully taxable. Exempt input tax refers to both the input tax directly attributable to exempt supplies and to the non-deductible amount of residual input tax. This amount of £625 per month (that is, £7,500 per annum) is normally referred to as the de minimis limit (VAT Regulations 1995, reg 106).

5.81 For a business submitting quarterly returns, therefore, provided that exempt input tax is less than £1,875 per quarter and less than half of the total input tax incurred in the quarter, that business will be able provisionally to deduct all of its input tax (other than VAT on non-deductibles). The annual adjustment is considered in detail in **Chapter 6**. However, it is worth noting at this stage that it is possible for a business to be able provisionally to deduct all of its deductible input tax as falling within the de minimis limits in say three quarters out of four, and yet fail to fall within the de minimis limit for the year as a whole or vice versa. Businesses which are close to the de minimis limits must therefore pay special attention to whether all of the residual input tax is deductible on a provisional or annual basis.

5.82 For a business incurring input tax both in respect of UK supplies and in respect of out-of-country or specified supplies the total amount of input tax deductible will be:

- input tax directly attributable to taxable supplies;
- a recoverable proportion of residual input tax (which may be 100 per cent if de minimis limits are met);
- a recoverable quantum of input tax relating to out-of-country and specified supplies under reg 103 (dealt with at paras **5.171–5.178** below).

5.83 Because the standard method can be more beneficial than an agreed or directed special method, or vice versa, it is sometimes disputed whether a special method has been agreed or withdrawn. Absent a special method, the standard method is used. Therefore, it is vital that the method in place at a given date is known. This will be considered further at **5.94–5.96** below.

5.84 It is also the case that the deduction referred to above is a provisional deduction which may be affected both by the annual adjustment or by other adjustments, such as the standard method override or a change of use adjustment (dealt with in **Chapter 6**) or a capital items scheme adjustment (dealt with in **Chapter 7**).

Special methods

5.85 A taxpayer can seek a special partial exemption method as an alternative to applying the standard method (reg 102). Clearly there are situations where it is sensible to do so, such as when a partly exempt taxpayer incurs input tax in one year which he is going to use to make substantially increased proportions of taxable supplies, but is unable to recover an increased proportion under the standard method override. Even if the standard method override did provide a solution, the timing of the deduction of VAT would be delayed and represent a cash flow cost to the business.

5.86 There are many business sectors where the operation of special methods is commonplace, for example in the financial and education sectors.

5.87 Customs and Excise also have the power to direct the use of a special method where they believe that the standard method does not lead to a fair and reasonable attribution of input tax to taxable supplies.

5.88 The standard method uses a values-based method to attribute and apportion input tax to the making of taxable supplies. A special method may use a values-based method or may use some other determinant of use such as floor areas (for example with property businesses) or transaction counts (for example with financial services businesses).

5.89 A special method may well be based entirely on a value-based apportionment, with the difference being that the values-based apportionment is carried out on a cost centre by cost centre basis.

5.90 The standard method uses a single global calculation to determine the deductibility of residual input tax. A special method is not restricted to a single global calculation and may, therefore, have several different sectors with different methods of determining use in different sectors.

5.91 Special partial exemption methods have to deal with a number of issues. In particular the taxpayer will have to determine the most appropriate measures of use for different parts of the business.

5.92 Historically, methods agreed usually included a clause that a method be used for a period of two years. However, as methods need to lead to a fair and reasonable attribution, changes could be contemplated at shorter intervals if required. Understandably, Customs and Excise might refuse to consent to frequent minor changes to a method.

5.93 Any method should also include provision for revising the method in the event of substantial changes to the business operations.

5.94 It is Customs and Excise's policy not to allow retrospective adoption of a special partial exemption method. They will, however, allow a method to be backdated so as to take effect from the beginning of a tax year (see *A J Barrett (as provisional liquidator for Rafidain Bank) (1993) VAT decision 11016* in which a Tribunal held that Customs and Excise had not acted unreasonably in applying this policy).

5.95 It is therefore important that taxable persons for whom the standard method does not provide a fair and reasonable attribution of input tax to taxable supplies, ensure that a special partial exemption method is agreed prior to the end of the tax year in question.

5.96 A practical difficulty, nonetheless, can arise when the taxpayer commences negotiations of a special partial exemption method in one tax year and yet the special method is not agreed with Customs and Excise until a later tax year. The courts have yet to determine whether, in such circumstances, the special method, once agreed, commences in the tax year in which negotiations commenced or the tax year in which the special method was agreed.

5.97 Failure to agree a special partial exemption method can lead to an increased and unnecessary irrecoverable VAT burden. In any situation where residual input tax is going to be used for an anticipated increase in level of taxable supplies and in situations where the standard method override will not provide an increase in recovery of residual input tax, a special partial exemption method should be sought.

Finding the right method

5.98 The usual reason for adopting a special partial exemption method is that an outputs-based method does not accurately reflect the extent to which inputs are used to make taxable supplies. The specific reasons why a turnover method may not achieve a reasonable measure of use can vary widely. Some of the reasons may include:

- The taxpayer is in a start-up position and therefore there are very few taxable outputs but there are large inputs referable to taxable activity. If the taxpayer also makes exempt supplies, an outputs-based method will not properly reflect the use to which the inputs are put.

- The margins on exempt transactions may be lower than the margins on taxable activities (or vice versa) meaning that there is a disproportionate use of inputs by the lower margin activity.

- An activity may be so incidental as to make it more appropriate to apply a 'tunnelling' method and so not apportion any overhead VAT to such activities (the equivalent of applying the incidental test under the standard method).

5.99 It is possible that a special method might be requested simply because the collection of data needed to operate the method might be easier. For example, a group of companies with considerable inter-company turnover might find it more difficult to determine properly the relative turnovers needed to apply the standard method.

5.100 Since the introduction of the standard method override, a business may seek a special partial exemption method simply to avoid having to consider whether any adjustments are required under that provision. However, since 1 January 2004 a special method override has also been introduced. The operation of the special method override is dealt with in Chapter 6 below. The combined effect of the special method override and the standard method override is that a use based apportionment can be required of all partly exempt taxpayers in circumstances where either override applies.

5.101 In constructing a special partial exemption method there are two variables that can be altered; the attribution process and the apportionment process. Input tax can be attributed to particular parts of a business and recovered according to the use in that specific part of the business. The method of apportionment can also differ, being a use-based or a values-based method. In addition, there can be different apportionment methods applied to different parts of the business.

5.102 Nonetheless, the method has to be readily verifiable by Customs and Excise and so, whilst a method can be constructed that appears quite complex, it has to be verifiable so that Customs and Excise can satisfy themselves that the method provides a fair and reasonable attribution of input tax.

Sectorisation and other techniques

5.103 In some circumstances, the recovery of residual input tax by reference to a single global calculation on all of the business's residual input tax would not accurately reflect the use to which the residual input tax was put. This may well be the case where different activities have different cost profiles. A sectorised method allows for residual input tax to be allocated to sectors where the costs are used similarly to make supplies. In other words, there are several 'pots' on which a calculation of the amount of deductible input tax is calculated, and the results are added together to compute the total deductible residual input tax. As has been mentioned at **5.101** above, there is no requirement that the same method of calculating the deductible proportion is used on each sector's pot.

5.104 Sectorised methods are common in several business sectors, such as in the banking and education sectors. Where businesses carry on a number of different business activities such an approach may lead to a more accurate reflection of use of residual input tax.

5.105 Businesses may sometimes decide that it is not worth the effort to calculate what residual input tax can be claimed. In such cases, they may use a method known as 'tunnelling'. Should it become worthwhile doing the calculation, then subject to VAT Regulations 1995, reg 29, the taxpayer would be able to start recovering residual input tax and also, subject to the three-year cap, recover any back input tax (see *University of Edinburgh (1991) VAT decision 6569* and *Ampleforth Abbey Trust (1998) VAT decision 15763*).

5.106 In tunnelling, Customs and Excise can allow activities to be dealt with separately and a formula-based approach (that is, a percentage of output tax can be recovered as if it were input tax) can be applied to each activity's separate cost centre. For example, in higher education establishments, Customs and Excise historically agreed a recovery rate of 20 per cent of output tax as if it were input tax in respect of accommodation and catering activities.

Agreeing a method with Customs

5.107 The process of agreeing a special partial exemption method can be difficult and time consuming. Perhaps this is unsurprising in that a taxpayer will usually only seek a special partial exemption method where one of two circumstances applies. The first is that the operation of the proposed special method will give a greater deduction of VAT than could be obtained under the standard method. The second is where Customs and Excise have required the taxpayer to take steps to agree a method because they believe that the standard method does not achieve a fair and reasonable measurement of use. However, provided that the business applying for a special method is aware of Customs and Excise's internal guidelines, this process may be made somewhat easier by ensuring that the method is readily verifiable by Customs and Excise officers and that the method chosen permits the deduction of input tax only to the extent that it is incurred in making taxable supplies.

5.108 Difficulties occasionally arise because Customs and Excise believe that a particular industry should have a particular typical level of VAT recovery and may baulk at a method that appears to allow significantly more than their benchmark figure. However, in any individual case, a business may operate in a completely different manner to its peers. The taxpayer needs to be aware of any perceptions of what recovery should be achieved and be able to justify any apparent departure from what is expected.

Example 1

A casino is negotiating a special method with Customs and Excise. It suggests a method that achieves a 25 per cent recovery of residual input tax. Taxable turnover is just eight per cent of total turnover. Customs and Excise argue that the method cannot be fair and reasonable because the recovery rate is so much greater than a turnover-based method. Suggest possible reasons for the difference.

Some possible reasons will be that:

- a restaurant will inherently incur more taxable expenditure than the gambling activities because of the nature of its business;
- in addition to VAT disallowed under the method, there is also likely to be VAT disallowed as business entertainment that increases the real amount of VAT disallowed above the headline rate of 75 per cent; or
- much of the VAT disallowed on the casino activities may be wholly attributable to the exempt supplies, so again the 25 per cent recovery may not give the full picture.

5.109 One of the other areas which Customs and Excise will insist upon in a special partial exemption method is that the method excludes any values which are distortive. It is clear in the operation of the standard method that certain high value incidental financial and land transactions are excluded from the calculation of the deductible proportion. Similarly, the agreement of a special partial exemption method will necessitate exclusion of distortive transactions. It is not only Customs and Excise that can suggest that supplies be ignored because their inclusion would be distortive – the taxpayer can do so as well.

5.110 In contrast with the standard method, whereby the global calculation of the deductible proportion is rounded up to the next whole number, special partial exemption methods are meant to obtain a more accurate reflection of use. The usual practice is, therefore, to take the calculation to two or more decimal places. However, if the special method employs a single outputs based apportionment calculation then, as with the standard method, the calculation should usually be rounded up to the nearest whole figure.

The negotiation process

5.111 As a taxpayer defaults to the standard method unless a special method is agreed, the negotiation process usually commences with either oral or written discussions between the taxpayer (and their advisors where retained) and Customs and Excise. However, there are occasions when Customs and Excise might commence the process by writing to a taxpayer or body representing taxpayers suggesting that the taxpayer or taxpayers concerned should commence negotiations for a special method. It is usual for Customs and Excise to allow the taxpayer to suggest a method before resorting to its powers to impose a method by a direction.

5.112 However, a special partial exemption method has to be agreed before it is legally in place. Knowing when the special method has been approved is, therefore, vitally important.

5.113 Often the taxpayer drafts a proposed special method and then a process of negotiation develops on the content of the draft method. Customs and Excise's silence should not be regarded as approval of the method. In the usual course of events, a special partial exemption method letter is sent by Customs and Excise to the taxpayer containing details of the method approved. The taxpayer is requested to sign and return a copy of the special partial exemption method letter. This letter can then be retained as proof that the method to be used has been approved.

5.114 It is vitally important to recognise that a special partial exemption method can only be approved by Customs and Excise prospectively. There can be no retrospective approval of a special partial exemption method (although see **5.94** above, as it is possible to backdate a special method to the beginning of the tax year in which the special method is agreed). Taxpayers and Customs and Excise alike can sometimes be confused by cases whereby the operation of an existing method has been faulty (such as failing to include input tax in a particular recovery calculation) and the retrospective agreement of a special method. Clearly a business is entitled (subject to any legitimate restriction on input tax recovery by operation of the three-year cap) to recover input tax erroneously excluded from the special partial exemption method calculation. However, amending the method is not permitted retrospectively, save for the same comments regarding backdating to the beginning of a tax year in which the amendment is agreed.

5.115 In *Pearl Assurance plc (1999) VAT decision 15960*, the taxpayer argued that notwithstanding its special partial exemption method, it could include figures in its calculation of residual input tax recovery that were distortive (in respect of property and securities transactions). The taxpayer argued that the special method adopted had never been approved or directed. Alternatively, the taxpayer argued that the approval or direction was invalid under the Sixth Directive, art 17(5). The Tribunal found that the method had been approved by the local VAT office and was authorised by art 17(5).

5.116 What has and has not been agreed in respect of special partial exemption methods has been the subject of a multitude of cases. In *Hellesdon Developments Ltd (VAT decision 16833) (2000) SWTI 222* for example, the Tribunal found that the correspondence between Customs and Excise and the taxpayer did not constitute the agreement of a special method.

5.117 If a taxpayer submits an acceptable special method, Customs and Excise guidance suggests that an acceptable method may be approved from the date that the trader became partly exempt. However taxpayers should not assume that this will be approved by the Tribunal or higher courts (see *Chard Bowling Club (VAT decision 15114) [1997] SWTI 1371* where Customs and Excise refused to approve a method retrospectively).

5.118 In cases where a special partial exemption letter is received from, and returned to, Customs and Excise there can be little doubt that the method has been approved. However, where this does not happen there can be an issue as to whether the method has in fact been approved. This issue arises as there is no procedure set out in the legislation as to how a special partial exemption method is to be approved. Indeed in a recent case, a special partial exemption method was approved by an officer for 48 hours until a superior Customs and Excise officer withdrew the method (*Living Design (Home Improvements) Ltd (2002) VAT decision 17874*).

5.119 In certain cases, where the taxpayer has knowingly adopted or sought a special partial exemption method and Customs and Excise are aware of what the taxpayer was doing or seeking to do it may be the case that the Tribunal would consider that a special partial exemption method has been approved. Indeed it may be difficult for Customs and Excise to deny approval of the method if a visiting officer has seen the partial exemption method being used by the taxpayer and has taken no action to question the use of that method (*Wellington Private Hospital Ltd [1993] VATTR 109*). However, it is preferable that there is no doubt that the method in place has been specifically approved in writing, as described above, rather than the taxpayer being a hostage to fortune.

5.120 As the negotiation process can take a material length of time, businesses seeking a special partial exemption method should apply for a special method well in advance of the end of the tax year in which it is intended to be applied.

5.121 In certain circumstances, Customs and Excise will direct the use of a special partial exemption method as they are empowered to do under VAT Regulations 1995, reg 102. However, if Customs and Excise direct a method which is ambiguous, such a method is void (*Kwik Fit (GB) Ltd v Customs and Excise Comrs [1998] STC 159*).

Failure to agree a special partial exemption method

5.122 Customs and Excise are not obliged to approve a special method. If Customs and Excise decide that a proposed special method does not lead to a fair and reasonable attribution of input tax to taxable supplies or if the accuracy of operating the special method is not readily verifiable by visiting officers, Customs and Excise may refuse approval of the proposed method.

5.123 A taxpayer can seek reconsideration of any decision to refuse approval of the proposed method and the decision would be appealable to the VAT and Duties

Tribunal. The jurisdiction of the Tribunal is limited to a supervisory view of whether a Customs and Excise's decision was 'reasonable'. There can be practical difficulties in persuading a Tribunal that Customs and Excise's failure to agree a proposed method was unreasonable. However, in situations where a taxpayer believes that the proposed method does provide a fair and reasonable attribution of input tax, a taxpayer may consider that an appeal to the Tribunal is worthwhile.

5.124 If a special method is not approved, the existing method in place (whether that is the standard method or a previously agreed special method) remains effective.

Amending or terminating a special partial exemption method

5.125 It is not possible for a taxpayer unilaterally to terminate a special partial exemption method without seeking agreement from Customs and Excise (See *Dean and Chapter of the Cathedral Church of St Peter (1989) VAT decision 3591*).

5.126 A method approved or directed by Customs and Excise remains in place until Customs and Excise approve or direct the termination of the method (VAT Regulations 1995, reg 102(3)). Termination of a method can only be prospective (reg 102(4)).

5.127 In *University of Exeter (VAT decision 18117) [2003] SWTI 1514*, Custom and Excise sought to withdraw a special method from a University and replace that method with an alternative method which would be backdated once agreed. However, the Tribunal held that the correspondence did not constitute a direction of a new special method. The Tribunal (following a similar decision in *Merchant Navy Officers Pension Fund Trustees (VAT decision 14262) [1996] SWTI 1538*) held that Customs and Excise were not able to withdraw approval of a special method if the result is to force the taxpayer to use a less satisfactory method.

5.128 Taxpayers seeking to leave a special partial exemption method must therefore open negotiations in the same manner as when they sought approval for the method. They must seek permission to terminate the method well in advance of the end of the tax year from which the method is sought to be no longer applicable.

Implementing and operating a method

5.129 Once a method has been agreed the special method can be operated. Special methods once agreed can remain in force for many years. However, most special partial exemption method approval letters contain a provision that the taxpayer must notify Customs and Excise of any changes in their business which could affect input tax recovery.

5.130 Apart from any provision within the method regarding notification of changes, the operation of a special partial exemption method is likely to be closely monitored by Customs and Excise on any assurance visits. Provided that the method adopted is capable of verification, the operation of the method, whilst it may be complex, should nonetheless be straightforward.

5.131 The key issue for both the taxable person and Customs and Excise alike, is ensuring that the method in place keeps pace with the changes taking place within the business. For example, when new activities are undertaken, does the existing method deal adequately with those new activities? Can any new activities be incorporated into an existing sector in a sectorised method, or is a new sector required?

5.132 In short, the operation of any special method should be reviewed regularly and in particular should be reconsidered when any new major additions or revisions to the taxable person's business operations are contemplated or enacted. Since 1 January 2004, the special method override permits Customs and Excise and businesses alike to issue a notice and effectively move to a use based method (see Chapter 6 below). It remains to be seen whether businesses adapting to rapidly changing circumstances will use notices under the special method override to move more quickly to a use based method rather than applying to Customs and Excise for a change in the existing special method. The speed at which such a change can be made by the business will also depend whether Customs and Excise accept any special method override notice issued by the business.

5.133 Because of the complexity of some special methods and the fact that in a sectorised method there are varying rates of recovery on different sector's 'pots' of residual input tax, the taxable person should undertake regular systems checks to ensure that input tax is being correctly allocated under the terms of the method.

5.134 One area which can cause difficulties is situations where a review of the operation of the method highlights that an error has been made. If the error highlights a quantum of under-recovered input tax, the usual mechanism for correcting an error under VAT Regulations 1995, regs 34 or 35 should be adopted. However, such claims can lead to discussions as to whether what has happened is that the agreed method has been operated incorrectly, in which case such retrospective claims for underclaimed input tax should be recovered, subject to the three-year capping provisions (in VATA 1994, s 80 or VAT Regulations 1995, reg 29(1A) respectively). However, if the 'error' is not in operation of the method but is in fact a request for a retrospective change to the agreed special method, such a claim is likely to be rejected.

5.135 In the same manner as retrospective agreement of a partial exemption special method is not permitted, a retrospective change in an agreed partial exemption method will also not be agreed, save that a change may be backdated to the commencement of the tax year in which the change has been agreed.

VAT accounting periods

5.136 The partial exemption regulations apply on a period by period basis. In each period in which a taxable person has to submit a VAT return and any VAT payable, the taxable person has to consider whether he is partly exempt and how much VAT he is able to deduct. This initial deduction of VAT in the period in which it is incurred is a provisional deduction, that is to say the deduction may be revised (up or down) at a later date.

5.137 The period in which a taxable person has to submit a VAT return and thus make any partial exemption calculations is usually a 'prescribed accounting period'. For most taxpayers this is a period of three months, with each period ending on the dates notified to him by Customs and Excise; but it can be some other period allowed or directed by Customs and Excise, eg monthly (VAT Regulations 1995, reg 99(1)(b)).

5.138 In certain circumstances a special accounting period may arise, that is to say a period of less or more than three months. This most commonly arises for newly registered businesses (VAT Regulations 1995, reg 99(1)(c)).

5.139 Where a taxable person is partly exempt, several periods are combined together to create a longer period, which is usually a tax year of 12 months commencing on the first day of either April, May or June, or a period of 12 months commencing on the day following the end of the previous tax year (VAT Regulations 1995, reg 99(1)(d) and 99(4)).

5.140 For a newly registered business, the longer period commences on the date he first incurs exempt input tax and ends on the day before the first tax year (VAT Regulations 1995, reg 99(5)).

5.141 For businesses which cease trading during a longer period, the longer period ends when the taxable person ceases to be taxable (VAT Regulations 1995, reg 99(6)).

5.142 The provisional deduction, either using the standard method or a special method, is thus carried out either during the prescribed accounting period or during the longer accounting period. The significance of the longer period is that an adjustment to the provisional deduction may be required at the end of the longer period. This 'annual adjustment' is considered further in **Chapter 6**.

5.143 Apart from the annual adjustment, further adjustments may be required to the provisional deduction. For businesses operating the standard method, a standard method override adjustment may be required at the same time as the annual adjustment. In circumstances where input tax has been provisionally deducted on the basis of intended use, and before the goods or services have been used the intended use changes within a six-year period, a further adjustment is required.

5.144 In addition, in the case of capital items falling within the capital goods scheme, a capital goods scheme adjustment is required.

Special situations

5.145 There are a number of transactions that call for special mention in the context of partial exemption. These are:

- the disposal of a business;
- the acquisition of a business;
- the sale of shares in a company;
- the purchase of shares in a company;
- entry and exit into VAT groups; and
- credit notes.

5.146 There are special considerations where a business carries out transactions that are excluded from being regarded as a supply, eg the transfer of a going concern. In particular, in *Abbey National plc v C & E Comrs [2001] STC 297* (**Case Summary** 39), the European Court of Justice concluded that costs incurred on the disposal of a going concern could not be attributed to supplies because there were no supplies to which it could be related. However, the costs were linked with that part of the business that was disposed of. The transactions in the list at **5.145** above (other than the sale of shares) need to be considered in light of such principle.

Disposal of a business

5.147 As noted, the disposal of the assets of a business as part of a going concern will not be a supply. Any input tax incurred on costs associated with disposing of the business or part of the business will be treated as an overhead either of:

- the business as a whole; or
- the part of the business being disposed where it is an identifiable separate business.

5.148 The recovery of that input tax will depend on how overheads of the business or the part of the business are recovered. As the *Abbey National* decision (see **5.146** above) demonstrates, the input tax will be:

- deductible in full if the business or part of the business being disposed of is wholly taxable;
- wholly non-deductible where the business or part of the business being disposed of is wholly exempt or non-taxable; or
- deductible as residual input tax deductible (according to whatever partial exemption method is applicable) where the business or part of the business being disposed of is partly exempt.

5.149 In addition to dealing with any input tax on the disposal, it is also possible that the business may have to make adjustments under the capital items scheme. The adjustments required under the capital items scheme are discussed in **Chapter 7**.

5.150 It is possible that some assets might not meet the criteria of being a transfer of a going concern. This is particularly the case with land and buildings, since special rules have to be met for such sales to be treated as a transfer of a going concern. Where assets are not part of the transfer as a going concern, the sale is likely to be exempt, taxable or possibly an out-of-country supply. The normal attribution rules will apply to such assets, but because they are likely to be capital assets, they may be excluded from account in any outputs based partial exemption method.

Example 2

A taxpayer sells his business for £2 million. Included in the sale is a building valued at £1 million. The taxpayer has opted to tax but the purchaser refused to opt and consequently the building is excluded from being part of the going concern and will be treated as a taxable supply.

The consequences of the above are:

- input tax referable to the half of the transaction which is a going concern will be overhead VAT and will need to be apportioned based on the business's partial exemption method;
- input tax referable to the building sale will be wholly deductible because the sale is a taxable sale;
- the business may also have to make capital items scheme adjustments in respect of the building; and
- the sale of the building may be considered to be an 'incidental supply' under VAT Regulations 1995, reg 101(3)(b) and so may not have to be taken into account for the purposes of determining the VAT deductible under the standard method, if applicable.

Acquisition of a business

5.151 When a partly exempt business acquires another business, the recoverability of input tax incurred in relation to the acquisition depends on whether the acquired business is itself to be used to make taxable or exempt supplies. Where the acquired business is to make taxable supplies, the overhead VAT incurred in relation to the acquisition will be recoverable (*C & E Comrs v UBAF Bank Ltd [1996] STC 372, CA*). Similarly, if the business is acquired in order to make exempt supplies, no deduction will be permitted. Where a business is acquired partly to make exempt supplies and partly to make taxable or other supplies giving right to a deduction, the input tax will be residual input tax and subject to apportionment.

5.152 However, the position is more complex when a taxpayer acquiring a business raises finance for the acquisition by issuing shares or debentures. As both the *RAP Group plc v Customs and Excise Comrs [2000] STC 980, Ch D* and *Southampton Leisure Holdings plc [2002] VAT decision 17716* (**Case Summary 44**) cases demonstrate, the input tax incurred will be used partly for the purposes of acquiring the business and partly for the purposes of issuing the shares. It will be for the taxpayer to arrive at an appropriate apportionment. One lesson that can be learnt from the *RAP Group plc* case is that it is important to ensure that the invoices dealing with any costs make the nature of the services performed clear. Without such evidence, it may be assumed by Customs and Excise or, on appeal, a tribunal or court that the whole of the VAT relates to the exempt issue of shares or similar non-taxable activity.

5.153 In *Halladale Group plc [2003] VAT decision 18218* case, the VAT and Duties Tribunal concluded that, where funds were raised by way of a listing on AIM, the input tax incurred in respect of the listing was not incurred solely for the purpose of making an exempt supply of shares. Apart from the issue of shares, the evidence showed that the appellant also incurred the input tax for general business purposes. Accordingly, the input tax was residual rather than solely attributable to exempt supplies.

Purchase of assets as a transfer of a going concern by a partly exempt VAT group

5.154 Where a partly exempt VAT group purchases assets by way of a transfer of a going concern ('TOGC') the representative member of the group purchasing those assets will have to treat the assets acquired as being supplied by himself to himself (VATA 1994, s 44). There is an exclusion for:

- assets, which were held by the vendor for more than three years prior to the day they are transferred;
- assets that are subject to the capital items scheme (because they are subject to adjustment under the capital items scheme); and
- goodwill (by concession).

5.155 The value of the self-supply will be the open market value of the assets (whatever price is paid for them). Assets, the disposal of which would fall to be zero-rated, and assets, the disposal of which would be exempt, are not subject to a VAT charge. Assets that would be subject to the reduced rate on disposal would similarly be subject to the reduced rate on a self-supply.

5.156 As with all other self-supplies, the representative member cannot directly attribute the input tax on the self-supply to the taxable self-supply, but rather has to treat the input tax incurred as residual input tax. There can therefore be a significant VAT cost in purchasing assets by way of TOGC by a partly exempt VAT group. Customs and Excise do have the power to reduce the value of the self-supply if the vendor was unable to deduct fully the input tax on the assets transferred.

VAT groups

5.157 Supplies made between members of a VAT group are disregarded. Therefore, the input tax on costs incurred by members of the group needs to be attributed to supplies made outside the group.It is therefore critical to know whether supplies are made or received at a time when the supplier or recipient is a member of a VAT group. There have been several significant disputes in situations where the issue of whether a supply has been made or received whilst the supplier or recipient respectively was or was not a member of a VAT group.

5.158–5.159 In the *J P Morgan Trading and Finance [1998] VAT decision 15373*, the issue was whether input tax incurred on the fitting out costs of a building was attributable to taxable supplies made by a company with which the appellant had previously been VAT grouped or whether the input tax was attributable in whole or in part to supplies made by the representative member of the VAT group. The Tribunal reduced Customs and Excise's assessment in that case but held that the costs had been used in part for the supplies made by the VAT group which the appellant had left and in part for taxable supplies it had made when no longer a member of the VAT group.

Joining or leaving a VAT group

5.160 For members of a VAT group all of the supplies made and received are treated as being made and received by the representative member of the VAT group. Therefore, it is the partial exemption method of the representative member which will determine recovery of VAT following a company's addition to a VAT group. Any changes to the composition of a VAT group must be notified to Customs and Excise. Customs and Excise will then either allow the existing special method to remain, or will request amendments to the special method. In the absence of agreed changes to the special method, if required by Customs and Excise, they may use their powers to direct a special method.

Credit notes

5.161 Credit notes that reduce the value of a taxable supply that was received will have an impact on the partial exemption calculations. Where the credit note affects a supply that took place within the same period as when the credit note was issued, there is no need to consider any adjustment.

5.162 However, where a credit note is issued in a subsequent period to the time when the original input tax was claimed, care will be required, as was shown in the case of *London International Financial Futures Exchange [1993] VAT decision 11611*. LIFFE incurred input tax on computer systems at a time when it was fully taxable. Its transactions subsequently became exempt because of a change in liability law. It recovered 100 per cent of the input tax claimed when the systems were acquired. It later received a substantial credit note reducing the price and netted the input tax credited against the input tax incurred in the subsequent period. The effect of this was to repay to Customs and Excise less than the VAT originally claimed. The

VAT and Duties Tribunal dismissed LIFFE's appeal against an assessment by Customs and Excise adjusting the clawback to 100 per cent to reflect the original input tax deducted.

Anti-avoidance and partial exemption

5.163 VAT can represent a significant cost to a business that is either not a taxable person or which makes exempt and non-taxable supplies. Inevitably therefore, taxpayers seeks to avoid tax while Customs and Excise seek to counter it.

5.164 The approach to tax avoidance can be broken down into a number of categories, ie:

- disputing the basis upon which the taxpayer's avoidance arrangement is based;
- introducing specific VAT avoidance legislation to counter measures used to avoid VAT;
- attacking the commercial rationale and seeking to show that the substance of the transaction is something other than that for which the taxpayer contends; and
- more recently, applying an interpretation to the transaction that counters any avoidance, such as the 'Halifax' doctrine (Case Summary 45).

5.165 A partly exempt taxpayer is usually concerned with mitigating non-deductible VAT. This can be achieved by removing VAT on costs incurred. There are a number of mechanisms that may be involved in attempting to achieve this objective and frequently arrangements involve the use of VAT groups, since supplies intra-VAT group are disregarded. As a consequence Customs and Excise have challenged several arrangements on the basis of the facts but have also persuaded the Government to introduce legislation to counter transactions which they perceive as avoidance.

5.166 Legislation that is intended to counter avoidance by exempt and partly exempt businesses includes:

- VATA 1994, Sch 6, para 1: this counters avoidance that is achieved by undervaluing taxable supplies made to a connected person who cannot recover all the tax charged;
- VATA 1994, s 44: this counters the use of transfers of going concerns into partly exempt VAT groups in order to avoid VAT on the purchase of capital assets (see **5.154–5.156** above);
- VATA 1994, Sch 9A: this prevents schemes that rely on entry and exit from VAT groups to avoid disallowable VAT (not only exempt input tax).

5.167 The Halifax doctrine is a recent addition to Customs and Excise's attacks on certain planning arrangements designed to mitigate non-deductible VAT. In the

Halifax case, a partly exempt business sought to recover input VAT in relation to procuring a new property. The arrangements involved a number of steps whereby construction services were supplied to and by subsidiary companies.

5.168 The Tribunal in the *Halifax* case has referred the following questions to the European Court of Justice:

> '(a) In the *relevant* circumstances [ie those pertaining in *Halifax*], do transactions—
>
> (i) effected by each participator with the intention solely of obtaining a tax advantage and
>
> (ii) which have no independent business purpose
>
> qualify for VAT purposes as supplies made by or to the participators in the course of their economic activities?
>
> (b) In the *relevant* circumstances, what factors should be considered in determining the identity of the recipients of the supplies made by the arm's-length builders?
>
> Does the doctrine of abuse of rights as developed by the Court operate to disallow the Appellants their *claims* for recovery of or relief for input tax arising from the implementation of the relevant transactions?'

5.169 It is apparent that the questions of whether or not a deduction can be denied because of the issues raised by Customs and Excise both in relation to whether an economic activity is being carried on which leads to an entitlement to deduction and whether it is possible to deny deduction on the basis of 'abuse of rights' will not be determined until the European Court of Justice has handed down judgment. Further questions have also been referred in the *University of Huddersfield Education Corp [2002] VAT decision 17854* although these are broadly the same as those referred in *Halifax*, save that the *Huddersfield* questions relate to the Sixth Directive, art 4(2) rather than art 4(1).

5.170 Taxpayers and their advisers are thus in a period of uncertainty in relation to deductions in situations where Customs and Excise may assert that avoidance is a primary motive. This is particularly the case in two decisions following the referral of the *Halifax* case where the courts have held that the Halifax arguments do not deny a deduction. In the case of *RBS Property Developments Ltd and Royal Bank Of Scotland Group plc (2002) VAT decision 17789*, the VAT and Duties Tribunal distinguished the *Halifax* case by finding that tax avoidance was not the sole motive for the transactions. In *WHA v C&E Comrs [2003] STC 648*, the High Court wished to have a further hearing solely on *Halifax* and abuse of rights issues, because the High Court had difficulty in applying these principles to ongoing transactions, such as those arising in that case, in contrast with the discrete nature of property transactions considered in the *Halifax* case. However, this further hearing never took place.

Customs and Excise's policy on reg 103

5.171 Where a taxable person makes supplies both within the UK and supplies outside the UK or certain 'specified supplies' (principally incidental financial transactions), then any residual input tax incurred may be referable either solely to UK supplies or in part to out-of-country or specified supplies and in part to UK supplies.

5.172 VAT Regulations 1995, reg 103 requires that a use-based method be used to determine the input tax that is deductible in making both foreign and specified supplies. The operation of the predecessor of reg 103 and its interaction with the standard partial exemption method provided for by the predecessor of reg 101 was considered by the House of Lords in *C & E Comrs v Liverpool Institute for Performing Arts [2001] STC 891* (**Case Summary 40**). The taxpayer made supplies of advertising to a German company. These supplies were outside the scope of VAT, the place of supply being the place where the customer belongs. However, such supplies of advertising would be taxable if made in the UK and thus input tax attributable to such supplies is deductible under what is now VAT Regulations 1995, reg 103.

5.173 However, the issue was whether, in calculating the deductible proportion of residual input tax under what is now VAT Regulations 1995, reg 101(2)(d), the value of the foreign advertising supplies should be included in the fraction as 'taxable supplies'. The House of Lords held that 'taxable supplies' meant taxable supplies made in the UK and thus the out-of-country taxable supplies of advertising were to be excluded from the fraction calculating the deductible proportion of input tax under what is now reg 101(2)(d). What is noteworthy is that Lord Scott considered that while 'taxable supplies' was restricted to supplies in the UK, 'exempt supplies' was not so restricted and thus foreign supplies which would be exempt if made in the UK were to be included in the fraction.

5.174 The difficulty following the *LIPA* judgment was how to deal with input tax incurred both for foreign and UK supplies. The apparent position was that reg 103 provided a mechanism for deducting input tax which was referable to foreign and specified supplies. Any residual input tax referable to both UK and foreign supplies not deducted under reg 103 was then thought to be included in residual input tax under reg 101(2)(d) so that the quantum attributable to UK taxable supplies could be determined.

5.175 However, in the recent tribunal decision in *Easyjet plc [2003] VAT decision 18230*, the taxpayer incurred input tax in respect of both specified and UK supplies. Customs and Excise argued in that case that all of the input tax used in part to make specified supplies was only to be apportioned using the use-based method provided for by VAT Regulations 1995, reg 103. By contrast, the appellant claimed that reg 103 only determined the recoverable amount of residual input tax under reg 103. The remaining residual input tax was then said by the taxpayer to fall to be apportioned under VAT Regulations 1995, reg 101(2)(d). Had the taxpayer succeeded in this argument, all of the input tax disputed in this case would have been recoverable.

5.176 The Tribunal held that VAT Regulations 1995, reg 103 was a self-contained provision and that any input tax attributed under reg 103 was apportioned on the basis of use in its entirety. This led to the somewhat surprising conclusion that the residual input tax relating to UK supplies which also related to specified supplies was all recovered on the same use basis leading to a markedly lower recovery of the residual input tax.

5.177 It remains to be seen whether the taxpayer in the *Easyjet plc* case will appeal this decision. However, it is worth noting that the decision implies that VAT Regulations 1995, reg 103 has an additional provision which requires a use-based recovery on residual input tax incurred in respect of UK supplies when such residual input tax relates both to foreign or specified supplies and UK supplies. On a plain reading of VAT Regulations 1995, reg 103 no such additional provision is apparent.

5.178 A further issue that arises with attribution to out-of-country and specified supplies under VAT Regulations 1995, reg 103, is whether a special partial exemption method can deal with reg 103 supplies or whether reg 103 requires input tax attributable to out-of-country and specified supplies always to be attributed and apportioned on the basis of use. The converse of this would be that Customs and Excise could allow a special partial exemption method that deals with input tax attributable to foreign and specified supplies on some basis other than on a use basis (for example on a values-based method). This issue is as yet untested before the courts.

Chapter 6

Adjustments to Input Tax Deductions

Introduction

6.1 There is an immediate right to deduct input tax when it is incurred (Sixth Directive, art 17(1); *Rompelman and Rompelman Van Deelen v Minister van Financiën (C-268/83) [1985] ECR 655* at *664, ECJ* **(Case Summary 4)**). Since the expenditure on which the VAT is incurred may be used for the purpose of an activity that takes place either over a period of time or at some time in the future, it follows that the expenditure may be used for different purposes to those that were contemplated when the expenditure was incurred and the VAT deducted. In such cases, in order to preserve fiscal neutrality and to ensure that input tax which is a cost component of taxable transactions is deductible and that input tax which is not a cost component of taxable transactions is not deducted, suitable adjustment mechanisms are required.

6.2 In addition, a business's balance of taxable and exempt supplies may fluctuate over time. Given that VAT returns cover a relatively short time period, it is quite likely that initial measures of use of supplies on which VAT is deducted may not accurately reflect actual use. Accordingly, adjustment is also necessary to even out the effects of time-related distortions.

Types of adjustment

6.3 This chapter deals with five of the six types of adjustment provided for in UK VAT law ie:

- The annual adjustment
- The standard method override
- The special method override
- Change of use adjustments
- The bad debts or late payments adjustment.

The sixth type of adjustment is the capital items scheme. This is dealt with in **Chapter 7**.

Annual adjustments

Summary

6.4 The initial deduction of input tax should take place in the period in which it is incurred (Advocate-General's opinion in *Terra Baubedarf-Handel GmbH v Finanzamt Osterholz-Scharmbeck (C-152/02)*. The period in which the initial deduction takes place will usually be either a month or a quarter. The deduction is regarded as provisional and may be subject to later adjustment. Only when input tax is no longer subject to adjustment can the deduction be said to be final.

6.5 The annual adjustment is meant to deal with any seasonal fluctuations in a taxpayer's business. It recognises that the measures of use can vary from one accounting period to another and that only by taking a longer period of time – usually a year – can a more accurate means of use be achieved. It is of course possible that a measure of use can be arrived at that does not vary from period to period, but in the vast majority of cases this will not be the case.

The longer period

6.6 The annual adjustment is calculated over the 'longer period'. This is defined in VAT Regulations 1995, reg 99 as follows:

> '(4) A taxable person who incurs exempt input tax during any tax year shall have applied to him a longer period which shall correspond with that tax year unless he did not incur exempt input tax during his immediately preceding tax year or registration period, in which case his longer period shall—
>
> (*a*) begin on the first day of the first prescribed accounting period in which he incurs exempt input tax, and
>
> (*b*) end on the last day of that tax year,
>
> except where he incurs exempt input tax only in the last prescribed accounting period of his tax year, in which case no longer period shall be applied to him in respect of that tax year.
>
> (5) A taxable person who incurs exempt input tax during his registration period shall have applied to him a longer period which shall begin on the first day on which he incurs exempt input tax and end on the day before the commencement of his first tax year.
>
> (6) In the case of a taxable person ceasing to be taxable during a longer period applicable to him, that longer period shall end on the day when he ceases to be taxable.'

6.7 It will be seen from the above therefore that the longer period normally corresponds with a tax year. However, if the taxpayer has not previously incurred 'exempt input tax', the longer period only commences in the period in which such exempt input tax is incurred. It will be recalled from para **5.4**, that exempt input tax is defined in VAT Regulations 1995, reg 99 as follows:

> ' "exempt input tax" means input tax incurred by a taxable person on goods imported or acquired by, or goods or services supplied to, him in so far as they are used by him or are to be used by him, or a successor of his, in making exempt supplies, or supplies outside the United Kingdom which would be exempt if made in the United Kingdom, other than any input tax which is allowable under regulation 103 or 103A.'

6.8 It should be noted that it is not necessary that the taxpayer makes any exempt supplies in the period concerned. It is sufficient that input tax be incurred on expenditure that is to be used to make exempt supplies or out-of-country supplies that would be exempt if made in the UK (except those out-of-country supplies for which a deduction is permitted under the VAT (Input Tax) (Specified Supplies) Order 1999.

6.9 The question arises as to how, when the longer period commences at a time when input tax would otherwise be exempt, input tax in a particular period is de minimis. It would appear that because such input tax is treated as taxable (VATA 1994, reg 106), there is no exempt input tax and the longer period must start at a later date. While there are unlikely to be many cases where this is an issue, it is conceivable that if in the first quarter very little exempt input tax is incurred so that it is de minimis and in the remaining one, two or three periods, the exempt input tax exceeds £1,875 per quarter or 50 per cent of all input tax. In such cases, a taxable person could be partly exempt for part of year when he would be de minimis if all four quarters are taken together. Other small anomalies are also possible.

How the annual adjustment works

6.10 The annual adjustment aggregates the residual input tax incurred over a period known as the 'longer period'. It then apportions that input tax by applying to it the normal measure of use taken over the same period. Thus, if turnover is used to measure use, as is the case in the standard partial exemption period, the turnover over the whole longer period will be taken into account to determine what input tax is deductible. Although an adjustment will usually have to be made in the case of the standard method, it is also common for special methods to provide for an annual adjustment.

6.11 The annual adjustment is provided for by the VAT General Regulations 1995, reg 107. Regulation 107(1) provides for the process of calculating the annual adjustment. Regulation 107(2) provides that the adjustment is to be included in the return following the longer period except where Customs and Excise allow another return to be used. In cases where a registration is cancelled before the expiry of the longer period, the adjustment is entered on the final return (reg 107(3)).

Example 1

Period		Value of supplies		Per cent	Residual input tax	Recoverable residual input tax
	A	*B*	*C*	*D*	*E*	*F*
	Taxable	*Exempt*	*Total*	*(A ÷ C)*		*(D x E)*
Q1	20,000	5,000	25,000	80	1,800	1,640
Q2	50,000	10,000	60,000	84	3,000	2,520
Q3	95,000	5,000	100,000	95	4,000	3,800
Q4	10,000	10,000	20,000	50	2,000	1,000
						8,960
Annual	175,000	30,000	205,000	86	10,800	9,288

It will be seen from the table that the percentage of taxable supplies fluctuates quite substantially – from 50 per cent to 95 per cent. Similarly, the amount of residual input tax incurred bears no relationship to the total supplies made. The annual adjustment smooths out the fluctuations.

		£
Total residual input tax deducted (Column F) in quarters 1 to 4	=	8,960
Total residual input tax that should be deducted (Column F)	=	9,288
Adjustment (additional input tax to be claimed)		328

Interaction of annual adjustments and de minimis limits

6.12 The annual adjustment can have an impact on the partial exemption de minimis limits. Thus, extending the example at **6.11** above, it should be assumed that the directly attributable input tax in each period is as shown in column X below.

Example 2

Period	Residual input tax	Recoverable residual input tax	Directly attributable exempt input tax	Total exempt input tax	Input tax restricted on return
	V	*W*	*X*	*Y*	*Z*
				(V – X + X)	
Q1	1,800	1,640	500	660	NIL
Q2	3,000	2,520	1,400	1,880	1,880
Q3	4,000	3,800	1,400	1,600	NIL
Q4	2,000	1,000	900	1,900	1,900
Annual	10,800	9,288	4,200	5,712	NIL

In Q2 and Q4 the provisional deduction is restricted as there is exempt input tax in excess of the de minimis limits (the lesser of £1,875 and 50 per cent of total input tax incurred). In Q1 and Q3 the quantum of exempt input tax is below the de minimis limit and in both cases is less than half of the residual input tax incurred (and must, therefore, be less than half of all of the input tax incurred) and so is recoverable in full. There is, therefore, no restriction of input tax in either period.

The annual adjustment shows that the total exempt input tax is below the de minimis limit, being the lesser of £7,500 per annum and 50 per cent of the total input tax incurred. There is a minimum of £15,000 of input tax (the £10,800 residual and the £4,200 attributable to exempt) and so the 50 per cent threshold must also be met. In this example, the business would be treated as fully taxable as a result of the annual adjustment. The additional input tax recoverable under the annual adjustment would be the amount entitled to be claimed over the full year less the amount already recovered. The VAT restricted in Q2 and Q4 (£1,880 plus £1,900) totalling £3,780 will therefore be recoverable from Customs and Excise.

The standard method override

Summary

6.13 The standard method override is a very recent addition to the partial exemption regulations, having only been introduced following the 2002 Budget. The stated purpose of the standard method over-ride is to target aggressive VAT avoidance by large businesses that use the standard method to deduct exempt input tax (see Information Sheet 4/02). However, the reality may be somewhat different as the secondary legislation governing annual adjustments under the standard partial exemption method has been revised and these revisions do not differentiate between the alleged large business VAT avoiders and the innocent or unwary.

6.14 It should be borne in mind that the standard method is the only method of determining what residual input tax is deductible on taxable supplies that does not necessarily involve determining the use of inputs. This is because, but for the standard method override, it might be merely a coincidence that the relationship between taxable turnover and exempt turnover actually bears any real relationship to the use of any supplies on which VAT is incurred. Thus, what the standard method override does is to require a use-based method in cases where the standard method does not actually result in a reasonably accurate measure of use.

6.15 It should also be noted that it is clear from the explanations given by Customs and Excise that they generally regard turnover as an accurate measure of use. The standard method override was aimed primarily at abuses of the system that resulted in input tax being incurred in a period where the proportion of taxable supply was high so as to generate a disproportionate deduction relative to the cost of taxable supplies. Be that as it may, the fact is that the legislation allows an adjustment both ways – ie it allows adjustment of significant understatements of input tax in just the same way as significant overstatements of input tax.

When does the standard method override operate?

6.16 Paragraphs **6.4–6.12** above outline the operation of the annual adjustment. The standard method override requires an additional calculation at the same time as the annual adjustment where the taxpayer uses the standard method. The override does not apply where the taxpayer uses a special method to determine the input tax he is entitled to deduct.

6.17 In cases where the taxpayer has no longer period (for instance where exempt input tax is first incurred in the last prescribed accounting period) in a tax year, the standard method override adjustment must be made in the prescribed accounting period following the one in which the provisional deduction was made.

6.18 The standard method override applies where the input tax provisionally deducted by a taxpayer using the standard method differs substantially from the deduction that would apply if it was determined on the basis of the use or intended use of the supplies on which the input tax was incurred. A difference is regarded as substantial if it exceeds:

- £50,000; or
- 50 per cent of the residual input tax incurred and £25,000.

Where the taxpayer is the representative member of a VAT group, only the £50,000 threshold applies (VAT Regulations 1995, reg 107C).

6.19 It will be apparent from the above that a taxable person will have to consider whether such a difference would arise if he were to calculate the input tax to which he is entitled based on actual use of the supplies on which the input tax is incurred. If the difference is substantial, the taxable person will have to make an adjustment on the same return as the annual adjustment, or if the taxpayer has no longer period, the return following the provisional deduction, or if the taxpayer has his registration cancelled, on his final return.

Considering use

6.20 Customs and Excise provide guidance on the standard method override in Notice 706/02, paras 5.1–5.11. It is clear from the Notice that Customs and Excise consider that taxable persons will need to keep evidence of their override calculation unless it is clear that no adjustment is required (see para 5.7, which advises keeping a copy in borderline cases).

6.21 The reference to 'use' in VAT Regulations 1995, regs 107A–107E means that, where the override applies, the deduction a taxable person is entitled to will be calculated in the same way as the deductions under reg 103 or 103A. Unlike a special method, there is no requirement that a taxable person agrees any method with Customs and Excise but, of course, if Customs and Excise do not consider that the method chosen results in a fair and reasonable attribution of input tax, they might seek to assess the taxable person for any perceived over-deduction. Any assessment would be subject to objection and appeal.

6.22 For further consideration of what is meant by the term 'use', see **Chapter 3**, paras **3.60–3.81**.

Examples of the operation of the standard method override

6.23 Examples of when a taxable person might be expected to operate the standard method override include the following.

6.24 A taxable person might be expected to operate the standard method override where the he incurs a large sum of residual input tax in a tax year when he is making predominantly taxable supplies but does not use the supplies on which the VAT was incurred until later tax years when he makes significantly more exempt supplies.

Example 3

'Example of an over-ride adjustment—VAT period that spans 18 April 2002

In this example a business with a tax year running from 1 June 2001 to 31 May 2002 incurs an abnormally high level of residual input tax in the weeks after 18 April on purchases for use in the next tax year in which the proportion of exempt supplies is planned to increase.

Standard method attribution

(*a*) Total input tax—£800,000

(*b*) Input tax which wholly relates to taxable supplies—£125,000

(*c*) Input tax which wholly relates to exempt supplies—£75,000

(*d*) Residual input tax—£600,000

(*e*) Value (excluding VAT) of all taxable supplies—£5,000,000

(*f*) Value of exempt supplies—£1,000,000

(*g*) Percentage of residual input tax deductible using the standard method is—84%

This is calculated by—

$$\frac{(e)}{(e) + (f)} = \frac{£5{,}000{,}000}{£5{,}000{,}000 + £1{,}000{,}000} = \frac{£5{,}000{,}000}{£6{,}000{,}000}$$

And the result is rounded up to 84%.

(*h*) Deductible residual input tax for the year is—£504,000

This is calculated by—(*d*) × (*g*) = £600,000 × 84%

(*i*) Total deductible input tax for the year is—£629,000

This is calculated by—(*b*) + (*h*) = £125,000 + £504,000

Calculating the over-ride adjustment

Is the business subject to the over-ride rule?

The business determines whether the over-ride applies by calculating the threshold limit for a period of only 44 days (18 April to 31 May 2002) and comparing that with the amount of residual input tax incurred in this period.

(*j*) Threshold limit for this period is—£6,027

This is calculated by—44 days / 365 days × £50,000

The business determines from its accounting records the following:

(*k*) Total input tax in this period—£325,000

(*l*) Input tax in this period which wholly relates to taxable supplies—£15,000

(*m*) Input tax in this period which wholly relates to exempt supplies—£10,000

(*n*) Residual input tax incurred on purchases for use this year—£100,000

(*o*) Residual input tax incurred on purchases for use in the next year—£200,000

The residual input tax incurred in the period is £300,000 (*n*) plus (*o*), which exceeds the threshold limit for the period of £6,027 (*j*) meaning the over-ride must be considered.

Is an over-ride adjustment needed?

Input tax deducted using the standard may not be a fair and reasonable reflection of use because many of the purchases on which it was incurred will not be used to make supplies until the next year when the deductible proportion may be very different. If this results in a substantial difference of deductible input tax then an over-ride adjustment must be made.

The business determines the input tax deductible for the period 18 April–31 May 2002 using the standard method.

(*p*) Deductible residual input tax for the period is—£252,000

This is calculated by—((*n*) + (*o*)) × (*g*) = £300,000 × 84%

(*q*) Total deductible input tax for the period is—£267,000

This is calculated by—(*l*) + (*p*) = £15,000 + £252,000

This is compared to an attribution based on use.

What would be a fair and reasonable attribution on the basis of use?

Dealing with this year's purchases separately from next year's purchases will provide for a fair and reasonable attribution based upon use. But to deal with next year's purchases, the business must project the level of taxable and exempt use.

(*r*) The percentage of deductible residual input tax in the next year 2002/03 based on forecast taxable and exempt supplies is—67%

This is calculated by—

$$\frac{[\text{forecast taxable supplies}]}{[\text{forecast total supplies}]} = \frac{£6{,}000{,}000}{£6{,}000{,}000 + £3{,}000{,}000} = \frac{£6{,}000{,}000}{£9{,}000{,}000}$$

And the result is rounded up to 67%.

(*s*) Input tax deductible against the purchases for next year, based on the forecast percentage of deduction is—£134,000

This is calculated by—(*o*) × (*r*) = £200,000 × 67%

(*t*) Balance of deductible residual input tax is—£84,000

This is calculated by—(*n*) × (*g*) = £100,000 × 84%

(*u*)Total deductible input tax on the basis of use is—£233,000

This is calculated by—(*l*) + (*s*) + (*t*) = £15,000 + £134,000 + £84,000

Therefore total input tax deductible in the period, using the standard method, is £267,000; whereas total input tax deductible for the period on the basis of use is £233,000.

Is the difference substantial?

A difference is substantial if it exceeds £50,000 or 50% of the residual input tax for the period but not less than £25,000. The lower of these two limits in this example is £50,000.

(*v*) The difference between input tax deducted using the standard method and the amount deductible on the basis of use is—£34,000

This is calculated by—(*q*) – (*u*) = £267,000 – £233,000

The difference of £34,000 is not substantial meaning that an over-ride adjustment is not required.'

(Customs and Excise Information Sheet 4/02, App 3.)

In the above example, it can be seen that only input tax incurred on or after the 18 April 2002 is subject to the standard method override.

6.25 The standard method override might apply where a turnover-based method of attributing input tax to taxable supplies is not accurate because of the differing margins on the different type of supplies. This could occur for example where taxable supplies include largely variable cost components while exempt supplies incur largely fixed costs.

Example 4

'Example of an over-ride adjustment—high value distorting transaction

This is an adaptation of the example given in the partial exemption public Notice 706. It illustrates how an over-ride adjustment is made when the standard method breaks down, which in this case is because of a high value taxable transaction consuming little or no inputs.

Standard method attribution

(*a*) Total input tax—£350,000

(*b*) Input tax which wholly relates only to taxable supplies—£125,000

(*c*) Input tax which wholly relates only to exempt supplies—£75,000

(*d*) Residual input tax—£150,000

(*e*) Value (excluding VAT) of all taxable supplies—£1,350,000

(*f*) Value of taxable transaction consuming little or no inputs—£1,000,000

(*g*) Value of exempt supplies—£550,000

(*h*) Value (excluding VAT) of machine used in the business and sold—£200,000

(*i*) Percentage of residual input tax deductible using the standard method is—68%

This is calculated by—

$$\frac{(e) - (f)}{(e) + (g) - (h)} = \frac{£1,350,000 - £200,000}{£1,350,000 + £550,000 - £200,000} = \frac{£1,150,000}{£1,700,000}$$

And the result is rounded up to 68%.

(*j*) Deductible residual input tax is—£102,000

This is calculated by—(*d*) × (*i*) = £150,000 x 68%

(*k*) Total deductible input tax is—£227,000

This is calculated by—(*b*) + (*j*) = £125,000 + £102,000

Calculating the over-ride adjustment

Is the business subject to the over-ride rule?

Yes. The business has incurred £150,000 residual input tax (*d*), which exceeds the threshold limit of £50,000.

Is an over-ride adjustment needed?

The input tax deducted using the standard method may not be fair and reasonable reflecting the extent to which purchases are used in making taxable supplies because few if any purchases are used in making the high value taxable transaction. The business must determine the amount of input tax deductible on the basis of use, and having compared that with the amount deductible on the basis of use, check whether the difference is substantial. If the difference is substantial an over-ride adjustment must be made.

What would be a fair and reasonable attribution on the basis of use?

In this example, all supplies other than the high value taxable transaction, consume purchases in proportion to their values. Accordingly, a fair and reasonable attribution can be achieved by excluding the value of the terminal market transaction from a calculation based on the standard method.

(*l*) Percentage of residual input tax deductible having first excluded the high value taxable transaction is—22%

This is calculated by—

$$\frac{(e) - (f) - (h)}{(e) + (g) - (f) - (h)} = \frac{£1{,}350{,}000 - £1{,}000{,}000 - £200{,}000}{£1{,}350{,}000 + £550{,}000 - £1{,}000{,}000 - £200{,}000}$$

And the result is rounded up to 22%.

(*m*) Deductible residual input tax is—£33,000

This is calculated by—(*d*) × (*l*) = £150,000 × 22%

(*n*) Total deductible input tax is—£158,000

This is calculated by—(*b*) + (*m*) = £125,000 + £33,000

Therefore, total input tax deductible on the basis of use is £158,000; whereas total input tax deductible using the standard method is £227,000.

Is the difference substantial?

A difference is substantial if it exceeds £50,000, or 50% of the residual input tax and £25,000.

(*o*) The difference between input tax deducted using the standard method and the amount deductible on the basis of use is—£69,000

This is calculated by—(*k*) – (*n*) = £227,000 – £158,000

This is a substantial difference for which an over-ride adjustment must be made. The sum of £69,000, which is deductible using the standard method, must be adjusted as an over claim by including it in the VAT return along with the annual adjustment.'

(Customs and Excise Information Sheet 4/02, App 2.)

6.26 A taxable person might be expected to operate the standard method override where there are deemed supplies, eg deemed taxable supplies under VATA 1994, Sch 6, para 10 – there is no value to the supplies but input tax is deductible on such supplies.

6.27 Prior to the introduction of the standard method override, once the annual adjustment had been completed there was no mechanism to adjust residual input tax, even if the ratio of taxable to exempt supplies moved from 99 per cent taxable to 99 per cent exempt or vice versa.

Interaction of the standard method override and the de minimis limits

6.28 In theory, the standard method override affects the operation of the de minimis calculation referred to in **6.12** above. The de minimis limits remain in place but the calculation of the standard method over-ride may have the effect of breaching the limit on an annual basis and thus making the business no longer fully taxable and having to suffer a restriction of input tax.

Interaction of standard method override and special methods

6.29 As already noted, the standard method override only applies to businesses operating the standard partial exemption method. It follows that a business that does not wish to apply for a special method could simply use the standard method and then adjust its input tax at the end of the year. Assuming that the standard method was advantageous to the taxable person, there could be a cash flow advantage in not applying for a special method. A number of issues need to be considered if this strategy is adopted, ie:

- Customs and Excise could direct that a special method be used;
- it is possible that the standard method override might not operate to best advantage and that the taxable person might end up with a less than optimum measure of use (if the difference was less than £50,000/£25,000 as the case might be); and
- Customs and Excise could contest the method used to adjust input tax under the standard method override, resulting in disputes, although it must be said that if Customs and Excise are likely to contest the method chosen, they may well also have contested the method adopted in a proposed special method.

6.30 It should be remembered that the standard method override operates both ways – ie if the difference is materially in favour of Customs and Excise, the override operates to require the taxpayer to pay back any over-deduction and vice versa.

6.31 It would appear that whether or not a special method is adopted or the override is used, an appeal against a decision by Customs and Excise will in both cases fall within VATA 1994,s 83(e) rather than s 83(c).

Interaction of the standard method override and the capital items scheme

6.32 The capital items scheme is considered in **Chapter 7**. Customs and Excise provide their view of the effect of the partial exemption override on the capital items scheme in Notice 706/02, para 5.10. It is clear that the override may operate in the initial period.

Example 5

A business purchases a building in February 2004 of its tax year to 31 March 2004 when it is fully taxable. It occupies 40 per cent of the building for own use but intends to let the building to a bank from 1 July 2004 without opting to tax the building.

Since 60 per cent of the building will be used for exempt supplies, if 60 per cent of the input tax on the building exceeds £50,000, the partial exemption override will apply.

The example above shows that the override might apply to the initial deduction to be made in relation to a capital item. The amount of input tax that falls to be adjusted under the capital items scheme in subsequent years is not affected by the override but it is possible that it will be used in determining the rate of recovery to be used in making any adjustment in subsequent years.

General

6.33 There is a potential anomaly where input tax is adjusted using income from a future year by operation of the standard method override, and that same income is used again in that future year to ascertain the taxable use of the item in a subsequent period. The same income therefore appears to have been used twice to determine the taxable use of the capital item, which is arguably not a proper method of determining deduction.

Special method override

6.33A With effect from 1 January 2004, where a partial exemption special method does not fairly and reasonably represent the extent to which goods or services are used or to be used by a taxable person in making taxable supplies, a Special Method Override Notice can be issued by either Customs and Excise or the taxable person (VAT Regulations 1995, regs 102A-C). The effect of the Notice is that, from the date of the Notice or a future date specified in the Notice, the taxable person must cease to use the partial exemption special method and must calculate deductible input tax according to a use-based apportionment. In Business Brief 27/2003 10 December 2003, Customs and Excise state that

> 'From time to time, for example when business circumstances change, a special method might no longer meet the principle of use and a new method must be found. Preparing a new special method can take time, especially for a large or complex business, and because a new method cannot normally be backdated Customs or the business can lose out as a result.
>
> ...
>
> A Notice allows either Customs or business to introduce an override with immediate effect, to correct the results of an unfair method until a replacement method is implemented. ... This means that neither Customs nor the business need be disadvantaged whilst a replacement special method is being prepared.'

The impression of fairness given by the Business Brief is undermined by the fact that, while Customs and Excise can serve a Notice which will have immediate effect without more, a Notice served by the taxable person cannot have effect until Customs and Excise have approved it.

Customs and Excise state (Business Brief 27/2003 10 December 2003) a Notice is intended to be a temporary measure and its use is expected to be rare.

A Notice will only be issued or approved where Customs and Excise:

- have clear evidence that the current special method does not fairly and reasonably reflect the principle of use; and
- are satisfied that a replacement method will not be agreed quickly; and
- are satisfied that either Customs and Excise or the business would otherwise lose out.

Even where the conditions for the issue of a Notice have been met, a Notice will only be served after Customs and Excise:

- have attempted, unsuccessfully, to persuade the business to comply, and have the evidence to show this; and;
- have decided that direction of a special method is not appropriate.

A Notice must specify:

- that it is a special method override notice;
- the date from which it takes effect; and,
- the reasons why the current special method does not reflect the principle of use.
- the Notice cannot take effect retrospectively

Approval of a Notice served by a business will be given in writing as soon as possible and ideally within 30 days of receipt. Decisions on serving a Notice will be taken by a central team.

A business can appeal to the VAT and Duties Tribunal against a decision by Customs and Excise to serve a Notice or not to approve a Notice served by a business and any VAT assessments made under a Notice.

Complying with a Notice

6.33B For each VAT return period (including any year end adjustment) from the date on which the Notice takes effect, a business must:

- determine the amount of deductible VAT using its current special method;
- determine the amount of deductible VAT in accordance with the principle of use; and,

- account for any difference between these amounts as a Notice correction.

The business must ensure that each time a VAT return is prepared, the amount of VAT deducted fairly and reasonably reflects the extent that costs and purchases are used or will be used in making taxable supplies (the principle of use). Failure to make corrections may result in a VAT assessment. A business can appeal to the VAT and Duties Tribunal against a decision by Customs and Excise to serve a Notice or not to approve a Notice served by a business and any VAT assessments made under a Notice.

Change of use adjustments

Summary

6.34 Input tax may be incurred for one intended purpose and yet be put to a different purpose in a later tax year. Regulations 108 and 109 deal with such changes. Regulations 108 and 109 are a means of implementing the Sixth Directive, art 20(1), which provides:

> '20.1The initial deduction shall be adjusted according to the procedures laid down by the Member States, in particular:
>
> (a) where that deduction was higher or lower than that to which the taxable person was entitled;
>
> (b) where, after the return is made some change occurs to the factors used to determine the amount to be deducted, in particular where purchases are cancelled or price reductions are obtained; however adjustment shall not be made in cases of transactions remaining totally or partially unpaid and of destruction, loss or theft of property duly proved or confirmed, nor in the case of applications for the purpose of making gifts of small value and giving samples specified in article 5(6). However, Member States may require adjustment in cases of transactions remaining totally or partially unpaid and of theft.'

Application of reg 108

6.35 VAT Regulations 1995, reg 108 deals with situations where input tax is initially deducted and it later turns out that some of that tax should not have been deducted. Regulation 109 (see **6.45** below) deals with the reverse situation, ie where input tax is initially restricted and it later turns out that the deduction should have been greater.

6.36 Regulation 108 provides:

> '108 (1) This regulation applies where a taxable person has deducted an amount of input tax which has been attributed to taxable supplies because he intended to use the goods or services in making either –
>
> (a) taxable supplies; or

(b) both taxable and exempt supplies,

and during a period of 6 years commencing on the first day of the prescribed accounting period in which the attribution was determined and before that intention is fulfilled, he uses or forms the intention to use the goods or services concerned in making exempt supplies, or, in the case of an attribution within sub-paragraph (a) above, in making both taxable and exempt supplies.

(2) Subject to regulation 110 and save as the Commissioners otherwise allow, where this regulation applies, the taxable person shall on the return for the prescribed accounting period in which the use occurs or the intention is formed, as the case may be, account for an amount equal to the input tax which has ceased to be attributable to taxable supplies in accordance with the method which he was required to use when the input tax was first attributed and he shall repay the same amount to the Commissioners.

(3) …'

6.37 The effect of the regulation can be illustrated in tabular form as follows:

Original use	*First use within 6 yrs*	*Adjustment required*
Taxable	Taxable and exempt	Yes
Taxable	Exempt	Yes
Taxable and exempt	Exempt	Yes

Therefore, until six years have elapsed from the first day of the prescribed accounting period in which the input tax was provisionally deducted, a clawback of input tax is possible under reg 108. It must be noted that it is only when the first use is other than the original intended use that an adjustment must be made. If the first use is the intended use, even if there is a change immediately thereafter, no adjustment is due.

6.38 As with all provisions that include references to use, the issues highlighted in **Chapter 3** will apply. Thus, if input tax has been used it is not available to be re-attributed under reg 108. This may sound self evident, but in practice whether or not input tax is available to be reattributed has been the cause of significant disputes.

6.39 For example, in *Cooper and Chapman Builders v C & E Comrs [1993] STC 1*, the company advertised flats as holiday accommodation (intended taxable supplies) but made an exempt supply of certain of the flats. The taxpayer contended that the advertising of the holiday accommodation evidenced that the intention had been fulfilled. However, the High Court held that the advertisement of the holiday accommodation did not mean that the intention to make taxable supplies had been fulfilled and an adjustment under the predecessor to reg 108 was required.

6.40 In *C & E Comrs v Briararch Ltd; C & E Comrs v Curtis Henderson Ltd [1992] STC 732, QB* (**Case Summary 14**) it was held that apportionment of input tax applied where a property is, or is intended to be, the subject of sequential supplies at different VAT liabilities. The companies had reclaimed input tax on renovating a listed building in full on the basis that the properties concerned would be the subject of taxable supplies but, when the building work was completed, they let the properties on short leases, an exempt supply, prior to fulfilling the intention of making taxable supplies. In circumstances such as these, where goods or services are put to an interim use different to that originally intended, provided the original intention is still retained, the input tax must be apportioned on a fair and reasonable basis. In *Briararch Ltd* the company let the property on a four-year exempt lease whilst still intending to make a taxable supply of a 25-year lease. The court held that $^{25}/_{29}$ of the input tax related to the intended taxable supply and that the clawback provisions of what is now reg 108 applied to $^{4}/_{29}$ of the provisionally deducted input tax.

6.41 When a project has been aborted due to circumstances outside the taxable person's control, the right to deduct under the Sixth Directive, art 17 remains secure (*Belgium v Ghent Coal Terminal NV (C-37/95)*). However, whether any adjustment to that deduction is required was not determined in that case, although many commentators have assumed that no adjustment to the deduction was necessary in the case of tax incurred in connection with the feasibility of building a coal terminal and presumably added no value to the property sold.

6.42 The issue of whether an adjustment is required in a situation where planned taxable supplies were thwarted arose again in *Tremerton Ltd v C & E Comrs (C-349/96) [1999] STC 270*. In that case, the taxpayer had intended to develop and sell residential accommodation. Its intention was thwarted as it was unable to raise the necessary finance. The taxpayer then sold the undeveloped land to a third party. The High Court confirmed that a reg 108 adjustment was necessary despite similarities with the *Ghent Coal* case as there was no basis for overriding the clear wording of reg 108.

6.43 For further consideration of the treatment of aborted transactions, see **Chapter 4**.

6.44 If an adjustment is required under reg 108, the adjustment must be made by the taxable person in the tax return for the period in which the changed use occurred.

Applications of reg 109

6.45 Where a taxable person provisionally attributes input tax to exempt supplies, but later uses that input tax to make taxable supplies (either in whole or part) before the original intention is fulfilled, input tax previously blocked can be deducted.

6.46 Regulation 109 provides for this adjustment in the following terms:

> '(1) This regulation applies where a taxable person has incurred an amount of input tax which has not been attributed to taxable supplies because he intended to use the goods or services in making either –

(*a*) exempt supplies, or

(*b*) both taxable and exempt supplies,

and during a period of 6 years commencing on the first day of the prescribed accounting period in which the attribution was determined and before that intention is fulfilled, he uses or forms an intention to use the goods or services concerned in making taxable supplies or, in the case of an attribution within sub-paragraph (a) above, in making both taxable and exempt supplies.

(2) Subject to regulation 110 and where this regulation applies, the Commissioners shall, on receipt of an application made by the taxable person in such form and manner and containing such particulars as they may direct, pay to him an amount equal to the input tax which has become attributable to taxable supplies in accordance with the method which he was required to use when the input tax was first attributed.

(3) …'

6.47 The position in reg 109 can be illustrated in tabular form as follows:

Original use	*Changed use*	*Eligible for refund*
Exempt	Taxable and exempt	Yes
Exempt	Taxable	Yes
Taxable and exempt	Taxable	Yes

6.48 There are thus similar issues as to whether a taxpayer can avail himself of an adjustment to input tax so as to deduct a further amount of input tax under reg 109 as those that arise in the clawback situation provided for by reg 108. That is:

- whether the original intention has been fulfilled; and
- whether as a matter of fact a change of use has actually occurred within the necessary time limit.

6.49 The difficulty in answering these seemingly simple questions was amply illustrated in *Royal and Sun Alliance Insurance Group plc v C & E Comrs [2003] UKHL 29, [2003] STC 832*. In that case, the Tribunal found for Customs and Excise, the High Court and Court of Appeal for the taxpayer and the House of Lords, by a three to two majority, for Customs and Excise. It is evident from such a passage through the courts, that such deceptively simple questions can nonetheless challenge the finest minds. The decision is considered in more detail in **Chapter 3, paras 3.71–3.81)** .

6.50 Lord Hoffman agreed with Customs and Excise's position, that in situations where input tax is incurred in a prescribed accounting period and attempts in that period are made to use the facilities for which the expenditure on which the input tax was incurred have failed, the input tax has been 'used up'. There was therefore no change in use as contemplated by VAT Regulations 1995, reg 109.

6.51 The difficulty with this position is that it is frequently the case with long-term property transactions that work is done in one period in relation to a future supply. Thus, it would have been eminently clear that if input tax was incurred on a building while it was made ready for occupation, the input tax is incurred on cost components on such future use. It is not clear from any of the decisions whether any evidence was given on what preparatory work was done during the 'void' periods. However, it is arguable that the House of Lords' decision should not be taken as meaning that it is impossible for input tax incurred on an apparently time-related supply not to be 'used' for a future supply so that the change of use adjustments may have to be considered in appropriate circumstances.

6.52 Unlike the case in reg 108, reg 109 does not permit the taxable person to make any adjustment for the tax to be repaid to him on his VAT return. Instead, he must currently make an application to Customs and Excise for a repayment at the local VAT business centre.

Definitions

6.53 Regulations 108 and 109 refer only to taxable and exempt supplies. That would not achieve the requirements of the Sixth Directive, art 20. However, in both cases, VAT Regulations 1995, reg 110 gives an extended meaning to the terms 'taxable supply' and 'exempt supply'.

6.54 Regulation 110 provides as follows:

> '110(1) Subject to paragraph (2) below, in this regulation, in regulations 108 and 109 above and in Part XV of these Regulations—
>
> (a) "exempt supplies" includes supplies outside the United Kingdom which would be exempt if made in the United Kingdom, other than supplies of a description falling within sub-paragraph (b) below; and
>
> (b) "taxable supplies" includes supplies of a description falling within regulation 103(1) above.
>
> (2) Subject to paragraph (3) below, for the purposes of identifying the use, or intended use, of goods and services in regulations 108 and 109 above and in Part XV of these Regulations—
>
> (a) "exempt supplies" shall be construed as including supplies of a description falling within regulation 103A(1) above, but only to the extent that there is, or would be, no credit for input tax on goods and services under that regulation; and
>
> (b) "taxable supplies" shall be construed as including supplies of a description falling within regulation 103A(1) above, but only to the extent that there is, or would be, credit for input tax on goods and services under that regulation.
>
> (3) Any adjustment under regulations 108 and 109 above shall not cause any more or any less input tax to be credited, as the case may be, in respect of

supplies of a description falling within regulation 103A(1) above than would be allowed or required under that regulation.

(4) Subject to regulation 103, where—

(a) regulation 108 or 109 applies,

(b) the use to which the goods or services concerned are put, or to which they are intended to be put, includes the making of any supplies outside the United Kingdom, and

(c) at the time when the taxable person was first required to attribute the input tax he was not required to use a method approved or directed under regulation 102 or that method did not provide expressly for the attribution of input tax attributable to supplies outside the United Kingdom,

the amount for which the taxable person shall be liable to account under regulation 108 or the amount which he is entitled to be paid under regulation 109, as the case may be, shall be calculated by reference to the extent to which the goods or services concerned are used or intended to be used in making taxable supplies, expressed as a proportion of the whole use or intended use.'

6.55 Although supplies falling within reg 103(1) are regarded as taxable supplies for the purposes of the operation of regs 108 and 109, they are not taxable supplies for the purposes of applying the standard method under VAT Regulations 1995, reg 101(2)(d) – see *Customs and Excise Comrs v Liverpool Institute for Performing Arts [2001] UKHL 28, [2001] STC 891 (Case Summary 40).*

Change of use in situations where the legislation is amended

6.56 When a member state amends its legislation so that exempt supplies become taxable or vice versa, the question arises as to whether input tax incurred in advance of the change of the liability of the supplies needs to be reattributed.

6.57 The most recent cases dealing with the issue are the joined cases of *Gemeente Leusden v Staatssecretaris van Financiën (C-487/01)* and *Holin Groep BV c.s. v Staatssecretaris van Financiën (C-7/02)*. The second Advocate-General (there was an earlier opinion) has given an opinion that the principles of legal certainty and legitimate expectation are engaged. Accordingly, in circumstances where the taxpayer has incurred input tax with the intention of making taxable supplies (of property subject to the option to tax), but was thwarted from fulfilling that intention because of a change in legislation which made the ultimate supplies of the property exempt, there is no need for an adjustment of the deducted input tax. The Advocate-General's opinion appears to be a logical follow-through from the earlier decisions in *Belgian v Ghent Coal Terminal NV (C-37/95)* (**Case Summary 30**) and *Grundstückgemeinschaft Schloßstraße GbR v Finanzamt Paderborn (C-396/98)* (**Case Summary 34**).

6.58 It remains to be seen whether the European Court will follow the Advocate-General's opinion. However, if it does so, it may have a significant impact on certain transactions conducted in the UK.

6.59 There have been several situations where a change in the law has made input tax incurred in anticipation of making intended supplies of one description, actually used in making a different category (exempt or taxable) of supplies. These include, but are not limited to, transactions spanning changes to the disapplication of the option to tax, transactions dealing with certain financial services, provision of sports and physical education services and provision of certain outsourced services, all of which are also affected by partial exemption.

6.60 Thus a taxpayer may have deducted input tax on the basis of making intended taxable supplies, only to find that the actual supplies made were exempt, or vice versa.

6.61 The Advocate-General in the *Leusden* case appears to take the view that the input tax deduction is secure and does not require adjustment even if the supplies eventually made following the change of law are exempt. However, he has also indicated that member states, when changing the liability of transactions by legislative enactment, may introduce transitional measures if they wish.

Adjustments in relation to late payments of debt

6.62 The Sixth Directive, art 11C(1) provides that:

> 'In the case of cancellation, refusal or total or partial non-payment, or where the price is reduced after the supply takes place, the taxable amount shall be reduced accordingly under conditions which shall be determined by the member states.
>
> However, in the case of total or partial non-payment, member states may derogate from this rule.'

6.63 The relief for bad debts could result in a mismatch between VAT collected and VAT claimed as a deduction where the debtor does not pay the creditor. Accordingly, art 20(1) authorises member states to require taxable persons to make adjustments in cases where a debt remains wholly or partly unpaid or in the case of theft. The UK has therefore implemented provisions that require a debtor to repay any input tax deducted where he has not paid the debt due within a specified period.

6.64 The clawback provision is contained in VAT Regulations 1995, reg 172H, which reads:

> '172H (1) Subject to paragraph (5) below, where a person–
>
> (a) has not paid the whole or any part of the consideration for a supply by the end of the relevant period; and
>
> (b) has claimed deduction of the whole or part of the VAT on the supply as input tax ("the deduction"),
>
> he shall make an entry in his VAT account in accordance with paragraphs (2) and (3) below.

(2) The person shall make a negative entry in the VAT allowable portion of that part of his VAT account which relates to the prescribed accounting period of his in which the end of the relevant period falls.

(3) The amount of the negative entry referred to in paragraph (2) above shall be such amount as is found by multiplying the amount of the deduction by a fraction of which the numerator is the amount of the consideration for the supply which has not been paid before the end of the relevant period and the denominator is the total consideration for the supply.

(4) …'

6.65 Previously, the creditor had to inform the debtor of any claim for bad debt relief. However, since 1 January 2003, the debtor has to adjust his input tax automatically where the following conditions are fulfilled:

- he has claimed input tax on a supply;
- he has not paid the creditor for all or part of the supply; and
- a period of six months has elapsed between the time when the supply was made or, if later, the time when the payment for the supply became due.

Where a business incurs input tax but does not pay for the supply, historically no adjustment to the input tax was required unless the supplier notified the business that it was making a claim for bad debt relief. For supplies made after 31 December 2002, VATA 1994, s 26A requires all businesses to make an adjustment to input tax when the consideration remains unpaid at the end of the period of six months following:

- the date of the supply; or
- if later, the date on which the sum became payable.

6.66 The adjustment has to be made in respect of the VAT accounting period when the relevant period has elapsed by reducing the taxable person's input tax by the amount of input tax outstanding on the unpaid portion of the supply. Unlike the mirror image of this provision for bad debt relief, the regulation does not make specific provision as to how the outstanding proportion is to be determined. This is no doubt because, under normal circumstances, the allocation of payments to supplies lies with the debtor, so that arguably the debtor always knows which supply or part of a supply he is paying for.

6.67 The taxable person is allowed to reclaim the input tax that he has added back in the VAT accounting period in which he makes the payment (VAT Regulations 1995, reg 172I).

Transfer of going concerns and adjustments

6.68 Where a business is sold by way of a transfer of a going concern, input tax incurred that was originally intended to be used for a specific purpose may now be used for a different purpose by the person who purchases the business ('the successor').

6.69 However, adjustments may be required by businesses operating the standard method where the successor, or any subsequent successor uses input tax for a substantially different purpose than the one on which the original deduction was based. In that case, the provisions of the standard method override may apply (see **6.13–6.34** above) (reg 107D).

6.70 In other situations, where the standard method override or special method override does not apply, it would appear that in practice, any subsequent change of use (other than in the case of capital items) is ignored. Whether any adjustment is technically required may be a matter for debate, but following the *Royal and Sun Alliance* case (see **6.49** above) for any inputs which have been consumed in the period in which the input tax was deducted, the input tax would not be available to be reattributed.

VAT groups

6.71 Similar situations arises when a company joins or leaves a group. There are no specific provisions relating to reg 108 or 109 adjustments with respect to VAT groups. For input tax on inputs that are or are deemed to be immediately consumed, there is no need for any change of use adjustment. However, there is the theoretical position that a change of use adjustment could be required, where on leaving a VAT group, input tax deducted by the representative member but referable to the entity leaving the VAT group is used by that entity to make a different liability of supply once outside the VAT group.

6.72 In *C & E Comrs v Svenska International plc [1999] STC 406* the case involved a situation where supplies were thought by the taxpayer to have been received and consumed at a time when the recipient was outside a VAT group and were provisionally attributed to taxable supplies. On joining the VAT group the representative member made predominantly exempt supplies. The issue was therefore whether there was a reattribution of the inputs to exempt supplies. However, the case was decided on its facts in that the inputs in question were continuous supplies and under the time of supply rules had never actually been received until the company was within the VAT group. The initial attribution was therefore incorrect and the correct attribution was held to be to exempt supplies.

Chapter 7

The Capital Items Scheme

Introduction

7.1 Chapter 1 describes the circumstances in which a taxable person might be required to make an adjustment to the VAT that he had provisionally deducted. One such circumstance is the VAT incurred on 'capital items'.

The vires for the adjustment is found in the Sixth Directive, art 20(2)–20(5).

Key features of that article are:

- The article applies to capital goods. There is no definition of what constitutes capital goods. Instead, art 20.4 allows member states to determine the 'concept' of capital goods. See, however, *Verbond van Nederlandse Ondernemingen (51/76), [1977] 1 CMLR 413, [1977] ECR 113* (**Case Summary 1**) – **7.13** below.
- The adjustment period is set at five years from date of acquisition or manufacture but, in the case of immovable property, member states have a discretion to extend the adjustment period to a maximum of 20 years.
- Member states can also provide that the adjustment period must commence on first use rather than on acquisition.
- It is open to member states to allow administrative simplifications including the application of de minimis limits.
- On a disposal within the adjustment period, the Sixth Directive requires a single adjustment in respect of the whole of the remaining period.

7.2 The Sixth Directive does not contain any explicit provisions on how adjustments must be made but it should be borne in mind that the legislation is part of the whole deductions system. The basic principles of the deduction system will therefore apply in interpreting the provisions of the adjustment process. The adjustment process must therefore ensure that the VAT on cost components that are used in the making of taxable supplies and certain other supplies such as 'out-of-country supplies' is deductible and VAT that is not incurred on such cost components is not.

7.3 Since capital goods are used over a period of time, the VAT incurred should be spread over the period of their use. However, the system recognises that it would be extremely onerous to require deductions to be made over the real life of an asset such as a building, which might exceed a hundred years, and hence provides an arbitrary period of five years (or up to twenty if member states decide to require adjustments over a longer period).

7.4 It should be noted that, in respect of the UK legislation, whether or not a supply or other transaction is a capital item is relevant not only to the question of whether or not the VAT deducted on an item has to be adjusted but also determines the application of:

- the anti-avoidance provisions that disapply the option to tax land and buildings that are used for exempt purposes; and
- the anti-avoidance provisions of VAT Regulations 1995, reg 93 to construction services.

The nature of capital items

7.5 The UK legislation refers to 'capital items' rather than 'capital goods', although Notice 706/02 is titled Capital Goods Scheme. It defines capital items by reference to two main criteria:

(i) an item that is intended solely for resale is not a capital item (VAT Regulations 1995, reg 112); and

(ii) only:

- certain computers and computer equipment; and
- certain land and buildings or construction works in relation to land and buildings, can be capital items.The effect of the definition is therefore to exclude from the adjustment process a large range of items that would be regarded as capital in accounting terms, including furniture and equipment (other than computers and computer equipment that are included within the scheme), motor vehicles of any kind and other means of transport, eg aircraft and ships.

Computers

7.6 Individual computers and items of computer equipment are subject to adjustment, but only where the item costs £50,000 or more, exclusive of VAT (VAT Regulations 1995, reg 113(a)). The £50,000 limit includes delivery and installation costs. Where an item is imported, the customs duty value will be used instead and any delivery not included in the customs value and installation costs must be added. Customs and Excise Notice 706/2/02 does not provide guidance on the treatment of in-house costs (eg use of internal IT staff to install a computer), but since they will not bear any VAT it is submitted that such costs are not taken into account in determining whether a computer is a capital item.

7.7 Also excluded is any software. It is important to note that it is the value of each item that is taken into account and not the total value of the invoice. Thus, if a taxpayer received an invoice for 60 personal computers at a cost of £900 each exclusive of VAT, the fact that the invoice price totalled more than £50,000 would not bring the equipment into the capital items scheme. This would be the case even where the computers are bought with a server and other equipment and are linked together as part of a single network.

7.8 It is common for computer suppliers to sell systems as a package. Because all items in the package are standard rated, it might normally be unimportant to decide whether, applying the principles in *Card Protection Plan Ltd v C & E Comrs (C-349/96)[2001] STC 174*, there is a single supply or several supplies but it may be necessary to do so if the package costs more than £50,000. In *Card Protection Plan*, the Court held that the existence of a single consideration did not necessarily mean that there is a single supply. See also *Talacre Beach Caravan Sales Ltd [2004] EWHC 165 (Ch), [2004] STC* for an example of different elements of a single supply where legislation requires it.

Example 1 – Packaged goods

Capital plc purchases a computer storage unit costing £52,000 plus VAT. In the course of negotiations, the supplier agreed to provide maintenance of the system worth £1,500 and networking equipment necessary to connect the storage to the existing system worth £750. Is the equipment within the capital items scheme?

Clearly, if the maintenance and networking equipment can be regarded as separate supplies from the storage unit, the cost of the unit will be £49,750 and will fall outside the scheme. The normal rules will have to be applied to decide whether or not there are separate supplies. Thus, assuming that the unit normally costs £52,000 and the supplier offered free maintenance and other equipment as an inducement, it might be argued that the unit costs £52,000 and the other items nothing.

If no allocation is made and the parties simply agree to a package, the normal principles will need to be applied to determine whether there is more than one supply or just a single supply. The networking equipment can be argued to be part of the wider system and not something required for the better use and enjoyment of the storage unit. Similarly, if the maintenance would normally be purchased separately, it may well be that what Capital plc has done is buy three pieces of equipment for £52,000 and the difference is a discount that reduces each item rateably, in which case the storage unit will not be a capital item (52,000/54,750 × £52,000 = £49,388).

Land and buildings

7.9 The specific items of land and buildings that are subject to the capital items scheme are as follows.

Table 1 – Items within the capital items scheme

Nature of interest in land	Details and legislation
Grants of interests in land	
1. The supply received comprising: • land; • a building or part of a building; • a civil engineering work or part of one.	(i) The value of the interest supplied to the owner (of the capital item) is £250,000 or more. (ii) The supply must be a taxable supply but not a zero-rated supply. (iii) The value of any rents payable by the recipient will be excluded provided that they are not invoiced more than twelve months in advance. (iv) Associated costs such as estate agent's costs are excluded. In effect, this means that it is largely the purchase of a freehold or equivalent interest or the premium in respect of a leasehold interest in land that will fall within the scheme. Note however that whilst properties occupied for rent only do not normally fall within this definition, if a prepayment of VATable rents exceeding 12 months of rentals is made, then this prepayment can create a capital item if it exceeds £250,000. (VAT Regulations 1995, reg 113(b))
Self-supply of building that qualified for zero-rating on change of use	
2. The self-supply of a building that was previously used either for a relevant residential purpose or a relevant charitable purpose.	The value of the self-supply must be £250,000 or more. The value of the self-supply is reduced by the number of years in the ten-year period within which adjustments can arise of use for a relevant residential purpose or relevant charitable purpose prior to the self-supply (see VATA 1994, Sch 10, para 1(4)–(6)). Therefore, a building that cost more than £250,000 may escape the application of the capital items scheme if there has been sufficient prior use to reduce the value of the self-supply below £250,000. Note that if such a building is leased and leased back prior to revised use, then a different form of clawback of original zero rating arises which is not caught by the capital items scheme (see VATA 1994, Sch 10, para 1(2)–(3)). (VAT Regulations 1995, reg 113(c))

Developer's self-supply

3. A building that was treated as supplied to a developer under the old 'Developer's self-supply rules'. These provisions ceased to have effect on 1 March 1997 although there will be items that fell within its provisions that are currently capital items by virtue of its provisions.	The value of the owner's interest in, right over, or licence to occupy the building must have been £250,000 or more. The value was determined in accordance with the provisions of VATA 1994, Sch 10, para 6(2). Broadly speaking the value was the aggregate of the land interest plus building costs. Unlike other provisions in relation to capital goods, the value of land was included even where it was not originally supplied as a taxable supply. (VAT Regulations 1995, reg 113(d))

Construction of a building

4. A building (other than one that falls within the self-supply provisions dealt with in item 2 above or is capable of falling within those provisions). In effect, this means any building other than one for a relevant charitable or residential purpose.	The aggregate value of the following must be £250,000 or above: (i) Any taxable supplies of the land on which the building is constructed, eg the supply of the freehold or a supply of a leasehold interest where the person granting such interest has exercised the option to tax. (ii) Any taxable (but not zero-rated) supplies of goods and services that are made or are to be made to the owner in connection with the construction of the building. (VAT Regulations 1995, reg 113(e))

Alterations, extensions and annexes

5. A building, which the owner alters, or an extension or annex, which the owner constructs.	(i) The alteration, extension or annex must create additional floor area of not less than 10 per cent of the original building. (ii) The value of taxable (but not zero-rated) supplies of goods and services made to or to be made to the owner must be £250,000 or more. (VAT Regulations 1995, reg 113(f))

Civil engineering works

6. A civil engineering work constructed by the owner (see **7.11** below in connection with the date this provision came into effect)	The aggregate value of the following must be £250,000 or above: (i) Any taxable supplies of the land on which the works are constructed, eg the supply of the freehold or a supply of a leasehold interest where the person granting such interest has exercised the option to tax. (ii) Any taxable (but not zero-rated) supplies of goods and services that are made or are to be made to the owner in connection with the construction of the building. (VAT Regulations 1995, reg 113(g))

Refurbishments

7. A building that the owner has refurbished.	The value of capital expenditure on taxable (but not zero-rated) supplies of services and goods affixed to the building in connection with the refurbishment must be £250,000 or above. (VAT Regulations 1995, reg 113(h))

Dates from when effective

7.10 The capital items scheme came into effect on 1 April 1990. In general, in determining whether or not the value of an item is £250,000 or more, only costs incurred after that date must be taken into account. It should be noted that an item can fall within the capital items scheme if some costs were incurred prior to 1 April 1990 and some after.

7.11 Civil engineering works and refurbishments were only brought within the capital items scheme with effect from 3 July 1997. Accordingly, in relation to those items set out in items 6 and 7 of the Table 1 above, only supplies received after that date must be taken into account when determining whether a refurbishment is a capital item. However, as with other capital items the fact that some costs are not taken into account in determining whether there is a capital item does not prevent the item from being a capital item if sufficient costs were incurred after that date.

Meaning of capital expenditure

7.12 The legislation in respect of refurbishments requires only 'capital expenditure' to be taken into account in determining whether or not a refurbishment is a capital item. There is no definition of what comprises capital expenditure. The guidance in Customs and Excise Notice 706/2/02, para 4.10 is that capital expenditure comprises those works that are of lasting benefit to a taxpayer's business or are likely to increase the value of the business assets. It also notes that if an asset is treated as capital expenditure for accounting purposes, the expenditure will be capital expenditure.

7.13 The European Court of Justice considered the question of what are capital goods in the case of *Verbond van Nederlandse Ondernemingen v Inspecteur der Invoerrechten en Accijnzen (51/76)* (**Case Summary 1**). The Court held that capital goods are those goods that are used for the purposes of a business and are distinguishable by their durable nature and their value. The Court also concluded that the acquisition costs of capital goods are written off over several years. The case was argued prior to the introduction of the Sixth Directive but is nevertheless relevant to the interpretation of art 20.

7.14 In general, therefore, the accounting treatment of expenditure is likely to have a significant effect in determining whether an asset is a capital item or not. However, the accounting treatment is not the sole determinant and all factors need to be considered in reaching a conclusion whether an item must be regarded as a capital item. Thus, it is possible that a large company might have an accounting policy whereby, say, refurbishments having a value of more than £250,000 are regarded as immaterial and are not capitalised. One issue that it is understood was raised with Customs and Excise when the capital items scheme was extended to refurbishments in 1997 was whether or not a refurbishment can validly be brought within the capital items scheme. It should be borne in mind that refurbishments will frequently comprise one or more supplies of services whereas the Sixth Directive, art 20(2) refers to 'capital goods'. The issue has not yet been raised before a VAT and Duties Tribunal. It would appear that the UK legislation relies on the fact that the Sixth Directive, art 20(4) allows member states to determine the concept of capital goods coupled with the fact that the work is undoubtedly done to what would comprise capital items. Further, if the refurbishments both have a durable nature and are capitalised in the accounts of a business, there are undoubtedly reasons why there should be some means for adjustment. As noted above, the European Court of Justice defined 'capital goods' as 'goods used for the purposes of some business activity and distinguishable by their durable nature and their value and such that the acquisition costs are not normally treated as current expenditure but written off over several years'.

7.15 It is therefore at least arguable that the definition refers to goods only. However, since no questions were asked about services, it cannot be conclusively concluded that the reference to goods in the Sixth Directive, art 20(2) excludes any reference to services applied to the production, maintenance or improvement of goods. It may be that, like so many transactions in VAT, the answer could depend on the exact nature of the refurbishment.

7.16 Where a refurbishment is treated as a revenue expense, it may not be a capital item. However, it may nevertheless be necessary for a taxpayer, who uses the standard method to determine his residual input tax recovery, to use a use-based method of determining his VAT recovery rather than the standard method where the benefit of the refurbishment is likely to extend over a period longer than the current VAT accounting period.

Meaning of 'goods affixed'

7.17 There is no definition of what comprises 'goods affixed' for the purposes of determining whether or not a refurbishment is a capital item. And accordingly the test of what 'goods affixed' means is likely to be whatever the man in the street would understand by the term. There does not appear to be any requirement that 'goods affixed' should be treated as part of any land under the relevant UK land law.

Apart from normal goods that are incorporated in buildings, including lifts, flooring and windows, the term is likely to include such items as:

- built-in cupboards and other permanently attached furniture;
- air conditioning and other permanently installed equipment; and
- lighting and electrical equipment.

In all cases, the common sense test of what a purchaser would expect to remain in a building is likely to arrive at a sensible application of the term.

7.18 Equipment, which by its nature is easily movable or which is secured to a building, but is not intended to be part of it, should not be regarded as 'goods affixed' to a building (see Notice 706/2/02, para 4.11). However, see *Rudolf Maierhofer v Finanzamt Augsburg-Land (C-315/00)*, in which the CJEC concluded that:

> '1. The letting of a building constructed from prefabricated components fixed to or in the ground in such a way that they cannot be easily dismantled or easily moved constitutes a letting of immovable property for the purposes of Article 13B(b) of Sixth Council Directive … even if the building is to be removed at the end of the lease and re-used on another site.'

7.19 For Customs and Excise's view on what are 'goods affixed', see Customs and Excise Notice 706/2/02, para 4.11.

Value of capital items comprising land, buildings and construction or civil engineering works

7.20 Since values are important in determining both whether an item is a capital item and also what input tax has to be adjusted, it is necessary to consider how the value of a capital item is determined. Customs and Excise's views are set out in Customs and Excise Notice 706/2/02, paras 4.1–4.15.

7.21 It will be seen from **7.61** below, that an item can become a capital item before it is physically completed. This can mean that the question of whether or not an item is a capital item may have to be determined before its full value is known. Customs and Excise Notice 706/2/02, para 4.2 advises taxpayers that they may need to estimate the value of an item in order to determine whether or not it is within the scheme. They give as examples construction projects and refurbishments where the costs on which input tax is incurred over time or contracts where there are retention clauses.

Example 2 – Estimation of the value of a capital item

A business contracts with a building firm to refurbish its premises. The refurbishment will add value to the building and the cost of the refurbishment will be capitalised and not written off against profit and loss account. The contract price is set at £180,000 plus the cost of materials marked up by 10 per cent plus VAT.

Whether the item is a capital item depends on whether or not the charge for materials (together with the uplift) will exceed £70,000. According to Customs and Excise Notice 706/2/02 the business therefore needs to estimate the cost of materials, add 10 per cent and, if this is more than £70,000, treat the costs incurred as a capital item.

7.22 Customs and Excise note that where it is estimated that the cost of an item will exceed £250,000 and it is therefore treated as a capital item, the fact that costs subsequently do not exceed the limit does not take the item out of the capital items scheme. Thus if in Example 2 above, the initial estimate of the cost of the materials was £64,000, the estimate of the cost of the refurbishment would be £250,400 (£64,000 + 10% of £64,000 + £180,000) and the item would have been treated as a capital item. If the material costs ultimately total £60,000, the final cost would be £246,000 but it would not take the item out of the scheme. The need to estimate is likely to be rare since there will be very few projects that are so borderline as to make this an issue. However it may be possible to challenge Customs and Excise in their view that a capital item can exist in circumstances where actual supplies made do not exceed £250,000.

7.23 A greater problem may lie in determining whether a series of works should be regarded as a single work or not. This may be relevant for one or more of three reasons:

- if an item is split so that it is regarded as comprising several individual 'items', it is possible that some or all such items will not exceed the limit and so fall outside the definition of being a capital item;
- even where each item is within the scheme, the date when the first interval commences for each item may be different and so the initial deduction and subsequent deductions in respect of each item may differ, leading to a different overall recovery than had all been regarded as one item;
- the question of what is a capital item and how it is used may affect the decision as to whether it falls within the anti-avoidance legislation referred to at **7.4** above.

7.24 The table below provides a summary of the costs that should be included in the value of an item for the purposes of determining, first, whether or not there is a capital item and, second, the amount of VAT that needs to be adjusted.

Table 2 – Value of capital items (other than computers)

Nature of item	What is included in its value
Grants of interests in land	
1. The supply received comprising of: • land; • a building or part of a building; • a civil engineering work or part of one.	The standard-rated value of the supply excluding associated costs such as legal or estate agency fees. From 3 July 1997, rent that is either prepaid or pre-invoiced for a period in excess of twelve months in advance must also be included. (Customs and Excise Notice 706/2/02, para 4.3)

Self-supply of building that qualified for zero-rating on change of use

2. The self-supply of a building that was previously used either for a relevant residential purpose or a relevant charitable purpose.	The value of the self-supply. This will be the value of the supplies received that were zero-rated because the building was to be used for a relevant purpose but is now to be used otherwise than for a relevant purpose. The value so obtained is reduced on a sliding scale based on the period of use for a relevant purpose. (Customs and Excise Notice 706/2/02, para 4.6)

Developer's self-supply

3. (Ceased to have effect in 1997).	The value of the self-supply.

Construction of a building

4. A building (other than one that falls within the self-supply provisions dealt with in item 2 above or is capable of falling within those provisions). In effect, this means any building other than one for a relevant charitable or residential purpose.	Aggregate of the VAT exclusive costs of the following taxable but not zero-rated supplies received (or to be received in the case of construction costs): ● any interest in the land (but not rents); ● construction costs (goods used in construction and services); ● other costs incurred in making the building ready for occupation, eg professional costs, demolition and site clearance, security, equipment hire, etc. (Customs and Excise Notice 706/2/02, para 4.4)

Alterations, extensions and annexes

5. A building, which the owner alters, or an extension or annex, which the owner constructs.	As for 4 above but excluding the land, which if recently purchased is likely to be a capital item already under 1 above. (Customs and Excise Notice 706/2/02, para 4.7)

Civil engineering works

6. A civil engineering work constructed by the owner (see **7.11** above in connection with the date this provision came into effect).	The standard-rated value of the supply excluding associated costs such as legal or estate agency fees. (Customs and Excise Notice 706/2/02, para 4.8)

Refurbishments	
7. A building that the owner has refurbished.	Broadly speaking the same as for the construction of a building but excluding the land, which is purchased as a taxable supply and will already be a capital item. (Customs and Excise Notice 706/2/02, para 4.9)

7.25 Customs and Excise comment (Customs and Excise Notice 706/2/02, para 4.5) that where a taxpayer purchases a piece of land and constructs a building on it, there is only one capital item and not two. While this will frequently be the case, it should be borne in mind that it is possible for land and existing buildings to be one capital item (if purchased and used as a taxable supply) and any subsequent alteration, extension, annex or refurbishment to be a further capital item. Similarly, it is possible for the purchase to be a capital item and any subsequent alteration, extension, annex or refurbishment not to be a capital item.

The adjustment process

General principles

7.26 The scheme requires that the VAT initially deducted on capital items be adjusted to reflect any change in use of the item in subsequent intervals.

7.27 The adjustment process can be expressed in the following steps:

- in the first interval, determine the VAT deductible in accordance with the normal rules (for example using the applicable partial exemption method if relevant);
- in subsequent intervals, calculate the VAT deductible for that interval on the basis of the formula:

$$\frac{\text{VAT on capital item} \times \text{Recoverable percentage for the interval concerned}}{\text{Number of intervals in adjustment period}}$$

  The recoverable percentage will normally be that used in calculating the 'longer period adjustment' under VAT Regulations 1995, reg 107. In other words it will normally be the partial exemption calculation for the tax year. However it should be noted that Customs and Excise have the power to allow or direct a method for calculating the recoverable percentage that differs from the partial exemption method;
- calculate the proportion of initial VAT attributable to the adjustment interval as follows:

$$\frac{\text{Initial VAT deducted in first interval}}{\text{Number of intervals in adjustment period}}$$

- if the relevant proportion of the original deduction exceeds the VAT attributable to the adjustment period, the difference will increase the VAT payable in the second VAT accounting period following the end of the interval concerned (ie the period following the longer period adjustment to be made under VAT Regulations 1995, reg 107). If the VAT deductible in the current period exceeds the relevant proportion of the VAT deducted in the initial period, the taxpayer can deduct the additional input tax in that period.

The adjustment period and adjustment intervals

7.28 The adjustment process takes place over a period called the 'adjustment period'. The adjustment period comprises five intervals in respect of computers and computer equipment and up to ten in respect of land, buildings and civil engineering works.

7.29 The adjustment period generally runs from one of the following events:

- the supply, acquisition or importation of a capital item;
- the date of the self-supply of the item; or
- the date of first use.

7.30 Adjustment intervals usually end at the end of successive VAT accounting years but there are exceptions. This section outlines the rules determining when the adjustment period begins and when each interval commences and ends.

Computers and computer equipment

7.31 The first interval in relation to computers or computer equipment commences on the date that a computer is first:

- supplied to the taxpayer;
- acquired by the taxpayer from a supplier in another EU member state; or
- imported into the UK by the taxpayer.

(VAT Regulations 1995, reg 114(4)(a).)

7.32 In each case, the date only applies where the computer or computer equipment is a capital item as defined (see **7.6** et seq above).

7.33 A computer or computer equipment could also have been acquired originally otherwise than as a capital item, eg as trading stock. Alternatively, it could have been manufactured by the taxpayer. In either case, it would not fall within the rules outlined at **7.31** above. In such cases, the first interval commences on the date of first application of the item in question to use as a capital item.

(VAT Regulations 1995, reg 114(4)(b).)

7.34 The first interval effectively ends on the last day of the tax year in which the first interval began. (Note: the legislation dealing with the date when the first interval ends actually refers to the 'day before the commencement of the tax year following that day' [the day of commencement]).

7.35 For the treatment of a computer that is transferred as a part of a going concern prior to the end of the first interval, see **7.111** et seq below.

7.36 For the treatment of a computer that is used as a capital item of a corporate body that either enters or leaves a VAT group during the first interval, see **7.116** below.

Land, buildings and civil engineering works

7.37 Most land, buildings and civil engineering works will become capital items either because:

- the taxpayer acquires them by way of a supply from another UK taxable person; or
- the taxpayer is involved in the construction, extension, alteration or refurbishment of the building, an annex or a civil engineering work.

7.38 However, as with computers, it is also possible that a building, annex or civil engineering work will become a capital item because there is a change in the use of an item, in particular:

- where an item which may have been trading stock is applied to use as a capital item; and
- where a building that was acquired for a relevant residential or relevant charitable purpose is applied to use in the course or furtherance of a business.

7.39 Where land, a building or civil engineering work is acquired by way of a taxable supply other than a zero-rated supply, the first interval commences on the date of the relevant supply.

(VAT Regulations 1995, reg 114(4)(a).)

7.40 The first interval of a building, annex or civil engineering work that is a capital item because it is constructed, altered, extended or refurbished by the taxpayer commences on the day that the building, annex, or civil engineering work is first used by the taxpayer.

(VAT Regulations 1995, reg 114(4)(e).)

7.41 Where a building, annex or civil engineering work that was held otherwise than as a capital item is applied to use as a capital item, the first interval commences on the date of first use.

(VAT Regulations 1995, reg 114(4)(b).)

7.42 The VAT and Duties Tribunal considered the question of what constitutes use in *East Kent Medical Services Ltd (1999) VAT decision 16095*. It concluded that 'use' in the context of the capital items scheme VAT Regulations 1995, reg 114(4)(e) did not refer solely to physical use. It could, and in that case did, refer to other use, in particular economic use, being the grant of an underlease by the appellant in a building. The issue has not been considered by the High Court.

The difficulty that arises in relation to this interpretation of what comprises 'use' can be seen by examining an example.

Example 3 – Commencement of adjustment period based on use

A taxpayer acquires land on 1 January 2003 for use in his business. At that date, some construction of a building has commenced. The taxpayer agrees to take assignment of the construction contract. The building was not a capital item in the vendor's hands as it was held for resale but becomes a capital item on purchase. The taxpayer's current business is 60 per cent taxable. Part of the new building will be let with the rest being used for the same business.

The taxpayer grants a lease to a third party on the same day as the land is acquired but occupation will only take place when the building is complete and rents will only be due from that date.

The building is completed on 31 December 2004 and occupation takes place on 1 January 2005 with rents commencing from the same date. The taxpayer's tax year commences and ends by agreement with Customs and Excise on 31 December of each year.

In the year commencing 1 January 2005, the taxpayer's actual recovery rate drops to 50 per cent.

Under the *East Kent* reasoning as to what constitutes use, it appears that the first adjustment period commences on 1 January 2003 because at that date there was part of a building and the taxpayer granted a lease over part of it. The first period ends on 31 December 2003 by which time no actual use has taken place since no supplies have been made and no physical occupation has taken place or indeed been possible. The VAT recoverable on any building costs in the first interval will be at 60 per cent based on intended supplies being both exempt and taxable, and 60 per cent being the partial exemption recovery rate for the period.

The second adjustment period (in the absence of any other intervening event) is from 1 January 2004 to 31 December 2004. Again, there has been no actual use (in terms of actual supplies) nor has there been any physical use. The VAT recovery on any costs in the second interval is also 60 per cent.

In the third interval (when actual use takes place), recovery drops to 50 per cent and an adjustment of 10 per cent or $\frac{1}{10}$ of the VAT on the capital item is made subsequently for that interval.

7.43 In the above example a mismatch arises. The effect of the *East Kent* interpretation of what is use is to match costs incurred in periods one to ten with revenue earned in periods one to ten despite the fact that the costs actually form part of the cost components of revenues arising in periods three to twelve. In a more extreme example, a lease could be granted ten years before rents flow or occupation commences, such that all intervals have expired before revenues derived from the building commence!

7.44 The Sixth Directive, art 20(2) does not require a use-based method of making adjustments – member states have an option to do so. The decision in *East Kent* raises a number of issues as to how the initial deduction must be calculated in certain cases. In the majority of cases, a building is likely to be acquired or constructed for a particular use and, apart from relatively small changes in the levels of use for different purposes, there may be no reason to believe that future use will be any different in principle to current use. However, the question arises as to what happens when use in the first and subsequent intervals is expected to vary?

7.45 It is possible to take the view that the initial recovery is still based on the level of use in the first interval and adjustments are then made in subsequent intervals to reflect changes. On the other hand, it is also possible to argue that the initial deduction should reflect expected use over the whole period of use (in accordance with the principles in *C & E v Briararch Ltd [1992] STC 732* (**Case Summary 13**). However, that case was decided in 1992 on facts that arose in 1987/88, ie prior to the introduction of the Capital Items Scheme. In 1996, the High Court appeared to reject the application of the *Briararch* principle on the basis that the Capital Items Scheme provided a statutory method of adjustment based on a ten-year adjustment period (see *C & E Comrs v R & R Pension Fund Trustees [1996] STC 889*). However, it is possible to argue that *R & R* dealt only with adjustments and not with the initial deduction.

7.46 The difference in treatment can be illustrated as follows.

Example 4 – Determining deduction in first interval

A business acquires a ten year taxable lease of a building for use for its taxable business. However, it also plans to move two divisions that use 50 per cent of the premises in five years time. The space occupied by those divisions will be let and because they will be let to financial services institutions, exemption will not be waived. It is possible to argue that either of two possible methods apply to the first interval with consequent changes to the following periods, ie:

	Applying Briararch	*Alternative*
First year deduction	75%	100%
Second to fifth years	No adjustment	No adjustment
Sixth to tenth years	No adjustment	Repay 5% pa

7.47 Under the *Briararch* principle, account has already been taken of the future use and so no adjustment is necessary unless the actual exempt use in years six to ten turns out to be different to 50 per cent. Under the alternative method, the actual use in the first interval is always used and adjustments are made later.

7.48 The *Briararch* approach adopted by Customs and Excise appears to rely on the wording of the UK legislation governing the right to deduct. This allows a deduction for input tax that is referable to 'supplies made or to be made by the taxable person in the course or furtherance of his business' (see VATA 1994, s 26(2)) and 'goods or services as are used or to be used by him exclusively in making taxable supplies' (see VAT Regulations 1995, reg 101(2)(b)).

7.49 The Sixth Directive uses slightly different wording and allows a deduction in respect of goods and services used for the purposes of the taxpayer's taxable transactions.

7.50 Either view can result in anomalies in different circumstances. Thus, the decision in *Rompelman and Rompelman Van Deelen v Minister van Financiën (C-268/83) [1985] 3 CMLR 202* (**Case Summary 4**), the European Court of Justice makes it clear that the principle of neutrality requires that a business that makes taxable supplies should be wholly relieved from the burden of input tax (including the financing of it). If the deduction system anticipates the subsequent making of exempt supplies, it is arguable that the principle of neutrality outlined in that case is not achieved.

7.51 A further inconsistency arises because the application of the *Briararch* principle to capital items would result in a difference in treatment between a taxable person that makes taxable supplies and then subsequently changes his intentions and makes exempt supplies and the taxable person who always intends to make taxable supplies followed by exempt supplies.

7.52 It should also be borne in mind that if future changes in use are taken into account in the initial interval, it is inevitable (because the initial use has been based on an average covering five or ten years) that the taxable person must apply to Customs and Excise to depart from the normal scheme of adjustments under reg 116. If he does not, the mathematical effect of using the normal method of calculating the adjustment will mean that the increased/reduced use is taken into account at the beginning and readjusted during the period. It is inherently contrary to the system of self-assessment that a taxable person should have to seek permission to adopt a method other than that laid down in the legislation to determine the VAT deductible on the cost components of his supplies.

7.53 However, the alternative view is also not free of problems. Clearly, if first use determines the initial deduction, there is greater scope for avoidance.

7.54 For the taxable person who wishes to avoid disputes, it would appear that it will be necessary to adopt the *Briararch* approach and determine both current and future use to determine his initial deduction. This may not be all bad news for taxable persons. Thus, a taxpayer who makes exempt and taxable supplies but intends to increase the extent of his taxable supplies will benefit from the principle. The problem that may well arise will be convincing Customs and Excise:

- where there is an initially high deduction followed by a clawback, that the subsequent change could not have been anticipated when the initial deduction was calculated; or
- where there is initially a low rate of deduction, that a higher deduction should be made in the first period because of the intention to increase taxable supplies in the future.

For most businesses, there should be no problems. However, businesses undergoing rapid change may well encounter difficulties.

The initial deduction

7.55 The Sixth Directive, art 17(1) provides that the right to deduct VAT arises when it is incurred. Accordingly, the initial deduction of VAT incurred on capital items will be made in the accounting period in which the VAT is incurred in the same way as any other VAT that is deductible.

7.56 It will also be the case that the amount of VAT that is deductible will be determined according to the normal rules, ie VAT will be deductible to the extent that it is used or to be used to make either taxable supplies or any other supply in respect of which a deduction is allowed. This will mean that any VAT that is input tax will be:

- deductible in full if the supply or supplies on which the VAT is incurred is used or to be used solely to make taxable supplies and other supplies in respect of which a deduction is permitted;
- subject to the normal rules dealing with residual input tax where it is only partly so used.

7.57 Where a business incurs VAT on a capital item and uses the standard method (VAT Regulations 1995, reg 102(d)) to determine the proportion of input tax to be deducted, the standard method override in VAT Regulations 1995, reg 107A may need to be used to adjust any initial deduction made.

7.58 It is important to understand how the partial exemption override applies to capital items in the initial period. In particular, it must be noted that the partial exemption override is not intended to make adjustments to the deduction of input tax in one year (the year when it is incurred) just because the use of the capital item will change over the period of use. The override adjusts initial VAT recovery only. Customs and Excise have stated that 'use' for the purpose of the override is only that use which could be anticipated in the tax year when input tax is initially incurred.

7.59 The special method override (see **6.35 et seq above**) applies similar principles to the standard method override to an attribution carried out using a special method. It follows that, as with the standard method override, if an adjustment had to be made under the special method override, this may affect the initial deduction under the capital items scheme.

7.60 In VAT Information Sheet 4/02 (which deals with the partial exemption override), Customs and Excise set out a number of examples as to how the legislation applies. Appendix 4 of Information Sheet 4/02 provides an example of how Customs and Excise consider the override should be applied to the purchase of a capital item. It is worth analysing the example (which is reproduced below) in more detail.

Example 5 – Operation of the partial exemption override

A fully taxable business acquires a building consisting of five equally sized floors on 1 December, one month before the end of its tax year, for £1 million plus VAT of £175,000. This is the first exempt input tax that it has ever incurred. It occupies the top floor for its own business with the intention of making an exempt letting of the remaining four floors. It does not find tenants until January and February in the next tax year.

The Information Sheet notes that the override applies because the standard method (which would give a 100 per cent deduction in the period when the VAT is incurred) does not provide a fair and reasonable method of determining the deductible VAT. The reason for this is because at the time the VAT is incurred, the intention is to use 80 per cent of the building to make exempt supplies. It is important to note that it is the intention to make exempt supplies with the remaining 80 per cent of the building that determines the need to make an override adjustment. The adjustment would have had to be made even if a tenant had only been found, say, in July, at a time when the actual intention would not have been fulfilled.

7.61 The rules determining when the adjustment period in relation to a capital item commences are such that it is possible to incur input tax on a capital item before the period actually starts. It is also possible (under the principles applied in *East Kent Medical Services* as to what comprises use (see Example 3 above) for an item to become a capital item before that item is physically used.

7.62 Customs and Excise's guidance on the partial exemption override, as set out in VAT Information Sheet 4/02, does not deal with such situations. It is conceivable that a business can incur VAT on a building, grant a lease (so that the building becomes a capital item) and yet have no means to measure that use because no income has accrued in respect of the building.

7.63 No problem arises in relation to a building that is wholly used (or it is intended that it will be so used) either for taxable purposes or exempt purposes. However, it would be possible for a taxpayer to start construction of a building to be used both for own use and for subletting and therefore have a clear indication that the input tax will be residual without knowing how to measure that use because actual physical use has not occurred. It could reasonably be expected in such circumstances that the override would not apply, and the standard method alone applies, unless that would not recognise exempt supplies in the interval concerned and would result in full VAT recovery.

7.64 The following example illustrates the situation where the override does not apply, but adjustment is made through the capital goods scheme.

Example 6 – Operation of capital items scheme

Computers Limited purchases a mainframe computer on 1 April 1999 for £100,000 plus VAT of £17,500. Its VAT accounting year ends on 31 March. In the year to 31 March 2000, its recoverable percentage is 80 per cent, and this reflects the computer's actual use. In the year to 31 March 2001, the recoverable percentage is only 60 per cent.

The initial deduction will be £14,000 (ie 80% × £17,500). The only further adjustments will fall due under the capital goods scheme in later intervals.

7.65 The rules as to when the adjustment period commences however can result in the situation where the initial deduction of VAT is determined prior to the start of the adjustment period.

Example 7 – Input tax incurred before commencement of adjustment period

Capital plc commences construction of a building on 1 April 2001. Construction continues until 31 March 2003. On 1 April 2003, Capital plc occupies the building. It incurs VAT on the construction of the building of £875,000 in the year to 31 March 2002 and £1,750,000 in the year to 31 March 2003.

The construction of a building is a capital item under VAT Regulations 1995, reg 113(d). The date the first interval commences is therefore determined by the provisions of VAT Regulations 1995, reg 114(4)(d). This is 1 April 2003. However, the VAT in respect of the capital item is incurred in the two years immediately prior to commencement of the first interval.

The normal deduction rules apply to capital items. It follows that Capital plc is entitled to deduct any VAT it incurs in the VAT accounting periods in which the VAT is incurred provided that the item is used or to be used for the purposes of making taxable supplies or any other supplies in respect of which a deduction is allowed. In determining what VAT is deductible, Capital plc must apply whatever method it normally uses to calculate what VAT is deductible.

7.66 If the item is used solely or is to be used to make supplies in respect of which a deduction is allowed, the whole of the VAT will be deductible. However, if the item is used or to be used to make both taxable and other supplies (ie it is residual input tax), the VAT to be deducted will be determined in accordance with the standard method (VAT Regulations 1995, reg 101(2)(d)) unless the taxpayer has been authorised or directed to use a special method by Customs and Excise (VAT Regulations 1995, reg 102). (See **5.85 et seq** above.)

7.67 As noted in **7.45–7.54** above, in determining use in the initial period, use both in that period and future periods may have to be taken into account. If the extent of use is not known at the time, it is intended use that must be taken into account. However, possible alternative arguments arise on the basis of the decision in *C & E Comrs v R & R Pension Fund Trustees.*

Subsequent intervals

7.68 In the second and subsequent intervals, the owner of a capital item must compare the input tax recovery he has achieved in the subsequent interval concerned with the input tax recovery he originally claimed. He must then adjust either one fifth of the input tax originally claimed, in the case of computers or land where the owner's interest ran for less than ten years at the date the adjustment period commenced, or one tenth, in the case of all other land.

Example 8 – Subsequent interval adjustment

The facts are as in Example 7 above.

The VAT incurred was £17,500 and the recovery in the first interval was 80 per cent. This gave VAT recovered of £14,000.

In the second interval, use is 60 per cent. The adjustment can be calculated in one of two methods, ie:

One fifth of original VAT deducted = 0.2 × 14,000	2,800
Actual VAT deductible = 0.2 × 17,500 × 60%	2,100
Adjustment (Pay to Customs and Excise)	700
Alternatively: (80% – 60%) × 0.2 × 17,500	700

Input tax incurred on capital items over more than one period – eg phased developments

7.69 More complex issues arise where the input tax on a capital item is incurred over more than one period. Three situations can be envisaged:

- the input tax is incurred in more than one period all of which precede the date on which the first interval commences;
- the input tax is incurred in one or more periods, one or more of which precedes the date on which the first interval commences and one or more of which follow that time; or
- the input tax is incurred after the date on which an item becomes a capital item, eg because the only supplies are continuous supplies and all of these take place after the item is first used.

7.70 Customs and Excise's Notice 706/2/02 suggests two methods of dealing with capital items. The first contemplates a rolling adjustment in which amounts incurred in different years are aggregated, and accumulated average recoveries are compared with actual use in any one year to determine what adjustment should be made. They refer to this as combined adjustments. The second method is to treat expenditure in each year as if it were a separate capital item. They refer to this as parallel adjustments. It should be noted that the two methods can give very different results. Further, in the combined method, the results can differ dependent on when the expenditure is incurred.

7.71 Examples 8, 9 and 10 below show how three different results can occur simply because the expenditure is incurred in different years. (The examples assume that the stage payments in a construction project differ, but in each case a lease is granted on 1 April 1999 so that the adjustment period and first interval commence on 1 April 1999.)

Example 9 – All input tax incurred before grant of the lease

Period ending	Interval	Input tax incurred	PE %	Input tax claimed
31–03-1998		60,000	80%	48,000

Period ending	Interval	Input tax incurred	PE %	Input tax claimed
31–03-1999		140,000	90%	126,000
31–03-2000	1		75%	
31–03-2001	2		75%	–2,400
31–03-2002	3		75%	–2,400
31–03-2003	4		75%	–2,400
31–03-2004	5		75%	–2,400
31–03-2005	6		85%	–400
31–03-2006	7		85%	–400
31–03-2007	8		85%	–400
31–03-2008	9		85%	–400
31–03-2009	10		85%	–400
				162,400

Example 10 – Input tax incurred both before and after the grant of the lease

Period ending	Interval	Input tax incurred	PE %	Input tax claimed
31–03-1998				
31–03-1999		60,000	90%	54,000
31–03-2000	1	140,000	75%	105,000
31–03-2001	2		80%	100
31–03-2002	3		75%	–900
31–03-2003	4		75%	–900
31–03-2004	5		75%	900
31–03-2005	6		85%	1,100
31–03-2006	7		85%	1,100
31–03-2007	8		85%	1,100
31–03-2008	9		85%	1,100
31–03-2009	10		85%	1,100
				161,900

Example 11 – Input tax incurred after the grant of the lease

Period ending	Interval	Input tax incurred	PE %	Input tax claimed
31–03-2000	1	60,000	75%	45,000
31–03-2001		140,000	75%	105,000

Period ending	Interval	Input tax incurred	PE %	Input tax claimed
31–03-2001	2		80%	1,000
31–03-2002	3		75%	0
31–03-2003	4		75%	0
31–03-2004	5		75%	0
31–03-2005	6		85%	2,000
31–03-2006	7		85%	2,000
31–03-2007	8		85%	2,000
31–03-2008	9		85%	2,000
31–03-2009	10		85%	2,000
				161,000

7.72 It will be observed that although economically the lease commences at the same time in each of the examples above, because the initial deduction is based on the recovery percentage in the period when the input tax was incurred, the initial deduction is different in each case and the adjustments in subsequent periods consequently also differ.

7.73 Of course, no difference would arise between the two methods if the taxable person knew in advance what use would be and applied the *Briararch* principle. However, in most cases, it is likely that the extent of future fluctuations in use would not be known and therefore differences can arise simply as a result of the timing of when the calculations have to be made. The partial exemption override may not apply for similar reasons.

7.74 The alternative method is the parallel adjustment method. Taking Example 11 above as a basis, the result would be:

Example 12 – Parallel adjustment method

Period ending	Interval	Input tax incurred	PE %	Input tax claimed
31–03-1999				
31–03-2000	1	60,000	75%	45,000
31–03-2001	2		80%	300
	1	140,000	80%	112,000
31–03-2002	3		75%	0
	2		75%	–700
31–03-2003	4		75%	0
	3		75%	–700
31–03-2004	5		75%	0

Period ending	Interval	Input tax incurred	PE %	Input tax claimed
	4		75%	–700
31–03-2005	6		85%	600
	5		85%	700
31–03-2006	7		85%	600
	6		85%	700
31–03-2007	8		85%	600
	7		85%	700
31–03-2008	9		85%	600
	8		85%	700
31–03-2009	10		85%	600
	9		85%	700
31–03-2010	11		90%	0
	10		90%	1,400
				163,100

Dealing with non-business use of an asset

7.75 Under the Sixth Directive, where an asset is acquired partly for business use and partly for non-business use, two possible treatments are possible. First, it is possible to allocate a part of the asset to non-business use and disallow the VAT incurred on that proportion. On a subsequent disposal of the assets, the proceeds attributable to the non-business part of the asset will be outside the scope of VAT (the *Armbrecht* principle) – see *Finanzamt Uelzen v Armbrecht (C-291/92) [1995] STC 997* (**Case Summary 19**). If such treatment is adopted, only that part of the cost of the asset that is for business use will fall within the capital items scheme. Any use of the private portion of the asset will not be taken into account in determining the taxable use of the asset.

7.76 The second possible treatment, is to treat the whole asset as used for business purposes and then treat the cost of any subsequent application to business use as a supply, whether taxable or otherwise, depending on the nature of the supply (the *Lennartz* principle – see *Lennartz v Finanzamt München III (C-97/90) [1995] STC 514* (**Case Summary 12**)). In such cases, the whole asset will be taken into account in determining whether there is a capital item or not. Similarly, any application to private use will be treated as a supply and will be taken into account in determining the extent of taxable use both in the first and subsequent intervals.

7.77 VATA 1994, Sch 4, para 5(4A) (inserted by FA 2003, s 22) effectively limits the application of the *Lennartz* principle under UK VAT law (see **Chapter 4**). However, prior to Royal Assent but subsequent to the 2003 Budget, the European Court of Justice delivered its opinion in the case of *Seeling v Finanzamt Starnberg (C-269/00) [2003] STC 805* (**Case Summary 48**). The Court rejected German arguments similar to those upon which the UK Government based its arguments that it was entitled to adopt para 5(4A). It remains to be seen whether the issue will cause sufficient practical and compliance problems to make it worthwhile for a taxable person to contest the validity of the clause. However, it appears that there could be problems where use changes as Example 13 below illustrates.

7.78 It is conceivable that the business or private use may be more or less than originally envisaged when the asset was acquired.

Example 13 – Private use of capital item

A taxpayer acquires a building as a hotel. He allocates a suite of rooms for the use of himself and his family and disallows any VAT referable to their acquisition. From time to time he allows other family members and friends to stay at the hotel and does not charge them for their stay. The cost of the occasional free use of the business part of the asset will be treated as a taxable supply and output tax will be due on the cost. The value of the supply is, however, also taken into account in determining the use under the capital items scheme.

7.79 It will be observed that under the new legislation, the taxpayer has to predict non-business use (even if occasional) when the VAT is incurred. There are no provisions under either EU VAT law or UK VAT law that allow VAT on non-business use to be re-allocated and treated as input tax once it has been regarded as VAT on private use.

Use before VAT registration

7.80 A person who carries on a business (in an every day rather than VAT sense of the phrase) but is not registered and is not required to be registered, may incur VAT on assets that would otherwise fall within the capital items scheme.

Example 14 – Use before VAT registration

A bank makes only exempt supplies of financial services and therefore does not register for VAT. It acquires a computer for £56,000 plus VAT and, since it is not registered, is unable to recover any VAT. A year after the purchase of the computer it expands its business to include leasing and hire purchase and registers for VAT.

7.81 In the circumstances outlined in Example 14 above, the original VAT incurred is not input tax since the bank was not a taxable person when it incurred it. However, VAT incurred on assets prior to registration that are still on hand at the date of registration may be treated as input tax (VAT Regulations 1995, reg 111(1)(a)).

7.82 VAT Regulations 1995, reg 112(2) defines a capital item as inter alia an item that a person 'uses in the course or furtherance of a business carried out by him'. Technically speaking, the asset cannot have been a capital item when the VAT was incurred because the taxpayer was not a taxable person either when the VAT was incurred or when the asset was first used. This would create an anomaly since reg 111 would appear to give a right to deduct the VAT incurred but reg 112 would appear not to bring the asset within the capital items scheme.

7.83 The anomaly can be resolved if the non-registration and subsequent registration is interpreted in accordance with the Sixth Directive, art 24 (Special scheme for small undertakings). Thus, technically speaking, a non-registered business carries on an economic activity (or undertakes a business in UK terms) but art 24 exempts a small businesses turnover from VAT. Accordingly, it would appear that an asset that was used in a business prior to registration and is subsequently used for taxable purposes after registration should be subject to adjustment under the capital items scheme.

7.84 Because the UK law does not appear to give the right to apply the capital items scheme in such circumstances, it would presumably be for the taxpayer to request the application of the capital items scheme under the principle of 'direct effect'.

What comprises use – physical v economic use?

7.85 A question arises as to what comprises 'use'. As noted at **7.42** above, this does not refer solely to physical use (see *East Kent Medical Services*).

7.86 However, as is evident from Examples 8 to 10 above, the fact that use can be considered to take place prior to the date when a building is first physically used can create some anomalous situations in the capital items scheme and, in particular, create situations where apportionment may not be based on actual use.

Disposals of capital items

Summary

7.87 VAT Regulations 1995, reg 115(3) deals with the disposal of capital items other than capital items that are disposed of as part of a going concern.

7.88 A taxpayer, who disposes of his entire interest in a capital item must make an adjustment in the interval in which the item is disposed of to reflect the change in use not only in that interval but also in any remaining intervals. The adjustment is therefore made up of two parts. In respect of the interval when the disposal takes place, the adjustment must be calculated on the basis of whatever partial exemption method is in place.

7.89 The legislation also provides that on the disposal of a capital item, the owner must calculate for each of the remaining complete intervals an adjustment on the basis that :

- if the disposal is a taxable supply, the whole of the input tax to be adjusted in the remaining periods is to be regarded as used for the purposes of making taxable supplies; but

- if the disposal is by way of an exempt supply, the whole of the input tax remaining to be adjusted in the remaining periods is to be regarded as used in making exempt supplies.

7.90 There is no specific guidance as to how the adjustment in respect of the interval in which the disposal takes place is to be made. However, it will be evident that unless the disposal is at the commencement or end of the interval, the actual use will usually comprise some use for whatever purpose the business normally carries on plus some use on the basis that part of the input tax for the period is referable to the disposal.

Example 15 – Disposal of capital item

Taking Example 6 above, assume that Computers Limited sells the mainframe computer on 31 March 2002. What adjustment must be made? The partial exemption recovery rate in that year is also 60 per cent.

The sale of the computer will be a taxable supply. The adjustment for the year to 31 March 2002 comprise:

Adjustment for the year to 31 March 2002 calculated as above	700
The VAT to be adjusted for the two periods is 20% × 17,500 × 2 =	7,000
The original deduction at 80% was 80% × 7,000 =	5,600
Therefore, a further 1,400 is deductible.	1,400
The net adjustment is, therefore, a further deduction of	700

7.91 If in Example 15 above, the sale took place on 30 September 2001 instead of on 31 March 2002, it would appear that use for six months of the final interval includes use for taxable purposes at 100 per cent rather than 60 per cent, so overall use should be 80 per cent (50% × 60% + 50% × 100%). This would mean that use in the interval was the same as that in the original period and no adjustment would be required in respect of the final interval although there would still be an adjustment in relation to the two unexpired intervals.

7.92 This will probably not create too much difficulty where a special method is in place. However, where the standard method is in use, the proceeds of the disposal of the property may have to be ignored as an incidental property transaction under VAT Regulations 1995, reg 102(3). Since the input tax to be adjusted may well be residual input tax, the adjustment may well over or under-state the proper deduction for the period. In such cases, it may be necessary to apply the partial exemption override to the adjustment on disposal.

7.93 It should also be noted that, where the adjustment does not result in a fair and reasonable attribution, it is open to the taxpayer to ask Customs and Excise to approve a special method for dealing with the adjustment (see VAT Regulations 1995, reg 116(2)).

What constitutes a disposal?

7.94 VAT Regulations 1995, reg 115(3) provides that, in addition to a normal disposal such as a sale of a property, deemed disposals are also to be regarded as disposals in applying the regulation. Accordingly, the following will also be treated as disposals–

- A capital item that is deemed to be a supply under the provisions of VATA 1994, Sch 4, para 8(1), ie a supply on deregistration of a business. The regulation also applies to a capital item that is on hand on deregistration but it is not treated as a disposal because it does not exceed the de minimis amount set out in that paragraph, currently £1,000.
- The outright application of the item to non-business purposes, eg own private use or disposal free of charge to a third party.

7.95 If a capital item is treated as being disposed of, an adjustment such as that described in paras **7.87–7.93** above will have to be made.

7.96 The question of how the disposal of a capital item is to be treated where it is disposed of by way of successive transactions has been referred to the European Court of Justice (*Centralan Properties Ltd v C & E Comrs [2003] EWHC 44 (Ch), [2003] STC 290*). The appellant had acquired a capital item. It disposed of a leasehold interest in the property in an interval subsequent to the first period and then shortly afterwards disposed of the remaining interest. The disposal of the leasehold interest was an exempt supply but the disposal of the remaining interest was a taxable supply. The two transactions were with separate companies. The taxpayer restricted its input tax in the interval that the leasehold interest was supplied but claimed to treat all the VAT attributable in the remaining intervals to the taxable supply of the remainder. Customs and Excise assessed the taxpayer on the basis that the remaining VAT should be treated as referable to both the leasehold interest and the taxable supply.

7.97 The appellant argued that VAT Regulations 1995, reg 115(3) contemplates that there can only be one disposal and on that disposal the whole of the remaining VAT referable to those intervals must be treated as referable to that last supply. The European Court decision, when handed down, will have little impact on future disposals because of the operation of the disposal test. (See **7.104** below.)

Loss, destruction, theft or other termination of an asset

7.98 VAT Regulations 1995, reg 115(4)(b) deals with the loss, destruction or theft of a capital item. Customs and Excise Notice 706/02/02, para 8.8 advises that a taxpayer should:

- calculate the adjustment for the interval in which it was lost stolen or destroyed on the basis that the item was used for the whole period of that interval; and
- make no further adjustments in respect of any remaining intervals.

7.99 The legislation does not appear to deal with the situation that arises where a lease over land on which a lessee has created a capital item by construction, refurbishment, etc, of a building, expires. It seems likely that the fact of expiry of the lease should have been taken into account in determining the number of intervals (bearing in mind that if an interest over land will expire in less than ten years, the number of intervals is reduced to five.

7.100 However, the building could have been constructed at a time when the period to run under the lease is less than five years and so the lease will expire prior to the end of the five-year period. It would appear that in such case, there is no adjustment.

Disposal prior to first use

7.101 Customs and Excise Notice 706/2/02 advises that where an asset is disposed of prior to first use, it is not regarded as being a capital item and therefore no adjustment has to be made (para 8.7).

7.102 It should be borne in mind that use in the context of the Capital Items Scheme has been held not to refer only to physical use – it can refer to economic and legal use (see comments on *East Kent Medical Services* at **7.42** above). It is therefore possible for an item to have been 'used' even though the building has not been physically occupied.

Example 16 – Disposal after first use but before physical use

A business commences construction of a property on 1 January 2002 and spends £2,000,000 plus VAT in the period to 30 June 2002. On 1 July 2002, it grants a lease of the uncompleted building for a premium of £1,800,000 plus rentals to be determined when final costs are known. On 1 January 2003, the building is completed but the business agrees with the lessee that it will sell the whole of the freehold to the lessee.

The effect of the transaction above is that the lessee never occupies the property prior to acquisition of the whole of the freehold. Under the *East Kent* reasoning, it is at least arguable that a capital item was created on 1 July 2002 followed by the disposal of the item thereafter.

7.103 The logical answer as to what VAT is deductible is that there is a single disposal of the freehold and all the costs of construction should be set against it. In effect, therefore, this is what Customs and Excise's advice says. However, it is at least to some extent at odds with the reasoning in *East Kent.*

The disposal test

7.104 The disposal test is set out in VAT Regulations 1995, reg 115(3A) and (3B). These regulations provide that the amount of VAT that can be deducted on disposal is to be limited by reference to the output tax chargeable on the disposal.

7.105 Although the legislation is worded in mandatory terms, Customs and Excise have a discretion to determine what adjustment is to be made. They have indicated that they will not apply the disposal test in certain circumstances and, when applying the disposal test, will limit any adjustment to that needed to counter any unjustified tax advantage (see VAT Notice 706/2/02 and Business Brief 30/97 dated 19 December 1997 for Customs and Excise's practice on adjustments on disposal).

7.106 VAT Notice 706/2/02 lists a number of examples where they will not usually apply the test as follows:

- sales of computer equipment;
- sales where the owner disposes of an item at a loss because of market conditions;
- where the value of the item has depreciated;
- where the value of an item is reduced for other reasons, eg as a result of having to accept a lower price to effect a quick sale;
- where the amount of output tax is lower than the input tax claimed only because of a change in VAT rate; and
- where the only use of the capital item throughout each interval of the adjustment period including the last when the disposal is made, is for taxable (including zero-rated) supplies.

7.107 VAT Notice 706/2/02 advises that the amount of the adjustment to make under the disposal test is such amount as will counter any unjustified tax advantage gained on the disposal. The Notice notes that this is a two-stage process, ie;

- calculate the net tax advantage; and
- calculate the portion of the advantage that is unjustified.

7.108 The Notice explains that the unjustified advantage is the overall benefit gained by the tax avoidance device, ie any input tax that would still be subject to adjustment under the scheme less any output tax payable under the scheme.

7.109 It should be noted that there is considerable scope for dispute on this issue. This arises because, even before any calculation is done, there may be a dispute over the method to be used. Thus, it is possible for the taxpayer to believe that there is no advantage or indeed tax avoidance device in the first place where Customs and Excise believe that there is. This is particularly so where an arrangement only has an impact on timing. Customs and Excise regard timing arrangements as being potentially VAT avoidance schemes whereas a taxpayer might not.

7.110 Given the scope for penalties on large amounts, it may be appropriate to advise Customs and Excise of any significant disposal where output tax is low enough potentially to bring the arrangement within the disposal test.

Specific issues

Transfer as a going concern

7.111 The disposal of assets as a transfer as a going concern (TOGC) under the VAT (Special Provisions) Order 1995, art 5 is not treated as a disposal in the same way as those described in paras **7.87–7.110** above. Instead, the recipient of the transfer 'inherits' the liability to make adjustments under the scheme.

7.112 Where the transferee takes over the existing registration, the adjustment periods remain the same and, apart from the change in ownership, there are no other consequences of the change. However, where the transfer is to a new taxpayer, a number of further consequences arise from the transfer.

7.113 In both cases, the immediate effect is that the transferee needs to ensure that he is provided with such information as will enable him to make the relevant adjustments. He will also no doubt wish to consider the extent of any potential adjustments prior to concluding any agreement for purchase of the business, as the amounts to be adjusted could represent a significant cost of the business acquired.

7.114 The following consequences also need to be considered where the transferee does not take over the existing registration number:

- If the transferor was the original person to acquire the capital item (ie was not himself a person who acquired the asset as part of a TOGC), then the disposal will terminate the current adjustment interval in respect of that item and the transferor will need to make an adjustment under the capital items scheme in respect of the period from the end of the last interval (or date of acquisition if the disposal is in the first interval) to the date of disposal.
- If the transferor acquired the capital item as part of a TOGC, he will not have to make any adjustment for, because the new transferee will have to make the adjustment (see below).
- Where the transferee is the first transferee (ie he acquires the item from the person who originally purchased, constructed or otherwise acquired the item), the date of acquisition will be the first day of a new adjustment interval. Thereafter, the remaining intervals will end on successive intervals of the first transfer. (VAT Regulations 1995, reg 114(5A)(c).)
- Where the transferee is a subsequent transferee (ie he acquires an item that has been subject to a previous TOGC), then the adjustment intervals will begin and end on previous anniversaries of the first transfer. (VAT Regulations 1995, reg 114(5A)(c).)

7.115 The impact of these rules mean that it is potentially possible for a transferee to have to make an adjustment for a period of use during which he was not the owner of the asset and therefore did not have any records that would enable him to calculate the adjustment. Apart from record keeping issues, the transferee needs to bear in mind that Customs and Excise may not share the previous owner's view of 'use' of the capital item, so there are potentially very substantial liabilities that might be incurred on a transfer.

VAT groups

7.116 Similar rules to those in relation to TOGCs apply to situations where:

- a company leaves a VAT group and either becomes registered in its own name or as part of a new VAT group; and
- a company enters a VAT group for the first time.

In each case, on the first time that the company becomes a member of a new VAT group or becomes registered on its own account, there will be a change in the date on which the adjustment intervals begin and end. Thereafter the adjustment intervals will begin and end on successive anniversaries of the first move.

TOGCs and groups combined

7.117 The same rules apply where, for example, an asset is first transferred as a going concern to a company and that company later enters a VAT group, or alternatively where a company leaves a VAT group and then subsequently transfers any capital item that was held at the time of the first movement as a going concern. The net result is that it is the first movement into or out of a VAT group or the first transfer of a going concern, whichever takes place first, that determines the beginning and end of subsequent adjustment intervals.

Other transfers under the VAT (Special Provisions) Order 1995

7.118 It is possible for a capital item to be repossessed and therefore to be excluded from being a supply under the provisions of the VAT Special Provisions Order 1995, art 5(4).

7.119 Unlike the provisions relating to TOGCs, there are no similar provisions relating to transfers under art 5(4). The purpose of art 5(4) is to prevent double taxation where an asset upon which VAT has already been charged is repossessed and sold by a financier.

7.120 It appears that there is no adjustment on actual repossession since that is not a disposal. The real disposal takes place if and when the financier disposes of the capital item. At that time, there is a disposal and an adjustment may be necessary.

Application to local authorities

7.121 Local authorities may have assets that fall within the capital items scheme. Such items may also be used for non-business purposes. A local authority is entitled to deduct the VAT it incurs for non-business purposes (VATA 1994, s 33).

7.122 Customs and Excise Notice 749 on local authorities advises local authorities that the normal rules requiring adjustments to be made apply to local authorities (at para 10.4).

7.123 In addition, Customs and Excise advise that non-business use should be treated as taxable use. There is no regulation specifically dealing with non-business use. There are ostensibly other ways in which non-business use could be dealt with but the advice in the Notice probably deals with non-business use as well as any other method might.

Interaction with change of use regulations (VAT Regulations 1995, regs 108, 109)

7.124 VAT Regulations 1995, regs 108 and 109 provide for the adjustment of the deduction of VAT deducted where there is a change in use of a supply between the time when the VAT is originally incurred and the time when the supply is first used (see **Chapter 6**).

7.125 Because a capital item can only come into existence when the asset in question is first used, it is not possible for regs 108 and 109 to operate once an asset has become a capital item. However, since input tax can be incurred prior to the time when an asset becomes a capital item, it is possible for regs 108 and 109 to apply to an item that will become a capital item.

Example 17 – Change of use

A company commences construction of a building on 1 April 2002. It incurs costs of £1,000,000 plus VAT in the VAT period to 30 June 2002. The company is fully taxable and claims all the VAT incurred in that period.

Following a down turn in business, it decides on 1 January 2003 that it will need to let the 20 per cent of the building temporarily and starts looking for a tenant. It finds a tenant in March 2003 and enters into a lease with effect from 1 April 2003. The company does not exercise the option to tax.

Both the tenant and the company occupy the building with effect from 1 April 2003.

The initial deduction will be 100 per cent, but when the company forms the intention to make both taxable and exempt supplies on 1 January 2003, it becomes liable to make an adjustment under VAT Regulations 1995, reg 108.

It must adjust 20 per cent of the tax it originally deducted, resulting in the initial recovery being 80 per cent rather than 100 per cent.

Termination of scheme on deregistration and other events

7.126 If an owner of a capital item ceases to be registered, then the provisions of VATA 1994, Sch 4, para 8 will apply. The taxpayer will then have to account for

VAT as if it were a disposal. If the asset concerned is a capital asset, the taxpayer will have to treat the capital item as if he had disposed of it.

Application during periods of non-use of asset

7.127 Customs and Excise advise that if a taxpayer ceases to use a capital asset, e g if it is 'mothballed' because it is not required for current use in the business, it is treated as continuing to be used to whatever extent it was used for prior to cessation of use. However, if the taxpayer ceases to use an asset and then forms an intention to use it for a different purpose, the new use will determine the extent of any use for subsequent intervals. Thus, if a taxpayer used a building for taxable purposes and then formed an intention to let the property (without opting to tax), the use subsequent to the change in intention would be exempt.

Customs and Excise's discretionary power

7.128 Customs and Excise have the power to allow or direct a different method to be used for the purposes of adjustments to be made in intervals subsequent to the first interval (VAT Regulations 1995, reg 116(2)). The regulation only refers to subsequent intervals because the normal deduction rules will apply to the initial deduction.

Other issues

Income and corporation tax

7.129 The Capital Allowances Act 2001 contains specific provisions determining how adjustments made under VAT Regulations 1995, reg 115 are to be treated for income tax or corporation tax purposes. The allowances which are most likely to interact with the capital items scheme are plant and machinery allowances, which are dealt with in ss 234–246, and industrial buildings allowances, which are dealt with in ss 345–351. Normally, where an industrial building includes plant and machinery (for example lift installations and air conditioning equipment), the expenditure will be dealt with as plant and machinery.

7.130 For the purposes of both plant and machinery and industrial buildings allowances, the initial qualifying expenditure will include any irrecoverable VAT, and exclude any recoverable VAT. If, in future accounting periods, further amounts of VAT become payable, that amount will be treated as additional qualifying expenditure in the period in which the additional VAT liability accrues.

7.131 On the other hand, if there is a rebate of VAT, the amount of the rebate is treated as disposal proceeds in the accounting period in which the rebate accrues.

7.132 For the purpose of calculating capital gains, computer equipment will normally be an exempt asset, but land will be a chargeable asset. When there is a chargeable disposal, the allowable expenditure will include any irrecoverable VAT, and exclude any recoverable VAT (see Inland Revenue Statement of Practice B1). This means that effect should be given to any VAT adjustments when the gain or loss is computed (see Inland Revenue Press Release, 20 March 1990).

Financial accounting issues

7.133 From an accounting perspective, an asset is recorded in the accounts of a business at its cost. This would normally be the net cost of the asset plus any VAT on the acquisition of that asset that is irrecoverable.

7.134 Those responsible for drawing up the accounts of a business will need to be aware that the non-deductible VAT on an asset will be determined over a period of ten years. However, the asset may well be depreciated or amortised over a considerably longer period. This may have implications for the financial accounting policies.

Example 18 – Non-deductible VAT capitalised

A new building is acquired for £10 million plus VAT at 17.5 per cent. In the first interval of the adjustment period, it is used wholly for taxable purposes and the whole of the VAT is recovered. In the second interval, the taxpayer acquires a new business and forecasts that the future VAT recovery will be only 60 per cent.

Assuming the building is used throughout the remaining nine intervals in the same way, VAT of £630,000 will be adjusted in annual instalments of £70,000 over the remaining nine years. However, since the building will probably have a life of at least 40 years, it may not be appropriate to write off the whole £70,000 each year and the taxpayer will need to consider what is the most appropriate method to deal with the capital items adjustment in the financial accounts.

7.135 It is quite possible and indeed probable that many adjustments will not be material from a financial accounting perspective. However, in some cases, the amounts may be material from a business's perspective and the appropriate accounting will need to be considered. It is beyond the scope of this work to advise on the correct method for dealing with adjustments in such circumstances.

7.136 Similar issues can arise where a taxpayer acquires a capital item as part of a going concern (see **7.111** above) or where a company moves out of a VAT group – whether into another VAT group or where it becomes registered in its own right.

Chapter 8

Transaction Specific Issues

Introduction

8.1 This chapter deals with the deductibility of input tax in a range of unusual or special circumstances, in particular those falling into the 'corporate finance' category: the issue, purchase or sale of shares and other securities; borrowing and other forms of financing; and the purchase or sale of a business.

8.2 The 'issue, transfer or receipt of, or any dealing with' any share (or any other form of security) is exempt under VATA 1994 Sch 9 Group 5 item 6, which means – at a very simplistic level – that, in principle, any VAT incurred in making that supply ought not to be recoverable. In practice, a number of factors come into play and the amount of VAT recovery can be anywhere in the range from zero to 100%. Not surprisingly, given that the amounts of input tax involved are often very large, this has been an area of keen interest and debate for many years. Successive decisions of the courts, both in the UK and in Europe, have clarified one aspect of the debate, only for the argument to move on to another. There is no sign of this level of activity abating in the near future.

The main issues: a potted history

8.3 A number of cases, over the years, have considered whether the input tax incurred on the costs of these transactions should be attributed to taxable or exempt supplies, or merely regarded as part of the general overheads of the business. The arguments have included an interesting debate over whether an issue or sale of shares is a supply at all; how the inputs are used; and how the partial exemption rules should be applied where the use is mixed.

8.4 The decision of the European Court of Justice in the case of *Polysar Investments Netherlands BV v Inspecteur der Invoerrechten en Accijnzen te Arnhem (C-60/90) [1993] STC 222* (**Case Summary 11**). This case concerned a Dutch intermediate holding company which owned shares in a number of foreign companies and had no income other than dividends. *Polysar* seemed to establish as a principle that the costs incurred by such companies should be regarded as used in a non-taxable activity and thus non-deductible. The actual decision however is not so sweeping: the Court held that the receipt of dividend income was not the consideration for anything done by the holding company but was an entitlement arising from the ownership of the shares. Accordingly, a business that did no more than passively hold shares was not carrying on an activity within the scope of the tax. In the UK, Customs initially interpreted this decision as meaning that no holding company should be allowed to recover any part of its input tax. After some months of lively debate Customs were persuaded to moderate this approach and accepted that there should be a distinction between 'passive holding companies' whose activities (or lack of activity) did not give rise to any entitlement to deduct, and others who took a more active role in the management of trading subsidiaries and/or actively traded their investment portfolio.

8.5 The decision of the ECJ in *BLP Group plc v Customs and Excise Comrs (C-4/94) [1995] STC 424* (**Case Summary 18**) killed off the argument that a business should be entitled to look through the immediate transaction – the sale of shares in a subsidiary – to the 'real' (taxable) business purpose for which the funds were intended. This was followed by the decision in *Wellcome Trust Ltd [1996] STC 945* (**Case Summary 23**), where the investment portfolio of a charitable foundation was found to be more similar to the investments of a private individual than a business activity within the scope of the tax.

8.6 In the UK, the taxpayer's entitlement to input tax recovery was restricted by a Court of Appeal decision in *Trinity Mirror plc [2001] EWCA Civ 65, [2001] STC 192* (**Case Summary 38**), which held that an issue of shares must be seen as an exempt supply rather than a 'non-event' and thus that input tax could not bypass the share issue and be attributed to the general business activities. More recent decisions, however, such as *Halladale*, *RAP Holdings* and *Southampton Leisure* (see below), have established that input tax recovery is still possible where it can be demonstrated that the inputs are not exclusively used in the share issue itself but in the surrounding events.

8.7 Although Customs have described the outcome of some of the leading cases (in particular *RAP*) as 'anomalous', it is clear that this treatment is in keeping with the intentions of the legislation, particularly if it is accepted that the share issue is not (as explained above) an end in itself but one of the steps involved in securing the primary objectives of the transaction. The decisions of the VAT Tribunal and the courts indicate, not that the input tax is wholly used in making taxable supplies, but that the inputs have a connection with the whole business.

8.8 Some ten years after *Polysar*, this is still a live issue; and cases outside the UK have given new life to the argument that *Trinity Mirror plc* seemed to have laid to rest. In particular, the decision of the ECJ in *KapHag* (see below) has re-ignited the debate on this point. These cases are discussed in more detail later in this chapter.

Partial exemption rules

8.9 As explained in **Chapter 2** above, the partial exemption regulations provide for a 'standard method' that applies by default to any trader who has not specifically agreed a 'special method' with Customs. The rules for the standard method are set out in reg 101, but if any overseas supplies are involved it is also necessary to refer to reg 103.

8.10 Many VAT cases on the recovery of input tax on share issues revolved around the application of the standard method. This is not surprising given that for many businesses the issue of shares is the only significant exempt supply that they make, so they have had no need to discuss a method with Customs. Under the standard method, if it can be established that input tax is not directly attributable to either taxable or exempt supplies it falls by default into the 'pot' and is apportioned. This apportionment is the familiar 'total value of taxable supplies divided by total value of all supplies' calculation.

8.11 Regulation 101(3)(b)(ii) excludes from the pro-rata calculation at 101(2)(d) 'any sum received by the taxable person in respect of [...] any supply which falls within Group 5 of Schedule 9' 'where such supplies are incidental to one or more of his business activities'. Therefore, under the standard method, the large (and thus distortive) exempt supply represented by the proceeds of the share issue is excluded from this calculation. If no other significant exempt supplies have taken place, the result is that the input tax is fully recoverable. This may appear, particularly to Customs, to be a 'wrong' result: recovering, as it were through the back door, input tax incurred in the course of making a large and important exempt supply. The introduction of the 'Standard Method Override' (**see Chapter 5**) may go some way to dealing with this perceived anomaly, since, where the override applies, the taxpayer is required to recalculate the recoverable amount on the basis of use rather than the simple mathematical formula set out in regulation 101(2)(d). It is possible however that Customs will be looking to make further changes to the partial exemption rules so that input tax that falls into the 'dual intention' category has to be more accurately apportioned between those intended uses. The wording of reg 103(2) may be an indicator as to how such a provision might look.

8.12 The effect of reg 103 is to require the taxpayer to attribute input tax on a share issue to taxable supplies to the extent that the goods and services are used in issuing shares to persons outside the EU, 'expressed as a proportion of the whole use or intended use'. Under reg 103 (2) this requirement applies to all traders 'notwithstanding any provision of any method that the taxable person is required or allowed to use under this Part of these Regulations which purports to have the contrary effect'. This does not necessarily mean a calculation based simply on the number of shares issued; it is for the taxpayer to determine the use. It is not difficult to imagine a situation where the costs involved in securing an overseas investor would be significantly greater than those needed to issue shares to local institutions who were already familiar with the business in question.

8.13 If the share issuer already has a special method then the letter setting out Customs' approval should in principle provide a mechanism for dealing with input tax on the share issue. However, there are two potential difficulties: first, very few special method approval letters make any clear provision for such events and secondly the terms of reg 103 can override the agreed method.

Analysis of the transaction

8.14 It is often said that VAT is a transaction-driven tax; what this means is that to arrive at the correct VAT result it may be necessary to analyse every step in the transaction rather than looking to the overall effect. This principle can be seen in the findings of the ECJ in *BLP*; see also *Robert Gordon's College [1995] STC 1093*. However, this does not mean that the underlying purpose or purposes of the parties to the transaction can be ignored. The legislation governing the deductibility of input tax relies on determining the use to which the goods and services concerned are put. Customs like to use the term 'cost component' (from the *BLP* case); but this implies that the components of an intangible supply of services can be identified in the same way as the parts used in the manufacture of (say) a bicycle. Attempting to apply the 'cost component' principle to transactions in financial services is not necessarily helpful. When considering corporate financing, mergers and acquisitions, it must be noted that the structure is often dictated by tax, regulatory and other concerns and it is easy to mistake the form for the substance.

8.15 Unlike most business transactions, a share issue is rarely an end in itself; it is not surprising therefore that the circumstances in which securities are issued can have an influence on the recoverability of the input tax.

8.16 The first question to be addressed is whether there is a supply at all. In the UK, Customs are firmly of the opinion that all transactions in securities of all kinds, including the issue of new shares, are exempt supplies. Where a business, acting as such, generates profits by buying and selling securities that are quoted on an exchange, it is difficult to avoid the conclusion that it is making supplies. Even where the transaction involves the exchange of one financial commodity for another, the existence of profit (or the potential for profit) would appear to distinguish the activity from a 'passive' investment portfolio such as that of Wellcome Trust. Any doubt that might have lingered on this point must have been removed by the decision of the ECJ in *First National Bank of Chicago (Case 172/96) [1998] STC 850* which concerned a bank, trading as a market maker in the international foreign exchange markets. The bank claimed that there was no difference in principle between trading in the foreign exchange markets and trading in any other form of financial instrument; it was therefore entitled to deduct input tax to the extent that it was attributable to FX trades with persons outside the EU. Customs were concerned at the difficulty of valuing the supply – which they said suggested that there was no clear connection between what was done and the supposed consideration; they also argued that the FX trade could not be differentiated from the situation where money in the same currency was exchanged for other notes or coins. The ECJ found in favour of the bank. The ECJ found that the difficulty in evaluating the consideration did not mean that none existed; and the fact that the bank quoted a spread between its bid and offer prices was sufficient proof that it did.

8.17 Taken together, these cases would appear to indicate that it is not the subject matter of the transaction, or the nature of the commodity or asset underlying the trade, that determines whether there is a supply to which input tax should be attributed; the purpose(s) and intention(s) of the business are more important.

8.18 Where a business, not a financial trader, sells existing securities (e g some or all of the shares in a subsidiary) there would appear to more room for debate, since the facts are closer to those of *Wellcome Trust than First National Bank of Chicago*. The leading case concerning such a sale is *BLP*, but in that case the ECJ was not asked to and did not debate the question of whether the sale of the subsidiary was a supply. It was accepted between the parties that it was. It seems likely, given the logic and the outcome of *First National Bank of Chicago,* that the sale of one of a group of trading companies, by the parent or holding company, would be seen as a supply. It is less certain that this would be the result if the vendor company was more passive, took little or no part in the management of the subsidiaries' businesses, and had as its main objective the generation of a long-term capital gain; or indeed if the vendor was disposing of a minority interest.

8.19 Whether a share *issue* is a supply is an even more complex question. Shares may be issued when the company is first formed, or in order to admit further investors, or to bring in additional capital; or new shares may be issued in the course of a merger or acquisition, in exchange for the shares of another company. *BLP* tells us that we cannot look *through* the transaction, to the ultimate purpose for which the funds are intended; but that does not mean that the circumstances surrounding the issue are of no consequence. It is possible to imagine that a court would find the issue of new shares to the public, by an open-ended investment company, not to be a supply, while the issue of shares as consideration for a takeover might be seen differently.

8.20 The question was given short shrift in the 1992 decision of the Tribunal in *Swallowfield plc [1992] VATTR 212*. The argument advanced in that case was that the issue could not be a supply because the subject matter (the various rights to profit, participation etc attaching to the shares) did not exist at the time of the transaction; the Tribunal was not swayed by this and concluded that there was a sufficiently clear nexus between the payment and the shareholder's rights received in return to constitute a supply within the meaning of the legislation.

8.21 In the *Trinity Mirror plc v C & E Comrs [2001] EWCA Civ 65, STC 192* (**Case Summary** 38) case the distinction between an issue of new shares and the purchase or sale of existing shares was again raised, but the taxpayer was unsuccessful at Tribunal, with the decision being finally upheld at the Court of Appeal in January 2001. The Court of Appeal held that the issue of shares is an exempt supply. *Trinity Mirror* had argued unsuccessfully that an issue of shares should not be regarded as a supply by the issuing company. The Court of Appeal did not think it necessary to make a reference to the ECJ and so the judgment is, in the UK and for the moment at least, the last word on the point.

8.22 For VAT purposes, a share issue (if it is a supply at all) is a supply of services – but only because it is not a supply of goods (see VATA 1994, s 5(6)). It is hard to see a supply of shares as the performance of a service in the normal sense of these words: an action performed for someone else. It could be said that a sale of shares has some of the characteristics of a supply of goods – the ownership of some thing, albeit not necessarily something tangible, is transferred and can be supplied on in the same state.

The use of the inputs: whether the costs are directly attributable to the share transaction

8.23 There are no significant physical components of a share issue, other than perhaps the cost of printing the certificates, or a prospectus in the case of a Public Offer. The more substantial costs are all in the form of services; and in many cases they are not used directly or exclusively in making the share issue but in dealing with the surrounding business concerns. The process of issuing shares is not particularly difficult or expensive. To understand the high level of costs that are often involved it is necessary to look at the circumstances surrounding the issue. Very often this reveals that the difficulties, the obstacles that need to be overcome, are related to the other side of the transaction. For example, when one company bids for control of another, the complicated and uncertain part of the transaction is securing the agreement of the existing owners of the shares. The new shares that are to be issued are no more than the consideration for the acquisition that is the sole purpose for which the advisers have been engaged and the costs incurred. Indeed, if the bid is not successful the new shares will not come into existence.

8.24 The process of acquiring a target company's shares, for a consideration in the form of cash, does not involve any exempt supply by the purchaser and should not therefore affect his entitlement to input tax deduction. Similarly, if the purchaser borrows money to fund the acquisition, he has not made an exempt supply (although he has received one) and the costs are regarded as general business overheads. If the business is fully taxable the input tax on related costs can be recovered in full, subject to the normal rules.

8.25 The position becomes more complicated as soon as the consideration takes the form of any kind of security. 'Share for share' transactions are very common in mergers and acquisitions, but the same VAT problems apply to issues of loan notes and other similar instruments. Although the essential nature of the transaction may seem very similar, there is now an exempt supply made by the purchaser in the course of the transaction. *BLP* tells us that we cannot 'look through' this supply but Customs tend to go further and argue that much if not all of the input tax must relate to the shares issued by the purchaser, apparently on the basis that this is the only supply that the purchaser makes. This simplistic approach does not stand up to scrutiny (and has been defeated at the Tribunal, as discussed below).

RAP Group plc

8.26 In *RAP Group plc v C & E Comrs [2000] STC 980* (**Case Summary 36**), RAP offered for, and acquired, the issued share capital of W plc. The acquisition was funded by the issue of new RAP shares for W plc shares and the issue of placing shares to RAP's existing shareholders. RAP claimed input tax on the supplies of services by its accountants, KPMG, its solicitors, TSB, and its stockbrokers, WdB, in relation to its acquisition of W plc. The Commissioners disallowed the deduction and issued an assessment. RAP appealed. The relevant part of the invoice from KPMG referred only to 'placing and open offer' and 'offer for W plc'. The invoice from WdB was in similar terms. The invoice from TSB included details such as: advising on the financing of the transaction; preparing service contracts for executive directors; preparing a due diligence report on W plc; investigating title to W plc's properties and preparing papers for its annual general meeting following the acquisition. RAP contended that, as a matter of law, part of the cost of the advisers' services was a cost component of its taxable transactions in the form of management services supplied to W plc once it was part of the RAP group and that there was a direct and immediate link between the advisory services received and the management services supplied. The tribunal dismissed the appeal. RAP appealed. The High Court held that the question in the instant case was whether the services were used for the exempt transaction or for that and some other taxable supplies. That was a question of fact. There was nothing in the evidence which prevented the Tribunal from finding that the services of KPMG and WdB were used for the exempt supply of the issue of shares. The Tribunal had been wrong, however, to ignore the clear terms of the invoice from TSB and to treat all the work as limited to the issue of shares. Accordingly, RAP's appeal was allowed in so far as it related to the input tax on the invoice of TSB. In respect of the input tax on the invoices of KPMG and WdB, the appeal was dismissed.

Southampton Leisure Holdings plc

8.27 *In Southampton Leisure Holdings plc v C & E Comrs [2002] VAT decision 17716* (**Case Summary 44**), Southampton Leisure Holdings plc ('SLH') acquired Southampton Football Club (SFC), issuing its own shares in exchange for those of SFC. The case concerned whether professional services incurred on the transaction were attributable to exempt supplies (i.e. the shares issued by SLH) or, as the taxpayer contended, both taxable and exempt supplies. SLH challenged an assessment issued by the Commissioners to disallow input tax claimed in respect of professional fees incurred on the issue of its shares to the shareholders of SFC in consideration for the transfer by SFC to the appellant of its shares. Both parties accepted that the issue by SLH of its own shares was an exempt supply under item 6, Group 5 and that any input tax wholly attributable to the exempt share issue was non-deductible. However, SLH argued that its intention in acquiring SFC was to make taxable supplies of management services, and so the input tax should be apportioned under the Regulations. The tribunal considered three points: whether there was a direct and immediate link between the professional services and the taxable supplies of management services; whether the professional services had a direct and immediate link to the appellant's business as a whole, or only to the exempt supply of shares; and whether, if the professional services had a link to the supply of shares, all of the professional services were used by the appellant in connection with that share issue. The Tribunal held, following *Cibo Participations* (see below), that there was no direct and immediate link between the professional services and the management services. The Tribunal also found that, as a matter of law and following *Cibo*, if there had been no issue of shares by the appellant, the professional services would have had the required link with the appellant's business as a whole. However, in this case, the services were used for the exempt issue of shares. The services supplied by one adviser were not wholly used by SLH in connection with its own shares and, therefore, qualified for apportionment as residual input tax. The remaining professional services related wholly to the exempt share issue and the attributable VAT was therefore non-deductible.

8.28 This 2002 decision by the VAT Tribunal forced a significant climb-down by Customs. Despite the clear findings of the earlier *RAP Group* case, Customs had maintained their resistance to the recovery of VAT in transactions where shares were issued. The *Southampton Leisure* Tribunal, however, held that many of the costs incurred at the time of such a transaction were not – as Customs had argued – used solely in making the exempt supply but had a direct link with other activities of the business.

8.29 Customs responded by issuing Business Brief Number 23/2002, which confirmed that services of 'acting as financial advisor, the drafting of service contracts for the directors, the due diligence review of the target company's affairs, the investigation of title and/or the valuation of that company's property and co-ordinating the transaction' were not used exclusively in making the exempt supply of the issue of shares. As a result, the tax incurred on those supplies should be treated as residual input tax.

8.30 Unfortunately, the Business Brief goes on to say that the decision has no application where shares are issued for subscription, for example in an initial public offer or rights issue. 'In these instances, the taxed professional services relating to the offer are used exclusively for the purposes of the exempt supply of an issue of shares.' This assertion was not part of the Tribunal's findings and may well be open to challenge, particularly in the light of *Halladale* (see below).

Halladale Group plc

8.31 An interesting development in the debate arose in the Scottish case of *Halladale Group plc v C & E Comrs [2003] VAT decision 18218* (**Case Summary 50**). The arguments in this case took a different turn from those dealt with in *RAP Group* and *Southampton Leisure*. The company traded and developed properties and incurred various professional costs in connection with an application for listing on the Alternative Investment Market (AIM). The Tribunal accepted as fact the evidence of the company's Finance Director that its main purpose in seeking an AIM listing was not the raising of funds (which could have been achieved at less expense through bank borrowing) but the prestige of being a quoted company. In other words, the Tribunal accepted that, *even where the share issue was the only supply made,* the taxpayer could have a dual purpose or intention to which the input tax could be attributed.

8.32 The *Halladale* decision has not been appealed by Customs, who apparently took the view that an appeal would be difficult once the finance director's evidence had been accepted as fact by the Tribunal. Customs have therefore adjusted their policy to acknowledge the *Halladale* decision – whilst asserting that in most cases the VAT will still be seen as attributable to the share issue. In Business Brief 30/03 they say:

> 'Costs incurred on a Stock Exchange listing are normally treated as wholly related to a share issue. This is because at the time of the listing or after wards, there is an intention to issue shares to raise capital. This is established Customs policy and is supported by the Tribunal decision in Actinic plc. But, on some occasions these costs can be treated as residual even though some shares are issued. This represents a change in policy and reflects the decision of the Tribunal in Halladale Group plc.'

The Business Brief goes on to say:

> 'Each case will be considered on its facts having regard to the circumstances of the share issue. However, it is likely the costs will be considered general overheads if, for example:

- The number of shares issued is small compared to the number listed; and
- The capital raised by the issue is minor compared with the costs incurred.'

It is clear therefore that Customs (and, probably, the courts) will feel free to distinguish the facts in other cases from those that supported the decision in *Halladale*. Nevertheless, the fact that a dual intention can sometimes be demonstrated represents progress of a sort.

EasyJet plc

8.33 Another aspect of 'mixed use' that has caused disagreements over the years is where the shares are issued or sold to persons both inside and outside the EU. The interaction of the partial exemption regulations and the Specified Supplies Order had already been considered by the House of Lords in *Liverpool Institute of Performing Arts ('LIPA')* (see **Chapter 5 and Case Summary 40**); in *EasyJet plc v C & E Comrs* the Tribunal tried to find a coherent interpretation of those provisions that would also cater for an international share issue.

8.34 Following the line taken in *LIPA*, Customs persuaded the Tribunal that reg 103 – in this case, 103(2) – should be interpreted as a self-contained separate regime for dealing with any input tax that was used to any extent in making a supply of shares to a person outside the EU. The effect of this was that the taxable person could not obtain the same result as *RAP Group* and *Southampton Leisure* where taking the input tax out of the category where it was directly attributable to exempt supplies meant that the tax was by default attributed to the general taxable activities of the business. As the Tribunal chairman put it:

> '… the fortuitous combination of the share-related services with other services would have enabled a substantial input tax recovery to be made, … (following RAP Group plc).'

The Tribunal accepted Customs' argument that such a result would have been 'anomalous'. However, it seems to have been assumed without much debate in *EasyJet* that the accounting services in question were primarily used in relation to the share issue. Whether the Tribunal would have been more receptive to an argument such as that advanced in *Halladale* (see above) is not clear.

The Irish Appeal Commissioners

8.35 Finally, a number of commentators have raised an eyebrow at a case decided by the Irish Appeal Commissioners. The case, reference number 1 AC 2003, concerned a computer software company (not named in the report) that sought to raise funds by means of a share issue. The transaction did not go through but the company nevertheless incurred professional fees and claimed the input tax on those fees. The Appeal Commissioners referred to the Sixth Directive and the cases of *Polysar*, *BLP*, *Wellcome Trust* and *Harnas & Helm*. They went on to compare the treatment of input tax incurred in connection with a loan to the treatment of input tax on a share issue and to discuss the 'commercial reality' of both.

8.36 The Commissioners commented that:

> 'When the company issues shares it does not bind itself in the same way as it does when it enters into contracts with other parties, regardless of whether it is supplying goods or services or receiving them. The issue of shares is a transaction which implements the wishes of a shareholder or shareholders acting in a capacity which is external to the company's activities. In the course of the issue of shares the company may receive funds to enable it to finance its activities but the person who contributed the funds is of no interest to the company; no more than the identity of or the number of shareholders in the company is of any concern to it.
>
> In the case of a bank loan the borrower is not treated as borrowing money to enter into the loan agreement, he enters into the agreement to enable him to make use of the funds for his own purposes. Similarly, when a company receives cash from a share issue, it has done so to enable it to make use of the proceeds for the purpose of its business / taxable supplies.
>
> In summary, the issue of shares by the company does nothing more, so far as the company is concerned, than recognise who the shareholders of the company are. The company suffers no depletion of its resources.'

8.37 The Appeal Commissioners saw a clear distinction between the circumstances of this case and those in *BLP*:

> 'The acceptance by *BLP* that it was making exempt supplies clearly distinguishes it from the present case. Further, the sale of shares acquired by *BLP* as an investment is not equivalent to the proposed issue of a company's own shares in return for cash.'

Holding companies that also supply services

8.38 *Floridienne SA and Berginvest SA v Belgian State* (*C-142/99) [2000] STC 1044* (**Case Summary 37**) concerned holding companies which provided taxable services to their subsidiaries, such as management, technical assistance, accounting and advisory services. They also provided loans to the subsidiaries. The Belgian tax authorities sought to restrict the input tax recovered by *Floridienne and Berginvest*.

The ECJ endorsed the approach in *Polysar [1993] STC 222* (**Case Summary 11**) that holding shares in companies is an economic activity where the holding is accompanied by direct or indirect involvement in the management of such companies. The ECJ also stated that a holding company whose sole purpose is to acquire holdings in other undertakings, without involving itself directly or indirectly in the management of those companies is not a taxable person and cannot deduct input VAT. As *Floridienne and Berginvest* were involved directly in the subsidiaries the input tax relating to those activities would be treated as residual and could be recovered in accordance with the partial exemption calculation.

8.39 In *Cibo Participations SA v Directeur régional des impots du Nord-Pas-de-Calais (C-16/00) [2002] STC 460* (**Case Summary 41**), the appellant was a holding company which owned significant shareholdings in three undertakings specialising in bicycles. *Cibo* challenged the French tax authority's refusal to allow *Cibo* to deduct input VAT on various services in connection with the acquisition of shares in its subsidiaries. The services in question included the auditing of the companies, assistance with the negotiation of the purchase price of the shares, organising the take-over of the companies and legal and tax services.

8.40 The first question considered by the ECJ was: what are the criteria for establishing whether the involvement of a holding company in the management of companies in which it has acquired a shareholding constitutes an economic activity? The ECJ held that, following *Floridienne* (above), the involvement of a holding company in the management of companies in which it has acquired a shareholding constitutes an economic activity where it entails carrying out transactions such as the supply by a holding company to its subsidiaries of administrative, financial, commercial and technical services.

8.41 The second question considered by the ECJ was whether a holding company may deduct VAT charged on expenditure incurred on services obtained in connection with the acquisition of a shareholding in a subsidiary. The ECJ held that, although there was no direct and immediate link between the services and any output transaction in respect of which VAT is deductible, the costs of those services are part of the taxable person's general costs and are, as such, cost components of an undertaking's products. Such services have, in principle, a direct and immediate link with the taxable person's business as a whole and are deductible in accordance with its partial exemption position.

The Hoge Raad Case

8.42 Case 38253 – judgment 14 March 2003 of the Hoge Raad (Dutch Supreme Court) concerned a Dutch holding company ('HoldCo') which owned 50% of the shares in another Dutch company ('SubCo'). HoldCo provided SubCo with various management services in return for management fees on which HoldCo charged VAT. In 1998, HoldCo sold its shares in SubCo to a third party and incurred VAT on professional services in relation to the sale of the shares. HoldCo sought to deduct the VAT but the Dutch tax authorities rejected the claim. HoldCo appealed to the Tax Court in the Hague which, following the *BLP* case

(*BLP Group plc v C & E Comrs (C-4/94) [1995] STC 424)*, held that the input tax was directly linked to the sale of the shares and was, accordingly, not deductible. HoldCo appealed to the Hoge Raad.

8.43 Without referring to the *BLP* case, the Hoge Raad held that, although the services in relation to the sale of the shares were directly linked to the business, the proceeds of the sale of the shares should be treated in the same way as dividends; that is, as outside the scope of VAT. The Hoge Raad concluded that the costs of the share sale were general expenses of the business of HoldCo and, accordingly, the input VAT fell to be deducted in accordance with HoldCo's partial exemption method. The principal conclusions of the Hoge Raad were set out in para 3.3.4 of the judgment as follows (unofficial translation):

> 'The relevant documents do not allow a conclusion other than that HoldCo did not sell the participation in the capacity of stock broker. In addition, there is no doubt that HoldCo took part in the management of the subsidiary by means of management activities performed against payment. … From the case law of the ECJ, in particular paragraphs 27 to 35 of *Cibo Participations SA,* it follows that the costs of these services form part of the general expenses of HoldCo and that, in general, there is a direct link between these services and all of the business activities of HoldCo. Whether the entire amount of input VAT can then be deducted, depends on the answer to the question as to whether, prior to the transfer of the participation, HoldCo carried out-wholly or partly-activities for which no right to a deduction existed. In this respect, it is important to note that-which may not reasonably be doubted – it follows from the ECJ's case law that the sales price for the participation, no more than dividends received in respect of such participation (as dealt with in this case law), does not fall with the scope of VAT, so that this price must not be included in the pro rata as laid down in Article 17(5) Sixth Directive.'

8.44 The Hoge Raad did not decide what amount of input VAT is deductible by HoldCo but referred the case to a lower court to investigate the facts, establish HoldCo's pro rata for the relevant year and determine the deductible amount.

8.45 Many commentators considered that the Hoge Raad had made an error in not referring to the *BLP* case. However, there are two reasons why the Hoge Raad may have felt that the *BLP* case was not relevant. First, the ECJ in *BLP* did not decide that a sale of shares by a holding company is exempt for VAT purposes. The liability of such a share sale was an assumption not a question in the reference by the UK High Court in *BLP* ('those services are used by B for an exempt transaction (sale of shares)'). The ECJ in *BLP* only addressed whether or not costs relating to an exempt transaction could be deducted. The ECJ in *BLP* did not consider whether or not the transaction itself was exempt. This seems an unlikely explanation as the ECJ often rephrases or rewrites reference questions to deal with points which are unclear or just wrong (for example, see *Marks and Spencer plc v C & E Comrs (C-62/00) [2002] STC 1036).* A better reason perhaps is that HoldCo's case differs factually from that of *BLP* in that the Hoge Raad held there was a direct link between the expenses of the share sale and the general business activities of HoldCo whereas the only direct link in the *BLP* case was with the share sale. Therefore, the Hoge Raad may have ignored the *BLP* decision on purpose because it was irrelevant to the circumstances of HoldCo's case. In a neatly symmetrical response, the Dutch tax authorities have said that they are going to ignore the judgment of the Dutch Supreme Court in this case. Another appeal, probably with a reference to the ECJ, on this point can be expected at some time. With the benefit of the ECJ's decision in *KapHag* (see **8.46** below), it now appears that the Hoge Raad may have been right to ignore or distinguish *BLP*.

Is a new issue of shares a supply?

KapHag

8.46 In *KapHag Renditefonds 35 Spreecenter Berlin-Hellersdorf 3. Tranche GbR v Finanzamt Charlottenburg (C-442/01) [2003], All ER (D) 362* (**Case Summary 49**) the ECJ held that a partnership does not make a supply of services for consideration when it admits a partner in consideration of payment of a contribution in cash.

The case concerned the admission of a new member to a partnership, in consideration of a payment in cash. The questions put to the Court were:

- whether the admission of a new partner represented a supply within the meaning of art 2 of the Sixth Directive and, if so –
- whether it should be regarded as an incidental transaction for the purposes of the partial exemption calculation set out in art 19.

8.47 The partnership in question was set up in the form of a closed property fund. The structure itself was complex and the case started out as a dispute over the deduction of VAT on the legal fees incurred in setting up the partnership itself. The Bundeshof took the view that the input tax was attributable to an exempt supply, the supply in question being the admission of a new partner. Both the taxpayer and the German Government's submissions to the Court drew comparisons between the admission of a new partner and the issue of shares by a company.

8.48 The European Commission's submission to the Court pointed out that, according to settled case law (*Wellcome, Polysar* etc) the mere acquisition and holding of shares did not constitute an economic activity for VAT purposes. They then raised the interesting point that the exemption for share transactions, as set out in arts 13B(d)5, was not intended to apply to the creation of new shares but to transactions in shares that were already in existence. The Court noted this comment (para 33) without expressly confirming whether or not it was correct.

8.49 The Court followed its earlier decisions, in *Polysar and Harnas & Helm*, and confirmed that the mere taking or holding of an interest in a company did not represent an economic activity on the part of the investor (or partner in this case).

8.50 According to the Court, it followed from that principle that neither the transfer of such an interest or the creation of a new interest could be a supply either; but this last step in the argument is not really explained in the decision. Having ruled that contributing cash and entering into a partnership is not an economic activity on the part of the new partner, the ECJ stated, at paras 40 and 41, that:

> 'If the taking of shares does not in itself constitute an economic activity within the meaning of the Sixth Directive, the same must be true of activities consisting in the transfer of such shares (*Case C-155/94 Wellcome Trust [1996] ECR I-3013, paragraph 33).*
>
> The admission of a new partner into a partnership does not therefore constitute a supply of services to him.'

8.51 Some observers have commented that this decision is hard to reconcile with the decision of the same Court in the *BLP* case, where it was assumed that a sale of shares by a holding company was an exempt supply. A closer look at *BLP* however reveals that the point was not disputed between the parties and did not therefore need to be considered by the Court. *BLP*, moreover, concerned the sale of existing shares rather than a new issue. More importantly, the fact that *KapHag* deals with the admission of a new investor to a partnership, and not with a body corporate, may be a key distinguishing point. Certainly, as far as the UK is concerned, Customs may be expected to take the line that *KapHag* is entirely consistent with their treatment of partnerships and therefore of no immediate relevance to the UK.

8.52 In *Wellcome Trust*, at para 33, the ECJ had stated that:

> 'As the Commission appositely pointed out, if such activities do not in themselves constitute an economic activity within the meaning of the Sixth Directive, the same must be true of activities consisting in the sale of such holdings.'

This is potentially confusing as the transfer of shares referred to in *Wellcome* was the transfer of shares in companies held by the investor whereas the transfer of shares referred to by the ECJ in *KapHag* is the transfer by the company or partnership of its own shares to the investor or partner.

8.53 Nevertheless paragraph 41 and the conclusion of the judgment in *KapHag* are unequivocal: the grant of [a right to] a share in the partnership in return for payment of a contribution in cash is not a supply of services. It is arguable that the same analysis must apply to the issue of shares by a company. The ECJ, however, did not actually say so. *KapHag* is a form of partnership, and some of the references in this case to 'shares' are merely describing the part-ownership of that entity. The Court heard that the partnership itself could not be said to own the rights to participate in future profits that the incoming partner wished to acquire: accordingly it could not be said to have supplied them. To extend this principle to a transaction involving the issue of securities however would almost certainly require a further ECJ case and a Court in Austria has made a reference on this specific point; and in the UK in the meantime Customs will continue to rely on *Trinity Mirror*.

Treatment of fees – other points to consider

8.54 Given the continuing resistance from Customs to the recovery of VAT on deal fees, it is essential to make sure that they are exempted wherever possible. The second step, before entering into the more theoretical aspects discussed above, is to ensure that all of the normal conditions for input tax recovery have been met.

One normal rule that is sometimes forgotten in such circumstances is that the VAT must be properly charged in the first place: so, if the purchaser's advisers' supply services that fall within one of the exemptions (eg by arranging or negotiating the deal) Customs would disallow the VAT. Another pitfall is attempting to recover input tax where the supply was made to someone else (eg the shareholders, or one of the advisers, rather than the company) – see Tripartite Arrangements, below.

Tripartite arrangements

8.55 In business it is very common for a number of parties involved in a transaction to come to an arrangement about the sharing and reimbursement of costs. This may arise, for example, where it is a condition of a loan that the borrower meets the costs of an accountant or a valuer instructed by the lending bank to confirm that there is adequate security for the proposed loan; or where meeting the cost provides an incentive to the other party as in a 'soft commission' arrangement. However, it is a precondition of VAT deduction that the taxable person has actually received the supply; who pays is of less importance. Two important cases have considered the problem of identifying the recipient of services: *C & E Comrs v Redrow Group plc [1999] STC 161 and British Airways plc v C & E [2000] V & DR 74.*

8.56 The decision of the House of Lords in *Redrow* provides guidance on how to identify the recipient of a supply of services where the services are supplied to more than one person. The Court set out four questions for a person claiming to deduct the input VAT:

(a) did that person instruct the supplier to do something?

(b) was something done for or obtained by that person?

(c) did that person use that something in the course or furtherance of its business?

(d) did that person pay consideration for the something which included VAT?

If the answer to all four questions is yes, then the person can treat all the VAT which it has paid as its input VAT.

8.57 The fact that someone else (who has not paid for it) also receives a service as part of the same transaction does not deprive the person who paid of the right to deduct. Even the apportionment of benefit between recipients of services does not matter as Lord Millett emphasised when he formulated one of the questions of the new test as 'did he obtain anything – anything at all – used or to be used for the purposes of his business in return for that payment?'

Customs' interpretation of the *Redrow* decision is contained in Business Brief 27/99 of 21 December 1999. Customs' view is that the decision only applies where the circumstances are similar to the *Redrow* case, i e where there is a claim to input tax credit by a taxable person who has commissioned goods or services and contracted with the supplier for them. Customs specifically reject the idea that payment for a supply means that the payer is a recipient of a supply. Usefully, Customs also state that they do not accept that a taxable person must have paid for a supply in order to be entitled to recover the input tax.

8.58 The *Redrow* case was applied by the VAT Tribunal in a re-hearing of the High Court case of *British Airways plc v C & E Comrs [1996] STC 1127* (meals provided to delayed airline passengers were held to be supplied to the passengers rather than the airline company). The Tribunal held that British Airways received a supply of services (the right to have the delayed passengers fed at its expense) from the restaurants and could treat the tax charged as input tax. The Tribunal held that in order to give rise to an input tax deduction under *Redrow*, there must be a prior agreement that goods or services should be supplied to a third party; and the agreement and supplies must be for the purposes of the paying party's business.

The treatment of loans and other forms of business finance

8.59 One of the arguments put forward in *BLP*, and dismissed by the ECJ, was that raising funds by a share sale was commercially very similar to raising funds by means of bank borrowing. It was confirmed therefore that where a business borrows money it is not engaged in any activity that in itself affects the entitlement to input tax recovery.

8.60 However, this does not mean that all 'debt' transactions can be disregarded. A popular tool in corporate finance is the loan note; and this (pending further developments in the courts) must be regarded as the issue or sale of a financial instrument and thus an exempt supply by the borrower.

8.61 Other matters of interest in connection with loans arise from the way in which certain advisers – e g valuers and accountants – are used. Typically these services are commissioned by the lending bank but the cost is passed on to the borrower.

8.62 The *Redrow* case was considered but not applied in *Poladon Ltd v C & E Comrs [2000] (VAT decision 16825) [2001] SWTI 180*. Poladon was a construction company which entered into a loan agreement with a bank. It was a condition of the loan that the bank required Poladon to pay for services of solicitors, valuers and quantity surveyors instructed by the bank to provide reports to the bank in relation to the activities of Poladon. The professional services firms issued VAT invoices addressed to the bank. The bank paid the fees and looked to Poladon for payment.

Poladon claimed the VAT on the invoices as input tax. Customs disallowed the claim and Poladon appealed to the VATand Duties Tribunal. Poladon looked to rely on *Redrow*. The Tribunal found that *Redrow* had no application to the facts of Poladon's appeal. The Tribunal found that Poladon had obtained some benefit from the professional services in question, namely the grant and continuation of the loan and lending facilities. Crucially, however, Poladon had never incurred any liability to the professional services firms to pay for their services. Only the bank was liable. The Tribunal held that Poladon was not entitled to credit for input tax in relation to the supplies by the professional services firms.

8.63 The appeal by Poladon might have had a different outcome if Poladon, together with the bank, had instructed the professional services firms and incurred some liability, perhaps jointly with the bank, to pay their fees.

Hedging and the corporate treasurer

Hedging or trading

8.64 All businesses need to manage their cash-flows and plan for possible movements in interest rates or currency prices. The process of managing such risks is known as 'hedging' or the 'laying off' of risk. The business may give the responsibility of managing such financial risks to a specialist treasury department. The treasury department will then act as an interface with the financial markets. The primary focus of the in-house treasury is to manage the businesses' cash-flows and borrowing requirements and to minimise losses through exchange rate and interest rate fluctuations.

8.65 The banks sell their hedging strategies as products to their corporate customers. In commercial terms, the investment banks are the suppliers and their corporate counter- parties, even those who are also financial businesses, are the customers. This is because the essential nature of these transactions is that the customer is seeking to remove an element of risk from his business arrangements, and the bank is prepared to assume that risk, in return for either a direct reward (such as a fee or commission) or an indirect reward (a dealing turn or a spread).

VAT treatment

8.66 It must be said that the VAT treatment does not always reflect the commercial reality described above. Customs' approach to determining the VAT treatment of the financial instruments used in hedging arrangements has typically been to look for cash flows moving between the parties involved and to treat these payments as indicating a supply. Therefore the VAT treatment of some of these hedging mechanisms can appear illogical. For example, under a single swap agreement the customer might (depending on market movements) be seen as making a supply to the bank on one settlement date and receiving a supply the next time around. A better approach would be to first establish whether any service is supplied and only then look to see if any identifiable consideration arises. It is difficult to see the corporate customer as doing anything of value to the bank.

8.67 The prices quoted by the banks in an FX trade incorporate a bid/offer spread that gives them the opportunity to generate a profit. This is the consideration for the service supplied by the bank. The corporate treasurer may or may not make a profit on his FX dealings but the key difference is the absence of anything that could be construed as consideration payable by the bank for anything done by the company. This reinforces the argument that the corporate treasurer is merely the recipient of the service. Similar arguments can be made in respect of options, futures and FRAs (Forward Rate Agreements).

Partial exemption implications

8.68 If the above analysis is correct it may mean that the treasury activity does not involve making exempt supplies and therefore that no input tax restriction is required. However, if there is clearly a business activity which is separate and distinct from whatever else the company does, Customs can still argue that this is an 'activity other than the making of taxable supplies' (using the wording of Regulation 101) and will expect any related input tax to be disallowed. A 'Treasury Department' employing several full-time dealers would be convincing evidence of such a non-taxable activity, whereas a few transactions handled by the Finance Director in his spare time should not.

8.69 Where it can be demonstrated that the corporate treasury does not constitute a separate activity of the business, it should be possible to treat its exempt transactions as 'incidental' so that they have little or no impact on the recovery of input tax. In such a company one would expect to find little or no input tax that was directly attributable to the hedging transactions and no compelling reason to allocate any part of the residual or general overheads there either. Clearly, other corporate treasuries are profit-centres in their own right and Customs would expect this to be recognised in determining the overall input tax recovery of the business. The concern in such cases would be to ensure that only an appropriate amount of input tax is attributed to the Treasury Department and that its high-value trades do not distort the level of VAT recovery elsewhere. One way of managing this would be to segregate the costs attributable to the treasury by using a sectorised special method.

Where the supply takes place: nominees

Water Hall Group plc

8.70 Following *Trinity Mirror* the issue of shares in the UK is firmly regarded as an exempt supply of services. Input tax attributable to an exempt supply is not recoverable except for exempt supplies specified by Treasury order. The VAT (Input Tax) (Specified Supplies) Order 1999 specifies, among other things, supplies to persons outside the EU which would be exempt financial services if made in the UK. It follows that the input tax in respect of professional fees relating to a share issue is recoverable only to the extent that the recipients of the supply of the shares (if an issue of shares is a supply) are persons belonging outside the EU (see *Water Hall Group plc v C&E Comrs [2003] VAT decision 18007, para 16*).

8.71 Water Hall is listed on the London Stock Exchange. In March 1999, Water Hall issued shares to raise equity finance. Approximately 37 per cent of the shares issued by Water Hall were issued to a nominee which held the shares on behalf of beneficial owners belonging outside the EU. The nominee company belonged in the UK. The Tribunal found (para 9) that:

> '(a) the nominee company held legal title to the shares on behalf of the beneficial owners;
>
> the nominee company's name is listed on Water Hall's register of members;
>
> the nominee company's name is recorded on the share certificate or CREST record;
>
> the nominee company is appointed by the beneficial owner and must act at all times in accordance with his instructions when dealing with the shares;
>
> ...'

The Tribunal also found that the beneficial owner of the shares made decisions as to how the nominee company should respond to communications from the company.

8.72 Water Hall claimed deduction of input tax on professional fees incurred in connection with the issue of shares to the UK nominee on behalf of non-EU beneficial owners. Water Hall knew at the time of the issue of the shares that the nominee company was merely a nominee and that it acted on behalf of beneficial owners established outside the EU. Water Hall argued that, for VAT purposes, nominees and bare trustees should be disregarded and only the beneficial owner should be seen as the recipient of the shares. Customs argued that the shares were issued to the nominee company, a person belonging in the UK. The fact that the nominee company only had legal title and held the beneficial interest in the shares on behalf of a non-EU person did not affect the analysis.

8.73 The Tribunal's shortly-stated conclusion was set out as follows:

> 'Our conclusions are that, in the case of nominees, the VAT legislation does not permit "looking through" to the underlying beneficial owner. This may be a lacuna in the legislation which needs correction but, as it stands, there is no provision which permits it.
>
> ...
>
> It does seem to us anomalous that the position is as we have stated above. The VAT position should not depend on the country of residence of a nominee.'

8.74 Although unfortunate for Water Hall, the Tribunal's decision could be a boon for everyone else. The use of nominees established outside the EU would seem to be a simple way to ensure recovery of input VAT in relation to share issues and, possibly, many other financial services. It might seem difficult for Customs to challenge an analysis which they proposed but note that Customs also have anti-avoidance arguments (non-economic activity and abuse of rights) which they would deploy if it appeared that transactions were being created (or re-routed) in order to secure a tax advantage.

Note: where a share issue is taken up by investors both inside and outside the EU the decision in *EasyJet plc* should also be considered (see **8.33** above).

The Transfer of a Business as a Going Concern

8.75 The basic rules and conditions are explained in **chapter 1**.

8.76 The legislation provides that the transfer of a business or part-business as a going concern ('TOGC') shall be treated as 'neither a supply of goods nor a supply of services'. This treatment is convenient for the taxpayer and for Customs. However, the legislation is silent as to effect of this deeming provision on the taxpayer's entitlement to input tax deduction. Clearly, if the transaction is not a supply then input tax cannot be attributed to it. The wording of the regulations however disallows deduction of input tax where it is used or to be used '... in making exempt supplies, or in carrying on any activity other than the making of taxable supplies'.

8.77 Customs do not suggest however that the input tax cannot be deducted; it is accepted that the transaction is disregarded and the inputs therefore fall to be apportioned as part of the general overheads. This was at one time an untested concession on the part of Customs, based on the idea that to disallow input tax would remove much of the intended benefit of the TOGC provisions.

8.78 The principle has now been placed on a firmer footing by the *Abbey National* (*Scottish Mutual*) case at the ECJ (*Abbey National v C & E Comrs [2001] STC 297* (**Case Summary 39**)). Scottish Mutual, a life assurance company, was a wholly owned subsidiary of Abbey National, which represented it for VAT purposes. In addition to its insurance business, Scottish Mutual carried on a business leasing premises for professional or commercial use. As part of that activity, it held a 125-year lease of Atholl House, Aberdeen which it sublet to commercial tenants. Scottish Mutual had opted to charge VAT on the rent it received for Atholl House and was thus able to recover all the input VAT paid on the costs connected with ownership of the building. In 1992, Scottish Mutual sold its rights under the lease and its rights in the sub-lease to a company outside the group. Customs agreed that the sale constituted a TOGC and that no VAT was therefore due on the sale price. Scottish Mutual incurred professional fees in connection with the sale; Customs considered that only part of the input VAT paid on those costs could be recovered. Abbey National contended that it was entitled to recover all the VAT and appealed to the Tribunal. When that application was unsuccessful, Abbey National appealed to the High Court which referred to the ECJ the question whether, where no supply of goods or services had taken place on the transfer of a totality of assets or part thereof within art 5(8) of the Sixth Directive, the taxpayer, on the proper interpretation of arts 5(8) and 17(2), could deduct the whole of the input tax in respect of costs attributable to the transfer.

8.79 The ECJ held that:

1 In principle, the existence of a direct and immediate link between a particular input transaction and a particular output transaction or transactions giving rise to the right to deduct was necessary before the taxable person was entitled to deduct input VAT and in order to determine the extent of such entitlement. A TOGC was not subject to VAT and consequently could not constitute a taxable transaction within the meaning of art 17(2). It followed that the various services acquired by the transferor in order to effect the transfer of a totality of assets or part thereof did not have a direct and immediate link with one or more output transactions giving rise to the right to deduct.

2 However, the costs of those services formed part of the taxable person's overheads, and as such are cost components of the products of a business. Even in the case of a transfer of a totality of assets, where the taxable person no longer effected transactions after using those services, their costs had to be regarded as part of the economic activity of the business as a whole before the transfer. Thus, in principle the various services used by the transferor for the purposes of the transfer of a totality of assets or part thereof had a direct and immediate link with the whole economic activity of that taxable person. It followed from art 17(5) that a taxable person who effected both transactions in respect of which VAT was deductible and transactions in respect of which it was not could deduct only that proportion of the VAT which was attributable to the former transactions. But if the various services acquired by the transferor in order to effect the transfer of a totality of assets or part thereof had a direct and immediate link with a clearly defined part of his economic activities, so that the costs of those services formed part of the overheads of that part of the business, and all the transactions relating to that part were subject to VAT, he could deduct all the VAT charged on his costs of acquiring those services.

8.80 If the taxpayer had had a sectorised special method, however, it is likely that the input tax would have been attributed to the property leasing activity rather than the taxpayer or the Court having to choose between direct attribution on the one hand and purely residual treatment on the other.

Deemed supplies under section 44

8.81 Section 44 sets out one of the oldest anti-avoidance provisions in the UK VAT legislation. It creates a charge to tax on assets transferred into a VAT group under the TOGC rules. The charge works on a self-supply basis and is applied to the open market value of the chargeable assets at the time of the transfer. The taxable person (ie the representative member of the group) must account for output tax on the deemed supply and can then treat that same tax amount as input tax, which is recoverable subject to the normal rules. The value of the deemed supply is excluded (by virtue of reg 101(3)) from the pro-rata calculation in 101(2)(d).

8.82 No special provision is made to deal with the deductibility of this input tax; but s 44 provides for full or partial relief (at Customs' discretion) from the charge for assets on which the taxable person was not able to deduct the input tax when they were first acquired. Certain other assets are excluded from the charge: those subject to the Capital Items Adjustment rules (the 'Capital Goods Scheme') and certain intangibles such as goodwill.

8.83 The requirement to account for the open market value of an asset is potentially beneficial: for example, if the asset consists of bespoke software which is of limited use to any other business, or new computer equipment which tends to lose value rapidly as new, faster and often cheaper products become available.

Examples of corporate finance transactions

8.84 The following hypothetical examples illustrate the above points.

Example1: acquisition (agreed) of a taxable trading business by a quoted holding company, consideration in cash and loan notes

The sole purpose of the transaction is for the bidder to take ownership of the target company. If this cannot be achieved the fees charged by the professional advisers will be waived or much reduced.

The fees will probably relate to such matters as the tax position of the vendor shareholders, retaining key staff, due diligence, negotiating the terms of the deal and the drafting of agreements and other documentation. These are not 'cost components' of the issue of loan notes but necessary steps towards the acquisition of the new subsidiary. It is arguable that the issue of the loan notes is one of the most straightforward aspects of the whole transaction and one which would not of itself require the services of the lawyers, tax accountants and valuers.

Example 2: a management buy-out

The MBO team forms one or more new companies, which will issue shares or other securities to a venture capital firm and other investors. Professional advisers are involved in the production of a Business Plan a report on the value of the business being acquired and its real estate and other assets, advice on taxation, negotiations with the bankers, the investors and the vendor, the recruitment of additional directors and non-execs, advice on the staff pension scheme, etc. On the successful completion of all of these services (but not otherwise) the transaction goes ahead, the investors receive their shares and the funds are used to buy the business from its former owner.

The acquisition may be of the business itself or the business may have been 'hived down' into a new company whose shares are then sold to the MBO vehicle. In these circumstances there must be a very strong argument that the share issue is only an ancillary part of the deal structure; it is a means to an end and cannot realistically be seen as the whole point of the arrangements. The treatment of the input tax should reflect this.

Example 3: a contested take-over

Like the agreed take-over or the MBO described above, a contested take-over will involve due diligence and a number of other services designed to minimise the risks to the purchaser. In addition, however, there might be a major public relations campaign, if the target company's shares are quoted on an exchange, and extensive negotiations with the reluctant vendors and with the management. Any services that consist of negotiation however are likely to be exempt. The PR services will carry VAT and are closely connected to the intended transfer of the shares and – if the consideration includes shares in the bidder-will include elements designed to enhance the perceived value of the bidder's shares. Even here, however, it should not be assumed that the fees relate entirely to the shares that are to be issued since their main purpose is to secure the agreement of the vendors to the sale of the target's shares. Many 'share for share' offers will include an underwritten cash alternative and the fees will also relate to this aspect of the deal.

8.85 These arguments as to the use of the services received should not be confused with those advanced unsuccessfully in the *BLP* and *Trinity Mirror* cases. Rather than arguing that the share issue is not a supply, or that it should be disregarded, a better case can often be made by examining the nature of the services received and the expertise brought by the advisers. Some of these services may have no connection with the share issue itself.

The fallacy of attributing the input tax to the share issue can be further illustrated by comparing two similar situations where the VAT result under Customs' current thinking would be very different. In the first, Company A acquires the shares in Company B, making a successful share-for-share offer underpinned by a cash alternative. Customs would take the view that Company A had made an exempt supply in the course of the transaction and would expect much of the input tax to be attributed to it and thus disallowed. In the second case, Company A issues shares to a group of investors before making the bid and only then engages a team of advisers to assist it in carrying out the acquisition; Company A will then be allowed to recover all of the VAT on their fees. The main purpose of the transaction, and the use to which the advisers' services are put, is the same in each case, but the VAT recovery position is changed by an arguably insignificant detail.

Planning

8.86 Given the range of possible outcomes, the first step in planning for the VAT costs in a corporate finance transaction must be to ensure that the facts are clearly understood. This is not an area where generalisations or assumptions can be safely relied upon. Before going further, therefore, it is essential to have a clear understanding of the transaction itself and the relationships between the various parties.

8.87 The second stage in planning is to ensure, before venturing into the uncertain and shifting terrain of non-supplies, dual intentions and use-based attributions, that all of the basic points have been covered. The suppliers and advisers' invoices should be examined, together if necessary with the underlying contract or engagement letter that defines the nature of the services and the identity of the recipient. Any VAT charged on a supply of financial services that is related to a transaction in securities, or lending or borrowing, should be challenged. Any VAT charged on a supply to anyone other than the taxable person in question cannot be recovered even if the taxable person is responsible, directly or indirectly, for meeting the cost.

8.88 Having eliminated the VAT that is not input tax or not properly charged, the remainder must be reviewed in the light of the regulations and of course any special method that has been approved by Customs. If the special method is clear and unambiguous and its terms cover all input tax incurred by the taxpayer, then it is the special method that dictates the rules of engagement and it is of no use arguing for substance over form, 'commercial reality' or invoking the underlying principles of the First and Sixth Directives.

8.89 If there is no special method, or its terms are of no assistance, we must turn to the various decided cases. Again, the best approach is to start with the simpler (or more settled) issues before entering into any dispute that relies on unresolved principles such as the application of the *KapHag* or *Halladale* decisions. For example, it is now settled VAT law that the costs incurred in connection with a share transaction need not be wholly attributed to that supply. Following *BLP*, it is not possible to ignore the exempt supply, but *RAP Holdings* and *Southampton Leisure* have confirmed that the taxpayer can have more than one intention when the costs are incurred, and if a service is not wholly used in making the exempt supply it must be considered to be attributable to the business activities in general. However, the days when full recovery could be achieved merely by demonstrating that the input tax is not directly attributable to the exempt supply of shares ended in April 2002 with the introduction of the Standard Method Override. If it has been established that the input tax is residual, the taxpayer is required to substitute a use-based attribution for the simple formula of reg 101. Determining the use may involve no more than confirming that the reg 101 formula gives a fair and reasonable result in the particular circumstances; it remains to be seen how the Tribunal will handle cases where Customs disagree with the taxpayer's view of that use.

8.90 Finally, and if all else fails, there is now a respectable argument that an issue of new shares, or the sale of existing shares by a person who is not in the business of generating profits from such trades, is not an economic activity within the scope of the tax. For the time being, this is uncharted territory and only those with the patience and the determination to blaze a trail through to the ECJ should contemplate challenging Customs and the UK courts.

Chapter 9

Business Specific Issues

Banking

Introduction

9.1 Banks are involved in a wide range of activities, some of which are discussed later in this chapter; their corporate finance services and the VAT implications of such transactions on the banks and their customers are discussed at length in **Chapter 8**.

9.2 This section considers the VAT issues arising from banks' mainstream 'retail' and corporate banking operations: lending, the provision of account facilities and the clearing and handling of cheques. With very few exceptions, these services are exempt from VAT and tend to be provided to customers in the same location. The result is that banks typically obtain very little input tax recovery; what they do recover relies on their non-core activities and their dealings in the international markets.

9.3 The British Bankers' Association publishes a 'Blue Book' which provides detailed guidance on the VAT treatment of banking activities. The contents of the Blue Book have been agreed with Customs and updated several times; the latest (2002) edition is available on CD-ROM.

Legislation

9.4 The exemptions applicable to banking activities are set out in art 13 B(d)1 of the Sixth VAT Directive (which covers lending); (d)3 (which covers the provision of 'deposit and current accounts, payments, transfers, debts, cheques and other negotiable instruments …'); and (d)4 (which covers 'transactions concerning currency, bank notes and coins used as legal tender …').

9.5 In the UK these exemptions are set out in VATA 1994, Sch 9, Group 5, items 1, 2, 3, 4 and 8.

Account operations

9.6 In providing a bank account to a customer the bank is clearly supplying a service for VAT. However in many banks this service is free, or at least free of overt charges while the account is in credit. The bank is willing to operate the account on this basis because it anticipates selling other services to the customer; the bank can also obtain income from the money markets for the time that it holds its customers' funds.

9.7 Customs ran the argument, in the case of *Governor and Company of the Bank of Scotland v C & E Comrs (1996) VAT decision 13854*, that the provision of a free account was not a service supplied for consideration, was therefore not an economic activity and no part of the attributable input tax could be recovered.

9.8 The Tribunal had no difficulty in dismissing this view, commenting that:

> 'Once the account is in credit (or debit) the legal relationship becomes that of debtor and creditor; and unless anything is agreed to the contrary the bank, in common with bankers generally, has a general lien over securities, etc deposited by the customer. The provision of "free" banking facility can not, in my view, be severed from the debtor and creditor relationship that subsists when the facility, eg the current account, is in operation. Whether one looks at the agreement for the current account facility or at the debtor and creditor relationship once the facility is used by the customer or at both there is a bilateral legal relationship under which both sides give consideration.'

9.9 Following *Bank of Scotland*, there can be no doubt (if there ever was) that banking is an exempt activity within the scope of the tax. Some VAT recovery is therefore possible under the normal partial exemption principles.

Electronic and online banking services

9.10 Services such as debiting and crediting transfers between accounts, standing charges and the supply of information concerning bank accounts are now often provided via automated teller machines ('ATMs') or the Internet. They remain exempt, being regarded as the provision of normal banking services by electronic means.

9.11 Since an online bank account can be accessed from anywhere in the world it is possible that there will be a gradual increase in the number of customers outside the EU and a corresponding increase in the amount of input tax that can be deducted.

Lending

9.12 'The making of any advance or the granting of any credit' is exempt under item 2 of Group 5. The value of the exempt supply is the gross interest or other sum received by the person making the loan or granting credit. This covers almost all forms of bank lending to business or retail customers, including mortgages, charges for an overdraft or excess borrowing and lending via a credit card.

9.13 An exception to this general rule is the supply of credit (and the arrangement of loans) to exporters where the services are in connection with the export or transhipment of goods to destinations outside the EU. Such supplies are outside the scope with credit, even for UK/EU customers.

9.14 Hire purchase or instalment credit finance is covered separately by items 3 and 4. HP involves two supplies: the supply of the goods and a supply of credit. The VAT due on the supply of goods is charged up front; the sums received over the term of the contract are in respect of the loan.

9.15 The management of credit is exempted but under note 2A to Group 5 this is restricted to 'such a supply made by the person granting the credit'. This can lead to difficulties where a portfolio of loans, or the right to the interest income, is transferred by the lender to another party – for example a securitisation vehicle.

9.16 In most cases, VAT deduction in respect of lending activities depends on the extent to which the services are supplied to persons outside the EU. In practice, most lending is to clients in the same country as the bank, but banks do also lend across borders, assign debts to offshore buyers (for example in a securitisation) and enter into various additional transactions in order to manage their own risks and that of the borrower; these additional 'hedging' transactions may be ancillary to the main lending activity but (depending on the partial exemption method) cannot be left out of the calculations.

Mortgagees in possession

9.17 One special arrangement exists for 'mortgagees in possession'. Following a lengthy consultation with mortgage lenders and other interested parties Customs agreed that a mortgage lender who repossesses a property and sells it to recover the debt can be regarded as the agent of the borrower; accordingly the bank can recover the VAT on certain related costs (such as the costs of securing the property and arranging the sale). This relies on a combination of the agency rules and the bad debt relief system and is set out in Customs' Business Brief 24/94.

Exceptions – taxable supplies

9.18 Banks do make some taxable supplies in the course of their mainstream activities. For example, the provision of bank statements is normally free of charge and seen as an integral part of the bank account service. However, a charge for supplying copies of old statements would be a separate taxable supply.

9.19 Other taxable supplies include:

- safekeeping services (unless part of a 'global custody' arrangement);
- trustee services; and
- any charge specifically for financial advice, if it is not provided in the course of lending.

Partial exemption

9.20 Banks have over the years adopted a variety of special methods to determine the recoverable amount. The *Bank of Scotland* case includes a detailed description of one that was until recently the normal method for a clearing bank in the UK; this would separate the large pool of input tax between 'services' and 'lending'. By segregating the 'lending' activity, the banks found that they could achieve a higher recovery rate in the 'services' side where most of the costs of running their systems and branch networks were allocated.

9.21 More recent methods involve a much more detailed allocation of input tax between the different sectors of the business. In some banks this goes down to the level of cost centres, each of which might be no larger than a trading desk or a small team. Customs tend to favour this approach because the scope for distortion of the overall result is much reduced. The basis of input tax allocation between sectors may simply follow the posting of the underlying cost, or an agreed basis of apportionment such as the number of staff in each sector.

Direct attribution: the Midland Bank case

9.22 Under any partial exemption method there is a requirement to identify input tax on any goods or services that are used, or to be used, exclusively in making either taxable or exempt supplies; such input tax is then recovered or disallowed in full, as appropriate. This step is usually called 'direct attribution' (see **Chapter 5** *Partial exemption*).

9.23 The case of *Midland Bank plc v C & E Comrs (C-98/98) [2000] STC 501* (**Case Summary 35**), concerned the attribution of input tax to a taxable supply of corporate finance advice. After the transaction a dispute arose, in which the bank was alleged to have misrepresented certain facts, and the case dealt with the bank's entitlement to directly attribute the input tax on its legal costs to the taxable supplies it had made in the course of the transaction. The case was eventually decided by the ECJ. Customs took the view that the legal services could not be cost components (using the term adopted by the European Court of Justice in *BLP*) of the bank's advice and that the bank's use of the inputs was more closely connected with defending its reputation. The ECJ agreed that, to be a cost component, it was not necessary for the expenditure to be incurred before the supply was made. However, the Court went on to hold that:

> '… a taxable person cannot deduct in its entirety the VAT charged on input services where they have been utilised not for the purpose of carrying out a deductible transaction but in the context of activities which are no more than the consequence of making such a transaction, unless that person can show by means of objective evidence that the expenditure involved in the acquisition of such services is part of the various cost components of the output transaction.'

Advice v intermediary services

9.24 It is sometimes difficult to determine whether a bank is acting as an adviser or as an intermediary. In practice these roles overlap and complement one another.

The way in which the remuneration is arranged can give a clue to interpretation but is not necessarily determinative. One would typically expect an adviser to be paid a fee and an intermediary to receive a commission; but an adviser can be paid by results or by reference to the value of the underlying transaction, while an intermediary may be paid a flat fee rather than a commission. Advisers (including lawyers) may take an active part in negotiations.

9.25 The documentation of the relationship is of critical importance. The engagement letter should make clear the nature of the services to be provided and if both intermediary and advisory elements are present it is helpful to provide for separate remuneration for each of them. It is not as convincing to do this only at the invoicing stage.

9.26 The implications for VAT recovery can be significant. Most corporate banking clients will be able to recover most of the VAT they pay on their costs. By identifying taxable elements in its services therefore the bank may be able to improve its own VAT position at no cost to the client.

Recharged expenses

9.27 A common problem in banking transactions is the treatment of recharged expenses. For example, a lending bank might instruct a professional adviser to prepare a report on the prospective borrower's financial position, or a valuation of assets. The cost of the report or valuation is passed on to the borrower. If the borrower is in business they might ask for the adviser's invoice to be made out in their name so that they can recover the VAT; but this does not assist unless it can be shown that the supply was made to the borrower. Where the bank has merely received and used the adviser's services in the course of making an exempt supply to the borrower, the bank must seek reimbursement of the whole, VAT-inclusive, cost from the borrower.

9.28 A possible solution in some circumstances is to have both parties instruct the advisor. Customs have accepted that certain services, for example a viability study, can be supplied either to the lending bank or the prospective borrower, depending on the facts. Customs' internal guidance (Customs Manual V1, Part 13, Chapter 2A, paragraph 18.4) suggests that they will place great importance on who instructs the adviser and receives his report; if both parties commission the work and receive a copy Customs say that the adviser should split the cost between the two and invoice half to each (although whether Customs are entitled to comment on the proportion to be invoiced is questionable).

9.29 Note that Customs also say:

> 'Where the company commissions the work but does not receive any report, the accountant's supply is made to the company but is not used by the company for the purpose of its business. Therefore neither the bank nor the company is entitled to recover any input tax.'

9.30 This arguably goes too far but does reinforce the need to distinguish between 'who pays' and 'who receives the supply'.

9.31 See also **Chapter 8**, on the *Redrow* and *Poladon* cases.

Clearing services

9.32 Cheque clearing services operated by a bank are an integral part of their operations and are exempt under item 8 or items 1 and 6. It has always been accepted that cheque clearing carried out by one bank for another is also exempt under these items.

9.33 However, the position was put in doubt by a Danish case, *Spaerkassernes Datacenter v Skatteministeriet (C–2/95) [1997] STC 932, ECJ*, which was referred to the European Court of Justice on the question of whether outsourced cheque clearing and payment processing services fell within the exemption. The view of the Danish Government was that these supplies were beyond the scope of the exemption and should be standard rated as data processing. The Advocate-General's opinion was that the exemption did not apply unless the taxable person carrying out the service had a direct connection with the bank's customer. However the Court held that a direct legal relationship with the end customer was not essential, and

> 'The fact that a transaction covered by those provisions is effected by a third party but appears to the end customer to be a service provided by the bank does not preclude exemption for the transaction.'

9.34 Therefore, the services of the data centre could be exempt 'if those operations are distinct in character and are specific to, and essential for, the exempt transactions'. The application of the decision to other types of outsourcing in the financial sector is still being debated; see *CSC Financial Services Ltd v C & E Comrs (C-235/00) [2002] STC 57, ECJ* and *C & E Comrs v FDR Ltd [2000] STC 672, CA.*

Credit card operations

9.35 Any interest or fee charged to a UK customer in respect of a credit card account is exempt under item 2 of Group 5.

9.36 Under note 4 to Group 5, the 'merchant charge' made by the acquiring bank to a retailer who accepts the card in payment for goods is also exempt. This typically takes the form of a discount, or a commission, on the price of the goods.

9.37 Charges passing between the banks and the various 'umbrella organisations' such as Visa International for clearing and settling credit card payments are exempt under item 5. The decision in *FDR* confirmed that charges by specialist outsourcers could also be covered by the exemption. Outsourcing however remains a contentious area.

Structured finance

9.38 Some banks employ specialist 'structured finance' teams to devise new financial products, or combinations of different financing techniques, to meet the particular needs of a client. A deal might involve, for example, an equity swap (which is effectively a sale and repurchase of securities) together with currency and interest-rate swaps and more traditional lending. Each of these elements must be treated, for VAT purposes, as a separate transaction.

(The treatment of swaps etc is covered under 'Capital Markets' at **9.74**.)

Insurance

Introduction

9.39 Insurance and reinsurance transactions of all kinds are exempt from VAT. This includes 'related services' such as claims handling and certain insurance-linked financial products such as pension schemes. Insurance companies and insurance brokers cannot therefore recover much, if any, of their input tax. The insurance companies also tend to operate in their local markets, so there may be little or no non-EU business to improve the recovery rate. The reinsurance and underwriting markets, by contrast, are worldwide.

9.40 Even for UK-based life assurance companies, however, the provision of insurance to their customers is only part of the picture. A life insurance or assurance company is also an investment company with an actively managed portfolio of investments in the stock markets and other assets including property. Customs tend to regard these activities as separate, and potentially distortive if included in a partial exemption method; however they do offer some scope for recovering part of the input tax suffered.

VAT legislation

9.41 The basis for the exemption of insurance and insurance-related services is set out in art 13B(a) of the Sixth Directive, which covers:

> 'insurance and reinsurance transactions, including related services performed by insurance brokers and insurance agents.'

9.42 In the UK this is reflected at rather greater length by VATA 1994, Sch 9, Group 2. The notes to Group 2 are longer than the text of the four items of the group itself, and contain detailed guidance on their interpretation. Most of the case law in this area has considered the meaning and application of the 'related services' and some of the notes can be traced to specific cases.

9.43 The role of an insurance intermediary is defined by notes 1 and 2 as:

'(1) For the purposes of item 4 services are services of an insurance intermediary if they fall within any of the following paragraphs–

(a) the bringing together, with a view to the insurance or reinsurance of risks, of–

(i) persons who are or may be seeking insurance or reinsurance, and

(ii) persons who provide insurance or reinsurance;

(b) the carrying out of work preparatory to the conclusion of contracts of insurance or reinsurance;

(c) the provision of assistance in the administration and performance of such contracts, including the handling of claims;

(d) the collection of premiums.

(2) For the purposes of item 4 an insurance broker or insurance agent is acting "in an intermediary capacity" wherever he is acting as an intermediary, or one of the intermediaries, between–

(a) a person who provides any insurance or reinsurance the provision of which falls within item 1, 2 or 3, and

(b) a person who is or may be seeking insurance or reinsurance or is an insured person.'

Insurance brokers and agents

9.44 The definitions in item 4 and notes (1) and (2) to Group 2 acknowledge that an intermediary is not just the person who sets up an insurance arrangement in the first place. The insurance contract runs over a period of time and any interaction with the insured person during that period can be seen as related to the policy.

9.45 An insurance intermediary whose business is all within the EU would not expect to recover much, if any, of his input tax. However, the recipient of the broker's service is not necessarily the insured person. Examination of the contracts may well indicate that the service is supplied to the insurer. The broker may spend the majority of his time dealing with actual and potential customers in his local market, but he typically does so as agent for one or more insurance companies; not all of them are in the UK, and some are outside the EU. The insured person does not normally pay the broker for his services (except for certain businesses who engage a broker specifically to provide advice); so where the broker collects the premium he normally does so as the agent of the insurer.

9.46 Insurance businesses incur significant amounts of input tax on their marketing costs. They have therefore been keen to see these services, wherever possible, as falling within the exemption as insurance-related services. Under note 7 to Group 2, however, the exemption does not apply to any supply of 'market research, product design, advertising, promotional or similar services', or to 'the collection, collation and provision of information for use in connection with' such services. The current guidelines place great emphasis on whether the person supplying the marketing service has the authority to bind the insurance company to the contract – ie do they (like a broker) have the power to create a contract, or does the service stop short at attracting the attention of potential customers (like an advertiser)? Merely sending out a mailshot falls short of being an intermediary service; but if the marketing company also handles the responses and puts the insurer in contact with the customer it can be said to be fulfilling a part of the role of 'an insurance broker or insurance agent'.

9.47 Customs say that they will accept an intermediary's services as falling within the exemption '... where the following three criteria are met:

- they are paid per successful take-up of an insurance policy;
- they are targeting their own customer base; and
- the intermediary endorses the product or the insurer.'

9.48 These elements are not necessarily the only indicators that an intermediary service qualifies for exemption; and they may not be determinative in all cases.

Claims

9.49 The payment of money, or the provision of replacement goods, under an insurance contract is not seen as the consideration for a supply and thus has no impact on the VAT deductions of either party.

9.50 Insurance claims by VAT-registered businesses will normally be settled on a VAT-exclusive basis, since the VAT-registered business can recover some or all of the VAT on the replacement goods (or repair services, as the case may be).

9.51 Claims handling is exempt from VAT, but this does not extend to all services that might be involved in a claim. Loss adjusters specialise in reviewing insurance claims, on behalf of the insurer. Their services are exempt, but only if they have delegated authority to settle the claim; otherwise the supply is seen as effectively one of information or advice. The services of 'other experts' in connection with insurance policies or claims follow the same guidelines: if the expert is merely valuing an item, or assessing the damage sustained in an accident, the service will probably be taxable, but if the expert is contracted to handle or settle the claim exemption should apply.

Warranties

9.52 Warranties, such as those sold with new kitchen equipment and new or used cars, are regarded as insurance products. Following a spate of avoidance cases, where retailers were perceived as shifting value from the taxable goods to the exempt warranty, these products are now subject to Insurance Premium Tax, at a rate set to match the standard rate of VAT.

9.53 The case of WHA (*WHA Ltd v C & E Comrs [2003] EWHC 305 (Ch), [2003] STC 648*) concerned a VAT planning structure which sought to recover the VAT on car repairs and parts supplied when a driver made a claim under the warranty. WHA happened to be providing the warranties under an arrangement with Viscount, a Gibraltar-based insurance company. For the planning to be effective, it had to be demonstrated both that the input goods and services were supplied to WHA (rather than the car owner) and that WHA used the inputs in making 'specified supplies' to Viscount. Alternatively, if the services of WHA were taxable, Viscount sought to recover the VAT under the 13th Directive, on the basis that Viscount itself was using the input services in making supplies to another non-EU insurer.

9.54 Customs won at Tribunal, where it was held that the garages made their supplies of replacement parts and repair services to the car owners and not to WHA. The Tribunal also found that WHA supplied two distinct services – claims handling (exempt) and arranging the repairs (taxable). The Tribunal further held that Viscount could not claim under the Thirteenth Directive because the provisions of the Specified Supplies Order did not apply to Thirteenth Directive claims.

9.55 WHA was successful on appeal to the High Court. Taking into consideration the *Redrow* decision, the Court found that WHA did receive a benefit from the garages' services which enabled WHA to perform its obligations to Viscount. The Court saw WHA as 'procuring the garage to do the necessary work', as part of a single supply of claims handling services. The claims handling services fell within the exemption under Sch 9, Group 2, and accordingly qualified for input tax deduction when supplied to a person outside the EU.

Reinsurance

9.56 Insurers usually lay off at least part of their risk by purchasing cover from a reinsurance company. The supply of reinsurance is exempt, the consideration being the premium paid. The reinsurance market is international, so reinsurance companies may have a significant level of non-EU income.

9.57 The case of *C & E Comrs v Deutsche Ruck UK Reinsurance Co [1995] STC 495* concerned the deduction of VAT on legal costs that arose some time after the reinsurance contract to which they related. The reinsurance contract was a non-EU supply and the company claimed full recovery on the basis that the input tax was directly attributable to that contract. Customs argued that the input tax was residual and the debate turned on whether the legal services could be a cost component of a supply that had already taken place before the legal dispute arose. Customs contended that 'the provision of insurance cover consisted only in the promise to pay money or confer some other benefit on the occurrence of any event specified in the contract and in the maintenance of that cover, not in the actual payment of money or other benefit in the event of the occurrence of any such event'. The Court found in favour of the company, on the basis that the reinsurance contract gave rise to obligations that remained in place for years and 'a supply of insurance services consisted both in entering into the contractual obligation and in fulfilling it'. Accordingly the company was correct in directly attributing the legal costs to the disputed contracts.

9.58 The Court found for the company because of the special characteristics of reinsurance. The case is not however a general authority for retrospective 'direct attribution', as can be seen by comparing the outcome to *C & E v Midland Bank plc (see* **9.23** *above).*

Partial exemption methods

9.59 Most of the recurring costs of an insurance business fall into the category of general overheads. Of those that relate specifically to individual contracts of insurance, many are exempt. Insurance companies are however major users of computer equipment and related software and support services. Some of these are undoubtedly used predominantly in connection with the company's dealings with its insurance customers. Others may be wholly or partly used in managing the insurance company's property or investment portfolios.

9.60 In contrast to the banks, who traditionally treated most of their input tax as residual, most insurers seem to have conceded that their inputs are wholly or predominantly used in making exempt supplies. Their partial exemption methods have therefore been an exercise in identifying departments or activities where some VAT recovery is possible (the staff restaurant, or the property portfolio) and deducting only the input tax that can be shown to be attributable to those departments. Many insurance companies posted costs to departments on a VAT-inclusive basis and thus had little or no idea how much VAT they were incurring. This has started to change, as insurance companies incur greater amounts of VAT on computer and other technology and make use of that technology in their accounting systems. However, moving away from the position where all of the input VAT is assumed to relate to exempt supplies of insurance is difficult. Customs' starting point appears to be that insurance is a wholly exempt business and that the taxable and non-EU activities should be seen as separate; and it is almost impossible to cancel an agreed partial exemption method until Customs can be convinced that the proposed new method is more accurate (but see **Chapter 6** paragraphs **6.33A** and **6.33B** on the Special Method Override Notice). One way to overcome this would be to split the business into sectors, to show that the taxable and non-EU activities do not distort the recovery of a large residual pot.

Capital markets

9.61 The term 'capital markets' is used here as a convenient shorthand for the national and international markets in shares and other such securities, derivatives, bonds, currencies, loans and deposits. This section therefore concentrates on transactions falling within items 1 and 6 of Group 5 of the exemption schedule and the various issues affecting VAT deduction in this sector.

9.62 The most important factor in securing any VAT recovery in respect of capital markets transactions is to establish whether the supply or any part of it qualifies as a 'specified supply' under VATA 1994, s 26 and the VAT (Input Tax) (Specified Supplies) Order 1999, art 3. Where securities are issued or sold as principal this is simply a question of identifying where the buyer is established; if the buyer is outside the EU then input tax is recoverable.

Intermediary services

9.63 In some markets (such as foreign exchange, or futures and options) participants contract as principal to principal and traders who – in commercial terms – might be regarded as brokers, are in fact riskless principals. In other markets, such as the stock markets, brokers arrange and execute transactions in return for a commission. The services of a broker or intermediary qualify as 'specified supplies' where either the client is outside the EU or the broker arranges a transaction where the client sells to a buyer outside the EU. This 'second bite of the cherry' is often forgotten, possibly because the necessary data is not collected automatically.

9.64 The transaction charges levied by exchanges such as LIFFE and the Stock Exchange, or the clearing services provided by the London Clearing House or Euroclear, are also exempted as intermediary services. Therefore, transaction charges on commodities trades are taxable but transaction charges in respect of trades in shares, bonds, and financial futures are exempt.

The 'non-supply' argument and identifying the consideration

9.65 In the early years of VAT, in the UK at least, the treatment of transactions on these markets varied considerably. Many supplies of these financial instruments were regarded by Customs as 'outside the scope' of VAT, for one reason or another. This had the convenient effect that the high values of such transactions could be left out of partial exemption calculations, thus preventing distortion at a time when only a limited number and variety of partial exemption methods were available. The other side of that coin however was that no part of any input tax that was attributable to such trading was recoverable, even if all or most of the customers were outside the EU. In practice many traders were allowed to look through or disregard these trades, with the result that the input tax was effectively attributed to other parts of their business.

9.66 It was always accepted that transactions in securities (which included shares, bonds, Certificates of Deposit and notes other than promissory notes) were exempt supplies. However, where bonds or commercial paper were traded at a price that was calculated as a discount against a nominal value, Customs considered that there was no consideration. No cases were ever heard on this but over the years it became clear that this was not well-founded and Customs gradually accepted that the consideration was whatever the buyer paid, irrespective of the nominal value. By 1995 therefore the only form of financial trading that was still officially regarded as outside the scope was Foreign Exchange. Customs acknowledged that there was some doubt on this, but their discussions with the industry failed to reach a consensus and they continued to maintain their 'no supply' policy until it was overturned by the case of *C & E Comrs v The First National Bank of Chicago (C-172/96) [1998] STC 850, ECJ*. The bank in this case acted as a market maker in the foreign exchange markets and a significant percentage of its counterparties were outside the EU. The bank had agreed a 'sectorised' special method with Customs, under which the input tax was first allocated between the different trading departments and then apportioned between that which was attributable to non-EU transactions by using a transaction count. This made FNBC an ideal test case, since it meant that the courts could be asked to rule on the fundamental question of whether FX trading of itself was an economic activity within the scope of the tax, without also having to address the even more perplexing question of how, if it was a supply, such a supply could be valued. In 1998 the case was decided by the ECJ, who held that FX trading by a market maker such as FNBC was indeed an economic activity. The key facts that led to this conclusion were that the bank, in holding itself ready to buy or sell at its quoted prices, was clearly performing a service; and the fact that it obtained a profit was incompatible with the idea that there was no consideration.

9.67 The second question addressed to the Court was to determine what, if such trading was a supply for consideration, was 'the nature of the consideration'. The Court found that this lay in the difference between the bid and offer prices quoted by such businesses, which created the potential for profit. However, the Court also ventured an opinion on how such consideration should be valued, even though his was of no relevance to FNBC itself, and concluded that this was the amount of profit achieved over a given period of time. This would always be a net figure of profits minus losses, and could not therefore be split between EU and non-EU trades. Since in most cases the only reason to place a value on such a supply would be to work out the non-EU percentage for partial exemption purposes, this was not particularly helpful. Indeed, since this was at odds with the treatment of all of the other forms of financial trading where bid and offer spreads are used, it had the potential to cause more problems than it solved. In practice the UK has effectively ignored this aspect of the decision.

9.68 In the UK, most businesses involved in the capital markets on a regular basis now use a special method similar in principle to that of FNBC at the time of the case: sectorisation (ie allocating the input tax between sectors of the business) followed by a transaction count to determine the relative volumes of EU and non-EU trades. The idea of counting the number, rather than the values, of supplies made in the period has the advantage that it may avoid distortion that could otherwise arise where trades of different kinds are carried out by the same department. This approach has its roots in the stockbroking sector and dates back to the days (before 1990) when stockbrokers' services were taxable and their only exempt supplies were 'error bargains' where they were obliged to enter into the market in their own name, as a principal, in order to correct a long or short position that had arisen through a mistake.

9.69 Transaction counts however are not without problems of their own. It is important to define clearly whether the method consists of counting supplies, counting deal tickets, or literally counting all transactions – including those where the taxable person is not making a supply but receiving one. Because FNBC was a market maker, it could be said to be supplying a service in every transaction; but other participants in the FX market are clearly acting as supplier when dealing with their clients and as a customer when they cover their positions by dealing with the market makers. In the futures markets, there is the question of whether a trade between members of the exchange, which is not regarded as a supply because there is no consideration, should nevertheless be regarded as a transaction for partial exemption purposes. Also, many futures traders may find it more convenient to count the number of lots traded than the number of occasions when a trade takes place.

'Not an economic activity'

9.70 Notwithstanding *First National Bank of Chicago*, there are still situations or activities within the capital markets where the taxable person may not be making a supply. One example would be the investment activities of a company (or other body) that did not actively buy and sell securities (etc) on a sufficiently regular basis to be regarded as carrying on an economic activity – see *Wellcome Trust Ltd v C & E Comrs (C-155/94) [1998] STC 945, ECJ* (**Case Summary 23**). In the UK, Customs' comments immediately following *Wellcome Trust* suggested that the decision would be relevant only to a similar charitable body and not, for example, to the investments of a pension fund, a unit trust or an investment company. This assertion has not been challenged, and it would not appear to be in anyone's interests to do so; however some of the observations made to (and by) the ECJ in *KapHag* (see **Chapter 8** and **Case Summary 49**) might prompt a tax authority in another member state to take a further case.

Not making a supply but receiving one

9.71 Another example where a taxable person might participate in the markets without making supplies arises from the special arrangements on the futures exchanges. A financial futures or options contract is not, strictly, a fungible instrument – that is, it cannot be bought and sold in the way that a share can. If a client wishes to take a position in the financial futures market, he goes to a member of the relevant exchange who then sells him a futures contract. When the client wants to close out his position, he must buy another contract with matching but opposite terms, from the same exchange member or another; the two positions are then matched by the Clearing House and (effectively) cancelled by setting one against the other. The client, unless he is also a member of the exchange, cannot 'sell' any futures contract and is always the recipient of the supply. Input tax need not therefore be attributed to these trades.

9.72 Customs also say (in Notice 701/9) that trades between members of a futures exchange such as LIFFE do not represent supplies for consideration unless a dealing turn or commission is shown. However, given the outcome of *First National Bank of Chicago* and the similarities between the markets in futures and foreign exchange, this is almost certainly incorrect. As with foreign exchange, the consideration lies in the differential between the prices at which the trader is prepared to buy and sell, which creates the opportunity to generate profit.

Options

9.73 Similar principles hold for options. An option conveys the right, but not the obligation, to buy or sell a specified quantity of a specified asset on a particular date or between a range of dates. The option contract is non-assignable: despite the name, even 'traded options' are not capable of being sold on. The person who creates or grants the rights pertaining to the option is the option writer; his exposure is theoretically unlimited, although in practice he will normally balance his trading book by entering into other contracts. The other party is the recipient of the supply and pays a premium for the rights acquired; the option buyer can only lose the amount paid on acquiring the option. The option buyer therefore does not make a supply in respect of that transaction, although he may of course make one if he himself writes options, or if in exercising the option he makes a supply of the underlying security.

Swaps and FRAs

9.74 Commercially, one might expect the same logic to extend to trading in swaps and Forward Rate Agreements (FRAs). Swaps and FRAs are financial products, and are sold as such by banks and other specialists; they are bought by businesses or investors who use them to manage interest rate or currency exposures. The swap buyer typically pays a premium on entering into the contract, which on the face of it would appear to indicate that this is a supply of services by the bank. However, the swap also involves a payment or series of payments at predetermined settlement dates, and these payments can go in either direction. Customs currently see the receipt of such a payment, by either party, as consideration for an exempt supply. A more realistic approach would be to accept that the consideration lies in the premium paid, and/or in the interest-rate differential built into the price; the sums changing hands on the settlement dates should probably be regarded as outside the scope in the same way as the payments made following an insurance claim or a winning bet.

New issues

9.75 A new issue of bonds or other financial instruments in the capital markets can be a very substantial transaction with considerable costs. The deduction of the related VAT is discussed in **Chapter 8**, along with the intriguing question of whether the issue of new shares should be regarded as a supply for VAT purposes. All of the concerns that have been debated by the courts in respect of share issues and share transactions apply with equal force to issues of other forms of financial instrument.

Finance houses, hire purchase and factoring

Finance houses

9.76 A finance house offers a range of financing options to business and private purchasers. The most common transactions are hire purchase and leasing, although there are many variations. In VAT terms, the finance house might appear to be primarily concerned with the exempt, credit-related aspects of these transactions, but it also makes supplies of goods (in a HP transaction, or when disposing of repossessed goods) and taxable services (under an operating lease).

9.77 Until the changes in the partial exemption rules in 1984, finance houses were regarded as fully taxable. Following those changes, Customs and the Finance Houses Association (now part of the Finance and Leasing association or FLA) agreed on some general principles as to how the association's members should treat their input tax. This allows members to split their input tax between HP, leasing and exempt lending operations. All of the input tax on leasing should be recoverable but none of the input tax on lending. In the HP sector of the method, the business can recover all of the input VAT on goods bought for sale in the same state and 15% of the residual input tax. The agreement is now rather dated and makes no provision for dealing with input tax on cross-border supplies, but could still be used as the basis for a special method.

Hire purchase

9.78 When a finance house provides funds to finance the purchase of goods in a HP transaction, the finance house becomes the owner of the goods. There is a supply of goods by the retailer or dealer to the finance house, and then two supplies, one of goods and one of exempt lending, from the finance house to the customer. The finance house is making taxable supplies in such circumstances and is liable to notify and be registered in the normal way.

9.79 HP companies may pay commission to retailers who introduce customers to their finance service. The commission is exempt – provided that the retailer acts as an intermediary; car dealers and furniture retailers typically sit their customer down and complete the application form with them but the position is not always so clear-cut. For example, if the retailer merely hands the customer a leaflet or provides a link on its website the introduction could fall outside the intermediary definitions.

Block discounting

9.80 A common feature in high street credit operations is 'block discounting'. This involves the finance house buying a number of rental agreements (for example in respect of televisions) for an up-front, discounted amount. At one time these were seen as exempt assignments of debts by the retailer/dealer to the finance house, but following discussions with the FLA Customs noted that in most cases these transactions also included the transfer of title to the goods. It was therefore agreed that, with effect from 1 December 1992, block discount trades should be treated as taxable supplies of goods, while the finance houses would now be seen as making taxable supplies of goods to the rental customers. In practice, the retailer would usually continue to collect the customer's payments but would now be seen as doing so as the agent of the finance house.

9.81 From the retailer's perspective the new VAT treatment would make little difference, since the 'assignments' would in most cases have been disregarded as 'incidental' under reg 101(2)(d). For the finance house, however, this clearly had the potential to substantially improve the recovery of input tax.

Factoring

9.82 Factoring, along with debt collection, is specifically excluded from exemption under Art 13B(d)(3) of the Sixth Directive (*Finanzamt Gross-Gerau v MKG Kraftfahrzeuge-Factoring GmbH (C-305/01) [2003] STC 951*). However, the assignment of debt which is an essential part of most factoring arrangements is exempt; and there are many forms of factoring, each with subtly (or significantly) different VAT issues.

9.83 The position of a factor who purchases debts from the original supplier, with no recourse to the assignor in the event of non-payment, has a further complication. On one analysis, his actions after taking ownership of the debts consist of collecting money for himself rather than supplying a service to anyone else; but a recent decision of the ECJ found otherwise (see **9.88** below).

9.84 The first question asked is usually whether the factoring arrangement is with or without recourse; that is, whether the risk of non-payment remains with the original supplier or passes to the factoring company.

9.85 The factor makes a living by purchasing the debts at a discount from their face value; the level of discount will reflect the risks involved and thus will be much higher if the factor has taken on the exposure to bad debts. The factor may pay some or all of the agreed value of the debts up front, or may settle at the end of an agreed period of time; sums released up front may be seen as effectively the same as a loan and are typically subject to interest. The factor may charge separately for maintaining the client's sales and debtors ledgers and for other administrative or advisory services; all of these are taxable. Some (non-recourse) factors also make supplies of goods that have been repossessed. Any assignment of debts back to the client under a 'with-recourse' factoring arrangement is disregarded (that is, it is regarded as a partial cancellation of the initial assignment rather than a new exempt supply).

Partial exemption implications

9.86 The client's VAT deduction entitlement is normally unaffected by the factoring arrangement. The assignment of debt is an exempt supply, but one that can be treated as 'incidental' under the standard partial exemption method. Any input tax that relates wholly to the assignment would in principle be irrecoverable, but in most cases this would appear to be de minimis.

9.87 The partial exemption position of the factor can be very complex. Customs agreed a set of ground rules with the Association of British Factors and Discounters (ABFD), full details of which can be found in Notice 700/57 (or on Customs' website). The main features of this are a requirement to separate the input tax between 'invoice discounting factoring' and 'mainline factoring' and the identification of certain transactions that are seen as fully attributable to either taxable or exempt supplies in this business. It should be noted that the agreement is not binding on individual businesses; nor does it constitute a special method.

The MKG case

9.88 On 26 June 2003 the ECJ released its decision on the case of *Finanzamt Gross-Gerau v MKG-Kraftfahrzeuge-Factory GmbH (C-305/01) [2003] STC 951, ECJ*. The Court drew a distinction between 'true factoring', where the debts and all associated risks were passed to the factor, and 'quasi-factoring' where the client retained the liability for non-payment. The German tax authority took the view that true factoring, as performed by MKG, was not an economic activity and denied input tax recovery to the company. The Finanzamt argued that the activity was comparable to the passive investment activity of *Polysar* (Case Summary 11). The ECJ disagreed, holding that true factoring represented a supply to the client (relieving them of the risk of non-payment and the work of collection and administration); the consideration for the supply was in the difference between the face value of the debts and the discounted value at which they were transferred. (In *MKG* the discount was actually described as a fee plus a commission, and VAT was charged because the service was seen as essentially one of debt collection). The supply thus identified did not fall into any of the exemptions (and as noted above is specifically excluded from art 13B(d)3); it was therefore taxable and the factor's input tax was recoverable under art 17.

9.89 The ramifications of this decision have yet to be seen. In Germany it appears that the decision is to be applied only narrowly, seeing the taxable activity as represented by the commission charged by the factor. In the UK, the case has led to a reappraisal of the current VAT treatment and ongoing discussions between Customs and trade bodies. It may be that the contractual position in the UK factoring industry is distinguishable from the German example considered by the Court.

9.90 The case does also raise the question of whether the treatment of other assignments of debts (or receivables) should be reviewed. The transfer of a stream of property rentals as security for a loan, or an assignment in the course of a securitisation, for example, could perhaps now be seen as supplies by the assignee.

Funds and investment management

Overview

9.91 Most readers will be aware that the services of fund managers are mainly taxable, while the activities of the various forms of collective investment scheme are mainly exempt. In practice, of course, very little about the VAT treatment of this sector is as simple as that sounds. Depending on the circumstances, on the nature of the investments, on the legal relationship between the manager and the owner of the assets, and on the way in which the activity is conducted, the ownership and the management of investments can be taxable, exempt, outside the country, or a non-business activity. Getting the entitlement to VAT deduction right is therefore no easy matter.

9.92 The participants in the market range from individual shareholders, through informal investment clubs and family trusts to the various kinds of investment company and some very large institutions. They are all involved in buying, holding and selling shares and other financial instruments, which on the face of it is an exempt activity. Even that simple statement however needs to be qualified. The *Polysar* (Case Summary 11) and *Wellcome Trust* (Case Summary 23) cases show that investment is not necessarily an economic activity at all, even when undertaken by a company, or on a large scale; on the other hand, in cases where it is a business activity, a sale of securities to a buyer outside the EU counts as a 'specified supply' for the purposes of VATA 1994, s 26(2)(c) and the related input tax can be recovered.

Investment management

9.93 Investment managers' services range from handling short-term cash deposits and quoted shares to managing open-ended investment companies ('OEICs'), hedge funds, investment trusts, unit trusts and other forms of individual or collective investment. The role of the fund manager varies, depending on the needs of the client, the nature of the assets and the degree of discretion he can exercise and the VAT treatment of his services changes accordingly. Some or all of the manager's functions may be sub-contracted out.

9.94 Fund managers are typically paid a periodic fee based on the value of funds under management; but they may also charge according to the volume of transactions undertaken for their client. The fund manager's fees may be paid by the fund itself or by the individual investors.

9.95 The fund manager's services will typically involve some or all of the following elements: investment advice; arranging the purchase or sale of investments; the administration of an investment fund (or trust); and managing a Unit Trust or an OEIC. In VAT terms therefore the manager makes both taxable and exempt supplies.

Investment advice

9.96 Investment advice and other fund management services, including administration, are standard-rated unless they relate directly to arranging specific transactions or the client is a unit trust or an OEIC, in which case the services will normally be exempt. If the client belongs overseas, the services may be outside the scope of UK VAT. It should be noted that fees charged to clients within the EU who are not in business remain standard rated. Therefore, a fee for managing an investment portfolio for (say) a Belgian individual would carry UK VAT, but managing the assets of a pension fund in Ireland would not.

9.97 The manager can recover input tax to the extent that it relates to taxable services, but is also entitled to recover input tax on the costs incurred in making 'specified supplies' – which include services to overseas clients that would have been taxable within the UK and all financial services supplied to persons outside the EU. See below for the unusual position regarding cross-border management of OEICs and unit trusts.

Arranging transactions

9.98 The 'issue, transfer or receipt of, or any dealing with' shares or other securities within the UK is an exempt supply under item 6, Group 5. This includes the issue or transfer or sale of units in a unit trust or the shares issued by an investment company or investment trust. Therefore, when an investment manager is paid for introducing an investor to one of these collective investment schemes his services are exempt.

9.99 If the recipient of the supply belongs outside the EU, or is in business and belongs in the EU, however, the supply is outside the scope of VAT, respectively with and without the right to input tax recovery.

9.100 The investment manager will act in the capacity of an agent, arranging transactions on behalf of the fund or the investor (the fund's principal).

Administration

9.101 Any charge for administering a portfolio, or a trust or investment fund, will be subject to standard-rated VAT. In some cases these costs are absorbed by the fund manager and taken into account in setting transaction charges or annual management fees.

9.102 There are special rules affecting the VAT treatment of administering a pension fund. The service itself is standard-rated and the pension fund manager will therefore recover any related input tax; the question however is whether the supply is seen as being made to the pension fund itself or to the employing company. The sponsoring company will generally be able to recover the VAT as normal input tax, since the company incurs the cost in fulfilling its obligations to employees and pensioners. Most pension funds recover little or no input tax, because their activities are exempt (or possibly 'not economic activities').

9.103 The administration of a PEP or ISA is again a taxable service.

Unit trust and OEIC management

9.104 The management of an authorised Unit Trust is exempt. Art 13B(d)6 of the Sixth Directive exempts 'the management of special investment funds as defined by Member States'. In the UK this was restricted to the management of an authorised unit trust by the unit trust manager; it was extended to cover the services of an authorised corporate director ('ACD') to an OEIC with effect from 24 March 1997. From that date, the services of the ACD of an OEIC are exempt, when they consist of managing the company's scheme property.

9.105 Following defeat in *Abbey National plc v C & E Comrs (VAT decision 17506) [2002] SWTI 842,*and *Prudential Assurance Co Ltd v C & E Comrs (VAT decision 17030) [2001] SWTI 769*, Customs accepted that the exemption of 'the management' must be applied to any business whose services consist of the management of the assets of the fund.

9.106 Customs have now changed the legislation to reflect those decisions. The new wording of item 9 exempts 'the management of an authorised unit trust scheme or of a trust based scheme' without the qualification 'by the operator of the scheme'. The exemption therefore covers sub-contracted unit trust management services.

9.107 Item 10 now reads 'the management of the scheme property of an open-ended investment company' and the notes to Group 5 have been amended accordingly. Note 10 refers to the Financial Services and Markets Act 2000, s 236 to establish the meaning of 'open-ended investment company'.

9.108 Whereas the old wording of items 9 and 10 clearly tied the conditions for exemption to definitions set out in UK law, there is now nothing in the plain wording of the Group to restrict the exemption to the management of unit trusts and open-ended investment companies in the UK. Indeed, item 10 could be said to apply to other forms of collective investment schemes such as SICAFs. Customs have however confirmed (in Business Brief 10/2003) that they will apply the exemption only to funds established in the UK:

> 'The references to authorised unit trust schemes or trust based schemes in item 9, group 5, Sch 9 to the VATA 1994 are references solely to UK based schemes.
>
> The reference to open-ended investment companies in item 10, group 5, Sch 9 to the VATA 1994 is a reference solely to those incorporated in the UK.'

Custody and safekeeping services

9.109 Simple safekeeping services are taxable, but if the service is primarily concerned with handling money, including the collection of dividends, the whole supply may qualify for exemption. This is sometimes described as a 'Global Custody' arrangement.

Partial exemption

9.110 Businesses in the fund management sector have traditionally recovered most of their input tax, with the level of disallowance being determined by the relative size of their exempt unit trust and more recently OEIC management income. The exempt proportion has increased further, following the extension of the exemption to sub-contracted unit trust and OEIC management.

9.111 Because a unit trust manager also buys and sells units from the 'manager's box', as principal, the standard value-based partial exemption method would be unfavourably distorted. Unit trust managers are normally partly exempt with a very high proportion of exempt outputs. The Unit Trust Association (now merged with the IMA) agreed a special method for unit trust managers in 1990, but this is not compulsory.

9.112 Examples of the VAT treatment of investment management services supplied in different circumstances:

Services supplied to	VAT treatment of the service	Manager's input tax recoverable
UK Pension fund	taxable	Yes
UK individual	taxable	Yes
UK OEIC or Unit Trust	exempt	No
Luxembourg investment company	outside the scope – specified supply	Yes
French individual	taxable	Yes
Belgian local authority	taxable	Yes
Irish OEIC	outside the scope – NOT a specified supply	No
Luxembourg SICAF	outside the scope – specified supply	Yes
US pension fund	outside the scope – specified supply	Yes

Services supplied to	VAT treatment of the service	Manager's input tax recoverable
Swiss individual	outside the scope – specified supply	Yes

Unit trusts

9.113 A unit trust is defined by the Financial Services and Markets Act 2000, s 237(i) as 'a collective investment scheme under which the property is held on trust for the participants'. The unit trust sponsor – the company that effectively operates the fund – assembles the portfolio of securities but deposits them with trustees who are legally responsible for the conduct of the trust. The range of securities contained in any one fund may be narrow or wide, allowing the investor to make investment decisions whilst still enabling him to obtain diversification.

9.114 The investors' rights to participate in the income and capital of the trust will depend on the number of units held. Each unit represents an undivided interest in the aggregate value of the underlying portfolio of securities. Usually a fixed number of units will be issued to the public, or to underwriters, at the launch of the trust. Because unit trusts may only issue redeemable securities the unit trust manager makes a secondary market in units, buying from and selling to investors at a price based on the underlying value of the fund.

9.115 If the unit trust scheme is to be offered to the public, it must be 'authorised' (under the FSMA). Unauthorised unit trust schemes exist but may not be advertised or promoted, except between authorised persons, thus restricting their use to professional investors. The VAT exemption does not extend to the management of unauthorised trusts.

Investment trusts

9.116 An investment trust is a UK resident company with all classes of its ordinary share capital quoted on the Stock Exchange. Such a company is prohibited from distributing any capital profits from the sale of investments, but must distribute at least 85% of its income. The trust income must be derived 'wholly or mainly' from shares or securities. An investment trust is similar to a unit trust in that the trust's sole business is the acquisition and disposal of securities in order to reflect the requirements of its investors. Essentially the investment trust represents a large investment portfolio owned by many shareholders who share in the income, expenses and traded gains and losses in proportion to their own shareholdings. However, whereas a unit trust is run by trustees, an investment trust is essentially a trading company controlled by a board of directors.

9.117 Investors acquire shares in a trust that matches their own portfolio requirements. The number of shares in issue will fluctuate daily, along with the size of the shareholders' investment.

9.118 Investors in an investment trust typically pay an up-front fee of 5%. This is seen as the consideration for the issue of new shares and thus exempt from VAT.

OEICs

9.119 An open-ended investment company (OEIC) is a more recent form of collective investment scheme subject to similar controls as a unit trust. Under an OEIC scheme, the assets belong to a special purpose company which has as its purpose the investment of its funds in order to spread investment risk and give its shareholders access to expert fund management.

9.120 The supplies made by the investment company or trust will generally consist of transactions in securities. If the whole of an investment trust's business takes place in the EU it will be fully exempt and unable to register for VAT. It is likely however that securities will be sold to purchasers belonging both within and outside the EU. Input tax is recoverable to the extent that it can be shown to relate to non-EU sales.

9.121 Note that dividends received from investments are ignored in this calculation, as are the proceeds received when a bond is held to maturity.

9.122 Dealings in the units themselves are transactions in securities and exempt under item 6 of Group 5. Where new units are created, Customs do not recognise any supply by the manager of the trust to the trustees in arranging for the creation of the units. Any fee charged by the manager to the trust will thus be outside the scope of VAT.

Other collective investment schemes

9.123 Other EU countries have also defined certain collective investment vehicles as 'special investment funds' under art 13B(d)6. These schemes are sometimes known as 'UCITS', referring to the EC UCITS Directive. ('UCITS' stands for 'Undertakings for Collective Investment in Transferable Securities'.) The UCITS Directive is an EC Directive which sets out a number of requirements for such investment vehicles (EC Directive 85/61/EEC, as amended by Council Directive 88/220).

9.124 Luxembourg and Belgium operate a form of UCIT known as a SICAF, while Ireland has OEICs. (A SICAF is a 'Société d'investissements à Capitale Fixe'.)

Land and property

VAT liability of property transactions

9.125 Property transactions can be taxable at the standard rate, taxable at the zero rate or VAT exempt, thus giving rise to several degrees of uncertainty as to the extent to which VAT incurred on expenditure is deductible.

9.126 At the present time, there is no provision in UK VAT law for supplies of land and property to be liable to VAT at a reduced rate, but that may just be a matter of time, as the UK comes under pressure from the EC to reduce or even repeal completely the zero rates, and from some sections of the UK property industry to equalise the VAT differential between new domestic housing and housing which was dilapidated, or derelict, and has therefore been renovated.

Attribution of input tax

9.127 In property transactions, attribution of input tax is normally determined on a property-by-property basis. A person should be able to recover all the input tax directly attributable to a building in relation to which taxable supplies are made, or to be made, either if they make taxable supplies of the building by selling or leasing it, or if they occupy it to carry on a business which makes only taxable supplies.

9.128 This principle of attribution and recoverability of input tax applies to all input tax incurred, regardless of the underlying supply upon which the input vat is incurred. Thus, if VAT is incurred on a head-rent of a building or a piece of land, it will be recoverable depending on whether the building, or piece of land, is used for making taxable supplies.

9.129 Similarly, input vat incurred on site charges and other preliminary costs is recoverable – or not – depending on whether the land or buildings are used for making taxable supplies.

9.130 The same principle also applies to VAT incurred on reverse premiums and other inducements. The liability of the underlying supply for which a reverse premium, or inducement, is the consideration is a vexed issue, currently being hotly debated by businesses, Customs and Excise, lawyers and VAT advisers, and an explanation of why it is a vexed issue is beyond the scope of this book. However, when VAT is incurred on a reverse premium or inducement, it is recoverable – or not as the case may be – depending on the use to which the relevant land or buildings are put.

9.131 A person will not recover any input tax directly attributable to a building in relation to which only exempt supplies are made or to be made. Where a property is used to make both taxable and exempt supplies then under VAT Regulations 1995, SI 1995/2518, reg 101 only a proportion of the input tax is recoverable.

9.132 Where supplies are zero-rated or exempt (or take place outside the UK), no VAT is charged by the supplier to their customer. Moreover, provided the person making the supplies is registered for VAT, they are able to obtain credit for (or obtain repayment of) any input tax paid by them which is directly attributable to any supplies they make which are zero-rated or treated as taking place outside the UK provided they would be taxable if made in the UK. However, they cannot obtain credit for (or obtain repayment of) any input tax paid by them which is directly attributable to any exempt supplies they make, or to supplies which are made otherwise than in the course of business.

9.133 Thus, zero-rating is the most favourable VAT treatment as it does not require the supplier to charge VAT to their customers and does not restrict recovery of VAT input tax. The making of exempt supplies, however, will be less desirable because the input tax attributable to such supplies is not recoverable.

9.134 Is there, then, much more to say in this section, other than to consider which supplies of land and property fall within which category, and hence which give rise to the right to deduct VAT, and which do not?

9.135 The answer is of course, 'yes', but why? It is principally because supplies, which would otherwise be exempt, can become liable to VAT at the standard rate, through the ability of suppliers to elect to waive exemption, more commonly referred to as 'the option to tax' (see paragraph **9.147** below). But supplies which are standard-rated can suddenly, and sometimes quite unexpectedly become VAT exempt, either through the disapplication of the option to tax, or through the passage of time which happens when a new building ceases to be new for VAT purposes.

Changes in the VAT liability

9.136 The metamorphosis of an exempt supply into a standard rated supply, and perhaps subsequently back into an exempt supply, will of course play havoc with a supplier's ability to deduct VAT, and the matter of determining what VAT is deductible and when, and what has to be repaid to or clawed back by Customs and Excise can be a complex matter which often catches out even the experienced business or professional adviser.

9.137 Determining the deductibility of any VAT incurred is not assisted by the underlying UK national property legislation. The UK national legislation on land and property transactions has been evolving for almost a thousand years, and it should come as no surprise that in many cases, the fundamentals of UK land law and pan-European VAT law are at best uneasy bedfellows.

9.138 The European Court of Justice in the case of *Finanzamt Uelzen v Armbrecht (C-291/92), [1995] STC 997* (Case Summary 19) (a case which dealt with the sale of a building comprising both commercial and residential premises) recognised that the national legislation of Member States may contain fundamental requirements which do not sit at all comfortably with the structure of Value Added Tax. In its decision, the European Court of Justice limited the extent to which national property law can determine VAT liabilities and the resulting fiscal effects of those consequences. Nevertheless, a taxpayer is able to rely on national law if the national VAT legislation is based on it and it is to the taxpayer's advantage to do so. This view was also exploited in the case of *Aquarium Entertainments [1994]*

VATTR 61, but interestingly enough was not followed in the case of *Tall Pines Golf and Leisure Co Ltd (VAT decision 16538) [2002] SWTI 904*, although the tribunal chairman was invited to do so.

The mechanics of VAT recovery

9.139 Where VAT is eligible for recovery from Customs, this is done by setting it against the output tax which a taxpayer accounts for on their return or, if their input tax exceeds their output tax on that return, claiming a repayment. A credit or a repayment may be obtained or claimed in full in the return for the period in which the VAT is incurred: there is no need to wait until there is sufficient output tax to set against the input tax. The maximum period between a taxpayer paying VAT to a supplier and obtaining a credit or repayment, where the entitlement arises, should be about four months for a person with a quarterly accounting period.

9.140 In property transactions, attribution of input tax is normally determined on a transaction, or property-by-property, basis. Transactions in land and property can conveniently be split into two main categories, commercial and residential.

Commercial land and property transactions

9.141 Exemption could reasonably be regarded as the default for transactions in commercial land and property, and it is therefore appropriate to look at precisely what is exempt from VAT. There is one complete group within the exemption schedule to VATA 1994 which is devoted entirely to land and property: VATA 1994, Sch 9, Group 1.

9.142 The basic principle in VATA 1994, Sch 9, Group 1 is that the grant of any interest in or right over land or licence to occupy land is exempt unless it is:

(a) excluded from exemption (and therefore standard-rated) under Item 1, paras (a) to (n) of VATA 1994, Sch 9, Group 1; or

(b) zero-rated under either VATA 1994, Sch 8, Group 5 or Group 6; or

(c) standard-rated if the supplier has opted to tax the land in question (VATA 1994, Sch 10. Part 2).

9.143 So, quite simply, if expenditure is incurred in anticipation of a transaction in commercial land and property, none of the VAT incurred on that expenditure can be deducted unless the transaction can be made to fall outside VATA 1994, Sch 9, Group 1.

9.144 The statutory exclusions from exemption mentioned at (a) and (b) above are, in general terms, relatively straightforward, and are not considered further (but see *Tolley's Business by Business*, Chapter 25 'Property Development' for a more detailed explanation). With one exception dealt with at the next paragraph below, all that need be said is that when a transaction in land and property falls within the exclusion from exemption under (a) or (b) above, the VAT incurred on the related expenditure may be deducted.

New buildings

9.145 That one exception is not so much an exception, but more of a pitfall which can often be overlooked, and is the freehold sale of a new building. The key word here is 'new' because the freehold disposal of a new building is excluded from exemption under Item 1, para (a)(ii) to VATA 1994, Sch 9, Group 1. When is a commercial building new? Customs and Excise say that a commercial building is new for VAT purposes for three years from the date it is completed. This means that any sale of the fee simple (freehold) within that three-year period will be liable to VAT at the standard rate, and hence all of the VAT incurred can be deducted.

9.146 The freehold of a commercial building can be sold many times within a three-year period, and still, for VAT purposes, remain new, liable to VAT at the standard rate, and therefore giving rise to the right to deduct VAT incurred on expenditure.

The election to waive exemption

9.147 The more interesting, more problematic, and much more frequently encountered exclusion from exemption is (c) above, the 'option to tax' – which is effectively standard rating by choice. This provision, one of only two such in UK VAT law (the other being in respect of certain supplies of Gold), allows a supplier to exercise a degree of choice. Thus, the supply of a land or property which would otherwise fall to be VAT exempt by default, will be transformed into a supply which will give rise to an obligation on the supplier to charge VAT but which will also give rise to the right, by the supplier to deduct VAT incurred on associated expenditure.

9.148 The option to tax was brought into UK VAT law in 1989 shortly after the UK finally lost the legal battle to retain what had until then been a widespread application of the zero rate to supplies of land and property, and it was introduced into the UK VAT legislation purely to allow most businesses engaged in land and property transactions to continue to be able to deduct the VAT incurred on the expenditure relating to the supply.

9.149 The option to tax, or, to give it its more correct legal terminology, the election to waive exemption, is permissive (under both UK and EC law). This means that, as UK law currently stands, a supplier cannot be forced to opt to tax, but has the right to decide the VAT liability for himself. Significant commercial and other tax issues are likely to flow from such a decision, but these are beyond the scope of this book. But for a business that has incurred, or is contemplating incurring, significant amounts of VAT the option to tax provided some freedom of choice, and hence allows a business to contemplate arranging its land and property transactions such as to be able to deduct VAT on the related expenditure.

9.150 Input tax which is incurred before the option to tax has effect (but after 1 August 1989) and which is fairly and reasonably attributable to a taxable supply of the property is recoverable, even where the person who exercised the option had made exempt supplies in relation to the property before the option has effect, provided Customs permit the recovery of such input tax when authorising the election (this is dealt with in greater detail in **9.162** below.

The scope of the option to tax

9.151 There are exceptions to every rule, and it is no different with the option to tax. In some cases, vendors or landlords have no freedom of choice because there are some supplies over which they cannot opt to tax, and hence in respect of which the VAT is not deductible. (Technically, the correct position is that the option to tax can be made on any property, but in some cases it is disapplied and will have no effect.) The option to tax, even if made, does not have any effect on the following supplies of land or property, and hence in respect of these supplies, no VAT can be deducted:

(a) the sale or letting of a building or part of a building intended for use as a dwelling, or for use solely for relevant residential purposes (VATA 1994, Sch 10, part 2(2)(a));

(b) the sale or letting of a building or part of a building intended for use solely for relevant charitable purposes (VATA 1994, Sch 10, part 2(2)(b));

(c) the sale or letting of a pitch for a residential caravan (VATA 1994, Sch 10, para 2(2)(c));

(d) the sale or letting of facilities for the mooring of a residential houseboat, where the residents are not prevented from occupying the houseboat throughout the year by any restrictive covenant or other restriction (VATA 1994, Sch 10, para 2(2)(d));

(e) the sale or letting of a property to a registered housing association (now termed Registered Social Housing Landlords) which has provided a certificate to the vendor or landlord that it will, after any necessary demolition, construct a building or buildings for use as domestic residential accommodation or solely for relevant residential purposes (VATA 1994, Sch 10, para 2(3)(a));

(f) the sale or letting of a property to an individual who will, after any necessary demolition, construct a dwelling for his or her own occupation (the so-called DIY Housebuilders) (VATA 1994, Sch 10, para 2(3)(b));

(g) the sale or letting or property between two persons, legal or individual, where:

   1. the property is an asset which is or is expected to fall within the Capital Goods Scheme; and

   2. the person occupying the property will use the property wholly or mainly to make supplies on which recovery of input tax is restricted;

if, at the time that the interest was granted, the person occupying the property was:

(a) the person who granted the interest; or

(b) a person who directly or indirectly provided the finance for the acquisition or construction of the property; or

(c) a person connected with either the person referred to in (a) or (b) above.

9.152 This last category of restriction, category (g) is anti-avoidance legislation, introduced as a result of the 1996 Budget, and further amended in the 1999 Budget. It is exceptionally complex even by the standards of VAT land and property legislation, and contains many new terms and conditions, the ultimate effect and application of some of which are even now still being tested and determined by the VAT tribunals and the courts.

9.153 For a much more detailed consideration of the option to tax on land and property transactions, how it is made, and how is can be disapplied, *see Tolley's Business by Business* Chapter 25.

When the option is disapplied

9.154 A supplier may therefore opt to tax, and have that option take effect, only to have it forcibly disapplied if one of the above circumstances in (a) – (g) above prevails. What would otherwise then have been a taxable supply in respect of which VAT is likely to have been quite rightly and properly deducted, becomes exempt, and in consequence, the supplier will have to repay the VAT deducted to HM Customs.

9.155 If the land or property on which the option to tax is forcibly disapplied, is a capital item within the Capital Goods Scheme, then the VAT deducted will be repaid to Customs and Excise under the terms of that scheme. But if the Capital Goods Scheme does not apply, then the provisions of 'clawback' under the VAT Regulations 1995, SI 1995/2518, reg 108 come into play, and it is under those regulations that VAT already deducted has to be repaid. The difference between the two is essentially of a mechanical nature, and the essence is that VAT which will have been deducted can quite suddenly and unexpectedly have to be repaid to Customs and Excise.

VAT incurred before exercising the option to tax

9.156 The flip side of the coin is of course that where VAT has not been deducted because it was incurred in respect of the making of exempt supplies, a successful option to tax will result in the making of taxable supplies, and hence there will, in most cases (see the paragraph below for details of the most likely exception), be a right to deduct at least some of the VAT previously incurred. How the Capital Goods Scheme affects the deduction of VAT is discussed in more detail in **Chapter 7**, but in simple terms where property is a Capital Item within the Capital Goods Scheme, then any deduction which arises will be made under its terms. If the property is not a Capital item, then any right to deduct which arises as a result of the option to tax will be made under the provision of 'payback ' under the VAT Regulations 1995, SI 1995/2518, reg 109.

9.157 However, exercising the option to tax will not always result in a business then being able to deduct VAT previously incurred. In their decision in the case of *Royal and Sun Alliance Insurance Group plc [2003] UKHL 29, [2003] STC 832* (Case Summary 47), the Lords took the view that the VAT incurred by RSA on the head rent charged by RSA's landlord was not deductible.

9.158 RSA had a number of leasehold properties which were surplus to its requirements, and sought subtenants. In order to maximise its commercial flexibility, RSA took the decision not to opt to tax until subtenants had been found, believing that this would afford it the best chance of achieving sublets. Once subtenants had been found, where these subtenants were engaged in activities which would permit them to deduct VAT on the rent charged by RSA, RSA then opted to tax.

9.159 RSA then submitted a 'payback' claim under the VAT Regulations 1995, SI 1995/2518, reg 109 for the VAT that the head landlord had charged it, but which it had not previously deducted.

9.160 In a 3–2 majority decision, the Lords took the view that the VAT charged by RSA's headland lord could only be attributed to the supply or supplies that RSA could have made, on a real-time basis, in the time period to which the rent related. What this means is that where RSA incurred VAT on rent quarters pre-dating RSA's option to tax, the VAT it suffered could not be a cost component of an onward taxable supply which gives rise to the right to deduct, because at that point in time, RSA had not opted to tax.

9.161 Put another way, the VAT incurred by RSA each rent quarter was consumed by it during that rent quarter, and because there was no option to tax in place, the VAT consumed did not form a cost component of any onward taxable supply and hence could not be deducted. It was only after RSA opted to tax that the VAT on the head rents started to be consumed by RSA for the purposes of an onward taxable supply, and hence RSA's right to deduct VAT on rent only arose on those rents charged by the Landlord after RSA had opted.

The need to seek permission to opt to tax

9.162 One final aspect of the option to tax and its impact on the deduction of VAT incurred by a business is that in some circumstances a taxpayer must seek Customs and Excise's prior permission to exercise the option to tax (VATA 1994, Sch 10, para 3(9)). In essence, permission is required when a supplier has already made exempt supplies of the property. It is important to realise that this does not apply when a supplier has made VAT exempt supplies and has used the property to house his business (ie a bank which has always occupied a building for its own use and which has not made supplies of the property), but only applies when the property or part has itself been supplied, for example, by a letting or sub-letting of all or part of it.

9.163 Where permission is required, there is a specific sequence of events that must take place before the option can be effective, ie the taxpayer must seek the permission of Customs and Excise to opt to tax. Only then can the taxpayer take the decision to opt to tax and hence to avail himself of the ensuing right to deduct VAT previously incurred.

9.164 Fortunately, the circumstances where Customs and Excise's permission is required are straightforward, although in many cases obtaining that permission can be fraught with difficulties.

9.165 Where permission is required, Customs and Excise require the person making the option to provide proposals for determining how any VAT previously incurred which was not deducted because it was attributable to the making of exempt supplies is now to be calculated as deductible being attributable to both the exempt supplies (made prior to the option taking effect) and the taxable supplies (made after the option has taken effect). See VATA 1994, Sch 10, para 3(9).

9.166 If Customs and Excise are satisfied that the proposed attribution for determining deductibility is fair and reasonable, they will give their permission to opt to tax, and hence for deduction to be made. If the supplier then accepts Customs and Excise's permission and proceeds with the option, he can then deduct the amount of VAT which Customs and Excise have agreed is attributable to his future taxable supplies of the property.

9.167 Customs and Excise may not accept the proposals for deduction put forward by the supplier and if that happens, Customs and Excise are not under an obligation to suggest an alternative method, although it is not at all unusual for them to do so.

9.168 The ruling of the High Court in the case of *C & E Comrs v R & R Pension Fund Trustees [1996] STC 889*, has influenced Customs and Excise to the extent that, even in cases where the property concerned does not fall within the Capital Goods Scheme, Customs and Excise take the view that the calculation of the quantum of deductible VAT must be carried out as if it did. Such an approach favours Customs and Excise, and it is hard to understand how Customs and Excise justify this new approach as providing a fair and equitable result.

Automatic permissions

9.169 There are a few very limited circumstances when properties have been used in the making of exempt supplies where it is not necessary to seek Customs and Excise's prior permission to opt to tax. Automatic permission does not, however, relieve the landlord or property owner from the obligation to notify

Customs and Excise that the option has been made. The few exceptions which constitute automatic permission are listed in C & E Notice 742, and it is important to note that to qualify for automatic permission, a business may in some cases, have to give up any right to deduct some or all of the VAT previously incurred, or to be incurred in the future. At the time of writing, the conditions for automatic permission are:

(a) where the (opted) property is a mixed use development and the only exempt supplies (sales, leasing or lettings) have been in relation to the dwellings; or

(b) it is proposed that there will be no input tax recovery on expenditure made prior to the effective date of the option, and

- the only income received from the property has been by way of rent (ie no premium was paid by the tenant), and
- the only input tax to be recovered after the option takes effect is on day to day overheads (ie you will not recover any VAT on a refurbishment or redevelopment); or

(c) it is proposed that input tax incurred prior to the option will be recovered, but this input tax relates solely to tax charged by the tenant upon the surrender of a lease, and

- the building, or relevant part, has since been unoccupied; and
- there will be no further exempt supplies of the property; and
- you intend or expect that your occupation of the land or building will be for a fully taxable purpose; or

(d) the exempt supplies have been incidental to the main use of the property (eg the siting of an advertising hoarding within the curtilage of a building).

Domestic and other 'non-commercial' land and property transactions

9.170 Land and property which is occupied or 'consumed' for domestic dwellings, for certain other 'relevant residential purposes', or for certain 'relevant charitable purposes' is intended to be relieved of the immediate burden of VAT by virtue of being either zero-rated, or exempt.

Zero-rated transactions

9.171 Zero-rated supplies of land and property are dealt with in some depth in *Tolleys Business by Business,* Chapter 11 'Construction Industry', but it is appropriate to consider them briefly in this chapter.

9.172 A transaction in land and/or property can only be zero-rated in certain quite rigidly defined circumstances. The legislation found in VATA 1994, Sch 8, Groups 5 and 6, allows the first grant of a major interest to be zero-rated, when it is made by a person who:

(a) has constructed or is in the process of constructing a dwelling or other building which is intended solely for relevant residential use or for use by a charity for relevant charitable use; or

(b) has converted or is in the process of converting a commercial building, or part of a commercial building, into a dwelling or other building intended for relevant residential use; or

(c) has substantially reconstructed a protected building (listed building) which remains a dwelling.

9.173 From 1 August 2001, the zero rate of VAT also applies to the sale of renovated houses that have been empty for 10 years or more (VATA 1994, Sch 8, Group 5, Note 7).

9.174 When a supplier makes a zero-rated supply, then clearly he will be able to deduct all of the VAT incurred on the expenditure relating to that supply. However, it is important to recognise the significance of the fact that what is zero-rated is only the first grant of a major interest. For instance a housebuilder who zero-rates the freehold sale of a new house may commonly accept houses in part-exchange, and such a business may find itself taking in part-exchange a house which it had originally built some years previously. Thus, the VAT that the housebuilder incurs in constructing the brand new house is deductible by him, but his eventual re-sale of the second-hand house is always going to be a VAT exempt supply, and hence he cannot deduct any of the VAT he has incurred in respect of buying in and selling on that second-hand house.

9.175 Although the first grant of a major interest in a new dwelling is zero-rated, housebuilders are not able to deduct all the VAT they incur on building a new dwelling. This restriction is given statutory effect by the VAT (Input Tax) Order 1992, SI 1992/3222, art 6, which is an anti-avoidance measure, intended to ensure that the final consumer does not acquire certain domestic fixtures and fittings free of VAT, and housebuilders are not able to deduct VAT on some items which are sometimes supplied as part of a new house. In the main, these deductible items are some fitted furniture, some electrical appliances and carpets. The rationale for this is that VAT can be recovered only on items ordinarily installed by builders, in new houses. (See *Tolleys Business by Business*, Chapter 11 'Construction Industry' for a more detailed explanation.)

9.176 As discussed above, the zero rate applies to the supply of the first grant of a major interest in properties which are dwellings, and results in the right to deduct the VAT incurred. But a supply liable to VAT at the zero rate, with the consequent right to deduct VAT incurred on expenditure, can also be made in respect of property which is not a dwelling.

9.177 The zero rate also applies to the supply of the first grant of a major interest in property which is intended to be used for relevant residential and relevant charitable purposes. A relevant residential purpose is defined in VATA 1994, Sch 8, Group 5, note 4 and note 5 and a relevant charitable purpose is defined in VATA 1994, Sch 8, Group 5, note 6.

9.178 Thus if a business is able to make a zero-rated supply of relevant residential or relevant charitable use property, then the VAT incurred may be deducted.

Exempt supplies

9.179 But not all supplies of new dwellings and/or property used for relevant residential or relevant charitable purposes will be taxable supplies giving rise to the right to deduct VAT incurred on related expenditure. It is often the case that supplies of new dwellings and of property used for relevant residential or relevant charitable purposes are exempt.

9.180 There are two principal variants here. Firstly, exempt supplies will be made when there is never a supply of the first grant of a major interest because the person who has constructed the properties supplies them under a grant of a lease of less than 21 years duration. Where such properties are supplied under such 'short' leases all of the supplies made will be exempt from VAT, and thus the supplier will not be able to deduct any VAT incurred on constructing the property, or on the on-going costs of repairs and maintenance.

9.181 Secondly, where there is a zero-rated supply which is followed by exempt supplies, usually where the freehold is not sold, but properties are leased. Even when the lease is a first grant of a major interest by virtue of the granting of a lease for a period exceeding 21 years, exempt supplies will still be made. In fact, there will be a zero-rated supply followed by on-going exempt supplies. The premium, if any, for the lease exceeding 21 years, or in the absence of a premium, the first rent payable under the lease, will be the consideration for the zero-rated supply. Thus, a zero-rated supply will be made, and this gives rise to the right to deduct the VAT incurred on the construction of the properties. But further payments of rent will be due under the terms of the lease, and all such further payments are consideration for exempt supplies, and the VAT incurred in relation to those exempt supplies is not deductible.

9.182 In practice, this means that the VAT incurred on the construction costs remains deductible, and is, in effect, 'ring-fenced'. However, VAT incurred after the zero-rated supply is made is not deductible, as it is attributable to exempt supplies. Thus, VAT incurred on on-going repair and maintenance expenditure, even on dwellings and property used for relevant residential or relevant charitable use is not deductible.

Property transactions forming part of the transfer of a business as a going concern (TOGC)

9.183 The deduction of VAT incurred when a business, or part of a business, is sold as a going concern has already been discussed at **Chapter 3** and will not be repeated here. However, one aspect of a TOGC involving land and property transactions is worthy of a passing mention.

9.184 With regard to deduction of VAT on the costs of disposal of properties by way of TOGC, the ECJ, in the case of *Abbey National plc (Case C-408/98) [2001] STC 297, ECJ* (**Case Summary 39**), has ruled that when a property business was transferred which had been operated as a fully taxable part of a business, the VAT on the costs of the TOGC were fully deductible. Had the property business been an exempt business, the VAT on the costs would not have been deductible.

DIY house and self-build projects by voluntary bodies

9.185 Specific legislation (VATA 1994, s 35) permits recovery of input tax on building materials by persons carrying out certain works other than in the course or furtherance of a business. This scheme puts such persons in a similar position to a developer building houses or flats for sale, who can obtain input recovery by virtue of the zero-rating of the first sale. Under the scheme, the person undertaking the building works need not be VAT registered to recover the VAT incurred. Recovery of VAT is permitted on building materials used for the purpose of:

- construction of buildings designed as dwellings;
- construction of a building for use solely for a relevant residential purpose or relevant charitable purpose;
- conversion of a non-residential building (or a non-residential part of a building) into dwellings or into a building intended for use solely for a relevant residential purpose (but not a relevant charitable purpose).

9.186 On a conversion within (c), VAT on services provided by a contractor (other than an architect, surveyor etc) is also recoverable. Services within (a) and (b) are normally zero-rated so recovery is not necessary.

Summary

9.187 To summarise, the basic rule for property transactions is that disposals and grants of interests in land are exempt. This means that no VAT is charged to the purchaser or tenant but input tax is not deductible by the supplier (the vendor or landlord). There is a facility, applicable to the non-residential sector, to treat otherwise exempt transactions as taxable (the 'option to tax'), and hence VAT incurred usually becomes deductible as a result.

9.188 Zero-rating is available in respect of certain supplies relating to qualifying buildings (relevant residential and relevant charitable use), and in such cases the VAT incurred on the related expenditure can be deducted.

Betting and gaming

Summary

9.189 VATA 1994, Sch 9, Group 4 exempts from VAT:

'The provision of any facilities for the placing of bets or the playing of any games of chance; and

The granting of a right to take part in a lottery.'

9.190–191 However, certain activities are excluded from the exemption, notably admission to premises, the provision of a right to participate in a game in respect of which a charge may be made, certain membership subscriptions and the provision of gaming machines.

9.192 In addition, most betting and gaming premises also contain other facilities, in particular catering and/or bar facilities. The net result is that taxable persons who provide betting and gaming facilities are likely to make both taxable and exempt supplies and will therefore be partly exempt.

9.193 A number of other features of betting and gaming businesses are worth noting, ie:

- In addition to catering for customers, gaming businesses usually also have to provide meals and refreshments to staff because of the unsocial hours they have to work;
- Many businesses will give away considerable amounts of meals and drinks in order to ensure that customers stay on premises and continue to participate in the core gambling activities;
- There are often admission charges to premises.

9.194 It should be noted that some gambling premises may form part of another business eg a hotel in which case even more complex issues may arise.

9.195 Where betting and gaming businesses make both taxable and exempt supplies, it will be necessary to carry out some method of apportionment in order to determine the VAT that is deductible.

Business entertainment

9.196 The VAT on business entertainment is not deductible (see **Chapter 4**). The amount of VAT to be disallowed is the VAT on the cost of providing such entertainment. However, the cost of providing meals to staff is not business entertainment (see **9.198–9.201** below).

9.197 It should be noted that the cost of the staff employed in providing the business entertainment is not treated as part of the cost – there are no self-supplies in relation to business entertainment since the UK has chosen not to implement the provisions of the EC Sixth VAT Directive, art 6(3).

Staff meals

9.198 VATA 1994, Sch 6, para 10 provides that where an employer provides catering and accommodation services to staff, there is a supply (which is taxable because there is no provision exempting such supplies). The value of the supply is limited to the cash actually paid and is taken as nil if no payment has to be made by the staff.

9.199 Even where no payment is received, the VAT on making such supplies is nevertheless deductible – provided that the taxable person is able to determine the VAT incurred on the provision of such services.

9.200 However, given that the value of the service may be reduced (if meals are subsidised) or may even be nil, if free, an outputs based method of determining the VAT deductible on staff meals is unlikely to result in a proper attribution of the input tax to these taxable supplies. It should be remembered that since the VAT on costs may be attributable to taxable supplies to customers, business entertainment and supplies to staff, some form of apportionment is inevitable.

9.201 Nevertheless, as will be seen below, that apportionment is likely to have to be made on a holistic basis.

Partial exemption

9.202 Businesses that undertake betting and gaming activities may need to apply for a special method to attribute input tax to taxable supplies. This will in part be due to the fact that in the absence of a special method, no input tax would be attributed to the nil value supply of staff meals. However, it is also the case that turnover may not represent a correct measure of the use of inputs to make taxable supplies in say a restaurant as opposed to what might be used to run a betting and gaming session. A further problem arises because the activities of a restaurant may be largely intended to support the activities of the gambling activities as in some casinos This is by no means always the case since there are casinos attached to fully fledged catering businesses e g a hotel where the restaurant is a business in its own right and not merely some supporting function of the gambling activities.

9.203 Notwithstanding the fact that turnover may be a poor measure of use, it is likely that Customs and Excise will use turnover-based methods as a yardstick against which to judge whether a special method is fair and accordingly a gaming business may well have to justify any alternative approach that it wishes to adopt. In *Aspinall's Club Ltd (VAT decision 17797) [2003] SWTI 314,* the taxable person was unable to convince a VAT and Duties Tribunal that a method based on floor area was fair. The evidence showed that taxable turnover represented 1% of the total turnover whereas the suggested method would have given a 55% recovery. It is obviously not possible to comment on the correctness or otherwise of a tribunal decision without having the same information to hand as that presented before the Tribunal. However, as noted, there are two fairly obvious reasons why a recovery of 1% was probably also not fair. However, it needs to be borne in mind that in the absence of agreement to a special method, a taxpayer will be stuck with the standard method. It follows that if a special method is advanced, the taxable person needs to make sure that he is able to demonstrate it is both fairer than the standard method and, if an alternative method has been advanced by Customs and Excise, fairer than that method as well.

9.204 The introduction of the standard method override can however limit the damage that will be incurred by not agreeing a suitable method. This will be clear when it is considered that the turnover of say a casino can fluctuate substantially without affecting the mainly fixed costs involved in operating a casino It just depends on how much punters are prepared to spend. On the other hand, if a restaurant is attached to the casino, there is more likely to be a physical limit to the value of meals and drinks that can be served. Thus, if the business neglected to apply for a special method or was refused one, it could use the standard method override to arrive at a fairer method.

Educational institutions

Summary

9.205 The supply of education by an eligible body is exempt from VAT. Eligible bodies include:

- schools;
- universities and other higher education institutions;
- further education colleges;
- public bodies; and
- not for profit organisations.

9.206 A body that is not within the above but teaches English as a foreign language will be an eligible body in respect of its supplies of English as a foreign language (including certain incidental supplies) but not in respect of other unrelated activities.

9.207 In addition to education, the supply of research by one eligible body to another is also exempt although it must be noted that the CJEC held that by exempting similar supplies of research from VAT, the Federal Republic of Germany was in breach of its obligations under the EC Sixth VAT Directive. (See *EC Commission v Germany (C-287/00) [2002] STC 982, ECJ*.)

9.208 Other activities of an educational institution will follow the normal rules. Supplies of education by a body that is not an eligible body will not be exempt.

9.209 Because an educational body makes both exempt and taxable supplies, it will have to restrict the amount of input tax it is entitled to deduct. In addition, it should be noted that Customs and Excise consider that certain grant-funded activities of higher education institutions are not business activities. In addition, the nature of some educational institutions' activities is such that they will carry on non-business activity. While this has some advantages in terms of certain zero-rate and reduced rate reliefs an educational institution can gain, it also means that an educational institution may also have to restrict the deduction of VAT it incurs on the grounds that it is not input tax but tax on supplies attributable to non-business activities.

Non-business supplies generally

9.210 As noted, certain educational institutions make non-business supplies. Thus, for example, sixth form colleges, tertiary colleges and colleges of further education normally provide education for no charge to students who are 19 (18 in Scotland) years or under at the start of their courses. This education is regarded as non-business. Other activities for which they make a charge eg for education provided to students over that age or to foreign nationals is regarded as an exempt supply.

9.211 The main differences in the impact of VAT between the provision of non-business supplies and exempt supplies are:

- Local authority funded schools can recover the VAT that they incur on expenditure on non-business activities. This is because the governors of such schools in fact incur such expenditure as agents for the local authorities and the expenditure therefore ranks for a refund under VATA 1994, s 33 (see **Chapter 1**). It should be noted that the right to recover the VAT only arises if the expenditure is by the local authority. Thus, expenditure paid for out of donations to say a parents' association will not qualify unless the money is donated to the local authority and the local authority incurs the expenditure.
- Schools that are not funded by local authorities are not eligible to recover VAT under VATA 1994, s 33. Even if the section did apply to them, since they make charges for education, their supplies would be exempt rather than non-business and therefore would still not be non-business activities even though the schools are in fact charities.
- Certain expenditure eg on fuel and power incurred by education institutions that are charities will be subject to the lower rate of VAT if certain conditions are met. The VAT so incurred will be subject to restriction but because the amount of VAT will be less, the net VAT cost will also be less;
- Certain construction services supplied to education institutions that are charities will not be subject to VAT because the supplies may be zero-rated as supplies for relevant residential or relevant charitable use. The question of whether or not VAT is deducted on such costs will therefore only arise if there is a change of use and a self-supply charge arises.

9.212 Apart from issues arising from the application of VATA 1994, s 33 – considered above – the normal rules relate to non-business expenditure of educational institutions. Thus, in principle, there may be a choice as to whether to treat the VAT incurred on non-business activities as deductible when it is incurred and then to account for output tax on any subsequent application to non-business use or to restrict the VAT incurred on non-business activities when it is incurred.

9.213 As noted in **Chapter 3**, FA 2003, s 22 purports to require that a business that incurs VAT on property-related expenditure related to both business and non-business activities must apportion the VAT incurred between both activities when it is incurred rather than deduct the VAT incurred and then account for output tax on non-business activities. Further, such legislation may be argued to be ultra vires European VAT law.

9.214 The effect of the legislation is that, for the education institution that does not consider it worth disputing the legislation, it will be necessary to restrict VAT incurred on non-business activities when it is incurred (estimating future use if necessary).

The significance of grant-funded activities on deductions

9.215 An issue that arises in respect of both business and non-business activities is the treatment of grant-funded activities. Customs and Excise take the view that some grants are outside the scope of VAT and are therefore relate to a non-business activity. However, just because there is non-business funding does not necessarily mean that the entire activity is non-business. Thus, research activity may be in part funded by grant and in part funded in other ways. The fact that is not entirely a non-business activity might mean that the benefit of reduced or zero-rates may not apply to expenditure that would otherwise be eligible for such relief. Customs and Excise would nevertheless expect a non-business apportionment to be carried out and some VAT disallowed as relating to the non-business activity. The normal rules would apply to that part of the activity funded in other ways.

9.216 Other grants may be regarded as consideration for a supply (see for example *Keeping Newcastle Warm Ltd v C & Excise Comrs (C-353/00) [2002] STC 943, ECJ*). This is the case notwithstanding the fact that the UK does not contain specific legislation implementing the last part of EC Sixth VAT Directive, art 11A.1(a), which reads:

> '1 The taxable amount shall be:
>
> (a) in respect of supplies of goods and services other than those referred to in (b), (c) and (d) below, everything which constitutes the consideration which has been or is to be obtained by the supplier from the purchaser, the customer or a third party for such *supplies including subsidies directly linked to the price of such supplies* [emphasis added];'

9.217 The consequences of the receipt of grants or subsidies on the right to deduct by educational institutions may therefore be summarised as follows:

- If the grant or subsidy is taxable as part of the consideration in respect of a supply, as in *Keeping Newcastle Warm* (see above), it will increase the value of taxable supplies in any turnover based partial exemption method;
- If the grant or subsidy is effectively a 'no strings attached' donation funding non-business activities, it may be necessary to restrict any VAT incurred that relates to that activity but it should be borne in mind that there may be no

relationship between the amount received and the costs referable to the receipt. It will therefore be necessary to determine an appropriate method to calculate the VAT, if any, referable to the grant or subsidy;

- It is also possible that a grant or subsidy could be part of the consideration for an exempt supply and, in such cases, the same principles apply – ie it may be necessary to take into account the fact of such subsidy in determining how much VAT is deductible.

9.218 Although the principles above are fairly clear, the actual application of the principles has been the subject of some doubt. Thus, Customs and Excise have taken the view that grants or subsidies have to be included in the denominator of any values based method. However, as noted above, the value of a grant or subsidy may not be an appropriate measure of the use any inputs. This has led to some disputes – particularly among universities as to how to determine the input tax deductible.

9.219 If a taxable activity is part-funded by grant, it is arguable that all the VAT on such activity should be recoverable. For example, a university enters into some research to develop a medical cure. The research is funded in part by grant but the intellectual property remains with the university and, if successful, it intends to sell the rights in order to earn taxable income.

Partial exemption generally

9.220 The normal partial exemption rules apply to educational institutions. Apart from non-business, taxable and exempt activities, some educational institutions may also make supplies to persons outside the UK that are outside the scope of VAT with the right to deduct any VAT incurred on such activities. It follows that an educational institution may have to undertake all the processes discussed in earlier chapters relating to the establishment of what VAT can be deducted ie:

- determine what VAT is incurred;
- determine the extent to which any VAT incurred is referable to non-business activities and restrict such VAT from deduction unless it is deductible under VATA 1994, s 33;
- determine the extent of any input tax deductible under VAT Regulations 1995, reg 103;
- determine the input tax deductible under either VAT Regulations 1995, reg 101 (standard method) or VAT Regulations 1995, reg 102 (special method).

9.221 In addition to the above, the partial exemption override may apply where the standard method is used and any capital items will be subject to adjustment under the capital items scheme (see **Chapter 7**).

Charities

Summary

9.222 The VAT treatment of charities is complex because they will usually have non-business and business supplies and, in addition, also have a mix between taxable and exempt supplies. Charities include a number of different types of organisations such as:

- churches and religious organisations;
- educational institutions;
- organisations that promote health and welfare or otherwise are involved in the protection of vulnerable people;
- sports and cultural organisations;
- museums and galleries.

9.223 Not all such organisations undertake activities that are outside the scope of VAT or are exempt but those that do may have to pay particular attention to how they determine the VAT they are entitled to deduct.

9.224 In some cases, the business activities may be hived off into a subsidiary (mainly for corporation tax reasons). However, even then some taxable supplies may remain in the charity and it may therefore still have to register for VAT. Further, even if a charity uses one or more subsidiary companies to undertake its business activities, if the charity is a corporate body (which many are) the subsidiaries can and may therefore be grouped with the charity. It is almost inevitable in such cases that the group will have taxable, exempt and non-business activities.

9.225 The basic steps a charity will need to carry out in respect of VAT deductions may be summarised as follows:

- identify what VAT has been incurred;
- exclude from deduction the VAT incurred on non-business activity – the balance of VAT is input tax;
- exclude from deduction any input tax such as that on cars that is never deductible;
- exclude from deduction any input tax wholly referable to exempt supplies and other non-taxable business activity;
- deduct all input tax referable to taxable activity and certain activity that is outside the scope of VAT but in respect of which there is a right to deduct;
- apportion any remaining input tax.

Exclusion from deduction of VAT on non-business activity

9.226 Donations, which are the main source of income for many charities, are not consideration for a business activity. Because they are not consideration, there is no supply and no right to deduct VAT incurred in raising such income. Some, but not all grants may also be in the nature of donations and therefore also not be consideration for any supply (For a case in which grants were considered to be consideration for taxable supplies, see *Keeping Newcastle Warm (C-353/00) [2002] STC 943, ECJ*).

9.227 Customs and Excise Notice 700, para 33 provides Customs and Excise guidance on how VAT attributable to non-business activity should be determined. The Notice sets out an example of a turnover method but also points out that it is open to a taxable person to use another method. In fact, it will frequently be the case that a turnover method is either inappropriate or cannot be applied.

Example 1

Assume that a charity acquires a building. It uses the building both as its headquarters and as the office of its very substantial taxable subsidiary, which is included in its VAT group. Apart from a few staff whose role is solely related to its charitable activities, most of the staff work on both the charity's and the subsidiary's affairs. The financial statements show that donations and legacies (the main source of its non-business income) fluctuate substantially and can range from 20% of total income to 60%.

In the circumstances above, it is clear that turnover is not an accurate measurement of use of the building. This is in fact the case for most donations and legacies since the amount of effort involved in securing a donation may be the same whether a person donates £100 or £100,000. This is even truer of legacies where very little effort may be involved at all. It follows that the size of non-business income may not be an appropriate measure of use.

9.228 In some cases, the apportionment of the VAT may be almost arbitrary eg:

- In *Dean and Chapter of Hereford Cathedral [1994] VATTR 159*, the VAT Tribunal concluded that VAT on the church infrastructure was incurred in part to support the taxable activities of the Church that raised funds for its maintenance and accepted a 50% attribution of VAT to taxable activities;
- However, in *Dean and Chapter of Bristol Cathedral [1997] VAT decision 14591, SWTI 242*, the VAT and Duties Tribunal only accepted a 25% apportionment to taxable activities.

9.229 It is perhaps also worth noting that because of the volatile nature of charitable activities, it will frequently be impossible even to estimate future use for business v non-business purposes. Accordingly, it is arguable that the measures included in FA 2003, s 22 (see **Chapters 3** and **11**) both fail to both comply with the EC Sixth VAT Directive and to meet the test of being capable of being applied whereas the application of the rules contained in EC Sixth VAT Directive, art 6(2) are eminently capable of being applied.

9.230 A charity will therefore need to determine what the best means is of measuring non-business use of both revenue expenditure and, if it does not wish to dispute the validity of VATA 1994, Sch 4, para 5(4A), the use of any assets on which VAT is incurred.

9.231 A key point to note is that there are no statutory provisions that require a charity to adopt a particular method. Indeed, there would appear to be no provision within EC VAT law that lays down any method for measuring VAT that is not being incurred in the capacity as taxable person. It does not matter that there may be another valid method that results in a greater restriction of VAT. It follows that a charity does not have to seek permission to adopt a particular method and indeed there is no authority that allows the attribution to be regarded as part of a special method under VAT Regulations 1995, reg 102. In the event of a dispute, Customs and Excise's remedy would be to assess and take their chances in a VAT and Duties Tribunal should the charity appeal.

9.232 An issue that arises in respect of charities is the treatment of investments. In general terms, charities are not allowed to conduct a trade. It follows that their investment activities will usually be non-business activities and will not give rise to an entitlement to deduct VAT on such activities. (See eg *National Society for the Prevention of Cruelty to Children (1993) VAT decision 9325* and *Wellcome Trust Ltd v C & E Comrs (C-155/94) [1996] STC 945, ECJ* (Case Summary 23).) It also follows that it may be necessary to regard some VAT on such activities as non-business VAT.

9.233 Because of the impact of VAT on non-business activities, it is generally beneficial if a charity can convert non-business activity to business activity provided that the person providing the money for whatever services are provided is able to deduct any VAT charged (eg a local authority). (See for examples *Hillingdon Legal Resources Centre Ltd [1991] VATTR 39*; *Whitechapel Art Gallery v C & E Comrs [1986] STC 156; Pre-School Learning Alliance (VAT decision 17737) [2003] SWTI 220*).

9.234 A further point of note is that if a charity adopts a particular method of measuring non-business use, it is not able to subsequently seek to adjust the method just because it identifies a better method of determining non-business use (see, for example, *Victoria and Albert Museum Trustees [1996] STC 1016*). It follows that great care should be taken in deciding what measure should be used.

Exclude from deduction any input tax such as that on cars that is never deductible

9.235 As with other businesses, the VAT on expenditure such as motor cars and business entertainment is not deductible and therefore any such input tax must be identified and disallowed in accordance with the rules set out in **Chapter 4**.

Partial exemption

9.236 Charities are entitled to a number of exemptions (see eg VATA 1994, Sch 9, Groups 7, 10, 12 and 13). The VAT referable to such supplies is accordingly not deductible. If the charity makes both taxable and exempt supplies, it will need to apportion any VAT that is referable to both taxable and exempt supplies in the same way as any other business (see **Chapter 5**).

9.237 As already discussed above, the partial exemption calculation must normally be done after any non-business VAT and input tax that is solely referable to taxable or exempt supplies has been identified. Some charities will also have VAT that is only deductible in accordance with VAT Regulations 1995, reg 103 – eg supplies that are made outside the UK.. Indeed the leading case on the application of this regulation involved a charity (*C & E Comrs v Liverpool Institute for the Performing Arts [2001] STC 891* (Case Summary 40)). Such input VAT will also need to be dealt with prior to the application of the partial exemption rules.

9.238 An issue that may arise with charities but would not arise in the case of most ordinary businesses is the treatment of subsidies. Customs and Excise have taken the view that the block grant or subsidy received by higher education institutions should be included in the denominator in any partial exemption method based on turnover. The rationale behind this view is that the subsidy is intended to pay for expenditure that is referable to exempt supplies and is therefore, in part, a measure of use for exempt or non-business supplies. However, this may not be entirely true. As part of their function, institutions may carry out activities that are taxable. To some extent the ability to win such work can depend on the ability of the university to undertake a particular line of study more efficiently (from the user's perspective) than elsewhere. Accordingly, it may equally be argued that the subsidies support taxable supplies and are therefore in part a measure of such use. It is likely that in most cases, institutions may have to undertake some 'horse-trading' with Customs and Excise to reach an agreement that provides a fair attribution of input tax without causing excessive administration burdens.

Museums and galleries

9.239 Among the range of organisations that may be charities are museums and galleries. Certain of their activities may be non-business activities and the VAT on such activities potentially subject to restriction as discussed in **9.225** above.

9.240 However, VATA 1994, s 33A provides that certain museums and galleries are entitled to a deduction for tax incurred on their non-business activities, ie where they provide free admission. Not all museums and galleries are exempt – only those specified by order. The order that sets out which museums are entitled to exemption is VAT (Refund of tax to Museums and Galleries) Order 2001, SI 2001/2879.

9.241 The existence of the refund provision does not necessarily mean that there is no requirement to carry out an apportionment since an apportionment may be a necessary preliminary step to carrying out a partial exemption calculation to deal with taxable and exempt activities.

Health and welfare

9.242 In so far as they are, in ordinary English usage, related topics 'Health' and 'Welfare' sit very comfortably together, and this close association extends to matters concerning the deduction of VAT. In VATA 1994, Sch 9, Group 7 is actually entitled 'Health and Welfare', and the relationship between the two, for VAT purposes, over and above the obvious ordinary synergy is that in general, the supply of 'health' related services and 'welfare' related services are exempt from VAT.

9.243 It is accepted wisdom that the VAT on costs incurred in respect of the supply of services which are exempt from VAT, is not deductible. Irrecoverable VAT therefore falls to be an additional cost to the business, which is quite right and proper, and in full accordance with both UK and EC VAT legislation.

9.244 However, matters are seldom quite so black and white in the world of VAT, and the area of health and welfare is no exception. Although the two topics have much in common, they also have some significant differences and it is therefore appropriate to consider them in turn.

Health

9.245 Health of course cannot be supplied; health is a state of physical and mental well-being, which is enjoyed – or not as the case may be – in differing degrees by individuals. What can be supplied to those individuals are the services of medical practitioners and institutions whose business rests in the care and healing of the sick and injured and the prevention of disease and infirmity.

9.246 Although the majority of this section will consider health and welfare services, the EC Sixth Directive (77/388), art 13A(1)(d) brings supplies of human organs, human blood and human milk, which are supplies of goods, within the exemption. But given that most health and welfare transactions will be supplies of services, art 13A(1)(b), (c) and (e) provides exemption from VAT for the provision of medical care in the exercise of the medical or paramedical professions as defined by the Member States concerned.

9.247 But it is not the case that the services supplied by all of the individual practitioners working in the health industry are exempt from VAT. This of course is a rather fundamental point and one which needs to be addressed in order to determine whether VAT on expenditure is deductible, and indeed, whether health industry practitioners may register for VAT in the first instance.

9.248 The relevant UK legislation, VATA 1994, Sch 9, Group 7, items 1, 2 and 3, lays down the list of those persons whose services, when supplied by way of business, are exempt from VAT, and these are:

> 1 The supply of services by a person registered or enrolled in any of the following—
>
> (a) the register of medical practitioners or the register of medical practitioners with limited registration;
>
> (b) either of the registers of ophthalmic opticians or the register of dispensing opticians kept under the Opticians Act 1989 or either of the lists kept under section 9 of that Act of bodies corporate carrying on business as ophthalmic opticians or as dispensing opticians;
>
> [(c) the register kept under the Health Professions Order 2001;]
>
> [(ca) the register of osteopaths maintained in accordance with the provisions of the Osteopaths Act 1993;]
>
> [(cb) the register of chiropractors maintained in accordance with the provisions of the Chiropractors Act 1994;]
>
> *(d) the register of qualified nurses, midwives and health visitors kept under [section 7 of the Nurses, Midwives and Health Visitors Act 1997];*
>
> [(d) the register of qualified nurses and midwives maintained under article 5 of the Nursing and Midwifery Order 2001;]
>
> (e) the register of dispensers of hearing aids or the register of persons employing such dispensers maintained under section 2 of the Hearing Aid Council Act 1968.
>
> 2 The supply of any services or dental prostheses by—
>
> (a) a person registered in the dentists' register;
>
> (b) a person enrolled in any roll of dental auxiliaries having effect under section 45 of the Dentists Act 1984; or
>
> (c) a dental technician.
>
> 3 The supply of any services by a person registered in the register of pharmaceutical chemists kept under the Pharmacy Act 1954 or the Pharmacy (Northern Ireland) Order 1976.

9.249 The list is very much as one would expect to find it in that it specifies most of the health care practitioners whom the general public would regard as providing healthcare services, but the list is not static, and has been amended several times since 1994, to reflect changing social and political attitudes. The services of registered Osteopaths and registered Chiropractors, to name but two, were not included in the original legislation, in 1994.

9.250 The services of the practitioners listed in the legislation are therefore exempt from VAT, and as a result, VAT incurred on the expenditure which forms a cost component of their exempt supplies cannot be deducted. But it is not automatically the case that services provided by persons who are not so registered are liable to VAT. Legal notes 2 and 4 of Group 7 also extend the exemption to related services performed by non-registered persons in certain circumstances.

9.251 Legal Note 2 brings within the scope of exemption services performed by non-registered persons where the services they provide are wholly performed or directly supervised by someone who is registered. However, once again this provision does not exempt every possible service – the services of the unregistered person must be of a type that would be provided by the registered medical practitioner in the course of his profession, in order to qualify for the exemption. The services performed by the unqualified staff must be of a nature that requires supervision. The exemption does not extend to services performed by unqualified staff for which no supervision is required and services which are not broadly of a medical or caring nature cannot gain exemption simply by the use of a qualified individual in a supervisory or managerial role. Nor can exemption apply where supervision takes place via a third party — for the exemption to apply the supervisor must always be in a direct relationship with the unqualified staff (see *Parkinson (Mrs MG) VAT decision 6017* and *Elder Home Care Ltd (1994) VAT decision 11185)*).

9.252 So, there is always a risk that non-registered persons working or practising in the healthcare sector may nevertheless find that their services will fall within the scope of the exemption, and hence they will be unable to deduct VAT on the expenditure they incur in relation to the supplies they make.

9.253 Legal Note 4 is much more precisely focussed than legal note 2, and is intended to apply in very limited circumstances where an EC practitioner who would be eligible to be registered under the visiting EEC practitioners list, but who is not so registered, performs services of an urgent or emergency nature. Without note 4, any charge made by such a visiting practitioner which is within the scope of UK VAT would otherwise be liable to VAT at the standard rate, assuming that the VAT registration threshold had been breached and the place of supply was the UK. This Note allows such charges to be exempt from VAT, thus relieving the recipient of the burden of paying the tax on health services received, but of course the visiting EC practitioner is rendered unable deduct VAT on the expenditure they incur in relation to the supplies he or she makes.

9.254 A further complication, albeit much less unwelcome, is the fact that despite all that has been said above, it is not the case that all the services provided by a person registered or enrolled on any of the registers specified in the legislation will be exempt from VAT.

9.255 It is perfectly possible for a registered person to provide services which are liable to VAT, and hence give rise to the right to deduct VAT on the expenditure they incur in relation to the supplies made.

9.256 For instance, a registered osteopath may supplement his or her income by freelancing in writing computer software. This would be a supply of services, and would be made by someone registered on the register of osteopaths, but the supply would not fall within the exemption, and the osteopath would be entitled to deduct VAT on related expenditure.

9.257 Another, perhaps more credible, example is where a registered medical doctor provides an expert opinion on a medical or health matter, for an insurance company, or as an expert witness in a legal dispute. It is clear in this second example that the services being provided are much more directly dependent on the professional medical/healthcare skills and qualifications that the doctor possesses. Because of this nexus, in the past Customs and Excise took the view that such medico-legal services were also exempt. However, as a result of the rulings of the ECJ in the cases of *Unterpertinger v Pensionsversicherungsanstalt der Arbeiter (C-212/01 [2003] All ER (D) 276 (Nov),* and *d'Ambrumenil v C & E Comrs (C-307/01) [2003] All ER (D) 281 (Nov),* which dealt with the liability of supplies made when medical doctors acted as expert witnesses and/or prepared medical certificates or reports designed to establish medical fitness and whether particular legal claims were satisfied, Customs and Excise have now changed their policy and accept that services which are predominantly legal, as opposed to medical, are liable to VAT at the standard rate.

9.258 The above change applied retrospectively back to 20 January 1997. Therefore, from that date, many healthcare professionals may be entitled or required to be registered for VAT and may deduct any related input tax (subject to the normal rules). However, services provided by a healthcare professional in the course of his normal 'doctor/patient' relationship, and services which are pre-dominantly medical and not legal (for example, medical reports for employers and life assurance policies), continue to be exempt from VAT (C & E Business Brief 26/96, 19 December 1996), and hence VAT incurred in relation to the provision of those services cannot be deducted.

9.259 A loophole – now closed – which has in the past allowed medical practitioners to become registered for VAT, and therefore to be able to deduct at least a proportion of the VAT they incurred in the making of exempt supplies, was commonly referred to as the 'toothbrush' scheme.

9.260 In very brief and simple terms, a dentist (the scheme applied equally well to doctors) would, in addition to providing exempt medical services, sell to patients such items as toothbrushes, toothpaste, mouthwashes, other oral hygiene products and the like, and as a result, would seek voluntary registration for VAT on the basis that taxable supplies were made by way of business.

9.261 Having become VAT registered, the dentist would then seek to take advantage of the then extant partial exemption de minimis rules which allowed a partly exempt business to treat itself as fully taxable if the amount of exempt input vat incurred was on average, less than £625 a month (there was another element to this test, but it was not relevant to the 'toothbrush' scheme). Thus, with some careful budgeting and expenditure planning, per annum up to £7,500 of exempt input VAT, i e VAT which was incurred in the making of exempt supplies, could be recovered.

9.262 This loophole was closed as a result of an amendment to Value Added Tax Regulations, SI 1995/2518, art 106(2) which introduced an additional condition in that to be able to treat itself as fully taxable, the average £625 or less of exempt input tax had to be less than half of all of the input tax incurred in the period. In simple terms, this meant that the vat incurred on the toothbrushes etc for resale had to be more than 50% of all of the VAT incurred, and in practice, virtually all doctors and dentists who had managed to treat themselves as fully taxable could no longer do so.

9.263 Healthcare practitioners will therefore very often supply goods, as well as services, in the provision of healthcare. For example, the supply of medical goods by a doctor will fall within the exemption if the goods are a minor, incidental or inseparable part of the overall service of medical care. For example, the bandages and dressings and the materials needed to inject drugs can be treated as part of the service of exempt medical care and thus any VAT incurred cannot be deducted.

9.264 Exemption will also apply to a supply of goods if the goods are used as an inseparable part of the course of treatment. For example, a dentist will exempt supplies of mouthwashes and teeth-braces and will not be able to deduct VAT incurred on their purchase. However, exemption does not include the sale of other related oral hygiene products held out as separate sales, such as toothpaste and toothbrushes. In the case of *O-Pro Ltd (VAT decision 16780) [2000] SWTI 1772,* Customs and Excise sought to standard-rate the whole price charged in respect of mouth guards supplied for children. The Tribunal heard evidence that a dentist took moulds of the child's mouth and they were produced by a dental technician from the mould. The guards were constructed by a dental technician and then returned to the dentist for fitting. The cost of the guards was substantially more than the cost of non-custom-made guards available from sports shops. Applying the tests set out in *Card Protection Plan Ltd v C & E Comrs, (C-349/96) [1999] STC 270, ECJ* the Tribunal concluded that it would be artificial to regard the mouthpiece as the principal supply. There were two supplies—the mouthpiece (in respect of which VAT on costs could be deducted) and the professional services (in respect of which VAT could not be deducted).

9.265 Drugs are often almost prohibitively expensive, and items such as artificial joints and other prostheses used in surgical procedures can be of significant value. For such high value goods, the VAT incurred in their purchase is likely to be significant, and hence suppliers of healthcare services will wish to be able to deduct VAT whenever possible. The case of *C & E Comrs v British United Provident Association (BUPA) [1997] STC 445, CA* clarified whether or not VAT on such items was deductible by determining that certain prostheses (for example, hip joint replacements, heart pacemakers and heart valve replacements) were not always automatically part of an exempt composite supply of medical care and, depending on the circumstances, could fall to be zero-rated under the provisions of VATA 1994, Sch 8, Group 12 (Drugs, Medicines, Aids for the Handicapped, etc), and in consequence, give rise to the right to deduct the VAT incurred on their purchase. It is, however, important to note that the clarification of how the legislation should be applied did not define that the supply of all such goods would be as part of, or ancillary to, exempt healthcare.

9.266 Having dealt so far with the ability of individuals, who make supplies of healthcare services, to deduct VAT it is appropriate to consider the position of corporates and other bodies, who as legally separate and independent entities, also provide healthcare services.

9.267 It is a moot point as to whether the repeated use of the term 'person' in VATA 1994, Sch 9, Group 7 applies to legal persons as well as to real, living, persons. Certainly, it is difficult to perceive how a corporate body could be a medical practitioner included on the register of medical practitioners. However, the point is not one on which it is necessary to dwell overlong. Item 4 of Group 7 brings within the exemption the provision of care and/or medical treatment and/or surgical treatment (including the supply of any goods) in any hospital or state regulated institution.

9.268 A hospital or state regulated institution may of course be owned and/or operated by an individual in which case it is perfectly possible that supplies of healthcare would be by the individual, and hence clearly fall within the scope of the exemption as discussed above.

9.269 But it is far more likely in practice that hospitals and institutions will be owned and/or operated by a corporate body, or other organisation. The very broadly drafted scope of Item 4 of Group 7 – 'The provision of care or medical or surgical treatment. In connection with it, the supply of goods, in any hospital or state-regulated institution' – ensures that VAT exemption, and following from it a restriction of the ability to deduct VAT on expenditure, applies to the supplies of healthcare services that corporate bodies and other legal individuals make in just the same way as it applies to supplies of healthcare services made by 'real' individuals or persons.

9.270 Thus, to all intents and purposes, the issues regarding the liability of supplies made, and hence the ability to deduct VAT incurred on costs related to the making of those supplies, are the same for corporates and legal individuals, as they are for individual persons.

Welfare

9.271 In respect of VAT deduction, welfare, as a topic, appears to be somewhat less problematic than Health. VATA 1994, Sch 9, Group 7, Item 9 exempts the supply of welfare services, and goods supplied in conjunction with those services, but only to the extent that the supply of those welfare services is made by a charity, or a state-regulated private welfare institution, or a public body.

9.272 Thus if a welfare service of any kind is supplied by an organisation which is neither a charity nor a state regulated private welfare institution nor a public body, then its supplies are liable to VAT at the standard rate, and as a consequence, it can deduct the VAT it incurs on its expenditure.

9.273 A charity providing welfare services may often do so for a fee or other form of remuneration, but may well choose to provide welfare services free of charge. If it provides welfare services free of charge, or for a charge which is consistently below cost, then its supplies are regarded not as exempt, but as non-business.

9.274 The difference between exempt business and non-business is, in this context, irrelevant, as in both cases, the charity will not have any entitlement to deduct VAT.

9.275 The term 'state regulated' requires definition, and that is provided by Legal Note 8 to VATA 1994, Sch 9, Group 7, which lays down that it means 'approved, licensed, registered or exempted from registration by any Minister or other authority pursuant to a provision of a public General Act, other than a provision that is capable of being brought into effect at different times in relation to different local authority areas'.

9.276 This legislation was introduced to take effect from 21 March 2002, as a result of *Kingscrest Associates Ltd and Montecello Ltd t/a Kingscrest Residential Care Homes [2003] V & DR 201; [2002] EWHC 410 (Ch), [2002] STC 490*. The taxpayer in that case argued that its supplies were liable to VAT at the standard rate because it was aware that its customer, a local authority, would be able to recover the VAT it incurred under the special refund provisions of VATA, 1994, s 33 (for further details of the refunds available under s 33 see **9.351**). Kingscrest, in its successful arguments, achieved a position whereby it could deduct all of the VAT it incurred on the basis that all of its expenditure was a cost component of an onward taxable supply. The local authority in turn, although not able to deduct the VAT as input VAT, nevertheless received a special 's 33' refund, and therefore did not suffer any irrecoverable VAT.

9.277 This apparently highly desirable situation achieved VAT neutrality in the particular circumstances of the *Kingscrest* case, but of course not every customer of such a supplier would be eligible for a s 33 refund. Therefore to ensure that the particular circumstances in *Kingscrest* could not be repeated in future, the exemption was extended to defined state regulated bodies, and its effect is both to ensure that charges levied by such suppliers are not subject to VAT and that such suppliers cannot deduct the VAT they incur on their related expenditure.

9.278 At the present time, Kingscrest are continuing their challenge to this position, albeit through a slightly different route in that they are challenging Customs and Excise's decision to refuse to allow them to register for VAT. It is therefore possible that this area of the exemption, and hence this particular 'block' on the ability to deduct VAT, will change again in the relatively near future.

9.279 The final category of organisations brought within the scope of the exemption is that of a 'public body'. A public body is defined as

> 'a government department within the meaning of [VATA 1994], s 41(6);
>
> a local authority;
>
> a body which acts under any enactment or instrument for public purposes and not for its own profit and which performs functions similar to those of a government department or local authority.'

9.280 Many of the activities carried on by the State are not business activities, and are subject to special rules and regulations (for a more detailed consideration of how and when VAT may be deducted or otherwise recovered by public bodies, see **9.323**. Notwithstanding that, it can be seen that this category is intended to ensure that when welfare services are provided by the State by way of business, through any particular state owned organisation, then the supplies it makes will be exempt.

9.281 Thus public bodies supplying welfare services by way of business are brought within the scope of the exemption, and can neither charge VAT on any fees or charges they levy, nor can they deduct VAT on any of the costs they incur in providing the services.

9.282 Finally, it will be appropriate to spend a few moments looking at the definition of 'welfare services'. Legal Note 6 to VATA 1994, Sch 9, Group 7A gives the definition as:

> 'services which are directly connected with –
>
> (a) the provision of care, treatment or instruction designed to promote the physical or mental welfare of elderly, sick or disabled persons,
>
> (b) the care or protection of children and young persons, or
>
> (c) the provision of spiritual welfare by a religious institution as part of a course of instruction or a retreat, not being in a course or a retreat designed primarily to provide recreation or a holiday.'

9.283 The definition is unsurprising, and brings into the scope of exemption a broad spectrum of services that the man in the street would ordinarily expect would be regarded as welfare services. Although a detailed consideration of what falls within the definition of welfare services may be found in Chapter **9.24** of *Tolley's VAT Business by Business*, it would be appropriate to mention one service which is now accepted as falling within the definition, and hence suppliers of those services are not able to deduct VAT they incur on related expenditure.

9.284 Supplies of domestic home help services such as cooking, cleaning and shopping were previously held by Customs and Excise to fall outside the exemption, and hence suppliers of these services were able to deduct VAT. However, in its decision in the case of *Watford and District Old People's Housing Association Ltd (t/a Watford Help in the Home Service)(VAT decision 15660) [1998] SWTI 1529*, the VAT and Duties Tribunal found that such services could constitute welfare services when supplied to those who need such services in order to remain resident in their own private homes. Consequently, suppliers of such domestic welfare services are no longer able to deduct the VAT they incur.

Sports bodies

Introduction

9.285 Eligible sports bodies are entitled to exempt from VAT certain but not all of their supplies of the provision of sports and physical recreation facilities. A discussion of what comprises an eligible body is beyond the scope of this work. Broadly speaking, it is only clubs that are managed on an essentially voluntary and not for profit basis that can exempt sports and physical recreation facilities. However, where a sports body is subject to 'commercial influence', effectively where a commercial entity or private individual is able to extract monies from the sports body (for example by way of charges for rent of facilities), that sports body will not be eligible for exemption. Commercial companies establishing not for profit bodies are not able to use the exemption unless the act of establishing a sports body seeking exemption is purely philanthropic (see *De Vere Golf and Leisure Ltd (VAT decision 18078) [2003] SWTI 1428* and *Messenger Leisure Developments Ltd (VAT decision 18300) [2003] SWTI 2204*).

9.286 Sports bodies that are not eligible bodies may have some exempt supplies in the form of the certain grants of the right to use sports facilities (see VATA 1994, Sch 9, Group 1, note 16) but otherwise should be substantially taxable businesses. In other cases, providers of sports and physical recreation may be able to provide services which are exempt supplies of education (eg taught classes such as swimming lessons and exercise to music classes supplied by local authorities). Most of the issues mentioned in **9.302 et seq** of this chapter relating to clubs and associations will also apply to sporting bodies. However, some further issues arise.

9.287 Eligible sports bodies that operate a membership scheme are only able to exempt supplies of sports services to members. Eligible sports bodies that do not operate a membership scheme are able to exempt supplies to individuals. Therefore membership clubs can make both taxable and exempt supplies of the identical services (exempt to members, standard-rated to non-members (see *Keswick Golf Club (VAT decision 15493) [1998] SWTI 1296*). Non membership bodies (such as recreational charities), are only able to exempt sports services to individuals and standard-rate supplies to groups, companies or associations (unless such supplies fall to be exempt under the land exemption for series of lettings or hire of facilities for periods exceeding 24 hours for playing sports).

The nature of expenditure incurred by sports bodies

9.288 The expenditure of sports bodies can generally be classified into two groups:

- expenditure relating to the sports and physical recreation facilities of the body;
- expenditure on other activities eg social and other recreational facilities of the club.

9.289 It is likely that a substantial proportion of expenditure will be of a capital nature ie expenditure on facilities, the club house and sports equipment.

Apportioning expenditure and the VAT thereon to supplies of sport and recreation

Expenditure on sports facilities

9.290 As already noted, it is likely that a sports body will make both taxable and exempt supplies of sporting facilities. It should also be borne in mind that sports bodies with a membership scheme can have different ways in which subscriptions are paid for eg a member might pay a subscription but in other cases the club might have a debenture scheme under which in return for an interest-free loan, the lender gains the advantages of membership. In such cases, although there will be 'payment' for the sports facilities, it will not be reflected in any turnover.

9.291 The result is that in many cases, the relative values of income from members in respect of sports facilities and those of non-members will not be an appropriate measure of the use of the expenditure incurred. Since there may also be other exempt income eg the hire of sports facilities that falls within the exemption in VATA 1994, Sch 9, Group 1, item 16), it is likely that many membership sports bodies might be wise to negotiate a special method in order to apportion the costs relating to sports facilities between exempt and taxable supplies.

9.292 One possible measure of use might be the relative numbers of users although even this could be distortive if there are a substantial number of days when the facilities are let on an exempt basis to third parties. However, many membership eligible sports bodies may wish to operate the simplest method possible due to lack of management resources.

9.293 Non-membership bodies may find that most of the input tax incurred in respect of sports activities is residual input tax, when operating the standard method, if they make supplies to individuals and to groups, associations or companies.

Expenditure on other facilities

9.294 Perhaps the most common facility that a sports body will have other than its sports facilities will be restaurant and bar facilities. Such facilities are usually intended to earn money to be ploughed back into the development of the club, unlike the restaurants and bars in the case of *Aspinall's Club Ltd (VAT decision 17797) [2003] SWTI 314*, and are probably not to be regarded as supporting the exempt activities of the club.

9.295 The input tax referable to such activities will be deductible. To arrive at such input tax, It will be necessary to do an apportionment eg an apportionment of building costs where the club buildings house both those premises such as the bar used for taxable activities and the change and other rooms associated with the sporting facilities. Such apportionments might be on the basis of floor area but could also be on other bases as well bearing in mind that the relative costs of the sports facilities could be greater or less per square foot than those of the other facilities.

9.296 The brief points above show that in many sports clubs, it is likely that a special method will be required to deal with partial exemption since a method based on turnover will not be fair and reasonable. While in larger clubs, the partial exemption override might conveniently be used to correct any distortion caused by using a turnover based method, this will not be the case for smaller clubs.

Capital items

9.297 The capital items scheme will apply to some capital goods of a club. However, bearing in mind the very large number of small sports bodies, it is quite conceivable that there will be a large number of construction works as well as the purchase of equipment that does not fall within the capital items scheme. VAT will be incurred on these items and there will be a one-off deduction when the VAT is incurred with no possibility of adjusting the deduction later (However, see the Consultation Paper on making input tax recovery fairer announced in the 2003 Budget.)

9.298 The problem that arises with this can be illustrated by reference to the VAT and Duties Tribunal decision in *Chard Bowling Club (VAT decision 15114) [1997] SWTI 1371*. In that case, the club incurred input tax on constructing a clubhouse which would lead to an increase in the proportion of taxable supplies. However, as the club had not requested a special partial exemption method, the input tax was recoverable according to the standard method. This resulted in a low level of recovery, based on the supplies made by the Club, before the Clubhouse had even been used. *Chard* was decided prior to the partial exemption override but even the existence of such provisions might not have made a difference in view of the £50,000 de minimis limits. It follows that care is needed when determining the deduction on large items whose use will continue into future periods. The result may be that it is necessary to use a special method that applies the *Briararch* principles.

9.299 Lottery projects can also cause special problems. In *Milnathort Golf Club (1998) VAT decision 17889*, Customs and Excise argued that input tax incurred in respect of constructing a clubhouse was only recoverable as residual input tax, even though one phase of the project related to the making of taxable supplies via a bar and kitchen facility. The Tribunal held that certain input tax was directly attributable to the making of taxable supplies.

9.300 In other situations, sports bodies may make applications for lottery funding in conjunction with local authorities. Special issues then arise, and professional advice should be sought. In *West Devon Borough Council [2001] STC 1282* for example, an unanticipated VAT cost arose for the local authority supporting a community project. It is therefore vital that prior to any lottery application being submitted, the VAT recovery in respect of the project is fully considered.

9.301 Where the sports body provides its sporting facilities free of charge, there is the likelihood that any VAT incurred on capital items will not be deductible. In *Clwb Rygbi Nant Conwy (VAT decision 16376) [2000] SWTI 316*, Customs and Excise sought to disallow input tax incurred on construction of a clubhouse as the club did not charge the players a playing subscription, but did make specific taxable supplies. The Tribunal allowed the appeal and thus the deduction on the specific facts in that case, although sports bodies providing sporting activities free of charge are forewarned that input tax deduction on facilities will not be deductible, in whole or in part, unless there is the necessary direct and immediate link with taxable supplies.

Summary

9.302 Sports bodies face complex problems because of the differing liabilities of the supplies they make. This is complicated further by the fact that turnover may not be the best measure of use of any goods and services received. The complexity of VAT deduction for sports bodies may be difficult for voluntary committee members and trustees to maximise the deduction of VAT incurred. Whenever sports bodies are planning to incur major items of expenditure, professional advice should be sought.

Clubs and associations

Summary

9.303 This section deals with clubs and associations other than sports clubs. Clubs and associations include a variety of bodies having objects determined by their members. Until 1 December 1999, many not for profit clubs and associations were not regarded as carrying on a business in respect of any benefits of membership. However, following the repeal of VATA 1994, s 94(3) it is generally the case that membership subscriptions are regarded as consideration for the benefits of membership.

9.304 Although subscriptions are consideration for a supply, those of certain non-profit making organisations may be exempt under VATA 1994, Sch 9, Group 9 'Subscriptions to trade unions, professional associations and public interest bodies'. There is an extra-statutory concession that allows such bodies to apportion part of any subscription income to the supply of 'free' club journals that might otherwise be regarded as ancillary to the principal (exempt) supply.

9.305 Although the main form of exempt income of non-profit making clubs and associations is likely to be subscription income or a proportion thereof there might also be other forms of exempt income eg a club or association formed to promote the arts might also earn exempt income from cultural activities.

9.306 Other common forms of income include sponsorship and donations. Some sponsorship might in fact be donations. However, it is also possible that sponsorship might be consideration for a supply.

9.307 It is also possible that clubs and associations will entertain members. This raises the question of whether or not the VAT on such entertainment is to be regarded as business entertainment or not.

9.308 It is important to note that many clubs are owned by businesses and are run for profit. These are likely to have little if any exempt income (a possible exception being income such as hall hire) although they might have activities such as business entertainment on which VAT may have to be restricted.

Non-business activities and non-deductible VAT

9.309 A key issue will be to identify any non-business activities. As outlined in **Chapter 3**, there are two possible treatments of the VAT incurred on non-business activities. Under the first, no VAT is restricted and instead and output tax charge is made. Under the second, an apportionment of any VAT incurred has to be done and that incurred on non-business activities is not deducted.

Business entertainment

9.310 While VAT on business entertainment is normally not deductible, it must be borne in mind that business entertainment is defined as follows:

> '(3) For the purposes of this article, 'business entertainment' means entertainment including hospitality of any kind provided by a taxable person in connection with a business carried on by him, but does not include the provision of any such entertainment for either or both-
>
> (a) employees of the taxable person;
>
> (b) if the taxable person is a body corporate, its directors or persons otherwise engaged in its management,

unless the provision of entertainment for persons such as are mentioned in sub-paragraph (a) and (b) above is incidental to its provisions for others (VAT (Input Tax) Order 1993, art 5).

9.311 A club or association may well entertain members. Whether or not this is business entertainment may depend on the circumstances. Thus, where it is provided to all members, it may be regarded as a part of the services supplied to members. If so, there will be no separate non-business apportionment of VAT on the grounds that it is business entertainment. Instead the deductibility of such VAT will depend on whether or not the subscriptions are taxable or exempt.

9.312 A further exception to the rule that VAT on business entertainment is non deductible that might be encountered by a club or association is reciprocal hospitality. This tends to occur more in the case of sporting clubs (see **9.293**) but is something that may need to be considered by other clubs and associations (see *Celtic Football and Athletic Co v C & E Comrs [1983] STC 470*).

9.313 Of course, the fact that business entertainment is regarded as an integral part of another supply, does not necessarily mean that the VAT incurred is deductible. It simply means that the question of whether or not it is deductible must be considered under the normal rule that requires the taxable person to consider whether or not the business entertainment is a cost component of another supply eg membership subscriptions. Thus, if entertainment is regarded as supplied to members as part of the benefits of membership, deductibility will rest on whether or not the subscription itself is taxable or not.

Donations and sponsorship

9.314 A club or association may receive donations, sponsorship and legacies for its activities. In the case of sponsorship, a question will first arise as to whether or not there is a supply. The liability of such income is beyond the scope of this book. However, where amounts received by way of donations, sponsorship or legacies are not part of the consideration for a supply, it will be necessary to consider whether or not any VAT incurred was incurred in order to receive such income and if so the extent to which it was so incurred. That VAT will not be deductible. Thus, it is common for bodies to employ fund-raisers who take a percentage of any funds raised as a fee. Any VAT incurred on such fees will not be deductible and, in addition, it may be that some of the VAT incurred on overheads must be apportioned and not deducted.

9.315 A turnover based method of determining the VAT deducted on non-business entertainment may not always be the most appropriate method. Further, once a method is used to determine the VAT that cannot be deducted as being referable to business supplies, that method cannot be corrected retrospectively (although it may be corrected prospectively).

Motor cars

9.316 The normal rules apply to VAT incurred on the purchase or leasing of motor cars – ie there will be a restriction of VAT even if the car(s) are used wholly for business purposes unless the cars are not available for non-business use, including any non-business objectives of the club or association.

The importance of recognising the difference between non-business VAT and exempt input tax

9.317 It might appear unimportant to separate VAT that is not deductible because it is referable to a non-business activity and VAT that is non deductible because it is exempt input tax. However, in the case of small clubs, it can have an impact of up to £7,500 per annum because of the operation of the de minimis limits.

9.318 The reason for this is that the de minimis limits in VAT Regulations 1995, reg 106 refer to relevant **input tax** and not VAT. Accordingly, a club or association might be regarded as fully taxable even though the input tax on taxable supplies is less than 50% of all VAT and non-deductible VAT exceeds £625 per month on average.

Example 2

A club carries out an apportionment of VAT and determines that VAT has been incurred on the following activities:

	£
Non-business activities	10,000
Taxable supplies	8,000
Exempt supplies	7,000
Total VAT	25,000

9.319 In the example above, the VAT on exempt supplies is less than £625 per month on average (£7,500 per annum) and is also less than 50% of all input tax (£8,000 plus £7,000) so the amount of VAT deductible is £15,000 and not just £8,000.

9.320 It should be borne in mind that the question of whether or not a business is fully taxable can be relevant to other issues eg whether or not the grant of a lease can be opted or not.

Partial exemption

9.321 As with other organisations, a club or association may have to carry out an apportionment of the VAT it incurs on its business activities including any carried on outside the UK, to determine whether or not it must restrict any input tax as being referable to exempt supplies.

9.322 When deciding what method to use to apportion any VAT, it should be borne in mind that the subscriptions may include an element of gratuity intended to assist the body subsidise its non-business activities. If the VAT on the non-business activities has already been restricted using an appropriate method, it is possible that a turnover-based method will not result in a fair and reasonable attribution of input tax. Bearing in mind that the partial exemption override only applies to exempt input tax and further that in any event it does not apply where the input tax does not exceed £50,000, it may be necessary that a club or association seeks a special method to determine what input tax is deductible.

Public bodies

9.323 An examination of the VAT recovery issues for public sector bodies inevitably gives rise to three fundamental questions:

(a) what is a 'public body';

(b) which of its activities are business, and which of its activities are non-business; and

(c) is there any kind of special VAT recovery or refund mechanism which applies to public sector bodies.

What is a public body?

9.324 As to what are public bodies for UK VAT purposes, some degree of general illumination can be had from of EC Council Directive 77/388 (the Sixth VAT Directive), Art 4.5. Article 4.5 does not in itself either list, or define public bodies, but it is nevertheless useful in that the first indent to Art 4.5 does make it quite clear that:

> 'States, regional and local government authorities and other bodies governed by public law shall not be considered to be taxable persons in respect of the activities or transactions in which they engage as public authorities, even when they collect dues, fees, contributions or payments in connection with these activities or transactions.'

9.325 A thorough exploration of the bodies and organisations which may be found in the UK which fall under the broad heading of 'states, regional and local government authorities and other bodies governed by public law' would very quickly take the reader into a detailed study of the UK's constitutional law, and such an exercise is far beyond the scope of this text. The following organisations have therefore been chosen for inclusion in this section:

(a) government departments;

(b) executive agencies;

(c) NHS trusts and health authorities;

(d) local authorities;

(e) non departmental public bodies (NDPBS – sometimes also known as quangos (quasi autonomous non governmental organisations) although that latter term is less often used these days; and

(f) museums and galleries.

9.326 A very brief mention is also made of a few 'other bodies' – organisations such as Embassies and Consulates, Overseas Military Forces and International Organisations – although strictly speaking they do not fall squarely within the concept of what is a UK 'public body'.

9.327 The issue of what is business and what is non-business is especially important for public bodies because the basic principle that VAT suffered on expenditure incurred for the purposes of making taxable supplies is deductible, applies to public bodies (regardless of how such are defined) in just the same way as it does to private sector organisations.

9.328 In para **9.324** above, it was explained that the first indent of art 4.5 lays down a basic principle that most public bodies are not taxable persons when they engage in their public authority functions. However, the second, and third indents provide exceptions to this rule, and define when these bodies are taxable persons, even when they engage in public authority functions:

> 'However, when they engage in such activities or transactions, they shall be considered taxable persons in respect of these activities or transactions where treatment as non-taxable persons would lead to significant distortions of competition.
>
> In any case, these bodies shall be considered taxable persons in relation to the activities listed in Annex D, provided they are not carried out on such a small scale as to be negligible.'

9.329 The second indent therefore allows a degree of distortion of competition in favour of Public Bodies, unless that distortion is considered significant. Unfortunately the term 'significant' is not defined, and Customs and Excise are able to use their discretion in applying this rule.

9.330 Annex D referred to in the third indent specifies those activities of Public Bodies which shall always be taken to be business activities, even when a Public Body undertakes any of those activities as a Public Authority; the activities listed in Annex D are:

1 telecommunications

2 the supply of water, gas, electricity and steam

3 the transport of goods

4 port and airport services

5 passenger transport

6 supply of new goods manufactured for sale

7 the transactions of agricultural intervention agencies in respect of agricultural products carried out pursuant to regulations on the common organisation of the market in these products

8 the running of trade fairs and exhibitions

9 warehousing

10 the activities of commercial publicity bodies

11 the activities of travel agencies

12 the running of staff shops, co-operatives and industrial canteens and similar institutions

13 transactions other than those specified in Art 13a(1)(q), of radio and television bodies.

9.331 Public bodies do therefore make a wide range of taxable supplies, and this bold but basic statement applies to all the organisations which are considered to be public bodies for the purposes of this section.

Government departments and executive agencies

9.332 There is no single or simple definition of what constitutes a Government department, but neither do we need one for the purposes of this section. Government departments are brought within the scope of the VATA 1994 by virtue of s 41(1) which states quite clearly that VAT shall apply to the Crown as it applies to taxable supplies made by taxable persons. Customs and Excise require that all Government departments that make taxable supplies shall be VAT registered – there is no VAT registration limit. The same applies to Executive Agencies, some of whom may be separately VAT registered; those Executive Agencies who are not separately VAT registered fall to be dealt with under the VAT registration number of their parent Government department.

9.333 If supplies made by a Government department or Executive Agency might not be taken to be business activities, then under the authority of VATA 1994, s 41(2), HM Treasury may, by Direction, specify such supplies as being supplies made by way of business. This Direction, often colloquially referred to as the 'Taxing Direction' is issued on an approximately annual basis, and is published in the London, Edinburgh and Belfast Gazettes. Although the Direction is issued by and under the legal authority of the Treasury, it is to all practical intents and purposes, drafted, administered and controlled by Customs and Excise.

9.334 The current Taxing Direction was issued on 7 June 2002 and took effect on 23 May 2002. Thus, in respect of all of their business activities, Government departments and Executive Agencies will be able to recover input tax, from Customs and Excise, in exactly the same way as a private sector business – ie by completing and submitting a VAT return.

9.335 In addition to being able to recover input VAT according to the normal rules and regulations which apply to private sector businesses, VATA 1994, s 41(3) allows Government departments to claim, from Customs and Excise, a refund of VAT which they have incurred on goods and services which they have bought in for their non-business activities.

9.336 VAT incurred on expenditure for non-business activities is not, of course, input VAT as defined in s 24 (1), and hence the refunds that Government departments are able to claim under s 41(3) are not governed by the rules and regulations that apply to input tax claims.

9.337 Section 41(3) allows the Treasury to make a Direction specifying the extent to which such refunds may be made and also gives Customs and Excise the power to determine the form and manner of how they require such claims to be made to them. This Direction, often colloquially termed the 'COS refund Direction' is of course a different Direction to the Taxing Direction issued under s 41(2), as referred to at **9.332** above. The term 'COS refund' derives from the fact that these are refunds were originally available to Government departments who contracted out services which were traditionally performed in-house, to private sector providers.

9.338 Customs and Excise are responsible for the day to day administration of the COS refund Direction, but unlike the Taxing Direction, the Treasury take a much more active role in drafting its terms and in setting the policy on how the COS refund Direction is to be administered.

9.339 Although s 41(3) permits Customs and Excise to make refunds to Government departments and Executive agencies of VAT incurred in respect of the purchase or acquisition of goods for non-business purposes, the COS Direction restricts the refund to the VAT incurred on services. In practice Government departments are permitted to claim a refund of VAT incurred on goods when those goods are incidental to the services purchased. An example often cited by Customs and Excise is the consumable goods which are subsumed into a supply of cleaning services.

9.340 The COS Direction also lists the services upon which VAT incurred may be reclaimed – there are currently 75 services which are listed as having been approved for refund claims. New COS Directions are issued by HM Treasury on a periodic basis, and since their inception in 1984, have been issued annually. However, in the last few years, new COS Directions have been published on a rather less regular basis. The current COS Direction was issued on 10 January 2003 and took effect on 2 December 2002.

9.341 Section 41(4) provides Customs and Excise with the necessary authority to require Government departments to keep specific records relating to these claims, and to produce these records to them for inspection and approval.

NHS trusts and health authorities

9.342 For VAT purposes, NHS trusts and health authorities have the same status as Government departments. This means that NHS trusts and health authorities have the ability to reclaim input VAT on their business activities in exactly the same way as Government departments, according to the normal rules and regulations.

9.343 The mechanics of submitting such claims to Customs and Excise and receiving repayments are broadly similar to how Customs and Excise administer VAT for private sector businesses, but in recognition of the importance and uniqueness of the administration of VAT in the NHS, Customs have set up a specialist NHS Administration Unit in London, in their Dorset House offices, to deal with NHS VAT issues.

9.344 Although the provision of NHS healthcare is not a business activity, the NHS does carry on a wide range of business activities and where these activities are taxable activities – the provision of private health care is quite obviously an exempt business activity – the NHS may recover input VAT in the same way as any VAT registered entity.

9.345 In respect of its non-business activities, the NHS is also able to claim contracted out services VAT refunds from Customs and Excise. Although, in practice, Customs and Excise internal administration of the processing and approval of these refunds distinguishes between Government departments and the NHS there is no other difference between the two, and the Directions and legal requirements arising from s 41 apply equally to Government departments and the NHS.

Local authorities

9.346 Local authorities engage in a wide range of activities, some of which will be business activities, and some of which will be non-business.

9.347 For their business activities, local authorities recover VAT incurred on their expenditure in exactly the same way, and subject to the same rules and regulations as a private sector body, with one very valuable exception, which arises in respect of their exempt business activities. This exception allows local authorities to recover more VAT, sometimes much more, than would otherwise be the case.

9.348 The Partial Exemption Regulations, regs 99–111, VAT Regulations 1995, SI 1995/2518, apply to local authorities in the same way as to any other VAT registered body. Regulation 106(1) introduces a de minimis provision which allows a VAT registered body to recover all of the VAT it incurs on expenditure related to exempt activities when the VAT incurred on exempt activities is below certain monetary limits.

9.349 Local authorities are not precluded from enjoying the benefits of reg 106(1), but they enjoy a much more generous de minimis provision under the terms of VATA 1994, s 33(2)(b). Section 33(2)(b) allows local authorities to reclaim input VAT which is attributable to exempt supplies if, in the opinion of Customs and Excise, it is an insignificant proportion of all of the VAT incurred by a local authority on its business activities.

9.350 Customs and Excise have, since the inception of s 33 and its predecessor sections, taken the view that 5% will be an insignificant proportion, for the purposes of applying s 33(2)(b). Thus, if the VAT incurred by a local authority on its exempt business activities is 5% or less of its total input VAT, it is able to treat itself as fully taxable and recover all of its input VAT. This is an important and hugely valuable provision for local authorities, because Customs and Excise have not sought to define a maximum monetary limit on this 'insignificant' exempt input VAT. For some of the larger regional local authorities and the metropolitan local authorities, 5% can amount to a very large sum indeed and they will manage their exempt business activities very carefully to ensure that they do not breach the 5% limit.

9.351 If a local authority does breach the 5% limit, then it must revert back to the ordinary partial exemption de minimis limits as per reg 106(1) to determine what amount of exempt input tax that it can recover.

9.352 VATA 1994, s 33 does not just serve to confer a VAT recovery benefit to Local Authorities in respect of their exempt input tax. In much the same way as VATA 1994, s 41 makes various provisions for government departments, executive agencies and the NHS to claim refunds of VAT incurred on expenditure for non-business activities, s 33 makes provisions for local authorities to claim refunds of the VAT they incur on their non business expenditure.

9.353 There, however, the similarity ends and the refund mechanism derived from s 33 is far less prescriptive that that derived from s 41. Section 33(1) requires that Customs and Excise shall refund to a local authority (and to any other body which falls within the scope of the section) all of the VAT it incurs on expenditure which is not for the purpose of any business carried on by it.

9.354 Thus, under s 33, a local authority is able to reclaim the VAT incurred on the purchase of any goods and on any service, for non-business purposes. For a s 33 refund, unlike a s 41 refund, there is no requirement that the goods have to be incidental to a service or that services have to be designated under a Treasury Direction.

9.355 Customs and Excise do have powers under s 33(1) to determine the form and manner of how local authorities shall make claims, but in practice the use of this power is imperceptible as local authorities make such claims as part of their ordinary VAT returns.

9.356 Where a local authority is not registered for VAT, and despite the fact that there is no VAT registration limit for local authorities this does happen in the case of some of the very smallest local authorities who make no taxable supplies at all, Customs and Excise will still make refunds to them of the VAT they incur on non-business expenditure. Customs and Excise have imposed some administrative conditions and limitations purely on the mechanics of how an unregistered local authority should claim a refund of VAT under s 33 and these are explained in some detail in *Tolley's VAT,* **CHAPTER 43.9**.

Non-departmental public bodies and quangos

9.357 NDPBs, or quangos as they have been referred to in the past, are very much part of the administrative machinery of Government in the UK. Once again, their legal basis and the mechanism by which they are brought into existence, interesting though it might be, is beyond the scope of this section.

9.358 NDPBs also carry out a wide range of functions, some of which will be business activities and some of which will be non-business. In that respect they may be thought of as being similar to Government departments and local authorities. However, unlike Government departments or local authorities, NDPBs do not enjoy any special VAT refunds. This is an important point, as NDPBs often fail to appreciate that they are eligible neither for s 41 refunds nor for s 33 refunds.

9.359 Where an NDPB undertakes a business activity, then it will be able to reclaim input tax under the normal rules and regulations. But where an NDPB undertakes non-business activities, then it is not able to recover the VAT incurred, which must be treated as an overhead cost.

Museums and galleries

9.360 For the purposes of input tax recovery, it is convenient to divide Museums and Galleries into two distinct types, specified and non-specified.

9.361 Non–specified museums and galleries, which comprise the vast majority of the UK's museums and galleries, do not qualify for any kind of special treatment as far as recovery of VAT is concerned. These bodies will only be able to deduct VAT under the normal input tax recovery rules and regulations. Many of them are able to, or are required to, treat their admission charges as VAT exempt. Where their admission charges are exempt, a museum or gallery will, by virtue of the fact that it is also likely to make taxable supplies, be partly exempt. Consequently, some input VAT may be recoverable according to the partial exemption method which is being used. However, it is likely that the majority of ordinary museums and galleries throughout the UK will only be able to recover a relatively small proportion of the VAT that they incur.

9.362 A singular distinguishing factor between specified museums and galleries and their counterparts who are not specified (other than the specified status itself) is the fact that they do not charge any entry or admission fee. Ordinarily, Customs would take the view that a museum or gallery which does not charge for admission is not in business for VAT purposes, and hence such a body would not be able to recover much, if any at all, of the VAT it incurs on its expenditure.

9.363 But under VATA 1994, s 33A, 'relevant' museums and galleries enjoy a special VAT recovery regime and s 33A(2) obliges Customs and Excise to make a refund of VAT incurred by a specified museum or gallery on expenditure incurred on the provision of free admission. Section 33(A), which was introduced under the Finance Act 2000, s 98(2), came into force from 1 September 2001. Section 33A(9), which paradoxically came into force rather earlier on 11 May 2001, empowers HM Treasury to specify, by Treasury Order, those museums and galleries which are given relevant body status for the purposes of the s 33A special refund of VAT.

9.364 Such a Treasury Order has been made and The VAT (Refund of Tax to Museums and Galleries) Order 2001, SI 2001/2879 lists those museums and galleries which have been given relevant-body status. Over 40 museums and galleries now have relevant body status and are entitled to claim VAT refunds from Customs and Excise.

9.365 As is the case for all public bodies that are able to enjoy a special refund of VAT, Museums and galleries are only able to claim their special refund where the VAT incurred does not relate to a business activity. Where relevant museums and galleries have business activities, they are required to attribute the VAT they incur directly to those business activities, and recover it – or not as the case may be – according to the normal rules which govern input VAT recovery.

9.366 If a relevant museum or gallery is not itself able to carry out such an attribution, then s 33A(7) allows Customs and Excise to determine how much VAT should be attributed to business activities and to exclude that amount from the VAT which is refunded to the museum or gallery under s 33A(2).

Other bodies

9.367 This is, of necessity, a catch all category, and carries no specific or statutory definition. Organisations such as NATO, Foreign Embassies and Consulates, Visiting Forces, the UN and its various off-shoots, the EU Commission and recognised international organisations (one such example is the International Maritime Satellite Organisation, but there are many others) are not of themselves, UK Public Bodies. Some of them are entitled to a relief from VAT under the Sixth VAT Directive, art 15(10) and hence are not charged VAT on certain supplies made to them.

9.368 Because the UK has not directly implemented Art 15.10 in domestic VAT legislation, bodies entitled to relief from VAT under art 15.10 of the EC Sixth Directive may be relieved from paying VAT on supplies they receive, or alternatively, may have to pay VAT, but may then receive a rebate from the UK Government. The UK Government usually makes whatever arrangements are necessary directly with the organisations concerned, so further consideration of their VAT recovery position is beyond the scope of this book.

9.369 Others, such as US Visiting Forces and Foreign Embassies and consulates, are entitled to relief from local taxes within the UK under treaties or agreements which have nothing to do with either UK or EU law. In general, the UK Government makes special arrangements to relieve such bodies from the impact of local taxes and as these reliefs are not part of the UK's VAT system, they are also beyond the scope of this section.

Retailers

Summary

9.370 There are probably very few retail businesses that have no exempt supplies and therefore do not need to consider whether or not they have to apply the partial exemption rules. Indeed, many larger retailers now have significant financial services businesses including banking, insurance, credit cards and loans. It is not the intention of this section to deal with retailers that are also significant financial services providers in their own right. Their financial service activities need to be considered on the basis that they are financial service providers and the issues relating to their partial exemption methods in respect of such businesses are dealt with elsewhere within this chapter.

9.371 On the other end of the scale, there are a vast number of small businesses owned by small or medium companies, sole proprietors or partnerships. In the past, such businesses would have had few if any exempt supplies. However, the advent of the National Lottery, the siting of cash machines in shops and the use of retailers to collect payments on behalf of others has meant that even the smallest corner shop may be partly exempt. In addition of course, such businesses will frequently also need to deal with private use of goods purchased in the business leading to a need to decide whether or not to restrict the deduction of VAT or whether to account for output tax on such use (**Chapters 4** and **11**).

Typical exempt supplies and non-taxable activities of retailers

9.372 Typical exempt supplies by retailers include:

- bank interest received;
- commissions for arranging insurance, loans and finance (including fees for accepting credit card payments);
- interest on credit granted, including on late payments of accounts;
- National Lottery and similar commissions;
- payments received for dealing with payments on behalf of third parties;
- rentals of property (unless opted);
- sales of postage stamps.

9.373 Individual taxable persons will frequently buy goods or services for private use from business suppliers or will apply goods already purchased to private use. Since only VAT incurred in the course or furtherance of a business is deductible, the retailer that does purchase goods or services for or applies goods or services to private use must account for VAT on such private use. This is considered below.

9.374 Special mention should be made of post offices. The Post Office appoints retailers to act as postmasters. The person appointed to act as postmaster receives a payment from the Post Office for acting as such. That payment is not consideration for a supply – it is regarded as a salary (see *H & V Patel (VAT decision 14956) [1997] SWTI 1216*). Further, even though a taxable person might enter into an arrangement to run a sub-post office with the intention of benefiting its retail business, the VAT charged by the Post Office is not regarded as in anyway attributable to the retail business see *H & V Patel (No 2) (VAT decision 15328) [1998] SWTI 644,* and a number of subsequent cases, most recently *N & S Chauban (2001) (VAT decision 17160*). The 2001 decision appears to be right – it is clear that the Post Office agrees to allow an individual or individuals to act as postmaster(s) and charges a fee for acting as such. The VAT is therefore not incurred in the capacity as taxable person and cannot be input tax no matter what the motive of the person or persons concerned.

Non-business

9.375 As already noted, there are two basic methods of accounting for VAT on non-business activity (see **9.308** above). In the first, the application of supplies of goods and services purchased for the purposes of a business activity but applied to a non-business activity is treated as a supply for consideration. The retailer must in such cases account for VAT on the cost of the goods or services applied. It is important to note that it is only the cost subject to VAT that is treated as the value of the supply for consideration and not the cost plus any related overheads that may not be subject to VAT.

9.376 The second method used is simply to disallow the VAT at the time it is incurred. Customs and Excise have referred to this as the 'normal method'. However, it is clear from cases such as *Lennartz v Finanzamt München III (C-97/90) [1995] STC 514, ECJ* (**Case Summary 12**), and *Seeling v Finanzamt Starnberg (C-269/00) [2003] STC 805, ECJ* (**Case Summary 48**), that in fact the first treatment is the preferred method under the EC Sixth VAT Directive albeit that the latter method is also permitted (see *Finanzamt Uelzen v Armbrecht (C-291/92) [1995] STC 997, ECJ* (**Case Summary 19**)). Of course, if goods or services are acquired other than in the capacity as taxable person, no VAT is deductible. It is implicit in the judgment in *Enkler v Finanzamt Homburg (C-230/94) [1996] STC 1316, ECJ* (**Case Summary 25**), that tax authorities do nevertheless have the right to consider whether in all the circumstances, an asset was acquired for a business purpose in the first place. If it was not acquired in the capacity of taxable person, no initial right to deduct arises.

9.377 Most retailers will also own motor cars or motor vans. As will be noted from **Chapter 4**, there are special rules dealing with the private use of motor cars.

If a motor car is purchased, then no VAT can be deducted unless it is not available for private use. It does not matter that the retailer does not intend to use any motor car for private use – the test is of intention to make available, not to actually use the car for private use.

9.378 In relation to leased cars, the retailer may only deduct 50% of the VAT on lease payments (assuming he is fully taxable) but does not have to account for any VAT on private use since the 50% restriction is regarded as covering all private use (see *C & E Comrs v Upton (t/a Fagomatic) [2002] EWCA Civ 520, [2002] STC 640*). Special rules apply to petrol supplied to employees for private use (see **Chapter 4**).

9.379 It is perhaps worth noting that there is a dichotomy between the treatment of private use under Income Tax rules and that under VAT rules. Under Income Tax rules, a retailer would have to account for Income Tax on private use on the retail value and not cost. This seemingly minor difference does of course mean that there is a further element of complexity in accounting for private use by a retailer.

Methods of dealing with VAT referable to exempt supplies

9.380 A taxable person who is a retailer must in principle disallow any input tax incurred on any exempt activities. He will be allowed to deduct all his input tax including that referable to the exempt activities provided that the input tax referable to those exempt activities is de minimis, i e it does not exceed £625 per month on average nor does it exceed 50% of all input tax.

Application of the standard method to retailers

9.381 Unless a retailer obtains approval to operate a special method, he will have to apply the standard method. In applying the method, certain incidental supplies can be ignored. The exempt supplies that will usually be capable of being ignored by a retailer will include:

- bank and other interest;
- commissions for arranging credit, eg the amount received from a financier in respect of consumer credit;
- property rental where the property activity is incidental to the retail activity eg rent received from a business that is allowed to operate a shop within a shop (except where the retailer has opted to tax).

9.382 Although there is no specific legislation allowing it, Customs and Excise apparently allow retailers to ignore sales of postage stamps in applying the standard method – presumably on the basis that in reality no input tax is truly referable to their sale.

9.383 This means that in principle certain exempt supplies will always have to be taken into account in the standard method eg:

- Lottery commissions;
- commissions for arranging insurance.

9.384 In small businesses, the VAT referable to lottery commissions and arranging insurance even using the standard method may be small enough to be ignored under the de minimis rules. However, retail taxable persons may need to consider a special method where lottery and other commissions that cannot be ignored as incidental are significant.

Special methods

9.385 There is no single way in which a special partial exemption method must be put together. However, it has to be fair and reasonable and must also broadly speaking achieve a result that ensures that input tax is deducted only to the extent that it is referable to taxable supplies.

9.386 Thus, for example, if a shop was fortunate enough to have very significant lottery income, this might result in a greater degree of input tax on overhead expenditure such as rent being disallowed notwithstanding that the lottery equipment occupies no more than a few square feet of the shop. A possible solution might be a method that ignores the lottery turnover but disallows a fixed amount of VAT on rent etc to take into account the real use of taxable inputs for exempt lottery commissions. Indeed, it is probably the case that 'tunnelling' methods, i e those which simply identify the non-core exempt or non-taxable activities and disallow any input tax directly attributable to those activities, possibly with an additional fixed amount to take account of the small proportion of fixed overheads that might be referable to the non-core exempt activity, are both simpler and fair. (Of course, in many cases, the de minimis limits may result in no input tax having to be disallowed at all.)

Second hand goods

9.387 One retail activity that merits brief consideration is the sale of second hand goods. Under the second hand goods scheme, a retailer is not permitted to deduct any VAT on the cost of second hand goods acquired – and indeed, the retailer is unlikely to have a tax invoice in any event. However, he is also not taxed on the full value of the supply and is instead taxed on the difference between the proceeds received and the cost of the goods.

9.388 There are, in fact, two schemes of accounting for second hand goods. The margin on goods having a having a high value (over £500) must be accounted for individually. This has one principal implication in relation to the deduction of VAT and that is that it is necessary when recording the cost of such goods to ensure that the non-deductible VAT is included in the cost and entered in the second hand records as such. Motor cars and certain other means of transport are always regarded as within this category even if they have a lower value than £500.

9.389 The global scheme applies in other cases. Under this method, it is still necessary to include the VAT on the cost of such goods in the value taken account in determining the margin on such sales. However, the margin is calculated on the basis of the aggregate margin and it is therefore not necessary to match costs and sales on an individual basis.

9.390 It should be noted that the cost of repairs to goods and overhead costs are not part of the cost of the goods and the input tax on such costs ranks for deduction in the normal way.

Motor cars and other assets on which VAT has been blocked

9.391 No input tax is allowed on the purchase, acquisition or import of motor cars that are available for private use. A consequence of this is that the disposal of such assets will also be exempt (or non-taxable if used for non-business purposes). The VAT on costs associated with such disposal will not be deductible.

Motor dealers

Introduction

9.392 Motor dealers core business is selling cars, either new 'qualifying cars' or used cars taxable under the second hand margin scheme. However, they may also make exempt supplies of cars on which input tax has been blocked (following *EC Commission v Ital (C-45/95) [1997] STC 1062, ECJ*, and the introduction of VATA 1994, Sch 9, Group 14). Because of the specific input tax block on cars (when, broadly speaking, made available for private use, or let on hire at less than an open market value), there is a significant likelihood of exempt supplies of cars. However, where motor dealers have 'stock in trade' cars (where a motor dealer intends to sell the car within 12 months of supply, acquisition or importation), these stock in trade cars are not subject to input tax blocking and thus do not give rise to partial exemption issues.

9.393 Apart from the core activity of selling cars, Motor dealers may also receive exempt commissions in respect of finance arrangements or insurance arrangements where the dealer acts as an intermediary between the car purchaser and the finance company or insurance company respectively. Whilst these commissions may be subsidiary to the core activity of trading in motor cars, they may nonetheless represent a significant stream of income for a motor dealer.

Partial exemption issues for motor dealers

9.394 In practice, many motor dealers, whilst making exempt supplies as described above, manage to remain 'fully taxable' by virtue of the partial exemption de minimis limits. By operating the standard method, the outputs values of cars can be significant (whilst the profit margins may be very slim) in comparison with the exempt income from finance and insurance commissions (although such commissions may be a significant contributor to profitability). However, the de minimis limits need to be closely monitored to ensure that they are not exceeded either in a given prescribed accounting period or over a tax year.

9.395 Historically input tax incurred in making exempt finance or insurance commissions would have been treated as attributable to taxable supplies under reg 105. However, that regulation was revoked with effect from 10 March 1999. It may still be possible to contend that such commissions should be excluded from the partial exemption calculation under the standard method as 'incidental supplies' (reg 101(3)(b)). However, the facts would need to support this as an incidental activity and where such income streams were a core part of the business, arguing that the income is incidental may be more difficult.

9.396 In *JDL Ltd [2002] STC 1*, the High Court confirmed that where a car dealer had sold demonstrator cars which had been depreciated in the accounts, such sales were sales of capital assets and excluded from the partial exemption calculation under the standard method (reg 101(3)(a)). It can be seen therefore that motor dealers may also be able to exclude the values of exempt supplies of cars from the standard method partial exemption fraction in situations where such cars are capital assets.

General business activities

9.397 Motor dealers can also be involved in other general business activities which affect the deduction of VAT. The current regulatory revisions for the sale of motor cars and associated services (the removal of the so-called 'block exemption'), may lead to increased merger and acquisition activity in the sector. The issues relating to raising finance (such as the question of whether input tax is deductible in situations where a business issues shares), and to reorganisations and restructuring will therefore need to be addressed by many motor dealers.

Business promotions activities

9.398 Motor dealers may be involved with business promotions activities although these are commonly driven via the manufacturers or distributors. If a motor dealer arranges its own promotional activities (such as track days), the blocking of input tax on expenditure incurred in relation to business entertainment must be considered in costing such activities (see for example *BMW (GB) Ltd v C & E Comrs [1997] STC 824* (**Case Summary 27**)).

Tour operators

Summary

9.399 Special rules apply to Tour Operators (see VAT (Tour Operators) Order 1987, SI 1987/1806). Because Tour Operators are only taxed on the margin between the amounts they charge to their customers and the costs incurred in making those supplies, the VAT on the costs that are taken into account in calculating the margin is not deductible.

9.400 It is common for tour operators to make other supplies such as the sale of insurance as agent. Since insurance is an exempt supply and (in these circumstances) is not one of those supplies that can be ignored as an incidental supply under the 'incidental rules' in VAT Regulations 1995, reg 101(3), it follows that, in principle, a tour operator may be partly exempt.

Margin scheme supplies

Basic rules

9.401 In general, margin scheme supplies are those supplies that the tour operator sells as undisclosed agent i e the agent buys in one or more supplies such as accommodation and sells them on to a customer in his own name. However, tour operators are able to exclude certain supplies that would otherwise be within the scheme from the operation of the margin scheme.

9.402 The margin subject to VAT is calculated by deducting the total costs of supplies purchased for the direct benefit of the travel from the total value of margin scheme supplies. The VAT on such costs is not recoverable. However, the VAT on overhead costs is deductible, subject to the normal rules.

Example 3

A tour operator purchases a block of accommodation in a hotel in Edinburgh during the annual festival. He also hires a coach and driver and sells travel and accommodation as a package. Some of the passengers request the tour operator to acquire tickets for certain shows on their behalf. His costs and revenues are as follows:

Revenue and expenditure

	£
80 packages at £250 each	20,000
82 rooms (2 for bus driver and tour guide)	12,300
Hire of bus	770
Meals (includes for bus driver and tour guide) 75)	3,075
Tickets sold to travellers	2,350
Tickets bought on behalf of	2,350
Calculation of margin	
Designated supplies	20,000
Cost of accommodation	–12,000
Cost of meals	–3,000
C ost of transport	–770
Margin	4230
VAT on margin	630

9.403 The sale of tickets has been excluded but it is also possible that they would be margin scheme supplies if the tour operator acted as undisclosed agency. The result would however be the same. The VAT on the costs of accommodation and meals for travellers is not deductible except for the VAT on the costs of the driver and tour guide as these are overhead costs. On the figures above, the VAT deductible would be:

$$\frac{17.5}{117.5} \times (300 + 75) = £\,56$$

The business exception

9.404 If a tour operator supplies a package to a business, he will be able to exclude such supplies from the tour operators' margin scheme and account for VAT in the normal way. Thus in the above examples, assume that 10% of the packages were sold to persons who showed that they were businesses. The result of this would be that the turnover would be reduced by £1,200 and VAT on such supplies would have to be accounted for in the normal way (remembering that there would be both standard rated and zero-rated supplies). The VAT on the accommodation and meals would be deductible in the normal way, thus VAT on £1,200 and £300 would be deductible.

9.405 The key point to note here is that it might be necessary to apportion the costs of creating a tour operator's package as between supplies to taxable persons and those to final travellers.

9.406 Where the business customer is also a tour operator, there is an option to account for VAT on wholesale margin scheme supplies (see VAT Notice

709/5/1998, para 4.2). If that option is exercised, no VAT would be deductible on the costs of the wholesale supplies but the VAT on the turnover would be restricted to VAT on the margin.

Exempt supplies of insurance and other exempt supplies

9.407 As noted, a tour operator may make other supplies, some of which are exempt. Exempt supplies would include arranging insurance, foreign exchange and possibly other financial transactions. Some costs may be referable to these supplies and will also not be within the exclusions from the standard method contained in VAT Regulations 1995, reg 101(3)(c). If so, in principle, the tour operator must apportion any directly and indirectly attributable input tax to such exempt supplies. If the exempt input tax so calculated is not de minimis (see **Chapter 1**), the VAT will have to be disallowed. If it is (which is likely to be the case in all but the larger tour operators, the VAT will have to be restricted.

9.408 It may be the case that it will be necessary to apply for a special method to apportion VAT to exempt supplies as it is possible that the margin will be higher on the exempt supplies (meaning that less input tax is referable to them) than is referable to the core business of selling taxable packages.

Non deductible VAT

9.409 It is also probable that tour operators might incur some input tax that is not deductible (eg VAT on business entertainment). The rules outlined in **Chapter 4** will apply in this case.

9.410 It should be noted that gifts such as promotional travel bags are not likely to be regarded as being supplied free of charge but are in fact part of the cost of packages since they are for the benefit of the travellers and are therefore cost components of the package.

Pension funds

Introduction

9.411 VAT law makes no special provision for pension funds. The normal rules apply. The first issue to consider is whether and to what extent a pension fund acts as a taxable person. To the extent that it does, it may have a liability or right to register for VAT and correspondingly a right to deduct any VAT incurred in respect of its taxable activities and activities (if any) outside the UK in respect of which a deduction is permitted. Even if the fund itself has no taxable activities, the employer or employers of members of the fund may have a right to deduct VAT in respect of the fund's activities.

9.412 Most pension funds are set up in the form of trusts. The funds will have one or more trustees who manage the funds. The duties of a trustee are threefold ie:

- To collect and manage contributions to the fund;
- To make payment of pensions when members become entitled to benefits;
- To invest any monies not immediately required to pay benefits and to manage those investments.

9.413 The leading case on pension funds is that of *C & E Comrs v British Railways Board [1976] STC 359, CA*. The Court there concluded that British Rail Board received certain services in relation to the first type of activity noted above and that there was no justification for concluding that when the board acted as sole trustee of the pension fund, it acted otherwise than in the capacity of employer of the beneficiaries. The Court agreed with the VAT Tribunal's view that the contribution to pensions, the management of the fund generally and the execution of the trust deed were matters (ie the first two activities mentioned above) which were part of the board's functions as employer.

9.414 It should be noted that the Court stressed that the decision had been reached on the facts of the case and in the particular case made reference to the legislation governing the board that made specific provision in relation to pensions. However, it is nevertheless the case that Customs and Excise's view is that part of the activities carried out by a pension fund are in fact activities of the employer and not of the trustees acting in a fiduciary capacity on behalf of the members. On the other hand, investment activities are activities of the fund and the normal rules apply to that activity.

Who must register for VAT?

9.415 To the extent that the activities are regarded as those of the employer (see **9.418–9.420** below), there will be no separate liability to register. However, if the fund carries out any investment activities that give rise to a liability to register for VAT (eg taxable property investment) or an entitlement to recover VAT (eg investing outside the EU), it may be required or entitled to register in the name of the trustees. It is perhaps worth pointing out that in *Wellcome Trust Ltd v C & E Comrs (C-155/94) [1996] STC 945* (**Case Summary 23**), the European Court of Justice considered that the investment activities of the Appellant were not business activities despite the scale and professionalism with which they had been carried out. However, it is likely that, in most funded pension funds, the fact that the trustees take an active role in management of investments and seek to maximise returns not only from earning income but from growth in the value of investments means that most pension funds do carry out a taxable activity in respect of their investments.

9.416 Customs and Excise take the view that if the employer is the sole trustee, then both the employer activities considered in **9.418–9.420** below and those of investment are to be regarded as undertaken by the employer so that no separate liability to register arises. The main impact of this on the deduction of VAT is that the employer may then become partly exempt as a result of the exempt activities of the fund being attributed to the employer and would almost certainly need to apply for a special method to determine its input tax entitlement if the volume of investment activity were substantial.

9.417 The view of Customs and Excise appears to be based on the *British Railways Board* case (see **9.413** above). However, the view is arguably misplaced. The Court in *British Railways Board* decided that the Tribunal had reached the right conclusion on the particular facts of the case. There is a great deal of difference between a person that acts in his own capacity as distinct and one who acts on behalf of another. An employer, who acts as corporate trustee of a fund might therefore be entitled to argue that the company should be registered separately in its fiduciary capacity as distinct from when acting in its own name.

Activities that are considered to be those of the employer

9.418 Customs and Excise set out in *Notice 700/17/02 – Funded pension schemes at para 2.3* the activities that they regard as part of the employer's business activities rather than those of the fund. These include:

- Making arrangements for setting up a fund;
- Management of the scheme, ie collecting contributions and payment of pensions;
- professional services such as audit and accountancy, actuarial and other advisory services;
- Work in connection with the provision of statistics in connection with the performance of a fund's investments or properties.

9.419 On the other hand, Customs and Excise do not regard services that relate to investments as being activities of the employer and therefore do not regard any VAT on such services as input tax of the employer.

9.420 Given the recent and current concerns of employers about the liability that they incur in relation to pension funds, there are likely to be circumstances where advice on investments of funds should be regarded as having been provided to the employer and not to the fund where the expenses are incurred and paid for by the employer. In such circumstances, the employer would be able to deduct the VAT following the principles established in *C & E Comrs v Redrow Group plc [1999] STC 161, HL* (**Case Summary 31**). The basis for this would be that the employer needs to monitor its liabilities under the scheme in order that it can make appropriate financial and accounting provision for any unfunded benefits and also to agree the level of future contributions to the fund necessary to pay employee pensions. To do this it requires the same sort of advice about investment as the fund itself. As in *Redrow* it is irrelevant that the fund gets a benefit out of the expenditure as well.

Pension funds that have several 'employer' firms

9.421 Most pension funds serve a group of companies and therefore there may be several employers of members of a single fund. However, bills for services will typically be issued in the name of the fund or of the main employer. This raises potential problems with deductions since clearly, to the extent that any VAT relates to services relating to the other companies' activities, it is not strictly deductible by the principal employer. The solution will frequently be that one employer will incur the VAT and deduct it and then will recharge the services to other employers.

VAT groups

9.422 Customs and Excise Notice 700/17/02 advises that a company that is the sole trustee of a pension fund can be part of a group registration. The implications of this are that any input tax would be regarded as input tax of the representative member. Further, the deduction allowed would be determined by the group partial exemption method. This could mean that the fund gets more or less of a deduction than had it been registered on its own account.

9.423 A difficulty lies with this concept since a trustee of a fund acts in a fiduciary capacity and therefore should not do anything that would result in the fund bearing a cost that it should not. It follows that the employer may need to make arrangements with the fund to reimburse costs incurred as a direct result of group registration.

9.424 As with the Customs and Excise view that a sole corporate trustee carries out the activities of a fund in its own name, the question of whether or not a corporate trustee can be regarded as acting on its own account for VAT is open to doubt. The decision in *Michaels v Harley House (Marylebone) Ltd [1999] 1 All ER 356, CA* suggests that where one company acts in a trustee capacity in relation to another company that person cannot be regarded as having sufficient control of the other company for the two to be regarded as part of a corporate group. Since VAT grouping depends on such control being present, it appears that there may be no eligibility for VAT grouping in such circumstances.

Evidence of input tax

9.425 Customs and Excise advise in Notice 700/17/02 that, in order to claim input tax deductions, an employer must hold an invoice for the expenditure made out in its name. It follows that it may be important when contracting with suppliers of services in relation to a pension fund to specify those services that are to be regarded as supplied to the employer and therefore invoiced to it and those that are supplied to the fund and invoiced to it.

9.426 Customs and Excise are prepared to accept that 30 per cent of the VAT on a supplier's services to a fund is related to the employer's rather than the fund's business in the absence of any alternative evidence. There is, however, no basis in law for this allocation and, as noted above, it is open to an employer to agree a different method of apportionment of charges as between employer and fund – even one in which the employer bears the whole cost of management.

Partial exemption – the position of the fund

9.427 It is likely that most pension funds will invest in UK securities and will as a result have some, usually substantial, exempt income. However, fund managers tend to spread investments and are also likely to invest in offshore securities including non-EU securities. Subject to the investment activities being regarded as carried out in the course of a business, investment in non-EU securities will carry a right to deduct VAT. The method of determining the deduction will be that set out in VAT Regulations 1995. reg 103 ie a use based apportionment will have to be applied.

9.428 Many pension funds also invest in property, particularly commercial and industrial property and so might have UK taxable activities. Where this is the case, it is quite likely that a turnover values based method of apportioning input tax will not be appropriate to the fund and a special method (see **Chapter 5**) will need to be used in order to secure a fair and reasonable attribution of input tax.

9.429 It is perhaps worth noting that a pension fund might be regarded as a connected party in relation to an employer. As a result, if any grant is made by a pension fund to an employer connected with the fund that might fall within the disapplication of the option to tax rules and result in exempt rather than taxable supplies being made and irrecoverable VAT being incurred.

Partial exemption – the position of the employer

9.430 Any input tax incurred by the employer in relation to the management of a pension fund will be subject to the same rules as those that relate to other input tax incurred. Thus, if it is possible to attribute input tax to specific supplies or groups of supplies, it may be possible to carry out a direct attribution. However, in most cases, since the expenditure on which the VAT is incurred will relate to all employees of the firm, it is more likely that the input tax will be residual. It will therefore have to be apportioned using a combination of a use-based method under VAT Regulations 1995, reg 103, the standard method under VAT Regulations 1995, reg 101 or a special method under VAT Regulations 1995, reg 102.

Chapter 10

Basic Planning

Introduction

10.1 There are a number of basic rules to any VAT planning. These are:

- determining the VAT liability of supplies and applying the lowest rate possible (or exempt the activity);
- accounting for output VAT as late as possible;
- ensuring that VAT is reclaimable; and
- reclaiming input tax as early as possible.

It is the last two aspects that are to be examined in this chapter, ensuring that any VAT that can be claimed is claimed and accelerating the input tax claim.

10.2 This chapter will not be examining any esoteric VAT planning, or what Customs and Excise may call unacceptable avoidance. Thus, planning such as that seen in cases like *Halifax plc [2002] VAT decision 17721, STC 402* are not discussed in this chapter. The concept of economic activity is discussed in **Chapter 2**. It should be noted, however, that Customs and Excise may regard any VAT planning or mitigation as unacceptable avoidance and professional advice should be sought to ensure that any planning mentioned is acceptable and not subject to challenge. In addition, planning that may have been acceptable in the past, may now be regarded as unacceptable as Customs and Excise seek to achieve their target of extra VAT to be collected (current target of an extra £2 billion to be collected per annum).

Obtaining proper tax Invoices

10.3 Input tax claims must be supported by a tax invoice (see Sixth Directive, art 18), though other documentary evidence needs to be obtained for certain other acquisitions such as imports, acquisitions from member states etc. The need to retain an invoice is a strict requirement within EU legislation and is seen as essential to prevent fraud. The UK has slightly less strict requirements. Regulations made under VATA 1994, s 24(6)(a) may treat VAT as input tax only to the extent that the VAT claimed is evidenced and quantified by reference to documents as specified in the regulations (and these are detailed in Value Added Tax (General) Regulations 1995/2518) or as the Commissioners may allow. VAT Regulations, reg 29(2) requires (amongst other things) the person claiming the input tax in respect of a supply from another taxable person to hold the document that is required to be provided under the VAT Regulations, reg 14. It is, therefore, important to know what is acceptable to Customs and Excise and the different types of invoice that may be issued by different types of taxpayer. Consequently, some of the following information has been extracted from Customs and Excise Internal Guidance and Public Notices. In particular, it should be noted that an invoice is not required for each deduction for VAT. For instance, supplies of leases may have one invoice to cover 12 monthly payments and there may be only one invoice to support these payments. It is essential in these circumstances that a memo cross reference is included in the accounts to the location of the supporting invoice. Often such invoices are kept in one folder so that they can be recalled with ease to support the claim. Alternatively a copy of the invoice may be made and placed within the invoice run where the deduction is made to provide evidence of input tax deduction. The exact method of filing and retrieval will be determined by the business's own systems, but thought must be given to how these invoices are to be retrieved for inspection by visiting VAT officers.

10.4 It should, however, be noted that a person may be entitled to reclaim input tax even where a VAT invoice has not been issued or retained. Customs and Excise can exercise their discretion to allow input tax to be reclaimed in other circumstances or where other evidence is held (see eg, VAT Regulations, 1995 reg 29(2), SI 1995/2518). The recent Advocate General's opinion in *Finanzamt Gummersbach v Bockemühl (C-90/02)*, however, has confirmed the need for a tax invoice to allow input tax to be deducted as a strict requirement. Should the ECJ confirm this opinion the UK may find that the discretion of Customs and Excise may become more limited.

10.5 The right to deduct not being limited to cases where output tax has been paid, but also where it is payable *Croydon Hotel and Leisure Co Ltd [1997] V & DR 254*. Conversely, holding a VAT invoice does not automatically entitle a person to reclaim VAT if a supply has not been received *Bond House Systems Ltd (VAT decision 18100) [2003] SWTI 1431*. Where the amount of VAT charged is not the correct amount, only the amount that should have been charged is deductible, even if the incorrect amount is shown on the invoice (see *Podium Investments Ltd [1997] VATTR 121* and *Genius Holdings BV v Staatssecretaris van Financiën (C-342/87) [1991] STC 239, ECJ)*. Customs and Excise will, however, often exercise their discretion and allow the input tax to be deducted where none or less should have been charged, if the party that has charged the VAT has accounted for the amount shown as VAT. Thus, it can clearly be seen that it is an important issue to determine whether a supply has been made or received to obtain an entitlement to input tax deduction and this is supported by the tax invoice.

10.6 These cases, however, are exceptional and it is normal for an invoice to be accepted as evidence of input tax having being incurred and for input tax not to be allowed unless there is a VAT invoice. Whilst a full tax invoice should be obtained wherever possible to support the input tax claim, Customs and Excise officers will often exercise their discretion and allow VAT to be reclaimed where there is a receipt rather than an invoice where it is clear that VAT would have been charged (that is, on a taxable supply by a nationally known entity that would be VAT registered). It is, however, better not to rely on the officer's discretion.

10.7 The Invoicing Directive (2001/1151EC) harmonises the requirements of an invoice throughout the European Union and was implemented by all member states by 1 January 2004. The details of this, the transitional regime and the UK's invoicing requirements are included in detail in **Chapter 12**. Customs and Excise have issued VAT Information Sheet 16/03, November 2003 regarding the transition to the new invoicing regime.

Where some of the information required on an invoice is missing, it is not a proper tax invoice and the strict position is that the VAT incurred cannot be reclaimed. There are occasions where input tax will be allowed without an invoice where the cost is incidental (see below) or in some restricted circumstances (see *Croydon Hotel and Leisure Co Ltd* above) or where a full invoice is not held, see below regarding less detailed tax invoices and other types of invoice. These are, however, exceptions and if a cost is in excess of £250 (£100 before 1 January 2004) a full tax invoice should be obtained. Where the amount is less than £250 and the supply is from a retailer, a retailer's or less detailed tax invoice can be used as evidence for a claim for input tax (see **Chapter 12**).

10.8 It is, however, common for some of the required information to be missing (for instance, an invoice rarely details the type of supply made which was a requirement before 1 January 2004) but such minor inconsistencies do not prevent VAT from being reclaimed and officers regularly exercise their discretion to allow input tax recovery. This, however, should not prevent a business from making every effort to obtain full or proper tax invoices to secure their input tax deduction.

10.9 Customs and Excise allow duplicate evidence or substitute evidence on occasion for input tax deduction. The variations to tax invoices are discussed in **Chapter 12** and other variations are detailed below.

Corporate Procurement Cards

10.10 The use of corporate credit cards or procurement cards can improve the administration of corporate purchasing, control of expenses and deduction of VAT. The use of these cards removes the need to deal with mountains of paperwork and small purchase invoices. The credit card company can provide all the necessary information electronically. This clearly would not be sufficient to support a claim for input tax. Customs and Excise have, however, exercised their discretionary powers under VAT Regulations, reg 14 to vary the requirements for an invoice to deal with these cards. The necessary details are provided in VAT Public Notice 701/48/02 and it is not necessary to reproduce them in detail at this point.

10.11 Although no actual invoice is produced, the credit card company passes the necessary information to the purchaser electronically and a VAT invoice report is produced. Two different types of invoice detail may be produced. This will either be line item detail invoices which provide detailed, itemised information on a line-by-line basis or simplified or summary VAT invoices which provide less detailed information at a summary level only.

10.12 Where line-by-line invoices are produced, Customs and Excise have agreed to waive the requirement to show the date of issue. The tax point becomes the date of processing. The invoice report issued to the purchaser must, however, show the transmission date for each transaction, so the purchaser will know the date input tax can be claimed. This data must be retained for the normal six-year period as if it is an invoice.

10.13 Where summary VAT invoices are produced only summary VAT information is provided. Customs and Excise will accept summary VAT invoice reports in support of input tax claims if it contains the following information:

- the value of the supply;
- the VAT amount charged;
- the VAT rate;
- the time of supply;
- a description of the goods;
- the supplier's name, address and VAT number; and
- the customer's name and address.

Where the value of a single transaction exceeds £5,000 a VAT invoice must be issued. A single transaction is the total value of purchases made using a card at any one time from one 'swipe' of the card.

Photocopy Tax Invoices

10.14 Customs and Excise will accept a photocopy of an original invoice as evidence for an input tax claim where the business requires the original tax invoice to be sent to a place which is not the same as the registered address for VAT (eg where invoices are kept at a warehouse some distance from the main accounting function). A number of conditions are imposed and these are:

- each photocopy must be certified as being a true copy of the original;
- the original invoice must be produced for inspection by Customs upon request; and
- all conditions and requirements of a tax invoice will be applicable to the photocopy.

Customs and Excise regard this as a concession that must be agreed in writing (see Internal Guidance V1–13, Chapter 2, s 8.8).

10.15 Customs and Excise do not accept a photocopied invoice if the original is lost (but see alternative evidence below). These conditions may seem overly strict but are required to prevent fraud or inadvertent double claiming of input tax.

10.16 A copied purchase invoice can be used as a sales invoice provided the invoice is annotated to provide the full requirements of a tax invoice. This would include information such as:

- the new supplier's VAT number, name and address;
- the new customer's name and address;
- the new date of supply; and
- a unique reference number.

See Customs and Excise Internal Guidance V1–24 Part A Section 2.27.

Electronic Invoicing

10.17 Electronic invoices can be used to support an input tax claim. The rules for electronic invoicing have been modified slightly due to the Invoicing Directive. All Member States must now allow electronic invoicing using an advanced electronic signature (a method of verifying data has not been altered during transmission), or Electronic Data Interchange (EDI) (a computer-to-computer exchange of structured data that permits automatic processing by the recipient). This will assist cross border invoicing.

10.18 In Information Sheet 16/03, Customs and Excise have stated that they are keen to facilitate the development of electronic invoicing systems. The criteria for e-invoicing are set out in Notice 700/63 Electronic Invoicing. Providing that a particular invoicing system meets the criteria in that Notice it can be used to transmit VAT invoices. Customs and Excise give examples of systems that are allowable:

Internet based systems (including EDI via Internet) such as:

(a) XML/XSL (extensible Mark-up/Style-sheet Language) messages, transmitted using http (hyper text transfer protocol);

(b) EDI files sent under FTP (File Transfer Protocol) or as attachments to e-mail; or

(c) Free format or structured text messages sent by Internet e-mail.

Intermediary service providers. Such services are capable of receiving messages in a wide variety of electronic standards (eg EDI, XML/XSL, CSV [comma separated variables] etc) that are most convenient to suppliers, undertaking intermediary translation, then passing them on to customers in a different format (as required by the customer). Usually these are Internet-based, and run on secured websites that are access controlled (I/Ds and password). Provision is made for both message encryption and electronic signatures, if users so require.

Bill presentment. Where invoices are 'presented' on websites, hosted either by suppliers or their agents. Customers simply access these websites to view their invoices.

10.19 Businesses intending to use electronic invoicing must give Customs and Excise at least 30 days written notice of intent (and current approvals continue). Customs and Excise will issue a letter outlining the conditions under which electronic invoicing can be used. Prior to 1 January 2004, this included control over the integrity of the invoice transfer process, completeness, accuracy and audit trail requirements. Invoices can be provided on magnetic tape or disc, or transmitted by electronic means. Customs and Excise permit the sending of invoices by e-mail or fax without any need for an electronic signature or handwritten signature. In addition, 'bill presentment' on a web site does not and will not require any form of signature.

VAT Fraction

10.20 Where less detailed tax invoices are issued, the amount of VAT that can be reclaimed is not specified. The VAT element must be extracted from the gross figure. This is achieved by multiplying the gross figure by the VAT fraction. The VAT fraction is the rate of VAT divided by 100 plus the rate of VAT.

10.21 Thus where the rate of VAT shown on the less detailed VAT invoice is 5 percent, the VAT fraction is $5/105$. This can be reduced down to $1/21$. Thus, if an item purchased is £210 and the VAT rate is shown as 5 percent, then the VAT embedded in the £210 is:

£210 × $1/21$ = £10.

This can be checked by multiplying the net figure (the gross amount less the VAT) by the 5 percent VAT rate and adding it to the net. This should give the gross figure.

Net figure is £210 less the VAT (£10) = £200
£200 × 5% = £10.
Net plus VAT = Gross £200 + £10 = £210

Where the rate of VAT shown on the less detailed VAT invoice is 17.5 percent, the VAT fraction is $17.5/117.5$. This can be reduced down to $7/47$. Thus, if an item purchased is £235 and the VAT rate is shown as 17.5 percent, then the VAT embedded in the £235 is:

£235 × $7/47$ = £35

Incomplete Tax Invoices

10.22 VAT cannot be claimed where a business does not have a valid tax invoice. On occasions, however, a tax invoice is held, but it is incomplete in some respect. It may be thought that as the VAT regulations have not been complied with that the VAT incurred cannot be reclaimed. An invoice is the evidence for input tax deduction. Customs and Excise can, however, exercise its discretion and allow a VAT deduction where incomplete evidence is held where other evidence can be provided to demonstrate that VAT has been incurred. Customs and Excise's views regarding this are detailed in their Internal Guidance V1–13, Chapter 2, s 8.7–8.11.

10.23 Where an invoice is complete other than for a few minor details, such as the identifying number or the customer's name and address it will usually be accepted as satisfactory evidence for input tax deduction. Customs and Excise will also accept that a date on an invoice can be taken to be the tax point if no other tax point is shown.

Alternative Evidence

10.24 Input tax can only be claimed where proper evidence to support the claim can be produced. Customs and Excise will not, however, just disallow a claim for input tax if a proper tax invoice is not held. It will consider what alternative evidence is available – see Internal Guidance V1–13, Chapter 2, s 8.11. The authority to accept alternative evidence is contained in VAT Regulations, reg 29 . What constitutes acceptable alternative evidence is not specified in these regulations. It is, therefore, a matter of discretion and judgement of the officer and VAT tribunals expect both of these to be exercised in a sensible and reasonable manner. Frequently, Customs and Excise will accept photocopy invoices as alternative evidence, despite the comments made above.

10.25 When Customs and Excise considers whether or not to accept alternative evidence it will consider:

- what documentation is held (eg order forms, delivery notes, stock records, proof of payment etc.)?
- Were the supplies in question received from a taxable person and liable to VAT at the standard rate?
- Does the business have a good compliance history?
- Do the sums involved make it reasonable to expect the business to obtain a duplicate tax invoice from the supplier concerned?

10.26 This final point is of importance when considering claims for employee expenses. Often some invoices will be missing, but alternative evidence can be made available and the values of the invoices make it unreasonable to expect duplicates to be obtained.

A leading case on missing invoices is *Vaughan [1996] V & DR 95* which concerned an appeal against an assessment disallowing input tax for renovations to a farm building for which the appellant held no invoices. The appeal was allowed as it could be seen that supplies had been received and paid for, some duplicates were obtained and the bookkeeper was able to give evidence regarding the entry of the original invoices into the records.

10.27 It should be noted that this discretion also extends to invoices that are false as well as to missing invoices. The appeal of *Ellen Garage (Oldham) Ltd [1994] VATTR 392* concerned VAT disallowed on the construction of four industrial units but the invoice number and supplier details were false. There was evidence that work had been done and cash withdrawals from the Bank exactly matched payments said to have been made.

No Invoice Required

10.28 Input tax can be claimed without a tax invoice (or other form of receipt) for individual purchases of £25 or less (including tax) where it is common for no invoice to be issued (VAT Public Notice 700, para 19(7)(5)). For instance, this will apply to:

- telephone calls made from public or private telephones;
- purchases through coin operated machines;
- car parking charges; and
- road and bridge tolls.

10.29 It should be noted, however, that it is necessary to ensure that the costs bear VAT. For instance, on-street parking meters and public authority tolls are not subject to VAT. Also, the expense must have been incurred for business purposes. Claims without an invoice are allowable on a discretionary basis and as such Customs and Excise expect the extent of such purchases to be reasonable in relation to the business activity. This provision is not carte blanche to reclaim input tax with no invoice. Frequently, Customs and Excise will expect to see other documentary evidence (expense claim forms etc) to support the claim.

Business Gifts

10.30 The recipient of a gift can reclaim any VAT charged (subject to the normal rules). A VAT invoice cannot, however, be issued by the supplier/donor as there is no consideration, but a VAT certificate can be issued to support the claim for input tax deduction. This is essentially the same as a VAT invoice but must bear the words 'VAT Certificate' instead of 'VAT Invoice', and state: 'No payment is due on the supply of the goods. Output tax has been accounted for on the supply.' Most Customs and Excise officers will accept a 'VAT only invoice' even though it is not actually correct.

Mileage allowances

10.31 VAT can also be reclaimed where an employee (or third party) is reimbursed for the actual cost of the fuel expense or where an amount is paid by way of a mileage allowance, see Value Added Tax (Input Tax) (Person Supplies) Order 1991/2306. The mileage allowance paid to the employee is to be determined by the distance travelled and the cylinder capacity of the vehicle used. It should be noted that there is an element of approximation in using a mileage allowance. Customs and Excise often state that the mileage rate to be used is that of the AA, RAC or other similar bodies. This is not a legislative requirement, but a good reason for using a different rate than these independently produced figures should be available to substantiate the claim. Where the mileage rate is for petrol, repairs, cost of the car etc, only the element relating to the petrol (or other road fuel) can be reclaimed as a mileage allowance.

10.32 The rates produced by the AA for 2003 are (in pence per mile):

Diesel

up to 1tr	to 1.3 ltr	1.31 to 2ltr	2.01ltr to 3 ltr	over 3tlr
7.24	7.89	8.26	9.10	12.24

Where diesel costs 78.1 pence per litre.

For every penny more or less, subtract or add to the cost:

0.09	0.10	0.11	0.12	0.16

Petrol

up to 1tr	to 1.3 ltr	1.31 to 2ltr	2.01ltr to 3 ltr	over 3tlr
7.73	9.66	11.59	12.42	16.56

Where petrol costs 76.5 pence per litre.

For every penny more or less, subtract or add to the cost and adjust the VAT amount

0.10	0.13	0.15	0.16	0.22

To calculate the VAT element, multiply the pence per mile rate by $7/47$.

Thus, if a petrol car of 2000 cc is used, a VAT claim can be made of 12.42p X $7/47$ = 1.85 pence per mile. Accurate mileage records must be kept, and these can be based on the employee expense forms.

(reference: http://www.theaa.com/allaboutcars/advice/advice_rcosts_diesel_table.jsp and http://www.theaa.com/allaboutcars/advice/advice_rcosts_petrol_table.jsp)

10.33 It was held in *EC Commission v Netherlands (C-338/98) [2001] STC 1506, ECJ* that the Netherlands had failed to comply with the Sixth Directive by allowing VAT to be claimed on a mileage allowance for the business use of a car. This has led many commentators to believe that the current UK provision will eventually have to be withdrawn. There are, however, differences between the UK and the Netherlands position. In the Netherlands the amount was paid for the use of a car and this car had not been supplied to a taxable person (but to the employee). Also, the sums were amounts paid in aggregate and did not take into account variations in consumption between the use and type of vehicles. In the UK, the VAT can only be reclaimed for a mileage allowance for the petrol element and it does vary according to the type of car. This and the lack of purchase invoices, however, may not be sufficient for the European Commission and it may take infraction proceedings against the UK at a later date. Such infraction proceedings may also affect the entitlement of a business to recover VAT on other supplies, eg hotel expenses, made to employees. However, until that time the mileage allowance can be used to substantiate a VAT reclaim.

It is also noteworthy that there is neither need for an invoice for a mileage allowance nor any need for a business/private apportionment. Many officers believe that the Department's prior permission needs to be obtained before using this method of input tax recovery. Clearly this is not the case as it is a statutory provision. (See also, Customs and Excise Internal Guidance V1–13, Chapter 2A, s 11.40).

10.34 Where a mileage allowance is not paid to employees, it may be difficult to substantiate the re-imbursement of the actual fuel expense. If Customs and Excise believe that any private motoring as well as business motoring has been paid for, the scale charge will apply. Tax invoices must also be obtained from employees as evidence to support input tax claims (invoices addressed to employees are acceptable) where an actual reimbursement is paid.

Reverse Charges

10.35 A tax invoice is not produced where there is a reverse charge and the recipient has to account for VAT on a supply received. It was in the Advocate General's opinion in *Finanzamt Gummersbach v Bockemühl (C-90/02)* that there is a need for an invoice from the supplier that complies with the normal invoicing rules to allow input tax to be deducted. The ECJ, however, held that a person is not obliged to be in possession of an invoice in order to be able to deduct the input tax arising from the reverse charge. A taxable person should ensure that the VAT is claimed (as well as output tax paid). There should be sufficient memo information recorded to ensure that the VAT reclaim can be justified.

10.36 Where an invoice is issued by the supplier, the invoice must be marked that the recipient is to account for the VAT, that the reverse charge procedure is to apply or an exemption applies.

Foreign Currency Invoices

10.37 Where an invoice is issued in a foreign currency the VAT value must be converted into sterling, otherwise the VAT is non-deductible.

Not a Tax Invoice

10.38 Requests for payment, delivery notes, consignment notes and proforma invoices are not VAT invoices. These should all be marked 'This is not a VAT Invoice'.

Employee Expenses

10.39 One of the most difficult areas for maximising input tax recovery is employee expenses. Too frequently staff do not obtain invoices or the invoices obtained are not proper tax invoices. The only real solution to this is to create a culture within the business that no expense will be paid unless a proper invoice is obtained. In addition, clear guidelines have to be given in respect of what constitutes a proper tax invoice and where VAT cannot be reclaimed. Staff guidelines in respect of employee expenditure usually concentrate on what type of hotel can be used and the level of expenditure on meals that is allowable. Guidance should also be given in respect of VAT deduction, obtaining invoices and non-deductible items.

10.40 Persons responsible for checking employee expenses should be made aware what is not an invoice (and guidelines can be obtained by using the information given earlier in this chapter) and what VAT is non-deductible (see **Chapter 4**). A further check needs to be introduced to ensure that an expense is not claimed where the expenditure is private or personal. Thus, even though an expense may be regarded as a business expense, there may be insufficient nexus between the expenditure and the business to allow input tax deduction (again, see **Chapter 4**).

10.41 When Customs and Excise review employee expenditure this will usually be undertaken through a sampling process. The visiting officer may review a particular period or branch for expenditure. The error rate found will then be applied to all employee expenses. It should be agreed with Customs and Excise what period or branch (or other selection criteria) is suitable and it should be ensured that this is a representative sample. For instance, a sample of the advertising or media branch is unlikely to be wholly representative as they may incur more entertainment than an engineering branch. A sample including the Christmas period is also likely to be unrepresentative. Should Customs and Excise insist on examining an area that is non-representative (for example, travelling salesmen), any assessment should be restricted to the expenses of similar groups and not applied to all employee expenses.

10.42 Where there are a large number of employees and employee expenditure, it is likely that there will be errors and Customs and Excise will raise an assessment on a review. Any assessment raised by Customs and Excise should be reviewed and the same period checked. If significant errors in Customs and Excise's assessment or proposed assessment are found (for instance, it is likely that visiting officers will disallow input tax where no invoice is held where there is no requirement to hold an invoice) the assessment should be disputed. Depending on the level of error, it may be necessary to conduct a further review of another representative period and obtain Customs and Excise's agreement to substitute that error rate for the one found by Customs and Excise.

10.43 Once agreed that the sample is representative it will, however, be difficult to reduce any assessment unless the sample checked by Customs and Excise is re-checked by the taxable person to find if Customs and Excise have erred in their assessment.

10.44 It should be noted that VAT incurred abroad can be reclaimed if it is incurred by a taxable person that is not in business in that country. **Chapter 13** gives details of VAT that is incurred in other member states of the EU that can be reclaimed. VAT can also be reclaimed in most other countries that have a VAT type system (eg Australia, Canada, Switzerland, Norway).

Procurement Companies

10.45 A procurement company is a company that purchases goods and services for other companies (though goods are normally purchased and not services). The objective of a procurement company (at least as far as VAT planning is concerned) is to accelerate the VAT that can be reclaimed by a taxable person, anticipate a rate change or supply items that are acquired subject to a positive VAT rate but sold at the zero-rate (see Net Repayment Companies below). There are many other reasons for a procurement company, such as centralisation of functions to provide expertise, obtaining bulk purchase discounts and better control of purchasing etc. These issues are not discussed in this chapter, but are all part of the commercial reasoning for a procurement company. Procurement companies may be regarded as being used for avoidance (eg where there is a rate change and a taxable person pre-orders goods to obtain goods at a lower rate) and Customs and Excise may take action to prevent the tax advantage being achieved, though there is no specific legislation to prevent such advantages arising. The taxable person's intention will be examined in these circumstances to determine if the intention is VAT avoidance or if there is a commercial reason for the purchase. It should also be noted that pre-payment is not restricted to taxable persons. When VAT was imposed on fuel and power at a positive rate, many private individuals pre-paid their fuel bills to ensure future supplies of fuel and power at the zero-rate.

Use of Procurement Companies by Exempt Businesses or Non-Taxable Persons

10.46 Taxable persons or entities that cannot reclaim any or most of the VAT that they incur (referred to as exempt persons in this section) may use a procurement company to delay the VAT cost. Without a procurement company the exempt person purchases the goods, incurs the VAT and stores the goods until they are used. The VAT incurred cannot be reclaimed and is an immediate cost. Where a procurement company is used the goods are bought by a procurement company and this company can reclaim the VAT charged to it. The procurement company would then store the goods VAT-free until required by the exempt person. The procurement company would account for the VAT when goods are sold to the exempt person, but that VAT will not be charged until the goods are actually delivered for use by the exempt person. Thus, the cost of funding the VAT whilst goods are stored is removed.

10.47 This advantage can be enhanced by using the goods on consignment rules and the continuous supply of services rules. The procurement company can provide goods on a sale or return basis. The goods held by the exempt company remain the property of the procurement company until adopted by the exempt person. Thus, the goods can be stored at the exempt person's premises. A periodic stock check will need to be made to determine the value of the stock taken (adopted) so that the procurement company can account for the VAT on that stock. It should be noted that any goods that remain in stock for 12 months are deemed to have been adopted and VAT is due on this stock. It should further be noted that a payment does not necessarily create a tax point; the tax point is the date of issue of an invoice, or the date of adoption. See VATA 1994, ss 6(2)(c) and 6(4).

10.48 Where continuous services are provided (for instance supplies of staff, leases, construction services etc.), the tax point is the date of payment or the date an invoice is raised. Thus, a procurement company may be formed to arrange the supply of temporary staff to an exempt person. The procurement company can reclaim the VAT that it is charged by the 'temp' agencies and does not need to charge VAT until it either raises an invoice or gets paid by the exempt person. VAT is, however, due within twelve months if no payment is made or invoice issued. See VAT Regulations 1995, SI 1995/2518, reg. 90.

Use of Procurement Companies by Persons Able to Deduct all Input VAT

10.49 Persons able to reclaim all input VAT may also use procurement companies. The procurement company will usually have a VAT stagger period that differs from the main taxable person. Thus, if the taxable person's VAT periods are quarterly periods and they end 31 March, 30 June, 30 September and 31 December. The procurement company could apply to have a VAT period that ends on 28 February, 31 May, 31 August and 30 November. The procurement company could then sell to the taxable person in the first month of its VAT quarter. The VAT charged will be deductible by the taxable person on its period ending 31 March (for sales made in March). The procurement company will not need to account for VAT until the 31 May return (payable on 30 June). The procurement company could also raise an invoice for its expected sales in April and May on the 31 March return. The VAT could again be reclaimed by the taxable person on the 31 March return (usually submitted by 30 April), but the VAT would not be payable by the procurement company until the 31 May return, due on 30 June. As can be seen the taxable person receives the VAT payable by the procurement company from Customs and Excise two months prior to payment. Customs and Excise may challenge such planning and it would be essential that such transactions were confined to real goods and services sold and that the procurement company takes title to the goods and responsibility for them. Also all invoices must be made to the procurement company, and it must be accurate in its invoicing to the taxable person. Customs and Excise may, in any instance, argue that real supplies are not made and that this is not economic activity.

Prepayments

10.50 Where a VAT rate is due to increase, it is common to use a procurement company to 'avoid' the VAT increase. Where there is to be a VAT rate increase or VAT is to be imposed upon a zero-rated or exempt item, the VAT cost can be avoided by paying a supplier for the goods or service before the increased VAT charge is imposed. This creates the tax point for the supply, even though no goods or services have yet been supplied VATA 1994, s 6(4). A VAT invoice could be issued where the VAT rate is to be increased as this will also create a tax point, and there would be no need for money to change hands. This is particularly important for taxable persons or businesses that cannot deduct VAT. It is arguable that the VAT is not actually avoided as none is due (or it is due at a reduced rate), when the tax point arises – even where the payment is made to an associated entity.

10.51 In such arrangements the supplier may want payment for the VAT that it will be required to pay to Customs and Excise on the issue of the invoice, but this VAT will be deductible as input tax by the recipient, subject to the normal rules. Where the supply is zero-rated or exempt, the issue of an invoice will not create a tax point, so pre-payments must be made.

10.52 *C & E Comrs v Faith Construction Ltd [1989] STC 539, CA* is the leading case on pre-payment schemes. It had the added feature that there was circularity of payments and Customs and Excise attempted also to apply the principles established in *Craven (Inspector of Taxes) v White [1988] STC 476, HL* and *Furniss (Inspector of Taxes) v Dawson [1984] STC 153, HL*. The case concerned the pre-payment of alterations works for Company D pre-1 June 1984 as such work was to become standard rated from that date. The works were to be undertaken by an associated company (F). To enable the prepayment to be made an arrangement was entered into where F received the money and lent it back to D. D then repaid the loan as the work proceeded. It was contended by Customs and Excise that the arrangement meant that payment had not actually been made, so there was no tax point created prior to 1 June 1984. The Tribunal and Court of Appeal held that a genuine contract payment had been made and that it (or they) were not entitled to disregard the legal effect of this payment. Thus, the prepayment was effective and enabled the transaction to be treated as zero-rated.

10.53 For many years it has been accepted that where genuine prepayments have been made (or invoices issued where the VAT rate is a positive rate of tax) the tax point would be created and the VAT liability position was 'frozen' at the time the payment was made (or invoice issued if appropriate). With the tide seemingly turning against VAT avoidance in the Courts, there can be no guarantee that such transactions, especially involving related parties, would continue to be accepted.

Exit Schemes

10.54 An attempt was made to utilise the combination of procurement companies and VAT grouping to allow input tax to be deducted either where VAT was non-deductible (for example on the purchase of motor vehicles) or where the taxable person was unable to reclaim the majority of the VAT that they incurred (e.g. a mainly exempt taxable person). The leading case in such transactions was *Thorn Materials Supply [1998] STC 725, HL*. A procurement company (or in *Thorn's* case, two companies) in a group would enter into an arrangement with the ultimate recipient company (also a group member) to purchase cars. The VAT on the purchase of these cars would not normally have been deductible. 90 per cent of the purchase price was paid to the procurement company (and this money was lent back to the recipient company). After making the payment, the procurement company or companies left the VAT group. The procurement company then acquired the cars from the third party supplier, reclaimed the input tax and supplied the cars to the recipient company (that has remained in the VAT group). The recipient company paid the remaining 10% due and the procurement company accounted for the VAT on this 10 per cent.

10.55 The VAT would not normally have been deductible on the cars purchased, but as the procurement companies were acquiring the cars for resale it was thought that the VAT could be reclaimed, though VAT would not be due on 90 per cent of the sale value as this part of the transaction occurred whilst the procurement company was grouped with the recipient company. It was held by the Courts that the planning was ineffective as the grouping provisions were for the facilitation of the collection of the tax and did not confer exemption or relief. VAT Act 1994, s 43 (1) may have the effect of deferring the charge to tax until the goods were subject to a supply outside the group, but did not prevent that charge to VAT.

10.56 *BUPA Purchasing Ltd v C & E Comrs [2003] EWHC 1957 (Ch), [2003] STC 1203* was another avoidance scheme where subsidiary companies in the group received substantial prepayments for future services whilst in the VAT group with the ultimate recipient of the supplies. The procurement companies subsequently left the VAT group and were separately registered and made substantial claims for input tax, although no, or little VAT was accounted for on the supplies made to the recipient companies in the VAT group. The High Court upheld the Tribunal decision 17815, in favour of Customs and Excise. The Tribunal had held, applying the principles laid down by Lord Nolan in *Thorn Materials Supply Ltd [1998] STC 725, HL*, 'the substantial prepayments made under the "Prepayment Supply Agreements" must be disregarded for tax purposes'. The fundamental purpose of the EC VAT legislation was 'to achieve neutrality'... 'there has to be a fiscal balance between the right to deduct the VAT paid on the goods and services bought in by a trader for the purposes of his business and his liability to pay VAT on the goods and services he supplies in his business and for which he bought in those goods and services. That neutrality is not achieved if the full value of VAT on inputs is available as credits while only a negligible portion of the value of the outputs to which the inputs are directly linked is taxed. VATA 1994, s 24(5) was to be interpreted 'purposively to permit a restriction of the input tax credit that can be allowed in a group exit scheme such as this to a portion that reflects that small fraction of the full acknowledged value of the services supplied that is alone subject to output tax'. As only 2 per cent of the services supplied by the recipient company were subject to VAT it was thought logical that 98 per cent of the input tax claimed was not deductible.

10.57 Prior to the *Thorn* case being heard Customs and Excise introduced the anti-avoidance provisions in VATA 1994, Sch 9A to prevent such exit schemes being effective in relation to supplies after 28 November 1995. Interestingly this anti-avoidance legislation contains a motive test, which is unusual in English or UK anti-avoidance legislation. Of further interest is the fact that this piece of legislation remains even though it would appear to be otiose following the *Thorn* and *BUPA* decisions and, as far as can be seen from Tribunal decisions, has never been used.

Net Repayment Companies

10.58 Taxable persons that are in a repayment position will be able to submit monthly VAT returns. This will mean that the taxable person will be able to reclaim VAT incurred on expenses two to three months quicker than they would if they were using quarterly VAT returns. In addition, if it is known that repayment returns are to be made, then resources can be diverted to this entity at the beginning of each month to produce the VAT return as soon as possible. Customs and Excise will repay the VAT owing, usually within a fortnight, and do not delay payment until the due date.

10.59 It may also be possible to split a business into separate entities so that a repayment company can be created to improve the cash-flow of both entities. This repayment taxable person will make monthly VAT returns. This can receive supplies from the main taxable person that are subject to VAT. The VAT can be deducted by the repayment company and this VAT can be reclaimed from Customs and Excise before the main trading entity has paid the VAT due to Customs and Excise as this taxable person will be submitting quarterly VAT returns.

Example 1

Main Trading Entity	Repayment Company
VAT period:	*VAT periods:*
1 January to 31 March	1 January to 31 January
	1 February to 28 February
	1 March to 31 March
VAT return submitted:	*VAT returns submitted:*
30 April	3 February
	3 March
	3 April

Main Trading Entity	Repayment Company
VAT Paid:	*Reclaim paid by C & E:*
30 April	14 February
	14 March
	14 April

This is a cash-flow gain of (14 + 31 + 30) + (17 + 30) + (16) days = 138 days.
If the VAT claimed is £100,000 each month, and interest rates are 5 per cent, then the gain is:
£100,000 X {(75/365 X 5%) + (47/365 X 5%) + (16/365 X 5%)} = £1,890.
Clearly this calculation can be altered easily for differing amounts. Thus, if the interest rate is 4 per cent, the gain is ⅘ of £1,890.

10.60 A common example of this type of company is the export company. Where a business exports goods (or dispatches goods), it can either reduce its VAT payment each quarter (as it will have correspondingly less VAT to pay as output tax if a proportion of sales are outside the UK), or it could sell all goods destined for export or dispatch to its own subsidiary export company. VAT will be charged to this export company. The export company will not charge VAT on its exports or dispatches but will be able to deduct the VAT that it incurs. This type of arrangement was tested in *Philips Exports Ltd, [1990] STC 508, QB*. Whilst this type of arrangement was clearly regarded as acceptable in 1990, it is not absolutely certain whether this will now be regarded as avoidance that is not acceptable and subject to challenge as an artificial arrangement, abuse of right, or even a *Halifax* type arrangement.

Early VAT registration

10.61 A person does not need to register for VAT until its turnover exceeds the VAT registration threshold. The current limit (w.e.f. 1 April 2004) is £58,000. Early VAT registration means either registering before taxable turnover reaches this threshold (voluntary registration) or before any taxable supplies have been made (intending 'trader' registration). Early registration is vital to ensure that VAT incurred on expenses can be deducted. Early registration ensures that VAT incurred is claimed as soon as possible. In addition, it protects the VAT deduction position. VAT cannot be reclaimed on goods on hand that were acquired up to three years prior to registration or on services incurred more than six months prior to registration. Customs and Excise will only back date VAT registration three years (where there has been taxable activity), so a maximum of six years worth of VAT on goods and three years six months of VAT on services can be reclaimed. If a project has taken longer than these periods before the date of VAT registration then this VAT is lost. In addition, if an entity does not register for VAT and fails to make any taxable supplies, the VAT incurred cannot be reclaimed. Where 'economic' activity is undertaken (see **Chapter 2**) the VAT incurred on the expenditure is deductible, but it is necessary to register to enable deduction to be made. Where an entity has failed to register and economic activity has ceased then no VAT can be deducted, as it is no longer possible to register for VAT.

10.62 Early registration is not usually advisable where persons that cannot reclaim VAT are supplied, as this will either increase the charge to these persons or will mean the margin obtained by the supplier is reduced. A judgement needs to be made as to whether the amount of input tax lost by not registering is greater or less than the reduced profit achieved if early registration causes fewer sales or/and reduced margins. As a general rule, however, where supplies are made to a person that is not able to deduct VAT, registration should be notified as late as possible.

Voluntary registration

10.63 A voluntary registration is where a person registers and taxable turnover is below the VAT registration threshold. This is usually an advantage where other taxable persons are being supplied, as the recipient of the supplies will be able to deduct the VAT charged. The voluntarily registering taxable person will be able to add output VAT to his charge for goods or services and be able to deduct VAT incurred on expenditure. It is usually quite easy to register as a voluntary taxpayer as the taxable person can prove to Customs and Excise that taxable supplies are being made, and registration is permitted. Customs and Excise cannot refuse to register such persons.

Intending 'Trader' Registration

10.64 An intending trader may have greater difficulties in demonstrating to Customs and Excise that they are intending to make taxable supplies. Customs and Excise are required to register persons that are undertaking economic activity, but this has to be proved to the satisfaction of Customs and Excise before registration takes place. Registration is normally not difficult to progress where there are bank accounts, contracts, purchase and sales orders, evidence of purchases of equipment, employment contracts etc. Customs and Excise, however, are wary of allowing such registrations, as their registration units are the first line of defence against VAT frauds and they wish to prevent fraudulent persons from obtaining VAT registrations. In addition, it is common for businesses not to have sufficient information to prove to Customs and Excise's satisfaction that they are 'intending to trade'. This is particularly the case where matters are at an early stage, i.e. prior to contracts being signed for acquisitions or purchases. Customs and Excise are understandably reluctant to issue VAT registration numbers in such instances.

10.65 There is no simple solution to this impasse. Customs and Excise are reluctant to accept a draft sale contract for the purchase of a business, yet the vendors of the business may be unwilling to treat the sale as a transfer of a business as a going concern unless it can be demonstrated that the purchasing entity is VAT registered. Clearly there is a need for warranties and indemnities in such a case, but the registration process can be facilitated by both parties providing as much information as possible to Customs and Excise. Often information provided by the vendor of the business will assist in the registration of the purchaser.

10.66 Similarly, difficulties can arise where the intended business relates to property transactions. Customs and Excise are not to know that the property is to be used for a taxable purpose. Where a site is to be developed for dwellings, but is currently a commercial or bare land site, there will be little evidence of an intended taxable supply. Often at these early stages only planning applications, rather than planning approval, are available and Customs and Excise may not accept this as suitable evidence. The matter would be expedited if the taxable person elected to waive exemption, but they may not wish to do this in case the planning application is turned down and the site is used for a different purpose. It is often a matter of persuasion to facilitate the registration of the entity, together with the provision of as much supporting paperwork as possible. Any purchase invoices, surveyor's correspondence, architect's drawings (or quotes) etc, will all assist in showing that there is an intention to make taxable supplies.

Monthly returns

10.67 When a taxable person is first registered it may be incurring more input tax than the output tax it is due to pay. Thus, it may be sensible to ensure that an application is made on registration for monthly VAT periods. This will accelerate VAT reclaims. This application will have to be made separately from the VAT 1 VAT Registration form, unless it is indicated on the form that the taxable person expects to be in regular receipt of repayments. As soon as the taxable person becomes a payment trader, it should notify Customs and Excise so that it can be moved to quarterly returns.

Stagger codes and special periods

10.68 If a particular VAT period end is required an application should be made at the time of registration (though the stagger code can be changed at a later date if required). The stagger codes are:

Stagger code 1, quarterly periods ending 31 March (and every three months);

Stagger code 2, quarters ending 30 April (and every three months afterwards); and

Stagger Code 3, quarters ending 31 May (and every three months afterwards).

A period should be chosen that is appropriate for the taxable person.

Should the taxable person require special periods (e.g. 13 week periods, or non-month ends), an application should be made at registration, though again the application can be made at a later date if required.

Payments on account

10.69 In the UK all businesses submit quarterly VAT returns unless they receive regular repayments when they can opt for monthly VAT returns. To improve the Treasury's cash-flow, however, VATA 1994, s 28 provides that each taxable person with a VAT liability of more than £2 million must make payments on account. Although the taxable person only makes quarterly VAT returns, it is also obliged to make two payments on account each quarter (at the end of the second and third month of the VAT period) and a balancing payment of the VAT due (the VAT due for the period less the two payments made on account).

10.70 Payments on account are required to be made for quarterly VAT periods commencing after 31 March each year when liability to pay VAT in the year ending the previous 30 September (or 31 October, or 30 November) exceeded £2 million, or if the VAT liability in that period did not exceed £2 million, it has exceeded £2 million in the VAT periods ending in any subsequent period of one year. This period is called the basis period. The VAT liability is the amount declared on returns and voluntary disclosures plus any assessments made by Customs and Excise and is notified to the taxable person by Customs and Excise. If no notification is made, then no payments on account need be made.

10.71 Clearly the payment on account is an adverse cash-flow cost to the business. A business does have the alternative of rendering monthly VAT returns or accounting for the correct amount of VAT each month (without submitting a return), if it believes that this will be a lesser amount. This may arise where there are significant seasonal variations

10.72 A taxable person may be able to avoid being brought into the payments on account regime in a number of ways. It could, for instance, incur an input tax charge prior to end of the basis period to reduce the amount of VAT liability to below £2 million. Alternatively it could delay creating tax points for supplies made to reduce the VAT liability to less than £2 million, perhaps by issuing an invoice on 1 October instead of 30 September. It is likely, however, that this will only mean that instead of exceeding the VAT liability of £2 million in the year ending, it will exceed this limit in the period after, and payments on account will still be due. An alternative would be to split the taxable person into two taxable persons. This will reduce the VAT liability for the individual taxable persons even if the total liability for both is still in excess of £2 million. Where there is a group registration, separate registrations could be formed. A further alternative would be to register in Divisions as each Division is treated separately for payments on account purposes.

10.73 The amount payable as a payment on account can be reduced or cancelled if Customs and Excise are satisfied there will be a reduction of 20% of future liability.

Cash-flow planning

Business organisation

10.74 The first step in cash-flow planning is to look at the activities of the taxable person to determine if it can be organised in a better way. For instance, a construction business may have the following elements:

- construction of zero-rated dwellings;
- supply of standard rate labour;

- supply of standard rate materials; and
- letting of exempt properties.

10.75 If each of these separate elements were separate companies, the usual solution for such a structure would be to group them in a VAT group. Whilst this would give an administrative simplification, it could have a cash-flow cost.

10.76 The part that builds and sells dwellings could be separately registered and make monthly VAT returns, each of the other entities should make quarterly VAT returns. The labour company and materials company could act as procurement companies for the dwellings company (see above). The exempt entity though would not be able to register for VAT, as it is not a taxable person. The objective for this company is not to incur VAT, as it cannot be deducted. Thus, it should either have its own labour force, or those who work in the labour company should have joint contracts of employment with the exempt company. This will mean that VAT will not be charged on supplies of labour (as there is no separate supply). Where a taxable person that is closely associated with the exempt company (i.e. one controls the other, or both are controlled by another person) provides services or goods to the exempt company, grouping should be considered. VAT will not be charged on the supplies made in the group, but there needs to be consideration how much VAT cannot be deducted on overhead costs, and if the exempt supplies made will adversely effect the fully taxable person that is a member of the group with the exempt company (see below).

10.77 Other methods of reducing the VAT cost to the exempt entity will be detailed below. Although some methods are methods of delaying the output tax charge, they are important cash-flow considerations when supplies are made to an associated taxable person that cannot reclaim all of the VAT that it incurs.

Stagger codes

10.78 An advantage can be gained through the use of differing stagger codes. For instance if the materials company supplied goods to the labour hire company for them to use in their construction activities, it could be arranged for the VAT periods of the labour hire company to end on 31 March (and quarterly thereafter) and for the materials company to end on 31 May (and quarterly thereafter). If the materials company invoiced all of its sales in March, the VAT could be deducted by the labour company on its March return, but would not be accounted for by the materials company until it submitted its May return.

Timing of sales invoices

10.79 It has been mentioned above that a significant advantage can be gained by careful timing of invoices. An invoice issued early in the month or VAT period gives a longer period for it to be collected before the VAT is due to be paid by Customs and Excise. Thus, if the VAT period of the taxable person ends 30 September, the invoice can be issued on 1 October and this gives an extra three months to collect payment before the VAT due is payable to Customs and Excise. Many businesses do not want to delay raising the invoice in this way as it is thought that the customer will take a further month to pay the bill. This problem can be reduced by clearly marking the invoice as being for work performed in September. In addition, there is no reason why the invoice issued on 1 October could not be for supplies for the month of October, and this early invoicing gives extra time to collect the debt. If an invoice is raised within 14 days after its tax point (or such longer period as is permitted by Customs and Excise), the invoice then becomes the tax point.

Proforma invoices

10.80 A proforma invoice does not create a right to deduct nor does it create a tax point where output tax must be accounted for. Thus, cash-flow can be improved by issuing proforma invoices and accounting for output tax on receipt of the cash. Where supplies are made to associated companies that cannot deduct VAT, the use of proforma invoices delays the time that the output tax has to be accounted for and assists cash-flow for the corporate group (not VAT Group).

Continuous supply of services

10.81 Where continuous supplies are made no tax point arises, until an invoice is issued or a payment is received (VAT Regulations,1995 SI 1995/2518, reg 90). Continuous supplies of services include leases, rents, hire staff etc. Supplies can be made to exempt business entities or taxable persons that cannot reclaim all of their VAT and as VAT is not charged, if no invoice is issued or payment made, cash-flow is improved. It should be noted that an entry in books of accounts would create a tax point as that is regarded as payment. In addition, from 1 October 2003 where supplies are made to an associated taxable person (or non-registered entities) that cannot reclaim all the VAT that is incurred, an annual tax point arises. This measure does not apply to zero-rated or exempt supplies or to supplies where the supplier can demonstrate that the recipient can deduct all the VAT incurred on the supply.

Goods on consignment

10.82 Where goods are supplied on approval or consignment then VAT is not due on the supply until an invoice is issued, the goods are adopted or 12 months has passed (VATA 1994, s 6 (2)(c) and s 6 (4)). The goods held by the exempt company (for instance, the property letting company in the example above) remain the property of the supplier (e g the materials company in the example above) until adopted by the exempt person. Thus, the goods can be stored at the exempt person's premises and no VAT will be due. A periodic stock check will need to be made to determine the value of the stock taken (adopted) so that the materials company can account for the VAT on stock taken. Any goods that remain in stock for twelve months are deemed to have been adopted and VAT is due on this stock.

Input tax accrual

10.83 It is unlikely that in any large organisation all purchase invoices are processed by the time that the period on the computer system is closed off and the VAT return is prepared. This means that input tax that is claimable is not claimed until a later period. The computer system may be able to identify invoices that are posted in a subsequent period but received earlier (particularly if the invoice date is posted onto the system). The VAT on these invoices is claimable, but must be reversed in the following VAT period to prevent a duplication of a claim. Where it is not possible to identify this VAT, a manual listing can be made of all invoices on hand. This will give a figure for invoices on hand and this VAT is deductible, but care must be taken to ensure that VAT for invoices relevant to the subsequent period is not claimed. Again this VAT claim must be reversed in the following period. It may prove tiresome to continually list this amount of VAT for invoices processed late. It is possible to obtain Customs and Excise's agreement that a figure can be estimated for input tax on invoices received but not processed. The estimate must take into account seasonal variations (if any) and be verified on a periodic basis. It is usual for the estimate to be slightly less than the amount that could be claimed to give certainty that there is no over claim. The agreement with Customs and Excise is usually shown as a percentage of input tax identified on invoices that have been processed in the period and any agreement must be made in writing.

Supply and leasing companies

10.84 Cash-flow can be improved by using companies to provide goods and services to taxable persons that cannot deduct all their VAT or are not registered for VAT. This is similar to the use of procurement companies mentioned above. These entities, however, tend to provide goods on a lease. For instance, a computer subsidiary may be formed to lease the computers to the taxable person that cannot deduct all their VAT. The computer company can reclaim all the VAT incurred on acquisition, but has to charge VAT on supplies to the (partly) exempt or (partly) non-business taxable person. This charge will have to be an open market value charge where the person making the supply is connected to the recipient and the recipient cannot reclaim all the VAT that it is charged. If an open market value is not charged, Customs and Excise can direct that the value shall be taken to be its open market value (VATA 1994, Sch 6, para 1).

10.85 This type of arrangement was commonly applied to property transactions, the properties being held in a property company and leased to the exempt or non-business entity. An election would be made to waive exemption so that the property company could deduct VAT on the property acquisition. Anti-avoidance legislation has, however, prevented this type of arrangement from working unless the property is not a capital item or a third party (which has not financed the transaction) is the taxable person leasing the property to the entity that cannot deduct all the VAT charged to it (VATA 1994, Sch 10).

Groups

10.86 As has been mentioned in the previous section of this chapter, grouping is not always the best solution for cash-flow planning. It is, however, a useful administrative relief, which allows taxable persons not to have to charge each other VAT on supplies, made and reduces the amount of work that needs to be undertaken to render returns. VAT grouping, however, is useful where a corporate body that cannot deduct all of its VAT can be included in the group. The requirements and effects of being in a group are discussed in **Chapter 2**. More details of the effects, consequences and impact of group treatment are discussed in that Chapter.

10.87 The principal benefit for cash-flow planning using a group is that VAT does not need to be charged to other members of the group. This means that there is no VAT that is non-deductible on these supplies where there is a taxable person in the group that cannot reclaim all of its VAT. The fact, however, that there is a member of the group that is making exempt or non-business supplies (or any other supplies that mean deductions are restricted) can cause a restriction of input tax of overheads. This loss of input tax has to be offset against the VAT that is not being charged to the taxable person that cannot deduct in full. To minimise this cost, it is necessary to ring fence as much input tax VAT as possible, as relating to the taxable activities. Any management costs needs to be apportioned as far as possible to these taxable activities. Further **information in respect of partial exemption, attribution and apportionment is detailed in Chapter 5**.

10.88 A further advantage of VAT grouping is that there will not be a cash-flow disadvantage on inter-company charges, if the stagger codes are unsuitable (see Stagger Codes above). As VAT is not charged, there can be no cash-flow loss if it is reclaimed after it has been paid by the taxable person making the supply. Conversely, of course, there is no cash-flow gain if the input tax can be deducted before the person making the supply has to account for the output tax.

Transfer of a going concern

10.89 It is often stated that one of the purposes of the Transfer Of a Going Concern (TOGC) regulations is to assist cash-flow. Whilst this may be one of the benefits of the TOGC regulations it was not their purpose. The purpose of the TOGC regulations is to prevent fraud. Under normal circumstances, a taxable person selling his business would be expected to account for VAT on the sale of most, if not all, assets (some exempt property sales, for instance, may be excluded). If VAT was charged, there would be a danger of this VAT not being declared and the person with possession of the VAT disappearing. Cash-flow, however, is an additional benefit.

10.90 Where a sale of a business is treated as a TOGC it is treated as not being a supply, no VAT is due and no VAT can be deducted (VAT (Special Provisions)

Order 1995, reg 5). If an amount representing VAT is charged, it is not VAT and is non-deductible. It is, therefore, vitally important to determine what is a TOGC and what is not a TOGC.

10.91 For a transaction to be treated as a TOGC it is necessary for:

- the assets sold to be used in carrying on the same kind of business;
- the transferee must be or must immediately become a taxable person;
- where there is a part transfer, that part must be capable of separate operation;
- the effect of the transfer is to put the new owner in possession of a business that can be operated as such;
- the business must be transferred as a 'going concern';
- there must not be a series of consecutive transfers of the business;and
- there should be no significant break in the normal trading pattern of the business.

10.92 There is a considerable body of case law in respect of TOGCs, but it would not be appropriate to enter into a detailed discussion of these here. What is essential, however, is that the purchaser acquires a business rather than a collection of assets. This will be a subjective judgement and it is necessary for both parties to the transaction to protect their position through warranties and indemnities. Where doubt does exist, it is sensible to obtain a ruling from Customs and Excise, but often Customs and Excise are unwilling to provide a specific ruling, particularly where they have given general guidance (such as when a sale of an investment property will be treated as a TOGC – Notice 700/9/02).

10.93 As has been mentioned there is an advantage of not charging VAT on a TOGC, as no VAT has to be accounted for on the transaction. This means that there is no possibility of one of the parties being out of pocket for the VAT element, either waiting for the purchaser to pay the VAT over when output tax has been accounted for, or more frequently, the purchaser waiting for Customs and Excise to repay the input tax deduction claimed. Also, where a property is sold as a TOGC, where no VAT is charged the Stamp Duty Land Tax charge will be less because SDLT is charged on the total consideration including VAT if chargeable. It should be noted, however, that this may become a decreasing problem as there is an increasing occurrence of companies that own properties being sold rather than properties, as the Stamp Duty cost is less.

10.94 In some instances, however, there may be a positive disadvantage in treating the transaction as a TOGC. For instance, where the purchaser can reclaim the VAT charged as a deduction before the vendor has to account for it as output tax, it would be advantageous to treat the transaction as not being a TOGC (assuming all other costs, particularly Stamp Duty remain the same). The simplest way to ensure that the transaction is not a TOGC is to purchase assets, though care needs to be exercised as the purchase of a single asset can be regarded as a TOGC (*Wrenshall (1992) VAT decision 10693*).

10.95 The input tax incurred on the sale (or purchase) of a business as a TOGC had originally been treated as residual VAT, deductible according to the business's partial exemption method. It was held in *C & E Comrs v UBAF Bank Ltd [1996] STC 372, CA* that there was a direct link between the purchase of a business and the making of supplies. Thus, if the business purchased was a taxable business then all the input tax incurred on the acquisition is recoverable; if it is an exempt business no VAT can be reclaimed on acquisition costs. The partial exemption status of the acquiring business was not seen as being relevant. Similarly, where a business is sold, it is the partial exemption status of the entity sold that is important not the entity making the sale as the costs of sale had a direct and immediate link with the business that was sold (*Abbey National plc v C & E Comrs (C-408/98) [2001] STC 297, ECJ*).

Chapter 11

Tax Avoidance

Introduction

11.1 The purpose of this chapter is to present an overview of the current landscape as regards VAT recovery and tax avoidance. It should perhaps be stressed at the outset that the landscape, which only a few years ago seemed relatively bright and clear, has recently become misty, if not clouded over, with complexity. In the light of this change, the best that can be achieved at the present time is to present a snapshot of the current terrain.

VAT avoidance should be seen in the context of the wider concept of VAT planning. In general terms, VAT planning does not involve complex schemes whose sole or main purpose is to avoid a VAT cost. The bedrock of VAT planning is more mundane – understanding the impact of VAT on the business, familiarity with the detailed procedures for invoicing and accounting for VAT, sustained and deep analysis of the taxpayer's partial exemption issues and attention to compliance detail.

11.2 There are however business contexts (outsourcing is a notable example) in which more aggressive VAT planning schemes may perhaps be called for. Thus we move from the area of general VAT planning to the more contentious and difficult area of VAT avoidance. It is worth stressing, perhaps, that VAT avoidance in this context refers to the organisation of a taxpayer's affairs with a view to reducing or eliminating the amount of VAT properly payable. In the context of input tax this may mean increasing the amount of VAT properly recoverable, rather than reducing the amount of VAT properly payable.

11.3 Despite sustained attempts by Customs and Excise to present the converse proposition as true, VAT avoidance is legal. It may legitimately be contrasted with VAT evasion, which is criminal. In this context, it is worthwhile quoting paragraph 33 of the ECJ judgment in *C & E Comrs v Cantor Fitzgerald International (C-108/99) [2001] STC 1453, ECJ*:

11.4

> '[The] court observes in that connection that, to facilitate the application of VAT, it is necessary to have regard, save in exceptional cases, to the objective character of the transaction in question. A taxable person who, for the purposes of achieving a particular economic goal, has a choice between exempt transactions and taxable transactions must therefore, in his own interest, duly take his decision while bearing in mind the neutral system of VAT … The principle of

the neutrality of VAT does not mean that a taxable person with a choice between two transactions may choose one of them and avail himself of the effects of the other.'

11.5 This important paragraph gives the ECJ's seal of approval to a taxpayer choosing a VAT efficient method of achieving his commercial objectives. The more detailed implications of the paragraph will be explored later in the chapter.

An overview of VAT avoidance schemes

11.6 In order to gain a coherent perspective on input tax and VAT avoidance issues, it is advisable to begin with a brief outline of how such avoidance schemes tend to arise. Typically, a partially exempt business such as a bank, insurance company or university, will be concerned to minimise the amount of irrecoverable VAT that it will incur on the purchase from a third party supplier of taxable goods or services. The VAT charged by the supplier would be wholly or partly irrecoverable in the hands of the end-user since it will be using the inbound supply for making outbound exempt supplies.

11.7 Several generic solutions to this VAT problem might be considered by the business. The most common solutions can be divided into four general categories.

11.8 The first category of solution inserts one or more special purpose vehicles (often referred to as 'SPVs') between the third party supplier and the taxpayer. Typically, these SPVs would take advantage of the time of supply and partial exemption rules in order to attempt to recover some or all of the VAT on the third party supplies whilst not having to charge VAT on the full value of the supplies to the partially exempt end-user. The key principle underlying this type of solution is that under VATA 1994, s 25(1), allowable input tax is determined by reference to the partial exemption regulations even if, in the circumstances, the attribution is not necessarily 'fair and reasonable'. This means that if one manipulates the time and value of the relevant supplies so that, under the partial exemption rules, an attractive (if unfair and unreasonable) attribution is achieved, then Customs and Excise or a court may not object on the basis that the purpose of the partial exemption rules is not thereby fulfilled.

11.9 The second category is suitable mainly for taxpayers who are receiving services that are deemed to take place where the customer belongs (i e VATA 1994, art 9(2)(e) or Sch 5 services). The central concept in this category involves inserting into the supply chain a non-UK SPV so that the supply from the third party supplier to the SPV is outside the scope of UK VAT. On the assumption that the supply would have been taxable if made in the UK, attributable input tax will be recoverable under VATA 1994, s 26(2)(b). The key problem with this type of solution is how to repatriate the services to the end-user in the UK without triggering the reverse charge mechanism (VATA 1994, s 8). Various possibilities are open to the taxpayer. Perhaps the most common is to attempt to re-characterise the services whilst they are offshore so that they no longer fall under art 9(2)(e), but under say art 9(1). Thus it is hoped that the inbound services will be treated as being made outside the UK and thus do not give rise to a reverse charge liability. Other solutions to the reverse charge issue involve the use of limited partnerships and/or VAT groups.

11.10 The first and second categories involve the insertion of one or more SPVs into the chain of supply. The success of these planning arrangement depends on the assumption that it is not permissible for Customs and Excise to take a 'global view' of the series of transactions in the chain of supply. The 'global view' issue is discussed in more detail below.

11.11 The third category relies upon the exempt end-user making, specifically for VAT recovery purposes, an outbound taxable (or exempt with right to refund) supply to which the problematic input tax may be attributed. Thus for example a bank may incur extensive legal costs which, without more, would be attributable to an exempt issue of shares. It may be possible for the bank to onward supply some of the legal advice, on a taxable supply thus shifting the input tax from being wholly irrecoverable to being residual. In the past, this category of VAT planning was widely used in two very different sets of circumstances.

11.12 First, the planning was used by universities constructing new buildings. Typically the university would contract with a third party builder to construct the building, opt to tax, and lease the property to an SPV which would in turn opt to tax and lease the property back to the university. The intended effect was that instead of the VAT on the capital cost of the project being irrecoverable at the outset (being attributed principally to the exempt supply of education), the VAT was recoverable by reference to the opted lease out to the SPV. The SPV would in turn recover the VAT on its inbound supplies and charge VAT back to the university. The net effect was that the VAT cost was 'drip fed' to the university on the rent payable to the SPV. Some of the schemes went further by arranging for the lease and leaseback structure to be collapsed after a few years, thus bringing to an end the drip-fed VAT cost. This sort of planning has effectively been closed down by the 'disapplication of the option to tax' provisions in VATA 1994, Sch 10, para 2(3AA).

11.13 The second set of circumstances was in relation to a business (generally with either a high or 100% recovery rate) which issued shares. Since, on the basis of current UK case law and practice, the issue of shares is an exempt supply, VAT incurred on legal and professional fees in respect of the share issue would, without more, be irrecoverable. The 'Golden Share' VAT avoidance scheme (as it was known) involved taxpayers issuing shares to EU customers selling, for VAT purposes, a single share to a non-EU resident. This would result in any input tax paid on the professional advisers' fees relating to the share issue being shifted from the exempt category into the residual category on the basis that non-EU supplies with an entitlement to input tax recovery were previously normally treated as 'true' UK supplies for partial exemption purposes. As receipts from the issue of shares would normally be treated as being 'incidental', they were ignored under the partial exemption standard method. This meant that the taxable person would then be able to recover the input tax on its advisers' services based on its residual recovery rate, thereby achieving a disproportionate recovery. The Golden Share scheme has been closed down by SI 1995/2518, reg 103(2).

11.14 The fourth category is now largely obsolete following the enactment of VATA 1994, Sch 9A. These arrangements attempted to make use of the VAT grouping rules to mitigate the irrecoverable VAT cost. Such schemes typically involved an associated company of the end-user entering or leaving the end-user's VAT group. The time of entering or leaving the group would be dictated by the intention that VAT charged by the third party supplier would be fully recoverable, whilst the VAT on the supplies by the company to the end-user would be mitigated by being partly sheltered by VAT grouping. Following the enactment of Sch 9A, such planning ideas are now effectively obsolete, although litigation in relation to pre-Sch 9A arrangements is ongoing.

Words of advice to potential VAT avoiders

11.15 Whilst this chapter is not designed to assist VAT avoidance, a few general words of warning to those considering entering into avoidance arrangements are perhaps in order. The first and perhaps most fundamental point is that the more moderate the arrangement, the greater the chance of success, whether in settling with Customs and Excise or in litigation. Excessive greed should be avoided if at all possible.

11.16 Secondly, VAT avoidance arrangements based on solid Community law principles are far more likely to stand up before the Tribunal and the courts than those which rely on the technical application of, for example, the UK's partial exemption, VAT grouping, or time of supply rules.

11.17 Thirdly, when entering into VAT avoidance arrangements there is often a tendency to buy into an arrangement suggested by professional advisers and then fail properly to implement the required steps. If the business does decide to enter into an avoidance scheme every effort should be made to ensure that contracts are properly executed (and not, for example, backdated) and that those charged with implementing the arrangements fully understand what is required of them. Where board decisions are required for particular steps in the arrangement, these should be given as much reality as possible, rather than being a rubber stamping of the 'VAT planning scheme'. At all times the taxpayer should bear in mind that the chances of success greatly increase if there is a coherent and credible narrative explaining the arrangements by reference to factors other than VAT. Of course, the outlook will be even more positive if the taxpayer is able to adduce cogent evidence to support this narrative. The taxpayer should give proper consideration to the practical implementation of the contractual arrangements. The reason for this is that a Tribunal (which one must assume will be seeking to strike down the arrangements) can be expected to be openly hostile to a scheme where, on the evidence, the reality of what happens in real life does not match the arrangements described in the contracts.

11.18 Finally, for a taxpayer to maintain in correspondence or discussions with Customs and Excise that there is a commercial purpose to a scheme, where this is self-evidently untrue, will only alienate a Tribunal, when (as it must) the day of reckoning comes and the true purpose of the arrangements has to be admitted before the Tribunal.

An analytical framework for the VAT issues

11.19 We turn now to the technical analysis of VAT avoidance schemes and input tax recovery. Since the issues are complex and interlocking, it is worthwhile, at the outset, to stand back from the detail and identify the key features which provide an analytical framework for the issues.

11.20 This chapter will adopt the following framework. First, we examine the key concept that VAT is a tax on transactions. This principle has broad and deep implications such as whether it is possible to take a 'global view' of the chain of supply and whether the term 'transactions' in this context is to be construed in a contractual or a commercial sense. The chapter then continues with an analysis of particular technical issues which may arise in the context of input VAT avoidance. These issues are dealt with in an order that reflects the conceptual framework of the Sixth Directive. The first specific technical issue discussed is the identity of the recipient of the supply (broadly based on art 2 of the Directive). Then the concept of economic activity is discussed (art 4), and this is followed by an analysis of the right to deduct itself (arts 17 to 20), in terms of attribution to business purposes, attribution of inputs to outputs and abuse of rights.

The key concept – a tax on transactions

11.21 As stated above, the conceptual starting point is the core principle of the VAT system. This is concisely set out in the First VAT Directive, art 2. This article states that VAT is a tax on *transactions*. In the current context, this principle has given rise to two related, contentious issues. The first is whether it is permissible to take a 'global view' of a series of transactions in the chain of supply. The second is whether the VAT analysis should be based on the relevant transaction in a contractual sense or, alternatively, on the underlying commercial reality. Each of these issues is dealt with in turn.

Is it permissible to take a 'global view' of a series of transactions?

11.22 As explained above, the first and second categories of planning technique involve the insertion of one or more SPVs in the chain of supply. If it is permissible for Customs and Excise to take a 'global view' of the series of transactions in the chain of supply, it will be possible for a court to disregard the SPV, with the consequence that the VAT avoidance arrangement would be defeated. It is in this context that the 'global view' issue has been dealt with by the courts.

11.23 The first relevant case is *BLP Group Ltd v C & E Comrs (C-4/94) [1995] STC 424, ECJ*. That case, which was not concerned with VAT avoidance arrangements, dealt with the deduction of professional fees in connection with the sale of shares carried out by a company in order to pay its debts. The company sought to attribute the fees to its underlying business which gave rise to the debts. By contrast Customs and Excise contended that the fees should be attributed to the exempt sale of the shares. The ECJ found in favour of Customs and Excise's interpretation. The judgment is authority for the proposition that one looks for an objective, direct and immediate linking of transactions, ignoring the taxpayer's ultimate aim in carrying them out.

11.24 The importance of this case for present purposes only became apparent when the above principle was considered and applied in the case of *Robert Gordon's College v C & E Comrs [1995] STC 1093, HL*. That case dealt with a college which provided exempt education and which wished to develop new playing fields and ancillary buildings. The college decided to use a form of VAT planning which falls neatly into the third category referred to above. It opted to tax and then let the property to a subsidiary. The subsidiary in turn opted to tax and licensed the College to use the property. The litigation concerning the VAT consequences of the arrangements reached the House of Lords. In the judgment the Lords decided that a self-supply charge was avoided because the College did not occupy the property as developer but rather as licensee of the subsidiary. Lord Hoffmann interpreted the *BLP* principle as follows: '… that decision [ie *BLP*] makes it clear that for the purposes of European value added tax legislation, it is not permissible to take a global view of a series of transactions in the chain of supply.'

11.25 This seems to be a clear and authoritative statement of the law. However the issue is slightly more complex than Lord Hoffmann's statement would indicate. This is because it is clear from numerous direct tax cases that a court, when faced with the task of analysing a tax planning scheme, must carry out two fundamental tasks. First, it must determine the legal nature of the transactions in question. Second, it must relate those transactions to the tax legislation.

11.26 In that context, the courts have adopted an approach which is loosely called 'the *Ramsay* principle'. This is a reference to the decision in *W T Ramsay Ltd v IRC [1981] STC 174, HL*. The *Ramsay* principle has been the subject of much judicial analysis, most notably in the recent House of Lords judgment in the case of *MacNiven (Inspector of Taxes) v Westmoreland Investments Ltd [2001] UKHL 6, [2001] STC 237*. Briefly and at the price of considerable oversimplification, the *Ramsay* principle states that in determining the legal nature of transactions, if there is a series or combination of transactions which are intended to operate as such, the court should have regard to that series or combination. Simply stated, each document and transaction should be viewed in the context to which it properly belongs.

11.27 Few would doubt that a sound VAT analysis should view documents and transactions in their proper context. However this issue has become confused with the prohibition of taking a global view of a series or combination of documents and transactions. If one cannot take a global view, then how can one determine the proper context of each document and transaction?

11.28 In the view of the author, however, the issue is clear. The two concepts are distinct. Viewing transactions in their proper context means that one does not blank out the background facts when considering a specific transaction; one does not view a transaction in isolation, but as part of a narrative. By contrast, taking a global view goes further by seeking to determine what overall change, if any, has been produced by a series of transactions. It is self-evident that the first principle is to be applied in the VAT system and clear on the basis of authority that the second principle is not.

Transactions: contract v commercial reality

11.29 A few words of introduction are necessary.

11.30 As explained above, the reason why businesses enter into VAT input tax planning schemes is because they wish to engage in a commercial transaction, but recognise that the commercial transaction will, without more, give rise to an input tax cost. To avoid this VAT cost, the taxpayer arranges the contractual relationships in a way which deviates from the underlying commercial reality. The contractual relationships which are entered into might seek to take advantage of VAT rules such as grouping, the time of supply or partial exemption rules in order to avoid an input tax cost. In simple terms, the arrangements entered into will be 'artificial'. Thus we must address the question of which of these, contract or commercial reality, forms the basis on which the VAT analysis is to be carried out.

11.31 One strategy which Customs and Excise may seek to adopt, when faced with a VAT avoidance scheme, is to argue that the 'artificial' contractual arrangements are ineffective even from a purely contractual perspective. In a commercial input tax scenario, where members of the public are not involved, the taxpayer should normally be able to ensure that the contracts are more or less watertight since the parties to the planning arrangement will be businesses who have bought into the scheme. Customs and Excise may then seek to argue that the VAT analysis should be based not on the contractual but rather on the commercial arrangements.

11.32 In terms of UK case law, perhaps the clearest support for stressing the commercial over the contractual is to be found in the reasoning of Laws J (as he then was) in *C & E Comrs v Reed Personnel Services Ltd [1995] STC 588*. The case, which did not involve VAT avoidance, dealt with the issue of whether an agency which provided temporary nursing staff to hospitals supplied nursing services. The oft-quoted judgment held that the concept of supply for VAT purposes may not be identical with that of contractual obligation. The terms of the relevant contracts might or might not determine the right VAT results; they did not necessarily do so. The House of Lords endorsed the *Reed Personnel* approach in *Eastbourne Town Radio Cars Associations v C & E Comrs [2001] STC 606*.

11.33 As regards the European basis for this approach, there are numerous references in ECJ judgments which support a commercial focus in relation to various fundamental categories within the VAT system. For example, it is clear that as a general principle the following issues are to be determined on a commercial basis: whether there is a single or multiple supply (*Card Protection Plan Ltd v C & E Comrs (C-349/96) [1999] STC 270, ECJ*); the value of a supply (*C & E Comrs v First National Bank of Chicago (C-172/96) [1998] STC 850, ECJ)*; and the place of a supply *(C & E Comrs v DFDS A/S (C-260/95) [1997] STC 384, ECJ).*

11.34 On the other hand in para 33 of the *Cantor Fitzgerald,* judgment quoted above, the possibility was canvassed of a taxpayer using one of two or more distinct legal arrangements in order to achieve a given economic result. This part of the judgment echoes paragraphs 25 and 26 of the *BLP* decision mentioned above. In *Cantor Fitzgerald* the ECJ held that the taxpayer is bound by the fiscal consequences of the transaction it actually enters into, even if an identical commercial result, achieved through another transaction, would be taxed differently. It seems to follow, arguably, that the legal form, rather than the commercial reality, is the key consideration.

11.35 There can be no doubt that the precise contractual obligations play an important role as the basis for the VAT analysis of a transaction. But how is this role to be defined? The issue is complex and one must beware of attempting a simplistic analysis. Having said this, the Tribunal in the case of *Debenhams Retail plc* (*VAT decision 18169) [2003] SWTI 1520* adopted the following (apparently reasonable) approach. The starting point for the VAT analysis must be the determination of the apparent contractual position. It is only if the totality of the evidence reveals something other than the apparent contractual position that it is legitimate to replace those contractual relationships with what is determined to have been 'the real deal'. Thus when the apparent contractual relationships show clearly and unequivocally a given supply for a particular consideration, it is not legitimate to disregard these relationships (save where they are a sham, see below). However, where the contract either does not tell the whole story, or is equivocal as to who is supplying what and to whom, it is permissible to substitute it with, or fill its gaps by reference to, the 'real deal'.

11.36 The lesson for any potential VAT avoiders is clear. One must strive to ensure that the contracts are drafted so as to be as clear, comprehensive and unambiguous as possible. Very careful thought and precise drafting skills are essential if the taxpayer is to deny a Tribunal the possibility of 'filling in the gaps' by reference to the 'real deal'.

Transactions: sham

11.37 We referred above to the concept of a sham and a brief parenthetical discussion of this concept is perhaps appropriate.

11.38 Customs and Excise sometimes contend that a transaction should be ignored for VAT purposes on the grounds that it is a sham. Briefly this means that the parties to the transaction intended to create one set of rights and obligations, but they performed acts or entered into documents which were designed to give the appearance of creating different rights and obligations. (based on Diplock LJ in *Snook v London and West Riding Investments Ltd [1967] 2 QB 786, CA).*

11.39 In more detail and so far as is relevant to VAT, the concept of a sham can be explained as follows. The parties must have two interlocking (subjective) intentions: first, an intention to create different rights and obligations from those appearing from the relevant document; and secondly, an intention to give a false impression of those rights and obligations to Customs and Excise. In determining whether these intentions exist, a court is not restricted to examining the document in question, but may examine external evidence such as the parties' explanations and circumstantial evidence (often the subsequent conduct of the parties).

11.40 It should be stressed that the sham doctrine is quite a narrow one. The fact that a document is uncommercial, or even artificial, does not mean that it is a sham. Furthermore, the fact that the parties subsequently depart from the agreement does not necessarily mean that they never intended the agreement to be effective – it may be that they have agreed to vary their agreement.

11.41 In broad terms, it is quite unusual for the sham doctrine to be invoked by Customs and Excise or the courts in relation to VAT avoidance schemes, and no more needs to be said about the concept in the context of the present chapter.

Identity of recipient of supply

11.42 Having dealt with the implications of the 'tax on transactions' concept, we turn now to particular technical issues which may arise in the context of input VAT avoidance schemes. The first issue which needs to be addressed in schemes which rely on the insertion of SPVs in the contractual chain is the identity of the recipient of the supplies made by the third party supplier. The issue arose in the context of the Tribunal decision in *Halifax plc, Countrywide Property Investments Ltd and Leeds Permanent Development Services Ltd [2001] V&S DR 73*. This decision marked a seismic shift in the approach of Customs and Excise and the Tribunal to VAT avoidance schemes. A number of concepts which had lain under the surface of the VAT system were brought out into the open and used against an aggressive VAT planning arrangement. The case is briefly summarised below.

11.43 Halifax was a bank which made mostly exempt supplies. It wanted to construct buildings for its business which would have meant suffering VAT on the inbound building supplies made by third party builders. This VAT would, without more, be largely irrecoverable. Halifax therefore entered into arrangements with three other companies in its group (we shall call these SPVs A, B and C) each of which was separately VAT registered.

11.44 Briefly stated, these arrangements were as follows. First Halifax made a loan to B to enable it to buy the relevant land and carry out the required building work. B then agreed with A that the latter would carry out the building work. A instructed third party builders to carry out the building work. The builders invoiced A who invoiced B. When the building work was complete B transferred its interest in the land on an exempt supply to C. C then granted exempt leases to Halifax. The scheme relied on certain aspects of the time of supply and partial exemption rules which we shall not discuss in the present context.

11.45 In due course A and B claimed input tax credit in respect of the inbound supplies of building works. This was refused by Customs and Excise on several grounds, one of these being that the third party builders' services were supplied directly to Halifax, rather than to A and then on to B and then on to Halifax.

11.46 For the reasons set out below, the Tribunal found that the sole reason for the insertion of A and B into the chain of supply was to avoid irrecoverable VAT. The transactions with the SPVs had no commercial purpose and were therefore outside the scope of VAT. In this context, the Tribunal held that Halifax received the taxable building supplies directly from the builders and not from B. In effect, the taxable supplies leapfrogged over A and B and passed directly to the Halifax, which, as recipient of the supplies, was largely unable to recover the associated VAT.

11.47 The basis of this conclusion was the judgment in *Reed Personnel Services*, referred to above. The Tribunal took this as authority for the proposition that the concept of making a supply for VAT purposes is not identical with the performance of an obligation under contract law. Where only two parties are involved there is generally little room for argument over who supplies what to whom. However where there are three or more parties, the contractual arrangements, although exhaustive for the purposes of their private law contractual obligations, may not define the VAT chain of supply.

11.48 The essence of the Tribunal's analysis is that where artificial transactions, such as those found by the Tribunal to have been undertaken by the SPVs, are interposed between an arm's length supplier and the ultimate recipient, the artificial transactions are 'collapsed' so as to leave the 'true' supply remaining. By applying the principle to the facts in the *Halifax* case, the Tribunal concluded that the arm's length suppliers were actually supplying directly to the Halifax, notwithstanding the contractual position ('the paperwork' in the words of the Tribunal).

11.49 As explained below, the original *Halifax* decision was quashed by the High Court and the case remitted to the Tribunal. The second time round, the Tribunal referred the issue of how to identify the recipient of a supply in the context of the scheme to the ECJ as the second part of the first question.

Economic activity – the Halifax principle

11.50 Prior to the *Halifax* case, Customs and Excise adopted two broad strategies for fighting VAT avoidance: (i) trying to import the *Ramsay* approach into the

VAT system, and (ii) targeted legislative changes to attack VAT avoidance schemes as and when they arose. With the *Halifax* decision, an entirely new approach came into its own.

11.51 This new approach focused on the Sixth Directive, art 4. As will be recalled from the discussion above, the Tribunal found that the sole reason for the insertion of B and A into the chain of supply was to avoid VAT. Accordingly, the Tribunal decided that the transactions with the SPVs had no business purpose and so were not an 'economic activity' as defined by art 4. The supplies were not therefore made by a taxable person acting as such and as such were not within the scope of VAT. On this basis, B made no taxable supplies of construction works to Halifax and obtained no taxable supplies from A. Thus A was not liable for output tax and B could not claim input tax.

11.52 In summary form, the *Halifax* principle states that where the sole reason for transactions is the avoidance of VAT, those transactions do not constitute economic activities, so that the supplies are not made by a taxable person acting as such and are therefore outside the scope of VAT. There has been much discussion on the issue of whether purpose is relevant to the classification of an activity as economic or non-economic and anyone interested in pursuing this issue can find detailed discussion in the series of post-*Halifax* Tribunal decisions. Some of the more relevant post-*Halifax* decisions are briefly described below.

11.53 The original *Halifax* Tribunal decision was issued in 2001. Proceedings in the High Court before Neuberger J (*Halifax plc [2002] STC 402*) determined that the reasons behind a participant's involvement in a scheme must be considered. It was not sufficient to consider only the motives of the 'prime mover' ie Halifax itself. The original decision was quashed and the matter was remitted to the Tribunal.

11.54 In Tribunal decision 17721, the Tribunal referred two questions to the ECJ. The first question fragments into two parts and relates to the *Halifax* principle. The first part essentially asks whether, in the context of a VAT avoidance arrangement, transactions effected by each participator with the intention solely of obtaining a tax advantage and which have no independent business purpose qualify for VAT purposes as supplies made by or to the participators in the course of their economic activities. The second part asks the ECJ to define the factors that should be considered in determining the identity of the recipients of the supplies made by the arm's-length builders. The second question relates to the abuse of rights principle, and is discussed below.

Post Halifax cases

11.55 The *Halifax* case has given rise to a series of related Tribunal decisions. Unfortunately, space does not allow for discussion of all of the cases, and only two of the most interesting are briefly summarised below.

11.56 The *Halifax* case was very quickly followed by a resounding victory for Customs and Excise in the VAT and Duties Tribunal in *BUPA Hospitals Limited and Goldsborough Developments Ltd (VAT decision 17588) [2002] SWTI 1175*.

11.57 The case revolved around arrangements whereby a significant pre-payment was made for the supply of drugs and prostheses in order to secure the deduction of input tax on that supply before the relevant law changed with effect from 1 January 1998. This change in the law removed the zero-rating that had until then applied to supplies of drugs and prostheses by private hospitals and replaced this zero-rating with exemption. This meant that private hospitals, such as those run by BUPA, would no longer be able to deduct attributable input tax.

11.58 The Tribunal approached the appeal by asking whether the BUPA companies concerned with the pre-payment transactions had made supplies in the course or furtherance of any business. The Tribunal, as it had done in the *Halifax* case, held that the purpose or motive in carrying on an activity is relevant to establishing whether it was an economic activity. Of particular interest is the Tribunal's reasoning that it was 'incumbent on the Appellants to demonstrate that they are not excluded on the grounds that tax avoidance was the motive or purpose for which the transactions were effected'.

11.59 The second Tribunal decision to follow *Halifax* was *Blackqueen Ltd (VAT decision 17680) [2002] SWTI 1409*. This was an appeal against Customs and Excise's refusal to refund sums under a series of Eighth Directive claims made by the Appellant. The claims were made as part of a complex planning scheme relating to the purchase and sale of cars. The scheme was designed so that the taxpayer's group recovered all of the input tax incurred on the purchase of cars whilst output tax on the sale of the cars would be based on the profit margin (if any) rather than on the full sale price.

11.60 Blackqueen was an Irish company whose role in the scheme was to buy the cars from a UK company, to make a supply of a lease for the use of the vehicles to a UK company, and then to sell the cars subject to the lease as a transfer of a going concern to another Irish company which was not UK VAT registered. The Eighth Directive claim was the mechanism by which Blackqueen attempted to recover all of the input tax incurred on the purchase of the vehicles.

11.61 One very interesting point (which is worthy of note for those contemplating litigation in relation to VAT avoidance arrangements) is that *Blackqueen* had consistently sought to maintain in both correspondence and discussions with Customs and in its witness statements that there was a commercial purpose to the scheme aside from VAT avoidance. However it had to concede at the outset of the Tribunal appeal hearing that the sole purpose of the scheme was VAT avoidance. Without doubt this about-turn alienated an already unsympathetic Tribunal.

11.62 So far as is relevant to this chapter, the Tribunal held that there were two issues which it had to address. The first was whether the Eighth Directive claims should be refused on the grounds that the supplies made to and by *Blackqueen* were not economic activities, and therefore, in accordance with the decision in *Halifax*, were outside the scope of VAT. The second, which we shall discuss at the end of the chapter, was whether the Eighth Directive claims should be refused as an abuse of rights in accordance with the decision in *BUPA*.

11.63 In relation to the first issue, the Tribunal concluded that the *Halifax* decision applied to both goods and services. It also confirmed that the *Halifax* principle provides that, where the sole reason for a transaction is the avoidance of VAT, the transacting entity does not have a business purpose and is therefore not engaged in an economic activity. The Tribunal stated that on an objective view, the scheme under consideration led to a distortion of competition as regards other like businesses and thereby ran counter to the principles of the Sixth Directive. The Tribunal concluded that where transactions do not have a business purpose, but rather are designed to manipulate the VAT system, they are not economic activities. Accordingly, the Tribunal found that the only taxable transactions in the scheme were the purchase of vehicles by the initial purchasing company from the manufacturers and the eventual sale of those vehicles to third party customers.

The right to deduct – attribution of VAT incurred to business purposes

11.64 Continuing with our analysis of particular technical issues, discussion now turns to the right to deduct in terms of attribution to business purposes.

Property used for non-business purposes

11.65 When goods are purchased partly for business use and partly for some other use, the taxpayer has, in theory, two options. First, he may claim input VAT on the proportion of the purchase price corresponding to the estimated extent of business use, and then make subsequent adjustments if appropriate. Alternatively, he may claim input VAT on the whole of the purchase price and then account for output VAT on the private-use element over time. This latter approach was sanctioned by the ECJ in the case of *Lennartz v Finanzamt München III (C-97/90) [1995] STC 514, ECJ* (**Case Summary 12**). The *Lennartz* principle, as it is commonly called, allows a trader acquiring goods partly for business and partly for non-business purposes to claim credit for the entire input tax incurred by him, but then to account for output tax on a proportion of the value of such goods as they are appropriated to non-business purposes.

11.66 In Customs and Excise's view this principle opened up a possibility of VAT avoidance. A taxpayer who could not otherwise recover VAT on the purchase of a building could artificially arrange to make use of the *Lennartz* principle to bolster VAT recovery. The slow depreciation of the buildings would mean that the corresponding output tax obligations would take a long time to counter the initial high recovery rate.

11.67 Finance Act 2003 included a measure (effective from 9 April, 2003) which aims to prevent the *Lennartz* approach being used for land and buildings where there is private or non-business use. The main legislative change is the addition of VATA 1994, Sch 4, para (4A). The intention of the legislation is that private and non-business use of land and buildings will in all cases be addressed by apportionment of the VAT incurred at time of purchase, so that only the business element counts as input tax and is recoverable.

11.68 It is highly questionable whether this provision is in compliance with the Sixth Directive as construed by the ECJ. The resolution of the issue involves difficult questions of EU and domestic law and the interaction between the two systems. The author fully expects a challenge to the validity of the new rules in the relatively near future – probably from an 'innocent' taxpayer, rather than a VAT avoider.

Attribution of inputs to outputs

11.69 The partial exemption rules contain a number of provisions which specifically target VAT avoidance schemes. For example, the 'Golden Share' scheme mentioned above, which aimed to shift VAT on professional fees in relation to a share issue from the exempt category into the residual category. The Golden Share scheme was closed down by SI 1995/2518, reg 103 (2). Unfortunately, the implications of this provision in the context of the interaction of Regulations 101 and 103 is left very unclear. This was demonstrated in the Tribunal decision of *EasyJet plc (VAT decision 18230) [2003] SWTI 1805*. Another provision targeting VAT avoidance was made in 1994. These changes to the de minimis input tax recovery rules in SI 1995/2518, reg 106 were the response to VAT planning arrangements implemented in the main by dentists (and thus known as the 'Toothbrush Scheme').

11.70 Perhaps the most relevant provision in the current context is the standard method override. By way of background to this provision, one recalls that in the case of input tax which cannot be attributed directly to taxable or exempt supplies the standard partial exemption method in SI 1995/2518, reg 101 seeks to achieve an equitable recovery rate by apportioning such VAT ('residual input tax') according to the values of outbound taxable and exempt supplies made in a period.

11.71 Over the past few years, many VAT avoidance schemes relied on the standard method to obtain input tax recovery greater than Customs and Excise considered fair and reasonable. The schemes often relied upon the principle that Customs and Excise may only direct that a company uses a special method (under SI 1995/2518, reg 102) prospectively. This meant that if the taxpayer could ensure that Customs and Excise found out about a scheme after the event, the taxpayer could rely on the standard method, with its broad brush approach to attribution. By manipulating the timing and the values of the inbound and outbound supplies, enormous VAT savings could be achieved.

11.72 When Customs and Excise finally decided to stop such arrangements, the method they came up with was aptly called a 'standard method override'. This provision, which is effective in relation to input tax incurred after 17 April 2002, requires businesses to override the standard method in cases where the result does not reflect the use made of the purchases. Naturally this includes cases of attempted VAT avoidance. The detailed rules of the override are complex and only an overview can be set out in this chapter.

11.73 Under SI 1995/2518, regs 106A and 107A-107E businesses are required to adjust the input tax deductible under the standard method at the end of their tax year if that amount is substantially different from an attribution based on the use of purchases. 'Substantially' is here defined as:

- £50,000 or greater; or
- 50% or more of the value of the residual input tax, but not less than £25,000.

11.74 Where the amount of residual input tax is less than £50,000 per year no override calculation is required and businesses can rely purely on the standard method. There is one exception to this: businesses that are defined as group undertakings by the Companies Act 1985 have to follow this new rule where their residual input tax is greater than £25,000 per year.

11.75 Any calculation of the 'extent of use' is acceptable as long as it produces a 'fair and reasonable' attribution of input tax according to the use, or intended use, of purchases in making taxable supplies. Customs and Excise advise that the easiest way to prepare a fair and reasonable calculation is to consider why the standard method breaks down and to correct for it.

11.76 Whilst there were initial queries as to the *vires* of the standard method override in EU law, these seem to have fallen away in the course of time. The override thus appears at this stage to be a relatively successful example of how Customs and Excise can target what they see as abuse through specific legislative changes.

Abuse of rights

11.77 The abuse of rights principle is perhaps the most controversial of all the recent case law developments. It is also the most difficult to evaluate in terms of whether it applies to VAT, and if so, to what extent. The issue is perhaps particularly difficult for those educated in the English legal tradition, and for whom the very concept of abusing a right is something of an abomination. If the law grants a taxpayer a right, then as a matter of principle the taxpayer is entitled to exercise that right. Either the concept of abuse of right is a legalistic way of limiting the scope of the right – a roundabout way of saying that the right does not exist in given circumstances – or it is meaningless.

11.78 Notwithstanding these apparently well-founded English law points, the abuse of rights principle is acknowledged in many legal systems. Furthermore, the principle has found its way into the Tribunal's mindset and is considered to be an integral part of the ECJ's stock of Community law principles. As mentioned above, the question of whether the principle is applicable to VAT has been referred to the ECJ.

11.79 Given the analytical complexity of the concept, only a cursory examination is appropriate for the purposes of this chapter. Discussion will therefore focus on the scope of the principle, its status, the circumstances in which the principle may apply and the specific conditions which must then be met for the principle to apply.

11.80 As far as the scope of the principle is concerned, the doctrine of abuse of rights states that Community law provisions are to be construed as permitting the denial of a right where, despite the formal conditions laid down being met, the exercise of the right would be abusive. As such, the principle is an aid to interpretation. The doctrine has been considered by the ECJ in several different contexts, but in all contexts the key issue is the purpose of the relevant Community provision.

11.81 The doctrine of abuse of rights was first raised by Customs and Excise in the *Halifax* case. The Tribunal concluded that the principle could not apply since the appellants gained no rights under the scheme and therefore, as a matter of logic, had no rights to abuse.

11.82 As far as the status of the principle is concerned, in the *BUPA* case the Tribunal concluded on the basis of the ECJ judgment in *Emsland-Stärke GmbH v Hauptzollamt Hamburg-Jonas (C-110/99) [2000] ECR I-11569* that the doctrine had become more than an aid to interpretation and had acquired the status of a general principle of Community law. The difference between the two approaches – aid to construction or principle of law is principally of theoretical interest and is unlikely to have any practical significance for those considering or implementing VAT avoidance schemes.

11.83 Turning now to the circumstances in which the principle may apply, the case law has identified three such sets of circumstances. These were summarised by the Tribunal in *Blackqueen* at paragraphs 115–116 as follows:

> 'The first situation covers the abusive use of Community law to circumvent national law where the application of a rule would run counter to the spirit and purpose of a directive and would be inimical to the effectiveness of other provisions of it … The second situation occurs where there has been an abuse of Community law to gain a financial advantage from Community funds …. The third situation occurs where Community law is used contrary to a national abuse of rights provision.'

11.84 The specific conditions which must be fulfilled before the principle is engaged were set out in *Emsland-Stärke GmbH.* The first condition is that there should be a combination of objective circumstances in which the purpose of the

Community rules is not achieved. The second condition is that there should be an intention to obtain an advantage from the Community rules by artificially creating the conditions for obtaining it.

11.85 One of the areas of uncertainty is whether the principle (assuming it exists and applies to VAT) is applicable to domestic law provisions which correctly implement EU law. The Sixth Directive does not purport to be the source of an individual's rights and obligations, but rather imposes on member states a duty to set up a VAT system in the domestic law which grants rights and imposes duties on individual taxpayers. If the domestic VAT law fails to carry out the terms of the Directive, then, and only then, will the individual have an enforceable Community right under the principle of direct effect. Only in such circumstances is the taxpayer purporting to exercise a Community law right, such that the abuse of rights principle may perhaps be engaged.

11.86 However this analysis potentially leads to a non-uniform application of VAT throughout the EU. To achieve neutrality, domestic courts should be required to interpret rights conferred by domestic implementing legislation in such a way that they do not exceed the rights which the taxpayer would have and could legitimately exercise under Community law. Arguably therefore the abuse of rights principle should apply equally whether or not the domestic law properly implements the Directive. Only time will tell how this exceedingly difficult legal quandary will be resolved.

Conclusion

11.87 At the outset, this chapter stressed that the landscape in relation to input tax and VAT avoidance has recently become clouded over with complexity. To a large extent this complexity derives from the series of cases following the *Halifax* Tribunal decision. Only in the course of time will the veil of uncertainty be lifted, and, hopefully, clarity will prevail.

Chapter 12

VAT Accounting and Administration

Introduction

12.1 The accounting system required to deal with VAT deductions may range from a very simple system to a very complex system. Complexity is likely to arise when a taxable person carries out a number of different activities, some of which give rise to a deduction and others of which do not.

12.2 Whatever the nature of the business, a taxable person needs to understand the issues in order to deal properly with VAT accounting for deductions. Apart from understanding the legal provisions relating to VAT deductions, a taxable person needs to understand the differences between financial and VAT accounting so that the financial accounting systems can be properly adapted to deal with VAT requirements.

12.3 This chapter first examines the legal framework in respect of VAT accounting. This is followed by consideration of differences between VAT and financial accounting and the practical consequences of this for systems dealing with VAT deductions.

The legal framework in relation to VAT accounting

European VAT Law

12.4 Apart from specific measures dealing with VAT invoicing and the evidence required by a taxable person in order to claim a VAT deduction, European VAT law does not specify what records a taxable person must keep in relation to VAT deductions.

12.5 Article 22 of the EC Sixth VAT Directive does however provide that taxable persons must:

> '... keep accounts in sufficient detail for value added tax to be applied and inspected by the tax authority' (art 22(2)(a)).

12.6 In addition, art 22(8) allows member states to:

> '... impose other obligations which they deem necessary for the correct collection of the tax and for the prevention of evasion, subject to the requirement of equal treatment for domestic transactions and transactions carried out

between Member States by taxable persons and provided that such obligations do not, in trade between Member States, give rise to formalities connected with the crossing of frontiers.'

12.7 Article 18 contains specific provisions relating to the records required in relation to VAT deductions. In essence, art 18:

- contains provisions specifying what evidence is required in order to deduct VAT (art 18(1));
- specifies the manner in which input tax is to be claimed (ie by set-off against output tax due);
- allows member states to provide what alternative evidence may be used if the evidence referred to in art 18(1) is not available;
- makes provision for repayment of input VAT that exceeds the output tax due.

12.8 However, the EC Invoicing Directive (2001/115/EC), which came into effect on 1 January 2004, lays down detailed requirements in respect of:

- the content of invoices;
- self-billing;
- requirements for e-invoicing; and
- electronic storage.

UK VAT law

12.9 The primary law in relation to VAT accounting is contained in VATA 1994, Sch 11. The primary legislation mainly comprises enabling provisions allowing the Commissioners to make regulations dealing with VAT accounting (VATA 1994, Sch 11, paras 2 and 6) and Customs and Excise's access to records (para 7).

12.10 In relation to VAT deductions, the principal regulations made under these provisions include:

- VAT Regulations 1995, Part III – VAT Invoices And Other Invoicing Requirements; and
- VAT Regulations 1995, Part V – Accounting, Payment And Records.

Within the VAT Regulations are a number of provisions giving the Commissioners powers to make certain directions, eg in relation to what records must be kept or to what evidence may be accepted as evidence of an input tax deduction.

Outline of records that have to be kept in relation to inputs

Summary

12.11 The accounting and record keeping requirements in relation to input tax can be considered in three parts:

- invoices and evidence of imports and acquisitions, including alternative evidence;
- the VAT accounting and audit trail; and
- the VAT return.

12.12 In addition, it is necessary to consider the manner in which records may be adjusted.

Invoices and evidence of imports and acquisitions

12.13 The integrity of the VAT deductions system is founded on the records that a taxable person is required to keep in relation to supplies, imports and acquisitions received. It is important to note that the system must not only keep records that evidence what VAT has been incurred (VAT Regulations 1995, reg 29(2)) but the purpose for which the supplies on which the VAT was incurred were acquired.

12.14 Regulation 29(2) allows Customs and Excise to allow a deduction on the basis of alternative evidence. Customs and Excise have also exercised their care and management powers to allow certain deductions to be made even though there is no documentary evidence, eg certain small supplies made by coin-operated machines.

12.15 The following sections set out details of the evidence that is required in order to deduct VAT on different types of transaction.

The responsibility of the taxpayer in relation to tax invoices

12.16 It should be borne in mind that it is the responsibility of the taxable person seeking to deduct VAT to ensure that he holds the required evidence. This is not an automatic or routine task. VAT case law contains several instances of taxpayers being denied a deduction because the document purporting to be a tax invoice was not valid.

12.17 In addition to the invoice being valid, it must be borne in mind that there must in fact be a supply. This issue has become even more important following the recent cases in *Bond House Systems Ltd, (VAT decision 18100) [2003] SWTI 1431,* and *Optigen Ltd and Fulcrum Trading Co (UK) Ltd (in liquidation) (VAT decisions 18112 and 18113) [2003] STI 1513.* In each case, the VAT and Duties Tribunal took the view that there was no underlying supply and therefore notwithstanding that the taxpayers in question held documents that purported to be tax invoices, no deduction was permitted.

12.18 The task of ensuring that an invoice is valid is not a mechanical task limited to ensuring that the details (which are described below) appear on the relevant document. The person claiming a deduction must also take reasonable steps to ensure that the person providing the invoice is a taxable person and that the transaction is a supply. Normally, this should present no difficulties because most suppliers will be known by the recipient of the supply or will be well known in their trade. However, Customs and Excise has denied deductions to taxpayers (and the Tribunal has upheld such decisions) in a number of cases. Reasons for refusing a deduction have included:

- the fact that the VAT number shown was fictitious;
- the fact that a company that had been registered for VAT was no longer registered when the VAT was charged;
- the fact that an invoice was described as 'pro-forma' and was not intended to be a tax invoice;
- the fact that a till strip issued by a retailer did not comply with the requirements necessary to be regarded as a tax invoice;
- where the supplier had self-billed a supplier, the fact that the customer was not in fact VAT registered;
- where a tax invoice was issued for a payment in advance but no actual supply was subsequently made; and
- where tax was charged on the transfer of a going concern (which is not a supply).

12.19 The key issue arising from these cases is that a taxable person seeking a deduction for input tax will need to take reasonable steps to ensure that an invoice complies with the formal requirements for a tax invoice, is issued by a taxable person and relates to a real supply. The formal requirements are considered below.

Evidence of receipt of a supply from a UK supplier – normal tax invoice

12.20 Subject to the exceptions mentioned above and dealt with further below, a taxable person must hold a tax invoice in order to deduct input tax on a supply received within the UK (VAT Regulations 1995, reg 29(2)(a)).

12.21 The requirements also apply to persons claiming refunds of VAT, whether under the Eighth or Thirteenth VAT Directives or the various UK provisions providing for special refunds (VATA 1994, ss 33, 33A and 41).

12.22 VAT Regulations 1995, reg 14(1) requires a tax invoice to contain the following details:

(*a*) an identifying number;

(*b*) the time of the supply;

(*c*) the date of the issue of the document;

(*d*) the name, address and registration number of the supplier;

(*e*) the name and address of the person to whom the goods or services are supplied;

(*f*) (until 31 December 2003 only) the type of supply by reference to the following categories:

- (i) a supply by sale;
- (ii) a supply on hire purchase or any similar transaction;
- (iii) a supply by loan;
- (iv) a supply by way of exchange;
- (v) a supply on hire, lease or rental,
- (vi) a supply of goods made from the customer's materials;
- (vii) a supply by sale on commission;
- (viii) a supply on sale or return or similar terms; or
- (ix) any other type of supply which the Commissioners may at any time by notice specify;

(g) a description sufficient to identify the goods or services supplied;

(h) for each description, the quantity of the goods or the extent of the services, and the rate of VAT and the amount payable, excluding VAT, expressed in any currency (sterling until 31 December 2003);

(i) the gross total amount payable, excluding VAT, expressed in any currency (sterling until 31 December 2003);

(j) the rate of any cash discount offered;

(k) (until 31 December 2003 only) each rate of VAT chargeable and the amount of VAT chargeable; expressed in sterling, at each such rate,

(l) the total amount of VAT chargeable, expressed in sterling; and

(m) the unit price.

12.23 The rules for invoices issued to customers in another member state are similar except that item (i) is not required and the requirements of (h) and (l) are modified to reflect the fact that supplies to non-UK taxable persons may not be subject to UK VAT. In addition, the VAT identification number of the UK supplier must contain the prefix GB.

(VAT Regulations 1995, reg 14.)

Evidence of receipt of a supply from a UK supplier – less detailed tax invoice

12.24 Customs and Excise allow (Notice 700, para 16(6)(1)) suppliers to issue a less detailed tax invoice provided that the amount of the invoice is less than £250. A less detailed tax invoice only needs to contain the following details:

- the name, address and VAT registration number of the supplier;
- the time of supply (tax point);
- a description which identifies the goods or services supplied; and
- for each VAT rate applicable, the total amount payable, including VAT and the VAT rate charged, shown in sterling.

A less detailed tax invoice may not include details of any exempt supplies.

A less detailed invoice may be used for fuel and power or derv (VAT Notice 700, para 17(1)).

Evidence of receipt of a supply from a UK supplier – modified tax invoice

12.25 A supplier can issue a modified tax invoice provided that the recipient of the supply agrees (VAT Notice 700, para 16(6)(2)). A modified tax invoice must include the following details:

- the VAT-inclusive value of each standard-rated or reduced-rate supply (instead of the VAT-exclusive values).
- at the foot of the invoice, separate totals of:
  - — the VAT-inclusive value of the standard-rated or reduced-rate supplies;
  - — the VAT payable on those supplies;
  - — the value, excluding VAT, of those supplies;
  - — the value of any zero-rated supplies included on the invoice; and
  - — the value of any exempt supplies included on the invoice.
- the name, address and VAT registration number of the supplier.

Evidence of receipt of a supply from a UK supplier – retailers' tax invoices

12.26 Where a taxable person purchases goods or services costing less than £100 (inclusive of VAT) from a retailer, he may be given an abbreviated tax invoice containing the following details:

(a) the name, address and registration number of the retailer;

(b) the time of the supply;

(c) a description sufficient to identify the goods or services supplied;

(d) the total amount payable including VAT; and

(e) for each rate of VAT chargeable, the gross amount payable including VAT and the VAT rate applicable.

(VAT Regulations 1995, reg 16.)

Evidence of receipt of a supply from a UK supplier – construction services

12.27 A taxable person, who receives certain construction services, will not be issued with a tax invoice by the supplier. Instead, the supplier is able to issue an 'authenticated receipt' provided that the receipt contains the same details as are set out at **12.22** above and also provided that he does not also issue a tax invoice or similar document.

(VAT Regulations 1995, reg 13(4) and VAT Notice 700, para 17(4)(2).)

Evidence of receipt of a supply from a UK supplier – cash and carry wholesalers

12.28 Customs and Excise also allow cash and carry wholesalers to adapt their till rolls to serve as a tax invoice. The following conditions must be met:

- the product coding system must clearly identify the different classes of goods sold. The system should be based on at least two or three digits;
- the wholesaler must be able to provide VAT-registered customers, ie those seeking to deduct VAT, with up to date copies of the lists;
- the till roll must include all the details required for a full VAT invoice as noted in at **12.22** above).

Unless all the conditions are met, the wholesaler must issue a full VAT invoice when a customer asks for one.

(VAT Notice 700, para 17(2).)

Evidence of receipt of a supply from a UK supplier – self-billing

12.29 A supplier may agree with a customer that the customer should make out an invoice and bill himself in place of the supplier. Such arrangements are particularly useful in the case of billing for supplies that depend on information in the possession of the customer, eg royalties payable in respect of the use of copyright, patents or other intellectual material where the value may be depend on the number of units published or produced by the customer. However, there are other reasons why a customer might prefer to issue the invoice and prevail upon the supplier to allow him to issue the invoice.

12.30 A taxable person that wishes a self-billed invoice to be treated as a VAT invoice can only do so if he enters into an agreement with the supplier and complies with certain conditions (VAT Regulations 1995, reg 13(3)). The EC Invoicing Directive means that with effect from 1 January 2004 approval for self-billing is no longer required although it is subject to certain conditions. The requirements of self billing agreements and other conditions relating to self-billing are contained in VAT Regulations 1995, regs 14(3A) – (3F). These require customers wishing to make use of self-billed tax invoices to:

- enter into an agreement with the supplier(s) agreeing to the use of self-billing. That agreement approval must include:
  - an undertaking not to issue a normal tax invoice;
  - details of the period for which the agreement is valid which may not be longer than one year or the term of the contract under which self-billed supplies will be made;
  - specify that the supplier will accept self-billed invoices in relation to supplies covered by the agreement; and
  - agree that the supplier will notify the customer if he ceases to be VAT registered;
- ensure that all the information that has to be shown on a normal tax invoice is shown on the self-billed invoice.

12.31 A self-billing agreement automatically terminates:

- When either the customer's or the supplier's business is transferred as a going concern;
- When the supplier ceases to be registered.

Self-billing can apply to intra-EU supplies (ie a supply made to a customer in another EU member state).

In addition, Customs and Excise have the power to make other conditions. It should be noted that the fact that a customer makes out the invoice for a supply does not necessarily mean that there is self-billing. In *Weldstruct Ltd [1977] VATTR 101*, the recipient of a supply had invoices printed on behalf of the supplier and with its agreement made out invoices to itself. The Tribunal rejected Customs and Excise's contention that VAT could not be deducted on the invoices because this was unauthorised self-billing. A similar situation arose in the case of *Ocean Leisure Ltd (VAT decision 13169)* and the same conclusion was reached. The main factor distinguishing the cases referred to above from self-billing is that in each, the invoices were issued on the supplier's own stationery – the recipient did not use its stationery – it simply acted as the equivalent of an invoice clerk of the supplier.

Where no evidence of receipt of a supply from a UK supplier

12.32 Customs and Excise do not require evidence in respect of certain small amounts (up to £25) on expenditure such as payphone calls or supplies from coin operated machines. However, before they will accept such a deduction, the taxpayer must be able to show that the supplier was registered for VAT. This should be relatively easy in the case of payphones operated by large household names but more difficult where the payphone is located in (say) a bed and breakfast enterprise or where there is no indication on a coin operated machine as to who the operator is.

Evidence of an acquisition from an EU member state (except UK)

12.33 A taxable person that wishes to deduct VAT incurred on acquisitions of goods from other member states must hold a document evidencing the acquisition.

12.34 If the acquisition is of new means of transport, the document will be one issued by the authority in the other member state from which the vehicle was acquired showing:

- the acquiring business's VAT registration number including the prefix 'GB';
- the VAT registration number of the supplier including the alphabetical code of the EC member state in which the supplier is registered;
- the consideration for the supply excluding VAT;
- the date when the document was issued; and
- a description sufficient to identify the acquisition as a new means of transport.

12.35 It should be remembered that VAT on a motor car can only be deducted if it is a qualifying vehicle, i e it is not available for private use (see **Chapter 4**).

12.36 The evidence required for other goods will be similar except that the description of goods will be different.

Evidence of an importation from outside the EU

12.37 A taxable person who imports goods will normally hold one of the following documents as evidence that goods have been imported from outside the EU and that VAT has been paid:

- a monthly certificate of imports (C79); or
- postal imports exceeding £2,000 – a single administration document (SAD); or
- postal imports not exceeding £2,000 – no document is issued showing the input tax paid;

- air or maritime imports – Customs and Excise authenticated invoice.

Alternative evidence

12.38 Customs and Excise have the power to accept alternative evidence where a taxable person seeking a deduction does not hold a tax invoice or equivalent evidence of a supply, acquisition or importation. In general terms, Customs and Excise are likely to wish to ensure that:

- there was an actual supply of goods or services. For example, the person may have a delivery note showing that goods were in fact delivered;
- consideration was given in respect of the supply. This might be evidenced by showing that payment was in fact made for the goods;
- the supplier was a taxable person. Thus, in the past, a Tribunal has taken the view that the fact that the value of a supply exceeded the compulsory registration limits was acceptable evidence that the supplier was a taxable person. (However, see *Bond House Systems Ltd (VAT decision 18100) [2003] SWTI 1431* and other cases – above.)

Additional evidence required in respect of fuel, telecommunications and IT equipment

12.39 In respect of fuel, telecommunications and IT equipment, Customs and Excise issued a consultation paper indicating that in respect of such supplies, they will require the taxable person to have undertaken additional steps to ensure that the supply was made by a genuine supplier. The provisions are part of an initiative aimed at preventing the 'carousel fraud' that took place in cases such as *Bond House Systems Ltd* and other cases – see above.

In essence, a person who purchases:

- alcohol;
- computer equipment;
- fuel and derv; or
- telecommunications equipment

will be expected to carry out additional checks to ensure that their purchase is a genuine purchase. The checks that need to be carried out include:

- checks to ensure that the VAT registration number of the supplier is a genuine registration;
- checks on the supplier to ensure that it is a genuine business capable of supplying the goods in question;
- checks on the goods themselves to ensure that they are genuine, that the prices are appropriate to their state and the market conditions at the time.

VAT records

12.40 VAT Regulations 1995, reg 31 sets out the records that a taxable person is required to maintain. In relation to inputs, a taxable person must keep the invoices and other documents described above, other normal business records and a VAT account.

The VAT account – what is due to or by Customs and Excise

12.41 VAT Notice 700/21/02 – 'Keeping records and accounts' provides guidance on what records and accounts must be kept. In relation to the VAT account, the Notice sets out an example of what information will be shown in the VAT account as follows:

Debits – VAT deductible (input tax)	*Credits – VAT payable (output tax)*
Acquisitions (see Notice 725 'The single market')	Sales
Purchases	Certain postal imports and imported services
Imports	Adjustments from special schemes
Adjustments from special schemes	Errors in earlier returns
Errors in earlier returns	Self-supplies
Bad debt relief.	Road fuel scale charges (see Notice 700/64 'Motoring expenses')

12.42 The VAT account in fact reflects what is due by and to Customs and Excise.

12.43 It is important to recognise that except where all VAT is recoverable, which will be rare, the accounting records will need to make provision to identify VAT that is recoverable and debit only that VAT to the VAT account.

The accounting process

12.44 The right to deduct VAT arises when it is incurred. As noted above, it is necessary to record not only the VAT incurred but also the use to which the supplies on which it was incurred were put. This is usually best done when it is incurred. Effectively therefore, the VAT entry should be made when an expense is accrued in the normal accounting records. Where VAT is wholly recoverable or wholly irrecoverable, the VAT accounting treatment is relatively straightforward. The VAT element of the expenditure will be debited either to the VAT account described at **12.41** above or will be charged directly to the relevant expenditure account – whether capital or revenue.

12.45 Where VAT is only partly recoverable, an apportionment must be made. There are two basic methods that can be used to deal with VAT on expenses that are only partly recoverable. In more sophisticated systems such as those that use relational databases to maintain details not only of the basic data but also of its relationship with other data, the VAT recovery rates may be determined and linked to specific cost centres and even specific accounts within the financial accounting records.

Example 1 – Allocation of input tax

A leasing and hire purchase business purchases a computer for £100,000 plus VAT. It has been agreed with Customs and Excise that 50% of the use is for taxable leasing purposes and 50% for the hire purchase business. In accordance with Customs and Excise's agreed method for hire purchase transactions, 15% of the input tax referable to the hire purchase business is to be treated as recoverable. The rate of VAT deduction allowed is:

Leasing	50.0%
Hire purchase 15% x 50% =	7.5%
Total	57.5%

Of the total VAT of £17,500 therefore, £10,062.50 is recoverable and £7,437.50 is not.

The accounting entry is therefore:

Debit Computer (Basic capital expenditure)	100,000.00
Debit Computer (Irrecoverable VAT)	7,437.50
Debit VAT account (Customs and Excise)	10,062.50
Credit Creditor (or cash if paid in cash)	17,500.00

12.46 The example above illustrates what might be done when the recovery rate is known or agreed at the time that the entry is made. This will seldom be the case.

12.47 Two methods are typically used to deal with the more normal situation where the recovery rate has to be calculated in retrospect. In more sophisticated accounting systems, the VAT incurred will be associated with the original account to which the supply on which the VAT was incurred is debited.

Example 2

Cost centre – 001

Net expense

VAT incurred

VAT deductible

Net cost

1.
Advertising

2,000
350
(175)
2,175

1.
Rental of property
– Taxable
– Exempt

10,000
4,000
1,750

(875)

10,875
4,000

1.

12.48 In Example 2, a record of the VAT incurred and recovered is associated with the relevant expense account for the relevant cost centre. The initial 50 per cent deduction is credited against the account and debited to the VAT account in **12.41** above. By ensuring that the link between the original account and cost centre are maintained, if the rate of recovery changes, it becomes easier to determine any adjustment. Thus, if at year end, the actual recovery rate turns out to be 40 per cent, it is easy enough to work out the adjustment as follows:

Original VAT deducted – 50% of £2,100 =	£1,050.00
VAT actually deductible – 40% of £2,100 =	£840.00
Adjustment	£210.00

12.49 There are several advantages in maintaining data showing the link between the VAT and the specific accounts and cost centres on which the VAT was incurred in the manner indicated above. From a financial accounting perspective, any non-deductible VAT is associated with the cost centre and account to which it actually relates. This allows for better financial budgetary control and ensures that those incurring the VAT cannot ignore the impact of VAT on the budgets for which they are responsible. From an Income and Corporation Tax perspective, the costs are associated with the appropriate accounts. This can be important from a perspective of, eg:

- the cost of assets for capital allowances purposes;

- the cost of benefits where an employee is taxed on a benefit by reference to its cost;
- the proper cost to be disallowed, e g in relation to non-business expenditure.

12.50 A more common method, particularly in small and medium businesses with less sophisticated VAT accounting systems, is to debit VAT to one or more 'pools'. In this method, the residual input tax (i e the VAT incurred other than that which is wholly deductible or wholly non-deductible) is accumulated in one or more separate VAT accounts. The appropriate method attributable to each pool is then used to determine the amount of VAT that is deductible and debited to the VAT account and that which is not. The balance is then written off to expenditure. By pooling the VAT, it can be more difficult to distinguish between capital and revenue and also to identify expenditure which is referable to specific expense.

Apportioning VAT between that which is recoverable and that which is not

12.51 In addition to determining what VAT is recoverable (as noted at **12.43** above), a taxable person also needs to maintain records of whatever is used to measure the use of supplies on which VAT is received. This may be turnover, numbers of transactions, floor area, staff hours or other data. This in itself can create problems e g because cash received creates a tax point whereas accounting records are based on an accruals system, the value of supplies can be distorted by abnormal receipts of cash or abnormal withholding of cash by customers.

12.52 Where residual input tax exceeds the de minimis limits for the standard method override to apply, it will also be necessary to collate information to show whether the actual use of goods and services received gives rise to an adjustment.

Accrual and estimation of VAT

12.53 Input tax is deductible when the VAT is incurred. In general Customs and Excise do not raise objections to deductions being claimed in a period other than that in which it is incurred but of course there are good commercial reasons why VAT should be deducted as soon as practicable. In addition, it should be borne in mind that there is a three-year period within which to claim any VAT that is deductible (see **12.90** below).

12.54 A key issue for taxable persons is that they are required to hold a tax invoice in order to deduct VAT. However, there can be a number of reasons why a business may not hold the relevant evidence. These range from problems with the taxable person's own systems to problems with suppliers and indeed the fact that the VAT regulations contain provisions that may cause delay. Examples include:

Example 3

- suppliers may not issue invoices at the time the supply is made, taking advantage of the VAT regulations that allow invoices to be issued up to 30 days (more if Customs and Excise agree) from the date of a supply – VAT Regulations 1995, reg 13(5);
- taxpayers may process invoices in batches leading to their being processed too late for inclusion in the VAT return; and
- in smaller businesses, invoices might only be processed when paid, leading to a permanent delay in claiming input tax.

12.55 Even if invoices are not processed in the financial records at the time the VAT return is processed, it is still permissible for the business to accrue the VAT incurred that is deductible in the VAT account and to include it in the relevant VAT return. One problem that can arise is that although it might be relatively easy to identify the VAT incurred, without coding and processing the expense and related VAT, it might be difficult to identify the actual extent to which the VAT is deductible. In principle, however, provided the VAT can be identified and the relevant proportion that is deductible in accordance with the business's partial exemption calculated, an accrual may be made. It should be emphasised that Customs and Excise's permission is not required to accrue deductible VAT. Accrual ensures that VAT is entered for deduction when it arises and is therefore in accordance with EC Sixth VAT Directive, art 17(1).

12.56 Greater difficulties arise where an invoice is not received. However, in principle, provided that a supply has actually been received, the relevant VAT is input tax and the VAT is deductible. Two possible methods can be used where no invoice is available, ie:

- seek permission of Customs and Excise to use alternative evidence of a supply if it appears unlikely that original evidence will be forthcoming, eg because a supplier is insolvent (see **12.38** above);
- seek permission of Customs and Excise to estimate the input tax that has been incurred but for which no evidence is available if the situation is temporary.

12.57 Although Customs and Excise have a discretion as to whether to accept alternative evidence or allow estimation, it seems unlikely that that discretion allows them to arbitrarily prevent the deduction of properly incurred input tax – particularly, for example, in those cases where the lack of a tax invoice is attributable to a direction by Customs and Excise allowing the supplier to extend the period within which an invoice must be issued. Indeed, the European Court of Justice in the case of *Schmeink (C-454/98)* held that:

> '… measures which a member state may adopt under Article 22(8) of the Sixth Directive in order to ensure the correct levying of the tax and for the prevention of fraud must not go further than is necessary to attain such objectives … They may not therefore be used in such a way that they would have the effect of

undermining the neutrality of VAT, which is a fundamental principle of the common system established by the relevant Community legislation.'

12.58 In the case of estimation, Customs and Excise normally require an appropriate adjustment to be made in the return for the period following that in which estimation is used.

Credit notes and debit notes

12.59 There is no specific provision in the primary VAT legislation or VAT regulations that specifies any requirements in relation to credit or debit notes. However, VAT Notice 700, para 18 deals with credits and debits. In essence, if there is an adjustment to the consideration for a supply, a credit note will normally be issued by the supplier.

12.60 An alternative treatment is that the recipient of the supply can, with the agreement of the supplier, issue a debit note reducing the consideration.

12.61 Whether a credit note or debit note is issued, it must comply with the requirements of para 18(2)(2) of Notice 700. Broadly speaking, a credit or debit note must:

- be issued in respect of a genuine supply;
- contain a heading describing it as a credit or debit note; and
- contain the following details:
  - the identifying number and date of issue;
  - the name, address and registration number of the supplier;
  - the name and address of the customer;
  - the reason for its issue—for example, 'returned goods';
  - a description which identifies the goods or services for which credit is being claimed or allowed;
  - the quantity and amount for each description;
  - the total amount credited, excluding VAT;
  - the rate and amount of VAT credited; and
  - details of the original VAT invoice or invoices in respect of which credit is being given or other means that demonstrate that VAT was accounted for on the original supply.

12.62 Where both the supplier and customer are fully taxable, there is no necessity for VAT to be accounted for on any adjustment provided both parties agree. It should be noted that even where both parties are taxable, there may be occasions when it is advantageous for the customer to receive a credit note eg where it results in a reduction of non-deductible VAT on say business entertainment expenditure.

12.63 Where a credit or debit note is issued, the result will be to reduce the VAT charged by the supplier and thereby the input tax deductible. The recipient of a credit note or the issuer of the debit note must make an entry in the VAT account in the period in which the consideration and input tax is reduced (not the original period when the input tax was claimed, if different).

12.64 Customs and Excise Notice 700, para 18(2)(4) states that an adjustment by way of credit or debit note can only be effective for VAT if the adjustment is made within three years of the original supply. This may be true where the credit note is issued to correct an error since such adjustments are made under the provisions of VAT Regulations 1995, reg 34 and sub-para (1A) does indeed require adjustments to be made within three years. The position might be different if the adjustment is by way of adjustment for a contingent event rather than by way of error, eg a discount. However, it seems unlikely that the point will be of great import since most adjustments would normally take place within a three-year period.

Discounts

12.65 From a VAT perspective, there are two methods of adjusting for discounts, ie:

- cash and settlement discounts reduce any consideration immediately (even when not taken). Accordingly, the taxable amount and the VAT thereon is reduced. Thus when entering the VAT in respect of a supply that is subject to a discount, it is the reduced amount that should be accounted for.
- in respect of all other discounts, the adjustment should be made by way of credit note or debit note (see **9.59** above) and accounted for in the period when the recipient of the supply becomes entitled to the discount.

12.66 From an accounting perspective therefore, cash and settlement discounts reduce the input tax to be accounted for on the original supply whereas all the others will usually be accounted for in a later period.

Adjustments for errors and voluntary disclosures

12.67 An error, whether in favour of Customs and Excise or in favour of the taxable person, that does not exceed £2,000 may be corrected in the VAT return in which the error is discovered. Error in this context refers to the net amount of over- and understatements of tax *(VAT Regulations 1995, reg 34)*.

12.68 Where the adjustment exceeds £2,000, a taxable person must correct his return in such time and in such manner as Customs and Excise direct. In order to avoid any misdeclaration penalty (VATA 1994, ss.63 and 64), a taxable person must make a voluntary disclosure of any error to Customs and Excise. A voluntary disclosure may be made on Form VAT 652 or by letter.

12.69 It is arguable that input tax may always be claimed late (provided it is claimed within the three-year time limits) because Customs and Excise have directed generally that input tax may be claimed late – see VAT Notice 700, para 10(5)(1). See also *Howard (VAT decision 5726)*, *Currie Group Ltd (VAT decision 5942)* and *Bulldog International Transport Express Ltd [1991] VATTR 515* in each of which cases, Customs and Excise asserted that input tax must be claimed and therefore input tax cannot be understated. It is arguable that the correct position is that input tax is correctly deductible when it is incurred. A taxable person may claim such input tax late if he chooses to avail himself of para 10(5)(1) but is also able to choose to have the error corrected in the correct period – which he may choose to do if he needs to offset an understatement in that period and so avoid penalties, interest or both.

Annual adjustments

12.70 Most partly exempt businesses will be required to make an annual adjustment. The manner in which the annual adjustment is calculated is set out in **Chapter 6**. From an accounting perspective, what is required is a system that ensures that the correct numbers from each quarter's returns are fed through into the annual adjustment.

- It should be borne in mind that in any given period it is possible that a business will have had either assessments by or will have made voluntary disclosures to Customs and Excise correcting returns either in the current year or in previous years. When correcting years in respect of which an annual adjustment has been made, it is likely that any assessment or voluntary disclosure would have been done on the basis of a re-worked annual adjustment. However, where an adjustment has been made in the current year, it is necessary to ensure that the numbers for the return to which the adjustment is relevant are amended and that the amended numbers are used in the calculation of the annual adjustment rather than the numbers used in the original return.
- It follows that all assessments made and voluntary disclosures accepted by Customs and Excise will need to be identified and brought to account in calculating the annual adjustment.

Example 4

VAT returns for the year ended 30 April 2003 (£'000s)

Input tax for the period to >>	*31-Jul-02*	*31-Oct-02*	*31-Jan-02*	*30-Apr-02*	*Voluntary disclosure*	*Total*
Directly attributable	1,732	1,856	2,317	710	40	6,655
Residual	112	176	187	90	–22	543
Total	*1,844*	*2,032*	*2,504*	*800*	*18*	*7,198*
Total residual	*280*	*320*	*440*	*200*	*–40*	*1,200*
Taxable turnover	4,000	4,400	5,100	1,350		14,850
Exempt turnover	6,000	3,600	6,900	1,650		18,150
Deductible proportion	40.0%	55.0%	42.5%	45.0%	55.0%	45.0%

Notes:
1. Error found in period 4 relating to period
2. Error is that £40k residual input tax was in fact fully taxable

12.71 The recovery rate for the annual adjustment is calculated as follows–

$$\frac{\text{Taxable turnover for the year} \times \text{Total residual input tax}}{\text{Total taxable and exempt turnover for the year}} = \frac{14,850}{18,150}$$

This gives a percentage of 45%.

The adjusted total residual input tax for the year is– 1,200

The adjusted residual input tax that is claimable is – 45% x 1,200 = 540

Since the total allowed was £543K, the business has to repay £3K to Customs and Excise.

The standard method and special method partial exemption overrides

12.72 The standard method partial exemption override (VAT Regulations 1995, regs 107A–107E) is considered in detail in **Chapter 6** above. It requires a taxable person to substitute a 'use' based method in place of the standard method if the standard method would not result in a fair attribution of input tax.

12.73 It would appear that Customs and Excise's main concern is that the timing of either the recognition of turnover or the time when input tax gives rise to a right to deduct may distort the operation of the partial exemption method. Thus, in most cases, the adjustment called for will be one of moving turnover from one period to another in order to ensure that turnover does give a proper reflection of the use of an expense that gives rise to an adjustment.

12.74 Although turnover may well be the best measure of use, subject only to better matching of costs and turnover, in some cases other factors will better measure use, eg floor area in the case of a building that has only been partly let following construction.

12.75 The accounting implications of the standard method partial exemption override may be summarised as follows:

- There will be a need to identify if the partial exemption override applies. Accordingly, a business that uses the standard method needs to have sufficient information in its records to calculate the disallowable VAT on a used-based method so as to determine its applicability. It is possible that this would mean having sufficient information to apply a special method;
- There will also need to be procedures to ensure that at the end of any partial exemption year, a review is made of the applicability of the partial exemption override.

12.76 The special method partial exemption override (VAT Regulations 1995, regs 102A–102C) differs from the standard method override because it contains no de minimis limits. If Customs and Excise consider that the method does not give a fair and reasonable attribution of input tax, they have to serve a notice on the taxpayer. This means that the taxpayer has no obligation to apply the method until a notice is served and therefore no reporting obligations arise until after such notice.

12.77 However, in the event that the method is unfair to the taxpayer (ie it understates the tax that should be deductible), it is for the taxpayer to serve a notice on Customs and Excise who may take steps to allow the taxable person to use a different method (specified in the notice) to achieve a fair and reasonable attribution. The main consequence of this is that the business may need to have a means of reporting any changes in what the business does or in specific transactions that might allow it to serve a notice on Customs and Excise so as to obtain a greater deduction of input tax.

The Capital Items Scheme

12.78 The VAT regulations do not contain specific rules dealing with what records must be kept in respect of capital items. However, every taxable person must keep such records as are required by Customs and Excise (see VATA 1994, Sch 11, para 6(1)).

Customs and Excise Notice 706/2/02, para 2.1 advises taxpayers that their records 'should include the following':

- a description of the capital item;
- the value of the item;
- the amount of input tax reclaimed on the item;
- the date of the start and end of each interval including the first;
- the date and value of any disposal (if the item is sold prior to the end of the adjustment period).

12.79 Although there are no specific requirements and Customs and Excise's Notice does not use words that suggest that para 2.1 has statutory effect, given the size of capital items, taxpayers should ensure that records are kept that will enable them to support the adjustments made in their VAT returns. Accordingly, other records such as partial exemption calculations showing how the rate of recovery in both the first and any subsequent adjustment intervals, will also be necessary.

12.80 Where a taxable person acquires the assets of a business as a going concern, he will have to ensure that he makes provision in any agreement of sale to gain access to records relating to any capital items since the responsibility for adjustments in any remaining adjustment interval will pass to the purchaser of any business. The same will be true where a taxpayer acquires a company that was a member of a VAT group since any capital item that remains in the company acquired will inherit the capital item's history of the previous representative member in relation to such item.

12.81 The normal rules apply in relation to the length of time that a taxable person must keep records, ie records must be kept for six years. This would normally mean that records of the purchase of a capital item must be kept for six years from the date or dates of purchase. However, Customs and Excise recommend in Notice 706/2/02, para 2.2 that records are kept long enough to show how each adjustment has been calculated.

VAT returns

12.82 From a perspective of accounting for VAT deductions on any VAT return, a taxable person needs to be able to determine the following numbers:

Box	Legend
2	VAT due in this period on acquisitions from other EC member states
4	VAT reclaimed in this period on purchases and other inputs (including acquisition from the EC)
7	Total purchases and inputs

12.83 The VAT included in box 2 is the output tax on acquisitions from the EU. The deduction for input tax, if any, is included in box 4. The value of purchases and other inputs in box 7 includes the values of any:

- imports;
- acquisitions from EC member states;
- 'reverse charge' transactions;
- gold transactions under the special accounting scheme;

- the full purchase amount of goods bought under the second hand schemes (even though it is the margin that represents the value of any taxable supply).

12.84 The value to be included in box 7 does not include:

- the VAT on the purchases etc;
- wages and salaries;
- PAYE and national insurance contributions;
- loans, dividends, and other payments of money that do not relate to supplies received;
- payments for MOT certificates, motor vehicle licence duty and local authority rates.

12.85 Because there are very few penalties relating to misdeclaration of the figures other than the VAT itself, the systems used to determine the numbers in box 7 are seldom as structured as those relating to boxes 2 and 4. The values may therefore not be accurate. Nevertheless, since the numbers may be used by Customs and Excise for credibility checks and, in addition, because it is a requirement that returns be accurate in all respects, systems are required to ensure that the correct numbers are inserted in the VAT return.

Agreements with Customs and Excise

12.86 Customs and Excise have the power under the Customs and Excise Management Act 1979 to enter into agreements in relation to the management and administration of VAT. Agreements are likely to be of two kinds, ie:

- those entered into with the taxpayer including agreements relating to partial exemption, which are authorised by VAT Regulations 1995, reg 102; and
- those entered into with trade bodies eg the agreement with the Finance House Leasing Association in relation to partial exemption calculations of hire purchase and leasing businesses.

12.87 Businesses need to maintain records of agreements that they have entered into with Customs and Excise and any amendments to them or correspondence interpreting them. No business is required to adopt a method that has been agreed by Customs and Excise with representative bodies of the Industry to which they belong. However, the application of a method agreement between a trade body and Customs and Excise to a business is not automatic. The business needs to notify Customs and Excise that it has adopted the method.

12.88 Customs and Excise have entered into the following agreements with the following trade bodies relating to the deduction of input tax:

- The Brewers Society – relates to tenanted estates (Notice 700/57/02, Part 4);

- Association of British Factors and Discounters – concerns the partial exemption method of factors (Notice 700/57/02 – but see comments in **Chapter 9** regarding case law on the liability of factoring.);
- Finance Houses Association Limited – regarding partial exemption of finance houses (Notice 700/57/02, Part 6);
- Association of British Insurers – concerning recovery of input tax relating to non-EU branches, i e recovery of VAT under VAT Regulations 1995, reg 103 (Notice 700/57/02, Part 7);
- Association of Investment Trust Companies – regarding partial exemption (Notice 700/57/02, Part 8).

12.89 Agreement with the Association of British Insurers, Lloyd's of London, The Institute of London Underwriters and the British Insurance and Investment Association – concerns the coding of supplies of marine, aviation and transport (MAT) insurance services and therefore affects the measurement of taxable and other supplies (Notice 700/57/02, Part 11).

The three-year cap and its impact on VAT accounting

12.90 VAT may only be recovered as input tax if it is claimed within the relevant time limits. Clearly, if a taxable person follows the correct procedures and accounts for input tax in time, the time limits will be of theoretical interest only. However, if input tax is not claimed in time, those responsible for accounting for VAT will need to be aware of the time limits.

12.91 At first glance, it might appear that if input tax has been underclaimed, the relevant rule is VAT Regulations 1995, reg 29. This provides that input tax must be claimed within three years of the date on which the return on which the VAT in question should have been declared was due.

12.92 Customs and Excise appear to have a different view. Thus, if the original return overstated a payment due to them and the effect of any failure to claim input tax is to show that a lesser amount was due, they consider that the claim is a claim for a repayment of tax overpaid falling within VATA 1994, s 80. The question was considered in *University of Sussex v C & E Comrs [2001] STC 1495*. However, Customs and Excise have not accepted the decision of the High Court and have indicated that they have appealed the decision to the Court of Appeal.

12.93 On the other hard, if the return showed a net repayment and output tax was overstated, the error is regarded as a claim under VAT Regulations 1995, reg 29.

12.94 The difference in treatment has some but not any major significance from a perspective of when the limits for a claim expire. In respect of both types of claim, there is a three-year limit. However, the limit runs from the time when the tax is paid whereas in respect of a claim under reg 29 the time limit runs from when the return was due – usually a matter of days.

12.95 One potentially significant issue is the matter of unjust enrichment. There is no provision in VAT Regulations 1995, reg 29 whereby a claim can be refused on the basis of unjust enrichment.

12.96 Arguably, a claim to deduct input tax – belatedly or otherwise, is always within VAT Regulations 1995, reg 29.

(See also VAT Regulations 1995, reg 34 dealing with amendment of returns.)

VAT groups

Summary

12.97 There are three principal issues relating to accounting in VAT groups:

- collection of data for returns;
- entry and exit from groups;
- non-tax issues.

Collection of data for returns

12.98 The EC Sixth VAT Directive, art 4 provides that member states may treat two or more legally separate entities that are bound together by economic, financial and organisational links as a single entity for VAT purposes.

This provision is enacted in VATA 1994, s 43. Sub-section (1) provides that certain consequences follow the registration of two or more entities as a group. These in turn have implications for VAT deductions accounting, ie:

- Supplies to or by any member of the group are treated as made to or by the representative member. The representative member therefore needs to be able to maintain details of all supplies made by or to members of the group in order to complete the group VAT return. If there is a single accounting system that is used to account for all companies within a group, this may not be too complex. However, if the accounting systems are devolved to different centres, it may be necessary to require each member to make returns (whether in paper form or in some electronic form) so that the consolidated return can be made.
- Because the group is treated as a single entity for VAT purposes, it follows that there will be only one partial exemption method that will apply to the whole group.
- Supplies between members of the group are disregarded. The result of this is that the normal link between inputs and outputs in a company will not

exist and the right to deduct must be determined by 'looking through' the disregarded transaction to the ultimate transaction made outside the group. This can be illustrated graphically as follows:

Thus, the supplies made to Group Co 1 must be attributed to the supplies made by Group Co 2 to its customers. However, this implies that when setting up the accounting systems of the two companies, it is necessary to ensure that there is a mechanism to ensure that VAT incurred by Group Co 1 is collated in an account and is then attributed to whatever supplies are made by Group Co 2. Clearly, it is possible to get to quite complex chains eg there could be more than one intermediate company.

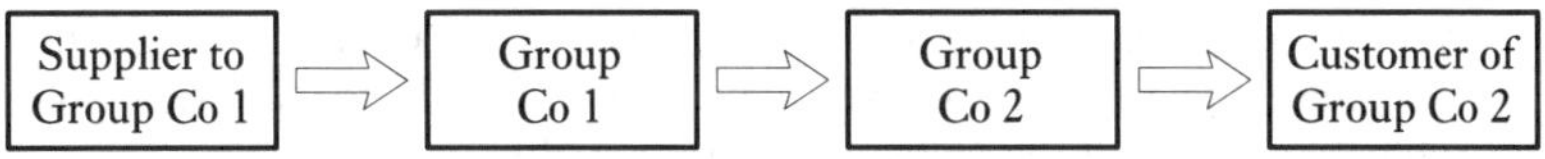

Fig. 3

A further consequence of this will be that VAT that might have been deductible had a group company been separately registered may become non-deductible as being referable to another company's exempt supplies. The company making the disregarded supply may therefore have to bear a VAT cost that it would otherwise not have incurred.

- Similar rules apply to imports and acquisitions by group members with similar consequences for accounting.

12.99 As noted, except where there is a single integrated accounting system covering all members of the VAT group, there will need to be a method of obtaining returns from each member of the group. In relation to VAT incurred, that return will have to show (as a minimum):

- the amount of VAT incurred and the accounts, cost centres or pools of VAT to which the VAT is referable so as to allow a proper apportionment of the VAT incurred;
- where supplies are made to a company within the same VAT group, the value of such supplies so that they can be eliminated from the values of supplies made to or by the group companies and also to assist in attributing the VAT incurred to supplies made by the various group companies.

Entry and exit from groups

12.100 Following the judgment of the Court of Appeal in *C & E Comrs v Barclays Bank plc [2001] EWCA Civ 1513, [2001] STC 1558* it is now the case that Customs and Excise can insist on a full 90 days' notice being given before a company can leave or enter a VAT group.

12.101 While Customs and Excise do not always insist on the full notice period (except where they perceive there to be avoidance), the fact that this notice has to be given has several implications including:

- On the acquisition of a company, if that company is not allowed to become a member of an existing VAT group immediately, the company will need to initially account for VAT on the basis of its being a separately registered company and later as part of the group. This can be disruptive from an accounting perspective.
- It is also possible that the company being acquired may not have been allowed to leave the previous VAT group of which it was a member. That can mean that it has to account for VAT to the previous and now unrelated group. This can have serious implications for confidentiality of information among other issues. Also, if the company is in a net repayment position, any repayment due to it would be collected by the old group with potential problems relating to the collection of money due.
- On leaving a VAT group, similar issues arise. Thus, a company disposing of a company that is part of a VAT group may have to continue accounting for that company's VAT despite having no legal power to get the requisite information, to carry out any audit or to collect any net VAT due.
- It is also the case that input tax deducted on the basis of a company being part of the VAT group may need to be adjusted if the company leaves the VAT Group since the act of entering or leaving the group can mean that the original supply does not take place and the provisions of VAT Regulations 1995, reg 108 or 109 apply.
- Entry into or exit from a VAT group can trigger capital items issues – see below.

Non-tax issues

12.102 It will be apparent that because VAT legislation makes no provision governing the relationship between members or ex-members of a VAT group, a number of issues may need to be resolved contractually.

Among the issues to be resolved will by agreement will be:

- Who bears the non-deductible VAT – the company making a disregarded supply or the company that makes the ultimate exempt supply that results in the input tax restriction? If the latter, there will need to be appropriate adjustments via inter-company accounts to transfer the non-deductible VAT to the correct company and cost centre.
- If a company enters a new corporate group but remains part of another VAT group, how can confidential information be protected, eg levels of sales? How can the company ensure that any credits due to the company are recovered (if there is a net repayment position)?

- Similarly, if a company leaves an existing corporate group but remains part of an existing VAT group, how will confidentiality be preserved?
- Agreement may be needed on other issues such as how to deal with capital items adjustments.

12.103 It is not possible to give an exhaustive list of issues because of the many different scenarios that can arise. It is sufficient to note that it is necessary to forecast the effects on deductions and make appropriate agreements to deal with any issues.

Disputes and appeals

12.104 In the event of a dispute with Customs and Excise, a taxable person has provisions under which he can appeal any decision relating to input tax. These include:

- VATA 1994, s 83(c) which allows a taxable person to appeal any decision relating to the amount of any input tax that can be credited;
- VATA 1994, s 83(e) the proportion of input tax allowable under s 26. This covers any method used to determine the amount of tax that is deductible.

There is no appeal against a decision relating to the amount of VAT that can be refunded under VATA 1994, s 33 (local authorities) or s 41 (government departments).

Corporation tax

Capital allowances

12.105 The Capital Allowances Act 2001 contains specific provisions determining how adjustments made under VAT Regulations 1995, reg 115 are to be treated for Income tax or Corporation tax purposes. The allowances which are most likely to interact with the capital items scheme are plant and machinery allowances, which are dealt with in CAA 2001, ss 234 – 246, and industrial buildings allowances, which are dealt with in ss 345 – 351. Normally where an industrial building includes plant and machinery (for example lift installations and air conditioning equipment) the expenditure will be dealt with as plant and machinery.

12.106 For the purposes of both plant and machinery and industrial buildings allowances, the initial qualifying expenditure will include any irrecoverable VAT, and exclude any recoverable VAT. If in future accounting periods further amounts of VAT become payable, that amount will be treated as additional qualifying expenditure in the period in which the additional VAT liability accrues.

12.107 On the other hand, if there is a rebate of VAT, the amount of the rebate is treated as disposal proceeds in the accounting period in which the rebate accrues.

For the purpose of calculating capital gains, computer equipment will normally be an exempt asset, but land will be a chargeable asset. When there is a chargeable disposal, the allowable expenditure will include any irrecoverable VAT, and exclude any recoverable VAT (see Inland Revenue Statement of Practice B1). This means that effect should be given to any VAT adjustments when the gain or loss is computed (see Inland Revenue Press Release, 20 March 1990).

Revenue expenditure

12.108 Income and corporation taxes are, in essence, tax on profits from trade. VAT deductions are relevant in calculating profits in that if the VAT is not deductible, the non-deductible cost will form part of the expenditure deducted in calculating profits or losses.

12.109 Where the underlying expenditure on which VAT is incurred is deductible in calculating profits or losses, the non-deductible VAT will also be deductible. However, where the VAT is non-deductible for income and corporation taxes purposes, the VAT should form part of the cost not allowed for direct tax purposes. Typical examples of expenditure that may not be deductible for income or corporation tax purposes and on which non-deductible VAT might be incurred include:

- business entertainment;
- lease payments on cars that have a value in excess of £12,000;
- expenditure of capital nature that also does not rank for capital allowances;
- some legal expenditure.

12.110 From an accounting perspective, as noted above, if the accounting system automatically associates the VAT with the relevant account, no further action will be required. However, if VAT is pooled and the deductible proportion only calculated in aggregate, further action may be needed to determine the extent to which any non-deductible VAT should be treated as non-deductible for corporation tax purposes. In most cases, the amounts may be immaterial – however, in other cases the amounts may be sufficiently significant to require action.

Other taxes

12.111 Similar issues to those that arise in relation to corporation tax may also arise in relation to other taxes. The question that will need to be considered is whether a VAT cost forms part of the tax base of a particular tax.

Financial accounting issues

12.112 From an accounting perspective, an asset is recorded in the accounts of a business at its cost. This would normally be the net cost of the asset plus any VAT on the acquisition of that asset that is irrecoverable.

12.113 Those responsible for drawing up the accounts of a business will need to be aware that the non-deductible VAT on an asset will be determined over a period of ten years. However, the asset may well be depreciated or amortised over a considerably longer period. This may have implications for the financial accounting policies.

Example 5 – Non-deductible VAT capitalised

1. A new building is acquired for £10 million plus VAT at 17.5%. In the first interval of the adjustment period, it is used wholly for taxable purposes and the whole of the VAT is recovered. In the second interval, the taxpayer acquires a new business and forecasts that the future VAT recovery will be only 60%.
2. Assuming the building is used throughout the remaining nine intervals in the same way, VAT of £630,000 will be adjusted in annual instalments of £70,000 over the remaining nine years. However, since the building will probably have a life of at least 40 years, it may not be appropriate to write off the whole £70,000 each year and the taxpayer will need to consider what is the most appropriate method to deal with the capital items adjustment in the financial accounts.

12.114 It is quite possible and indeed probable that many adjustments will not be material from a financial accounting perspective. However, in some cases, the amounts may be material from a business's perspective and the appropriate accounting will need to be considered. It is beyond the scope of this digest to advise on the correct method for dealing with adjustments in such circumstances.

12.115 Similar issues can arise where a taxpayer acquires a capital item as part of a going concern or where a company moves out of a VAT group – whether into another VAT group or where it becomes registered in its own right.

Chapter 13

Refunds to Businesses Established Outside the Member State

Introduction

13.1 A business that incurs VAT in a member state in which it is not established (this could be a non-EU business, or a taxable person established in a different member state than the one where the VAT was incurred) can reclaim the VAT incurred if it meets certain conditions. These conditions are detailed in the following sections. This repayment of VAT satisfies the need to ensure that VAT charged in the EU is not a burden upon a business. It may be thought that this repayment of VAT would be restricted to EU businesses (which was originally the case, Eighth Directive refunds are made to taxable persons established in member states only). The Thirteenth Directive, however, allows refunds to businesses established outside the EU, but only if the country where they are established allows reciprocal refunds to taxable persons established in the EU who incur VAT or similar turnover taxes in that country.

13.2 It should be noted that refunds will not be made to persons making taxable supplies in the member state. In such cases VAT can only be reclaimed by VAT registration. It is a common error for an overseas business to assume that because it does not have an establishment for direct tax purposes in the member state that it does not need to register for VAT. This is not the case. Although the VAT liability for some supplies can be passed to the customer (through the reverse charge mechanism), it may be necessary to register for VAT both to enable VAT to be reclaimed and also to comply with VAT accounting legislation and pay any VAT that is due on supplies made. Before any claim is made using the Eighth or Thirteenth Directive, a business or taxable person should ensure that it is not liable to register for VAT.

Claims by EU businesses – Eighth Directive

13.3 The Eighth Directive on Turnover Taxes (Directive 79/1072, 6 December 1979) required each member state to make refunds of VAT incurred in that member state to taxable persons established in other member states. The objective is to ensure that a taxable person does not bear an irrecoverable VAT cost as a cost component of supplies made by that person.

13.4 The recitals to the Eighth Directive contain certain principles which underpin the refund system. First, discrepancies between member states are to be abolished (this is an ongoing process). Second, there is an aim to prevent any incidence of double taxation. Third, the Directive was a further step towards economic integration. Fourth, the treatment of taxable persons from differing member states are not to differ (which is an important principle of neutrality). Finally, refunds and decisions relating to refunds are to be notified within six months of the date of application for the refund.

13.5 There are a number of conditions common to all member states for making refunds. These are:

- the person claiming the refund is not a taxable person (registered, or liable to be registered) in the member state where the claim is made;
- the person making the claim is a taxable person established in another member state (see below);
- VAT is to be refunded in respect of:
  - services;
  - movable property; or
  - goods imported

  to the extent that they are used:
  - for transactions relating to an economic activity in another member state and the VAT would have been deductible in that member state (where the VAT was incurred); or
  - for transactions relating to imports, exports or international goods traffic; and
  - for supplies of services where the VAT is accounted for by the person to whom the service is supplied (ie the VAT is accounted for by a reverse charge – note: items that can be accounted for using a reverse charge differ slightly between member states).

13.6 It should be noted that VAT is not refundable on immovable property. This is logical because the place of supply of immovable property is where it is located and ownership of such property will indicate a place of establishment for VAT purposes. In either case, supplies are made in the member state and the taxable person is not eligible to claim a refund under the Eighth Directive but must be registered instead. Also, where a business is partially exempt, the amount of refund should take into account the partial exemption restriction. There is, thus, a two-stage test before making a refund. First, is the expense one that gives a right to deduction in the country of refund? For instance, a hotel expense can be reclaimed in the UK, but if the expense is incurred in France, then the VAT cannot be reclaimed. Secondly, what transactions do the expenses relate to and do they give a right to deduction in the country where the taxable person is established? See *Ministre du Budget v Société Monte Dei Paschi di Siena (C-136/99) ECJ [2001] STC 1029, ECJ.*

13.7 A taxable person established in another member state is a person who is carrying on an economic activity but:

- has neither the seat of that economic activity, nor a fixed establishment (or in the absence of such a seat or fixed establishment, a domicile or normal place of residence); and
- does not supply any goods or services (except for transport connected to the international carriage of goods and related services, and 'reverse charge' services),

in the member state where the reclaim is being made.

13.8 A refund claim is made by submitting:

(1) A claim on the prescribed form to the relevant authority. These forms (a copy of which is at Annex A to the Eighth Directive) is the same form for each member state. Each member state's form, however, is in its own language. It should also be completed in BLOCK CAPITALS. Any language version can be used when making claims in other member states as each form is identical, but it must be completed in the language of the member state from which the refund is claimed. The UK form is the VAT 65 and this is obtainable from the National Advice Service (0845 010 9000), on Customs and Excise's web site at http://www.hmce.gov.uk/forms/formsvat/formsvat.htm.

(2) The original invoices that support the claim for VAT must be submitted with the claim form. Where a member state will accept claims for input tax from taxable persons established in the member state without original invoices, it must also allow Eighth Directive claims with similar supporting evidence as is allowed to taxable persons established in its own territory. Thus, as the UK allows claims without invoices for VAT incurred on supplies from coin-operated machines for UK established businesses, the same facility to make a claim without an invoice has to be given to persons making Eighth Directive reclaims. In addition, where the originals have been lost through no fault of the taxable person, the member state can accept claims without originals where there is no risk of fraud or duplicate claims (*Société Generale des Grandes Sources d'Eaux Minérales Françaises v Bundesamt für Finanzen (C-361/96) [1998] STC 981, ECJ*).

(3) A Certificate of Status. These certificates can be obtained from the local tax authority to show that the person making the claim is a taxable person. The certificate (a copy of which is at Annex B of the Eighth Directive) is valid for one year and does not need to be submitted for each claim (if multiple claims are made in the year), as long as the tax authority that is receiving the claim has an extant copy. A separate original certificate will need to be submitted to each member state where a claim is to be made. A copy for a UK VAT registered business can be obtained from:

National Registration Service
VAT 66 Section
Deansgate
62–70 Tettenhall Road
Wolverhampton WV1 4TZ

(4) A written declaration must be made that no goods or services have been supplied (other than the excepted supplies mentioned above) and an undertaking given that sums claimed in error will be repaid.

13.9 Claims are based upon the calendar year. A claim must be for a period of:

(a) no more than a year; and

(b) must be for a period of not less than three months (unless this period is for the remainder of the year).

13.10 An application for a refund relating to the period ending 31 December must be submitted by 30 June of the following year. There are minimum amounts that can be claimed which vary depending on whether a claim is made for the full year or for a shorter period.

13.11 The refund must be made, or the decision regarding the refund must be communicated to the claimant within six months of making the claim. Any refusal to pay the claim must be accompanied by reasons and appeals can be made on the same basis as a person that is established in that member state (so in the UK an appeal will be made to the VAT and Duties Tribunal). Payment will be made either in the country where the claim is being made or in the country where the applicant is established (and the claimant is required to pay the bank charges incurred for cross-border payments).

13.12 It is no longer necessary for EU taxable persons to appoint a local fiscal agent to deal with VAT affairs in any member state.

Non-refundable VAT

13.13 VAT cannot be reclaimed on the following items:

- immovable property;
- a supply that is not for the purpose of the business;
- any part of a supply that is used for non-business or exempt purposes;
- supplies that the taxable person intends to use for a supply in the member state where the claim is being made;
- a supply that has been exported or is intended to be exported; and
- supplies that relate to Tour Operator Margin Scheme costs.

13.14 Each member state also has its own list of non-deductible items that apply to taxable persons established in its own territory as well as to persons making Eighth Directive reclaims (see the sections below). Note, where supply is mentioned above, this also includes importation.

Claims by non-EU businesses – Thirteenth Directive

13.15 The Thirteenth Directive on Turnover Taxes (Directive 86/560, 17 November 1986) allows businesses established outside the EU to make a claim for VAT incurred in EU member states.

13.16 The basis for making claims is similar to the process for making claims under the Eighth Directive. The form to be used is similar to the Eighth Directive claim form. Each member state's form, however, is in its own language but as each form is identical any language version can be used when making claims in other member states, but it must be completed in the language of the member state from which the refund is claimed. It should also be completed in BLOCK CAPITALS. The UK form is the VAT 65A and this is obtainable from the National Advice Service (0845 010 9000), on Customs and Excise's website at http://www.hmce.gov.uk/forms/formsvat/formsvat.htm.

13.17 In addition a certificate of status is required to be obtained and submitted with the claim. These certificates can be obtained from the local tax authority to show that the person making the claim is a taxable person. The certificate is valid for one year and does not need to be submitted for each claim (if multiple claims are made in the year), as long as the tax authority that is receiving the claim has an extant copy. A separate original certificate will need to be submitted to each member state where a claim is to be made.

13.18 Similarly the original invoices and a statement that over claimed VAT will be repaid and no goods or services have been supplied in the EU must support the claim.

13.19 Claims will only be accepted from persons established in countries that have reciprocal arrangements. Thus, if a country has a turnover tax system and does not allow EU established businesses to make reclaims, then the EU member states will not make refunds to persons established in that country. It should be noted that none of the States of the USA (with, it is understood, one exception) make refunds of any Sales Tax charged. The EU will, however, refund VAT to persons established in the USA. This is presumably because Sales Tax is not regarded as being a turnover tax with credit. As no Sales Tax credits are given to persons established in the USA, EU taxable persons are not being discriminated against. In some countries it may be necessary to register for VAT (or the local turnover tax) in order to obtain a VAT refund in that country, even though supplies are not being made.

13.20 Taxable persons not established in any member state of the EU can make claims. A person who is a taxable person established outside the EU is a person who is carrying on an economic activity but:

- has neither the seat of that economic activity nor a fixed establishment, (or in the absence of such a seat or fixed establishment, a domicile or normal place of residence); and

- does not supply any goods or services (except for transport connected to the international carriage of goods and related services, and 'reverse charge' services)

in any member state of the EU.

13.21 Claims cannot be submitted if any supplies are made in the EU member state where the claim is being submitted other than transport (and ancillary services) supplies for the international carriage of goods or supplies that will be subject to the reverse charge.

13.22 It should be noted that non-established businesses making E-commerce supplies into the EU are required to register for VAT in one member state. This can be an electronic registration and returns can be rendered electronically, but VAT has to be accounted for at the rate applicable in each member state that supplies have been made in. This allows output tax only to be accounted for. Although supplies are being made in the EU any input tax on costs that are incurred in the EU must be claimed through the Thirteenth Directive mechanism.

13.23 VAT cannot be reclaimed on the following items:

- immovable property;
- a supply that is not for the purpose of the business;
- the part of a supply that is used for non-business or exempt purposes;
- supplies that the taxable person intends to use for a supply in the member state where the claim is being made;
- a supply that has been exported or is intended to be exported; and
- supplies that relate to Tour Operator Margin Scheme costs.

13.24 Each member state also has its own list of non-deductible items that apply to taxable persons established in its own territory as well as to persons in making Thirteenth Directive reclaims (see the sections below).

13.25 Member states may require the appointment of a tax representative. Each member state will determine their own arrangements for submitting claims, the time limits for claims, and the periods that these claims will cover and arrangements for refunds. These may differ from the conditions for Eighth Directive reclaims. For instance, in the UK the claim period is the 12 months ending 30 June each year, instead of the claim period being the calendar year as it is for the Eighth Directive. Claims in relation to the year ending 30 June must be made by 31 December of that year.

Claiming refunds in member states

13.26 The following outlines the rules regarding making claims in each of the member states and some other information useful to making Eighth or Thirteenth

Directive claims (for instance the format of VAT numbers so that proper invoices can be obtained). The information provided here is for the purposes of recovering VAT using the Eighth or Thirteenth Directive. Clearly it is limited in its scope and details are subject to change. For instance, there are many other addresses that may be required when dealing with any tax authority (such as for registration). Also, the non-deductible items listed cover items that may be purchased by most non-resident taxable persons, but there are certain other exclusions. For instance, VAT cannot be reclaimed when it relates to an exempt activity, but this is not listed as a separate item in each member state's details below. Also, specific details for intra-community trade invoices are not given as they are not required for the purpose of this chapter. Furthermore, whilst the Invoicing Directive is supposed to harmonise invoicing requirements, many member states still maintain local variations.

Austria

13.27

What is VAT called?

Mehrwertsteuer (Mwst). Umstatzsteuer (Umst)

Country code

AT

VAT registration numbers

(Umsatzsteuer – Identifikationsnummer)

U followed by 8 digits in one block (U12345678)

Contact details for information regarding the local VAT system

Bundesministerium fur Finanzen
Abteilung IV/9
Himmelpfortgasse 4–8
A – 1010 Vienna
Tel: (+43) 1 514 33/1561
Fax: (+43) 1 513 98 61
e-mail: PostIV/9@bmf.gv.at
web: www.bmf.gv.at
VAT Rules web: www.rdb.at

Tax representative details for non-EU claimants

Only where the taxable person is established in a non-EU State that has no mutual assistance agreement.

Contact details for Eighth Directive reclaims (and overseas businesses registrations)

Finanzamt Gradz Stadt
Referat fur auslandische Unternehmer
Conrad von HotzendorfstraBe 14–18
8018 Graz
Tel: (+43) 316 8810
Fax: (+43) 316 81 04 08
e-mail: post.068.fastmk@bmf.gv.at

Invoice details

There are no specific exemptions to invoicing and simplified invoices can be issued where the amount is less than €150.

Taxable persons are required to issue invoices if they carry out transactions with other taxable persons and they are requested to issue the invoice. VAT must be indicated separately on the invoice.

Electronic invoicing is not allowed.

Minimum claim

€36 in one year

€360 for part of a year

Non-deductible input tax

Vehicles, car hire, petrol, entertainment.

Belgium

13.28

What is VAT called?

French: Taxe sur la Valeur Ajoutée (TVA)

Flemish: Belasting over de Toegevoegde Waarde (BTW)

Country code

BE

VAT registration number

(le numero d'identification a la taxe sur la valeur ajoutée)

(BTW – identificatienummer)

Nine digits in one block (123456789)

Contact details for information regarding the local VAT system

Bureau central de TVA pour assussujettis étrangers (French)
Tour Sablon – 24th etage
Rue Stevens, 7
B – 1000 Brussels

Central BTW kantoor voor buitenlandse belasting-plichtigen (Flemish)
Terruggaven, Zaveltoren – 24ste verdieping
Stevensstraat, 7
1000 Brussel
Tel: (+32) 2 552 59 33 4
Fax: (+32) 2 552 55 41
web: minfin.fgov.be

Central tax authorities
Adminstration de la fiscalité des entreprises et des revenues
Tour Finances
Bd du Jardin Botanique No 50
Bte 61
B – 1010 Brussels
Tel: (+32) 2 210 29 11
Fax: (+32) 2 210 26 35

Tax representative details for non-EU claimants

Tax representatives are required before effecting any transactions in Belgium, other than where the VAT is accounted for under a reverse charge.

Contact details for Eighth Directive reclaims

Bureau central de TVA pour assussujettis étrangers
Remboursement
Tour Sablon – 25th etage
Rue Stevens, 7
B – 1000 Brussels

Central BTW kantoor voor buitenlandse belasting-plichtigen
Terruggaven, Zaveltoren – 25ste verdieping
Stevensstraat, 7
1000 Brussel
Tel: (+32) 2 552 59 77
Fax: (+32) 2 552 55 42

Invoice details

Taxable persons are required to issue invoices.

The invoice must be issued no later than the fifth working day of the month following that in which the VAT becomes payable.

The invoice must contain the following details:

- date of issue
- sales journal serial number
- taxable person's name, address, trade register number and VAT registration number
- name and address of recipient of the supply
- date of supply
- details to identify the transaction
- value, VAT at each rate and total VAT due
- legal provisions exempting the transaction from VAT
- reference to any previous invoices.

Invoices do not need to be issued to private individuals where the supply is intended for private use, other than for the supply of motor vehicles, yachts, aircraft, buildings, construction work, HP and leasing, goods that are usually supplied for business use, supplies by producers and wholesalers, supplies of parts and accessories where the VAT inclusive price exceeds €125, removal and storage of furniture, and supplies of gold.

Electronic invoicing is permitted on application to the Finance Ministry. Print outs of the invoices are not required other than for inspections.

Minimum claim

€25 in any one year

€200 for part of a year

Non-deductible input tax

Tobaccos, spirits, accommodation, meals and beverages under a catering or accommodation contract, entertainment costs. Maximum of 50% deduction for motor vehicles for passenger transport.

Denmark

13.29

What is VAT called?

Omsaetningafgift

Country code

DK

VAT registration numbers

(momsregistreringsnummer)

Eight digits in one block (12345678)

Contact details for information regarding the local VAT system

Told-og Skatteregion Sonderborg
Hilmar Finsens Gade 18
DK – 6400 Sonderborg
Tel: (+45) 74 12 73 00
Fax: (+45) 74 42 28 09
Email: soenderborg@toldskat.dk
Web: www.toldskat.dk (A VAT Guide for Foreign Enterprises is available on this site in English, Danish and French.)

Tax representative details for non-EU claimants

Only where the taxable person is resident in a country outside the EU that does not have a mutual assistance treaty with Denmark.

Contact details for Eighth Directive Reclaims

Told-og Skatteregion Sonderborg
Hilmar Finsens Gade 18
DK – 6400 Sonderborg
Tel: (+45) 74 12 73 00
Fax: (+45) 74 42 28 09
Email:soenderborg@toldskat.dk

Invoice details

An invoice is to be issued for each supply made at the time of the supply or immediately afterwards. Receipts can on occasion be substituted for invoices. Invoices, receipts and credit notes must be numbered in sequence. Each invoice must contain:

- date of issue
- seller's name, address, and VAT registration number
- purchaser's name and address
- nature of goods or services, the quantity and price
- VAT amount.

Invoices are not required for sales to private persons. Retailers and other persons normally supplying private consumers only need to issue an invoice when requested.

Electronic invoicing is permitted. Hard copies must be produced on request.

Minimum claim

DKr 200 per annum

DKr 1,500 for part of a year

Non-deductible input tax

Certain goods transport vehicles, Food for employees and owners of businesses, accommodation, payments in kind, nurseries, recreations centres, summer cottages for employees, entertainment, gifts, passenger vehicles designed for not more than nine people.

Finland

13.30

What is VAT called?

Arvonlisavero (ALV)

Country code

FI

VAT registration numbers

(arvonlisaverorekisterointinumero)

(Mervardesskatteregistreringsnummer)

(momsregistreringsnummer)

Eight in one block (12345678)

Contact details for information regarding the local VAT system

Uusimaa Regional Tax Office
Corporate Tax Office
Opastinsilta 12
PO Box 30
00052 VEROTUS
Tel: (+35) 8 20 466017
Fax: (+35) 8 9 73114392
Web: www.vero.fi
Finnish VAT Act and Regulations: www.finlex.fi
VAT Act in English: www.finlex.fi/pdf/saadkaan/E9931501.PDF

Tax representative details for non-EU claimants

A tax representative is required if VAT liable sales are to be made in Finland.

Contact details for Eighth Directive Reclaims and Registration of Overseas Businesses

Uudenmaan verovirasto (8th and 13th Directive Reclaims)
Yritsverotoimisto
PL 34
00521 Verotus
Tel:(+35) 8 973 114311
Fax:(+35) 8 0973 114392

Uusimaa Regional Tax Office (VAT Registration)
Corporate Tax Office
Opastinsilta 12
PO Box 30
00052 Verotus
Tel:(+35) 8 20 466017
Fax:(+35) 8 9 73114700
Web address for registration forms: www.ytj.fi

Invoice details

Taxable persons are required to issue invoices when making a supply to a taxable person or a non-taxable legal person. Invoices must contain:

- date
- serial number
- VAT registration number
- business identity code
- name and address of customer
- name and address of supplier
- description of the supply
- exclusive consideration
- amount of VAT for each VAT rate
- exempt supplies and reference to the exemption.

For cash transactions to consumers receipts can be issued instead of invoices.

Electronic invoicing is permitted.

Minimum claim

€25 in any one year

€200 for part of a year

Non-deductible input tax

Residential property, leisure facilities, kindergartens and related services, some public transport, entertainment, cars (including hire), motorcycles, light aircraft, vehicle fuel and repairs and all related supplies.

France

13.31

What is VAT called?

Taxe sur la Valeur Ajoutée (TVA)

Country code

FR

VAT registration numbers

(le numéro d'identification a la taxe sur la valeur ajoutée)

11 characters – all numbers, though Government and local authority Departments use some alpha characters for the first, second or first and second character.

Contact details for information regarding the local VAT system

Direction Genérale des Impots
Department de la Bercy
F-75012 Paris
Tel: (+33) 1 53 18 11 34
Web: www.impots.gouv.fr (Recent Tax Measures)
Web: www.finances.gouv.fr (Ministry of Finance)
Web: www.impots.gouv.fr (Taxation (English, French and German))

Tax representative details for non-EU claimants

A Tax Representative is required if VAT payments are due from a person not established or domiciled in the EU.

Contact details for Eighth Directive Reclaims and Registration of Overseas Persons

Direction Genérale des Impots des non-residents (8th and 13th Directive)
Service de remboursements de la TVA aux assujettis establis d l'étranger
Centre des Non-Residents
10 Rue D'Uzes
75080 Paris Cedex 02
Tel: (+33) 1 44 82 25 40
Fax: (+33) 1 40 41 05 36
E-mail: cinr@dresg.net

Direction Genérale des Impots des non-residents (Registration & Info)
Inspection TVA
9 Rue D'Uzes
TSA 39203
75094 Paris Cedex 02
Tel: (+33) 1 44 76 19 07 (or 08 or 09)
Fax: (+33) 1 44 76 19 43
E-mail: cinr@dresg.net

Invoice details

All taxable persons must issue an invoice, including those engaged on an occasional basis. The invoice is normally to be issued immediately the supply is made and the purchaser can demand an invoice. Each invoice must contain:

- name and address of the supplier
- name and address of the customer
- date of supply
- quantity and description of the supply
- unit price
- VAT exclusive total
- VAT amount for each rate of VAT
- VAT number of supplier.

Invoices are required to be issued in French, but certain invoices can be issued in another language where a certified translation is provided.

Electronic invoicing is permitted where the information sent and received is identical and hard copies can be produced and the system of transmission meets the standards set by the Minister for the Budget.

Minimum claim

€25 in any one year

€200 for part of a year

Non-deductible input tax

Accommodation, hotels, restaurants, vehicles, transport, gifts, petrol, 20% of VAT incurred on diesel fuel, 50% of VAT incurred on petroleum gas.

Germany

13.32

What is VAT called?

Mehrwertsteuer (Mwst)

Umstatzsteuer (Umst)

Country code

DE

VAT registration numbers

(Umsatzsteuer – Identifikationsnummer)

Nine digits (123456789)

Contact details for information regarding the local VAT system

Bunderesministerium der Finanzen
Referat Presse und Information
11016 Berlin
Fax: (+49) 30 22 42 – 32 60
Web: www.bundesfinanzministerium.de (General information on VAT Rules)
Web: www.bff-online.de (more detailed information, office addresses and forms)

Persons not established in the EU must register at:

Berlin Finanzamt Neukolln-Nord
Sonnenallee 223
12059 Berlin

Tax representative details for non-EU claimants

Use of a Tax Representative is not compulsory and is used only where a person represented in Germany effects non-taxable transactions and cannot deduct input tax.

Contact details for Eighth Directive Reclaims

Bundesamt fur Finanzen
Friedhofstrasse 1
53225 Bonn
Tel: (+49) 228 406 403
Fax: (+49) 228 406 2661

Invoice details

Any taxpayer is entitled to issue an invoice for supplies of goods or services.

An invoice is to contain the following:

- name and address of the supplier
- name and address of the recipient
- quantity and description of the goods or services
- date of supply
- consideration
- VAT payable.

Invoices issued after 30 June 2002 must detail the tax number assigned to the supplier. Invoices for reverse charge transactions must indicate this on the invoice. There is no rule requiring the invoice to be issued within a time period. Invoices do not have to be issued to non-taxable recipients. There are no simplification rules for invoices. Electronic invoices are permitted. This must contain an electronic signature.

Minimum claim

Taxable persons resident in the EU

€25 in any one year

€200 for part of a year

Taxable persons resident outside the EU

€250 in any one year

€500 for part of a year

Non-deductible input tax

Food and accommodation costs. Private household expenses, staff travel costs in staff vehicles, subsistence, private residence removal expenses. 50% of the input tax relating to the purchase, manufacture, hire or operation of vehicles used for private or other non-business purposes. Entertainment costs that are non-deductible for income tax purposes, which means that usually 80% of the VAT is non-recoverable. Full details of the expenditure must be provided to prevent full disallowance.

Greece

13.33

What is VAT called?

Arithmos Forologikou Mitroou (FPA)

Country code

EL

VAT registration numbers

(Arithmos Forologikou Mitroou (FPA))

Nine digits, commencing with a zero (012345678)

Contact details for information regarding the local VAT system

Ministry of Economic Affairs and Finance
Director-General for Taxation
Directorate 14 – VAT
Sina 2–4
10672 Athens
Tel: (+30210) 3647203 – 5
Fax: (+30210) 364413
e-mail: elvies@otenet.gr
web: www.gsis.gov.gr (details of Local Tax offices (DOYs) can be obtained at this site).

Tax representative details for non-EU claimants

Persons not established in Greece must appoint a tax representative if they are taxable persons not established in the EU or appoint a tax agent if they are taxable persons established in a member state of the EU.

A tax representative must be appointed where there is a supply of goods or services, import of goods or intra community acquisitions effected for consideration on Greek territory by a taxable persons established outside the EU.

Invoice details

An invoice is to contain the following:

- name, profession and address of the supplier
- identification of the recipient
- quantity and description of the goods or services
- date of issue
- consideration broken down by VAT rate
- any deductions
- serial number of any consignment notes
- tax number of supplier and the local tax office.

Invoices are not required for a number of asset sales, utilities, postal services, banking or where goods are sold to final consumers for a value of less than €50. A retail receipt instead of an invoice can be issued to final consumers.

Electronic invoicing is not prohibited, but pointless as a paper version is also required. It is expected that electronic invoicing will be permitted from 1 January 2004.

Contact details for Eighth Directive reclaims

Ministry of Economic Affairs and Finance
Director-General for Taxation
Directorate 14 – VAT
Sina 2–4
10672 Athens
Tel: (+30210) 3647203 – 5
Fax: (+30210) 364413

Minimum claim

€25 in any one year

€200 for part of a year

Non-deductible input tax

Tobacco, alcohol, entertainment, hospitality, accommodation, meals, beverages, transport and recreation of staff and taxable persons, private cars and other vehicles.

Ireland

13.34

What is VAT called?

Value Added Tax (VAT)

Country code

IE

VAT registration numbers

(Value Added Tax Identification Number)

Eight characters including one or two alpha numbers as the last or last and second character (1234567A or 1A34567B)

Contact details for information regarding the local VAT system

VAT Interpretation Branch
Office of the Revenue Commissioners
Stamping Building
Dublin Castle
Dublin 2
Tel: (+353) 1 647 5000
Fax: (+353) 1 679 5236
Email: vat@revenue.ie
Web: www.revenue.ie

Tax representative details for non-EU claimants

Not required

Contact details for Eighth Directive Reclaims

The Revenue Commissioners
VAT Repayment Section
Government Buildings
Ennis
County Clare
Tel: (+353) 65 412 00
Fax: (+353) 65 403 94

Invoice details

Invoices must be issued when supplies are made to taxable persons. These must contain:

- name and address of the supplier
- supplier's VAT registration number
- name and address of recipient
- date of issue
- date of supply
- full description of the supply
- quantity of supply
- VAT exclusive value
- rate (including zero-rate) and amount of VAT at each rate.

Invoices are not required to be issued to non-taxable persons unless they request an invoice in writing.

Invoices can be issued electronically where the integrity of the system is guaranteed. Details can be found on the Revenue's website.

Minimum claim

€25 in any one year

€200 for part of a year

Non-deductible input tax

Food, drink, accommodation, personal services for the taxable person, agents or employees, entertainment, purchase, lease or hire of passenger vehicles, petrol, work on goods that are non-deductible where such goods are handed over as part of the contract.

Italy

13.35

What is VAT called?

Imposta sur Valore Aggiunto (IVA)

Country code

IT

VAT registration numbers

(il numero di registrazione IVA)

Eleven digits (12345678901)

Contact details for information regarding the local VAT system

Ministero delle Finanze
Segretariato Generale
Ufficio Relazioni Internazionali
Viale dell' Aeronautica, 122
00144 Roma
Tel: (+39) 6 592 5967 or 6 543 94256
Fax: (+39) 6 591 2983
Web: www.finanze.it

Tax representative details for non-EU claimants

A representative may be appointed in order to meet Italian VAT obligations. There is a requirement to register the representative and is the subject of a record authenticated by a notary. The representative has the same rights and obligations as the person he represents.

Contact details for Eighth Directive Reclaims
Ufficio Entrate di Roma 6
Via Canton n.20
001144 Roma
Tel: (+39) 6 5207 4217
Fax: (+39) 6 520 3907

Invoice details

Taxable persons are required to issue invoices for each supply made at the time of supply or upon payment. The following information must be provided:

- date
- consecutive serial number
- name and address of the supplier
- VAT identification number
- quantity, type and description of the supply

- unit price
- tax exclusive total
- VAT charged at each separate rate.

Unless requested to do so, invoices do not need to be issued by retailers where they have given the VAT office prior notice, for supplies through vending machines, supplies by mail or to homes or supplies made by itinerant taxable persons, supplies by hotels, passenger transport supplies, finance services, or exempt transactions.

Minimum claim

€ 25 per annum

€ 200 for part of a year

Non-deductible input tax

Hotel accommodation, food, drink, travel expenses, motor vehicles and other transport vehicles, petrol, diesel, luxury goods such as furs and oriental carpets.

Luxembourg

13.36

What is VAT called?

Taxe sur la Valeur Ajoutée (TVA)

Country code

LU

VAT registration numbers

(le numéro d'identification a la taxe sur la valeur ajoutée)

Eight digits (12345678)

Contact details for information regarding the local VAT system

Bureau d'imposition X de l'Adminstration de l'Enregistrement et des Domaines
7, Rue Plebiscite
Boite postale 31
L – 2010 Luxembourg – Ville
Tel: (+352) 44905 – 1
Fax: (+352) 29 11 93
Web: http://saturn.etat.lu/etva/index.do (VAT forms) in French and German
Web: http://www.etat.lu/memorial (Legislation)

A consolidated version of the law at 12 February 1979 is available at

Editions de l'imprimerie St-Paul, Luxembourg
2, rue Christophe Plantin
L – 2988 Luxembourg
Tel: (+352) 49 93 1

Tax representative details for non-EU claimants

Not required

Contact details for Eighth Directive Reclaims

Adminstration de l'Enregistrement et des Domaines
Bureau d'Imposition XI
17 Ave Guillaume
BP 31
2010 Luxembourg
Tel: (+352) 44 905 455
Fax: (+352) 25 07 96

Note, although the official languages of Luxembourg are French, German and Luxembourgish, the forms must be completed in French.

Invoice details

Invoices must be issued when supplies are made to taxable persons. It must be issued by the 15th day of the month following that in which the supply was made. The invoice must show:

- date of issue
- name and address of the supplier
- name and address of recipient
- date of supply
- quantity and description of the supply

- price exclusive of VAT
- VAT rate and VAT amount (at each rate)
- reasons why VAT is not chargeable if appropriate.

An invoice can be either German or French.

Less detailed invoices can be issued where the invoiced amount is €50 or less, showing the following information:

- name and address of the supplier
- description of the supply
- price including VAT
- rate of VAT.

Invoices do not need to be issued to non-taxable persons.

Minimum claim

€ 25 per annum

€ 200 for part of a year

Non-deductible input tax

VAT incurred on items that are not of a strictly 'professional' nature, such as entertainment or recreation is non-deductible.

Netherlands

13.37

What is VAT called?

Omzebelasting (OB)

Belasting over de Toegevoegde Waarde (BTW)

Country code

NL

VAT registration numbers

(BTW – identifcatienummer)

Nine Digits and three characters in the range B01-B99 (1213456789B99)

Contact details for information regarding the local VAT system

Belastingdienst Particulieren/Ondernemingen Buitenland
Postbus 2865
NL – 6401 DJ Heerlen
Tel: (+31) 45 573 6666
Fax: (+31) 45 573 6684
Web: www.belastingdienst.nl

Tax representative details for non-EU claimants

Only required for distance selling or warehouse arrangements.

Contact details for Eighth Directive Reclaims

Belastingdienst Particulieren/Ondernemingen Buitenland
Postbus 2865
NL – 6401 DJ Heerlen
Tel: (+31) 45 573 6666
Fax: (+31) 45 573 6684

Invoice details

An invoice must be issued by the 15th day following the month of supply, or where there is a payment on account, before the payment takes place. The following details must be included:

- serial number
- VAT Number
- date
- date of supply
- name and address of the supplier
- name and address of the customer
- description of the supply
- quantity supplied
- consideration
- turnover tax payable.

Invoices do not need to be issued by small undertakings. In addition suppliers of public passenger transport and food and accommodation in hotels and restaurants do not need to issue invoices.

Minimum claim

€25 in any one year

€200 for part of a year

Non-deductible input tax

Food and drink supplied by hotels and restaurants, luxuries, amusements entertainments, gifts to persons that cannot deduct input tax, supplies to staff of housing, goods in kind, sport, recreational facilities, transport and other private consumption items.

Portugal

13.38

What is VAT called?

Imposto sobre o Valor Acrecentado (IVA)

Country code

PT

VAT registration numbers

(o numero de identificacao para efeitos do imposto sobre o valor acrescentado)

Nine digits (123456789)

Contact details for information regarding the local VAT system

Direccao-General Dos Impostos
Direccao De Servicos Do IVA
Avenida Joao XXI, 76
1049–065 Lisbon
Tel: (+351) 21 761 0000 (Switchboard)
Tel: (+351) 21 761 0337 (Direct)
Tel: (+351) 21 761 0338 (Direct)
Fax: (+351) 21 793 6508
e-mail: dsiva@dgci.min-financas.pt
web: www.dgci.min-financas.pt

Tax representative details for non-EU claimants

Tax representatives must be appointed by non-resident taxable persons. The tax representative must be a taxable person in Portugal.

Contact details for Eighth Directive Reclaims

Direccao-General Das Contribuicoes e Impostos
Direccao De Servicos de Reembolsos Do IVA
Avenida Joao XXI
Apartado 8220
1802 Lisbon Codex
Tel: (+351) 1 795 0102
Fax: (+351) 1 793 81 13

Invoice details

Invoices must be issued to taxable persons and exempt persons. Invoices must be issued for distance selling transactions. It must be issued no later than the fifth working day following that on which VAT is payable (or the 15th day following the month end for distance selling transactions). An invoice must contain:

- name and address of the supplier
- VAT identification number of the supplier
- name and address of the customer
- VAT Identification number of the customer
- quantity and description of the goods or services
- exclusive amount
- rates and tax payable
- reason if VAT is not charged.

Invoices do not need to be issued by retailers making supplies to private individuals.

Electronic invoicing is permitted, but authorisation must be obtained from the Director-General for Taxation

Minimum claim

€19–95 in any one year

€159–62 for part of a year

Non-deductible input tax

VAT cannot be reclaimed on vehicles (including coaches, motorcycles and aircraft), petrol, transport and travel of the taxable person and staff, accommodation, food and drink, leisure and luxury goods, 50% of the VAT incurred on diesel, LPG and gas, except where it is used in heavy passenger vehicles, public transport vehicles, road haulage vehicles and tractors, when all input tax incurred can be claimed.

Spain

13.39

What is VAT called?

Impuesto sobre el Valor Anadido (IVA)

Country code

ES

VAT registration numbers

(el numero de identificacion a efectos del Impuesto sobre el Valor Anadido)

Nine characters, with alpha characters either first, last, or first and last (X12345678, or X1234567Z, or 12345678Z)

Contact details for information regarding the local VAT system

General information

Subdireccion General de Informacion y Asistencia Tributaria del Departmento de Gestion de la Agencia Esatal de Adminstracion Tributaria
C/ Infanta Mercedes, 37
E – 28071 Madrid
Tel: (+34) 1 583 89 76

Detailed information

Subdireccion General de Impuestos sobre el Consumo. Direcccion General de Tributos
C/ Alcala, 5
E – 28014 Madrid
Web: www.aeat.es

Tax representative details for non-EU claimants

Required where a person is established in a country that does not have a mutual assistance treaty with Spain.

Contact details for Eighth Directive Reclaims

Delegacion Especial de Madrid de la Agencia Estatal de Adminstracion Tributaria
Dependencia Regional de Gestion
Seccion de Regimenes Especiales
C/ Guzman el Bueno, 139, Planta 1a
28071 Madrid
Tel: (+34) 1 582 67 39
Fax: (+34) 1 582 67 57

Invoice details

With the exceptions noted below, an invoice must be issued for all transactions and must be supplied within 30 days of the transaction. Each invoice should contain:

- consecutive numbering
- name and address of supplier
- tax registration number of the supplier
- name and address of the recipient
- tax registration number of the recipient
- if the recipient is a natural person, the person's identity card number
- date and place of issue

Invoices do not need to be issued for tolls, activities relating to the simplified VAT scheme, transactions authorised by tax authorities. Transactions by non-taxable persons for amounts of less than €90 may omit the particulars of the recipient. Suppliers of passenger transport, accommodation, catering services, parking, retail, entertainment, and telephone services may issue less detailed invoices.

Minimum claim

€25–34 in any one year

€201–34 for part of a year

Non-deductible input tax

Accommodation, meals, travel expenses, entertainment, car hire and fuel.

Sweden

13.40

What is VAT called?

Merardeskatt (MOMS)

Country code

SE

VAT registration numbers

(Mervardesskatteregistreringsnummer) (momsregistreringsnummer)

Twelve digits (123456789012)

Contact details for information regarding the local VAT system

Skattemyndigheten I Stockholms Ian
Skattekontor Riks
S-106 61 Stockholm
Tel: (+46) 8 694 1000
Fax: (+46) 8 642 9261
e-mail: skm@skm01.rsv.se
web: www.rsv.se

VAT Legislation available on these web site
www.riksdagen.se
www.notisum.se
http://www.lagrummet.gov.se

Tax representative details for non-EU claimants

Tax representatives are required where a taxable person is established in a country without a mutual assistance agreement with Sweden.

Contact details for Eighth Directive Reclaims
Sarskilda Skattekontoret
77183 Ludvika
Tel: (+46) 240 870 00
Fax: (+46) 240 103 40

Invoice details

An invoice should be issued for each supply and for prepayments. The invoice should contain the following details:

- amount payable
- VAT amount
- name and address of supplier (or other identifying information)
- name and address of the customer (or other identifying information)
- description of the transaction
- place the goods are received
- VAT registration number of the supplier.

Where the usual procedure is to round to the nearest Krona, VAT can be rounded to the nearest Krona.

On line and electronic invoicing is allowed in Sweden.

Minimum claim

SEK 250 in any one year

SEK 2,000 for part of a year

Non-deductible input tax

Entertainment and transport (unless exclusively for the business). 50% of the VAT can be reclaimed in car hire, unless exclusively for the business.

United Kingdom

13.41

What is VAT called?

Value Added Tax (VAT)

Country code

GB

VAT registration numbers

(Value Added Tax (VAT) registration number)

Nine digits (123456789)

Contact details for information regarding the local VAT system

Customs and Excise
Aberdeen Non-Established Taxable Persons Unit (NETPU)
Custom House
28 Guild Street
Aberdeen
AB9 2DY
Tel: (+44) 1224 844 653/4/5
Fax: (+44) 1224 844 611
e-mail: Ian.Davidson@hmce.gov.uk
Donna.Webster@hmce.gov.uk
Web: www.hmce.gov.uk
www.legislation.hmso.gov.uk

Tax representative details for non-EU claimants

Not obligatory

Contact details for Eighth Directive Reclaims

Customs and Excise
VAT Overseas Repayment Unit
Custom House
PO Box 34
Londonderry
BT48 7AE
Tel: (+44) 2871 372 600
Fax: (+44) 2871 372 520

Invoice details

VAT invoices are to be issued by taxable persons in the UK for taxable supplies in the UK or to persons in another member state within 30 days of the time of supply. The following details must be included on the invoice:

- identifying number
- time of supply
- date of issue
- name and address of supplier

- VAT number of the supplier
- name and address of the customer
- type of supply
- description of the supply
- rate of discount
- rate and amount of VAT
- total chargeable.

Less detailed tax invoices where the supply is less than £250 (€375) including VAT where issued by a retailer. This should show:

- name and address of the supplier
- VAT registration number or the supplier
- description of the supply
- total payable including VAT
- for each VAT rate, the total payable including VAT and the VAT rate.

Invoices do not need to be issued in relation to any supply:

(i) from a coin-operated machine;

(ii) a zero-rated supply to a customer in the UK; and

(iii) a supply to a person in the UK who is neither registered nor liable to be registered for VAT.

Electronic invoicing is permitted where Customs and Excise's audit trail requirements and authentication requirements are met.

Minimum claim

£16 in any one year

£130 for part of a year

Non-deductible input tax

VAT cannot be reclaimed on non-business purchases, cars, entertainment, goods installed in new dwellings and similar buildings, assets sold under the second-hand scheme. Only 50% of the VAT incurred on leased cars can be reclaimed. All VAT can be reclaimed on car purchases and hire where it is intended to be used exclusively for the business.

The information in following sections of this chapter was partly obtained from the European Commission document 'Application in the Member states, Facts for use by Administrations/Traders Information Networks etc'.

Minimum claims

13.42 There is no maximum amount that can be claimed. The following amounts are the minimum amounts that can be claimed. The figure for the whole year is a lower amount. Claims for part of a year (unless it is for the period at the year end) is a higher figure to ease administrative burdens on the taxation authority.

Country	Minimum claim per year	Minimum claim per quarter or period of less than a year
Austria	€36	€360
Belgium	€25	€200
Denmark	DKK200	DKK1,500
Finland	€25	€200
France	€25	€200
Germany *	€25	€200
Greece	€25	€200
Ireland	€25	€200
Italy	€25	€200
Luxembourg	€25	€200
Netherlands	€25	€200
Portugal	€19–95	€159–62
Spain	€25–34	€201–34
Sweden	SEK 250	SEK2,000
UK	£16	£130

Note, claims in Germany by non-EU resident taxable persons are a minimum of €250 for a claim for a year and €500 for claims for a part of a year.

VAT rates

13.43

Member state	Super reduced rate	Reduced rate	Standard rate	Parking rate
Austria	–	10	20	12
Belgium	–	6	21	12
Denmark	–	–	25	–
Finland	–	8 & 17	22	–
France	2.1	5.5	19.6	
Germany	–	7	16	–
Greece	4	8	18	–
Ireland	4.3	13.5	21	13.5
Italy	4	10	20	–
Luxem-bourg	3	6	15	12
Netherlands	–	6	19	–
Portugal	–	5 & 12	19	–
Spain	4	7	16	–
Sweden	–	6 & 12	25	–
UK	–	5	17.5	–

Note, several countries also have a zero-rate (exemption with credit).

VAT rates of commonly purchased items

13.44

Category	BE	DK	DE	EL	ES	FR	IE	IT	LU	NL	AT	PT	FI	SE	GB
Foodstuffs *ex = exemption*	6 12 21	25	7 16	8	4 7	5.5 19.6	0 4.3 13.5	4 10	3	6	10	5 12 19	17	12 25	0 17.5
Passenger transport	6 0 ex	ex 0	7 16	8	7	5.5	ex	10 ex	ex 3	ex 6 19	10	5	8	6 0	0
Books	6 21	25	7	4	4 16	5.5 19.6	0	4 20	3	6	10	5	8	6	0
Newspapers	6 6 21	0 25	7	4	4 16	2.1 19.6	13.5	4	3	3	10	5	0 22	6	0
Periodicals	0 6 21	25	7	4	4 16	2.1 19.6	13.5	4 20	3	6	10	5	0 22	ex 6	0
Hotel accommodation	6 ex	25	16	8	7	5.5	13.5	10	3	6	10	5	8	12	17.5
Sporting events	6 ex	25 ex	7 16	8	7 16	19.6	ex	10 20	3 ex	6	20	5	8 ex	6 ex	17.5
Cinema, theatre & cultural admissions	6 ex	25	Ex 7	4	7 ex	5.5 19.6	ex 13.5	10	3	6	ex 10	ex 5	8	6	17.5
Alcohol	21	25	16	18	16	19.6	21	20	15 12	19	20 12	19 12	22	25	17.5

Soft drinks	2	25	16	8	7	5.5	21	20	3	6	20	12 5	17	12	17.5
Road fuel	21	25	16	18	16	19.6	21	20	12	19	20	19 12	22	25	17.5
Restaurants	21	25	16	8	7	19.6	13.5	10	3	6	10	12	22	25	17.5

Country codes

13.45

Country	Country Code
Austria	AT
Belgium	BE
Denmark	DK
Finland	FI
France	FR
Germany	DE
Greece	EL
Ireland	IE
Italy	IT
Luxembourg	LU
Netherlands	NL
Portugal	PT
Spain	ES
Sweden	SE
UK	GB

Non-Deductible Items

13.46

Member state	Entertain-ments	Car hire	Petrol	Hotel ac-com	Restau-rant	Passen-ger trans-port
Austria	X	X	X			
Belgium	X	50%		X	X	
Denmark	X	X		X		
Finland	X	X	X			
France	X		X	X	X	X
Germany	80%	X		X	X	
Greece	X	X	X	X	X	
Ireland	X	X	X	X	X	
Italy	X	X	X	X	X	
Luxem-bourg	X					
Nether-lands	X	X	X		X	X
Portugal	X	X	X		X	
Spain	X	X	X	X	X	X
Sweden	X	50%				
UK	X	*				

X = Non-deductible

% shows percentage non-deductible

* Deductible, unless long-term hire when 50% deductible

Geographical features in respect of VAT

Denmark

13.47 The Faeroe Islands and Greenland are not part of the EU.

Germany

13.48 Heligoland and Busingen are not part of Germany for VAT purposes.

Greece

13.49 In Lesbos, Chios, Samos, the Dodecanese, the Cyclades, Thassos, Northern Sporades, Samothrace and Skiros the rates of 4%, 8% and 18% have been reduced by 30% to 3%, 6% and 13%. These preferential rates do not apply to tobacco products or means of transport.

Mount Athos is excluded from the scope of VAT.

Spain

13.50 The Canary Islands, Ceuta and Melilla are not part of Spain for VAT purposes.

France

13.51 Special rates apply in certain territories:

Corsica	0.90%	applies to some theatrical shows, sales of live meat and charcutere animals supplied to persons not liable to pay tax
	2.1%	applies to goods supplied in Corsica to which reduced rates apply in France
	8%	certain work on immovable property, agricultural equipment, sales for consumption on the premises, sales of low voltage electricity
	13%	petroleum products
Overseas departments		A reduced rate of 2.1% applies and a standard rate of 8.5%
Monaco		Treated as supplied in, to or from France

Italy

13.52 Livigno, Campione d'Italia and the territorial waters of Lake Lugano are excluded from the scope of VAT.

Austria

13.53 16% VAT rate applies in Jungholz and Mittelberg.

Portugal

13.54 Special rates apply in the Azores and Madeira:

4% Reduced rate

8% Parking rate

13% Standard Rate

Finland

13.55 Aaland is not part of the European Union.

United Kingdom

13.56 Supplies made to or from the Isle of Man are treated as having been made to or from the UK. The Isle of Man has some differing VAT rates. Certain hotel accommodation is subject to a reduced rate of VAT.

The Channel Islands are not part of the EU for VAT purposes.

Selected case summaries

1. Verbond van Nederlandse Ondernemingen v Inspecteur der Invoerrechten en Accijnzen

ECJ Case 51/76; [1977] ECR 113; [1977] 1 CMLR 413

Definition of 'capital goods'.

Facts

In a Dutch case, the appellant (V) had bought a printer and reply cards. The Dutch legislation adopted a derogation in the Second Directive allowing capital goods to be excluded from the VAT deduction system but the Dutch legislation excluded all business assets from deduction. V claimed that 'business assets' was a wider expression than 'capital goods' and that the Dutch legislation thus purported to exclude more than was authorised by art 17 of the Second Directive.

Issue

What is the meaning of 'capital goods'?

Decision

The ECJ defined 'capital goods' as 'goods used for the purposes of some business activity and distinguishable by their durable nature and their value and such that the acquisition costs are not normally treated as current expenditure but written off over several years'. However, the ECJ also held that the member states have a certain margin of discretion as regards the requirements which must be satisfied concerning the durability and value of the goods, together with the rules applicable for writing off, provided that they pay due regard to the existence of an essential difference between capital goods and the other goods used in the management and day to day running of undertakings.

Note

The case was argued on the provisions of the Second Directive but the decision is clearly relevant to the Sixth Directive and has been cited in this context in two Tribunal cases involving the Sixth Directive, namely *Trustees of the Mellerstain Trust v Customs and Excise Comrs (1989) VATTR 223* and *Scottish Homes v Customs and Excise Comrs (2000) VAT decision 16644*.

2. Customs and Excise Comrs v Lord Fisher

High Court [1981] STC 238; [1981] 2 All ER 147

Meaning of business.

Facts

A landowner (F), who was registered for VAT, organised the shooting of pheasants on his family estate. Originally, friends and relatives had been invited to shoot on the estate as family guests. F asked those he invited to make specified contributions towards the cost. He did not advertise for guests and only invited family friends and relatives. The contributions usually met about half the cost of the shooting. The Commissioners issued an assessment on the basis that F was making supplies for consideration. F appealed, contending that the running of the shoots did not amount to the carrying on of a business. The Tribunal accepted this contention and allowed F's appeal. The Commissioners appealed.

Issue

Whether pheasant shoots where the participants made contributions towards the cost is a business activity.

Decision

The High Court upheld the Tribunal's decision. The High Court listed six criteria which indicated that an activity is a business. The criteria were that the activity should:

(a) be a serious undertaking earnestly pursued, not necessarily a commercial or profit-making activity;

(b) have a reasonable or recognisable continuity;

(c) have a certain measure of substance, ie value;

(d) be conducted on sound and recognised business principles;

(e) be predominantly concerned with making taxable supplies for a consideration; and

(f) consist of making taxable supplies commonly made by those who seek to profit by them.

The six criteria should not be regarded as exhaustive and none of them is conclusive.

Note

The European Court of Justice has held that criterion (e) is not relevant in deciding whether or not an activity is an economic activity in the terms of art 4 of the Sixth VAT Directive and that the scale of the transaction is also irrelevant (*Wellcome Trust Ltd v Customs and Excise* – see **23**. below).

3. Celtic Football and Athletic Club Ltd v Customs and Excise Comrs

Court of Session [1983] STC 470

Whether VAT on hotel expenses of visiting football club met by host club incurred on 'business entertainment'.

Facts

A Scottish football club (Celtic) took part in the European Cup organised by the Union of European Football Associations, and played teams from Romania and Hungary in successive rounds. Two games were played in each round on a 'home' and 'away' basis, and the rules provided that the home club was to pay the hotel expenses of the visiting club. Celtic reclaimed input tax in respect of the hotel accommodation which it provided in Glasgow for the Romanian and Hungarian teams. The Commissioners issued an assessment to recover the tax, considering that the expenditure constituted 'business entertainment'. Celtic appealed.

Issue

What is meaning of 'entertainment'?

Decision

The Court of Session allowed Celtic's appeal, holding that 'entertainment' should be construed as meaning hospitality free to the recipient. Because of the reciprocal obligations under the competition rules, what the visiting teams enjoyed at Celtic's expenses was not free to them, since they were required to meet Celtic's hotel expenses for the other matches in the round. There was, therefore, no provision of 'business entertainment' within what is now the VAT (Input Tax) Order 1992, art 5.

4. DA Rompelman & EA Rompelman-van-Deelen v Minister van Financiën

ECJ Case 268/83: [1985] ECR 655; [1985] 3 CMLR 202

Whether a taxable person must make taxable supplies prior to being regarded as entitled to deduct input tax.

Facts

In a Dutch case, a couple acquired a future title to two units which were intended to be used as showrooms and which were under construction. They gave notice that the showrooms would be let to taxable persons and that they would opt for the supply to be taxable under the provisions of Dutch law. They applied for a refund of input tax incurred before the premises had been let. The Dutch authorities rejected the claim on the grounds that the couple had not, at that time, made any taxable supplies. The couple appealed, and the case was referred to the ECJ.

Issue

Whether the acquisition of an asset with a view to making supplies in the future is an economic activity within art 4(1) of the Sixth Directive.

Decision

The ECJ ruled that a person undertaking acts preparatory to the carrying on of an economic activity qualified as a 'taxable person' within art 4(1) of the Sixth Directive, and that input tax was recoverable in such circumstances. The purpose of the system whereby input tax could be deducted was to relieve a taxable person entirely of the burden of VAT suffered in the course of his economic activities, which included preparatory acts such as the purchase of immovable property.

5. Whitechapel Art Gallery v Customs and Excise Comrs

High Court [1986] STC 156; [1986] 1 CMLR 79

Apportionment of VAT incurred as between business and non-business activities – whether grants and donations to be included in denominator.

Facts

A registered charity operated an art gallery. It did not charge visitors for admission to the gallery but it received income from selling souvenirs, from organised tours and lectures, from the occasional hire of the gallery, and from charging admission fees to occasional exhibitions. The charity reclaimed the whole of its input tax, and the Commissioners issued an assessment to recover some of the tax, considering that the charity's entitlement to input tax should be restricted to the proportion which its taxable supplies bore to its total supplies, including grants and donations. The charity appealed. The Tribunal allowed the charity's appeal in part, holding that, since only some of the charity's activities constituted a business, the Commissioners were correct to seek an apportionment of the charity's input tax, but that they were not justified in including grants and donations in the computation. The charity appealed to the High Court.

Issue

Whether input tax can be apportioned between business and non-business activities.

Decision

The High Court upheld the Tribunal's decision. Applying the decision of the Court of Appeal in *Apple & Pear Development Council*, input tax was only recoverable if the goods or services were to be used for business purposes. The artistic services which the gallery gave to the public free of charge did not form part of a business activity on which taxable supplies were made. All of its other activities could properly be regarded as a business which it ran in association with its artistic activity. The High Court observed that most, if not all, of the input tax which the gallery claimed to be recoverable might well have been paid in respect of goods or services used or to be used for the purpose of its business.

6. Merseyside Cablevision Ltd v Customs and Excise Comrs

[1987] VATTR 134 (VTD 2419)

Whether activities of a company that intended to provide cable television services were an economic activity notwithstanding that the activity was aborted.

Facts

In 1982 a company (M) was incorporated to carry on the business of supplying cable television in the Merseyside area. It incurred considerable preliminary expenditure and applied to be registered for VAT to enable it to reclaim input tax on this expenditure. Initially, the Commissioners refused to register the company on the grounds that it was not trading. Subsequently M supplied consultancy services to another associated company and renewed its application for registration. It was registered in December 1983, the registration being backdated to May 1982 at its request. In January 1984 it submitted its first VAT return, covering the period from May 1982 to 31 December 1983, and reclaiming more than £33,000 as input tax. In August 1985, the Commissioners formally rejected the claim, ruling that M was not entitled to be registered under the legislation then in force (VATA 1983, Sch 1) and that the registration should be treated as void since M was not making taxable supplies. M appealed.

Issue

Whether tax on supplies intended for use in relation to taxable supplies, which did not take place, was input tax.

Decision

The Tribunal allowed M's appeal against this decision. Applying *Amministrazione delle Finanze dello Stato v Simmenthal SpA*, 'the law of the European Economic Community ... prevails over any contrary provision in national law'. Under art 4 of the Sixth Directive, any person carrying on an economic activity was a 'taxable person'. If goods or services were supplied to him by another taxable person, and he used those goods or services for the purposes of his taxable transactions, he was entitled to deduct the tax he had suffered on the supplies made to him from the tax for which he was accountable on the supplies made by him. Applying *Rompelman v Minister van Financien* (see **4**. above), a person who carried on activities which were preparatory to the carrying on of an economic activity was to be treated as a person carrying on that economic activity. M had had a fixed and continuing intention to operate a cable television service, which qualified it as a 'taxable person' within art 4(1) of the Sixth Directive. The fact that, under the UK legislation then in force, M was not entitled to be registered for VAT, did not alter the fact that, under Community law, it was a taxable person and was entitled to credit for the input tax it had suffered.

Note

The relevant provisions of VATA 1983, Sch 1 were subsequently amended by FA 1988.

7. Apple and Pear Development Council v Customs and Excise Comrs

ECJ Case 102/86; [1988] STC 221; [1988] 2 All ER 922 [1988] ECR 1443; [1988] 2 CMLR 394

Whether there was a direct and immediate link between compulsory charges and services provided.

Facts

The Apple and Pear Development Council was established in 1966 by a statutory instrument, with the principal object of promoting the sale of apples and pears in England and Wales. The Council comprised 14 members, appointed by the Minister for Agriculture, the majority of whom were growers nominated by the National Farmers Union. All commercial growers with two hectares or more and 50 or more trees, had to register with it and pay a compulsory annual charge, based on the area of their land, to meet its expenses. Initially the Commissioners accepted that its activities were business activities, on which it was entitled to reclaim input tax, and that its compulsory charges to growers were outside the scope of VAT. However, in 1981 the Commissioners issued a ruling that its activities did not constitute a business and that it was not entitled to reclaim input tax. The Council appealed to the VAT Tribunal, which allowed the appeal. The ruling of the Tribunal was the subject of successive appeals and finally came before the House of Lords which held that an activity could only constitute a 'business' if it involved the making of taxable supplies for consideration and referred the case to the ECJ.

Issue

Did the activities of the Apple and Pear Development Council and compulsory charges on growers constitute 'the supply of ... services effected for consideration'?

Decision

The ECJ held that, for a supply of services to be for consideration within art 2(1) of the Sixth Directive, there must be a direct link between the service provided and the consideration received. On the evidence, there was no relationship between the level of the benefits which individual growers obtained from the Council's services and the amount of the mandatory charges which they were obliged to pay. Accordingly, the compulsory annual charges did not constitute 'consideration' and the Council was not making supplies of services for consideration.

8. Leesportfeuille 'Intiem' CV v Staatssecretaris van Financiën

ECJ Case 165/86: [1988] ECR 1471; [1989] 2 CMLR 856

Whether VAT on petrol supplied to employees but invoiced to employer deductible by employer.

Facts

In a Dutch case, petrol was supplied to a company's employees, used exclusively for the purposes of the company's business and invoiced to the company. The company reclaimed input tax on the petrol and appealed against the Dutch authorities' refusal to allow the deduction. The Netherlands Supreme Court referred the case to the ECJ for a ruling on whether the fact that the petrol was supplied directly to the employees precluded the deduction by the employer of the VAT paid on the petrol.

Issue

Whether the rule that a taxable person can only deduct VAT due or paid in respect of goods and services supplied to him in the course of his business precludes the deduction of VAT where goods are purchased by the taxable person and, after being supplied to his employees, are used for the taxable person's business purposes.

Decision

The ECJ ruled that, although art 17(2)(a) of the Sixth Directive restricted a taxable person's right to deduct tax to amounts due or paid 'in respect of goods ... supplied to him', the purpose of that provision could not be to prevent such a person deducting VAT paid on goods which were sold to him for use in his business, albeit that the goods were actually physically delivered to his employees. Accordingly, VAT could be reclaimed by an employer in such circumstances.

9. Mol v Inspecteur der Invoerrechten en Accijnzen

ECJ Case 269/86; [1988] ECR 3627; [1989] 3 CMLR 729 [1989] BVC 205;

Vereniging Happy Family Rustenburgerstrat v Inspecteur der Omzetbelasting

ECJ Case 289/86: [1988] ECR 3655; [1989] 3 CMLR 743, [1989] BVC 216

Whether the illegal sale of drugs is an economic activity.

Facts

In two Dutch cases, the Dutch tax authorities assessed persons to VAT on the sale of drugs even though such sale was contrary to Dutch law. The persons appealed on the ground that the transactions in question were not liable to VAT because they were illegal.

Issue

Whether the unlawful supply of drugs for consideration is a supply of goods by a taxable person acting as such within art 2 of the Sixth Directive.

Decision

The ECJ held that the illegal sale of drugs such as amphetamines or hashish was not an 'economic activity' and thus not a supply for VAT purposes. While the principle of fiscal neutrality precluded 'a generalised differentiation between lawful and unlawful transactions', supplies of narcotic drugs were outside the scope of this principle, since 'because of their very nature, they are subject to a total prohibition on their being put into circulation in all the Member States, with the exception of strictly controlled economic channels for use for medical and scientific purposes'.

10. Kühne v Finanzamt München III

ECJ Case 50/88; [1990] STC 749; [1989] ECR 1925; [1990] 3 CMLR 287, Article 6(2) of Sixth Directive

Treatment of private use of goods as supply of services.

Facts

In a German case, the taxpayer had purchased a second-hand car from a non-taxable person. The car was purchased with the intention of being used for both private and business purposes. The German tax authority charged VAT on the private use, based on the depreciation of the car and the proportion to which it was used privately. The taxpayer appealed, contending that art 6(2) of the Sixth Directive only imposed a charge to output tax where the input tax had been wholly or partly deductible, and thus precluded a charge to tax where no tax had been deducted on the acquisition of the asset from a non-taxable person.

Issue

(a) Whether art 6(2)(a) of the Sixth Directive precludes taxation of the depreciation of business goods in respect of their private use where the VAT on such goods was not deductible because they were purchased from a non-taxable person.

(b) Whether the answer to (a) is different where, although the taxable person was not able to deduct the VAT in respect of the supply of the goods to him, he was able to deduct VAT on goods and services for the use and maintenance of the goods.

(c) Whether the member states' power to derogate from the rule in art 6(2)(a) allows them to refrain from taxing such use wholly or partly or allows them to tax such use whether or not the value added tax on such goods was wholly or partly deductible.

(d) Whether art 6(2) precludes national tax legislation imposing value added tax on the private use of business goods where the value added tax on those goods was not wholly or partly deductible.

(e) Whether art 6(2) is directly effective and can be relied upon by a taxpayer against any national provision which was incompatible with it.

(f) Whether the taxable amount in respect of the private use of business goods includes all the expenses incurred by the taxable person or merely the consideration for the supply of goods and services on which the value added tax is deductible.

Decision

The ECJ held that:

(a) Article 6(2)(a) of the Sixth Directive precludes taxation of the depreciation of business goods in respect of their private use where the value added tax on such goods was not deductible because they were purchased from a non-taxable person.

(b) The reply to (a) is the same where the taxable person can deduct the VAT on supplies of goods and services for the maintenance or use of the goods.

(c) Article 6(2) does not allow member states to tax the private use of business goods where the value added tax on such goods was not wholly or partly deductible.

(d) Article 6(2) precludes national tax legislation imposing value added tax on the private use of business goods where the value added tax on those goods was not wholly or partly deductible.

(e) Article 6(2) is directly effective and can be relied upon by a taxpayer against any national provision which was incompatible with it.

(f) VAT is not due on the depreciation of business goods in respect of their private use where the VAT on the goods was not deductible but VAT is chargeable on the expenses incurred for the maintenance and use of the goods in respect of which the taxable person is entitled to deduct tax.

Accordingly VAT was not chargeable in the circumstances of the case.

11. Polysar Investments Netherlands BV v Inspecteur der Invoerrechten en Accijnzen

ECJ Case C-60/90: [1991] 1 ECR I-3111; [1993] STC 222

Holding company – taxable person.

Facts

In a Dutch case, a company (P), which acted as a holding company, and did not carry on any commercial or management activity, reclaimed input tax. The Dutch authorities issued an assessment to recover the tax considering that, since the company did not carry on any commercial activity, it was not a taxable person and could not reclaim any input tax. P appealed and the case was referred to the ECJ.

Issue

Whether a holding company whose activities are concerned solely with the holding of shares in subsidiary companies may be classified as a taxable person.

Decision

The ECJ held that a holding company whose sole purpose was to hold shares in other undertakings, without any direct or indirect involvement in the management of those undertakings, was not a taxable person and had no right to deduct or reclaim input tax.

12. Lennartz v Finanzamt München III

ECJ Case C-97/90: [1991] 1 ECR 3795; [1993] 3 CMLR 689; [1995] STC 514

Capital goods scheme – non-business.

Facts

In a German case, a tax consultant purchased a car. Initially he used the car mainly for private purposes and did not reclaim any input tax on the purchase. In the following year, his business use of the car increased, and he reclaimed a proportion of the input tax incurred on the purchase of the car. The German tax authority refused to repay the tax, considering that the consultant should be treated as having initially bought the car wholly for private use and that he was not entitled to reclaim any input tax on the subsequent business use of the car. The consultant appealed and the German court referred the case to the ECJ for a ruling on whether input tax could be reclaimed under art 20(2) on a capital item which was not initially used for business purposes but was used for business purposes within five years from its acquisition.

Issue

Whether the capital goods scheme applies where a taxable person initially acquires goods wholly for private use but later uses them for business purposes during the adjustment period. What conditions must be met for the capital goods scheme to apply?

Decision

The ECJ held that the question of whether input tax was deductible was to be determined solely by reference to the capacity in which the purchaser of goods was acting at the time of the purchase. Article 20(2) did not itself contain any provisions as to the origin of the right to deduct but merely established the procedure for calculating adjustments to the initial deduction. Therefore, if a person purchased goods for private purposes but subsequently used them for business purposes, no input tax would be deductible. However, the immediate use of the goods for either taxable or exempt supplies was not of itself 'a condition for the application of art 20(2)'. The question of whether goods had been purchased for the purposes of an 'economic activity' was a question of fact which had to be determined in the light of all the relevant circumstances. Where goods were purchased partly for the purposes of taxable business transactions and partly for private purposes, the taxable person could reclaim the whole of the input tax but would then have to account for output tax on the private use.

13. Customs and Excise Comrs v Briararch Ltd

High Court [1992] STC 732

Grant of short tenancy pending sale of major interest in building – adjustment of attribution of input tax.

Facts

A company (B) restored a listed building with the intention of granting a 25-year leasehold interest in it. However, it was unable to find a lessee who would accept a long lease, which would have been a taxable supply, and granted a four-year tenancy to provide it with temporary rental income. It reclaimed the whole of the input tax incurred on the restoration. The Commissioners issued an assessment to recover the tax, considering that it should be wholly attributed to the four-year tenancy, which was an exempt supply. B appealed.

Issue

Whether, where it remained B's intention to grant a long lease (a taxable supply), the input tax should be apportioned between the exempt supply and the future taxable supply.

Decision

The Tribunal allowed B's appeal, holding that, since the Commissioners had accepted B's evidence that it intended to make a taxable supply of a 25-year lease in the building, it followed that 25/29 of the input tax which B had incurred related to this future taxable supply and was therefore deductible. The High Court upheld the Tribunal's decision. The regulations envisaged that input tax should be apportioned in such cases and such an apportionment was in accordance with art 20 of the Sixth Directive.

14. Finanzamt München III v Möhsche

ECJ Case C-193/91: [1993] ECR I-2615; [1997] STC 195

Taxation of the private use of goods.

Facts

In a German case, an assessment was made charging VAT on the private use of a car which had been treated as a business asset. The assessment included a proportion of certain expenses, such as garage rental and insurance, on which the owner had neither been charged nor had he deducted VAT. The owner appealed and the case was referred to the ECJ.

Issue

Whether a trader who uses a motor car belonging to his business for private purposes must account for tax, by way of a charge for private use, on the cost of various non-taxable or exempt items of expenditure incurred in connection with the maintenance or use of the car (in particular garage rental, tax, insurance and parking fees).

Decision

The ECJ held that art 6(2)(a) of the Sixth Directive had to be interpreted strictly and that therefore ancillary services relating to the private use of goods did not fall within its provisions. It should therefore be interpreted as precluding the taxation of goods and services where the owner of the goods had not been able to deduct input tax in respect of such services.

15. Sofitam SA (formerly Satam SA) v Ministre du Budget

ECJ Case C-333/91: [1993] ECR I-3513; [1997] STC 226

Economic activity – receipt of dividends – pro rata calculation.

Facts

In a French case, a company which had substantial income from dividends reclaimed the whole of its input tax. The French tax authorities issued an assessment computed on the basis that the company was only entitled to reclaim a proportion of its input tax, since the dividend income should be included in the denominator of the fraction laid down by art 19(1) of the Sixth Directive as turnover in respect of which input tax was not deductible. The company appealed, contending that dividends should not be taken into account in the denominator and the Conseil d'Etat referred the case to the ECJ.

Issue

Whether share dividends received by a taxable person must be included in or excluded from the denominator of the fraction used to calculate the deductible proportion.

Decision

The ECJ upheld the company's contention, holding that the receipt of dividends was not within the scope of VAT, since it did not amount to consideration for any economic activity. Consequently dividends on shares were to be excluded from the denominator of the fraction laid down by art 19(1) for the purposes of calculating the deductible proportion of input tax

16. Customs and Excise Comrs v Kingfisher plc

High Court, [1994] STC 63

Interpretation of VAT group registration provisions – whether the use of a credit card issued by one member of a VAT group to pay for sales by another member were to be regarded as payment by the cardholder to the retailer.

Facts

K was the representative member of a VAT group of companies trading as retailers which also included a company (T) that issued credit cards for use in shops owned by members of the group. K did not account for VAT on sales paid for by the credit cards issued by T until the users of the cards had paid the amounts in question to T. The Commissioners issued assessments on the basis that K should account for tax on the basis that the time of supply was when the sale took place, as with any other credit card. K appealed, contending that sales by means of T's credit cards should be self-financed credit as the credit had been provided by a member of the K VAT group which was a single taxable person and, therefore, VAT need not be accounted for until payment was received. The tribunal allowed K's appeal and the Commissioners appealed to the High Court.

Issue

Whether K should be treated as carrying on both T's credit business and the retail business in the group.

Decision

The High Court upheld the decision of the Tribunal. Popplewell J held that, under what is now VATA 1994, s 43, K was deemed to carry on the retail businesses of its retail subsidiaries and also T's credit business. Accordingly, K's deemed retail sales were financed by its deemed credit business and the sales in question were 'self-financed credit sales' and, as indicated in Notice No 727 (1987 edition), para 9, VAT need not be accounted until payment was received.

17. Customs and Excise Comrs v FW Rosner

High Court 1993, [1994] STC 228

Business purpose – private purposes.

Facts

The proprietor of a private educational establishment was convicted of conspiracy to defraud in relation to the provision of false information under the Immigration Act 1971 and in assisting overseas visitors to the UK in making false representations about whether they were genuine students. He was fined and ordered to pay the costs of the prosecution. He also paid the costs of an appeal by one of his students and incurred legal costs in negotiating with Customs and Excise for a compounded penalty to avoid criminal proceedings regarding evasion of VAT. He reclaimed input tax in respect of the legal costs incurred and the Commissioners issued an assessment to recover the tax, considering that the expenditure had not been incurred for the purposes of the business. The proprietor appealed, contending that the expenditure had been incurred for the purpose of his business since he had been liable to imprisonment and if he had been imprisoned for any length of time his business may have been forced to close.

Issue

Whether legal costs of sole taxable person charged with criminal offence deductible – distinction between whether services supplied to a business and services which benefit a business but are not supplied to it.

Decision

The High Court upheld the assessment, holding that the fact that the business had benefited from the expenditure was not conclusive since 'there must be a real connection, a nexus between the expenditure and the business'. On the evidence, there was no clear nexus between the expenditure in question and the business. Accordingly, the expenditure in question had not been incurred for the purpose of the business and none of the VAT was deductible.

18. BLP Group plc v Customs and Excise Comrs

ECJ Case C-4/94: [1995] STC 424; [1995] ECR-I 983; [1996] 1 WLR 174; [1995] All ER (EC) 401

Whether input tax on the sale of shares is deductible.

Facts

A holding company provided management services to a group of subsidiary trading companies. In 1991 it disposed of 95% of the shares in a German subsidiary company. It was accepted that this disposal was an exempt supply within what is now VATA 1994, Sch 9, Group 5. However, the company reclaimed input tax in respect of professional services supplied in relation to this disposal by a merchant bank, a firm of solicitors and a firm of accountants. The Commissioners issued an assessment to recover the tax, with the exception of a small proportion which they accepted as forming part of the company's general overhead expenses and as not being directly used for the disposal in question.

The company appealed. The Tribunal dismissed the company's appeal, holding that the tax was not deductible since it related entirely to the making of an exempt supply. The company appealed to the High Court which referred a preliminary question to the ECJ.

Issue

Is input tax incurred in relation to an exempt supply (sale of shares) deductible in whole or in part where the purpose and result was to raise money to discharge indebtedness?

Decision

The ECJ upheld the Tribunal's decision, holding that input tax was only deductible under art 17 of the Sixth Directive if the goods or services in question had a direct and immediate link with taxable transactions. The fact that the ultimate aim of the taxable person was the carrying out of a taxable transaction was irrelevant.

19. Finanzamt Ülzen v Armbrecht

ECJ Case C-291/92: [1995] STC 997; [1995] ECR-I 2775; [1995] All ER (EC) 882

Sale of property partly used for business purposes and partly used for private purposes – application of art 2(1) of Sixth Directive.

Facts

In a German case, an hotelier sold a guesthouse, part of which he had used for private purposes rather than for business purposes. He was assessed on the whole of the proceeds, and appealed, contending that he should only be required to account for tax on the proportion of the proceeds which was attributable to the part of the guesthouse which he had used for business purposes. The case was referred to the ECJ.

Issue

Whether, where a taxable person has appropriated part of a business property for his private use, he acts as a taxable person in relation to the sale of that part.

Decision

The ECJ ruled that where a taxable person sold property, part of which he had chosen to reserve for private use, the sale of that part was outside the scope of art 2(1) of the Sixth Directive.

20. Intercommunale voor Zeewaterontzilting (in liquidation) v Belgian

ECJ Case C-110/94: [1996] STC 569; [1996] ECR-I 857

Reclaiming input tax on costs of profitability study re developing processes for turning sea and brackish water into drinking water.

Facts

In a Belgian case, a company was established with the object of developing processes for turning sea and brackish water into drinking water. It reclaimed input tax on the costs of a profitability study, but went into liquidation without beginning to trade. The Belgian tax authority issued an assessment to recover the tax which the company had reclaimed. The liquidators of the company appealed, and the case was referred to the ECJ.

Issue

Whether the commissioning of a profitability study by a company which has declared its intention to make taxable supplies may be regarded as an economic activity. Whether the status of 'taxable person' may be withdrawn from that company retroactively, where, as a result of that study, it is decided to put the company into liquidation so that the envisaged economic activity does not give rise to any taxable transactions.

Decision

The ECJ held that initial investment expenditure incurred for the purposes of a business could in principle be regarded as an economic activity within art 4(2) of the Sixth Directive. However, art 4 did not preclude a tax authority from requiring objective evidence in support of a declared intention to commence economic activities which would give rise to taxable transactions. A taxable person only acquired that status definitively if he made such a declaration in good faith. In cases of fraud or abuse, a tax authority could claim repayment retrospectively on the ground that the deductions had been made on the basis of false declarations. Accordingly, the ECJ ruled that when a tax authority had accepted that a company which had declared an intention to begin an economic activity had the status of a taxable person, the commissioning of a profitability study could be regarded as an economic activity and the company's status as a taxable person could only be withdrawn 'in cases of fraud or abuse'.

21. Customs and Excise Comrs v UBAF Bank Ltd

Court of Appeal [1996] STC 372

Acquisition of shares and businesses – attribution.

Facts

A bank, which was partly exempt, had operated an equipment leasing business for several years. In 1987 this business had suffered losses. In 1990 and 1991 the bank acquired the share capital of three existing leasing companies. It took over the leasing businesses formerly operated by these companies, which became dormant subsidiaries. The bank reclaimed input tax on fees which it paid to solicitors and brokers relating to the acquisition of the companies. The Commissioners issued an assessment to recover some 28% of the tax, considering that it was partly attributable to exempt supplies. The bank appealed, contending that all the input tax should be treated as reclaimable, since it had acquired the companies for the purpose of making taxable supplies. The Tribunal accepted this contention and allowed the bank's appeal, holding that there was 'no need to distinguish between the share purchases and the subsequent purchases of the businesses'. The Commissioners appealed straight to the Court of Appeal.

Issue

Whether input tax incurred on acquisition of leasing companies and their businesses attributable to taxable supplies and deductible.

Decision

The Court of Appeal upheld this decision. On the evidence, the Tribunal had been entitled to find that there was a direct link between the acquisitions and the making of taxable supplies. *BLP Group plc*, (see 18 above) distinguished.

22. Gemeente Emmen v Belastingdienst Grote Ondernemingen

ECJ Case C-468/93: [1996] STC 496; [1996] ECR I-1721; [1996] All ER (EC) 372

Meaning of building land.

Facts

In a Dutch case, a local authority appealed against an assessment charging tax on a supply of land, contending that the land was not 'building land' within art 4(3)(b) of the Sixth Directive and that the supply was therefore exempt under art 13B(h). The case was referred to the ECJ.

Issue

What is the meaning of 'building land'?

Decision

The ECJ held that it was for the member states to define the concept of 'building land' within the meaning of art 4(3)(b) and art 13B(h). It was not for the court to specify what degree of improvement had to be exhibited by land which had not actually been built on in order to be categorised as within the definition of 'building land'.

23. Wellcome Trust Ltd v Customs and Excise Comrs

ECJ Case C-155/94: [1996] STC 945; [1996] ECR-I 3013; [1996] 2 CMLR 909; [1996] All ER (EC) 589

Economic activity – sale of shares and securities by charity – relevance of scale of activity.

Facts

A company, which was registered for VAT, acted as the sole trustee of a charitable trust. In 1992 it sold a large number of shares in a public company. The shares in question had been obtained by the trust in 1986 in exchange for shares which had been bequeathed to the trust in 1936. The company reclaimed input tax in respect of expenses incurred in relation to the sale of such shares to people resident outside the EU. The Commissioners rejected the claim on the grounds that the company's investment activities did not constitute a business. The company appealed, contending that its investment activities were carried out on such a large scale that they constituted an 'economic activity' within art 4(2) of the Sixth Directive. The tribunal referred the case to the ECJ.

Issue

Whether the purchase and sale of shares and other securities by a trustee in the course of the management of the assets of a charitable trust is an economic activity.

Decision

The ECJ held that the exercise of the right of ownership could not by itself be regarded as an economic activity. Neither the scale of a sale of shares nor the employment of consultancy undertakings in connection with it could constitute criteria for distinguishing between the activities of a private investor, which were outside the scope of VAT, and those of a larger investor. The question of whether or not the sale of shares and securities was the predominant concern of the activity in the course of which the sales took place could not affect the classification of investment activity. Accordingly, the concept of economic activities, within art 4(2) of the Sixth Directive, did not include an activity consisting in the purchase and sale of shares and other securities by a trustee in the course of the management of a charitable trust.

24. Régie Dauphinoise-Cabinet A Forest Sarl v Ministre du Budget

ECJ Case C-306/94: [1996] STC 1176; [1996] ECR-I 3695; [1996] 3 CMLR 193

Article 19(2) – pro rata calculation – incidental financial transactions.

Facts

In a French case, a company which carried on a property management business invested sums which it received as advances from co-owners and lessees and retained the interest which it received. This interest amounted to about 14% of the company's income. It reclaimed the whole of its input tax, including the input tax relating to such investments. The tax authority took the view that, because the interest was exempt from VAT under art 13B of the Sixth Directive, the effect of art 19(2) of the Directive was that only a proportion of the input tax was deductible and that the amount of interest received should be included in the denominator of the fraction used to calculate the deductible proportion of input tax. The company appealed, contending that the transactions were 'incidental financial transactions' for the purposes of art 19(2). The case was referred to the ECJ.

Issue

Whether interest received by a property management company on investments, made for its own account, of sums paid by owners or lessees must be included in the denominator of the fraction used to calculate the deductible proportion in art 19(2) of the Sixth Directive.

Decision

The ECJ ruled that the transactions were not 'incidental financial transactions' for the purposes of art 19(2), since the receipt of such interest was a 'direct, permanent and necessary extension of the taxable activity of property management companies'. Accordingly, the amount of interest received should be included in the denominator of the fraction used to calculate the deductible proportion of input tax. *Sofitam SA v Ministre du Budget* (see **15.** above) distinguished.

25. Enkler v Finanzamt Homburg

ECJ Case C-230/94: [1996] STC 1316; [1996] ECR I-4517; [1997] 1 CMLR 881

Whether caravan purchased to carry on an economic activity.

Facts

In a German case, a married woman (E) was employed by her husband who carried on business as a tax consultant. In 1984 she notified the tax authority that she was beginning a business of hiring out motor caravans. She purchased a caravan, reclaimed input tax and accounted for output tax, most of which represented payments from her husband. In 1986 she notified the tax authority that she intended to use the caravan for private purposes only. Subsequently the tax authority issued an assessment on the basis that E had never been acting as a taxable person. E appealed and the case was referred to the ECJ for rulings on the interpretation of art 4(2) and art 11A1(c) of the Sixth Directive.

Issue

(a) whether the hiring out of tangible property is to be regarded as an economic activity; and

(b) in what circumstances is the hiring out of tangible property such as a motor caravan to be regarded as being done for the purpose of obtaining income therefrom on a continuing basis.

Decision

The ECJ held that the hiring out of tangible property was an economic activity within art 4(2) of the Sixth Directive if it was 'done for the purpose of obtaining income therefrom on a continuing basis'. The question of 'whether the hiring out of tangible property such as a motor caravan is carried on with a view to obtaining income on a continuing basis' was 'for the national court to evaluate in all the circumstances of the particular case'. The Court also ruled on another matter not related to input tax deduction.

26. Harnas & Helm CV v Staatssecretaris van Financiën

ECJ Case C-80/95: [1997] STC 364; [1997] ECR-I 745; [1997] 1 CMLR 649; [1997] All ER (EC) 267

Economic activity – acquisition of shares and bonds by a partnership.

Facts

In a Dutch case, a limited partnership held shares and bonds. It reclaimed input tax which it had incurred in connection with loan transactions. The Dutch tax authority rejected the claim on the basis that the partnership was not carrying on any economic activity. The partnership appealed, and the case was referred to the ECJ.

Issue

Whether art 4(2) of the Sixth Directive is to be interpreted as meaning that the mere acquisition and the holding of bonds and the receipt of income therefrom are economic activities conferring on the person concerned the status of a taxable person.

Decision

The ECJ ruled that the mere acquisition and holding of bonds and the receipt of income therefrom were not to be regarded as economic activities within art 4(2) of the Sixth Directive. *Polysar Investments Netherlands BV v Inspecteur der Invoerrechten en Accijnzen* (see **11.** above) applied.

27. BMW (GB) Ltd v Customs and Excise Comrs

High Court [1997] STC 824

Business entertainment – cost of track days held by motor distributor.

Facts

A company (BMW) carried on business as an importer and distributor of motor-cars and motorcycles. It sold such vehicles to independent dealers, who in turn sold them to members of the public. In the course of its promotional activities it arranged 'track days', at which dealers and potential customers could test-drive its cars. Dealers were required to make payments ranging from £25 to £85 per person attending. BMW also arranged golfing days and curling days, and reclaimed input tax on the total costs of these activities. The Commissioners issued assessments on the basis that BMW could only recover the proportion of the input tax which equated to the proportion of the costs which was reimbursed by the dealers (ie 29% of the input tax on the 'track days', and 17% of the input tax on the 'curling days') but that the remainder of the input tax was not recoverable, since it was attributable to supplies of business entertainment. BMW appealed.

Issue

Whether there was a supply of business entertainment. Whether the supply of business entertainment by BMW was to dealers or to customers.

Decision

The Tribunal dismissed the appeal. The Tribunal observed that there were 'two quite distinct elements in the track days'. Expenditure on demonstrating BMW's products, such as test drives and brake demonstrations, was not within the definition of 'business entertainment'. However, BMW had also incurred substantial expenditure on 'hospitality'. This hospitality was supplied by BMW rather than by the dealers and only the percentage of the relevant input tax which was attributable to the supplies to the dealers was recoverable. The percentage which was attributable to the supplies to the potential customers was 'business entertainment' and was not recoverable. BMW appealed to the High Court which upheld the Tribunal's decision. On the evidence, the supply of facilities to the customers was distinguishable from the transaction between BMW and the dealers. There was a gratuitous provision of services by BMW to the customers, which was within the definition of 'business entertainment'.

28. Customs and Excise Comrs v Kilroy Television Co Ltd

High Court [1997] STC 901

Business entertainment – buffet meals for participants in television programme.

Facts

A company which produced television programmes provided modest buffet meals, costing less than £10 per head, for people who participated in the programmes. It reclaimed input tax on the cost of the meals. The Commissioners issued assessments to recover the tax, considering that the expenditure was within the definition of 'business entertainment' and the company appealed. The Tribunal allowed the company's appeal, finding that the company had placed itself under a legal obligation to provide the meals. The Commissioners appealed to the High Court.

Issue

Whether the food was provided pursuant to a legal obligation.

Decision

The High Court upheld this decision as one of fact. The case was 'on the borderline' but, on the evidence, the tribunal had been entitled to find that the meals did not constitute 'business entertainment'. Dicta in *Celtic Football & Athletic Club Ltd* (see **3.** above) applied.

29. Ernst & Young v Customs and Excise Comrs

[1997] V & DR 183 (VTD 15100)

Business entertainment – dinner dance for employees and guests.

Facts

An accountancy partnership reclaimed input tax in respect of a Christmas party and a dinner dance which it organised for its employees. For the Christmas party, each employee was required to pay £10 towards the cost and was entitled to bring one guest to the Christmas party but was required to pay a further £15. No guests attended the dinner dance, which took place after a conference attended by partners and employees. With regard to the Christmas party, the Commissioners issued an assessment to recover the tax on the amount by which the cost of the party exceeded the payments made by the employees. With regard to the dinner dance, the Commissioners issued an assessment to recover the whole of the tax attributable to the cost of the disco and to the cost of alcoholic drinks which were served before and after the meal and 50% of the tax attributable to the cost of the dinner. The partnership appealed, contending that its purpose in incurring the expenditure was to reward its staff and therefor the expenditure had been incurred for the purpose of its business.

Issue

Whether a dinner dance for employees of accountancy partnership was business entertainment.

Decision

The Tribunal allowed the appeal. The Tribunal specifically disapproved the Commissioners' practice, laid down in Leaflet 700/55/93, of allowing only 50% of input tax attributable to entertainment of employees. With regard to the guests of the employees, the Tribunal distinguished *KPMG (No 2)* on the grounds that in that case no charge had been made. Applying dicta of Keene J in *BMW (GB) Ltd* (see **27.** above), the Tribunal held that:

> 'the crucial characteristic of "entertainment" within the phrase "business entertainment" is that it is provided to a person or persons who enjoy it free of charge'.

Although the charge of £15 was considerably less than the cost of the party

> 'it was not so small that one can say that the meal was effectively supplied free of charge'.

The Tribunal held that the expenditure was not within VATA 1994, s 84(4) since that provision had to be read in the light of art 17(6) of the Sixth Directive. Alternatively, the Tribunal considered that even if the expenditure were deemed to be within s 84(4), the appeal would still be successful on the grounds that:

> 'the Commissioners were unreasonable in disallowing the expenditure because no reasonable body of Commissioners understanding the law as we have found it to be could consider that the expenditure was non-business'.

However, the Tribunal dismissed the appeal of the firm against a decision disallowing the VAT on a cabaret performed at a partners' conference on the ground that it was not incurred for use for the purpose of the appellants' business.

30. Belgium v Ghent Coal Terminal NV

ECJ Case C-37/95: [1998] STC 260; [1998] ECR 1; [1998] All ER (EC) 223

Whether input tax on aborted transaction must be repaid.

Facts

A company had purchased some land in Ghent in 1980. It had work carried out on the land and reclaimed input tax on these supplies. In 1983, it was required by Ghent Council to dispose of the land, without having ever used it for any taxable transactions. The Belgian government sought to recover the tax which the company had reclaimed and the company appealed and the case was referred to the ECJ for a ruling on the interpretation of art 17(2) of the Sixth Directive.

Issue

Whether a taxable person is entitled to deduct VAT on goods or services supplied to him for the purposes of investment work intended to be used in taxable transactions. If so, whether the right to deduct remains acquired where, by reason of circumstances beyond his control, the taxable person has never made use of that investment work in order to carry out taxable transactions.

Decision

The ECJ held that the right of deduction was exercisable and remained acquired where, by reason of circumstances beyond his control, the taxable person had never actually used the goods and services in question for the purposes of taxable transactions (while observing that such a supply might give rise to a subsequent adjustment under art 20).

31. Customs and Excise Comrs v Redrow Group plc

House of Lords [1999] STC 161; [1999] 2 All ER 1 [1999] 1 WLR 408;

Recipient of supply.

Facts

A group of house building companies instituted a scheme for prospective purchasers of its houses, whereby it nominated an estate agent to sell the houses already owned by such purchasers and paid the agent's fees. The scheme was instituted because most prospective purchasers could not proceed with a purchase until they had found a buyer for their existing homes. The group deducted input tax on the fees which it paid to the estate agents. The Commissioners issued an assessment to recover the tax, considering that the supplies were made to the owners of the houses rather than to the company. The representative member of the group appealed, contending that it was acting as a joint principal and was a joint recipient of the supply, so that it was entitled to deduct the input tax. The Tribunal accepted this contention and allowed the appeal, holding on the evidence that the agents' services were provided both to the company and to the potential purchaser. The Court of Appeal reversed this decision. The company appealed to the House of Lords.

Issue

Whether the house building company is entitled to deduct the VAT charged on the supply of its estate agents' services in arranging for sale of houses owned by prospective purchasers.

Decision

The House of Lords unanimously allowed the company's appeal and restored the decision of the Tribunal. Applying *Belgium v Ghent Coal Terminal NV* (see **30.** above), the House of Lords held that the supplies had been 'received in connection with the business activities of the taxable person, for the purpose of being incorporated within its economic activities'. Lord Hope observed that 'the fact that someone else – in this case, the prospective purchaser – also received a service as part of the same transaction does not deprive the person who instructed the service and who has had to pay for it of the benefit of the deduction'.

32. Tremerton Ltd v Customs and Excise Comrs

High Court [1999] STC 1039

VAT Regulations 1995, reg 108.

Facts

In 1995 a company (T) purchased a property with the intention of redeveloping it as residential accommodation. It obtained the necessary planning permission and reclaimed input tax on services supplied by planning consultants, engineers, surveyors, etc. relating to the proposed redevelopment. However, it was unable to raise the necessary finance to proceed with the redevelopment and, in May 1996, it made an exempt supply of the site (with the benefit of the planning permission) to a Jersey company. The Commissioners issued an assessment to recover the input tax which T had reclaimed. The Tribunal dismissed T's appeal, holding that the effect of VAT Regulations 1995, SI 1995 2518, reg 108 was that the input tax had to be attributed to the exempt supply which T had actually made, rather than to the taxable supply which it had originally intended to make. The provisions of reg 108 were consistent with art 20(1) of the Sixth Directive. The wording of art 20(1) was 'wide enough … to include a change of intention which results in a change of the VAT status of a transaction from taxable to exempt'. T appealed to the High Court.

Issue

Whether input tax reclaimed on expenditure relating to redevelopment of property must be repaid under reg 108 on subsequent exempt supply of property.

Decision

The High Court upheld the Tribunal's decision. Carnwath J observed that there had been a 'change … in the factors used to determine the amount to be deducted', within art 20(1)(b). The Tribunal had been entitled to find that there had been a sufficient direct and immediate link between the supplies which T received and the supply which it made for the input tax to be reattributed from the intended taxable supply to the actual exempt supply. *Belgium v Ghent Coal Terminal NV* (see **30.** above) distinguished.

33. Finanzamt Goslar v Breitsohl

ECJ Case C-400/98: [2001] STC 355

Taxable person – economic activity not started.

Facts

In a German case, a woman (B) registered as a car dealer and began building work with the aim of constructing a repair workshop. However, she was unable to complete the work for financial reasons and subsequently sold the partly completed building and the land on which it stood. She purported to waive exemption on the building but not the land with the intention of reclaiming input tax on the building work without having to account for output tax on the sale of the land.

Issue

What evidence is required for right to deduct where economic activity not started?

Decision

In relation to the right to deduct input tax, the ECJ held that a person who had the intention, confirmed by objective evidence, to commence independently an economic activity within the meaning of art 4 and who incurred the first investment expenditure for those purposes had to be regarded as a taxable person. Acting in that capacity he had therefore in accordance with art 17 the right immediately to deduct the VAT payable or paid on the investment expenditure incurred for the purposes of the transactions which he intended to carry out and which gave rise to the right to deduct. The taxable person did not have to wait for the actual exploitation of his business to begin. The right to deduct the VAT paid on the first investment expenditure was in no way dependent upon formal recognition of the status of taxable person by the tax authority.

However, art 4 did not preclude the tax authority from requiring objective evidence in support of the declared intention to commence economic activities giving rise to taxable transactions. A taxable person acquired that status definitively only if he made a declaration of intention to begin the envisaged economic activities in good faith. In the instant case it was for the national court, taking into account the circumstances of the case and in particular the progress of the building works in mid-May 1990, to check whether the declaration of the intention to commence economic activities giving rise to taxable transactions had been made in good faith and was borne out by objective evidence. Accordingly, the answer to the first question was that

> '… Articles 4 and 17 are to be interpreted as meaning that the right to deduct the VAT paid on transactions carried out with a view to the realisation of a planned economic activity still exists even where the tax authority is aware, from the time of the first tax assessment, that the economic activity envisaged, which was to give rise to taxable transactions, will not be taken up.'

34. Grundstückgemeinschaft Schloßstraße GbR v Finanzamt Paderborn

ECJ Case C-396/98: [2000] ECR I-4279

Right to deduct where legislation amended so as to retrospectively prevent the option to tax – principle of legitimate expectation.

Facts

In a German case, a company acquired development rights in respect of building land. It subsequently elected to waive exemption in respect of the land. It began construction work in January 1994 and reclaimed input tax. The tax authority issued assessments to recover the tax on the basis that the possibility of waiving exemption in such cases had been withdrawn by an amendment to German law which came into force on 1 January 1994 and had retrospective effect. The company appealed, contending that the retrospective restriction of its right to opt for taxation was a breach of the Community law principle of legitimate expectation. The case was referred to the ECJ.

Issue

Whether the right to deduct VAT paid on goods or services is retained where a change in law after the supply of such goods or services, but before they could be used to make taxable supplies, prevents a taxable person from electing to waive exemption and making taxable supplies.

Decision

The ECJ held that the effect of art 17 of the Sixth Directive was that input tax incurred on intended taxable supplies was deductible despite the subsequent change in the law. The ECJ observed that, under art 17(1), the right to deduct arose at the time when the deductible tax became chargeable. The ECJ held that 'in the absence of fraud or abuse and subject to any adjustments to be made' under the conditions laid down in art 20, the right of deduction was 'retained even if the taxable person has been unable to use the goods or services which gave rise to a deduction in the context of taxable transactions by reason of circumstances beyond his control'. In such circumstances, 'the taxable person is entitled immediately to deduct the VAT due or paid on the goods or services supplied with a view to the performance of the economic activities which it envisages carrying out'. The principles of the protection of legitimate expectations and of legal certainty 'preclude its being deprived retroactively of that right by a legislative amendment postdating the supply of those goods or services'.

35. Midland Bank plc v Customs and Excise Comrs

ECJ Case C-98/98, [2000] STC 501; [2000] All ER (EC) 673, [2000] 1 WLR 2080

Attribution.

Facts

A bank, which was partly exempt, incurred legal costs in defending a claim alleging negligent misrepresentation in relation to the sale of a company. The bank's client was a US corporation and its supplies to the client were accepted as zero-rated under the legislation then in force. The bank reclaimed the whole of the input tax relating to the claim. The Commissioners issued assessments on the basis that the tax should be apportioned between taxable supplies and exempt supplies. The bank appealed, contending that the tax was wholly attributable to the zero-rated taxable supplies which it had made to its US client. The High Court referred the case to the ECJ.

Issue

Whether there must be a direct and immediate link between a particular input transaction and a particular output transaction or transactions giving rise to entitlement to deduct before the taxable person is entitled to deduct input VAT and in order to determine the extent of such entitlement.

Decision

The ECJ held that input tax was only deductible if there was a direct and immediate link between a particular input transaction and a particular output transaction. It was for the national court to apply the 'direct and immediate link' test to the facts of each particular case. A taxable person could not deduct the full amount of input tax incurred on services which had been utilised:

> '… not for the purpose of carrying out a deductible transaction, but in the context of activities which are no more than the consequence of making such a transaction, unless that person can show by means of objective evidence that the expenditure involved in the acquisition of such services is part of the various cost components of the output transaction'.

36. RAP Group plc v Customs and Excise Comrs

High Court [2000] STC 980

Share issue – legal and accountancy services – invoices – apportionment of input tax.

Facts

RAP acquired the issued share capital of W plc. Each of W plc's shareholders was issued one new ordinary share in RAP plus a warrant in exchange for each 130 ordinary shares in W plc. RAP claimed input tax on the supplies of services by its accountants, KPMG, its solicitors, TSB, and its stockbrokers, WdB, in relation to its acquisition of W plc. The Commissioners disallowed the deduction on the ground that the input tax was used 'exclusively in making exempt supplies' within VAT Regulations 1995, reg 101(2)(c) and issued an assessment. RAP appealed to the Tribunal. The relevant part of the invoice from KPMG referred only to 'placing an open offer' and 'offer for W plc'. The invoice from WdB was in similar terms. The invoice from TSB included details such as: advising on the financing of the transaction; preparing service contracts for executive directors; preparing a due diligence report on W plc; investigating title to W plc's properties and preparing papers for its annual general meeting following the acquisition. RAP contended that, as a matter of law, part of the cost of the advisers' services was a cost component of its taxable transactions in the form of management services supplied to W plc once it was part of the RAP group and that there was a direct and immediate link between the advisory services received and the management services supplied so that the input tax should be apportioned under reg 101(2)(d). The Tribunal dismissed the appeal. RAP appealed to the High Court.

Issue

Whether the services, in respect of which the VAT was incurred, were used for an exempt supply (the share issue) or for that and some other taxable supplies (management services).

Decision

The High Court allowed the appeal in part. The High Court held that the question whether the services were used for an exempt supply or partly for that and partly for taxable supplies was a question of fact. There was nothing in the evidence which prevented the Tribunal from finding that the services of KPMG and WdB were used for an exempt supply. The Tribunal had been wrong, however, to ignore the clear terms of the invoice from TSB and to treat all the work as limited to the issue of shares. TSB's services had been partly used for the purposes of making taxable supplies, so that the tax shown on the invoice from TSB should be apportioned. Accordingly, RAP's appeal was allowed in so far as it related to the input tax on the invoice of TSB. In respect of the input tax on the invoices of KPMG and WdB, the appeal was dismissed.

37. Floridienne SA v Belgian

[2000] STC 1044, [2001] All ER (EC) 37

Deduction of input tax by holding company – whether dividends to be included in denominator in determining VAT deductible.

Facts

In a Belgian case, two holding companies that were directly or indirectly involved in the management of their subsidiaries received dividends and interest from them. The holding companies reclaimed the whole of their input tax. The Belgian authorities sought to recover some of the tax on the basis that it was partly attributable to the receipt of income which was exempt from VAT. The companies appealed and the case was referred to the ECJ.

Issue

Whether art 19 of the Sixth Directive must be interpreted as meaning that:

(1) dividends distributed by its subsidiaries to a holding company, which is subject to VAT in respect of other activities and which supplies management services to those subsidiaries, and

(2) interest paid by the subsidiaries to the holding company on account of loans it has made to them,

must be excluded from the denominator of the fraction used to calculate the deductible proportion.

Decision

The ECJ held that dividends paid by a subsidiary company to a holding company were outside the scope of VAT and had to be excluded from the denominator of the fraction used to calculate the deductible proportion of input tax. Interest paid on loans to subsidiaries should be similarly excluded where the relevant loans did not constitute 'an economic activity of the holding company', within art 4(2). Whether the relevant loans were within the charge to VAT was a question to be decided by the national court, applying the principles laid down in *Régie Dauphinoise-Cabinet A Forest Sarl v Ministre du Budget* (see **24.** above).

38. Trinity Mirror plc (formerly Mirror Group Newspapers Ltd) v Customs and Excise Comrs

Court of Appeal [2001] STC 192; [2001] EWCA Civ 65

Whether the issue of shares is a supply.

Facts

A company (Mirror) reclaimed input tax on professional fees relating to an issue of additional shares to raise finance for its business. The Commissioners ruled that the input tax relating to shares issued to people resident in the EU was irrecoverable. It was accepted that the company was entitled to reclaim input tax relating to sales of shares to people resident outside the EU. Mirror appealed, contending that the input tax should be treated as deductible since the issue of a company's own shares was not itself a supply and the purpose of the share issue was to facilitate its trading activities, in the course of which it made taxable supplies. The Tribunal dismissed the appeal. Mirror appealed to the High Court which upheld the decision of the Tribunal. Mirror appealed to the Court of Appeal.

Issue

Whether the issue by a taxable person of its own shares for the purpose of financing the expansion of its business constitutes a supply of services for VAT purposes.

Decision

The Court of Appeal upheld the decision of the lower courts. The issue of a company's shares was a supply of services within art 6(1) of the Sixth Directive. The supply was exempt from VAT and the expenditure in question was directly attributable to this exempt supply, so that the input tax in question was not deductible. The fact that the supply did not involve any depletion of the company's resources was not conclusive. The Court of Appeal did not think it necessary to make any reference to the ECJ.

39. Abbey National plc v Customs and Excise Comrs

ECJ Case C-408/98: [2001] STC 297; [2001] 1 WLR 769; [2001] All ER (EC) 385

Article 17(5) of Sixth Directive – Deduction of input tax on sale of a property as a going concern.

Facts

A company, which was a subsidiary member of a banking group, carried on an assurance business and held a number of let properties as investments. It sold a tenanted property in respect of which it had elected to waive exemption. The sale of the property was treated as the transfer of part of a business as a going concern. The company, which was the representative member of the group, reclaimed input tax on its solicitors' fees in relation to the transfer. The Commissioners issued an assessment on the basis that, since a transfer of a going concern was not a supply for VAT purposes, the input tax in question could not be directly attributed to taxable supplies and had to be treated as residual input tax within VAT Regulations 1995, SI 1995 2518, reg 101(2)(d). The company appealed and the High Court referred the case to the ECJ for a ruling on the interpretation of art 17(5) of the Sixth Directive.

Issue

Whether, where a transfer of a business or part of a business as a going concern is regarded as not being a supply of goods, the transferor may deduct the VAT on the costs of the services acquired in order to effect the transfer.

Decision

The ECJ ruled that where, in accordance with art 5(8) of the Sixth Directive,

> 'the transfer of a totality of assets or part thereof is regarded as not being a supply of goods, the costs incurred by the transferor for services acquired in order to effect that transfer form part of that taxable person's overheads. In principle, such services have a direct and immediate link with the whole of his economic activity. If, therefore, the transferor effects both transactions in respect of which value added tax is deductible and transactions in respect of which it is not, it follows from art 17(5) ... that he may deduct only that proportion of the value added tax which is attributable to the former transactions. However, if the various services acquired by the transferor in order to effect the transfer have a direct and immediate link with a clearly defined part of his economic activities, so that the costs of those services form part of the overheads of that part of the business, and all the transactions relating to that part of the business are subject to value added tax, he may deduct all the value added tax charged on his costs of acquiring those services.'

40. Customs and Excise Comrs v Liverpool Institute for Performing Arts

House of Lords [2001] UKHL 28; [2001] STC 891; [2001] 1 WLR 1187

Attribution – exempt, taxable and foreign supplies – standard method.

Facts

An educational institute (LIPA) made exempt supplies of educational services in the UK and taxable supplies of advertising and publicity services to a German company which were treated as made in Germany. The supplies to the German company would have attracted VAT if they had been made in the UK. LIPA used the standard method for attributing input tax to taxable supplies pursuant to the VAT to determine the amount of its deductible input tax. An issue arose between LIPA and the Commissioners as to the correct method of attributing residual input tax to taxable supplies, in particular with regard to the proper treatment of foreign supplies. The Commissioners ruled that these supplies were not to be treated as taxable supplies for the purposes of the partial exemption provisions but should be apportioned in accordance with what is now VAT Regulations 1995, reg 103. LIPA appealed to the Tribunal, contending that, even though the supplies were deemed to be made outside the UK, they should be treated as taxable supplies in the denominator of the fraction prescribed by what is now VAT Regulations 1995, reg 101(2)(d) so that LIPA could reclaim all or substantially all of its input tax. The Tribunal held that the foreign supplies should be treated as 'taxable supplies' for the purposes of the partial exemption fraction. The Commissioners appealed to the High Court. Carnwath J upheld the Tribunal's decision. The Commissioners appealed further to the Court of Appeal which overturned the decisions of the lower courts and allowed the Commissioners' appeal. LIPA appealed to the House of Lords.

Issue

Whether 'taxable supplies' includes out-of-country supplies and 'all supplies' means taxable supplies and exempt supplies and does not include foreign supplies.

Decision

The House of Lords unanimously dismissed LIPA's appeal. Lord Slynn of Hadley observed that what is now regulation 103 'provides a separate code for determining the amount of input tax relevant to the making of out-of-country supplies'. Lord Scott of Foscote observed that art 17(5)(c) allowed Member States to require a taxable person to calculate deductible input tax on the basis of the use of all or part of the goods or services. Further, art 17(5)(c) permitted a use-based apportionment in respect of the input tax on some of the goods or services and a value-based apportionment in respect of the input tax on other goods and services. The words 'all supplies' in what is now reg 101(2)(d) did not include foreign supplies that would, if made in the UK, have been taxable. Those supplies were dealt with under reg 103 which provided a separate regime for foreign supplies.

Note

For the Commissioners' practice following this decision, see Business Brief 12/01 issued on 11 September 2001.

41. Cibo Participations SA v Directeur régional des impôts du Nord-Pas-de-Calais

ECJ Case C-16/00 : [2002] STC 460

Holding company – VAT on costs of acquisition of shares in subsidiary – economic activity.

Facts

In a French case, a holding company, with three subsidiaries, reclaimed input tax. The French tax authority rejected the claim on the basis that the company was not carrying on any economic activity. The company appealed and the case was referred to the ECJ.

Issue

Whether VAT on costs relating to the acquisition of shares in a subsidiary relate to an economic activity and are deductible.

Decision

The ECJ held that the management of subsidiary companies could qualify as an 'economic activity' if it was accompanied by activities such as the 'performance of administrative, financial, commercial or technical services'. Costs relating to the acquisition of shares in a subsidiary company could be treated as general overhead costs. The ECJ also held that the receipt of dividends was outside the scope of VAT.

42. Customs and Excise Comrs v Barclays Bank plc

Court of Appeal [2001] STC 1558; [2001] EWCA Civ 1513

Date on which company ceases to be treated as part of group of companies.

Facts

On 27 February 1995 a banking company (B) gave the share capital of one of its subsidiaries (TDL) to a charitable trust. The Commissioners informed B that the subsidiary would be removed from B's group with effect from 1 July 1995. B appealed, contending that, as a matter of law, TDL had ceased to be a member of its group at the time of the transfer of the share capital. The Tribunal allowed B's appeal. The Commissioners appealed to the High Court which dismissed their appeal. The Commissioners further appealed to the Court of Appeal.

Issue

Whether TDL automatically ceased to be a member of the Barclays VAT group on the change of control on 28 February 1995 or on 1 July 1995, as specified by the Commissioners.

Decision

The Court of Appeal unanimously overturned the decisions of the lower courts and upheld the Commissioners' ruling. The Court of Appeal held that exit from a VAT group was not automatic but dependent on an application by the company or a notice from the Commissioners and there was nothing in art 4(4) of the Sixth VAT Directive to preclude that interpretation. Sir Andrew Morritt V-C observed that there was an obligation to notify the Commissioners of any change in the constitution or ownership of a company which might necessitate the variation of the register. If the Commissioners ascertained that the relevant control had ceased, they were required to give a notice terminating the group treatment from such a date as they might specify. Group treatment did not 'begin with the onset of eligibility but with the beginning of a prescribed accounting period. The express provisions for the termination of such treatment do not provide that it should be coterminous with the cesser of eligibility either.'

Notes

(1) The decision discusses VATA 1994, s 43(6), which was repealed with effect from 27 July 1999 by FA 1999, Sch 2. Similar provisions are, however, contained in the new VATA 1994, s 43C(3), (4).

(2) The House of Lords rejected the company's application for leave to appeal against this decision.

43. Customs and Excise Comrs v Upton (t/a Fagomatic)

Court of Appeal [2002] EWCA Civ 520; [2002] STC 640

Motor car – available for private use – blocked input tax.

Facts

A taxable person (U), who lived in Central London, carried on the business of supplying and servicing cigarette vending machines in public houses. He reclaimed input tax on the purchase of a Lamborghini. The Commissioners rejected the claim on the basis that the Lamborghini was available for private use. U appealed to the Tribunal which allowed his appeal. The Commissioners appealed to the High Court which allowed their appeal. U appealed to the Court of Appeal.

Issue

Whether motor car to be regarded as available for private use so that input tax on purchase blocked.

Decision

The Court of Appeal unanimously dismissed U's appeal. Peter Gibson LJ observed that:

> 'the intention specified in para (2E)(a) [of VAT (Input Tax) Order 1992, art 7], viz. to use, is not synonymous with the intention specified in para (2G)(b), viz. to make available for use, nor does an intention to use a car exclusively for business purposes exclude the possibility of an intention to make the car available for private use'.

Where an individual taxable person acquired a car,

> 'the very fact of his deliberate acquisition of the car whereby he makes himself the owner of the car and controller of it means that at least ordinarily he must intend to make it available to himself for private use, even if he never intends to use it privately'.

On the evidence, the result of the taxable person's:

> 'deliberate action in acquiring the car and obtaining insurance permitting private use was to make the car available to himself for private use and … he must be taken to have intended that result in the absence of evidence to the contrary, even if he did not intend to use the car privately'.

Accordingly, the effect of art 7(2G) was that the tax was not deductible.

44. Southampton Leisure Holdings plc v Customs and Excise Comrs

[2002] V & DR 235 (VTD 17716)

Acquisition of shares in subsidiary company – attribution – apportionment.

Facts

A company (SLH), which was partly exempt, acquired the share capital of a company (F) which traded as Southampton Football Club. SLH issued shares to F's shareholders in exchange for their own shares in F. SLH and F remained separately registered for VAT. SLH incurred VAT on professional fees which it sought to recover in part on the basis that the input VAT was attributable in part to management services provided by SLH to F and was residual tax within VAT Regulations 1995, reg 101(2)(d). The Commissioners issued an assessment on the basis that the tax was wholly attributable to the exempt supply of shares. SLH appealed.

Issue

Whether the supplies of professional services were used in making both taxable and exempt supplies or were used exclusively in making exempt supplies.

Decision

The Tribunal allowed the appeal in part. The Tribunal held the appeal raised three questions, namely:

(a) Was there a direct link between the services supplied to SLH and the supply of management services by SLH?

(b) Was there a direct link between the services supplied to SLH and SLH's business as a whole?

(c) Were all the services used by SLH for the share issue?

In relation to the first issue, the Tribunal accepted that *Cibo Participations* (see **40** above) was a binding decision that there is no direct and immediate link between the costs of acquiring a subsidiary company and a subsequent supply of management services. In relation to the second issue, the Commissioners argued that an exempt supply of shares prior to making an acquisition constituted a chain-breaking event as a result of which there was a direct link between the services and the exempt supply of the shares. The Tribunal held, following *Cibo*, that if there had been only an acquisition without any issue of shares then the services would have been directly linked to SLH's business as a whole allowing SLH to treat the input VAT as residual input tax. The final issue was whether the services were wholly used in connection with the share issue. The Tribunal followed *RAP* (see **36**. above) and looked at each of the invoices in turn and concluded that the services of all but two suppliers were not used exclusively in the exempt supply of shares and should therefore be treated as part of SLH's residual input tax.

45. Halifax plc (and related appeals) v Customs and Excise Comrs

[2002] VATDR 117 (VTD 17721)

Tax avoidance – whether transactions constituted supplies for VAT purposes – abuse of rights.

Facts

A bank (H) wished to construct a number of 'call centres'. If it had arranged for this itself, most of the input tax would have been attributed to its exempt supplies and would have been irrecoverable. It therefore granted a leasehold interest in the relevant sites to an associated company (L), which was not a member of its VAT group. L then arranged for another associated company (C) to carry out the work. C engaged builders to undertake the construction. C reclaimed input tax on the amounts charged by the builders and charged output tax to L, which reclaimed these amounts as input tax. The Commissioners rejected the claims on the basis that the builders had actually supplied their services to H rather than to C, and that the purported supplies between L, C and H did not constitute 'supplies' for VAT purposes, and should be disregarded. H, L and C appealed.

Issue

Whether transactions with associated companies carried out for tax avoidance purposes were supplies for VAT purposes. Whether the principle of abuse of rights prevents a tax advantage being obtained.

Decision

The Tribunal dismissed the companies' appeals, finding that H's 'sole purpose in arranging for the insertion of (L) and (C) contractually between itself and the arm's length construction contractors was to procure (in group terms) the recovery of substantially all the VAT on the construction works, when otherwise most of that VAT would have been irrecoverable'. On the evidence, there was no 'business or 'commercial' rationale' for the relevant transactions. Applying dicta of the ECJ in *Direct Cosmetics Ltd v Customs and Excise Comrs (No 2)*, the scheme constituted 'tax avoidance'. Applying dicta of Advocate-General Lenz in *The Wellcome Trust Ltd* (see **23.** above) in deciding whether an activity was an 'economic activity', it was 'the inherent nature of the activity itself that is the vital consideration'. The inherent nature of the transactions here was tax avoidance, and there was 'no business purpose'. Applying the principles laid down by Laws J in *Reed Personnel Ltd*, 'the supplies of construction works were made by the arm's length builders direct to (H)'. Accordingly L and C were not entitled to reclaim input tax. The Tribunal observed that H could reclaim a proportion of the relevant input tax, applying the partial exemption provisions.

The companies appealed to the High Court, which remitted the case back to the Tribunal. Neuberger J held that the Tribunal had erred in concentrating solely on the intention of H in entering the transactions and that there was 'real doubt as to whether the Tribunal considered the subjective reasons of (L) and (C) for entering into the transactions, and in particular whether the sole subjective reason in each case was for the purpose of avoiding or mitigating VAT liability'.

In the second proceedings before it, the Tribunal reviewed the case and made a specific finding that 'the sole purpose of (C) and (L) in entering into the relevant transactions was VAT avoidance'. The Tribunal directed that the case should be referred to the ECJ for rulings on whether 'transactions, effected by each participator with the intention solely of obtaining a tax advantage and which have no independent business purpose, qualify for VAT purposes as supplies made by or to the participators in the course of their economic activities' and on whether the doctrine of 'abuse of rights' should 'operate to disallow the appellants their claims for recovery of or relief for input tax arising from the implementation of the relevant transactions'.

46. Centralan Property Ltd v Customs and Excise Comrs

High Court [2003] STC 290; [2003] EWHC 44(Ch)

Capital goods scheme – leaseback transaction – effect of VAT Regulations 1995, reg 115.

Facts

A university constructed a building in 1994. It sold it to a subsidiary company (C) and leased it back. Since the sale to C was standard-rated, the university reclaimed all the input tax which it had incurred on constructing the building. In 1996, C granted an exempt 999-year lease to another subsidiary company (H), which was not registered for VAT. Three days later, C also sold the freehold to the university for a minimal sum and then deregistered for VAT. The Commissioners issued an assessment on C to recover input tax of £796,250, on the basis that the building was a 'capital item' and that C had supplied the whole of its interest in that item, so that the provisions of VAT Regulations 1995, SI 1995 2518, reg 115 applied. C appealed to the Tribunal contending that, because there had been a three-day gap between the grant of the lease to H and the subsequent sale of the freehold, the provisions of reg 115(3) did not apply and that the only necessary adjustment was under reg 115(2) to take account of three days of exempt supplies. The Tribunal rejected this contention and dismissed the appeal (except that it reduced the assessment from £796,250 to £796,090). C appealed to the High Court.

Issue

What is the proper interpretation of art 20(3) of the Sixth VAT Directive in relation to supplies of immovable property?

Decision

The High Court directed that the case should be referred to the ECJ for a ruling on whether, in the circumstances of the case, art 20(3) of the Sixth Directive should be interpreted so that:

'(a) the capital good is regarded until the expiry of the period of adjustment as if it had been applied for business activities which are presumed to be fully taxed;

(b) the capital good is regarded until the expiry of the period of adjustment as if it had been applied for business activities which are presumed to be fully exempt; or

(c) the capital good is regarded until the expiry of the period of adjustment as if it had been applied for business activities which are presumed to be partly taxed and partly exempt in the proportion of the respective values of the taxed sale of the freehold reversion and the exempt grant of the 999 year lease'.

Sir Andrew Morritt V-C observed that 'the proper interpretation and application of art 20(3) in relation to immovable property must accommodate the various and varied systems of land law applicable in individual Member States. Not all of them differentiate between immovable property and estates or interests in it ... this is essentially a question for the European Court of Justice.'

Note

The UK legislation in question, VAT Regulations 1995, SI 1995/2518, reg 115, was subsequently amended by VAT (Amendment) (No 3) Regulations 1997,

SI 1997/1614, reg 12, with effect from 1 May 1997 so that the arrangements in place in this case are unlikely to be repeated.

47. Customs and Excise Comrs v Royal & Sun Alliance Insurance Group plc

House of Lords [2003] STC 832; [2003] UKHL 29; [2003] 1 WLR 1387; [2003] 2 All ER 1073

Election to waive exemption – subsequent claim for adjustment of attribution under VAT Regulations, 109.

Facts

A group of insurance companies held the leasehold of a number of properties. The group had originally used the properties for the purposes of its insurance business but subsequently vacated them and decided to sublet them. In 1995, it elected to waive exemption in respect of the properties. It subsequently claimed a repayment of input tax incurred on rents and service charges relating to the properties prior to the election, while they were vacant, although it had initially attributed this input tax to exempt supplies. The Commissioners rejected the claim and the representative member of the group (RSA) appealed, contending that it was entitled to make an adjustment under reg 109 of the VAT Regulations 1995, SI 1995/2518. The Tribunal rejected this contention and dismissed the appeal, finding that the input tax in dispute related to a period when R was actively seeking to sublet the properties and holding that any such supplies would be exempt because R had not elected to waive exemption at the relevant time. The High Court reversed the Tribunal's decision. The Commissioners appealed to the Court of Appeal which, by a majority, upheld the High Court's decision. The Commissioners appealed to the House of Lords.

Issue

Whether input tax incurred in relation to vacant unelected properties becomes deductible after an election to waive exemption has been made.

Decision

The House of Lords allowed the Commissioners' appeal and restored the Tribunal's decision (by a 3–2 majority, Lord Woolf and Lord Clyde dissenting).

Lord Hoffmann observed that:

> 'in order to come within reg 109 … RSA must have first had an intention to use the inputs in supplying exempt sub-leases and then used them, or formed an intention to use them, in supplying taxable sub-leases'.

On the evidence, RSA:

> 'was not carrying on an economic activity for the purpose of making taxable outputs'.

Applying the principles in *Belgium v Ghent Coal Terminal NV* (see **30.** above):

> 'just as a failure to make taxable supplies does not destroy a right of deduction, so a failure to make exempt supplies does not create one'.

RSA were in the same position as someone:

> 'who decided to change from an activity which involved making exempt supplies to a different activity making taxable supplies. If there are still inputs around from the previous activity which can be used in the new taxable activity, like a building which has been constructed for exempt letting and is then used, after an election, for taxable letting, the taxpayer will be entitled to an adjustment ... but he cannot rewrite history.'

Lord Walker of Gestingthorpe observed that:

> 'it is an inescapable consequence of the general structure of VAT that a taxable person who makes partially exempt and partially taxable supplies (or who switches from exempt to taxable supplies) cannot expect precisely the same treatment as one who makes taxable supplies throughout. That would be pressing the principle of fiscal neutrality too far.'

48. Seeling v Finanzamt Starnberg

ECJ Case C-269/00: [2003] STC 805

Capital goods – business and private use – apportionment.

An exempt supply so that input tax referable thereto not deductible.

Facts

In a German case, a taxable person constructed a building which he used partly for business purposes and partly for residential purposes. He deducted the whole of the input tax on its construction on the grounds that it was a business asset and accounted for output tax in respect of his private use of part of the building, on the lines laid down by *Lennartz v Finanzamt München III* (see **12.** above). The tax authority rejected his claim to deduct the whole of the input tax. He appealed and the case was referred to the ECJ for guidance on the interpretation of arts 6(2) and 13B(b) of the Sixth Directive.

Issue

Whether a national law which treats the private use by a taxable person of part of a building, which is part of the assets of his business, as an exempt supply of the leasing or letting of immovable property within art 13B(b), is precluded by arts 6(2)(a) and 13B(b) of the Sixth Directive.

Decision

The ECJ held that, where a taxable person 'chooses to treat capital goods used both for business and private purposes as business goods, the VAT due as input tax on the acquisition of those goods is in principle wholly and immediately deductible'. The effect of arts 6(2)(a) and 11A1(c) was that the use of such capital goods for private purposes was treated as a supply of services. Accordingly, the taxable person was entitled to deduct the whole of the input tax and was required to account for output tax. Article 13B(b) had no application to 'the private use by a taxable person of part of a building which is treated as forming, in its entirety, part of the assets of his business'.

49. KapHag Renditefonds 35 Spreecenter Berlin-Hellersdorf 3 Tanche GbR v Finanzamt Charlottenburg

ECJ Case C-442/01: [2003] All ER(D) 362(Jun)

Supply of services – economic activity – payments to partnership by new partner.

Facts

A German partnership admitted a new partner in return for a payment to the partnership. The partnership reclaimed input tax on legal fees relating to the admission of the new partner. The tax authority rejected the claim on the basis that the fees related to an exempt supply of services. The partnership appealed and the case was referred to the ECJ.

Issue

Whether a partnership makes a supply of services for consideration when it admits a new partner in consideration for a payment of a contribution in cash.

Decision

The ECJ ruled that:

> 'A partnership which admits a partner in consideration of payment of a contribution in cash does not effect towards that person a supply of services for consideration within the meaning of art 2(1) of Sixth Council Directive …'.

50. Halladale Group plc v Customs and Excise Comrs

(VTD 18218) [2003] SWTI 1803

Share issue and listing – attribution to taxable supplies – apportionment.

Facts

A property company reclaimed input tax on professional fees relating to an issue of shares and to the listing of its shares on the London Stock Exchange Alternative Investment Market. The Commissioners issued a ruling that the input tax was used 'exclusively in making exempt supplies' within VAT Regulations 1995, reg 101(2)(c). The company appealed, contending that the fees relating to the listing on the Alternative Investment Market were partly attributable to making future taxable supplies, so that the tax should be apportioned under reg 101(2)(d).

Issue

Whether professional services on which VAT was incurred were used exclusively for the purposes of the exempt transaction (issue of shares) or partly for an exempt transaction and partly for the general purpose of the business (future taxable supplies).

Decision

The Tribunal accepted the company's contention and allowed the appeal. The Tribunal held that 'the AIM listing was in part for the general business purposes of the appellants and was not an essential element of the issue of shares'. The expenditure had 'a dual purpose'.

51. Customs and Excise Comrs v Southern Primary Housing Ltd

Court of Appeal [2003] EWCA Civ 1662; [2004] STC 209

Attribution – apportionment.

Facts

In February 2002 a company (S) purchased some land with the intention of obtaining planning permission for the construction of flats on the land and then selling the land to a housing association. VAT was charged on this transaction because the vendor had elected to waive exemption in respect of the land. Two months later S agreed to sell the land to a housing association under a contract whereby it also agreed to build 24 flats on the land. It treated the sale as exempt but treated the input tax on its purchase of the land as partly attributable to taxable supplies of building work. Subsequently, the Commissioners issued an assessment on the basis that the tax was wholly attributable to S's resale of the land, which was an exempt supply. S appealed to the Tribunal which allowed S's appeal, holding that S Ltd had made joint supplies of land and building services and had never made a separate supply of land. The Commissioners appealed to the High Court which upheld the decision of the Tribunal and dismissed the Commissioners' appeal. The Commissioners appealed to the Court of Appeal.

Issue

Whether input tax incurred on purchase of land is attributable to the exempt sale of land by company or to the exempt sale and the taxable building work provided in relation to the land.

Decision

The Court of Appeal unanimously upheld the assessment, holding that the input tax on the cost of buying the land was not a 'cost component' of the contract for the development of the land. Jacob LJ observed that:

> 'there is nothing about the development contract as such which makes the land purchase and sale essential. If the housing association had already owned the land or had bought it from some third party, the inputs of the development contract would have been just the costs of carrying it out. The fact that there were commercially linked land transactions does not mean that those transactions are directly linked to the costs of the development contract. One would not say that the cost of buying the land was a cost of the development contract itself. It follows that the input tax on that cost is not a cost of the contract.'

Index of case summaries

Title of case	
1.	*Verbond van Nederlandse Ondernemingen v Inspecteur der Invoerrechten en Accijnzen*
2.	*Customs and Excise Comrs v Lord Fisher*
3.	*Celtic Football & Athletic Club Ltd v Customs and Excise Comrs*
4.	*DA Rompelman & EA Rompelman-van-Deelen v Minister van Financiën*
5.	*Whitechapel Art Gallery v Customs and Excise Comrs*
6.	*Merseyside Cablevision Ltd*
7.	*Apple & Pear Development Council v Customs and Excise Comrs*
8.	*Leesportfeuille 'Inteim' CV v Staatssecretaris van Financiën*
9.	*Mol v Inspecteur der Invoerrechten en Accijnzen* *Vereniging Happy Family Rustenburgerstrat v Inspecteur der Omzetbelasting*
10.	*Kühne v Finanzamt München III*
11.	*Polysar Investments Netherlands BV v Inspecteur der Invoerrechten en Accijnzen*
12.	*Lennartz v Finanzamt München III*
13.	*Customs and Excise Comrs v Briararch Ltd*
14.	*Finanzamt München III v Mohsche*
15.	*Sofitam SA (aka Satam SA) v Ministre du Budget*
16.	*Customs and Excise Comrs v Kingfisher plc*
17.	*Customs and Excise Comrs v FW Rosner*
18.	*BLP Group plc v Customs and Excise Comrs*
19.	*Finanzamt Ülzen v Ambrecht*
20.	*Intercommunale voor Zeewaterontzilting (in liquidation) v Belgian State*
21.	*Customs and Excise Comrs v UBAF Bank Ltd*

	Title of case
22.	*Gemeente Emmen v Belastingdienst Grote Ondernemingen*
23.	*The Wellcome Trust Ltd v Customs and Excise Comrs*
24.	*Régie Dauphinoise-Cabinet A Forest Sarl v Ministre du Budget*
25.	*Enkler v Finanzamt Homburg*
26.	*Harnas & Helm CV v Staatssecretaris van Financiën*
27.	*BMW (GB) Ltd v Customs and Excise Comrs*
28.	*Customs and Excise Comrs v Kilroy Television Co Ltd*
29.	*Ernst & Young v Customs and Excise Comrs*
30.	*Belgium v Ghent Coal Terminal NV*
31.	*Customs and Excise Comrs v Redrow Group plc*
32.	*Tremerton Ltd v Customs and Excise Comrs*
33.	*Finanzamt Goslar v Breitsohl*
34.	*Grundstückgemeinschaft Scholßstraße GbR v Finanzamt Paderborn*
35.	*Customs and Excise Comrs v Midland Bank plc*
36.	*RAP Group plc v Customs and Excise Comrs*
37.	*Floridienne SA v Belgian State*
38.	*Trinity Mirror plc (aka Mirror Group Newspapers Ltd) v Customs and Excise Comrs*
39.	*Abbey National plc v Customs and Excise Comrs*
40.	*Customs and Excise Comrs v Liverpool Institute for Performing Arts*
41.	*Cibo Participations SA v Directeur régional des impôts du Nord-Pas-de-Calais*
42.	*Customs and Excise Comrs v Barclays Bank plc*
43.	*Customs and Excise Comrs v CM Upton (t/a Fagomatic)*
44.	*Southampton Leisure Holdings plc v Customs and Excise Comrs*
45.	*Halifax plc (and related appeals) v Customs and Excise Comrs*
46.	*Centralan Property Ltd v Customs and Excise Comrs*

Title of case	
47.	*Customs and Excise Comrs v Royal & Sun Alliance Insurance Group plc*
48.	*Seeling v Finanzamt Starnberg*
49.	*KapHag Renditefonds 35 Spreecenter Berlin-Hellersdorf 3 Tanche GbR v Finanzamt Charlottenburg*
50.	*Halladale Group plc*
51.	*Southern Primary Housing Ltd v Customs and Excise Comrs*

EU – UK Legislation Comparative Table

Sixth Directive Article		UK Legislation	
Article	Sub-Article	Primary	Secondary
17	(1)	VATA 1994 s25(1), 26(1)	
17	(2) a)	VATA 1994 s24(1), (5), 26(2), 25(6), (7)	
17	(2) b)	VATA 1994 s24(1), (5), 26(2) 25(6), (7)	
17	(2) c)	VATA 1994 s24(1), (5), 26(2), 25(6), (7)	
17	(2) d)	VATA 1994 s24(1), (5), 26(2), 25(6), (7)	
17	(3) a)	VATA 1994 s26(2)	
17	(3) b)		
17	(3 c)	VATA 1994 s26(2)	SI 1995 No 2518 Reg 103 SI 1999 No 3121
17	(4) indent 1 1st indent	VATA 1994 s39	SI 1995 No 2518 Regs 173–184
17	(4) indent 1 2nd indent	VATA 1994 s39	SI 1995 No. 2518 Regs 185–197
17	(4) indent 2 a)	VATA 1994 s39	SI 1995 No 2518 Regs 185–197
17	(4) indent 2 b)	VATA 1994 s39	SI 1995 No 2518 Regs 185–197

Sixth Directive Article		UK Legislation	
17	(4) indent 2 c)	VATA 1994 s39	SI 1995 No 2518 Regs 185–197
17	(5) indent 1	VATA 1994 s24(5)	SI 1995 No 2518 Regs 99–111
17	(5) indent 2	VATA 1994 s24(5)	SI 1995 No 2518 Regs 99–111
17	(5) indent 3 a)		SI 1995 No 2518 Regs 102
17	(5) indent 3 b)		
17	(5) indent 3 c)		SI 1995 No 2518 Reg 101
17	(5) indent 3 d)		SI 1995 No 2518 Reg 101
17	(5) indent 3 e)		SI 1995 No 2518 Reg 106
17	(6) indent 1	VATA 1994 s25(2)	
17	(6) indent 2		
17	(7)	VATA 1994 s34	SI 1995 No 2518 Regs 112–116
18	(1) a)	VATA 1994 s24(6)	SI 1995 No 2518 Reg 29
18	(1) b)	VATA 1994 s24(6)	SI 1995 No 2518 Reg 29
18	(1 c)	VATA 1994 s24(6)	SI 1995 No 2518 Reg 29
18	(1) d)	VATA 1994 s8	
18	(1) e)		SI 1995 No 2518 Regs 25, 26

Sixth Directive Article		UK Legislation	
18	(2) indent 1		SI 1995 No 2518 Regs 24–43
18	(2) indent 2		
18	(3)		SI 1995 No 2518 Reg 29(3)
18	(3a)		SI 1995 No 2518 Reg 29(2)
18	(4) indent 1		SI 1995 No 2518 Reg 25(3), (4), (5)
18	(4) indent 2		
19	(1) indent 1 1st indent	VATA 1994 s26(3)	SI 1995 No 2518 Reg 101
19	(1) indent 1 2nd indent		SI 1995 No 2518 Reg 101
19	(1) indent 2		SI 1995 No 2518 Reg 101
19	(2)		SI 1995 No 2518 Reg 101
19	(3) indent 1		
19	(3) indent 2		
20	(1) a)	VATA 1994 s26(3) (6)	SI 1995 No 2518 Regs 107–110
20	(1) b)	VATA 1994 s26(3) (6)	SI 1995 No 2518 Regs 107–110
20	(2) indent 1	VATA 1994 s34	SI 1995 No 2518 Regs 112–116
20	(2) indent 2	VATA 1994 s34	SI 1995 No 2518 Regs 112–116
20	(2) indent 3	VATA 1994 s34	SI 1995 No 2518 Regs 112–116
20	(3) indent 1	VATA 1994 s34	SI 1995 No 2518 Regs 112–116

Sixth Directive Article		UK Legislation	
20	(3) indent 2	VATA 1994 s34	SI 1995 No 2518 Regs 112–116
20	(4) 1st indent	VATA 1994 s34	SI 1995 No 2518 Regs 112–116
20	(4) 2nd indent	VATA 1994 s34	SI 1995 No 2518 Regs 112–116
20	(4) 3rd indent	VATA 1994 s34	SI 1995 No 2518 Regs 112–116
20	(4) 4th indent	VATA 1994 s34	SI 1995 No 2518 Regs 112–116
20	(5)		
20	(6)		
21	(1) a) indent 1	VATA 1994 s1(2)	
21	(1) a) indent 2	VATA 1994 s48	SI 1995 No 2518 Reg 10
21	(1) a) indent 3	VATA 1994 s14	SI 1995 No 2518 Regs 11, 12
21	(1) a) indent 4		
21	(1) a) indent 5	VATA 1994 s43, 47	
21	(1) b)	VATA 1994 s8	
21	(1) c)	VATA 1994 Schedule 11	
21	(1) d)	VATA 1994 s1(3)	

Index

C

E

F

I

J

K

L

M

N

O

P

T